Klaas Bentein, Mark Janse (Eds.)
Varieties of Post-classical and Byzantine Greek

Trends in Linguistics
Studies and Monographs

Editors
Chiara Gianollo
Daniël Van Olmen

Editorial Board
Walter Bisang
Tine Breban
Volker Gast
Hans Henrich Hock
Karen Lahousse
Natalia Levshina
Caterina Mauri
Heiko Narrog
Salvador Pons
Niina Ning Zhang
Amir Zeldes

Editor responsible for this volume
Chiara Gianollo

Volume 331

Varieties of Post-classical and Byzantine Greek

Edited by
Klaas Bentein and Mark Janse

ISBN 978-3-11-099154-3
e-ISBN (PDF) 978-3-11-061440-4
e-ISBN (EPUB) 978-3-11-061463-3
ISSN 1861-4302

Library of Congress Control Number: 2020941600

Bibliographic information published by the Deutsche Nationalbibliothek
The Deutsche Nationalbibliothek lists this publication in the Deutsche Nationalbibliografie;
detailed bibliographic data are available on the Internet at http://dnb.dnb.de.

© 2022 Walter de Gruyter GmbH, Berlin/Boston
This volume is text- and page-identical with the hardback published in 2021.
Typesetting: Integra Software Services Pvt. Ltd.
Printing and binding: CPI books GmbH, Leck

www.degruyter.com

Acknowledgments

ὥσπερ ξένοι χαίρουσιν ἰδεῖν π(ατ)ρίδ(α)·
οὕτως καὶ οἱ γρά(φοντες) βιβλίου τέλος +
(DBBE 346; Oxford, Bodl. Libr., Barocci 102, f. 210v.)

This volume contains selected and thoroughly revised versions of papers presented at the international conference on 'Varieties of Post-Classical and Byzantine Greek' which took place at the Royal Academy of Dutch Language and Literature (KANTL) in Gent on December 1st and 2nd, 2016, with the financial support of the Research Foundation – Flanders (FWO), de Gruyter Mouton, the Commission Scientific Research (CWO) of Ghent University and our research group Diachronic & Diatopic Linguistics (ΔiaLing). We would like to thank our junior colleagues from the Greek section at Ghent University for their enthousiastic practical support before, during and after the conference.

The volume has been a very long time in the making: μέγα βιβλίον, μέγα κακόν (although Callimachus surely did not have edited volumes in mind when he coined his saying). We would like to thank the many people who have contributed to its completion: Chiara Gianollo, Barbara Karlson, Julie Miess and Uri Tadmor (now at Brill) of de Gruyter for their patience and support; our meticulous copy-editors Eline Daveloose, Cleo Janse and Febe Schollaert; the anonymous reviewer from de Gruyter for her or his useful remarks and suggestions; the contributors to this volume, for their patience, support and, most importantly, for accepting to each review one chapter according to his or her expertise; and, last but not least, our respective families for bearing with us during yet another academic elephant's gestation period including the corona pandemic lockdown during the Spring of 2020: *finit corona opus*.

https://doi.org/10.1515/9783110614404-202

Contents

Acknowledgments —— V

List of contributors —— XI

The Greek Alphabet —— XV

List of abbreviations —— XVII

Klaas Bentein and Mark Janse
1 Varieties of Post-classical and Byzantine Greek: Novel questions and approaches —— 1

Part I: VARIETIES OF POST-CLASSICAL AND BYZANTINE GREEK

Martti Leiwo
2 Tracking down lects in Roman Egypt —— 17

Marja Vierros
3 Idiolect in focus: Two brothers in the Memphis Sarapieion (II BCE) —— 39

Aikaterini Koroli
4 Imposing psychological pressure in papyrus request letters: A case study of six Byzantine letters written in an ecclesiastical context (VI–VII CE) —— 75

Victoria Fendel
5 Greek in Egypt or Egyptian Greek? Syntactic regionalisms (IV CE) —— 115

Sofía Torallas Tovar
6 In search of an Egyptian Greek lexicon in Ptolemaic and Roman Egypt —— 141

Geoffrey Horrocks
7 Byzantine literature in "classicised" genres: Some grammatical realities (V–XIV CE) —— 163

Martin Hinterberger
8   From highly classicizing to common prose (XIII–XIV CE): The
    Metaphrasis of Niketas Choniates' *History* —— 179

Mark Janse
9   Back to the future: Akritic light on diachronic variation in
    Cappadocian (East Asia Minor Greek) —— 201

Part II: DIMENSIONS OF VARIATION IN POST-CLASSICAL AND BYZANTINE GREEK

Carla Bruno
10 Tense variation in Ptolemaic papyri: Towards a grammar of
    epistolary dialogue —— 243

Jerneja Kavčič
11 The Classical norm and varieties of Post-classical Greek:
    Expressions of anteriority and posteriority in a corpus of
    official documents (I–II CE) —— 265

Joanne Vera Stolk
12 Orthographic variation and register in the corpus of Greek
    documentary papyri (300 BCE–800 CE) —— 299

Emilio Crespo
13 The Greek phonology of a tax collector in Egypt in the first century CE —— 327

Julie Boeten
14 Metrical variation in Byzantine colophons (XI–XV CE):
    The example of ἡ μὲν χεὶρ ἡ γράψασα —— 353

Staffan Wahlgren
15 Arguing and narrating: Text type and linguistic variation in tenth-
    century Greek —— 369

Klaas Bentein
16 The distinctiveness of syntax for varieties of Post-classical and Byzantine Greek: Linguistic upgrading from the third century BCE to the tenth century CE —— 381

Index locorum —— 415

Index nominum —— 423

Index rerum —— 425

List of contributors

Klaas Bentein is Associate Research Professor at Ghent University and Principal Investigator of the ERC project "Everyday writing in Greco-Roman and Late Antique Egypt. A socio-semiotic study of communicative variation" (2018–2023). He has worked as a visiting research fellow at Macquarie University (2012), the University of Michigan (2013–2014) and Harvard's Center for Hellenic Studies (2017–2018). His main research interests include Ancient Greek linguistics, historical sociolinguistics, social semiotics, and papyrology. He is the author of *Verbal Periphrasis in Ancient Greek: Have- and Be- Constructions* (OUP, 2016) and editor of *Variation and Change in Ancient Greek Tense, Aspect and Modality* (Brill, 2017).

Julie Boeten is currently a PhD student in Greek linguistics at Ghent University, with a master's degree in Greek and Latin Language and Literature. Her research is funded by the Flemish Fund for Scientific Research (FWO). Her work is also affiliated with the Database of Byzantine Book Epigrams (DBBE), which is hosted by Ghent University at www.dbbe.ugent.be.

Carla Bruno is Associate Professor at the University for Foreigners of Siena where, after her degree in Historical linguistics from the University of Pisa, she received her PhD in 2003. She teaches General and Historical linguistics. Her reasearch is focused on morpho-synctactic aspects of the Indo-European languages (especially Ancient Greek) from both a synchronic and a diachronic perspective, with special attention to linguistic variation and change.

Emilio Crespo is Professor of Greek Philology at the Universidad Autónoma de Madrid and President of the Pastor Foundation for Classical Studies (Madrid). An Honorary Doctor from the Aristotle University of Thessaloniki, he is co-author of *Sintaxis del griego clásico* (Gredos, 2003), associate editor of the *Encyclopedia of Ancient Greek Language and Linguistics* (Brill, 2014) and author of a widely known Spanish translation of Homer's *Iliad* (Gredos, 2010). His most recent publications deal with discourse markers and with dialect contacts in the north of Ancient Greece. He is currently working on politeness in Homeric diction.

Victoria Fendel completed her DPhil in Classical Languages and Literature at the University of Oxford (Lady Margaret Hall) in 2018 with a thesis on language contact between Greek and Coptic and her MPhil in Theoretical and Applied Linguistics at the University of Cambridge (Peterhouse) in 2019.

Martin Hinterberger is Professor at the University of Cyprus, where he teaches Byzantine Literature. His major research interests are emotions in Byzantine literature and society (particularly envy, jealousy, arrogance, shame), *metaphraseis*, Byzantine hagiographical literature, autobiography, and the history of Medieval Greek, especially as a literary language. He is editor of *The Language of Byzantine Learned Literature* (Brepols, 2014).

Geoffrey Horrocks is Professor Emeritus of Comparative Philology at the University of Cambridge and a Fellow of St John's College. He was educated at the Manchester Grammar School and Downing College Cambridge (1969–1972) before embarking on a brief career in industry. After returning to Cambridge for his PhD, he was first a Research Fellow at Downing College (1976–1977) and then a University Lecturer in the Linguistics Department of the

School of Oriental and African Studies, University of London (1977–1983). He came back to Cambridge in 1983 as a University Lecturer in Classics (Philology and Linguistics) and was elected to the established chair of Comparative Philology in 1997. He retired in 2016. He holds an Honorary Doctorate from the University of Athens (2012), and is the author or co-author, *inter alia*, of *Space and Time in Homer* (1981), *Generative Grammar* (1987), *Greek: A History of the Language and its Speakers* (2nd ed. 2010), the *Blackwell History of the Latin Language* (2007), and the *Cambridge Grammar of Medieval and Early Modern Greek* (2019).

Mark Janse is BOF-ZAP Research Professor in Ancient & Asia Minor Greek at Ghent University and Associate in Greek Linguistics of Harvard's Center for Hellenic Studies. He is a former Visiting Fellow of All Souls College (Oxford), the Onassis Foundation (Athens) and Harvard's Center for Hellenic Studies (Washington, DC) and a former Onassis Senior Visiting Scholar at Harvard, Princeton, Stanford and the University of Arizona. His research interests include Ancient, Medieval and Modern Greek linguistics, with particular attention to Cappadocian and other Asia Minor Greek varieties. He is associate editor of Brill's *Encyclopedia of Greek Language and Linguistics* and (co)editor of *Studies in General and Descriptive Linguistics in Honor of E.M. Uhlenbeck* (1998), *Bilingualism in Ancient Society* (2002), *Language Death and Language Maintenance* (2003), *Studies in Modern Greek Dialects and Linguistic Theory* (2011), *The Diachrony of Gender Marking* (2011), and *Variation and Change in Ancient Greek Tense, Aspect and Modality* (2017).

Jerneja Kavčič is an Associate Professor of Greek at the University of Ljubljana, Slovenia. Her research interests concern Greek in all its historical stages (Ancient, Byzantine, and Modern Greek) as well as linguistic theory (mostly syntax). She authored a volume on the syntax of the infinitive and the participle in Early Byzantine Greek (2005), compiled the first Modern Greek-Slovenian dictionary (2006) and wrote the first Modern Greek grammar in Slovenian (2011).

Aikaterini Koroli is a papyrologist, philologist and linguist. She studied Greek Philology at the University of Athens. She is a holder of a Master's degree in Educational Linguistics and of a doctorate in Classics and Papyrology from the same University. The topic of her thesis, which was published in 2016, is the text-linguistic analysis of the speech-act of requesting in the private correspondence preserved on papyri and ostraka of the Roman, Byzantine and Early Arab periods of Egypt. From September 2015 to January 2019 she worked as a researcher at the FWF project "Text and Textiles from Late Antique Egypt" (with Prof. Dr. Bernhard Palme and Mag. Ines Bogensperger) in affiliation with the Austrian Academy of Sciences. She currently holds a Hertha-Firnberg postdoctoral fellowship at the University of Wien, and is working on a project entitled "Business Letters from Byzantine Egypt. First Edition and Linguistic Analysis of twenty five Greek Papyri". Her publications so far deal with Greek papyrology, Ancient and Late Antique Greek literature (with emphasis on post-classical Greek epistolography), applied linguistics (text-linguistics, sociolinguistics, teaching Greek as a second language), social and economic history, as well as the material culture of Late Antiquity.

Martti Leiwo is Adjunct Professor and Senior Lecturer at the University of Helsinki, Department of Languages and Adjunct Professor of Ancient languages at the University of Turku. He is member of the Board of the MA and PhD programmes of languages, University of Helsinki and principal investigator of the project "Act of the Scribe: transmitting linguistic knowledge and scribal practices in Graeco-Roman Antiquity", funded by the Academy of Finland. He is also the editor-in-chief of *Arctos. Acta philologica Fennica*. He has been Professor of Greek Language and Literature, University of Helsinki, and Director of the Finnish Institute at Athens, Greece. His research interest are bi- and multilingualism, language variation and change and, generally, historical sociolinguistics.

Joanne Vera Stolk is a postdoctoral fellow of the Research Foundation Flanders at Ghent University and a Marie Curie postdoctoral fellow (NFR COFUND) for the University of Oslo. Her current projects focus on scribal corrections in documentary papyri and linguistic norms in Graeco-Roman Egypt. She also teaches Greek papyrology at the universities of Ghent and Leiden and is working on editions of Greek and Coptic papyri from the papyrus collections of the Oslo University Library and the Leiden Papyrological Institute.

Sofía Torallas Tovar is Professor in the Department of Classics and Near Eastern Languages and Civilizations, and the Oriental Institute at the University of Chicago and Associated faculty at the Divinity School (PhD Universidad Complutense de Madrid 1995). Her area of specialization is Greek and Coptic papyrology, and the study of Greco-Roman and Late Antique Egypt. She works at the crossroads between the material study of written objects – papyri, ostraca, mummy labels, and inscriptions – and the analysis of the information provided by the wealth of Egyptian documentation.

Marja Vierros is an Associate Professor of Classical Philology at the University of Helsinki and the Principal Investigator of the ERC project "Digital Grammar of Greek Documentary Papyri" (2018–2023). She received her PhD in 2011. She has been long-time member the Finnish team (lead by prof. Jaakko Frösén) editing and publishing the dossier of carbonized early Byzantine papyri found in Petra, Jordan. She has worked as a Visiting Research Scholar at the Institute for the Study of the Ancient World (New York University) and as a postdoctoral scholar in two projects funded by the Academy of Finland.

Staffan Wahlgren is Professor of Classical Philology at the Norwegian University of Science and Technology in Trondheim. His research interests include Greek linguistics, textual criticism and Digital Humanities.

The Greek Alphabet

The Greek alphabet is used throughout this volume, because the actual pronunciation varies enormously, both diachronically and diatopically, which would have resulted in different transcriptions for same or similar words from different periods. For the benefit of readers who are unfamiliar with the Greek alphabet or unfamiliar with either the ancient (5th–4th c. BC) or the modern pronunciation we provide here a comparative table of both. The modern pronunciation is basically the same as that of the LMedGr, barring diatopic variation. The successive changes in the pronunciation of the Greek vowels and diphthongs are the most complex. For detailed information on these changes with further bibliographical references we refer the interested reader to Horrocks (2010).[1] The following tables are based on Horrocks (2010: xviii–xx).

Greek letter			Ancient pronunciation	Modern pronunciation
Α	α	alpha	[a], [a:]	[a]
Β	β	beta	[b]	[v]
Γ	γ	gamma	[g]	[ɣ], [j]
Δ	δ	delta	[d]	[ð]
Ε	ε	epsilon	[e]	[e]
Ζ	ζ	zeta	[dz], [zd]	[z]
Η	η	eta	[ɛ:]	[i]
Θ	θ	theta	[tʰ]	[θ]
Ι	ι	iota	[i], [i:]	[i]
Κ	κ	kappa	[k]	[k], [c]
Λ	λ	lambda	[l]	[l]
Μ	μ	mu	[m]	[m]
Ν	ν	nu	[n]	[n]
Ξ	ξ	xi	[ks]	[ks]
Ο	ο	omikron	[o]	[o]
Π	π	pi	[p]	[p]
Ρ	ρ	rho	[r]	[r]
Σ	σ, ς	sigma	[s]	[s]
Τ	τ	tau	[t]	[t]
Υ	υ	upsilon	[y], [y:]	[i]
Φ	φ	phi	[pʰ]	[f]

---

[1] Horrocks, Geoffrey C. 2010. *Greek: A history of the language and its speakers*, 2nd ed. Malden: Wiley-Blackwell.

https://doi.org/10.1515/9783110614404-205

Χ	χ	khi	[kʰ]		[x], [ç]
Ψ	ψ	psi	[ps]		[ps]
Ω	ω	omega	[oː]		[o]

Digraphs	**Ancient pronunciation**	**Modern pronunciation**
αι	[aɪ]	[e]
αυ	[au]	[af], [av]
ει	[eː]	[i]
ευ	[eu]	[ef], [ev]
οι	[oɪ]	[i]
ου	[uː]	[u]
ᾳ	[aːɪ]	[a]
ῃ	[ɛːɪ]	[i]
ῳ	[oːɪ]	[o]
γγ	[ŋg]	[(ŋ)g]
γκ	[ŋk]	[(ŋ)g]
γχ	[ŋkʰ]	[ŋx], [ŋç]
μπ	[mp]	[(m)b]
ντ	[nt]	[(n)d]

Diacritics		**Ancient pronunciation**	**Modern pronunciation**
’	smooth breathing	Ø	Ø
‘	rough breathing	[h]	Ø
´	acute accent	[rise + fall on next syllable]	[stress]
`	grave accent	[absence of rise]	[stress]
~	circumflex	[rise-fall]	[stress]

List of abbreviations

Abbreviations in interlinear glosses are in accordance with the Leipzig Glossing Rules

APIS	Advanced Papyrological Information System: quod.lib.umich.edu/a/apis
BDAG	Montanari, Franco. 2015. *The Brill Dictionary of Ancient Greek*. Leiden: Brill.
CGCG	Emde Boas, Evert van, Albert Rijksbaron, Luuk Huitink & Mathieu de Bakker. 2019. *The Cambridge Grammar of Classical Greek*. Cambridge: Cambridge University Press.
CGMG	Holton, David, Geoffrey Horrocks, Marjolijne Janssen, Tina Lendari, Io Manolessou & Notis Toufexis. 2019. *The Cambridge Grammar of Medieval and Early Modern Greek*. Vol. 1–4. Cambridge: Cambridge University Press.
DBBE	Database of Byzantine Book Epigrams: www.dbbe.ugent.be
DDbDP	Duke Database of Documentary Papyri: papyri.info
DGE	Adrados, Francisco Rodríguez. 1980–. *Diccionario Griego-Español*. Madrid: Consejo Superior de Investigaciones Científica
EAGLL	Giannakis, Georgios (general ed.). 2014. *Encyclopedia of Ancient Greek Language and Linguistics*. Leiden: Brill: brill.com/view/db/eglo.
HGV	Heidelberger Gesamtverzeichnis der Griechischen Papyrusurkunden Ägyptens: aquila.zaw.uni-heidelberg.de
LBG	Trapp, Erich (ed.). 1994–2017. *Lexikon zur byzantinischen Gräzität: besonders des 9.-12. Jahrhunderts*. Wien: Verlag der Österreichischen Akademie der Wissenschaften: stephanus.tlg.uci.edu/lbg
LME	Kriaras, Emmanuel. 1968–. *Λεξικό της μεσαιωνικής ελληνικής δημώδους γραμματείας, 1100–1669*. Thessaloniki: Κέντρο Ελληνικής Γλώσσας.
LSJ	Liddell, Henry Georg & Robert Scott. 1940. *A Greek-English Lexicon*. Revised and augmented throughout by Henry Stuart Jones with the assistance of Roderick McKenzie. Oxford: Clarendon Press: stephanus.tlg.uci.edu/lsj
Mayser	Mayser, Edwin. 1926–1938. *Grammatik der griechischen Papyri aus der Ptolemäerzeit mit Einschluss der gleichzeitigen Ostraka und der in Ägypten verfasten Inschriften. Bd. 1: Laut- und Wortlehre. 2. Teil: Flexionslehre*, 2nd ed. 3. Teil: *Stammbildung*, 2nd ed. Bd. 2: *Satzlehre*. 1. Teil: *Analytischer Teil: Erste Hälfte*. 2. Teil: *Analytischer Teil: Zweite Hälfte*. 3. Teil: *Synthetischer Teil*. Leipzig: Teubner (1970 reprint Berlin: de Gruyter).
Mayser-Schmoll	Mayser, Edwin & Hans Schmoll. 1970. *Grammatik der griechischen Papyri aus der Ptolemäerzeit mit Einschluss der gleichzeitigen Ostraka und der in Ägypten verfasten Inschriften. Bd. 1. Laut- und Wortlehre. 1. Teil. Einleitung und Lautlehre*, 2nd ed. Berlin: de Gruyter.
OCD	Whitmarsh, Tim. 2020. *Oxford Classical Dictionary*. Oxford: Oxford UP: oxfordre.com/classics
ODB	Kazhdan, Alexander. 1991. *The Oxford Dictionary of Byzantium*. Oxford: Oxford University Press.

PGL	Lampe, G.W.H. 1961. *A Patristic Greek lexicon*. Oxford: Clarendon Press.
PN	Papyrological Navigator: papyri.info
TLG	Thesaurus Linguae Graecae: stephanus.tlg.uci.edu
TM	Trismegistos: trismegistos.org
TM Archives	Trismegistos Archives: www.trismegistos.org/arch
TMTI	Trismegistos Text Irregularities: www.trismegistos.org/textirregularities

Klaas Bentein and Mark Janse
1 Varieties of Post-classical and Byzantine Greek: Novel questions and approaches

Abstract: This chapter draws attention to the importance of studying not only linguistic variation in language, but also the patterned heterogeneity that can be related to it – in other words, linguistic varieties. Whereas the presence of varieties such as foreigner talk, female speech, colloquial language, etc. in the Classical period has received considerable attention, much less work has been done on the Post-classical and Byzantine periods, a situation which this edited volume hopes to remedy. Before outlining the contributions to the volume, we address a couple of central theoretical questions to research on linguistic varieties, such as the relationship between concepts like 'variant', 'variety' and 'variation', the modeling of varieties in terms of a 'variational space', the relationship between varieties, and the different methodologies that can be adopted to study linguistic varieties.

> "The most novel and difficult contribution of sociolinguistic description must be to identify the rules, patterns, purposes, and consequences of language use, and to account for their interrelations." (Hymes 1974: 75)

1 Introduction

For a long time, linguistic variation was conceived of as a problem, rather than a topic worthy of scholarly attention. Under the impulse of William Labov and others, however, scholars came to recognize the central importance of heterogeneity in language, which in turn led to the establishment of sociolinguistics as a discipline. Scholars working within this discipline have investigated the correlation between linguistic variants and contextual variables such as age, gender, social class, social distance, etc. Of course, in actual language use, variants (and to some extent, variables) do not occur in an isolated fashion; rather, there is patterned heterogeneity. In this spirit, scholars have turned their attention to the description of linguistic varieties or "lects", such as chronolects, dialects, idiolects, ethnolects, genderlects, regiolects, sociolects, technolects, etc. in a great number of languages.[1]

---
[1] For good introductions to linguistic varieties see Kiesling (2011), Sinner (2013); for an encyclopedic overview see Ammon et al. (2004–2006).

https://doi.org/10.1515/9783110614404-001

The main aim of this volume is to explore varieties of Post-classical and Byzantine Greek. When it comes to Classical Greek, varieties have received quite some attention: scholars have discussed varieties such as scientific and medical language, female speech, foreigner talk, religious language, colloquial language, profane and obscene language, etc.[2] Studies have also been written on individual authors and linguistic features, such as Thesleff (1967) on registers in Plato, Trenkner (1960) on paratactic structuring, and Dickey (1996) on forms of address. In comparison with Classical Greek, relatively little research has been done on Post-classical and Byzantine Greek, with the exception of Biblical Greek.[3] This is rather remarkable, since, as one of us has written in the past, "the situational characteristics of our Post-classical textual witnesses diverge to a much greater extent than what is the case for Classical Greek, making Post-classical Greek more suitable for diachronic (register-based) research" (Bentein 2013: 35).

In recent years, a number of edited volumes have appeared, which have started to rectify this situation: these include Evans and Obbink's (2010) *The language of the papyri*, Leiwo et al.'s (2012) *Variation and change in Greek and Latin*, Hinterberger's (2014) *The language of Byzantine learned literature*, and our own *Variation and change in Ancient Greek tense, aspect and modality* (Bentein, Janse & Soltic 2017). The present book is intended to complement these volumes, which mostly deal with linguistic features, rather than patterns of linguistic features, that is, linguistic varieties. In addition to the discussion of specific varieties, this book explores a number of key research questions:
- Which linguistic models can be used for the description and analysis of varieties?
- What is the relationship between different dimensions of variation, for example between the diachronic and the diastratic dimension?
- What role do idiolects play for the description of language variation?
- To what extent do non-congruent features (i.e. features belonging to different, or even opposed varieties) occur in texts?
- What is the relevance of and relationship between documentary and literary texts as sources of variation?
- At which linguistic levels (phonological, morphological, syntactic, lexical) can varieties be described?

---

2 See, e.g., Bain (1984), Lopez Eire (1996), van der Eijck (1997), Willi (2003), Fögen (2009), Schironi (2010), Janse (2014) and corresponding entries in *EAGLL*; for general overviews see Clackson (2015), Janse (2020).
3 On the Greek of the New Testament see e.g. Janse (2007). On the Greek of the Fathers, see e.g. Bentein (2015).

2 Theoretical background

Space does not permit us to fully discuss the broad topic of linguistic variation, more specifically linguistic varieties, but we do want to briefly outline some of the key issues which are immediately relevant to the contributions to this volume, and which will remain essential for future students of linguistic varieties. In what follows, we address the following four questions: (i) how do the notions of (linguistic) "variant", "variety" and "variation" relate to each other?, (ii) can the notion of variety be theorized in a more precise way?, (iii) how do varieties relate to each other?, and (iv) what methodology should one adopt when studying linguistic varieties?

2.1 Variant, variety, variation

Our first point concerns the key notions (linguistic) "variant", "variety" and "variation". As scholars have argued, both variants and varieties are indicative of linguistic variation, that is, "differences in linguistic form without (apparent) changes in meaning" (Walker 2010: 16). As Hudson's (1996: 22) definition of linguistic variety indicates, however, variety forms a more global category, which generalizes over individual speakers and individual linguistic items: "we may define a variety of language as *a set of linguistic items with similar social distribution*" (Hudson 1996: 22). Well-known in this regard is Halliday's (1978) distinction between two major types of varieties, that is, varieties according to user ("dialects") and varieties according to use ("registers").

Many questions surround the two key notions of linguistic variety and linguistic variation: for example, scholars have discussed whether there are sufficient criteria to be able to speak about a variety, and how to draw boundaries between varieties, questions well known from dialectology. The distinction between dialects and registers, too, does not seem absolute: several scholars have proposed to recognize "social dialects". These and other difficulties have led Hudson (1996: 68) to even completely deny the validity of the notion "variety": "we have come to essentially negative conclusions about varieties... We have suggested that the only way to solve these problems is to avoid the notion 'variety' altogether as an analytical or theoretical concept." Hudson (1996: 48–49) opposes an "item-based" approach (focusing on linguistic variants) to a "variety-based approach" (focusing on linguistic varieties), heavily favoring the first type of approach.⁴ Evidently, we do not support Hudson's (1996) proposal to completely abandon varieties, and to focus on an item-based approach.

Linguistic variants are not without difficulty either: for example, sociolinguistic studies typically posit as a working principle the semantic equivalence of the variants that together make up a variable, but scholars have questioned the existence/possibility of complete semantic equivalency.⁵ We feel it is important to be aware of these and other theoretical difficulties, and to combine both types of approaches as much as possible.

2.2 Variational space

The second issue which we want to address here is how we can theorize varieties and the situational dimensions that go behind them in a more precise way. A useful starting point in this regard is the German notion of *Variationsraum* or "variational space". Klein provides the following definition:⁶ "Diese Dimensionen [der Variation] können sehr unterschiedlicher Art sein; sie bilden insgesamt so etwas wie einen Raum, in dem sich die sprachliche Variation bewegt; diesen Raum bezeichne ich als Varietätenraum" (1976: 29) .

Sociolinguistic research has attempted to define language's variational space more precisely: since the 1960s, various proposals have been made by scholars such as Coseriu (1969), Halliday (1978), Dittmar (1997) and Berruto (2004). According to the model first introduced by Coseriu (1969), four general dimensions can be distinguished: (a) the "diachronic" dimension (variation in time), (b) the "diatopic" dimension (variation in space),⁷ (c) the "diastratic" dimension (variation according to the speaker's social status), and (d) the "diaphasic" dimension (variation in communicative settings).⁸ If and how these general dimensions can be further

---

4 So e.g. Hudson (1996: 49): "the notion 'linguistic variety' is an optional extra, available when needed to capture generalisations that apply to very large collections of linguistic items, but by no means the only mechanism, or even the most important mechanism, for linking linguistic items to their social context".
5 Lavandera (1978: 181), for example, has proposed to relax the condition that the referential meaning of all variants must be *identical*, and has suggested to replace it with a condition of "functional comparability".
6 See more recently Lange, Weber & Wolf (2012: 1) "a variational space depicts the sum total of all varieties of a single language."
7 This is probably the best studied dimension; see now Auer & Schmidt (2010).
8 Other scholars have proposed to add a "diamesic" dimension.

subdistinguished⁹ is a matter of discussion, especially when it comes to the diastratic and diaphasic dimensions. Some scholars have attempted to do so by referring to the notion "lect", which stems from dialect, and offers a convenient way of describing varieties. Berruto (1987: 21), for example, specifies different types of varieties by positing them along three axes (diaphasic, diamesic, and diastratic).

Berruto's (1987) model has often been referred to in variationist studies. Whether it could be applied to Ancient Greek (Post-classical and Byzantine Greek in particular) remains to be seen. Future scholarship will need to be wary of simply applying a model developed for one language to another language. As Lüdtke and Mattheier (2005) have noted, certain variationist dimensions are more important in one language than the other:

> So kann mann etwa zeigen, dass die französische Spracharchitektur wesentlich deutlicher durch die diastratische und die diaphasische Dimension geprägt ist als die deutsche, bei der (immer noch) die diatopische Dimension im Vordergund steht. Im britischen English wäre ähnlich wie im Französischen die diastratische und die diaphasische Dimension und ähnlich wie im Deutschen die diatopische Dimension zu berücksichtigen (Lüdtke & Mattheier 2005: 34)¹⁰

Another issue that needs to be sorted out is the role of the notion "idiolect". Berruto (1987) does not take this type of lect into account, even though modern-day studies have claimed a central role for it.¹¹ In recent years, scholars working on the language of Ancient Greek documentary sources, too, have come to stress its central importance.¹²

2.3 Varieties and variants: Interrelationships

Our next point concerns the relationship between linguistic varieties, and the social dimensions that go behind them. Coseriu (1980), among others, confronted

---

9 Cf. Berruto (2004: 193): "weiter gibt es diesen Dimensionen untergeordnete, spezifischere Faktoren, die für detailliertere Klassifikationen zu berücksichtigen sind." ["Furthermore, there are subordinate, more specific factors to these dimensions that must be considered for more detailed classifications."]
10 "So, for example, one can show that the linguistic architecture of French is much more clearly characterized by the diastratic and the diaphasic dimensions than that of German, where the diatopic dimension is (still) in the foreground. In British English, one would have to take into account the diastratic and the diaphasic dimension, similar to French, and the diatopic dimension, similar to German."
11 Cf. Oksaar (2000).
12 See e.g. Evans (2015), Nachtergaele (2015), Leiwo (2017).

this problem by arguing for a hierarchical relationship between three types of varieties, which he calls *Dialekt* (a "syntopic" unit), *Sprachniveau* (a "synstratic" unit [also called "sociolect"]) and *Sprachstil* (a "synphasic" unit [also called "register"]). Berruto (1993: 11) subsequently elaborated Coseriu's model, by arguing that diatopic varieties can also serve as diastratic varieties, diastratic varieties as diaphasic varieties, and diaphasic as diamesic varieties, but not the other way around (cf. Sinner 2013: 73).

As one can see, Coseriu's (1980) and Berruto's (1993) treatments do not take into account the diachronic dimension, which is not uncommon, as noted by Sinner (2013: 231):

> Die diachrone Perspektive wurde in vielen varietätenlinguistischen Arbeiten und Darstellungen von Varietätengefügen lange Zeit nur am Rande erwähnt. Manchmal wird dies damit begründet, dass die historische Perspektive ein zu umfangreiches oder ein zu komplexes Thema darstelle, manchmal wird deutlich gemacht, dass der Grund darin liegt, dass die diachrone Perspektive mit den anderen Varietätendimensionen nicht vergleichbar sei, weil es nicht um Varietäten, sondern ihren Wandel gehe.[13]

Clearly, future studies need to better integrate diachronic change in their modelling of varieties. Nabrings (1981: 38) has suggested that this can be thought of in terms of the succession of "zeitlich aufeinanderfolgende 'homogene' sprachliche Systeme",[14] but whether the distinction between diachronic layers is so simple is questionable.[15]

Next to the interrelationship of varieties, one can also inquire about the interrelationship between the linguistic features that characterize varieties: at which levels can these features be found, and to what extent do they co-occur? Is it true that the morpho-syntactic dimension is the least characterizing for linguistic varieties, as scholars have claimed?[16] Do we posit "co-textual congruence" as a prerequisite, or can we also allow for "non- or fractional congruence"?[17] James (2014: 14) has noted that non-congruence is often the case between the orthographic/phonological and syntactic level, but perhaps similar observations can be made inside one and the same level, as suggested by Halla-aho (2010: 172): "even within one

---

13 "The diachronic perspective has long been mentioned only marginally in many variationist-linguistic works and representations of varieties. On some occasions this is justified by the fact that the historical perspective is too extensive or too complex a topic, whereas on others it is made clear that the reason is that the diachronic perspective is not comparable with the other variational dimensions, because it is not about varieties, but about their change."
14 "Chronologically successive 'homogeneous' linguistic systems."
15 Cf. Sinner (2013: 232).
16 Cf. Hudson (1996: 43–45), Berruto (2004: 193), Bentein (this volume).
17 Cf. Agha (2007).

level, e.g. syntactic, it may be possible to identify different registers occurring next to each other, for example typical letter phrases and colloquial syntax". How problematic this is for the study of varieties remains to be studied.

2.4 Methodology

To conclude this discussion, we briefly want to go into methodology. Two main approaches are typically distinguished, referred to as "quantitative" vs. "qualitative". Whereas William Labov is generally acknowledged to be the main proponent of the quantitative approach, known as "variationist sociolinguistics",[18] John Gumperz has formed the leading figure of the qualitative approach, known as "interactional sociolinguistics".[19] When it comes to Ancient Greek, some attempts have been made for a quantitative approach to the study of variation and varieties, but by and large scholars tend to adopt an interpretative, qualitative approach, among others because creating statistics is a hugely time-consuming task, and it is not always clear what it contributes.

Horrocks (2007: 630–631), for example, has proposed a classification of writing styles in Post-classical Greek, distinguishing between three major styles, called "basic/non-literary"[20], "official and scientific/technical"[21], and "literary"[22]. We both find this an original and impressive proposal, but we can't help wondering what the classification would look like if we let the data speak for themselves, that is, when we ask the computer to analyze which features most often accompany each other. This is the approach propagated by Biber (1994), which has had very few followers in Greek linguistics so far.

Another methodological point that is worth considering is which sources to use for our investigations, and how to approach them. Ancient Greek is a corpus language, so out of necessity we have to work with texts. This does not mean that we do not have choices, however: older works, such as Browning's (1983) *Medieval and Modern Greek*, limit themselves to texts that are "spoken-like" – "authentic",

---

18 E.g. Labov (1994–2010).
19 E.g. Gumperz (1982).
20 Characterized, for example, by the use of ἀπό to mark the agent in passive constructions, the use of ἵνα after verbs of commanding, the use of the genitive articular, infinitives in a final sense, etc.
21 Characterized, for example, by the frequent use of τυγχάνω in the sense of 'to be', the use of φημί with an accusative and infinitive, the use of ὅτι after verbs of thinking, etc.
22 Characterized, for example, by the use of the optative in subordinate clauses after past-tense main verbs, the personal passive construction, a general effort to preserve the classical future and the perfect in all their forms, etc.

to use a term introduced by Joseph (2000) – such as documentary sources, hagiographical texts, etc. More recent works, on the other hand, such as Horrocks (2010), have argued for the importance of an inclusive approach, taking into consideration higher-register works as well. For the study of varieties, this definitely seems the best way to go.

A second, perhaps even more important methodological distinction is that between texts which report directly on the social value of linguistic features, such as stylistic manuals, scribal corrections, manuscript additions, etc., and texts which merely testify to actual language in use. Do we consider the first type of testimonies to be worthy of study? Or do we agree with modern-day observations that speakers form bad observers of social distinctions?[23] Recent research has explored the value of the first type of source for both Post-classical and Byzantine Greek,[24] and has come to some very interesting findings.

3 Outline of the volume

Linguistic varieties in Post-classical and Byzantine Greek constitute a very broad topic, which can be approached from many different angles. This is reflected by the contributions to this volume, which deal with different time periods, different dimensions and domains of variation, and use different methodologies. Broadly speaking, however, one can say that this volume consists of two main parts.

The first part of the volume (chs. 2–8) deals with linguistic varieties more narrowly speaking. Many of the contributions to this part deal with Greek in Egypt. Martti Leiwo (ch. 2) takes a broad approach, and investigates which varieties or "lects" can be distinguished. Focusing on the Roman period, Leiwo zooms in on a couple of geographical areas, in particular the Eastern desert, where the context of writing was quite different than for example in the Fayum, with a strong presence of the Roman army, the absence of scribes, and *ostraca* forming the standard writing material. Leiwo characterizes what he calls the "ostraca variety" as a mix of different varieties and registers, including ethnolects, idiolects, and doculects. Marja Vierros (ch. 3) specifically looks into one

---

23 Cf. Sinner (2013: 127–8): "es ist auch zu bedenken, dass trotz anderslautender ansichten in der sprachwissenschaft sprecher wohl i.d.r. nicht wissen, wass sie selbst – in sprachlicher hinsicht – tun oder nicht tun, und normalerweise nicht einmal in der Lage sind, von ihnen selbst Gesagtes im genauen Wortlaut zu wiederholen." ["One must also consider that, despite different views in linguistics, speakers usually do not know - in linguistic terms - what they are or are not doing and are usually not even able to accurately repeat what they have said themselves."]
24 See e.g. Luiselli (2010), Cuomo (2017), Bentein (this volume).

of the varieties mentioned by Leiwo, namely idiolect. Focusing on the archive of the Katochoi of the Sarapeion, she draws attention to several documents that are written in the own hands of the brothers Apollonius and Ptolemaeus, the archive's main figures. Vierros investigates whether it is possible to identify the idiolects of the two brothers through these autograph texts. Aikaterini Koroli (ch. 4) asks whether it is possible to speak of an "ecclesiastical" style of letter writing. She focuses on a corpus of request letters from the Late Antique period, and analyzes which strategies people use to achieve their communicative goal, that is, the satisfaction of the request. She concludes that although there are clear differences between the writers of the letters, politeness in general seems to be a priority. Victoria Fendel (ch. 5) discusses whether it is possible to identify features in the areas of verbal, nominal and discourse syntax that can be qualified as characteristic of Egyptian Greek. She argues that two of the three constructions investigated, the support verb construction χάριν ὁμολογέω 'to be grateful' and the predicative possessive pattern with ὑπό 'by', can be qualified as regionalisms. Multifunctional καί 'and', on the other hand, is better qualified as a "colloquialism". Sofia Torallas Tovar (ch. 6) also deals with Egyptian Greek, attempting to define more accurately the Egyptian Greek lexicon. Torallas Tovar extensively discusses the sources available for such a definition, distinguishing between documentary papyri and literary sources, and outlining some of the difficulties associated with these sources. The last three contributions to the first part of the volume deal with Byzantine Greek. Geoffrey Horrocks (ch. 7), addresses the question of how Byzantine writers used "Classical" Greek. Focusing on expressions of futurity and modality, Horrocks argues that these writers were subject to interference from their natural speech, especially in more abstract areas of grammar such as syntax and semantics. He concludes that high-register Byzantine Greek should be considered a variety of its own, rather than an exact copy of Classical Greek. Martin Hinterberger (ch. 8) also explores the question of high-register classicizing Greek, but from a different angle. He juxtaposes Nicetas Choniates' (XIII CE) *History*, which was written in high-register classicizing prose, with its *metaphrasis*, which is composed in a much simpler variety of Greek, sometimes called "Byzantine written koiné". Hinterberger explores the differences between these two texts at different linguistic levels, but also notes that there are shared linguistic characteristics, which leads him to question how these varieties can be accurately defined and distinguished. Mark Janse (ch. 9) analyzes the linguistic differences of two variants of a traditional medieval song from Cappadocia as evidence for diachronic variation in Medieval and Cappadocian Greek. He shows how the largely formulaic language of such traditional songs allows for the retention of archaisms as well as the insertion of innovative forms. Apart from loanwords and grammatical patterns borrowed from Turkish, the so-called 'Byzantine residue' of Cappadocian offers a unique and hitherto unexplored glimpse of language variation in Medieval Greek.

The second part of the volume (chs. 10–16) addresses the linguistic features that are indicative of varieties of Post-classical and Byzantine Greek, taking into consideration different linguistic levels. Carla Bruno (ch. 10) discusses tense variation in a small corpus of Ptolemaic private papyri, focusing on the use of the present, aorist and perfect indicative, framing her observations in the concept of the "epistolary dialogue" and noting that the deictic center of the statement cannot only be anchored to the time of writing (the addressor's perspective) but also to the time of reading (the addressee's perspective). Jerneja Kavčič (ch. 11) also goes into tense usage, but in a different context: she studies expressions of anteriority and posteriority in infinitive clauses, and analyzes to what extent official papyrus texts reflect the "Attic" norm (that is, Classical Greek). Whereas the frequent use of the perfect infinitive in official papyrus texts cannot be called an influence of Classical Greek, that of the future infinitive may be. Joanne Vera Stolk (ch. 12) concentrates on orthographic variation in documentary sources, which she tries to relate to the register of the text. After proposing a general classification of the different types of documentary sources, she shows that there seem to be convincing correlations between orthography and social context. She argues, however, that there may also be conflicts between orthography and social context, for which the *Sitz im Leben* of the document needs to be taken into account. Emilio Crespo (ch. 13) also studies orthographic variation, but on a much smaller scale, focusing on a single archive, that of the tax collector Nemesion. Crespo poses the question whether the orthographic variation in this archive is best interpreted in terms of idiolect, register, dialect, or sociolect. He argues that we are most likely dealing with a sociolect of Koinè Greek which is characterized by a pronunciation with interference from Coptic. Julie Boeten (ch. 14) discusses metrical variation in a hitherto completely ignored corpus of texts, Byzantine poetic colophons or book epigrams. Focusing on the ἡ μὲν χεὶρ ἡ γράψασα colophon, she argues that metrical variants do not simply represent mistakes by the scribe. Referring to the notion of "information unit", she suggests that the stringing together of units was, perhaps, deemed more important than the resulting number of syllables. Staffan Wahlgren (ch. 15) takes into account different types of syntactic variation, concerning verb forms, subordination, particles and case syntax. Focusing on the oeuvre of Symeon the Logothete (X CE), Wahlgren analyzes and compares the use of these different linguistic features in descriptive, narrative and argumentative sections. In the final chapter to this volume, Klaas Bentein (ch. 16) also takes a broad approach, by investigating whether variation at the syntactic level should be considered distinct from variation at other linguistic levels. For this purpose, he compares different types of sources from different time periods, proposing a distinction between "user-centered sources" and "observer-centered sources".

References

Agha, A. 2007. *Language and social relations: Structure, use and social significance.* Cambridge: Cambridge University Press.
Ammon, Ulrich, Norbert Dittmar, Klaus J. Mattheier & Peter Trudgill (eds.). 2004–2006. *Sociolinguistics: An international handbook of the science of language and society,* 2nd ed. Berlin: de Gruyter.
Auer, Peter & Jürgen Erich Schmidt (eds.). 2010. *Language and space: An international handbook of linguistic variation.* Vol. 1. *Theories and methods.* Berlin: de Gruyter Mouton.
Bain, David. 1984. Female speech in Menander. *Antichthon* 18. 24–42.
Bentein, Klaas. 2013. Register and the diachrony of Post-classical and Early Byzantine Greek. *Revue Belge de Philologie et d'Histoire* 91. 5–44.
Bentein, Klaas. 2015. The Greek of the Fathers. In Ken Perry (ed.), *The Wiley-Blackwell companion to Patristics,* 456–470. Oxford: Wiley-Blackwell.
Bentein, Klaas, Mark Janse & Jorie Soltic (eds.). 2017. *Variation and change in Ancient Greek tense, aspect and modality.* Leiden: Brill.
Berruto, Gaetano. 1987. *Sociolinguistica dell'italiano contemporaneo.* Roma: Carocci.
Berruto, Gaetano. 1993. Varietà diamesiche, diastratiche, diafasiche. In Antonio A. Sobrero (ed.), *Introduzione all'italiano contemporaneo,* 37–92. Bari: Laterza.
Berruto, G. 2004. Sprachvarietät – Sprache (Gesamtsprache, historische Sprache). In Ulrich Ammon, Norbert Dittmar, Klaus J. Mattheier & Peter Trudgill (eds.), *Sociolinguistics: An international handbook of the science of language and society,* 2nd ed. (2004–2006), vol. 1, 188–195. Berlin: de Gruyter.
Biber, Douglas. 1994. An analytical framework for register studies. In Douglas Biber & Edward Finegan (eds.), *Sociolinguistic perspectives on register,* 31–56. Oxford: Oxford University Press.
Browning, Robert. 1983. *Medieval and Modern Greek,* 2nd ed. Cambridge: Cambridge University Press.
Clackson, James. 2015. *Language and society in the Greek and Roman worlds.* Cambridge: Cambridge University Press.
Coseriu, Eugenio. 1969. *Einführung in die strukturelle Linguistik.* Tübingen: Narr.
Coseriu, Eugenio. 1980. 'Historische Sprache' und 'Dialekt'. In Joachim Göschel, Pavle Ivic & Kurt Kehr (eds.), *Dialekt und Dialektologie: Ergebnisse des Internationalen Symposions 'Zur Theorie des Dialekts', Marburg/Lahn, 5–10 September 1977,* 106–122. Wiesbaden: Steiner.
Cuomo, Andrea Massimo. 2017. Medieval textbooks as a major source for historical sociolinguistic studies of (high register) Medieval Greek. *Open Linguistics* 3. 442–455.
Dickey, Eleanor. 1996. *Greek forms of address: From Herodotus to Lucian.* Oxford: Oxford University Press.
Dittmar, Norbert. 1997. *Grundlagen der Soziolinguistik.* Tübingen: Narr.

Eijk, Philip J. van der. 1997. Towards a rhetoric of ancient scientific discourse. In Egbert
    J. Bakker (ed.), *Grammar as interpretation: Greek literature in its linguistic contexts*,
    77–129. Leiden: Brill.
Evans, Trevor V. & Dirk D. Obbink (eds.). 2010. *The language of the papyri*. Oxford: Oxford
    University Press.
Evans, Trevor V. 2015. Idiolect and aspectual choice in Ancient Greek: Evidence from the
    Zenon Archive and the Greek Pentateuch. In James K. Aitken & Trevor V. Evans (eds.),
    Biblical Greek in context: essays in honour of John A. L. Lee, 59–90. Leuven: Peeters.
Fögen, Torsten. 2010. Female speech. In Egbert J. Bakker (ed.), *A companion to the Ancient
    Greek language*, 311–326. Malden: Wiley-Blackwell.
Gumperz, John J. 1982. *Discourse strategies*. Cambridge: Cambridge University Press.
Halla-aho, Hilla. 2010. Linguistic varieties and language level in Latin non-literary letters. In
    Trevor V. Evans & Dirk D. Obbink (eds.), *The language of the papyri*, 171–183. Oxford:
    Oxford University Press.
Halliday, M.A.K. 1978. *Language as social semiotic: The social interpretation of language and
    meaning*. London: Arnold.
Hinterberger, Martin (ed.). 2014. *The language of Byzantine learned literature*. Turnhout:
    Brepols.
Horrocks, Geoffrey C. 2007. Syntax: from Classical Greek to the Koine. In A.-F. Christidis (ed.),
    A history of Ancient Greek: From the beginnings to Late Antiquity, 618–631. Cambridge:
    Cambridge University Press.
Horrocks, Geoffrey C. 2010. *Greek: A history of the language and its speakers*, 2nd ed. Malden:
    Wiley-Blackwell.
Hudson, Richard A. 1996. *Sociolinguistics*, 2nd ed. Cambridge: Cambridge University Press.
Hymes, Dell H. 1974. *Foundations in sociolinguistics: An ethnographic approach*. Philadelphia:
    University of Pennsylvania Press.
James, Patrick. 2014. Papyri, language of. *EAGLL* [online edition].
Janse, Mark. 2007. The Greek of the New Testament. In A.-F. Christidis (ed.), *A history of
    Ancient Greek: From the beginnings to Late Antiquity*, 646–653. Cambridge: Cambridge
    University Press.
Janse, Mark. 2014. Aischrology. *EAGLL* [online edition].
Janse, Mark. 2020. The sociolinguistic study of Ancient Greek and Latin. *Arctos* 54, in press.
Joseph, Brian D. 2000. Textual authenticity: Evidence from Medieval Greek. In Susan
    C. Herring, Pieter van Reenen & Lene Schøsler (eds.), *Textual parameters in older
    languages*, 309–29. Amsterdam: Benjamins.
Kiesling, Scott F. 2011. *Linguistic variation and change*. Edingburgh: Edinburgh University
    Press.
Klein, Wolfgang. 1976. Sprachliche Variation. *Studium Linguistik* 1. 29–46.
Labov, William. 1994–2010. *Principles of linguistic change*. Vol. 1–3. Malden: Blackwell.
Lange, Claudia, Beatrix Weber & Göran Wolf. 2012. Introduction. In Claudia Lange, Beatrix
    Weber & Göran Wolf (eds.), *Communicative spaces: Variation, contact, and change:
    Papers in honour of Ursula Schaefer*, 1–6. Frankfurt am Main: Lang.
Lavandera, Beatriz. 1978. Where does the sociolinguistic variable stop? *Language in Society* 7.
    171–182.
Leiwo, Martti. 2017. Confusion of moods in Greek private letters of Roman Egypt. In Klaas
    Bentein, Mark Janse & Jorie Soltic (eds.), *Variation and change in Ancient Greek tense,
    aspect and modality*, 242–260. Leiden: Brill.

Leiwo, Martti, Hilla Halla-aho & Marja Vierros (eds.). 2012. *Variation and change in Greek and Latin*. Helsinki: Suomen Ateenan-Instituutin säätiö.
López Eire, Antonio. 1996. *La lengua coloquial de la comedia aristofánica*. Murcia: Universidad de Murcia.
Lüdtke, Jens & Klaus J. Mattheier. 2005. Variation – Varietäten – Standardsprachen. Wege für die Forschung. In Alexandra N. Lenz & Klaus J. Mattheier (eds.), *Varietäten – Theorie und Empirie*, 13–38. Frankfurt am Main: Lang.
Luiselli, Raffaele. 2010. Authorial revision of linguistic style in Greek papyrus letters and petitions (AD I–IV). In Trevor V. Evans & Dirk D. Obbink (eds.), *The language of the papyri*, 71–96. Oxford: Oxford University Press.
Nabrings, Kirsten. 1981. *Sprachliche Varietäten*. Tübingen: Narr.
Nachtergaele, Delphine. 2015. Three new letters in the Thermouthas dossier. *Mnemosyne* 68, 53–67.
Oksaar, Els. 2000. Idiolekt als Grundlage der variationsorientierten Linguistik. *Sociolinguistica* 14, 37–42.
Schironi, Francesca. 2010. Technical languages: Science and medicine. In Egbert J. Bakker (ed.), *A companion to the Ancient Greek language*, 338–353. Malden: Wiley-Blackwell.
Sinner, Carsten. 2013. *Varietätenlinguistik: eine Einführung*. Tübingen: Narr.
Thesleff, Holger. 1967. *Studies in the styles of Plato*. Helsinki: Societas Philosophica Fennica.
Trenkner, Sophie. 1960. *Le style καί dans le récit attique oral*. Asse: van Gorcumn.
Walker, James A. 2010. *Variation in linguistic systems*. New York: Routledge.
Willi, Andreas. 2003. *The languages of Aristophanes: Aspects of linguistic variation in Classical Attic Greek*. Oxford: Oxford University Press.

Part I: **VARIETIES OF POST-CLASSICAL AND BYZANTINE GREEK**

Martti Leiwo
2 Tracking down lects in Roman Egypt

Abstract: This paper deals with different varieties of Greek in Egypt setting them in their social and linguistic context and identifying their distinctive characteristics. It offers a description of chosen varieties in a given context explaining the language usage and common features of the variety. In addition to this, the paper combines extra-linguistic contextual information with language usage.

The scribes had diverse educational backgrounds and the documents had different functions, which had an impact on the linguistic output. Different educational background produced variation even inside the same genre and register. The overall analysis ultimately seeks to illustrate and understand the rate of language change in various linguistic situations. The main areas of study are the Oxyrhynchites and the Fayum area on the one hand and the Eastern Desert on the other, which represent very different linguistic areas. The Fayum with the nearby Nile valley was the most Hellenized area in Egypt, with many L1 Greek speakers. Thus, it is an area where we might expect to meet the highest number of professional Greek L1 scribes. The second area differs both linguistically and contextually from the Fayum and the Nile Valley. The Eastern Desert included a caravan route from the south to the Nile Valley, but there were also military routes with numerous *praesidia*, Roman forts, between the Red Sea and the Nile. The crucial difference between these two areas was the availability of professional scribes. The residents of the *praesidia* either had to write themselves or use anyone who had some writing skills. These Roman forts were lodged by many L2 Greek speakers, for whom their L1 produced contact-induced effects when writing L2 Greek.

> "It is useful to have a term for any variety of a language which can be identified in a speech community – whether this be on personal, regional, social, occupational, or other grounds" (Crystal 1997: 24)

1 Introduction

I will deal with different varieties of Greek in Egypt, and set them in their social and linguistic context, identifying their distinctive characteristics, and, ultimately, giving them a label, using the concept of "lect".[1] By choosing to name them lects, however, I do not mean to take a stand on methodological or terminological discussions, but rather to offer an easy description of a variety, if that seems reasonable in a given context, thus explaining the language usage and common features of the variety.[2] In addition to this, the paper aims, as far as possible, to combine extra-linguistic contextual information with situated and dynamic language usage.[3] The scribes working in the speech communities had diverse educational backgrounds and the documents written in the communities had different functions, which means that all of this had an impact on the linguistic output. Different educational background produced variation even inside the same genre and register. The overall analysis ultimately seeks to illustrate and understand the rate of language change, proceeding from individual to general language usage. I am interested in all linguistic levels, but my focus is on phonology and morphology, especially seen through the lens of orthography.

In the study of variation and ongoing changes of Greek in Egypt, the existence of a special Egyptian variety of Greek has been suggested.[4] Following this idea, Sonja Dahlgren (2016) has investigated the phonology of Greek in Egypt, where she indeed has found evidence for an Egyptian Greek variety. As a side path of my main topics, I will also try to find additional support for this in my data. As a whole, I will focus on documentary varieties, combining linguistic analysis with extra-linguistic context. The main areas are the Oxyrhynchites and the Fayum area on one side and the Eastern Desert on the other, which represent very different linguistic areas.

My starting point is the assumption that individuals are essential in a sociolinguistic study of language, as their language use may uncover practices which cannot be seen to happen systematically in every register. But at the same time "this unique object, the individual speaker, can only be understood as the product of a unique social history, and the intersection of the linguistic patterns of all the social groups and categories that define that individual . . . However, each individual shows a personal profile of the comparative use of resources made available by the speech community." (Labov 2001: 34).

---

[1] This contribution has been written within the project "Act of the Scribe: Transmitting Linguistic Knowledge and Scribal Practices in Graeco-Roman Antiquity" funded by the Academy of Finland (287386). I would like to express my gratitude to Mark Shackleton for the revision of my English.
[2] I am unwilling to participate in the terminological discussion, but I am well aware of it. My aim is to use such terminology that does not need special knowledge of any specific linguistic theory. More information can be obtained from, e.g., Trudgill (2003, 2011), Eggins (2004), Bentein (2015); see also Willi (2017) for register variation in Greek.
[3] See also Bubenik (2014: 1.a).
[4] Horrocks (2010: 111–113).

There is no doubt that ancient authors knew and understood sociolinguistic registers,[5] and as evidence we can quote, e.g. Aristotle and Isidorus. Aristotle commented, among others:[6]

(1) οὐ γὰρ ταὐτὰ οὐδ' ὡσαύτως ἀγροῖκος ἂν καὶ πεπαιδευμένος εἴπειεν

'for the uneducated man would not say the same things and in the same way as the educated'
(Aristot., *Rh.* 1480a; IV BCE)

More than nine hundred years later Isidorus (ca. 560–636 CE) used almost the exact words with which Lasswell (1948) and Fishman (1965) brought social context into the study of communication and linguistics:

(2) *In quo genere dictionis illa sunt maxime cogitanda, quis loquatur et apud quem, de quo et ubi et quo tempore.*

'In all kinds of speech, one has to observe especially these things: *who speaks and in what situation, about what, where and when.*'
(Isid., *Orig.* 2.14.1–2)

Compare Isidorus' comment on the maxims of the first modern communication theory by Lasswell (1948): "Who says what in which channel to whom with what effect?" and to Fishman's legendary paper (1965): "Who speaks what language to whom and when?" Isidorus (together with earlier rhetoricians) knew, it seems, almost exactly the role of communication and its sociolinguistic aspects. Thus, from the late fifth century BCE onwards, in advanced rhetorical teaching, registers were indeed appreciated. This can also be seen in various corrections that scribes themselves made to their text.[7] In the examples below the corrections above the line are marked like this: \ὅλως/. Therefore, we can obtain more linguistic information if we are able to observe and take into account several questions before tackling linguistic analysis or any kind of theoretical approach. Among the most important questions are, in my opinion, the following:
- Who was responsible for the language of the document?
- What is the standard with which a given document is written and to what should it be compared?
- What deviations from the (pre-defined) standard exist and what are the potential reasons behind nonstandard variants (apart from simple faults)?

---

5 Cf. Müller (2001: 17–18); Willi (2017: 261–262).
6 Translations are mine, if not otherwise stated.
7 See e.g. Luiselli (2010: 72).

- Is there an internal change in process, or can the variation be contact-induced, or both at the same time?
- If contact-induced variation can be observed, what is the native language of the writer and could the variety in question be characterized as an ethnolect?
- What linguistic clues directly point to general scribal usage – a doculect – versus individual usage – an idiolect?
- Can we make a typology of identified hands and their linguistic identities?
- And, finally, are there significant differences between drafts, copies and originals, and if so, can these be traced?

It is obvious that not all of these questions can be answered in the course of the study, but in my view they should be considered on every single occasion. It must be also emphasized that many editors provide a great deal of useful information in their editions about papyri, ostraka and tablets. Below I will, at first, outline the social setting in Egypt regarding linguistic attitudes, writing and language use.

2 Ethnic practices and attitudes

2.1 Egyptian or Greek scribes?

In early documents Greek written with a typical instrument for Demotic writing, a brush-like rush, meant that the writer was Egyptian. However, after 230 BCE, the use of a brush in writing Greek was quickly abandoned.[8] This signified that even Egyptians used the *kalamos* in writing Greek, so there was no external difference in writing anymore, and the L1 of the scribe could not be surmised from the strokes of the letters. But even if technical equipment was standardized, prejudice and discrimination seemed to prevail in social and political discourse. The attitudes set up ethnic stereotypes, as we can see by Aristophanes of Byzantion: ἐθνῶν μὲν οἷον κιλικίζειν καὶ αἰγυπτιάζειν τὸ πονηρεύεσθαι, καὶ κρητίζειν τὸ ψεύδεσθαι 'of ethnic names, for example "to Cilicize" and "to Egyptianize" mean "to be a crook", and "to Cretanize" is "to lie"' (*fr.* 24).

Imperfect command of Greek combined with foreign looks were also reasons for discrimination, at least during the Hellenistic period. A famous example of discrimination is a complaint of racist treatment:

(3) ἀλλὰ κατεγνώκασίμ μου ὅτι εἰμὶ βάρβαρος. δέομαι οὖν σου \εἴ σοι δοκεῖ/ συντάξαι αὐτοῖς ὅπως τὰ ὀφειλόμενα κομίσωμαι καὶ τοῦ λοιποῦ εὐτάκτωσίν μοι ἵνα μὴ τῶι

---

[8] Clarysse (1993: 190, 193).

λιμῶι παραπόλωμαι ὅτι οὐκ ἐπίσταμαι ἑλληνίζειν. σὺ ο\ὖ/ν καλῶς ἂν ποιήσαις ἐπιστροφήν μου ποιησάμενος.

'They have treated me with scorn *because I am a foreigner*. I beg you therefore, if it seems good to you, to give them orders that I am to obtain what is owing and that in future they pay me in full, in order that I may not perish of hunger, *because I do not know how to act the Hellene*. Please, therefore, kindly cause a change in attitude toward me.'
(P.Col. IV 66 = Zenon papyri; 256–255 BCE. [Editors' translation])

The editors, Westermann, Keyes and Liebesny (1940: 16–17), comment on this passage: "his connection with the camels suggesting he was an Arab... In its grammatical structure the letter is not bad, and the writer certainly had some knowledge of an official complaint (*enteuksis*). Nevertheless, the letter cannot be that of a scribe, who would have followed a better word order and would have avoided the repetition of simple phrases which is here so noticeable." I agree with the editors that the letter is not written by a professional scribe, but if the sender wrote it himself, he had quite a good command of the register needed for such a document. A few corrections made by the writer, e.g. awareness of expressions of politeness adding εἴ σοι δοκεῖ 'if it seems good for you' above the line as well as correcting an incorrect spelling from ον to ο\ὖ/ν 'so', in basically a good standard style of complaint clearly show that the variety is not an "ethnolect", even if the writer may be writing in his L2.

2.2 Varieties at Oxyrhynchites and the Fayum

The Fayum with the nearby Nile valley was the most Hellenized area in Egypt, with many L1 Greek speakers.[9] Thus, it is an area where we might expect to meet the highest number of L1 Greek speakers as well as good professional Greek scribes. This, in fact, can be clearly seen in the documents. In this area, we can identify a great deal of variation between formal, informal and "colloquial" registers.[10] All registers show, it would seem, little effect of language contact unlike areas further south and east, but there are marks of internal

---

9 See e.g. Lewis (1983).
10 For concepts such as "formal" or "colloquial" see Dickey (2010: 3–6), Clackson (2010: 7–11). I use the term "colloquial" here to denote a variety that shows signs of phonetic spellings and obvious uncertainty with Classic Attic orthography.

ongoing changes, especially vowel-raising. An example of a very refined bureaucratic variety, real officialese, is (4), a proclamation of a *strategos*:

(4) Αὐρήλιος Ποσειδώ-
νιος στρα(τηγὸς) Ὀξυρυγχ(ίτου)·
παραγγέλλεται τοῖς
ἀπὸ τῶν μελλόντων
λειτουργεῖν τῷ εἰσιόν-   5
τι ἔτει ἀμφόδων συν-
ελθε[ῖ]ν σήμερον ἐν
τῷ συνήθει τόπῳ κα[ὶ]
ὀνομάσαι ὃν ἐὰν αἱρῶν-
ται φύλαρχον ὄ[ν]τα   10
εὔπορον καὶ ἐπιτήδει-
ον κατὰ τὰ κελευ-
σθέντα ὑπὸ τῶν τὸ
ἀπότακτον συστη-
σαμένων, πρ[ὸ]ς τὸ   15
δύνασθαι αὐτὸν
τοῦ χρόνου ἐνστάν-
τος ὑγιῶς καὶ πιστῶς
ἀντιλαβέσθαι τῆς
λειτουργίας.   20

'From Aurelius Posidonius, strategus of the Oxyrynchite nome. Notice is given to the inhabitants of the quarters about to serve in the coming year to assemble today at the accustomed place and to name whomever they choose as phylarch, being a person of means and suited for the post in accordance with the orders of those who constituted the appointed office (?) in order that when the time comes he may be able to perform the duty honestly and faithfully. . .'
(P.Oxy. IX 1187, Oxyrhynchus; 254 CE) [tr. A. Hunt]

This is typical officialese, which is orthographically immaculate. The notice consists of one syntactically well-governed sentence. It is constructed around the only finite verb, παραγγέλλεται 'it is announced', with well-built but rigid syntax. When compared to the common unofficial letter register, the difference is considerable as can be seen in examples (5), (6) and (7).

Example (5) is a letter dated to the reign of Tiberius.[11] The sender was Hermogenes, who addressed his letter to a prophet called Haryetes. The letter shows phonetic spellings with internal vowel change typical of many private documents, basically with variation in spelling the phonemes /i/ and /e/ as well

---

[11] Cf. Grenfell & Hunt (P.Oxy. XII, 1916: 238): "An incorrectly spelled letter, written in the reign of Tiberius to a prophet by a friend."

as preferring the Attic variant ποέω rather than ποιέω 'I do'.¹² A very typical variation in this area is uncertainty in writing the phoneme that was depicted by the letters υ <y> and οι <oi>. This graphic uncertainty is due to the merger of the phonemes represented by these letters, thus creating a sound that did not have its own letter.¹³ The phoneme behind these letters is not of interest here, but it produced serious difficulties to many scribes in this area.¹⁴

Above some lines the writer has also corrected a few misspellings, e.g. Τιβεροω to Τιβεριου 'of Tiberius', thus revealing that correct spelling was important for the scribe. The letter was written more than two hundred years earlier than (4), clearly indicating that the date alone is not always a useful criterion for analysing the rate of linguistic change from Greek documents. The scribe, the social context, the register and the genre all play a crucial role in the analysis, whereas the date often has more to do with phraseological than with grammatical changes:

(5) Ἑρμογένης Ἁρυώτῃ
τῷ προφήτῃ καὶ φιλ-
τάτῳ πλῖστα χαί(ρειν)
καὶ διὰ παντὸς ὑγιε(νειν).
οὐκ ἠμέλησα περὶ   5
οὗ μοι ἐπιτέταχας.
ἐπορεύθην πρὸς
Ἑρμογένην τὸν κω-
μογρ[α]μματέαν, καὶ
ὁμολόγησέ μοι ποῆσε   10
τὴν ἀναβολήν. πεπόη-
τε εἰς τὸν ἐκλογιστήν.
λυπὸν ἠὰν δύνῃ ἐ[π]ισ-
τολὴν λαβῖν παρ' αὐ-
τοῦ τοῦ ἐκλογισ[τοῦ]   15
ὡς Ἑρμογένει, ἵν[α]
μὴ σχῇ τ[. . .]..[. . .]

'Hermogenes to Haryotes the prophet, my dear friend, greeting and best wishes for your continual health. I did not neglect your instructions: I went to Hermogenes the komogrammateus, and he consented to make a delay. He has made it as far as the eklogistes is concerned (?). For the rest, if you can get a letter from the eklogistes himself for Hermogenes, in order that he may not keep the . . .'
(P.Oxy. XII 1480 = White 1986: no. 81; Oxyrhynchus; 32 CE) [tr. Grenfell]

---

12 Cf. Mayser-Schmoll (87–88); see also Clarysse (2010: 40–41).
13 Cf. Mayser-Schmoll (89–90); Horrocks (2010: 162–163); Bubenik (2014: 3b); Dahlgren (2016: 81–82).
14 Cf. ex. (5) l. 13 λυπόν ~ λοιπόν. For the phoneme, see Horrocks (2010: 167), Dahlgren (2016: 81–82).

I continue with the same genre, a letter, but in a different register. A competent scribe wrote (6), which is a letter written in familiar register from a son, Theonas, to his mother, Tetheus.[15] The scribe has copied the lively and casual style of the son, although taking care that the letter is otherwise formally correct although it has some spelling variation, such as, for example, ἤμι (εἰμι) 'I am', λοιποῦ (λυποῦ) 'do not grieve' and ἐλοιπήθην (ἐλυπήθην) 'I was grieved':

> (6) Θεωνᾶς Τεθεῦτι τῆι μητρὶ καὶ κυρίᾳ πλεῖστα χαί(ρειν).
> γεινώσκειν σ[ε] θέλω ὅτι διὰ τοσούτου χρόνου οὐκ ἀ-
> πέσταλκά σοι ἐπιστόλιον διότι ἐν παρεμβολῇ ἤμι καὶ
> οὐ δι' ἀσθένε[ι]αν, ὥστε μὴ λοιποῦ. λείαν δ' ἐλοιπήθην
> ἀκούσας ὅτι ἤκουσας. οὐ γὰρ δεινῶς ἠσθένησα. μέμ-   5
> φομαι δὲ τὸν εἴπαντα σοι. μὴ ὀχλοῦ δὲ πέμπειν τι ἡ-
> μῖν. ἐκομισάμεθα δὲ τὰ θαλλία παρὰ τοῦ {τοῦ} Ἡρακλεί-
> δου. Διονυτᾶς δὲ ὁ ἀδελφός μου ἤνεγκέ μοι τὸν θαλ-
> λὸν κα[ὶ τὴν] ἐπιστολήν [σου] ἐ[κο]μισά[μ]ην.

> 'Theonas to Tetheus his lady mother, many greetings. I would have you know that the reason why I have been such a long time without sending you a letter is that I am in camp, and not that I am ill; so do not grieve about me. I was much grieved to hear that you heard about me, for I was not seriously ill; and I blame the person who told you. Do not trouble to send me anything. I received the presents from Heraclides. Dionytas my brother brought me the present, and I received your letter.'
> (P.Oxy. XII 1481 = White 1986: no. 102; Oxyrhynchus; II CE) [tr. Grenfell]

The scribe has unquestionable improved the syntax of this letter, twice with participles in lines 5 and 6, ἀκούσας 'having heard', τὸν εἴπαντα 'the one who has told' (see also Vierros, this volume). The accusative singular of the latter participle is a Great Attic Koiné innovation and has been levelled to the paradigm of the aorist 1 (weak aorist) with the vowel /a/ instead of /o/, creating εἴπας (Nom.), εἴπαντα (Acc.) rather than εἰπών, εἰπόντα.[16] The editors did not comment on the form at all. There are a few similar examples of this verb, all from Oxyrynchites. P.Mich. XVIII 774 is a very early complaint (193/4 BCE) that has a participle εἰπάντων, showing that paradigm levelling was going on during the Hellenistic period. A later, but even more interesting example is P.Alex. 28, l. 22 (III CE), which has the aorist indicative 1st person εἶπαν (standard εἶπον) with the letter η <ê>, but the vowel /a/ by analogy to the sigmatic aorist -σα 'I said', as well as a levelled ἠμῆν (standard Attic ἦν) 'I was' with the regular ending -μην of the imperfect 1st

---

15 See also Clarysse (2017: 67) about the expression of emotions in this letter.
16 See e.g. Bubenik (2014: 1c–d, 2c).

person. The last example is in a collection of four *Hypomnematismoi* (SB XIV 12139; II–III CE), in this case briefings for a judge offered as precedents supporting a desired judgment. Their register is official and the orthography is quite good, but the aorist indicative, third person plural, is εἶπαν (standard εἶπον) 'they said'. In this case the form is corrected to εἶπον in the apparatus.

Another interesting form is ἤμι (l. 3) for εἰμι. Through a search with Paratypa[17] I found only three other examples of this spelling, of which two were in the same letter (P.Tebt. II 420, l. 4 and l. 26; III CE) and one was in an account of property of a woman (BGU IV 1069, l. 8; 243/4 CE), both from the Fayum area. As these four attestations are geographically close with each other, there is a slight possibility that the spelling reflects a dialectal pronunciation.

An example of a private letter that has probably been written by the sender himself is example (7). The sender is obviously not a professional scribe, as can be seen from the spelling. The editors, Grenfell and Hunt (1916: 241), comment: "On the verso is a letter to the same Epimachus from a friend called Morus, who together with Panares had been winnowing some barley under difficulties caused by the weather. The script is the rude uncial of an illiterate writer, who makes numerous mistakes of spelling in spite of several corrections." This comment is typical of many early editions, but here we should be more accurate and analytical. First, the writer is not illiterate, quite the opposite in fact, as he is quite expressive in lines 6 and 7. He also knows how to write quite fluently, having minor difficulties though in combining phonology/phonetics and accurate spelling. Accordingly, he has made several corrections above the line aiming at standard Hellenistic Koiné. This ambition to correct spellings is a clear sign that the writer is conscious of the importance of orthography:

(7) Μῶρος Ἐπιμάχῳ τῶι κυρίωι μου
χαίρειν.
γράφω σοι ἵν' ἰδῇς ὅτι λελικμήκαμεν
τὴν κριθὴν τοῦ Αὐασίτου τῇ η, καὶ οὐ
οὕτως αὐτὴν λελικμήκαμεν μετὰ   5
κόπου. ὁ Ζεὺς γὰρ ἔβρεχε καὶ ἀμάχητος
ἦν ὁ ἄνεμος, καὶ Πάρες οἶδε ὅσα πεποκα-
μεν \ἵ/να εἰσχύσωμεν \ὅλως/ μετενέγκαι τὰ ἄλλα
σὺν θεοῖς. ἐξέβησαν δὲ \τοῦ ὅλου/ ἀρτάβαι λη χυνικε δ·
τ<ο>ύτων κατέφθακα ἀρτάβας ιβ χύνικα(ς) η.   10

---

17 papygreek.hum.helsinki.fi

ἐξήτασα δὲ περὶ τῆς θειμῆς τοῦ χόρτου
τοῦ ἐφετινοῦ, ἐπράθη δ\ὲ/ ἐν τῇ κώμῃ ἐξ
ἑπτὰ δραχμῶν τὸ ἀγώγιν. καὶ Πάρες δὲ
οἶδε. πολλὰ δὲ ἐκξετάσας εὗρον ξη[ρὰ]
καὶ οὐκ εὐθύχαλκα, ἀλλὰ μετὰ τετρά- 15
μηνον. δοκιμάσις δὲ [σὺ] πῶς σε βαστα-
ζι καὶ ἂν σύ δοκῇ γράψις μοι περὶ τούτων,
καὶ πόστον μέρος καταφθάνω τοῦ μεγάλου
κληρου\ς/, καὶ ἡ θέλις μεῖξαι [αὐ]τὰ τοῦ Αὐασίτου μετὰ τῶν ἄλλων. ἐν τῷ δὲ τόπῳ πα- 20
τρός σου ἀποτέθεικα τὴ\ν/ μερίδαν μου.
τὸ προσκοίνημά συ ποιῶ καὶ τῶν τέκνων
σο̣υ̣ π[ά]ν̣των [καὶ] τ̣ῶν ἀδελφῶ[ν] σο̣υ̣ [πάντων]

'Morus to my lord Epimachus, greeting. I write to inform you that we have winnowed the barley of the man from the Oasis on the 8th, and we never had so much trouble in winnowing it; for it rained and the wind was irresistible, and Panares knows how we worked to succeed in transferring all the rest with the help of the gods. The total result was 38 artabae 4 choenices; of these I have disposed beforehand of 12,5 art. 8 choen. I made inquiries about the price of annual grass: it was sold in the village at 7 drachmae the load, as Panares too knows. After many inquiries I found some that was dry, and not to be paid for in ready money, but after four months. You will examine the question how you are to transport it, and, if you please, write to me about this, and say what proportion I am to dispose of beforehand from the large holding, and whether you want me to mix what belongs to the man from the Oasis with the rest. I have stored my share in the room belonging to your father. I supplicate on behalf of you and all your children and all your brothers'
(P.Oxy. XII 1482, Oxyrynchus; 120–160 CE) [tr. Grenfell]

In addition to the corrections marked above the line, there are several others made on the letter, as well as deletions (marked as ⟦ ⟧); for example ω is corrected from ο, in line 8: εἰσχύσομεν to εἰσχύσωμεν '(in order to) succeed' and the name from Πάρας to Πάρες (of which the correct form is Πανάρης). In addition, εκζητησας 'after many inquiries' (l. 14) is corrected to ἐκξετάσας, and μέρον 'proportion' (l. 18) to μερος, and in line 16 σύ is deleted as well as αυ in the word αὐτά in line 19. We can see that, in addition to corrections, the writer had difficulties even with common spellings, as for example the ει-ι, οι-υ variation, where the writer preferred to choose ει and υ. This latter variation might give a false assumption that the writer did not always use the dative case according to the standard, for example συ = σοι 'to you' with δοκῇ '(if) it seems' in line 17.[18] Also, the second singular personal pronoun συ in line 22 τὸ προσκοίνημά **συ** ποιῶ καὶ τῶν τέκνων σο̣υ π̣[ά]ν̣τω̣ν 'I supplicate on behalf of you and all your children and all your brothers' should be analysed as the dative (=σοι, just as in line 17) rather than the genitive σου, even if the genitive is the standard.[19] As we can see, the dative is used without problems in the letter in line 9 σὺν θεοῖς 'with the help of the gods', line 12 ἐν τῇ κώμῃ 'in the village', and line 20 ἐν τῷ δὲ τόπῳ 'in the room'.

In line 11 the writer has written θειμης instead of τειμης (=τιμῆς) '(of) the price', but although this is typical of Egyptian speakers' L2 Greek, I cannot find other clues of Egyptian Greek variety in the letter. On the contrary, the variety seems to be that of an Egyptian L1 Greek speaker,[20] although not a real expert in style and syntax. However, the writer has good knowledge of verbal morphology, his syntax is fluent, if not even better than many other letter writers. In his linguistic competence, we may note the interchange of the imperfect, the perfect and the aorist indicative, the use of the infinitive (line 8 μετενέγκαι 'to transfer', line 19 μεῖξαι 'to mix') and the use of the subjunctive. One can, finally, note the levelled accusative singular μερίδαν (= μερίδα) 'share' (l. 21) typical of the period.[21]

3 The Eastern Desert and "ostraka culture"

The second area in my analysis differs both linguistically and contextually from the Fayum and the Nile Valley. The Eastern Desert included a caravan route from the south to the Nile Valley, but there were also military routes between the Red Sea and the Nile. Because of the mineral riches in these parts, it was in the Emperor's personal interest to keep the routes safe and, therefore, the

---

18 The line has the dative μοι, and the writer knows that μοι is different from the nominative (ἐγώ), whereas there seems to be no difference in pronunciation between συ and σοι, which makes the confusion obvious.
19 The standard is τὸ προσκύνημά σου ποιῶ, but the writer does not seem to confuse ου <oy> and υ <y>. The editors correct συ to the genitive σ<o>υ, but that seems improbable to me. The dative σοι with the *proskynema* phrase seems to be mostly used in the ostraka of the Eastern Desert, where the speech communities were multilingual (Leiwo 2018), see, for example, O.Claud. II 278; 302 and O.Did. 379; 382 (both by Filokles, see below). Unfortunately, the genitive σου in τῶν τέκνων σο̣υ is not very legible, and has dots under the letters.
20 For example οι <oi> for υ <y>, ἐξήτασα for ἐκζήτασα; cf. Horrocks (2010: 111–113), Dahlgren (2017).
21 Cf. Bubenik (2014: 2c).

Romans developed a strong security system in the area. It is surprising how large the Roman network of roads really was. The results of numerous desert surveys indicate that the Roman route system in the Eastern Desert was elaborate and sophisticated.[22] The roads were unpaved dirt roads, *viae terrenae,* and their width varied from about 5.1 to even 32.3 metres. The widest attested section of road is a short segment near the Mons Porphyrites quarry[23], which has a stunning width of 53m.[24] The road from Myos Hormos by the Red Sea to Koptos by the Nile is about 180 km long and the road from the regional capital Berenike by the Red Sea to Koptos is approximately 380 km.[25] Both roads were strongly fortified and there was a Roman military post or *praesidium* every 30 km along both roads. The soldiers and civilians at these forts communicated by writing on potsherds, *ostraka.* All letter writers along the roads were linked to the Roman army in some respect, and many of them were auxiliaries, i.e. mainly Egyptians during the first and early second century CE, when the mining activity was at its peak.

As regards writing letters, the greatest difference between the Eastern Desert on the one hand and the Fayum and the Nile Valley on the other was the availability of competent scribes. The residents of the *praesidia* either had to write themselves or use anyone who had – even very modest – writing skills. Professional scribes were seldom available. The writing material was almost without exception ostraka rather than papyri.[26] Even *curatores* of the *praesidia* used ostraka. Only the most official correspondence, for instance that with the central administration in Berenike, was written on papyrus. Private use of papyrus was rare, though occasionally there was a need for papyrus as well.[27]

---

22 Sidebotham (2011: 136).
23 It was the only place in the world where imperial porphyry was quarried and then transferred to Rome using titanic machinery.
24 Sidebotham (2011: 138).
25 Sidebotham (2011: 128); cf. Maxfield (2005).
26 Cf. Maxfield (2003).
27 O.Claud. II 239, ll. 1–9 (126–175 CE): Πίσων Ζήνωνι καὶ Ὡρίωνι τοῖς ἀδελφοῖς πολλὰ χαίρειν. προσδέχομαι ὑμᾶς ἐν ταῖς κα[λ]άνδαις. ἵνα οὖν πέμψῃ<ς> μοι μίκκον χαρτάριον καὶ στημόνιν. μὴ ἀμελήσῃς. πέμψον μοι διὰ τοῦ ἀναδίδοντός σοι τὴν ἐπιστολήν. Ὡρίωνι ταῦτα λέγω. ['Piso to Zenon and Horion his brothers, many greetings. I expect you on the first of the month. Send me a bit of papyrus and some string. Don't forget. Send it to me by the person who brings you this letter. This I say to Horion.']. Papyrus was also needed to make a copy of a book, O.Claud. II 299, ll. 5–9 (126–175 CE): καλῶς ποιήσις, ἢάν τὸν χάρτην ἀ[γ]οράσῃς, ἀπελθὼν πρὸς Δίδυμον τὸν καθηγητὴν καὶ δοὺς χαλκὸν ἵνα μεταγράφηταί μοι πέζον λόγον ['please, could you buy papyrus, take the professor to Didymus, and give him money so that he can copy me a prose work.']. See also Cuvigny (2003: 266) (= M1191): καὶ ἐὰν ἔχῃς χάρτης πένψων μοι ὃ ἔλαβες ὅτι

A typical ostrakon letter is written in a fluent hand, but difficulties in spelling and grammar are conspicuous. Only a few of the writers seem to have been professional (army)scribes, the majority were clearly private persons.

According to what we know of the auxiliaries and other residents of the *praesidia*, many letter writers were L2 speakers of Greek: among them Latin, Egyptian, Syrian, Aramaic, Arabic, Nabatean L1 speakers. Naturally, also L1 Greek speakers must have been part of the Roman army, but even they usually had a modest command of standard Attic or Koiné grammar. Some writers always follow their idiolectic spelling (see below), whereas others have much orthographic variation, even in the same letter, but share the same sociolect.

As the extralinguistic context was mainly the Roman army, we encounter many otherwise unattested Latin loans. At Krokodilό, for example, we have new loans in only 151 ostraka: τὰ πουπλικα = τὰ δημόσια 'public taxes' (O.Krok. 70, l. 4; 98–117 CE), οὐεσσιγατου = probably *vestigatum* (the supine) (O.Krok. 74, l. 6; 117–125 CE), σουκεσσορων = *successorum* (O.Krok. 96, ll. 9–10; 98–138 CE).

As it is, there were many non-native Greek speakers, for whom L1 phonology created difficulties when writing L2. L1 could cause difficulties in choosing letters from the L2 alphabet to correspond to those phonemes of L2 that are foreign to the L1 of the writer.[28] The situation clearly favoured an expansion of a contact variety of Greek. The formation of a contact variety, in general, begins with mixing, or with the creation of a feature pool[29] drawn from the language varieties present in the contact environment.[30] Various studies[31] indicate that contact environments are basic to linguistic change, creating a period of rapid change. One of the clearest L1 transfer features from Egyptian to Greek is the

---

χρείαν ἔχω ['and if you have papyrus, send what you get to me, as I need it.']. This letter was sent by Numerios Dioskoros to Felix, curator of the *praesidium* Maximianon.

28 On multilingualism see Fournet (2003: 430): "Victimes d'une véritable schizophrénie linguistique. . . les auxiliaires égyptiens parlent égyptien entre eux, mais doivent correspondre en grec, en tout cas quand ils peuvent maîtriser cette langue. Ils sont même sporadiquement confrontés au latin, qui . . . leur est plus encore étranger. Ce divorce entre langues parlée et écrite explique le très mauvais niveau de langue que manifeste la plus grande partie de notre documentation." ["Victims of a real linguistic schizophrenia . . . the Egyptian auxiliaries speak Egyptian among themselves, but must correspond in Greek, in any case when they can master this language. They are even sporadically confronted with Latin, which . . . is even more foreign to them. This split between spoken and written languages explains the very poor level of language that most of our documentation shows"].

29 The feature pool is "the total set of linguistic variables available to speakers in a contact environment in which a process of competition, selection and exaptation takes place" (Aboh & Ansaldo 2007: 44).

30 Mufwene (2001: 3), Aboh & Ansaldo (2007: 44), Operstein (2015: 4).

31 See Operstein (2015) for references.

merger of voiced and voiceless stops /k, p, t, g, b, d/. The phonetic process behind this merging is underdifferentiation.[32]

Example (8) describes a typical Egyptian variety of Greek, and could, therefore, be called an ethnolect of an Egyptian L2 Greek speaker:

(8) Ἰουλᾶς Λοκρητίῳ
τῷ γυρίῳ χαίριν. κα-
λῶς ποιήσας περὶ οὗ
σε ἠρώτηκα τερματίου
μικρὸν εἰς λαντάλια,   5
τῷ τρεπτῷ σου ποιή-
σον τῇ χάριταν. ἀσπά-
ζομαι Κάσσιν· καλῶς
ποιήσης τῶσις αὐτω,
Λονγίνῳ.

'Ioulas to Lucretius my lord, greetings. Please, could you do what I asked you (and send) some leather for sandals. Do this favour for your servant.[33] I send greetings to Kassis. Please, give this to Longinus.'
(O.Krok. I 73; ca. 109 CE)

This letter reveals various phonological characteristics that are typical of Greek in Egypt. In the first line, the name of the curator of the praesidium Krokodiló, Lucretius, is written with <o> rather than <ου>.[34] The variation between /o/ and /u/ (<ου>) is frequent in Egyptian Greek.[35] In principle, there is a general tendency to transfer native language phonology to L2.[36] It is precisely this tendency that created uncertainty in choosing the right letter for the unstressed /u/ or /o/, even if, in this case, the name Lucretius is a Latin one transcribed into Greek. This becomes clear from the other phonological variation in Ioulas's letter, since we can suggest with confidence that he was an Egyptian who uses Greek as his L2. Gignac (1976: 208) indicates that the majority of attestations of /o, u/ confusion occurs initially and medially, which means that this usage thus follows Coptic phonological rules.[37]

Among the most typical features of Egyptian Greek is the merger of voiced and voiceless stops. In example (8) this merger can be seen with rare clarity: γυρίῳ (κυρίῳ) 'to (my) lord' (l. 2), τερματίου (δερματίου) '(of) leather' (l. 4),

---

[32] Weinreich (1963: 18) lists underdifferentiation among the most frequent contact phenomena.
[33] On the meaning of this sentence see Cuvigny (2003: 370).
[34] Cuvigny (2003: 318).
[35] Gignac (1976: 208), Dahlgren (2017: 83–84).
[36] Clahsen et al. (2010: 22–28).
[37] Dahlgren (2017: 83).

λαντάλια (σανδάλια?) 'sandals' (l. 5), τώσις (δώσεις) 'you will give' (l. 9).³⁸ Since Coptic did not have an opposition between voiced and voiceless stops, they were frequently confused with one another as they represented a single phoneme for Egyptian L1 speakers.³⁹

Another quite common contact-induced variation is that between aspirated and unaspirated stops, here τρεππτῷ (θρεπτῷ) 'to (your) servant' (l. 6).⁴⁰ There is also another example from Krokodiló, the feminine τρεππτῇ (Cuvigny 2003: 371, K527). It seems that, at first, voiceless aspirates did not change into fricatives in L1 Greek in Egypt, though voiced plosives did, and the overall change to fricatives was, it seems, completed only by the 3rd/4th century CE.⁴¹ There is still one further variation worth discussing. The politeness formula καλῶς ποιήσεις 'please' is first written as καλῶς ποιήσας (l. 2–3) and then καλῶς ποιήσῃς (l. 8–9). In lines 2–3 he seems to be uncertain about the syntax of this politeness formula, using what looks like the aorist participle (ποιήσας). The standard syntactic construction of the idiom is καλῶς ποιήσεις + the aorist participle.⁴² However, the unstressed vowel was subject to contact-induced variation and may not have any morphological substance.⁴³ Also, the variation of ι <i>, ει <ei> and η <ê> is problematic, and may reflect language internal and contact-induced facts.⁴⁴ There is, therefore, no reason to suggest a modal confusion between the future indicative and the aorist subjunctive in the use of the form ποιήσῃς (in standard orthography ποιήσῃς is the aorist subjunctive). To me, this variation is phonological. Other linguistic variation in this letter is common elsewhere and is not specifically due to Egyptian contact or to being an ethnolect.

Above I have discussed varieties that belong to a certain genre, private letters, and show variation within the genre. I will now attempt to find varieties that might show more idiolectic language use, although this is possible only if there are enough letters that are written in the same hand. To trace these, one either has to have an autopsy as well as sufficient skills for an analysis of different hands, or to look for information given in editors' comments on handwriting.

---

38 The editor, Cuvigny, suggests a correction to δούς, but I prefer to keep τώσις (= δώσεις) αὐτὸ; cf. Leiwo (2010: 105, 112–113), Gonis (2009: 218).
39 Gignac (1976: 77), Horrocks (2010: 112), Dahlgren (2017: 58).
40 Horrocks (2010: 112).
41 Horrocks (2010: 170).
42 Leiwo (2010: 99–101).
43 Cf. Dahlgren (2017: 59–66).
44 For a detailed discussion see Dahlgren (2017: 103–104).

Fortunately, the editors have, indeed, suggested that some ostraka letters have been written by the same person. Even if their number is not very large, there are at least some that can give us hints about idiolectic usages. I have earlier dealt with two writers, Dioskoros and Petenephotes, both at Mons Claudianus (O.Claud. 224–242; O.Claud. 243–254, respectively; 126–175 CE), who seem to use idiolectic language.[45] Dioskoros had a trained hand, but a lot of morpho-syntactic non-standard idiosyncrasies. Petenephotes, for his part, had difficulties in writing unstressed vowels, thus creating what seems to be a modal confusion in the verb system.[46] Even other writers, however, had similar idiosyncrasies, but perhaps not as much the same ones as, for example, these two. A further example of another type of personal touch in the language usage is a letter by Longinus about money, transmission and rent concerning Sarapias, a prostitute:

(9) ἀπόδος Ἀπολιναρίῳ.
　　Λονγεῖνος Ἀπολιναρίῳ
　　Ἀπολιναρίῳ τῷ ἀδελφῷ μου
　　καὶ κυρίῳ πλῖστα χ(αίρειν) καὶ διὰ παντὸς
　　ὑγ<έ>νι<ν>. καλῶς ποιήςις, κύρι ἀδελφέ μου,　　5
　　πέμψον μοι Σαραπιᾶτι μετὰ Τιβεριᾶτι
　　ὅτι χρηςω αὐτήν. ἰ μὲν θέλις ἀφῖνε
　　αὐτὴν σατων ὥλων τὸν μῆνον, ἄφες
　　καὶ οὐδέν ἐστι χαλκόν. ἰ μὲν θέλις αὐτὴν
　　μισθῶσε παρὰ σέν, πέμψον μοι τὰς (δραχμὰς) οε　　10
　　καὶ γράψον μοι ὅτι ἔχω αὐτὴν ὡς ἐπίτρωπον.
　　ἰ μὲν εὕρηκες μίσθωμα αὐτὴν ἰς Διδύμους,
　　ἀσφάλισον σατω λίαν παρὰ πιστὸν ἄνθρωπο<ν>
　　ἵνα μὴ αὐτὴν ὑβρίςουσιν. ἐὰν ποιήςις μοι
　　μίκκόν τι, ἀνδαποδώςω σοι καὶ πάντοτε　　15
　　ἔχω τὴν ἐξουσίαν σου ὡς ἀδελφόν.
　　γράψον μοι περὶ τῆς σωτηρίας σου
　　ἀσπάςον Μάξιμος καὶ Τιβεριατ( )
　　καὶ Σκνῖφις καὶ Βαρβάραν.
　　ἔρρωσω　　　　　　　　　　　　20

'Give to Apollonaris. Longinus Apollinaris to Apollinaris, my brother and lord, many greetings and well-being forever. Please, my lord brother, send me Sarapias with Tiberias, because I need her. If you wish to send her away before the whole month is over, send her, and there will be no charge. If you wish to keep her hired by you, send me 75 drachmas, and write to me that "I have her as an executor." If you find her a job and a price at Didymoi, make it sure in front of a very reliable man that no violence is done to her. If you do me this small favour, I'll give it back to you, and I

---

45 Cf. Leiwo (2003: 83–84; 2005: 248–261; 2017: 255–258).
46 See Leiwo (2017).

will have your excellency as a brother forever. Write to me about your health. Greet Maksimos, Tiberias, Sknips and Barbara for me. Good health'
(Krokodiló, K227; Cuvigny 2003, 385; early II CE)

The same hand, probably that of Longinus Apollinaris himself, wrote several letters from Krokodiló and one from Persou.[47] The most striking phenomenon in his language use is his habit of taking a particular case for a personal name and subsequently always using it in the same case. It is quite common in ostraka letters not to inflect personal names, but to use only the nominative.[48] Longinus, however, used whatever case he encountered somewhere. In (9) the names Ἀπολιναρίῳ (l. 2, dative instead of nominative), Cαραπιᾶτι, Τιβεριᾶτι (both l. 6, dative instead of accusative), Μάξιμος, Τιβεριατ(ι) (both l. 18, nominative and dative instead of accusative,) Cκνῖφιc (l. 19, nominative instead of accusative), Βαρβάραν (l. 19, an accusative as it should be) have been taken as such, without any relation to phrase syntax. This habit is quite extraordinary, and according to H. Cuvigny (2003: 386) such idiosyncrasy is typical of Longinus.

The names in the letter connect Longinus to the circle of a certain Philokles, a pimp and businessman, active in Krokodiló and Didymoi.[49] Philokles was closely connected to the woman here mentioned – spelled Cκνῖφιc (Sknifis) – who probably was, for some time, his wife.[50] There is a great deal of variation in Philokles's spelling of this name. In the salutary formula of his letters we find the following: Φιλοκλῆc Cκιπν/Cκιφι/Cπιν (Skipn, Skiphi, Spin). The normal case in the salutary formula is, of course, the dative, but Philokles seems to have two accusatives Cκιπν and Cπιν, and one dative Cκιφι. All these instances show that he did not really know how to inflect this name in Greek. What we know from other letters, however, suggests that the correct form of her name in the nominative was Cκνιψ (Sknips), cf. O.Did. 386 (120–125 CE): Ειουλία Cκνιψ τῇ μη[τρί χαίρειν] ['Ioulia to her mother Sknips, greetings']. Iulia, who was probably the real daughter of Sknips and Philokles,[51] used a scribe, and, as is often the case, the name is not

---

47 His name is sometimes Longinus and sometime Longinus Apollinaris, but the hand is the same with both names, cf. Cuvigny (2003: 386–387).
48 Cf. Leiwo (2003: 85).
49 Over 100 letters are written by or to him (Bülow-Jacobsen, O.Did. [2012: 295]). He had a house and pigs at Krokodiló, where many letters concerning him were found. All letters by Philokles (O.Did.; O.Krok.) are written by the same hand except one, O.Did. 390, which is a business letter to an important client. A scribe is used to write this letter. Philokles also had many idiolectic features, for example very frequent use of the form οἶδες 'you know' (οἶσθα in Attic), and many spellings of his own, as for example O.Did. 393: ἐνθῖν, ἔνθη 'to come' (ἐλθεῖν, ἔλθῃ).
50 Bülow-Jacobsen (2012: 296).
51 Bülow-Jacobsen (2012: 310).

inflected, being in the nominative rather than the dative Σκνιπι (Sknipi), and is thus probably the name as it should be spelled. However, Philokles, who wrote himself, is careful to inflect the name, though differently on different occasions, regardless of the case that would be syntactically correct.[52]

There are also other details worth commenting on in example (9). Except for his use of personal names, Longinus seems to be quite confident in his use of cases and phonetics. His use of the dative is standard and voiced and voiceless stops as well as vowels are generally written as expected by an L1 speaker. We find in l. 15 ἀνδαποδώcω cοι καὶ πάντοτε . . . 'I will give it back and forever . . .', where the first /nt/ is written <nd> and the second <nt>. This combination may be normal language internal variation, as we know the phonetic result in Greek came to be [nd] or [d] in due course.

The honorary title in l. 16 ἔχω τὴν ἐξουcίαν cου ὡc ἀδελφόν 'I'll have your excellency as a brother' is an early example.[53] It suggests a Latin influence, where ἐξουcία is a translation of *auctoritas*. A quite good command of Greek morphosyntax and phraseology, obvious Latin influence in the honorary title together with a somewhat intended peculiar use of cases with personal names suggests to me either an L1 Greek speaker or, alternatively, a bilingual Latin/Greek speaker with a slight preference for the latter.

4 Conclusions

The language of the ostraka letters is somewhat different from that of the papyri in general. It is clearly constructed of memorized phraseology mixed with self-made clauses. These elements of everyday phonetics and morphology combined with learned orthography suggest a pool of phraseology from where suitable clauses for basic correspondence can be picked, but also difficulties immediately when such clauses do not exist. These difficulties emerge as hypercorrect forms as well as general difficulties in morphology and syntax. A basic education for writing seems to be a fact at the *praesidia,* since many correspondents could actually write and even poor writers made corrections. This is an important observation as it clearly shows that writing skills were considered useful in the Roman army. Altogether, the 'ostraka' variety seems to be like a cocktail of different colours mixed with ethnolects, idiolects and doculects, or, to put it another way, different varieties and registers in one and the same wrap, like Mexican food.

---

52 It is not possible to deal in detail with the letters of Philokles here.
53 LSJ s.v. gives as the first example P.Oxy. VIII 1103 from the fourth century CE.

To sum up: professional scribes tend to repeat the same formulas and the same spellings in their production, whereas non-professional writers may have a lot of variation even in one and the same letter, but still be very consistent with some spellings or structures. Some private writers were obviously more flexible with the ongoing changes than others, who try to follow standard Attic Koiné. Due to this, it is sometimes almost impossible to specify a form accurately. Obviously, there are multiple reasons for the opaqueness of the forms, because internal variation and contact-induced variation may have similar results. However, what seems to be obvious is the fact that there were evidently many L2 Greek speakers, which gave rise to rich variation. This must have had an effect on language change in general, making the rate of change faster than in basically L1 social contexts, thus giving support to theories of contact-based language change, according to which adult L2 speakers create rapid change.

References

Aboh, Enoch O. & Umberto Ansaldo. 2007. The role of typology in language creation: A descriptive take. In Umberto Ansaldo, Stephen Matthews & Lisa Lim (eds.), *Deconstructing creole*, 39–66. Amsterdam: Benjamins.

Bentein, Klaas. 2015. Particle-usage in documentary papyri (I–IV AD): An integrated, sociolinguistically informed approach. *Greek Roman and Byzantine Studies* 55. 721–753.

Bubenik, Vit. 2014. Koine, Origins of. *EAGLL* [online edition].

Bülow-Jacobsen, Adam. 2012. Private Letters. In Hélène Cuvigny (ed.), *Didymoi: Une garnison romaine dans le désert oriental d'Égypte*. Vol. 2: *Les textes*, 234–395. Le Caire: Institut français d'archéologie orientale.

Clackson, James. 2010. Colloquial language in linguistic studies. In Eleanor Dickey & Anna Chahoud (eds.), *Colloquial and literary Latin*, 7–11. Cambridge: Cambridge University Press.

Clahsen, Harald, Claudia Felser, Kathleen Neubauer, Mikako Sato & Renita Silva. 2010. Morphological structure in native and nonnative language processing. *Language Learning* 60. 21–43.

Clarysse, Willy. 1993. Egyptian scribes writing Greek. *Chronique d'Égypte* 68. 186–201.

Clarysse, Willy. 2010. Linguistic diversity in the archive of the engineers Kleon and Theodoros. In Trevor V. Evans & Dirk D. Obbink (eds.), *The language of the papyri*, 35–50. Oxford: Oxford University Press.

Clarysse, Willy. 2017. Emotions in Greek private letters. *Ancient Society* 47. 63–86.

Crystal, David. 1997. *The Cambridge encyclopedia of language*, 2nd ed. Cambridge: Cambridge University Press.

Cuvigny, Hélène. 2003. La société civile des *praesidia*. In Hélène Cuvigny (ed.), *La route de Myos Hormos: L'armée romaine dans le désert oriental d'Égypte*, 361–395. Le Caire: Institut français d'archéologie orientale.

Dahlgren, Sonja. 2016. Towards a definition of an Egyptian Greek Variety. *Papers in Historical Phonology* 1. 90–108.
Dahlgren, Sonja. 2017. *Outcome of long-term language contact: Transfer of Egyptian phonological features onto Greek in Graeco-Roman Egypt*. PhD dissertation, University of Helsinki.
Dickey, Eleanor. 2010. Introduction. In Eleanor Dickey & Anna Chahoud (eds.), *Colloquial and literary Latin*, 3–6. Cambridge: Cambridge University Press.
Eggins, Suzanne. 2004. *An introduction to systemic functional linguistics*, 2nd ed. London: Continuum.
Fishman, Joshua. 1965. Who speaks what language to whom and when? *La Linguistique* 2. 67–88.
Fournet, Jean-Luc. 2003. Langues, écritures et culture dans les *praesidia*. In Hélène Cuvigny (ed.), *La route de Myos Hormos: L'armée romaine dans le désert oriental d'Égypte*, 427–500. Le Caire: Institut français d'archéologie orientale.
Gignac, Francis T. 1976. *A grammar of the Greek papyri of the Roman and Byzantine periods*. Vol. 1: *Phonology*. Milano: La Goliardica.
Gonis, Nikolaos. 2009. Review of Cuvigny (2005). *Bulletin of the American Society of Papyrologists* 46. 217–218.
Horrocks, Geoffrey C. 2010. *Greek: A history of the language and its speakers*, 2nd ed. Malden: Wiley-Blackwell.
Labov, William. 2001. *Principles of linguistic change*. Vol. 2: *Social factors*. Malden: Blackwell.
Lasswell, Harold. 1948. The structure and function of communication in society: The communication of ideas. In Lyman Bryson (ed.), *The communication of ideas: a series of addresses*, 215–228. New York: Institute for Religious and Social Studies.
Leiwo, Martti. 2003. Both and all together: The meaning of ἀμφότεροι. *Arctos* 37. 81–99.
Leiwo, Martti. 2005. Substandard Greek: Remarks from Mons Claudianus. In Nigel M. Kennel & Jonathan E. Tomlinson (eds.), *Ancient Greece at the turn of the millennium: Recent work and future perspectives: Proceedings of the Athens symposion, 18–20 May 2001*, 237–261. Athens: Canadian Archaeological Institute at Athens.
Leiwo, Martti. 2010. Imperatives and other directives in the Greek letters from Mons Claudianus. In Trevor V. Evans & Dirk D. Obbink (eds.), *The language of the papyri*, 97–119. Oxford: Oxford University Press.
Leiwo, Martti 2017. Confusion of moods in Greek private letters of Roman Egypt. In Klaas Bentein, Mark Janse & Jorie Soltic (eds.), *Variation and change in Ancient Greek tense, aspect and modality*, 242–260. Leiden: Brill.
Leiwo, Martti. 2018. Multilingual military forts in Roman Egypt. *Lingue Antiche e Moderne* 7 [online: all.uniud.it/lam/lamrep/2018/LAM_7_2018_Leiwo.pdf].
Lewis, Naphtali. 1983. *Life in Egypt under Roman rule*. Oxford: Oxford University Press.
Luiselli, Raffaele. 2010. Authorial revision of linguistic style in Greek papyrus letters and petitions (AD I–IV). In Trevor V. Evans & Dirk D. Obbink (eds.), *The language of the papyri*, 71–96. Oxford: Oxford University Press.
Maxfield, Valerie A. 2003. Ostraca and the Roman army in the Eastern Desert. *Bulletin of the Institute of Classical Studies* 46. Supplement 81: *Documenting the Roman Army*, 153–173. London: University of London.
Maxfield, Valerie A. 2005. The Roman Army and the Road from Koptos to Myos Hormos. *Journal of Roman Archaeology* 18. 731–740.

Mufwene, Salikoko 2001. *The Ecology of Language Evolution*. Cambridge: Cambridge University Press.
Müller, Roman. 2001. *Sprachbewusstsein und Sprachvariation im lateinischen Schriftum der Antike*. München: Beck.
Operstein, Natalie. 2015. Contact-genetic linguistics: Toward a contact-based theory of language change. *Language Sciences* 48. 1–15.
Sidebotham, Steven E. 2011. *Berenike and the Ancient Maritime Spice Route*. Berkeley: University of California Press.
Trudgill, Peter. 2003. *A glossary of sociolinguistics*. Edinburgh: Edinburgh University Press.
Trudgill, Peter. 2011. *Sociolinguistic typology: Social determinants of linguistic complexity*. Oxford: Oxford University Press.
Weinreich, Uriel. 1963 [1953]. *Languages in contact: Findings and problems*. The Hague: Mouton.
White, John L. 1986. *Light from ancient letters*. Philadelphia, PA: Fortress Press.
Willi, Andreas. 2017. Register variation and tense/aspect/mood categories in Ancient Greek: Problems and perspectives. In Klaas Bentein, Mark Janse & Jorie Soltic (eds.), *Variation and change in Ancient Greek tense, aspect and modality*, 261–286. Leiden: Brill.

Marja Vierros
3 Idiolect in focus: Two brothers in the Memphis Sarapieion (II BCE)

Abstract: The chapter discusses the Katochoi archive from the point of view of idiolects. Several documents written in the hands of Apollonios and Ptolemaios, sons of Glaukias, can be identified within the archive, which comprises of several types of documents. I study whether these autograph texts can be said to represent the idiolects of Apollonios and Ptolemaios and how this perspective might change our interpretation of the interesting linguistic variation found in the whole archive. Apollonios, for example, wrote many drafts and copies which do not necessarily reflect his personal language use in the morphological or syntactic levels. However, the orthography reveals individual practices. I will present examples of language use by both brothers, comparing them to the scribal language use found in the same archive.

1 Idiolect: A definition and its relevance

Idiolect can be defined as a "dialect of an individual person at one time".[1, 2] The term implies that all speakers have their own style of speaking and producing language, but also that this style is subject to change over time. Such unique features can include vocabulary, grammar and pronunciation. Some scholars have argued that variationist linguists should not take idiolects into account, since "the grammars in which linguistic change occurs are grammars of the speech community" (Weinreich, Labov and Herzog 1968: 188).[3] Later, Labov (2001: 34) expanded on this, stating that the individual does not exist as a linguistic object but nonetheless shows a personal profile of the comparative use of resources made available by the speech community. He continues, however, to say that sociolinguists agree that the primary site for linguistic investigation is

---

1 This contribution has received funding from the Academy of Finland project "Act of the Scribe: Transmitting Linguistic Knowledge and Scribal Practices in Graeco-Roman Antiquity" (287386) and from the European Research Council (ERC) under the European Union's Horizon 2020 research and innovation programme (grant agreement No 758481 "Digital Grammar of Greek Documentary Papyri").
2 Britannica.com, s.v. "dialect".
3 Cf. Labov (2001: xi).

https://doi.org/10.1515/9783110614404-003

the individual's productions and interpretations. These should be used, in turn, as components to construct the principal target of study: the language of the speech community. Indeed, the study by Labov on linguistic change and variation in Philadelphia includes many profiles of individual language users, descriptions of their language use, and their potential role as linguistic innovators who disseminate their inventions within their networks. Therefore, it seems that the study of idiolect is warranted, but it should also lead to further understanding of variation within the speech community.

When studying historical languages where the available data is limited by ancient texts that have largely been preserved contingently, I feel that there is a special need to investigate the possibility of certain features being idiolectal rather than being shared by the whole speech community. However, quite often, this kind of investigation is not possible. With Greek documentary papyri from Egypt, for instance, this is possible only when we have a set of texts from the same place and time, often in the form of an archive.[4] The archives can contain several texts that have been written by one writer (identified either by handwriting or name – in the best cases, by both).[5] One further reason to study idiolects is that, by discerning the linguistic features typical of individuals, we may be able to identify some of the writers and/or authors of the texts, even if handwriting analysis is not possible. On the other hand, we may need to distinguish the writer from the author – that is, the person who wrote the text was not necessarily the same person who was in charge of –, e.g. the choice of words and the syntax.[6] The question of who was in charge of what parts of the language of a given text is complicated, and the pursuit to identify idiolects in this chapter is also an attempt to find some answers to this larger question.

An archive often also gives us more context on the speech community, people who produced the texts, the background of the community, families, language contact, etc. In the archive under investigation here, the family functions as a nuclear speech community. However, variation also occurs between family members, since the peer group from the larger speech community also exerts

---

[4] For a thorough introduction on papyrus archives, see Vandorpe (2009). Several Ptolemaic archives are presented in Vandorpe & Waebens (2009). Papyrus archives can conveniently be searched and studied via TM Archives.
[5] Cf. Evans (2010) on identifying the language of individuals in the Zenon archive in the third century BCE, and Leiwo (this volume) on idiolects in archives of ostraca in the Roman period.
[6] Cf. Evans (2010: 66–69) and Luiselli (2010: 73) (with bibliography).

an influence.⁷ While there are four brothers present in the archive, only two of them wrote most of the texts, and we do not have texts from other generations. Our brothers' language uses display both similarities and dissimilarities.

2 Context: The Katochoi archive and its documents

In this chapter, I will focus on the idiolects of two brothers on the basis of the documentary material found in the temple area of Sarapis in Memphis, Egypt, which is dated to the second century BCE. These texts have been preserved in the so-called "Katochoi of the Sarapieion" archive, published as a single volume by Ulrich Wilcken in 1927.⁸ The exact location of the papyrus find is unknown.⁹ These texts have fascinated both scholars and non-academic audience, because they tell a vivid tale about two girls, Taues and Taous, who are twins and protégées of the protagonists of the archive, and their hardships, including an evil mother figure. We know a great deal about the historical context of the multi-ethnic Memphis area thanks to the important monograph by Dorothy Thompson (2012), and the Katochoi archive has been studied extensively from the historical point of view. The language has been studied to a lesser degree, though already Wilcken (1927: iii) mentioned that the language requires future study from many different points of view. Now, the recent article by Bentein (2015) provides a linguistic analysis of many phenomena in the archive and discusses the influence of text type and status on the language. Indeed, the archive is a veritable source of material for further linguistic studies. I will give

---

7 See Hazen (2002).
8 Ca. 110 documentary Greek texts belonging to the archive are included in the UPZ I edition (Wilcken 1927). The main body of the archive is formed by documents **2–105** in UPZ I (the bold numbers in this chapter refer to the number assigned to the texts in UPZ I; non-bolded numbers may follow, indicating the line number). In addition, **110–111**, **144**, **145**, and **147** are included in the archive. The UPZ publication numbers do not correlate with the inner chronology of the archive. Some texts were not published in UPZ I – namely, the literary and Demotic Egyptian ones.
  See Trismegistos archive ID 119 (www.trismegistos.org/arch/detail.php?quick2=119) for the whole list; the total number of texts listed there is 127 (3 of which are uncertain).
9 According to Wilcken (1927: 1–3), the texts from Memphis were found by local inhabitants around 1820 and then distributed via at least three different antiquities dealers (Henry Salt, Bernardino Drovetti, Johann d'Anastasy) to Europe.

a brief overview of the context for the sake of better understanding the environment and background in which these brothers wrote their texts. I will also discuss different registers and text types, since they had an influence on language use that cannot be overlooked, but what I wish to add to Bentein's work, is tracking down the writer vs. author and their impact on the different levels of language as well as give more examples and actual numbers of the distribution of the phenomena. However, many interesting phenomena are still left for future studies.

Memphis was the second largest city of Ptolemaic Egypt and had a multi-ethnic population. Greeks had settled there already before the conquest of Egypt by Alexander the Great. That Greek population was called "Hellenomemphitai".[10] However, the protagonists of our archive came from the neighbouring Herakleopolite nome. Ptolemaios, the eldest son of Glaukias, was a recluse (*[en]katochos*) in the Sarapieion temple complex of Memphis since 172 BCE,[11] and his youngest brother, Apollonios, joined him after their father had died (before 164 BCE). Apollonios was perhaps born in 175 BCE,[12] so he was still in his teens when he was running errands and performing writing tasks for Ptolemaios and their other brothers between Memphis and Psichis in 164–158. In 158, he became a recluse himself for a few months. Ptolemaios was around twenty years his brother's senior, and Apollonios called him "father" in many occasions. They had two other brothers, Hippalos and Sarapion, who stayed in the village of Psichis, in the Herakleopolite nome, where the family owned a house. The house had been allotted to their father, Glaukias, who was a soldier-settler (*katoikos*).

---

10 Thompson (2012: 77). Cf. Herodotus (2.154.1–3), who speaks of Greek and Carian mercenaries who served under Psammetichos I (664–610 BCE) and their transfer to Memphis under the reign of Amasis (570–526 BCE). UPZ I **1** (Curse of Artemisia) is dated approximately to the fourth century BCE and evidences the mixed dialectal language use of the Hellenomemphitai.
11 What exactly is meant by a "recluse" or one who is "in detention" in the temple has not been finally determined; see the discussions in, e.g. Delekat (1964), Lewis (1986: 69–87), Legras (2011), Thompson (2012: 199ff). At any rate, these recluses lived in the area of the temple of Astarte within the Great Sarapieion and were not allowed to leave the temple area. Thompson (2012: 205–6) makes the interesting observation that the language of the cult Ptolemaios was involved in was neither Greek nor Egyptian but possibly Phoenician (based on the homeland of the goddess).
12 Thompson (2012: 228) assumes that Apollonios was 18 years old when Ptolemaios enrolled him in the army in 157 BCE (**14**); Wilcken (1927: 114) suggested the years 173 or 174 as Apollonios' year of birth. His day of birth was Hathyr 10 (i.e. the beginning of December in the years 175–173 BCE). He was referred as παιδάριον 'young boy' in texts written before Hathyr 10, 161 BCE.

Glaukias was entitled Macedonian and belonged to the esteemed group of *sungeneis* ('[king's] cousins', Lewis 1986: 74). Ptolemaios and Apollonios inherited their father's title of Macedonian. It is clear that Glaukias had Greek/Macedonian ancestry, and his son Ptolemaios appeals to the king in one of his petitions by emphasizing his Greek (*hellēn*) status.[13]

Both Apollonios and Ptolemaios wrote Greek texts. Wilcken identified their individual handwritings. Apollonios learnt how to write possibly in the Sarapieion, since a training alphabet written in his hand has been preserved (**147**). He wrote more documents than Ptolemaios, who only wrote accounts, dream descriptions, and one private letter and copied some poetry. He could have embarked on some sort of administrative career that required writing skills, since he drafted some and copied many petitions as a young boy, and his handwriting developed toward cursive already early on.[14] It must be noted that the copies of petitions as well as the copies of the receipts concerning twin's matters were originally written in ca. 163–161, i.e. when Apollonios was in his early teens.

We do not know for sure if he copied these petitions at the time when they were originally written or if he used them as a learning material in later years. The petitions concerning his own matters as well as the letters were written later, when he was 17 or 18 or more. Approximately half of the private letters in the archive were written by Apollonios – only one by Ptolemaios, since Apollonios wrote many of the letters on behalf of Ptolemaios. The documents written by Apollonios, Ptolemaios, and other hands are presented in Table 1, which is organized by text types.

---

13 UPZ I 7: παρὰ τὸ Ἑλληνά με εἶναι 'because I am Greek' (also in UPZ I **8**, a later version of the same petition). Veisse (2007) distinguishes the different aspects of Ptolemaios' designations: "Macedonian" was restricted to the official sphere; geographically, he was a "man of the Herakleopolite"; culturally, he was a "Hellene"; being a "recluse" was the defining element of his social identity. We must note, however, that Apollonios added the word "Macedonian" in the titulature of Ptolemaios in several draft petitions (but, in the scribal drafts, the title is often missing). Apollonios also added marginalia to a copy of Euripides' *Telephos*: "Apollonios, the Macedonian . . . a Macedonian, I say", perhaps comparing himself to Telephos, who laments his destiny as a Hellene among barbarians; see Thompson (2012: 242).
14 Wilcken (1927: 115) describes the handwriting of Apollonios as ugly and uneven but notes that, already as a young boy, his hand was half-cursive and had developed to cursive in basic training. Wilcken's view was that rapidity was the aim of Apollonios rather than beautiful handwriting.

Table 1: Documents in the Katochoi archive grouped by hand writing and genre.[15]

UPZ I documents	Ptolemaios	Apollonios	Scribal/other hands[16]
Petitions (final)			7, 20[17], 36(?)[18]
Petitions (drafts)		12+13, 18, 32, 44, 49+50, 52+53, 57	2, 3+4, 5+6, 8, 9+10+11, 15+16, 17, 19, 24, 40, 41, 42, 43+45, 46+47+48, 51
Petitions (copies)		14, 22, 33+34+35, 39	
Orders and reports		23, 26, 37, 38 (copies)	21, 25, 27, 28
Private letters	67	63, 65, 68, 69, 70, 73, 74, 75, 76 [72]; P.Mil. I 2, 28	59, 60, 61, 62, 64, 66, 71, 72
Receipts		29 (copy), 31 (draft?)	30
Accounts	56, 82–85, 86 3–12, 87, 88, 90 13, 15–17, 92, 94 iii–iv, 95–100, 101 1–16, 18–23, 103–105; P.Mil. I 2, 27	54, 55, 58 (frgs), 89, 91, 93 (letter), 94 I–II, 101 (marg), 102 1–6	

---

15 Versions of same text are joined together by the plus symbol (+). Some versions of the same text are in different cells in this table, see below, text groups.
16 This column contains the texts written by hands other than those of Apollonios or Ptolemaios. In the case of petitions, orders, and reports, they were mostly written by scribes with trained hands, but, in the case of private letters, it is more difficult to determine the actual writer.
17 Whether this text was the final version that was sent is difficult to determine. It was written in fine calligraphic script and seems to be the text that was actually sent as the petition; however, three subscriptions were copied in one hand at the end (ll. 74–78), and, before that, there are some lines in Ptolemaios's hand that have been erased. Perhaps two "final" copies were made, and **20** was the version that stayed with the petitioner; the official marks would have been copied on it, too, after the decisions had been made.
18 Text **36** has subscriptions in other hands signifying the receipt of the petition by officials and some instructions on how to proceed with the case; in that respect, it seems to be the version actually sent to the *hupodioikētēs* Sarapion. But it also has corrections added above the line and a part written in Apollonios's hand (Wilcken, 115, 234). Texts **33–35** are Apollonios's copies of this same text, while **43** has been written in an elegant hand with corrections in two different hands and marginalia in Apollonios's hand.

Table 1 (continued)

UPZ I documents	Ptolemaios	Apollonios	Scribal/other hands[16]
Marginalia/ additions	20 67–71 (m3)	21 24–5, 27, 36 (m4), 43 (m4)	
Dreams	77, 79, 80 (list only)	78	
Literature and educational material (copies)	Poseidippos's epigrams, part of a comic play	81 (Nectanebo), 147 (alphabet), writing exercises and Greek poetry	110 (Letter of Herodes), 111 (royal letter), 144 (model letter), 145 (model letter)[19]

Whether Apollonios could also write Demotic Egyptian has been debated among scholars. Some say that he was more fluent in Demotic than in Greek, but others do not believe he knew how to write Demotic at all.[20] The brothers lived in a temple area where most other people – their fellow recluses and the people they had to write petitions against – were Egyptians. The twin girls Taues and Taous became their protégées after their father Hargynoutis, Ptolemaios' Egyptian friend, died. To have been able to communicate in this environment, it is very likely that Ptolemaios and Apollonios were able to speak Egyptian.[21] Therefore, Apollonios could very well have also learnt to write Egyptian. As for bilingualism, one of the dream descriptions written by Ptolemaios (narrating a dream of a

---

19 Texts **110–111, 144–45** are on the other side of *Ars Eudoxi*, an astronomical treatise found in the archive.
20 Thompson (2012: 230): "Apollonios was equally familiar with Egyptian language and culture. His Greek has a strong Egyptian flavour and, if the Demotic record betrays the language of his dreams, he dreamed in Egyptian, too (P.Bologna dem. 3173, etc.)." Apollonios also wrote the Dream of Nectanebo (Koenen 1985), a Greek translation (or adaptation) of a Demotic literary text. Wilcken (1927: 350–351) expressed doubts about Apollonios' skills in Demotic, while Legras (2007) initially considered Apollonios to be biliteral but later (2011) changed his mind, with light arguments; cf. Vierros (2012b), Prada (2013).
21 It is possible that the mother of these two brothers was Egyptian (cf. Thompson 2012: 198) and, thus, they could have been completely bilingual. Greek was at least their father's tongue, but we have no way of knowing whether Glaukias was a first-generation immigrant or not. A Demotic ostracon seems to refer to Apollonios also by his Egyptian name, Peteharempi (P.Dem.Bol. 3173), though this interpretation can be disputed. In any case, the names of the brothers represent Hellenized names rather than "common" Greek names, Ptolemaios being a Hellenistic dynastic name and Sarapion a theophoric name from the Hellenistic god Sarapis; Apollonios was also very common among Hellenized Egyptians. See e.g. the discussion in Vierros (2012a: 45–49).

certain Nektembes) appears to evidence code-switching: possibly Egyptian words (written in the Greek alphabet) in the middle of otherwise Greek text.[22] Another dream describes the twins being in a school room of Thothes (**78** 8–9), which suggests that Egyptian education was available at the temple.

A great deal of evidence attesting to the copying and drafting texts and, therefore, also on the recycling of papyri is also present in this archive. In some cases, our main hint that a text is just a draft is the fact that a version of the same text has been written on the other side of the papyrus or that many different texts are written on the same papyrus, on the same or both sides. Table 2 indicates which papyri contain multiple Greek texts; some papyri even contain three or four texts. There are also Demotic texts (some of which may have been written by Apollonios) which perhaps served just as scrap papyrus, where Demotic was washed out and Greek accounts written over or in between Demotic texts.[23] Two example cases of the reuse of papyri may clarify the complexity of understanding the nature of any given text. It is good to be aware of the physical aspects of the texts, since they can sometimes help us to understand in which order some versions were written and whether it was visually possible to copy from one text directly to another (e.g., if the model text was on a separate papyrus sheet). Case 1 (Figure 1) is papyrus 406 [2] from the Leiden National Museum of Antiquities: Text **33** is a claim for oil, written in the hand of Apollonios, a draft which breaks off in the middle of l. 15; other versions of the same text are found on other papyri (**34**, **35**, and **36**). Text **49**, rotated 180°, is a petition on behalf of the twins; only the first four lines have been written, and the text breaks off in the middle of the first word of l. 5. The text has two orthographic mistakes that are corrected in **50**.[24] Text **50** is a version of **49**, this time the whole text, and was clearly written after **49**, because it does not fit in a single place, since the text of **49** had already been written on the papyrus first.

---

[22] **79** 3–5: τὸ δεύτερ[ον]· Φαφερεσιευρεηξ Παῦνι ἐν τῷ Βουβαστῳ χμεννι ἐν τῷ οἴκῳ τῷ Ἄμμωνος πελ λελ χασονχανι. ['The second (dream): Faferesienreēx month of Pauni in the Boubasteion chmenni in the house of Ammon pel lel chasonchani']. Wilcken (1927: 366) states that "diese barbarischen Lautgruppen in 4 und 5 können nach Lage der Dinge nichts anderes sein als griechische Transkriptionen von ägyptischen Wörtern" ["These barbaric sound groups in 4 and 5 can not be anything other than Greek transcriptions of Egyptian words"]. The meaning of these Egyptian words has not been deciphered as far as I know. On the other hand, they might represent some other language – e.g. Phoenician (cf. fn. 11) – or just gibberish. I follow here the original division of the transliterated Egyptian words in the papyrus, as did Prada (2013), who also discusses the language of the dreams and dream interpretation in general.

[23] A comprehensive list of all Demotic palimpsests is available in Clarysse & Vandorpe (2006).

[24] Text **47**, on a different papyrus, has the same beginning (but it differs from **50** at the end) and spans 25 lines but breaks off in the middle of a sentence.

Table 2: Reuse of papyri in the Katochoi archive.

recto	verso
UPZ I **2**: Petition of Harmais (163)	UPZ I **52**: Petition of Ptolemaios (draft) (161)
UPZ I **3**: Petition of Ptolemaios for Herakleia (164) P. L. Bat. 24 pp. 24–25 no. 113 descr. (Dem)	UPZ I **4**: Petition of Herakleia (same hand as that of *recto*) (164)
UPZ I **9**: Petition of Ptolemaios (161–160)	UPZ I **100**: Account (157)
UPZ I **12**: Petition of Apollonios (158)	UPZ I **13**: Petition of Apollonios (158–157)
UPZ I **14**: Petition of Ptolemaios; palimpsest (157)	Demotic?
UPZ I **15**: Petition of Ptolemaios (156)	UPZ I **16**: Petition of Ptolemaios (156)
UPZ I **17**: First petition to Sarapion (163)	UPZ I **86**: Account (161)
UPZ I **18**: Petition for the twins (163)	UPZ I **18v**: Beginning of a petition (162–161) UPZ I **82**: Account (163–161)
UPZ I **21**: Notice (162) UPZ I **75**: Beginning of a letter (after 162)	
UPZ I **23**: Report of Apollonios, γραμματεύς (162) UPZ I **26**: Order from Mennides to Theon (162) UPZ I **27**: Order from Theon to Dionysios (162)	
UPZ I **77**: Ptolemaios's dream descriptions (158) UPZ I **97**: Accounts (158) UPZ I **89**: Account of twins' food supplies (159)	UPZ I **31**: Receipt (162)

Table 2 (continued)

recto	verso
UPZ I 33 Initial oil claim (161) UPZ I 49: Petition for twins (beginning) (161) UPZ I 50: Petition for twins (161)	
UPZ I 43: Petition to Sarapion (161?)	UPZ I 34: Initial oil claim (161) UPZ I 44: Petition to Sarapion (3 lines) (162–161)
UPZ I 39: New oil claim (161) UPZ I 74: Private letter (161 or after)	
UPZ I 47: Petition for twins (162–161)	UPZ I 104: Account (162–161)
UPZ I 54: Account (161 or after)	UPZ I 55: Account (161 or after)
UPZ I 56: Bread account (106 or after)	Paris, Louvre 7171 + Paris, Louvre 7172 (literary; Pack 1965, 1435 = TM 59936), school texts
UPZ I 57: Petition (164–161) UPZ I 58: Notifications and fragments (163–162)	UPZ I 58: Notifications and fragments (163–162)
UPZ I 63 Letter/petition (158) UPZ I 80: List of dreams (158 or after) UPZ I 96: Accounts (158) (Demotic, washed away)	
UPZ I 67: Ptolemaios' letter (153–152)	UPZ I 103 Account (153)
UPZ I 78: Letter (dreams) (159 or after) (Demotic)	
P.Par. 2 (literary; Pack 1965, 246 = TM 59451)	UPZ I 79: Dream of Nektembes (159) UPZ I 90: Account (159) UPZ I 101: Account (156)
UPZ I 84: Account (160) (Demotic, washed away)	UPZ I 83: Account (161) Demotic, wisdom text
UPZ I 85: Account (160)	Demotic, wisdom text?

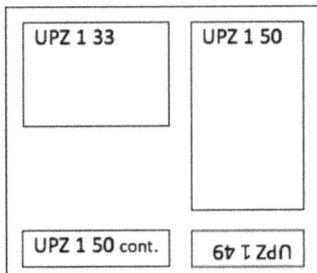

Figure 1: Positions of different documents in one papyrus sheet, Leiden 406 [2].

Case 2 (Figure 2) is taken from the Dresden papyrus (inventory number unknown): Text **43**, on the *recto*, is a petition in a scribal hand (other hands have made interlineal corrections and Apollonios' hand appears on the margins). Text **34**, on the *verso*, rotated 90 degrees to the right and written by Apollonios, is the second version of **33**. Text **44**, rotated 180°, contains only three lines of the petition (**43**) on the *recto*.

As e.g. **43** in Case 2 shows, the petitions written by scribal hands could also be drafts – i.e. they were still not the final versions of the text ready to be sent. We have very few cases where there is evidence that the petition was actually the one sent to officials. The ones that do are **7** and **36** (see Table 1); these bear the subscriptions that were made when the petition was received and are followed by a list of actions to be taken. Since **36** includes Apollonios' writing after the official response, we can assume that the petition had been returned to the petitioner. The existence of **7** in this archive also suggests the same (since the details of the papyrus finds remain unknown, however, it may be the case that the papyri were not all found at the same place; see above). Text **14** is a copy made in Apollonios' hand, but it includes the official markings, i.e. it represents a final, sent petition, but as a private copy. Distinguishing a copy from a draft is not always straightforward, but I attempted to make this distinction in Table 1 on the basis of Wilcken's judgements, corrections applied to the text, and differences between the versions (if several versions exist).

One approach for studying idiolect is to compare the versions of the same text written by different hands. They may be drafts or copies, sometimes with very similar wordings, but sometimes presenting significant development in composing the same text. I list below these versions, i.e. text groups, where one or more versions of the same text are by Apollonios' hand and some in scribal hands:[25]

---

[25] Texts **7** and **8** are also versions of the same, but apparently neither is in Apollonios' hand.

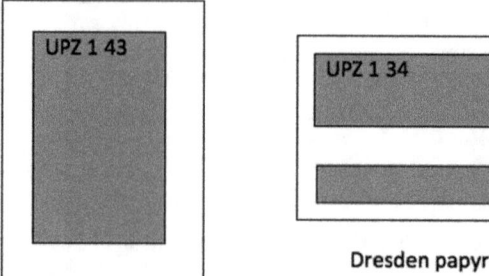

Figure 2: Positions of different documents in both sides of the Dresden papyrus.

Text group A:	**18** (Apollonios' hand)
	19 (scribal hand, same as in **9** and **24**)
Text group B:	**25** (scribal hand)
	26 (Apollonios' hand)
Text group C:	**33** (Apollonios' hand, unfinished)
	34 (Apollonios' hand)
	35 (Apollonios' hand)
	36 (scribal hand; hand 4 = Apollonios' hand)
Text group D:	**39** (Apollonios' hand)
	40 (scribal hand, similar to **28**)
Text group E:	**43** (scribal hand, same as **10**, **41**, **42**; hand 4 = Apollonios' hand)
	44 (Apollonios' hand, unfinished)
	45 (scribal hand?)
Text group F:	**46** (scribal hand?)
	47 (scribal hand, same as **2** and **8**?; unfinished)
	48 (scribal hand, unfinished)
	49 (Apollonios' hand; unfinished)
	50 (Apollonios' hand)

3 Linguistic material: Possible idiolectal features of Apollonios and Ptolemaios

I will consider several different levels of language in the search for the idiolectal features of Apollonios and Ptolemaios. I begin with the orthographic data, which often reveal issues relating to pronunciation and, therefore, ongoing phonological changes evidenced by misspellings. Orthography can also reveal aspects of education, i.e. the writing can be in accord with the standard spelling with certain words, but repeat certain idiosyncrasies with others. I will then look at some aspects of morphology and certain syntactic features – namely, the use of particles, participles, and conjunctions.

3.1 Phonology

The brothers are infamous for their poor ability to spell. Scholars have made statements such as that "[Ptolemaios'] spelling was purely phonetic, his grammar shaky at best" (Lewis 1986: 74) and that "[Apollonios'] spelling is notoriously poor. In particular, he has little sense for the quantitative distinctions of Greek vowels and diphthongs, a phenomenon which went hand in hand with the modification of the nature of the Greek accents" (Koenen 1985: 174, fn. 9).[26] Depauw and Stolk (2015: 209) also noted how the editorial regulations peak substantially in the mid-second century BCE due to the Katochoi archive, meaning that orthography was corrected by the papyrus editors to a significant amount.

The most common interchange of graphemes in Greek papyri in general, that between ι and ει, is expectedly also the most common in our archive.[27]

---

[26] Wilcken (1927: 115) also noted a difference in the orthography between the brothers; he describes Apollonios' orthography "noch vulgärer als die des Ptolemaios" ["even more vulgar than that of Ptolemaios"], mentioning his misspellings of ῥάυδος (for ῥάβδος 'rod'), ἐμβλεύσαντες (for ἐμβλέψαντες 'looking'), Σαραπιγῆωι 'Sarapieion', and κάαγω (κἀγώ 'and I') and examples of metatheses such as πόρσωπον for πρόσωπον 'face' and Ἀφορδίτη for Ἀφροδίτη 'Aphrodite'.

[27] Bentein (2015: 465–466). As Horrocks (2010: 161–162) presents it, the original diphthong ει had monophthongised already in the eighth–seventh century BCE, resulting in the new midhigh vowel /e:/. After the classical period, it was pulled towards /i:/ (affecting first the preconsonantal and word-final allophones, but then applying generally); approximately at the same time, the distinction between short and long vowels disappeared. In the table of sounds of the Egyptian Koine of the mid-second century BCE, Horrocks (2010: 167), following Teodorsson (1977), presents ει as /i/ before a consonant and a raised /e/ before a vowel. See also Mayser-Schmoll (60–70), Gignac (1976: 189–191).

The standard ι written as ει occurs 100 times[28] (of which only nine occurrences are in hands other than those of Apollonios or Ptolemaios). The standard ει written as ι occurs 131 times[29] (of which seventeen occurrences are in hands other than those of Apollonios or Ptolemaios). Based on this analysis, it was slightly more common to write ει as ι than vice versa. In Ptolemaios' case, a few words are repeatedly written in the same way, thus making the number bigger (e.g. χαλκῖα for χαλκεῖα 'copper coin' 11 times in the accounts **98** and **99**). In any case, even this very common interchange was mostly avoided by other writers in the archive (cf. the number of documents by other hands in Table 1), but our brothers betray a lack of education in their orthography and confirming that they probably pronounced ι and ει similarly. In the copies Apollonios made, he occasionally confuses these letters even when the scribal hand did not.[30] That means that he could not always follow the standard orthography even when copying.

Examples of standard ι written as ει are found in all positions and by all hand writing types: word-initially in 9 instances (e.g. εἰδού for ἰδού 'see:imp' in **77** 15 and **78** 25; εἵνα for ἵνα 'that' **18r** 23); word-finally in 20 instances (mostly Apollonios and Ptolemaios; once in a scribal hand, e.g. λέγουσει for λέγουσι 'they say' **77** 14; ἔτει 'year:dat' for ἔτι 'still' **18r** 15; περεὶ for περὶ 'about' **77** 1, **80** 1, 2, 3, 4, 6); in stressed syllable (e.g. τείθεσθαι for τίθεσθαι 'pay' **14** 71; ἐπεὶ for ἐπὶ 'upon' **77** 23); in unstressed syllable (e.g. βασιλεικοῦ for βασιλικοῦ 'royal' **23** 5; δειὰ for διὰ 'through' **77** 6; λίθεινα for λίθινα 'of stone' **57** 5); the ending -ιν was written as -ειν in 19 instances (e.g. πάλειν for πάλιν 'again' **18r** 26; πόλειν for

---

28 Analysis extracted with the aid of the Paratypa tool (see Henriksson, Dahlgren & Vierros forthcoming). Search description: select Deletions, then Original: ε (ends with), After ι (begins with), filtered by collection (only UPZ I) and time (second century BCE), acquired 15 Dec 2017: total results 106; some occurrences not being exactly ει instead of ι removed. The Trismegistos Text Irregularities (TMTI, see Depauw and Stolk 2015) database gives 83 results (ει instead of ι, restricted to second century BCE and then using the Find-function for the provenance L01 (i.e. Memphis, Saqqara, Serapeum)).

29 Paratypa search (Additions; standard: ε (ends with), After: ι (begins with), restricted by UPZ collection and second century BCE, acquired 15 Dec 2017 (total number is 136, but five instances must be cleaned out as irrelevant for this interchange; some cases where the type of interchange is difficult to judge are counted, e.g. Μέμφιν for Μέμφει 'Memphis:acc/dat'; see below on morphology). TMTI gives 108 hits for "ι instead of ει" with the same additional actions as in the previous footnote).

30 E.g. in text group B: **26** ἐπεισκεψάμενον, ἀρχεισωματοφύλακα against **25** ἐπισκεψάμενον 'to be inspected', ἀρχισωματοφύλακα 'chief of the body guard'; in group C: **33, 34, 35** χάρειν against **36** χάριν 'for the sake of'. However, in text goup F, Apollonios wrote correctly μεθ' ἱκετείας 'by supplication' in **50** whereas the scribal hand in **46** wrote μετ' εἰκετείας, but, at the same time making other confusions between ι and ει not present in **46** or **47**.

πόλιν 'city' **18r** 12; σύμταξειν/ σύνταξειν for σύνταξιν 'payment' **39** 7, **50** 21, 34, **53** 21; χάρειν for χάριν 'for the sake of' **33** 9, **34** 6, **35** 13 **110** 44; ἔστειν for ἐστιν 'is' **18r** 15, **77** 13).

As Dahlgren (2017: 101) noted in the data she retrieved from the Roman period, this direction of interchange happened most in certain phonetic environments: adjacent to /m, n/, back vowels, liquid /r/,[31] and /s/. When we look closer at the phonetic environment where this interchange occurs in the Katochoi archive, we find supporting evidence from the Ptolemaic period: the position after liquids /r/ and /l/ stand out with much higher numbers compared to other consonants (vowels did not yield results, thus agreeing with Horrocks' and Teodorsson's result that, before a vowel, ει was still a raised /e/).[32] The position before /n/ and /s/ also stand out (see above, the ending -ιν).[33] Examples of standard ει written as ι are also found in all positions:[34] word-initially in 31 instances (ἰ for εἰ **70** 3, 25, **110** 4; ἰκοστοῦ for εἰκοστοῦ 'twentieth' **35** 19; ἰλήφασι for εἰλήφασι 'receive:pf.3pl' **52** 14, 16, **53** 16, 18, **54** 3, 6, etc.); word-finally (e.g. λέγι for λέγει 'say:pr.3sg' **79** 3; ἐπὶ for ἐπεὶ 'upon' **23** 20, **26** 6, **32**, 19 etc.); in stressed syllable (e.g. γραμματῖς for γραμματεῖς 'scribes' **38** 15, 18, **39** 17, **57** 21; χρίας for χρείας 'needs' **4** 19, **110** 57); in unstressed syllable (e.g. πιράσεται for πειράσεται 'attempt:fut.3sg' **70** 14; θέλις for θέλεις 'want:pr.2sg' **68** 5); the ending -ειν was written as -ιν (e.g. πολῖν for πωλεῖν 'sell' **12** 20; φυγῖν for φυγεῖν 'flee' **79** 19; χαίριν for χαίρειν 'rejoice' **67** 2, **86** 1).

---

31 Liquids, however, can either raise or lower the quality of the vowel, depending on what the previous and following syllables contain (Dahlgren 2017: 96–97).
32 After /r/ 22 instances; after /l/ 14 instances, whereas, in other environments, there are no more than 10 instances. However, after /r/ cases include the same words several times, e.g. χάρειν written for χάριν 6 times, all in Apollonios' texts, and περεί written for περί 6 times (once, πρεί), all in Ptolemaios' texts. It therefore seems like Apollonios and Ptolemaios had their own mindset on how to write these particular words; pronunciation did not need to play a significant role, cf. Dahlgren (2017: 71) on semi-standard local variants. Apollonios wrote χάριν correctly only once, in his letter to Ptolemaios (**70**); Ptolemaios, on the other hand, managed to write περί correctly in two documents (**79, 101**).
33 Before /n/ 24 instance; before /s/ 11 instances; before /a/ 10 instances; others, fewer than 10 instances.
34 The phonetic environment in this direction differs from that of ει written for standard ι. Here the position after a stop /k, p, t/ is the most common (and, when coupled with the aspirated or voiced allophones, even more so; especially π_ and φ_ together total 38 instances). However, before the liquid /l/, the interchange is frequent (32 instances); in that position, /s/ (17 instances) and /n/ (19 instances) are also significant. In the position _λ, one recurring word dominates the result: ἰλήφασι(ν) written for εἰλήφασι(ν) 'receive:pf.3pl' occurs 19 times, all in Apollonios' texts; before /n/ and /s/, the cases are more varied.

Another very common confusion, that between *omicron* and *omega* tells that the loss of distinctive vowel length had already taken place.[35] For standard *omega*, the Katochoi papyri had *omicron* in 59 instances; in the opposite direction, 51 instances. Instances of expected ω written as ο came almost exclusively from the hand of Apollonios (only 4 times in Ptolemaios' hand and 3 times in those of others).[36] Note also his use of two omicrons for the long vowel; τοον for τῶν (**79** 2), a feature common in Coptic (Dahlgren 2017: 144). The other direction, expected ο written as ω, appears also 5 times in scribal hands (+**110**), 8 times in Ptolemaios' hand; and the rest of the 38 instances were in Apollonios' hand. This count includes also instances where the writer avoided declining nouns of the third declension in the genitive case – e.g. Μακεδών for Μακεδόνος 'Macedonian', see below 3.2. In both directions, Apollonios has confused *omicron* and *omega* also when the text he copied from had the standard form (e.g. in text group C, **34** against **36**). Standard ω was written as ο word-initially (e.g. ὁς for ὡς 'so that' **14** 76, ὅμην for ᾤμην 'believe:impf.1sg' **78** 36); word-finally (e.g. δο for δῷ[37] 'give:aor.3sg' **33** 8, κάτο for κάτω 'below' **54** 31, ἀξιο for ἀξιῶ 'request:pr.1sg' **12** 49); in stressed syllable (e.g. τον for τῶν 'the:gen.pl.' **34** 13, **110** 122, πόποτε for πώποτε 'ever' **70** 6, 24, **78** 28); in unstressed syllable (e.g. ἔδοκέ for ἔδωκέ 'give:aor.3sg' **78** 37, πολῖν for πωλεῖν **12** 17). Standard ο was written as ω word-initially (e.g. ὠνηλάται for ὀνηλάται 'donkeydrivers' **12** 40, ὥπως for ὅπως 'that' **110** 65); word-finally (τω for τό 'the:nom/acc.sg.' **32** 9, **34** 7; no other examples); in stressed syllable (e.g. βαπτιζώμεθα for βαπτιζόμεθα 'sink:pr.1pl' **70** 13, τώπους for τόπους 'places' **35** 18); in unstressed syllable (e.g. εὔγνωμων for εὔγνωμον 'sensible' **57** 18, σημαινωμένωι for σημαινομένωι 'aforementioned' **14** 12).

It is perhaps not as useful to review the phonetic environment when the overall figures of occurrences are relatively low, leaving more room for chance. Nevertheless, it could strengthen the idea that Egyptian was a relatively strong language for Apollonios. In the direction of standard ω written as ο, dentals received the highest score (τ_: 4, δ_: 12, θ_: 1). In the opposite direction, the highest scores were seen before nasals (_ν: 21, _μ: 8).[38]

---

35 Cf. Horrocks (2010: 167).
36 Twice in **110** (an administrative letter copied in a handwriting that seems to be unprofessional, see Wilcken 1927: 473–475 – i.e. perhaps material from scribal education) and once in a private letter (**72**) for which Wilcken did propose could be Apollonios' hand, but see below.
37 Similarly written in **36**, but not similarly corrected by the editor, see below on verbal inflection.
38 In Coptic, ω was higher than ο, and these phonetic environments can raise the quality of the vowel (Dahlgren 2017: 42–43, 59, 94). Coptic, of course, was not attested yet at this time, but the same phenomena may have already been present in the earlier phase of Egyptian.

Somewhat more interesting is the interchange of *eta* and *epsilon*, since this confusion would not occur with the commonly known raising of *eta* to /i/ but could rather simply reflect the loss of the distinctive vowel length of the /e/ sound combined with the slight raising of η (but not yet to /i/) as presented by Teodorsson and Horrocks.³⁹ However, it has also been suggested that this interchange was specific to Egyptian writers.⁴⁰ This would corroborate the bilingualism of Apollonios and Ptolemaios, whose texts repeat this confusion in spite of their emphasis on their Hellene identity and status. Mayser and Schmoll's lists (39–41) show that *eta* appears instead of *epsilon* in final position, before consonants and before vowels (α, η, ω, ου; the last especially in personal names ending -κλῆς and -ῆς),⁴¹ but *epsilon* instead of *eta* occurs only before consonants or in final position.⁴² Gignac lists several occurrences for the Roman and Byzantine period, and η > ε (standard η written as ε) is attested before or after a nasal or liquid (the latter only when unaccented), before /s/, and in final position. In the opposite direction, ε > η, back vowels and other positions also appear in the environment. Table 3 presents all examples of this interchange in our archive, categorized by hand. The first interesting feature is that Ptolemaios has not written *epsilon* instead of standard *eta* (η > ε) even once. He only ever replaces *epsilon* with *eta* (ε > η). In this direction, he has written ἕως 'until' quite persistently as ἥως – in total, 48 times. In contrast, his brother Apollonios wrote ἥως only once and ἕως correctly in ten documents (many of them copies of petitions). This particular word is also written correctly in most scribal hands. But Apollonios was not always capable of following the scribal hands, since in group F texts Apollonios copied δήοντα (**50**) even though the word was written δέοντα 're-quired' in **46, 47, 48**. In **14**, which is clearly a copy of a petition that has gone through the official rounds, Apollonios' version includes several confusions with *epsilon* and *eta*. It is presumable that they were present only in Apollonios' copy, not in the text he copied from (which is not preserved).

It is noteworthy that ε and η are confused in Apollonios' hand and the scribal hands also when *iota* adscripts (-ει instead of -ηι) apply. The long diphthong -ηι

---

39 Horrocks (2010: 161–162) on /ε:/ (η) first being pulled to the position abandoned by /e:/ (ει) and only afterward towards /i/. See also his table of Egyptian Koine in the second century (p. 167), wherein η was raised to /e/, while ε was pronounced just as /e/.
40 Clarysse (1993: 197). For a thorough discussion on Coptic *eta* having the quality of [e] see Dahlgren (2017: 106–112).
41 Mayser-Schmoll (39–41). In all papyri, in the centuries BCE 217 hits (Paratypa, 21 Dec 2017).
42 Mayser-Schmoll (46–49); before a vowel, only one special case is mentioned. In all papyri, in the centuries BCE, 249 hits (Paratypa 21 Dec 2017). The only vowels following this interchange are υ (5 times), ευ in initial position, and ι (e.g. η(ι) for ει); see below.

was, according to Teodorsson and Horrocks already merged with ει and raised to /i/ in the fifth century BCE.⁴³ It is therefore peculiar that the allegedly unpronounced

Table 3: All examples of the interchange between *eta* and *epsilon* in the Katochoi archive.

ε ~ η	Ptolemaios	Apollonios	Scribal/other hands
ε > η	πλῆρης (πλῆρες 'full') 77 14 ἐννήα (ἐννέα 'nine') 77 11 ἤαν (ἐάν 'if') 67 10 ἥως (ἕως) (48 times)⁴⁴ Ἡρακλήου (Ἡρακλέους 'Heracles') 84 80	δήοντα (δέοντα 'required') 50 10 εὐσήβειαν (εὐσέβειαν 'respect') 58 5 μητήνεκα (μετήνεγκα 'transfer') 14 110 ἤτη (ἔτος 'year') 18v 2 ἠζημίοται (ἐζημίωται 'cause loss') 70 18 ἥως (ἕως) 54 5 πατηρα (πάτερ 'father') 78 36 ἰπή (εἰπέ 'say') 78 44	ἥως (ἕως 'until') 21 9
η > ε		ἀπελλάγηνν (ἀπηλλάγην 'escape') 12 27 Διοσκουδει (Διοσκουρίδηι 'Dioskourides') 14 99, 53, 117, 123 ἀρχειπερέτην (ἀρχυπηρέτηι 'chief minister') 14 97, 121 διοικητε̄ι (διοικητῆι 'finance minister') 14 139 ἐγγλογίζεται (ἐγλογίζηται 'count') 14 41 γραφε̄ι (γραφῆι 'writing') 14 73 δειακονε̄ι (διακονῆι 'serve') 18r 23 ἐπιμελητε̄ι (ἐπιμελητῆι 'financial officer') 50 11 εἴε (εἴη 'be') 68 2 ἐπητρίᾳ (ἠπητρίᾳ 'mender') 91 16, 93, 10	ἐξερημωμένον (ἐξηρημωμένον 'desolated') 5 37 κατοχε̄ι (κατοχῆι 'detention') 6 36 διαλαβειν (διαλάβηι 'treat') 10 32, 11 28 (?)

---

43 Horrocks (2010: 112, 167); Dahlgren (2017: 111).
44 56 3, 4, 5, 9, 10, **77** 21, 25, **82** 24, **84** 16, 33, 49, 72, 92, **85** 39, **86** 2, **87** 9, **90** 8, 15, **92** 2, 4, **96** 25, 30, 31, 35, 45, 46, **98** 19, 53, 57, 78, 81, 140, **99** 15, 25, 26, 44, 47, **101** 5, 13, **104** 14, **105** 16. Document **103** 2 is the only instance in which Ptolemaios has written ἕως correctly, but, in the same document, l. 5, he has also written the word as ἧς.

written *iota* was not learned simply in connection with the letter η (and α and ω) in dative and subjunctive endings, but it also interfered with endings when they were mistakenly written with an *epsilon*. Apparently, the mute *iota* was learned on its own, connected to certain sounds /a, e, o/, not in connection with certain graphemes. In general, we can note that the variation ε > η took place before back vowels or consonants and in final position and, in the opposite direction, before a consonant or in final position. Thus, the results show the same tendency as the observations of Mayser and Schmoll and those of Gignac. Since the surrounding consonants are exactly the same as the ones Dahlgren (2017: 100–106, 160–161) talks about, the influence of Egyptian phonology in these coarticulate spellings has to be taken into account.

Apollonios was clearly aware of his own difficulties with the interchange of η and ε, since he made several corrections around these graphemes, e.g. in his draft **18r** (l. 3 μητρός 'mother' corrected from μετρος, l. 19 ἔλθη 'come' corrected from ηλθη, l. 28 ἀπῆλθεν 'go away' from απελθεν, μητέρα 'mother' from μητηρα).

Significantly rarer is the interchange of ε with αι. Both Apollonios and Ptolemaios wrote only once αι for ε and only once the other way around.[45] Supposedly these spellings were both pronounced /e/ by the second century BCE, but as an exception the Egyptian Greek variant is mentioned, where αι was more retracted.[46] Our brothers seem to use that variant. However, there is also one instance of Μαικεδόνος written by Apollonios (**53** 2), to be compared with his spelling of Μεκεδώνος (**13** 6). This indicates that the quality distinction between /a, e/ was not very clear to Apollonios in an unstressed syllable (cf. below).

The raising of /y/ to /i/ is attested in the interchange of υ and ι. These instances are not very frequent but appear in the writing of both brothers in either direction, for which see Table 4. The word for 'twins', δίδυμοι, appears frequently, and Apollonios writes the word correctly in over twenty documents.[47] Ptolemaios, however, writes the word correctly only around half the time.[48] At any rate, the words presented in Table 4 all have a bilabial nasal /m/ next to the confused sound. Other writers in the archive managed to adhere to

---

45 εὐφράνεσθαι for εὐφραίνεσθε 'rejoice:inf/2pl' **78** 39 and παλεοῦ for παλαιοῦ 'elder'. **94** 8 (Apollonios); ἔφαιρ for ἔφερε 'bring' **79** 7 and ἀνύγετε for ἀνοίγεται 'open:3sg' **79** 7 (Ptolemaios). Their brother Sarapion had also one example of the first interchange: εἰδῆται for εἰδῆτε 'know:2pl' **66** 4.
46 Horrocks (2010: 167).
47 In **22, 23, 26, 29, 31, 32, 33, 34, 35, 37, 38, 39** (corr. ex διδιμων), **44, 49, 50, 52, 53, 54, 55, 57, 78, 89.**
48 **56, 79, 85, 104** (**96** δειδυμῶν).

Table 4: Interchange of ι and υ.

ι ~ υ	Ptolemaios	Apollonios
υ > ι	ἰμεῖν for ὑμῖν 'you' **66** 4 δυδίμη for διδύμη 'twin' **77** 3, 11	διδιμῶν for διδυμῶν 'twins' **49** 3 ἥμυσι for ἥμισυ 'half' **52** 15
ι < υ	ἥμυσου for ἥμισυ **67** 5, 9 δυδίμη for διδύμη **77** 3, 11 δυδυμῶν for διδυμῶν **84** 1, 32, 56 **85** 2, 25	σησαμύνου for σησαμίνου 'of sesame' **33** 7 ἥμυσου for ἥμισυ **52** 12 **53** 15, 17, **54** 6, 7, 11, **55** 5 ἥμυσι for ἥμισυ **52** 15

standard orthography regarding υ and ι. In Apollonios' hand, there are two interesting examples of αι written for αυ (καιτῶν for αὐτῶν **44** 2, αἰταὶ for αὐταὶ **54** 31). In the first case, it is possible that there was simply a confusion as to how to perform the crasis with καί but with the latter example that is not the case; it seems that ι and υ were confused within the diphthongs αυ and αι. Apollonios has other examples of crases (**78** 15 κἀαγὼ for καὶ ἐγώ 'I too' **68** 1 καυτός for καὶ αὐτός 'myself' [similarly in **11** 29 by a scribal hand; in letters by other hands **61** 5, **64** 2 καυτοί for καὶ αὐτοί, **66** 2]).

Once, Apollonios wrote μου 'my' for μοι 'me' (**35** 22). Rather than confusion of /u/ and /y, i/, we should perhaps interpret this instance as a confusion between the genitive and the dative cases, since the dative case was sometimes difficult for Apollonios (see below). Or it was just a slip of the pen, since in the other version in Apollonios' hand, the word was written μοι (**34** 10). Another case of υ confusion was with the old diphthong οι, which developed through /y/ to /i/. By the first century BCE, it had gone through /y/.[49] We have only two instances of υ written instead of οι: ἀνύγωι for ἀνοίγω 'open:1sg' **78** 7 (Apollonios); ἀνύγετε for ἀνοίγεται 'open:3sg' **79** 7 (Ptolemaios). There are more instances in the opposite direction but only with one word: τὸ θρύον 'reed' in θροιοπόλιον for θρυοπώλιον 'rush-seller's shop' (**12** 13, Apollonios) and θροία for θρύα/θρύων (ca. 15 times in Ptolemaios' hand and once in Apollonios'). Furthermore, Apollonios occasionally wrote an additional γ in between vowels (representing a glide and relating to fricativization of γ), e.g. Σαραπίγηωι instead of Σαραπιείωι 'Sarapieion'.[50]

Interestingly one feature is missing from the brothers' writings that appears 15 times by scribal and other hands: the dropping of *iota* from different forms of

---

[49] Horrocks (2010: 167).
[50] Cf. Bentein (2015: 467), Gignac (1976: 71–72), Mayser-Schmoll (141–143). The twins' names, Taues and Taous, were written in many instances with a γ (Ταγης, Ταυγης, etc.).

ποιέω 'to do', e.g. πεποήμεθα for πεποιήμεθα (**17** 21, **19** 5) and ποήσασθαι for ποιήσασθαι (**10** 19, 23). The dropping of *iota* with this verb has been connected to the imitation of Attic orthography by some well-educated scribes.[51] Therefore, Apollonios, who always[52] writes this verb with *iota*, is apparently ignorant of Atticist pedantry. On the other hand, he has occasionally dropped the *eta* from this verb.[53] This feature may also be used as an argument for Apollonios not being the writer of one letter (**72**), which Wilcken marked to be by the hand of Apollonios with a question mark. The handwriting indeed bears similarities to the hand of Apollonios, and the text also shares several similar problems with orthography as Apollonios' texts. However, since Apollonios writes ποη- only once (against 6 documents with ποιε-/ποιη- and 10 with ποι-) and **72** has two instances of ποη- (ll. 8 and 16) and include no *iota* adscripts, which Apollonios usually writes (even hypercorrectly), it seems reasonable to conclude that this letter sent by Myrullas and Chalbas, who were titled as Arabs, was not written by him. In the opposite direction, there are few instances of the addition of *iota* in forms of βοηθός 'assistant' and βοήθεια 'help' both in texts by scribal hands (βοιηθείας **5** 53, βοιη[θ]òν **46** 19, βοιηθòν **47** 23) and in Apollonios' drafts/copies (βοιηθòν **50** 26, **52** 8, **53** 9).

Some other orthographic variants of the brothers can be seen as pointing to Egyptian influence in addition to the confusion of *eta* and *epsilon*, such as problems with the voiced and voiceless/aspirated consonants (see further below) and the confusion between ε - α - ο, due to the reduction of unstressed vowels to schwa.[54] Table 5 presents the instances of interchange between α and ε, showing that the occurrences happen in unstressed syllables and often in connection with retracting consonants.[55] Some of these instances may be due to morphological "equalization of the endings" in *-es/-as* (see 3.2 below). Confusion between ε and ο are few, but they more clearly show the reduction of unstressed syllable (not morphological confusion) – e.g. προσβυτέρου for πρεσβυτέρου 'elder' (**13** 13) by Apollonios, who also wrote προσβύτη (**78** 36), and ὑπογραψας for ὑπέγραψε 'subscribe:3sg' (**26** 18). Once, Ptolemaios wrote ἐργάσζοντος for ἐργάζοντες 'working' (**77** 21) (unlikely to be a mistake between genitive singular vs. nominative plural, since the subject is clearly plural: δυω ἄνθρωποι 'two people'). Other hands in the Katochoi archive did not confuse ο for ε (and, in the whole corpus

---

51 Clarysse (2010: 40–41).
52 With one exception: **57** 4 ἐπόησαν.
53 **14** 12, 18, 35, 37, 83, 114, **23** 13, **26** 16, **50** 12, **58** 4, **70** 21; πεποιμένος **12** 48–49; ποισάμενοι **13** 27, ποισης **73** 4, ποισις **74** 10.
54 Dahlgren (2017: 62–66).
55 Dahlgren (2017: 115).

Table 5: Interchange of ε and α.

ε ~ α	Ptolemaios	Apollonios	Scribal/other hands
ε > α		ἀπελθόντες 'go away' for ἐπελ-'come' **12** 29 ἀπέδωκα 'give' for ἐπέδ- 'give besides' **14** 104 (?), 105, 107 (?) ἐπέταξαν (-αξεν) 'order' **18r** 6 ὑπογραψας for ὑπέγραψε 'subscribe' **26** 18 ἀπάναγκον for ἐπάν- 'compulsory' **31** 10 ἀνανεκει for ἀνενεγκεῖν 'report back' **43** 22	Ἄραβας for Ἄραβες 'Arabs' **72** 2 ὑβρίζοντας for ὑβρίζοντες 'violating' **8** 21 τύπτοντας for τύπτοντες 'beating' **8** 22
α > ε	σινδόνες for σινδόνας 'linen cloth' **84** 4, **85** 7	Μεκεδώνος for Μακεδόνος 'Macedonian' **13** 6 ἐπέδοκα for ἀπέδωκα **52** 4, **53** 4 ἠνθρεκίσθαι for ἠνθρακίσθαι 'roast' **78** 33 φοίνικες for φοίνικας 'dates' **89** 16 θρίδακες for θρίδακας 'lettuce' **89** 3 ὄρνιθες for ὄρνιθας 'birds' **102** 4	ἐντρεπέντος for ἐντραπέντος 'notice' **5** 24 ἐπειρότατον for ἀπειρότ- 'most ignorant' **110** 54 προσεδρεύσετε for -σατε 'serve' **110** 138 ἐξαργυρίζοντες for -ζοντας 'turn into money' **110** 136 δηλώσαντες for -ντας 'make known' UPZ I p. 596 16

of papyri from the second century BCE, they have been confused only 27 times in total); the other direction (ε for o) is more commonly attested in the whole corpus (60 from the second century BCE), but, in the Katochoi archive, only Apollonios once writes ἔθες for ἔθος 'custom' (**12** 20). Scribal hands confused o and α twice (δύνομαι for δύναμαι 'to be able:1sg' in **9** 10 and **10** 22[56]) as well as Ptolemaios and Apollonios once each.[57] In the other direction, 3 instances are attested in Apollonios' hand and 3 in other hands.[58]

---

56 Texts **9** and **10** are both petitions about the same subject but were written by two different scribal hands.
57 The instances are not as clear: οἰδην for αἰδοῖον 'genitals' (**77** 30, Ptolemaios) and ἀμτος for ἄμητας 'milk cake' (**89** 9, Apollonios).
58 Apollonios: ταῖς 'the:fem.dat' for τοῖς 'the:masc.dat' **39** 31; ἀρχισωματαφύλακος for ἀρχισωματοφύλακος 'chief of the body guard' **14** 94, 118. Others: βολάμενοι for βουλόμενοι

As for consonants, the distinction of voiced stops from voiceless was not present in Egyptian; thus, the confusion of these in Greek can only point to an Egyptian influence.[59] For dentals, τ and δ were confused by Apollonios and Ptolemaios, but not very often (5 examples of τ > δ[60] and two of δ > τ[61]). Confusions of κ and γ are more numerous but concern mostly the preposition ἐκ either alone or in compounds – notably, only one of these instances occurs in Apollonios' hand; the remaining occur in scribal hands (the preposition alone and some compounds) and in Ptolemaios' (word 'napkin' repeatedly in **83–85**: ἐγμαγην/ἐγμαγῆα for ἐκμαγεῖον/ἐκμαγεῖα).[62] In all cases of the preposition alone, the following word begins with /m/. Thus, voicing of the previous sound can be expected without assuming Egyptian influence.

3.2 Morphology

Nominal inflection. The use of nominative plural ending *-es* for *-as* in accusative plural of athematic nouns is a commonly known feature of Koine Greek.[63] We find it, e.g. in **70**, a letter written by Apollonios: the nominative ending -ες was written instead of accusative ending -ας, even though the definite article shows that the writer's intention was to write the accusative (πρὸ\ς/ τοὺς τὴν ἀλήθειαν λέγοντες 'to those who speak the truth'). In an account written by Apollonios, several nouns are in nominative with the *-es* endings (written -ες or -ης). Other items in that list are in the neuter or in the accusative of the second

---

'willing' **72** 10, βουλαμένων for βουλομένων 'willing' **110** 124, μικρὰν 'small:fem' for μικρὸν 'small:masc/neut' **110** 201.

59 Mayser-Schmoll (143), Gignac (1976: 76–86), Horrocks (2010: 112), Dahlgren (2017: 58).

60 Apollonios: Ἀσταρδιδηνον for Ἀσταρτιείωι 'temple of Astarte' **13** 11, ἔδι for ἔτι 'yet' **33** 11, ἀνδαποδῷ for ἀνταποδῷ 'repay' **53** 30, δραπέδην for δραπέτην 'runaway' **69** 6; Ptolemaios: δοσαυτη for τοσαύτης 'that much' **67** 11.

61 Apollonios: βατίζειν for βαδίζειν 'walk' **78** 3; Ptolemaios: προστάτι for προστάδι 'vestibule' **77** 22. Other hands: τὲ for δὲ UPZ I p. 596, **110** 83, παρεφετρευόντων for παρεφεδρευόντων 'garrisoned' **110** 206. In addition, Apollonios apparently corrected himself in this respect: in **14** he wrote ἐπετοδοκα (for ἐπέδωκα) where, in Wilcken's view, the syllable το was corrected to δο without deleting the first erroneous one (cf. also ἀπέτωδωκα in line 100 in the same document).

62 ἐγ for ἐκ 'from': **3** 9, **19** 6 (corrected from ἐν 'in') **46** 11, **47** 15, **50** 15 (Apollonios), **110** 182; ἐγδοκὴν for ἐκδοχὴν 'understanding' **110** 86; ἐγλειπεῖν for ἐκλιπεῖν 'leave' **47** 14. On the case of διγνύοι for δεικνύοι 'point out' (**76** 5, Apollonios), cf. Bentein (2015: 467). This word does not come up in searches in Paratypa, since this correction is not included in the apparatus. Wilcken only mentions it in the commentary to **76**.

63 Bubenik (2014); Torallas Tovar (2014).

declension. Thus, it is likely that Apollonios meant to use the accusative throughout the list.[64] In a petition written by a scribe (**8**), -*as* was (hypercorrectly?) written instead of -*es* (ὑβρίζοντας καὶ τύπτοντας 'violating and beating up', ll. 21–22). The reason was probably not so much confusion of cases *per se*, but rather the quality of the vowel in an unstressed final syllable, most likely a *schwa*, which made the writer confuse which vowel to write in the plural accusative vs. nominative. In letter **72** 2, Ἄραβας is written instead of Ἄραβες 'Arabs', but this does not require us to identify Apollonios as the writer of the letter (cf. above).

Bentein (2015: 469–470) discusses a certain reluctance in this archive to decline third declension nouns, related to the "losses" in Greek declension of consonantal stems noted already by Jannaris ([1897] 1968). The examples Bentein gives come from scribal hands (**5, 43**), Apollonios (**18v, 57, 77**), and Ptolemaios (**77**). I would like to add that the nominative form Μακεδών 'Macedonian' appears instead of the genitive Μακεδόνος four times (**18v** 1, **34** 1, **43** 2, **20** 66); the latter two documents are otherwise from scribal hands, but these words have been added apparently in Apollonios' hand in **43** (between the lines) and **20** where a whole line was deleted; **18** and **34** are all in Apollonios' writing. In fact, **18v** is the docket on the back side of the draft petition and reads παρὰ Πτολεμαίου Γλαυκίου Μακ[ε]δ[ών] ὁ ἐν κατοχῇ. . . ('from Ptolemaios, son of Glaukias, Macedonian, who [is] in reclusion'). The ending of the word "Macedonian" is in a lacuna, so, in fact, it is difficult to say how the word was declined,[65] but the fact that the relative pronoun in the beginning of the second line is in the nominative suggests that the writer wanted to switch to the nominative here; most likely, therefore, he intentionally used the nominative also for the word 'Macedonian'. In **34**, the word is clearly left uninflected (as a parenthetical remark), just like in the additions in **43** and **20**. In **18r**, Apollonios, along the same line, uses nominative instead of dative in the title of a person.[66] This usage can be compared to the so-called phrase-initial inflection used by bilingual notaries in Upper Egypt, whose L1 Egyptian clearly had an influence on their habit of leaving latter parts of a phrase in the nominative case where Greek would have required agreement of all words in the phrase; very often this happened in the description of a person, like here.[67]

---

[64] **89** 3 θρίδακες for θρίδακας 'lettuce', 3, 13 σφλανγνίδης for σπλαγχνίδας 'entrails', 5 γονγυλίδης for γογγυλίδας 'turnips', 16 φοίνικες for φοίνικας 'dates'.

[65] The facsimile P.Paris pl. 26 shows that almost the entire word Macedonian is in a gap, in which a shorter version of the word admittedly seems to fit better.

[66] **18r** 4 Φιλίππωι Σωγένου στρατι[ώτ]ης (for στρατιώτῃ) 'to Philippos, son of Sogenes, soldier'.

[67] Vierros (2012a: 140–147).

The consonantal stem declension is seen avoided among some writers other than our brothers, e.g. with participles (private letter **64** 3 σημηνας 'reporting:nom' for σημήναντι 'reporting:dat', 11 παραγενηθεις 'be assisted:nom' for παραγενηθέντι 'be assisted: dat'). However, in a petition (**2**), two participles were used in accusative instead of genitive (3 διαζῶντα for διαζῶντος 'living through', 7 διαιτώμενον for διαιτωμένου 'living'), and the latter is not inflected in the third declension, so some other factor must play a role in the case confusion attested there.

Some case confusions may be caused by similarity in pronunciation combined with the factor of not knowing correct orthography. This can be behind most instances of confusions by Apollonios and Ptolemaios, but let us first examine the case which appears in other writers as well as in Apollonios' texts. It was more common to write the dative Μέμφει 'Memphis' instead of the accusative Μέμφιν in the phrase ἐν τῶι πρὸς Μέμφει μεγάλωι Σαραπιείωι ('in the Great Sarapieion at Memphis'). However, the accusative Μέμφιν was occasionally written by scribal hands (**3, 17, 47, 48**) and by Apollonios (**13, 52, 53, 58**). Since the preposition *pros* could also take the accusative case, this need not be understood as a mistake. However, the editors have mostly corrected the accusative into the dative. The phrase was indeed more common with the dative (at least in 14 documents in this archive). The weakness of the final /n/ is not unusual in papyrus Greek, and Bentein (2015: 468) also notes that it is quite often dropped; his examples all come from one document written by Ptolemaios (**77**) – the similar pronunciation of ι and ει was already discussed above. Therefore, it is not surprising to find these two forms confused. It is interesting, however, that when we compare the pair of petitions **12** and **13**, both drafts of the same text written by Apollonios, the word was written Μέμφι in **12** 9 and Μέμφιν in **13** 9 – i.e. if **12** was a later draft, as other factors also suggest, this would mean that Apollonios "corrected" the accusative into a form that resembles more the dative, even though it is not exactly written in the standard.[68] The fact that Apollonios seemingly added a hypercorrect *nu* into a dative form in **29** 6 (Κρατερῶν χειριστῆ τῷ pro Κρατερῷ χειριστῆ τῷ 'to Krateros, the manager'), suggests that he simply was able to occasionally add an extra *nu* in forms he still understood as datives. The genitive instead of dative in μου 'my' for μοι 'for me' (**35** 22) was mentioned

---

[68] The earlier petition (**13**) has been left unfinished in the middle of the text, whereas **12** is the entire petition (albeit without the greetings at the end). In **13** 26, Apollonios also wrote dative instead of accusative: οὐθένα (corr. ex ουθενι) κοσμωι (for κόσμον) ποιοάμενοι 'doing nothing decent', which was structured with a different verb with dative in **12** οὐθενὶ κόσμῳ χρησάμενο\ι/ 'using no decency'. In **13** 1–2, Apollonios wrote the name of the addressee Poseidonios in the genitive plural Ποσιδωνεων, probably attracted from the following title τῶν φίλων 'of friends', but corrected it to the dative in **12**: Ποσειδωνίωι τῶν φίλων.

already above ("Phonology"). Apollonios' sudden feminine nominative πασαι 'all' instead of masculine dative πᾶσι may just be a slip of the pen; the article τοῖς shows he is not addressing only females, in which case the pattern of phrase-initial inflections could explain this mistake (**74** 7 τοῖς ἐν οἰκο πασαι χαίρειν 'to all in the house, greetings').

A genitive used instead of the nominative ἡ δὲ οἰκίας (for οἰκία) τοῦ πατρός (**18** 8) ('father's house') could also be explained as a hypercorrect addition of final sigma, but the following possessive genitive could have attracted the case here. On the other hand, the definite article shows that Apollonios intended to write the nominative.

Several case confusions occur with names ending in -ις (gen. -ιος) or neuter nouns ending in -ιον (discussion in Vierros 2012a: 167–173), e.g. genitive instead of dative or nominative (**68** 3 Πετοσίριος for Πετοσίρει 'Petosiris' [first name of three, two others in the dative]; **65** 5–6 Πετευσοράπιος for Πετευσοράπις 'Peteusorapis'). Dative or accusative were written instead of genitive by Ptolemaios (**88** 2–4 παρὰ τω Σαράπει . . . Ἀφροδεισιωι 'from Sarapis:dat, . . . Aphrodisios:dat' for παρὰ τοῦ Σαράπιος . . . Ἀφροδεισίου 'from Sarapis:gen, . . . Aphrodisios:gen'; Ἀφροδισιω 'Aphrodisios:dat' for Ἀφροδεισίου 'Aphrodisios:gen' **84** 91 [with preposition παρά, **85** 23]; Σαραπίωνα Sarapion:acc' for Σαραπίωνος 'Sarapion:gen' **80** 4 with the preposition περί[69]). It is not surprising to find that the vocative was not used in **66** 6 (Ἀπολλώνιος 'Apollonios:nom' for Ἀπολλώνιε 'Apollonios:voc').

In the dream descriptions written by Ptolemaios (**77**), very few instances that could be interpreted as something other than phonological effect on orthography occur. However, some of these could be morphological as well. Especially three participle forms in the nominative in one sentence: οἴομαι τὴν Ταγῆν εὔφονον (for εὔφωνον) **οὖσα** (for οὖσαν) καὶ ἡδυτέραι τῇ φωνῇ καὶ εὖ **δειακειμενη** (for διακειμένην) καὶ ὁρῶ τὴν Ταοῦν **γελωσα** (for γελῶσαν) καὶ τὸν πόδα αὐτῆς μέγαν καθαρόν ['I seem to see Tages rather sweetly singing (?) and well disposed, and I see Taous laughing, and her foot is big and pure'] (col.1, 16–20).[70] The bolded nominative forms instead of accusatives could easily be explained with the weakness of the final nasal (see above), but, since Ptolemaios omits the final nasal in this text only in these words and writes it correctly dozens of times (8 times in this very sentence), we should rather assume that he has meant to write these participles in the nominative case. In fact, all his participles in this text are in the nominative even when the head is in the accusative (cf. Ταοῦν . . . προσπαιζουσα [for προσπαίζουσαν]

---

[69] Three items above in this same list are also nouns and names with the same preposition, all correctly inflected in the genitive.
[70] Translation by Rowlandson (1988: 103).

'Taous . . . joking' col.1, 24–25, Ἄμμωνα . . . τριτος ὢν [for τρίτον ὄντα] 'Ammon . . . being third (i.e. in his trinity?)' col.2, 25, βοῦν . . . οὐδεινουσα [for ὠδίνουσαν] 'cow . . . being in labour' col.2, 27).⁷¹ Therefore, this is more of a syntactic reanalysis of the participial complement as somehow outside the agreement pattern. The same phenomenon occurs in Apollonios' letter about a dream **78** 25 ἐμὲ δὲ ἄφες, εἰδού (for ἰδού), πολιὰς **ἔχων** (for ἔχοντα) 'release me, see, I have grey hair'.

Verbal inflection. Verbs were inflected in a surprisingly standard manner. Only occasionally and mostly from Apollonios do we find interparadigmatic leveling⁷² – e.g. weak aorist vs. strong aorist εἶπα Ἁρμάεις for εἶπον Ἁρμάει 'I told to Harmais' (**78** 21), εἶπάς 'you said' (**52** 5, **53** 6; not corrected in the *apparatus*); εἶπα and εἶπας also in **62** 14, 19, which was not written by Apollonios;⁷³ aorist ending in perfect stem: ἐνβέβληκαν instead of ἐνβεβλήκασιν 'they threw' (**70** 9; not corrected in the *apparatus*). In the pair of petitions **12+13**, Apollonios used the form ὕβριζαν, which should apparently be taken as the active aorist 3rd person plural (i.e. ὕβρισαν); however, in **12**, he corrected this from the imperfect ὕβριζον. Athematic verbs (*–mi*) were treated as thematic, which fits with expectations of this time: **70** 2–3 ὀμνύο (for ὀμνύω) instead of ὄμνυμι 'I swear'.⁷⁴ Future periphrasis μέλλομεν σωθῆναι 'we will be saved' is also found in **70** 12.⁷⁵ The scribe of **8** used infinitive forms instead of finite ones: ανωσαι for ἀνέωσάν 'thrust through:3pl' and σκυλαι for ἔσκυλαν 'stripped:3pl' (both l. 21), ανελειν for ἀνέλωσι 'take away:3pl' (l. 15). These can perhaps be better placed under the category of syntactic confusion – e.g. the writer had used *accusativus cum infinitivo* just before line 15.

The formation of participles was not always clear: Sarapion, the brother of Apollonios and Ptolemaios, wrote a participial form for an imperative: **66** 5 παραγενομενοῦ for παραγενοῦ 'be present'. One interesting correction is from present to perfect participle in a copy written by Apollonios: ἀντι[[λαμβανο]]λημμένου

---

71 One dubious case is on col. 1, 21–22: δυω ἄνθρωποι ἐργάσζοντος 'two people working', where the participle probably is meant to be plural nominative ἐργάζοντες, not singular genitive. The possibility of confusing ε and ο in instressed syllable, see above. In another dream account (**79**) written by Ptolemaios, there are participles in the accusative, e.g. ἔχοντα 'having' on l. 6.
72 Cf. Bubenik (2014: 2c).
73 Of course, the sigmatic aorist forms of εἶπον are also found in e.g. Ionic prose.
74 The athematic first person singular form (-μι) of this verb is quite rare in papyri: 31 hits of ομνυμι in all DDbDP, only three of which are from the Hellenistic period. The form was revived from the second century CE onwards. The search ομνυω# received 385 hits; 44 of them from the Hellenistic period. The form in –ω appears, in fact, already in Classical prose writers such as Herodotos, Xenophon, and Plato; see Jannaris (1897: 234), Gignac (1981: 375–377).
75 Cf. Bentein (2015: 471).

(read ἀντειλημμένου) 'assist' (**39** 4–5). In the scribal version of the same text, this word is not well preserved (ἀντε[ιλημμένου]), but, apparently, Apollonios first thought to use the present participle and then, perhaps after checking the exemplar, had to change the form to perfect participle. This suggests that he was not copying word by word. Another copy of a petition by Apollonios shows also that the copying process did not always result in similar forms: **35** has διδοῖ 'give:3sg' (l. 12) and λάμβανωσιν 'receive:pr.ind.3pl (l. 18) and νομίζαντα (l. νομίσαντα) 'thinking' (l. 20), whereas other copies of the same petition have δο (l. δῷ) 'give: subj.3sg', λάβωσιν 'receive:aor.subj.3pl', νομίσαντα 'thinking' (**33** 8, 13, 14) and δοι (l. δῶι)[76] 'give:subj.3sg', λάβωσιν, and νομίσαντα (**34** 5, 8, 9), and the possible final text (**36** 11, 16, 17) has δοῖ, λάβω\σιν/ and νομίσαντα, respectively.

3.3 Syntax

In Ancient Greek, a large group of small indeclinable function words are labelled as "particles".[77] As Revuelta (2014) points out, this is a "ghost term" and does not denote a homogenous word class, since it includes words with so many different functions (coordinating conjunctions, focusing devices, disjuncts, and discourse connectors). It has also been noticed that there was a general decline in the use of particles in Post-classical Greek, and, as Bentein (2015: 472) noted, this process is already visible in our archive. In general, documentary papyri provide good material for observing variation in so far as the use of particles. One question we might investigate is how these different function words were used by a second language speaker. If the actual spoken level of the language was not used in everyday discussions and if Greek literature was not read to a large extent, would an L2 user learn the nuances of the different connectors, disjuncts, and focusing devices? L2 users in general may be the driving force behind the diminishing use of particles. However, although our brothers were most likely bilingual, their Greek was in all probability on the L1 level. So how did they treat "particles"?

Bentein (2015: 472–474), for instance, noticed that "sentence connective particles" were quite frequent in petitions, but asyndeton is more commonly seen especially in the dreams texts. He also made the interesting observation that, in certain petitions, especially those addressed to the king, the highest

---

[76] It is strange that the editor has made this correction in **33** whereas in **36** the form δοῖ was not corrected.
[77] See, e.g. Denniston (1996 [1950²]) for Greek particles and Blomqvist (1969) for particles in Post-classical Greek.

addressee possible, particles may have been used to elevate the language in later drafts.[78] By comparing texts written by different hands, we can add further to this discussion. In Table 6, I have collected some of the most common particles in our archive, excluding, e.g. the sentence connector καί but focusing mostly on what Bentein called "sentence connective particles" and Revuelta calls "discourse connectors", the particle δέ being the most common example.

Table 6: Selection of particles in the Katochoi archive.

	Scribal hands (petitions)	Petitions + orders/reports (copied or drafted by Apollonios)	Letters (other hands)	Letters / dreams (Apollonios's hand)
δέ	ALL	ALL (not **44, 49**)	ALL	**68** 1; **69** (δ'); **78** 25, 26; **76**: [δὲ]
μέν	**6** 35; **7** 23; **8** 11, 15; **9** 6; **10** 21; **11** 21; **19** 13; **20** 29, 39, 43; **36** 10; **40** 5; **41** 4, 13; **42** 3, 14, 23; **43** 12 (m2); **45** 7; **46** 3, 11; **47** 5, 15; **48** 4;	**14** 7; **23** 10, 13; **32** 13, 19, 23; **33** 8; **34** 5; **35** 12; **37** 19; **38** 5; **39** 6; **50** 6, 15; **58** verso5	**59** 8; **71** 5, 15	**68** 4
τε	**2** 25; **6** 10; **8** 13, 14, 17; **9** 10, 16; **15** 8, 13, 42; **16** 14, (17), (27); **19** 3, (11); **20** 32, 49; **24** 24; **41** 21, 24; **42** 6, 11, 35, 36; **43** 17; **51** 11, 16	**12** 31; **14** 9, 13, 28; **31** 6, 9, 12	**59** 14; **60** 19, 21; **62** 6, 8; **71** 13	**78** 44
γάρ	**2** 5; **7** 14; **8** 8; **15** 23, 26; **16** 7, 8; **19** 6; **20** 15, 39; **42** 10; **46** 23	**32** 37; **50** 34	**60** 15; **62** 28, 29	**68** 6, 7; **70** 17; **71** 19
οὖν	**2** 24; **3** 10 (-v); **5** 10, 46; **6** 9; **7** 22, 29; **8** 28, **10** 20; **17** 20; **19** 30; **20** 21, 41; **24** 20; **25** 9 (-v); **36** 10; **40** 12; **41** 13; **42** 38; **46** 11; **47** 15; **51** 15	**13** 30; **23** 20; **26** 6 (-v); **32** 19; **33** 8; **34** 5; **38** 10, 17; **39** 16; **50** 15 (-v); **52** 6; **53** 7; **57** 10, 12, 19	**60** 20; **62** 25; **64** 6; **72** 16	**73** 4; **74** 10
δή	**39** 27	[**40** 19]		

---

78 Cf. Luiselli (2010: 88–94).

On this topic, the letters are the most interesting genre in the Katochoi archive: all letters written by other hands have instances of δέ, but, in Apollonios' letters, the word is quite rare. It occurs in three of his letters but not in his other five; in **76**, it was included but then later deleted by the writer.[79] Certain other particles (μέν, τε, γάρ, and οὖν) are quite well attested in the petitions. It is further noteworthy that, in Apollonios' drafts and copies, these particles feature less abundantly; μέν mostly appears in the copies (only **32** and **50** are drafts, in my opinion), οὖν appears in drafts and copies equally, and γάρ appears only in two drafts. In letters in general, these particles are used sparingly and by Apollonios even more so. It is an open question whether the reason for this was because the letter genre was less formal making asyndeton more acceptable, or perhaps it was due to the influence of the register; Apollonios' letters, for instance, are mostly addressed to the members of his family. It is also interesting to note that Apollonios uses γάρ four times; apparently, this was his favourite particle. Apollonios clearly knew how to use these small function words, since he had copied them in the petitions; however, he did not see the need to use them in his informal letters. Perhaps their function was not clear to him, or perhaps γάρ as presenting an argument[80] can be said to be heavier than, for example, οὖν (marks transition from a subsidiary to a main unit) or δέ (connecting units on the same hierarchical level), and it stuck with him for that reason.[81]

Participles were another way of elevating the tone of the petitions. Bentein (2015: 476) argued that, in certain petitions, participles were used to avoid use of finite present tense forms. Main events in the past were narrated by using participles, making for long, complex sentences. The example Bentein gives is a petition (**6**) written by a scribal hand. I will examine one pair of texts (**12+13**) to see how Apollonios used participles. Both of these texts seem to be drafts, as they explain the same situation, but **12** gives more background information on the events that drove Apollonios to write the petition. We do not know for sure which one he wrote first – that is, which direction he intended going: toward a more stripped-down or elaborate version, but, as I have argued above, **13**, which breaks off in the middle and has fewer particles, seems to be the earlier version. Apollonios is not simply copying here as with the earlier petitions concerning the twins. He is drafting the text about his own affairs. He was

---

79 The letter **72** is counted as not written by Apollonios in Table 6. It contains both δέ and οὖν.
80 Revuelta (2014).
81 As a postpositive particle, however, γάρ suffered the fate of all other such particles, eventually disappearing altogether from the modern form of the language, see Jannaris (1968 [1897]: 400, 409).

approximately 17 years old by the time of writing, and he had gained some practice on the petition formulae when copying the earlier petitions. We may still note that his orthography is not in a good state here, possibly because he is actually the composer of the text, not simply copying text written by professional scribes.

Below, we have two versions of the same event. The longer version in **12** has different sentence division and is considerably more verbose. Even in the first version, **13**, however, the predicate ὕβριζάν (see above for the form) is complemented by three participles referring to the malefactors (ἐπισελθόντες 'rushing in', ἔχοντες 'carrying', ποισάμενοι 'doing') and one genitive absolute structure that refers to Apollonios himself. In the longer version, there are multiple genitive absolutes in the first sentence, followed by several participles complementing ὕβριζάν.

(1) **ἐμοῦ** δὲ **καθημένου** ἔσω ἐν τῷ παστοφορίωι **ἐπισελθόντες** (for ἐπεισελθόντες) Τεεβήσιος υἱοὶ τρίτοι ὄντες Πεταῦς καὶ \Τεῶς/ καὶ Πετεαρτώτης ε[....] ῥαύδους (for ῥάβδους) **ἔχοντες** οὐθένα (corr. ex ουθενι) κοσμωι (for κόσμον) **ποισάμενοι** (for ποιησάμενοι) ὕβριζάν με.

'I was sitting inside the *pastophorion*, when Teebesis' sons, being three, Petaus and Teos and Peteartotes rushed in [. . .] carrying staves and violated me doing nothing decent.' (UPZ I 13, ll. 16–28; 158–157 BCE) [my translation]

(2) . . . ἔτους) κγ Παῦνι κε **ἐλθόντος μου** ἐπὶ τὸ θροιοπόλιον τὸ ὑπάρχον ἐν τῷ αὐ ἱερῶι ὥστε ὠνήσασθαι θροία, τοῦ δὲ **πολῶντος** μὴ **βολομένου** ἀποδώσθαι ἐξ ὧν ἔθες πασ [α] ι πολῖν, ἀλλὰ **βολομενένου** ἄλλα εὐτελεστεραν μοι δοῦνα, **ἐμοῦ** δὲ **βολομένου** τῶν χρησίμων ἀγωράσ(αι), ἔδωκέ μοι μετὰ ἀνατάσεως καὶ **λαβὼ\ν/** ἀπελλάγην\ν/ εἰς τὸ ἐμαυτοῦ παστοφορόριον. μετὰ δὲ ταῦτα **ἀπελθόντες** οἱ τοῦ\του/ ἀδελφοὶ Πεταυτός τε καὶ Τεῶς ῥαύδους **ἔχοντες** οὐθενὶ κόσμῳ χρησάμενο\ι/ {επη} **εἰσπηδήσαντες** εἰς τὸ παστοφόριον, ἐν ο καταλύω, ὕβριζάν με καὶ μαστικου [καὶ] ταῖς ρύδ [.] τοις ὠνηλάται **ὄντες** καὶ χρή[ματα α]**θροντες** ἐφ᾽ οἷς ἔχο\υ/σι χρήμασιν οὔτε τοῦ ἱεροῦ **στυχασάμενοι** οὔτε τοῦ καλῶς **ἔχοντος**.
13. l. θρυπώλιον 15. l. αὑ<τῷ> 16. corr. ex.. σαιθαι, l. θύρα 17. l. πωλοῦντος 18. l. βουλομένου 19. l. ἀποδόσθαι 20. l. ἔθος, l. πᾶσι, l. πωλεῖν 20a. l. βουλομένου 21. corr. ex ευτελεστερον, l. εὐτελέστερά 22. l. δοῦνα<ι> 23. l. βουλομένου 24–25. l. ἀγο|ράς 27. l. ἀπηλλάγην 28. l. παστοφόριον 20–30. l. ἐπελ|θόντες 32. l. ῥάβδους 34. corr. ex χρησαμενο [.] 37. corr. ex φαστοφοριον, l. ᾧ 38. corr. ex υβριζον 39. l. ἐμαστίγου<ν> 40. l. ῥάβδοις, l. ὀνηλάται 41–42. l. [ἀ] |θρ<οίζ>οντες 44. corr. ex χρημα [τεσ] σιν 45. l. στοχασάμενοι

'In year 23, 25th of Pauni I went to the bulrush-shop which is attached to the said shrine to buy some reeds; but the seller refused to sell the ones he normally sells to all his customers, trying to force on me others of substandard variety. I demanded to buy the decent ones, which he gave to me in a threatening manner; I took them and went back to my cell. Later, however, the shopkeeper's brothers, Petaus and Teos, arrived carrying staves, and without any decency charged into the cell where I live. They insulted me

and thrashed me with their staves, since they are donkey-boys, extorting money in addition to what they had already obtained. Neither the (sanctity of the) temple nor the law deterred them.'
(UPZ I 12, ll. 11–47; 158 BCE) [tr. Ray 2006]

I find it an important observation that this kind of participial style was attempted here, though it is not as elaborate as, for example, in the petition **6**, written by a scribe. When we compare the language of Apollonios in the petitions above to his letters written six years later (**68, 69, 70**) we may note that the sentences there are shorter and include finite verbs much more abundantly than in these petitions, and the use of participles is very moderate. In **68**, there are only two participles: ἀπόστιλόν (for ἀπόστειλόν) μοι ἐπιστόλιον ἔχων\τα/ (for ἔχοντα) Πολυδεύκην ('Send me a letter quickly by means of Polydeukes') (4–5) and βλέπω Μενέδημον κατατρέχοντά με ('I see Menedemos chasing me') (6). In **69**, there is one genitive absolute, ἀπόντος μου ('me being absent') (2), and one other participle (I do not count the two attributive participial forms), προσέχων μὴ εὕρῃ τι ('taking care that he finds nothing') (7). In **70**, the participles are used at the end of the letter: δύο ἡμέρας ποιεῖ ἐν τῶι Ἀνουβιείωι πίνων ('[the *strategos*] will spend two days in the Anubieum drinking') (21–23) and αὐτοὺς δεδώκαμεν καὶ ἀποπεπτώκαμεν πλανόμενοι (for πλανώμενοι) ὑπὸ τῶν θεῶν καὶ πιστεύοντες τὰ ἐνύπνια ('we have given ourselves away and have been deluded, led astray by the gods and trusting dreams') (26–30). Looking further at the genitive absolute structure, we have an interesting example of two versions of a bank receipt, one written by an official (**30**) and its copy written by Apollonios (**29** 6–12) from 162 BCE, i.e. when Apollonios was ca. 13 years old. The writer of the receipt[82] did not use the genitive absolute correctly i.e. did not inflect the participle in the genitive and Apollonios has copied the structure as such (but added a prepositional prefix for the verb for some reason): π(αρ)οντες Χρυσίππου καὶ Ἀρή(ου) (**30** 3–4) and συνπαροντες Χρυσίππου καὶ Ἀρήου (**29** 8–9); read (συν)παρόντων ('Chrysippos and Areos being present [together]'). A difference between the brothers should be noted: as mentioned above in connection with morphology, Ptolemaios chose the nominative case for all his participles in **77**, whereas Apollonios has not produced this type of syntactic reanalysis.

The use of tense in the letters is interesting. Present and perfect are generally the most common (cf. the use of aorist participles in **12** and **13**). In **68**, Apollonios uses perfect tense when telling past events in real life, but, at the end, when he refers to the ominous dream he has had, he uses the present tense. In the second

---

[82] According to Wilcken (1927: 221), hand of a certain Chrysippos, "a strongly abbreviating chancery hand".

letter (**69**), the future is also found on line 5 (παρέσομαι 'be present'), but there, too, when he refers to the dream about Menedemos, he uses the present. In the last letter (**70**), which is quite bitter and unhappy, he blames himself and his brother for believing the dreams, because they are now in trouble. Again, present and perfect tense are the most common, but note also the future πιράσεται 'try' on line 14 and, two lines above, the periphrastic μέλλομεν σωθῆναι 'we will be saved'. Future is not used, however, from line 19 onwards, when he speaks about the *strategos*, who will be coming "tomorrow" to the Sarapieion to drink for two days. Sadly, these texts are among the last from our brothers. We do not know if they survived their troubles or not.

In light of what we have seen above, we can conclude that the use of participles belonged very much to the stylistic genre of the petitions but are not totally avoided in the private written language register of individuals accustomed to using them, as Apollonios obviously was. The only letter written by Ptolemaios does not contain any participles, though it is also a very short letter. One of their brothers, Sarapion, wrote one participle form, but he obviously meant it as an imperative: παραγενομενοῦ for παραγενοῦ ('be present') (**66** 5).

The last point I will address is the use of final conjunctions ἵνα and ὅπως in purpose clauses. The latter is used more often than the former in the Katochoi archive, which is in accordance with Clarysse's (2010: 43–45) table describing the chronological distribution of these conjunctions: during the third and second centuries BCE, ὅπως was still used more often than ἵνα, but, in the Roman period, ἵνα had clearly replaced ὅπως. In Apollonios' case, there is a handful of instances of either,[83] though most occurrences come from scribal and other hands (14 ἵνα; 27 ὅπως). In a few instances, ὡς was used as a final conjunction by scribal hands (7 subscription Μενεδήμωι. προνοήθητι ὡς τεύξεται τῶν δικαίων ['To Menedemos. See to it that he receives justice']; cf. **9** 12, **19** 8/9, **45** [12]).

4 Conclusions

Writings by both Apollonios and Ptolemaios betray phonological spellings signalling some of the ongoing sound changes in Greek to a greater extent than what is evident from the scribes' writings. However, they also have some of their own peculiarities. These differences partly reflect their lack of education in orthography, but some can be considered idiolectal, since both brothers do not necessarily share the same idiosyncrasies. Some of these help in identifying

---

[83] ἵνα: **18r** 23 (εἵνα), **39** 33, **78** 35 (ἀ for ἵνα); ὅπως; **12** 52, **14** 27, 29, 40, **68** 7.

the writer (e.g. Ptolemaios' habit of writing ἤως instead of ἕως 'until'). Some of them also suggest that the brothers' other language, Egyptian, was one factor behind their orthographic fingerprints.

From the morphological features, there is some hint of possible idiolectal language use, like the use of nominative with, e.g. the title Macedonian. This may naturally also be a more commonly spread phenomenon among bilingual writers with less education,[84] but, in the Katochoi archive, it is not found in other hands. Lack of systematic education, especially in official petition jargon, might be one major force behind the tendency to omit particles by Apollonios and Ptolemaios in their letters, but these can also be considered personal preferences or matters of register. But since other letter writers do not avoid particles to the same extent, genre does not seem to be the determining factor.

In sum, one writer who wrote several types of documents could leave us traces of several different -lects, and they need not all be personal or individual, as in the case of Apollonios, who left many copies written in his hand but not drawn up by him. He was familiar with the scribal lect but could not, or chose not to use it in his private letters. Understanding the differences between document types help us trace actual individual language patterns. When we are able to identify these idiolects, we can better understand variation in the speech community. In our case, it becomes clear that the orthographic variation is due to the individual performing the writing even when he is copying a text that has more standard orthography. This individual's spellings may signal his own pronunciation possibly influenced by his bilingual background and at the same time the lack of scribal education. In other words, the whole speech community can share the features of similar pronunciation to some extent, but it is only visible to us through one or two individuals. Then again, the texts with non-standard orthography may be composed with complex syntax and morphological sophistication, if the text is a copy of a text composed by a professional scribe. Since the Katochoi archive provides the possibility to identify such copying and drafting processes, we no longer need to wonder about the seeming conflict between the orthographic and morphosyntactic levels of one text. Moreover, it is useful to see that the idiolects truly differ even between family members, i.e. between Ptolemaios and Apollonios who shared a father and similar growth milieu. Apollonios' predisposition in petition writing gave him the advantage to adopt some features of legal formulaic language even if it did not lead him in using, for example, discourse connectors to a greater extent in his private writing.

---

84 Cf. Vierros (2012a).

References

Bentein, Klaas. 2015. The Greek documentary papyri as a linguistically heterogeneous corpus: The case of the katochoi of the Sarapeion-archive. *Classical World* 108. 461–484.
Blomqvist, Jerker. 1969. *Greek particles in Hellenistic prose.* Lund: Gleerup.
Bubenik, Vit. 2014. Koine, Origins of. *EAGLL* [online edition].
Clarysse, Willy. 1993. Egyptian scribes writing Greek. *Chronique d'Égypte* 68. 186–201.
Clarysse, Willy & Katelijn Vandorpe. 2006. A Demotic lease of temple land reused in the katochoi archive (Louvre N 2328A). *Ancient Society* 36. 1–11.
Clarysse, Willy. 2010. Linguistic diversity in the archive of the engineers Kleon and Theodoros. In Trevor V. Evans & Dirk D. Obbink (eds.), *The language of the papyri*, 35–50. Oxford: Oxford University Press.
Dahlgren, Sonja. 2017. *Outcome of long-term language contact: transfer of Egyptian phonological features onto Greek in Graeco-Roman Egypt.* PhD dissertation, University of Helsinki.
Delekat, Lienhard. 1964. *Katoche, Hierodulie und Adoptionsfreilassung.* München: Beck.
Denniston, John Dewar. 1996 [1950]. *The Greek particles*, 2nd ed. revised by K.J. Dover. London: Duckworth.
Depauw, Mark & Joanne Vera Stolk. 2015. Linguistic variation in Greek papyri: Towards a new tool for quantitative study. *Greek, Roman & Byzantine Studies* 55. 196–220.
Evans, Trevor V. 2010. Identifying the language of the individual in the Zenon archive. In Trevor V. Evans & Dirk D. Obbink (eds.), *The language of the papyri*, 51–70. Oxford: Oxford University Press.
Gignac, Francis T. 1976. *A grammar of the Greek papyri of the Roman and Byzantine periods.* Vol. 1: *Phonology.* Milano: La Goliardica.
Gignac, Francis T. 1981. *A grammar of the Greek papyri of the Roman and Byzantine periods.* Vol. 2: *Morphology.* Milano: La Goliardica.
Hazen, Kirk. 2002. The Family. In J. K. Chambers, Peter Trudgill & Natalie Schilling-Estes (eds.), *The handbook of language variation and change*, 500–525. Malden: Blackwell.
Henriksson, Erik, Sonja Dahlgren & Marja Vierros. Forthcoming. *Orthographic variants and phonological change: A contextual search tool for Greek documentary papyri, ostraca and tablets.*
Horrocks, Geoffrey C. 2010. *Greek: A history of the language and its speakers*, 2nd ed. Malden: Wiley-Blackwell.
Jannaris, Antonius N. 1968 [1897]. *An historical Greek grammar chiefly of the Attic dialect as written and spoken from Classical Antiquity down to present time founded upon the ancient texts, inscriptions, papyri and present popular Greek.* Hildesheim: Georg Olms.
Koenen, Ludwig. 1985. The dream of Nektanebos. *Bulletin of the American Society of Papyrologists* 22. 171–194.
Labov, William. 2001. *Principles of linguistic change.* Vol. 2: *Social factors.* Malden: Blackwell.
Legras, Bernard. 2007. La diglossie des enkatochoi grecs du Sarapeion de Memphis (IIe siècle av. n. è.). *Ktema* 32, 251–264.
Legras, Bernard. 2011. *Les reclus grecs du Sarapeion de Memphis: Une enquête sur l'hellénisme égyptien.* Leuven: Peeters.
Lewis, Naphtali. 1986. *Greeks in Ptolemaic Egypt: Case studies in the social history of the Hellenistic world.* Oxford: Clarendon Press.

Luiselli, R. 2010. Authorial revision of linguistic style in Greek papyrus letters and petitions (AD I–IV). In Trevor V. Evans & Dirk D. Obbink (eds.), *The language of the papyri*, 71–96. Oxford: Oxford University Press.

Prada, Luigi. 2013. Dreams, bilingualism, and oneiromancy in Ptolemaic Egypt: Remarks on a recent study. *Zeitschrift für Papyrologie und Epigraphik* 184. 85–101.

Ray, John. 2006. The dreams of the twins in St. Petersburg. In Kasia Szpakowska (ed.), *Through a glass darkly: Magic, dreams and prophecy in Ancient Egypt*, 189–203. Swansea: The Classical Press of Wales.

Revuelta, Antonio. 2014. Particles, Syntactic features. *EAGLL* [online edition].

Rowlandson, Jane. 1988. *Women and society in Greek and Roman Egypt: A sourcebook.* Cambridge: Cambridge University Press.

Teodorsson, Sven-Tage. 1977. *The Phonology of Ptolemaic Koine*. Lund: Acta Universitatis Gothoburgensis.

Thompson, Dorothy. 2012. *Memphis after the Ptolemies*, 2nd ed. Princeton: Princeton University Press.

Torallas Tovar, Sofía. 2014. Koine, Features of. *EAGLL* [online edition].

Vandorpe, Katelijn. 2009. Archives and dossiers. In Roger S. Bagnall (ed.), *The Oxford handbook of papyrology*, 216–255. Oxford: Oxford University Press.

Vandorpe, Katelijn & Sofie Waebens. 2009. *Reconstructing Pathyris' archives: A multicultural community in Hellenistic Egypt*. Brussel: Koninklijke Vlaamse Akademie van België voor Wetenschappen en Kunsten.

Veisse, Anne-Emmanuelle. 2007. Les identités multiples de Ptolémaios, fils de Glaukias. *Ancient Society* 37. 69–87.

Vierros, Marja. 2012a. *Bilingual notaries in Hellenistic Egypt: A study of Greek as a second language*. Brussel: Koninklijke Vlaamse Akademie van België voor Wetenschappen en Kunsten.

Vierros, Marja. 2012b. Review of Legras 2011. *Bulletin of the American Society of Papyrologists* 49. 343–348.

Weinreich, Uriel, William Labov & Marvin Herzog. 1968. Empirical foundations for a theory of language change. In Winfred P. Lehman & Yakiv Malkiel (eds.), *Directions for historical linguistics*, 97–195. Austin: University of Texas Press.

Wilcken, Ulrich (ed.). 1927. *Urkunden der Ptolemäerzeit (Ältere Funde). Bd. I. Papyri aus Unterägypten mit 2 Tafeln*. Berlin: de Gruyter.

Aikaterini Koroli

4 Imposing psychological pressure in papyrus request letters: A case study of six Byzantine letters written in an ecclesiastical context (VI–VII CE)

Abstract: The present study deals with two kinds of linguistic strategies attested in private request letters on papyrus, namely politeness strategies and those giving the epistolary text an imperative tone. By means of these coexisting strategies the sender exercises psychological pressure on the recipient, so that the latter satisfies his/her request(s). The object of the offered analysis is a corpus of six well-preserved, already published private papyrus request letters, which are dated to the Byzantine period of Egypt (330–641 CE) and written in an ecclesiastical milieu, i.e. they are sent to and received by clerics or monks. The selected letters are examined from the perspective of the interaction between politeness and imperative tone strategies. My aim is to explore whether they bear common features that allow us to speak of a special, "ecclesiastical" style of Byzantine letter writing in the papyri.

1 Introduction

1.1 The aim of the study

The vast majority of private papyrus letters dated to the Byzantine period of Egypt (330–641 CE) fall into the category of request letters.[1] As such, we consider the letters in which requesting constitutes the primary communicative goal – or, at least, one of the main communicative goals – of their senders.[2] The latter resort to several

---

[1] The present paper is based on my thorough study of requesting in an extensive corpus of 7.836 private papyrus letters dated to the Roman (31 BCE–330 CE), Byzantine and Early Arab (641–799 CE) periods of Egypt (Koroli 2016).
[2] Private letters can be defined as the authentic letters preserved on the original writing materials, referring to various fields of private life and sent to private persons and not to the authorities (Koroli 2016: 37–48, esp. 48). Private papyrus letters can be divided in two broad categories on the basis of the main communicative goal(s) of the ancient writers: (a) request letters, and (b) letters where requesting is not included in the main communicative goals of the sender, even if

https://doi.org/10.1515/9783110614404-004

linguistic strategies in their effort to convince the recipients to satisfy their requests. Very often, they use a wide variety of politeness strategies or they give their request(s) an imperative tone. The present chapter offers a study of the two aforementioned categories of linguistic strategies.

The object of my analysis is a corpus of six well-preserved, already published private papyrus request letters, which are dated to the Byzantine period and written in an ecclesiastical milieu, i.e. they are sent to and received by clerics or monks. The state of preservation of the writing material, along with the amount of information available regarding the context of the selected letters,[3] enables comprehensive analysis. My ultimate aim is to explore whether and to what extent we are entitled to speak of a special, i.e. "ecclesiastical" style of letter writing on the basis of papyrological evidence.

1.2 Theoretical framework and methodology

Linguistic politeness denotes the variety of strategies used by the requesters to soften the burden[4] imposed on the persons invited to satisfy their request. In this way, they prevent the possibility of becoming disliked sabotaging the achievement of their goal. The complexity of this linguistic and cultural phenomenon lies in the fact that it is connected with the interlocutors' social features and relationship, the situational context of the text, as well as the general cultural framework, i.e. what is considered as (im)polite in a given speech community.[5] While analyzing courtesy expressions and imperative tone in papyrus request letters we are faced with one more factor of complexity: papyrus letters abound in markers of conventional politeness not necessarily connected to requesting, but to the writing of the letter *per se*. Φιλοφρόνησις, the expression of courtesy and friendly attitude towards the recipient of the letter, was considered by ancient epistolary theorists as the primary purpose of composing a

---

they contain stereotypical requests through which the senders express their concern for the recipient and his or her relatives. For this classification, see Koroli (2016: 193–202, 257–263). Private correspondence was connected to the practicalities of everyday life, as well as to the maintenance of family and social bonds. Therefore, the greater proportion of request letters among private papyrus letters should be attributed to the key role of requesting in all these aspects of private life (e.g. in sending and receiving goods, transactions, cooperating, problem solving, etc.).

3 See §4.
4 Or threat, according to Brown and Levinson's theoretical model (1987). When the beneficiary is not the sender, there is no such a burden.
5 Cf. Sifianou (1992: 38–39, 46–47, 200–219; 2014: 278–283).

letter and thus one of its inherent elements.[6] When it comes to papyrus request letters therefore, one must decide whether and to what extent this formulaic politeness should be connected to requesting or not. The analysis proposed will be completed in two stages:
a) Location of the politeness and imperative tone markers in the selected texts and study of the way they enhance the achievement of the writers' main communicative goal, i.e. the satisfaction of the request.
b) Comparative study of the linguistic data with certain social features of the writers, namely the fact that they are either monks or clergymen, as well as their place/status in the monastic order or the clerical hierarchy.

This text-driven analysis of papyrological evidence is based on theoretical and methodological concepts of text-linguistics and speech act theory.[7] The focus of study is not the use of single decontextualized linguistic elements but rather two sorts of interaction: on the one hand the interaction of various linguistic choices serving in conjunction the writer's intention and on the other hand the interaction of the text as a whole with its situational, inter-textual, and cultural context.

---

[6] For ancient epistolary theory, cf. Trapp (2003: 42–46), Muir (2009: 18–24), Koroli (2016: 48–51). Compare also the term *captatio benevolentiae* denoting the linguistic strategies used by the writer of ancient letters and petitions in order to gain the favour of the addressee; cf. Zilliacus (1949, 1953, 1967), Koskenniemi (1956: esp. 64–154), Papathomas (2007, 2009). One of the most common expressions of formulaic courtesy is the use of honorific names, cf. Hornickel (1930), Zilliacus (1949), Kim (2011: 52–57 *et passim*).

[7] The approach suggested here has some relevance to studies concerning the organization of textual information, e.g. Kim (1972), who analyzed directives in a small corpus of papyrus letters of introduction and Risselada's analysis of directives in a small corpus of Latin authors (1993), which is also based on speech act theory. Studies on some markers of politeness and imperative tone in private request letters are offered by Leiwo (2010) and Dickey (1996, 2001, 2010, 2016a). My starting point is the thorough, systematic analysis of the papyrological evidence and the classification of markers of politeness and imperative tone as (a) commonplace and unusual, (b) directly and indirectly connected to requesting, and finally (c) more helpful and less helpful as far as the achievement of the sender's goal is concerned.

In other words, I intend to create a framework of analysis applicable to the special features of papyrus letters. Modern analyses of linguistic politeness may enable more insight if we take into consideration the individualities of papyrus correspondence. For instance, it would be tempting to examine the wealth of information found in papyrus letters according to Brown and Levinson's (1987) notions of positive and negative politeness, of requesting as a threat, and of positive and negative politeness cultures. Also, to draw the line between the frequent, conventionalized or formulaic strategies and the unusual or unexpected ones on the basis of Terkourafi (2002, 2005, 2008), and Watts' (2003) theories. On the application of modern models of analysis on ancient sources, see Dickey (2016b).

1.3 Directive speech acts in papyrus private letters

Directives[8] in private papyrus letters can be analyzed according to speech act theory[9] as locutionary, illocutionary and perlocutionary acts.[10] For example, the sender of SB XIV 12123 (V–VI CE), asks the recipient to send him a bowl (φιάλιον), which is necessary because of the upcoming visit of the prefect:

(1) καταξιούτω ἡ ἀδελφική σου διάθεσις πέμψαι μοι διὰ τοῦ γραμματη| φόρου τὸ φιάλι<ο>ν, ἐπειδὴ χρεία γίνεται αὐτοῦ αὔριον· | ἤκουσα γὰρ ὅτι ἀνέρχεται ὁ κύριός μου ὁ ἄρχων. καὶ με<τὰ> τὴν | ἐπιδημίαν \αὐτοῦ/ πάλιν εἰ χρῄζεις λαμβάνεις· οἶδας γὰρ ὅτι ἄλλο | οὐκ ἔχω· εἰ γὰρ εἶχον, οὐκ ἂν ἐζήτουν, ὡς καὶ ἐπίστασαι.

> 'May your brotherly attitude deign to send me the bowl via the letter-carrier, as there will be need of it tomorrow; for I heard that my lord the prefect is coming up. And after his visit you can have it again if you need it. For you know that I don't have another one; for if I had, I would not have asked, as you understand'.[11]
> (SB XIV 12123, 1–5; V–VI CE) [tr.: Shelton (1977: 169)]

Since the intention of the scribe is to ask for an article that he needs, the illocutionary act performed is requesting. The formulation of the request, i.e. the locutionary act, is found at the beginning of the letter (καταξιούτω . . . φιάλι<ο>ν ['May . . . the bowl']). In the remainder of text the scribe not only explains the reasons for requesting this bowl (ἐπειδὴ . . . ὁ ἄρχων ['. . . as . . . the prefect']; οἶδας γὰρ . . . ἐπίστασαι ['For you know . . . you understand']) but also assures the recipient that he will give the bowl back when necessary (καὶ με<τὰ> . . . λαμβάνεις ['And after . . . you can have it']). The possible satisfaction of the request, that is the sending of the bowl by the recipient, constitutes the perlocutionary act.

Directives similar to this are attested in the main body of the papyrus private letters.[12] They concern a wide variety of everyday issues that can be classified according to the following (overlapping) thematic categories: financial and/or law

---

8 The terms "directive" and "request" are used indiscriminately as general terms denoting all kinds of directive speech acts (asking, begging, commanding, urging, etc.).
9 Searle (1969, 1976, 1981).
10 Koroli (2016: 89–99).
11 The English translation of the texts and passages cited in the present chapter is my own unless otherwise attested.
12 These directives are rarely submitted as postscripts, see Koroli (2016: 218–226). Furthermore, the verso also contains stereotypical requests, by means of which the sender asks the letter-carrier to give the letter to its addressee; e.g. P.Oxy. LVI 3869, 14 (VI–VII CE): ⳨ἐπίδ(ος) τῷ θαυμασ(ιωτάτῳ) vacat Ἀνοῦπ π(αρὰ) Ἰωάγγου ['Deliver to the most admirable Anup, from

issues, domestic and/or professional activities, health and/or illness, human relationships (family, friendships, cooperations), important events such as birth or death, justice and/or restoration of the order, ethics and/or religion (but no metaphysics), religious habits, obligations or events, and, of course, psychological and/or emotional issues. The object of requesting is either giving/sending or receiving (mostly goods, money, letters and individuals), or is related to other activities, such as the production of oral texts, for example, when the recipient is asked to submit a request to a third person, tasks related to professional life, social or emotional problems, and others. Finally, an important parameter of requesting is the number of persons involved, namely the requester(s), the recipient(s) of the request(s), the person(s) who will satisfy the request(s) and the beneficiary/-ies from the satisfaction of the request(s), as well as the relationship of these individuals.[13]

1.4 Direct and indirect directives

1.4.1 Direct requests

The majority of requests contained in papyrus private letters are direct, i.e. requests formulated in a manner which points directly to the writer's communicative goal. Direct requests are formulated mainly by means of grammatical markers of deontic modality.[14] Performative verbs such as ἐρωτῶ and παρακαλῶ (both meaning 'to entreat') are also very common. Alternatively, verbs such as γράφω ('to write') or πέμπω ('to send') are combined with subordinate clauses of purpose; in this case, the directiveness derives from the purposive value of the subordinate, which reveals in an explicit manner what is requested.[15]

John'; tr. Sirivianou (in Sirivianou et al. 1989: 158)]; on this type of request, see Koroli (2016: 227–230).
13 Koroli (2016: 93–97).
14 Mostly imperative or subjunctive mood, or rarely infinitive or simple future; the encodement of deontic modality in the lexicon, i.e. the use of deontic verbs such as the impersonal χρή ('it is necessary'), is much rarer.
15 On the various ways of formulating direct requests in private papyrus letters, see Koroli (2016: 100–126), where many examples and previous bibliography are offered; cf. also indicatively Ljungvik (1932: 94–98), Steen (1938: 131–138, 140–143, 146–147, 153–168). Deontic modality is very closely related to directives; cf. Iakovou (1999: 27–30).

Direct requests constitute the core of thematic-textual units including their thematically relevant co-text. The organization of these units is based on the following rhetorical pattern:

preparation for the directive – formulation of the directive – supplement of the directive

The framing of the requests, i.e. their thematically relevant co-text, functions as their preparation or their supplement in one or more of the following ways: A. informing the recipient; B. imposing psychological pressure on the recipient; C. in other ways, e.g. encouraging the recipient (assuring him/her that the satisfaction of the request is feasible). This organizational pattern varies, depending on whether it is complete, as well as on the function of the preparation and/or the supplement.

Many private papyrus letters contain more than one directive. These directives may concern the same topic or not. In the first case, they belong to the same thematic-textual unit, the structure of which is based on complicated versions of the above presented rhetorical schema. In the second case, they constitute the core of separate thematic-textual units. Sometimes, a directive plays a subsidiary role with regard to another request (basic directive). These supplementary directives increase the perlocutionary effect of the basic directives because they impose psychological pressure on the recipient either directly, e.g. by repeating the content of the basic request, or indirectly, e.g. by inquiring for the recipient's health.[16]

1.4.2 Indirect requests

The term "indirect request" is used in the present study to denote the directive which is not formulated by means of the recurrent linguistic elements presented in Section 1.4.1. These requests do not constitute the core of textual units based on the aforementioned tripartite organizational pattern. In the case of indirect requests the recipient has to detect the sender's communicative goal. Indirect directives are very rare in private papyrus letters. This should be attributed, first of all, to the utilitarian character of these letters, which are short texts concerning everyday issues. Moreover, the formulation of direct requests makes the sender's communicative goal easily conceivable by the recipient, which was important given the difficulties concerning the sending of the letters.

---

[16] Koroli (2016: 127–202).

Unlike modern languages like Modern Greek and English, indirect requesting is not necessarily connected to politeness. However, there are several letters where the sender chooses this method of requesting in order to be both discreet and polite. In this case, a variety of interacting linguistic choices are resorted to in order to submit the request.[17]

2 Politeness strategies vs. imperative tone in request papyrus letters

2.1 General remarks

Both markers of politeness and markers of imperative tone function as means of imposing psychological pressure on the recipient of the request letter, i.e. as means of increasing the perlocutionary result of requesting.[18] Specifically, politeness strategies function as means of imposing indirect – but not necessarily light – psychological pressure: their use is aimed at the moral engagement of the recipient. The sender attempts to seem pleasant to the recipient showing his/her respect, friendliness, admiration, or even his/her affection. By doing so, he/she tries to compensate for the burden laid upon the recipient due to requesting. In several request letters though polite tone is striking or even extreme. Finally, some of the politeness strategies attested in papyrus request letters are very frequently attested in the papyrological evidence, whereas others are rarely or even once attested.

The function of strategies giving the papyrus private letters an imperative tone is stronger or more direct in comparison with the function of politeness strategies. By using them, the writer expresses clearly his/her communicative goal; sometimes he/she expresses intensively his/her will and aims at the immediate activation of the recipient by causing a sense of responsibility or even negative feelings such as sadness, fear or guilt. In my opinion, there are three variations of such an imperative tone: A. the urgent tone due to a problematic situation; B. the strict tone (without necessarily blaming the recipient); C. the accusative or criticizing tone. Urgency, strictness and criticizing mood may well overlap. For example, the sender may adopt a strict attitude towards the recipient

---

17 P.Oxy. XVI 1868 (VI–VII CE) and P.Oxy. XVI 1869 (VI–VII CE) are such cases; see Papathomas and Koroli (2014), Koroli (2014: 50–52), Koroli (2016: 212–214).
18 See Koroli (2016: 231–256).

not only because he/she wants to be absolutely sure that the latter will satisfy the request and/or because his/her social status allows him/her to do so, but also because they want at the same time to blame the recipient for being negligent, inconsistent, irresponsible or, in general, for having caused a problem. In other cases, the sender may stress the urgency of solving a problem in the most polite way, because the recipient is not responsible for the problem in question and/or because the social status of the recipient is much higher than that of the sender. Similarly to politeness strategies, markers of imperative tone vary, depending on whether and to what extent they are commonplace or unusual. It should be noted that cursing was a very rare occurrence in private papyrus letters.[19]

To sum up, politeness is the antipode of requesting in the sense that requesting lays a burden on its recipient and politeness strategies compensate for this burden. Every choice of the sender putting emphasis on requesting itself is an imperative tone marker; every choice deriving from the sender's effort to lessen the burden of requesting and become pleasant for the recipient is a politeness marker. Imperative tone markers showing the sender's strict or accusative attitude towards the recipient could be also defined as 'impoliteness markers'. It is interesting to observe how politeness strategies interact with imperative tone markers.

2.2 The place of markers of politeness and of imperative tone in the main body of request papyrus letters

The position of markers of politeness and of imperative tone contained in the main body of the letter is either in the thematic-textual unit of the directive(s), or in the non-directive co-text which is not thematically related to a directive.[20] The markers of politeness or of imperative tone contained in the main body of the Byzantine letters interact with those contained in the verso.

---

19 SB XX 14463 (V CE) offers a very rare example of cursing: Οὐαλέριος vacat Ἀθανασίῳ [- - -] | κακόγηρε, προδότα, πορνοβοσκέ· τὸ πρᾶγμα τοῦτο.[- - - αὐ]|τῇ τῇ ὥρᾳ ἐνεχθῶσι αἱ ἑκατὸν σαργάναι του [- - - τί] | ἐστιν νεῦρα Οὐαλερίου. μὰ τὸν Χριστόν, δ<ε>ῖ με καῦσαί σε ο̣[- - -] ['Valerios to Athanasios . . . you, bloody old man (?), traitor, brothel-keeper! This thing . . . bring the one hundred baskets of . . . immediately . . . they are whips of Valerios. For Christ's sake, I must burn you . . .'].

20 This chapter includes only some of the recurrent or commonplace strategies. Given the topic of the present paper, the passages cited are extracted exclusively from Byzantine letters.

2.2.1 Markers of politeness or imperative tone in the textual unit of the directive — Some characteristic examples

Both politeness and imperative tone are codified, first and foremost, in the formulation of the request.[21] The use of the 2nd person plural or the 3rd person singular (usually with an honorific name as subject) is one of the recurrent politeness strategies.[22] The choice of the subjunctive instead of the imperative mood is also one of the most common markers of politeness. The use of θέλω ('to want') or καταξιόω ('to deign') in one of these two moods constitutes a more striking politeness strategy.[23] The use of performative verbs ἐρωτῶ and παρακαλῶ (also in the passive aorist) or formulas such as καλῶς or εὖ ποιέω (in the 2nd person, 'you will do well to. . .') also belong to the commonplace strategies of politeness.[24] Linguistic choices for the avoidance of the deontic markers (such as γράφω + purpose clause) discussed in Section 1.4.1 should also be considered as markers of politeness. Finally, the occurrence of conditional sentences, may lessen the deontic content.[25]

The use of the imperative mood or of the simple future instead of the subjunctive or παρακαλῶ are very common imperative tone markers. An equally common strategy is the increase of deontic modality;[26] this is achieved, for

---

21 Cf. Leiwo (2010); Dickey (2016a).
22 Cf. e.g. P.Cair.Masp. I 67064, 15–16 (ca. 538–547 CE; see HGV): κα[ὶ] ἀπ[ο]|πέμψατέ μοι τὰ αὐτὰ χαρτία ['and **send back** to me the same small leaves of papyri']; P.Oxy. XVI 1847, 2–4 (VI–VII CE): **παρασκευάσῃ** οὖν αὐτὸν | **ἡ σὴ γνησία ἀδελφ[ότη]ς** τὸ γραμμάτιον ἀποτεθῆν[αι] ἐν μέσῃ χειρὶ . . . | καὶ τὰ ὁλοκόττινα δοθῆναι τῇ γυναικί . . . ['**Will your true brotherliness** therefore **cause** the bond to be deposited by him . . . and the solidi to be given to the woman . . .'; tr.: Grenfell, Hunt & Bell (1924: 32)].
23 Cf. e.g. P.Hamb. III 228, 6–7 (VI CE): **θέλησον** δὲ **ἀνελθεῖν** πρὸς τὸν γεοῦχον καὶ παρακαλέσαι αὐτόν, ἵνα πέμψῃ | τὸν αὐτὸν μονοπωλάριον ἐνταῦθα πρῶτον. ['**Be so good as to go** to the landlord and ask him to send the same monopolarius here first'; for a German tr., see Kramer and Hagedorn (1984: 179)]; P.Ant. I 45, 2–4 (VI CE): **καταξιώσῃ ἡ σὴ ἀδελφότης ἐᾶσαι** | τὸν κύριον Οὐράνιον ἐν τῇ μεγάλῃ οἰκ{ε}ίᾳ | εἰς ὀλίγας ἡμέρας. ['**May your brotherliness condescend to let** the lord Ouranios be in the great house for a few days'; tr.: Roberts (1950: 103)].
24 Cf. e.g. P.Köln III 166, 14–15 (VI–VII century CE): **παρακληθήτω** οὖν ἡ ἐμὴ **δέσποινη** (l. **δέσποινα**) | συντόμως **δηλῶσαί** μοι τὴν ἀπόκρισιν ἢ τὴν τιμήν. ['**I ask my mistress to give me the answer** or the purchase price'; for a German tr., see Hübner (in Kramer, Erler, Hagedorn and Hübner 1980: 186–187)].
25 Cf. e.g. SB XVI 12573, 2–4 (mid-VI CE; see HGV): εἰ δοκεῖ τῷ ὑμετέρῳ μεγέθει, Ἀ[ν]τώνιο[ν] τὸν πεδιοφύλακα καὶ Παύλου (l. Παῦλον) | τὸν φυγό<ν>τα καταξιωσάτω τούτους ζητῆσαι καὶ συνευρεθῆναι μετὰ τῶν | ἄλλων. ['**Please / If you are fine with it**, may your highness condescend to seek out the guard of the estate Antonios and the escaped Paulos and make them stay with the others'; for a German tr., see Karlsson and Maehler (1979: 289)].
26 Koroli (2016: 106–112).

instance, by means of deontic adverbs, as well as adverbs or adverbial phrases denoting the manner, the quantity, or the time.[27] Furthermore, formulas like μὴ οὖν ἄλλως ποιήσῃς ('don't do it in other way') or directives with many parts are very frequently attested.[28]

Both politeness and imperative tone are expressed in various manners in the non-directive co-text, functioning as preparation for or supplements to the directive. For example, stressing the urgency undoubtedly accords the letter an imperative tone.[29] The reminders of older requests, not yet satisfied by the recipient and, in general, complaints or expression of anger or disappointment for promises not kept are common thematic motifs.[30] On the other hand, flattering the recipient before and/or after the formulation of the request is clearly a politeness strategy.[31] Furthermore, even the provision of detailed information to justify the submission of the request could be considered a sort of politeness strategy.

---

[27] Cf. CPR XXIV 31, 7–8 (mid- or second half of VII CE): λοιπὸν πέμψον **εὐθέω[ς** τὰ] | ὀφείλοντα ζητῆσαι <τ>αῦτα αὐτόθι. ['So ask **immediately** what is needed to be claimed on the spot'; for a tr. in German, see Palme (2002: 183)].

[28] A request has two or more parts when the object of what is asked is denoted by infinitives, participles or subordinate clauses which are dependent on the same verb or verbal periphrasis (see Koroli 2016: 123–125). In the following passage, not only is the formula πᾶν ποίησον used, but also the recipient is asked to proceed in three actions, all objects to the periphrasis: **πᾶν ποίησον** οὖν, κύριέ μου | ἀδελφέ, σοῦ κατερχομένου **λαβ<ε>ῖν** τὸ κέρμα | **καὶ ἀγοράσε** (l. ἀγοράσαι) μοι ἐντολικὸν **καὶ λαβ<ε>ῖν** | παρὰ τῆς Μεγάλης τὸ στιχάριον (P.Oxy. XIV 1775, 11–14; IV CE). ['Therefore, my lord brother, **make any possible effort to take** the money when you come **and carry out** the note of authorization, **and take** the tunic from Megale'; for an Italian translation, see Naldini (1998²: 275–277) [No 66]].

[29] For example, in the following passage, the choice of vocabulary clearly points to a problematic situation: P.Oxy. XVI 1849, 1–2 (VI–VII CE): καταξιώσῃ ἡ ὑμετέρα γνησία ἀδελφότης μίαν ὑπὲρ μίαν πέμψαι μοι ἐλεοσπάρακα (l. ἐλαιοσπάραγα), | ἐπειδὴ τὸ λάχανον ὅδε (l. ὧδε) **σαπρόν** ἐστι καὶ **σιαίνομε** (l. σιαίνομαι). ['Will your true brotherliness have the goodness to send me from day to day some asparangus, for the vegetables here are **rotten** and **disgust** me'; tr.: Grenfell, Hunt & Bell (1924: 33)].

[30] Cf. e.g. P.Oxy. XVI 1935, 2–5 (VI CE): καταξιώσῃ ἡ σὴ ἀδελφότης παρασκεύασον τοὺς ἀγροφύλακας | τοῦ κτήματος Μεσκανούνιος ἀναδοῦναι τὴν μηχανὴν τοῦ | θαυμασιωτάτου Παπνουθίου, **ὡς καὶ [ἄ]λλοτε εἴ[ρη]κα** | **τοῖς φροντισταῖς τοῦ αὐτοῦ κτήματος**. ['May your true brotherliness condescend to cause the land-guards to hand over the field / water-wheel of the most splendid Papnouthios, **as I have said at another time to the stewards of the same estate.**'].

[31] Cf. e.g. P.Herm. 17, 2–3 (late IV CE?; see BL X 86): **ἡ χρηστώτητά (l. χρηστότης) σου κατέλαβεν πάντας τοὺς μὺ (l. μὴ) δυναμένους·** | καμὲ φθάσι (l. φθάσῃ) ἡ ἐλεημωσύνην (l. ἐλεημοσύνη) σου, κύριε. ['**Your goodness embraces all those without resources**; and let your mercy extend to me too, my lord'; tr.: Bagnall and Cribiore (2006: 204); see also Rees (1964: 30)].

2.2.2 Coexisting directives

The formulation of subsidiary requests, repeating emphatically (either identically reproducing or paraphrasing) one or more basic requests is a recurrent linguistic strategy used to convey an imperative tone to the request letter. In most cases, these subsidiary requests are commonplace requests through which the sender asks the recipient not to be neglectful.[32] The coexistence of more than one request in many cases intensifies the imperative tone.[33]

At the other end of the scale, any stereotypical, commonplace request connoting that the sender cares about the recipient and/or his/her family, functions as a politeness strategy regarding the basic request(s) contained in the letter.[34]

2.2.3 Politeness strategies in the non-directive co-text, not thematically related to a directive

As already noted in Section 1.3, conventional politeness constitutes an integral part of letter-writing regardless of the main communicative goals of the senders. The use of strategies which are closely related to requests in terms of subject matter, can be attributed with certainty to the effort of the sender to enhance the satisfaction of the request. Politeness strategies which are not thematically connected to directives, are mostly common politeness markers occurring in all kinds of letters (not only in request letters) or even in other kinds of papyrus non-literary texts. The use of these commonly attested strategies in

---

32 Cf. e.g. PSI IV 318, 3–9 (IV CE?): παράσχου τῷ ἀδελ|φῷ μου Ἀμμωνίωνι | ἀφ' ὧν μου ἔχεις | ἀργυρίου μυριάδαν μίαν· | γί(νεται) ἀρ(γυρίου) (μυριάς) α. **ἀλλ' ὅρα μὴ | ἀμελήσῃς, κύριέ μου | ἄδελφε**. ['Provide my brother Ammonion ten thousand muriads of silver; total, 10.000 myriads of silver. **See that you won't be neglectful my lord brother.**'].
33 Cf. e.g. P.Oxy. XVI 1838, 1–5 (VI CE), which contains four directives: καὶ τὴν ὑποδοχὴν πᾶσαν τοῦ μακαρίου Ἰού[σ]του αὐτὸς **ὑπόδεξε (l. ὑπόδεξαι)**, | **καὶ μὴ ἐάσῃς** τὸν σῖτον ἐπάνω τῶν γεωργῶν. **ἔασον δὲ** | Φίβιν ἐγγὺς σοῦ, ἵνα διδάξῃ σε τὰ πράγματα ἕω[ς] ὅτε μάθω | ποῖον τύπον ὀφείλω δοῦναι αὐτῷ. τὸν **δὲ** σύμμαχον Ἰούστου **ἔ[α]σον** ἐγγὺς | σοῦ ἕως ὅτε πληρώσῃ τὸν ἐνιαυτὸν αὐτοῦ. ['**Receive** yourself all that the late Justus collected, **and do not leave** the corn in the hands of the cultivators. **Allow** Phibius to remain with you in order that he may instruct you in your duties until I learn what decision I am to give him. **Allow** the messenger of Justus to remain with you till he has completed this year'; tr.: Grenfell, Hunt & Bell (1924: 21)].
34 Cf. e.g. the request contained in ll. 27–28 of P.Oxy. LIX 4000 (late IV CE), a long letter, containing many directives: **ἄσπασον** τοὺς ἡμῶν | πάντας κατ' ὄνομα. ['**Greet** all your own people name by name'; tr.: Ioannidou (in Handley, Ioannidou, Parsons, and Whitehorn 1992: 156)]. Requests like this not only do not constitute a burden for the recipient, but also their formulation constitutes a politeness strategy.

request letters, however, has a special dynamic: similar to politeness strategies which are thematically related to requests, they function as compensatory strategies, only in a more indirect way.

Thus, any expression of deference, care, love or admiration contained in the main body of the letter, such as the commonplace expressions of greeting and wishing, or the expressions of thanking or positive evaluation of the recipient, can be considered as a strategy of politeness.[35]

2.3 The features of the Byzantine style of letter writing

In Byzantine correspondence on papyrus, the interaction of politeness and imperative tone becomes more interesting. In these letters, the emphasis on politeness is greater, even when the writer obviously has the intention of blaming the recipient. Furthermore, there are much more options codifying the intention of the ancient writers to seem polite in comparison with earlier periods. For instance, the sender can use the subjunctive mood instead of the imperative as well as the 2nd person plural of politeness or the 3rd person singular (with an honorific name as subject). Consequently, the complete absence of commonly used politeness strategies where their use is expected, is much more striking compared to letters dated to earlier times.[36] Furthermore, in private letters of this era, politeness is very closely related to religiousness and the display of Christian virtues, such as humbleness.[37] The increase of politeness strategies in private

---

[35] Cf. e.g. the beginning of the short request letter P.Ant. I 45, 1–2 with BL XI 7 (VI CE): πρὸ μὲν πάντων πολλὰ προσκυνῶ καὶ ἀσπάζομαι | τὰ ἴχνη σου. ['First of all I make obeisance to your countenance and salute your footsteps'; tr.: Roberts (1950: 103)].

[36] Cf. e.g. the case of P.Harr. I 159, 1–7 with BL III 83 (V–VI CE): ⳨ ἦλθεν ὁ καιρὸς τῆς καταβολῆς. φρόντισον οὖν μὴ ἀμελήσῃς, ἵνα μοὶ (l. μὴ) ὀχλήσῃς ἐνταῦθα, | καὶ μὴ ἀνέλθῃς ἐς τὴν πόλιν [πρὶν ἂν ποιήσῃς] τὴν καταβολήν, καὶ μὴ | ὡς ε‹ἰ›ς ἡμᾶς ἀσχημονῆσαι. οἱ δὲ σταυρ[οῖς ὕπ]ησιν (l. ὕπεισιν) τοῦ γεούχου καὶ τοῦ βοηθοῦ. ποίησόν | τινα δύο μουείων (l. μωίων) χόρτου ⸌ἐνεχθῆναι⸍ τοῦ ζῴου ταχέως. φρόντισον δὲ τὰ {ἐ}πέ‹ν›τε ὁλοκόττινα | τοῦ τέκτονος πεμ. [- - -] | (hand 2) λαβὲ καὶ τὸν σῖτον τοῖς πε[σί] (l. παισί). οἶδες (l. οἶδας) ὅτι ὁ κόμες (l. κόμης) ἀπεσ[πασε] ν[εωστὶ (?)] τὸν σῖτον | Μαλέου Κλέωνος· μὴ ἀμελήσῃς [οὖν]. ['The time for you to make the payment has come. So, take care that you don't disturb me here, that you don't return to the city before making the payment and you don't misbehave with us. Those who behave in this way are under the torment of the landowner and the assistant. Take care that the one of the two moia be quickly carried by the animal. Take care that the five solidi of the craftsman . . . Moreover, take the wheat from the slaves; you know that lately the comes took away the wheat of Maleos Kleon. Therefore, don't be neglectful. . .'; for a Spanish tr., see O'Callaghan (1963: 157–159) [No 42]].

[37] On private Christian letters on papyrus, see, among others, Tibiletti (1979), Naldini (1998²), Kim (2011), and Koroli (2016: 75–97).

letters dated to this period could be attributed to the gradual disappearance of the opening and closing formulas from the fourth and fifth centuries CE onwards.[38]

3 Classification of papyrus request letters on the basis of politeness and imperative tone

Linguistic (im)politeness is a very complex phenomenon. Therefore, several linguistic and extra-linguistic factors should be taken into consideration while analysing papyrus letters from this point of view. The most important parameter is the content of the text, namely what is requested and for whom. The interaction of various linguistic elements and strategies, i.e. the quantity, quality and originality of linguistic markers of politeness or of imperative tone markers, should also be examined carefully. Specifically, what should be examined is A. the combination and interaction of commonplace politeness strategies (e.g. the honorific names) with those less common; B. the combination and interaction of strategies making part of the thematic-textual unit(s) of the directive(s) with those found in other parts of the letter; C. the coexistence of politeness strategies with imperative tone markers and the way the former moderate the impact of the latter.

The social identity and the relationship of the correspondents are equally important factors. The reconstruction of the extra-linguistic context of papyrus letters is difficult if not impossible. Nevertheless, frequently the main body of the letter and/or the verso contain useful information concerning the correspondents' social status and their relationship (e.g. words or expressions denoting professions, titles or family relationships). Difficulties derive from damaged writing material, the ambiguity of the content and/or the use of polysemous words, such as κύριος/κυρία or δεσπότης/δέσποινα often used in addresses.[39] Finally, the dating of the papyrus letter plays a crucial role. For instance, it is absolutely necessary to consider the norm of letter writing established from the fifth century onwards (see §2.3).

Judging by the above-mentioned observations we could divide requesting in private papyrus letters into the following categories on the basis of the interaction between imperative tone and courtesy strategies, otherwise said of

---

38 Papathomas (2007: 507).
39 Dickey (1996, 2001); Papathomas (2007: 504–506).

the proportion between imperative tone and politeness strategies. These categories belong to a continuum starting from over-politeness and ending in impoliteness:

a) Requesting concerning an urgent situation. The sender appears to be absolutely dependent on the recipient's help. Over-politeness strategies and the expression of humbleness are the means to which he/she resorts in order to be convincing. In this case, we can speak of solicitation.
b) There is a problem to be solved, an urgency or even an accusation. The urgency or the critical mood of the sender though are obvious only from the content, since the sender refers to them in the most discreet way. This is because over-politeness is displayed as a compensation for the imperative tone deriving from the content, so that the sender does not seem offensive. In other words, the sender clearly relies on politeness strategies to be convincing but not because he/she is dependent on the recipient.
c) There is neither a problem nor any kind of urgency. Also, there is no emotional involvement. The tone is not at all imperative. The sender may use some conventional, i.e. common, politeness strategies, only because he/she does not want to spoil his/her request by seeming rude.
d) The tone is imperative by necessity due to an urgency and the sender may seem worried. Although politeness is not neglected and attention is paid to not being rude, he/she does not count as much on politeness strategies.
e) There is again an imperative tone due to urgency. The sender displays over-strictness but without blaming the recipient. Even if there are some politeness strategies, the sender certainly does not depend on them. The sender's social status or relationship with the recipient allows him/her to be indifferent to whether he/she seems particularly gentle or not.
f) There is a clear imperative tone due to the sender's intention to accuse the recipient of causing a problem and/or of his/her character in general. Although there are possibly a few politeness strategies, the imperative markers are dominant.
g) The irritation of the sender is very obvious. The tone of the letter is severely critical or even threatening. No politeness strategies are used. Even the very expected/conventional markers of politeness are absent.

In categories a–d, politeness is considered as a priority or even a necessity (in a and b), in categories e–f, politeness stops being a necessity, whereas in category g, politeness strategies are absent. Linguistic politeness and impoliteness are related to the social status of the correspondents. It seems, for example, that the complete lack of politeness strategies is possible only if the social status of the sender is higher and/or if he/she has authority over the recipient.

4 The selected texts

As already noted in Section 1.1, all six selected Byzantine letters allow us to examine politeness and imperative tone from a sound basis, given that their context is clear.[40] There is no doubt that they all date to the Byzantine period of Egypt, and therefore they bear the typical features of Byzantine letters (see §2.3). They were all produced in an ecclesiastical milieu: they were all sent to and received by clerics or monks.[41] Both their main body and verso allow us to make assumptions about the situational context, the social identity of the correspondents – namely their gender, their profession, and their status in the ecclesiastical community –, as well as the relationship between the sender and the recipient. The relevant remarks contained in the editions and in the secondary literature were of course taken into consideration. Finally, the letters in question are preserved on the same writing material, i.e. papyrus.

As already noted, only linguistic strategies found in the main body of the letter will be focused on. These strategies though interact with the politeness markers included in the verso of the papyrus, for example the plethora of honorific names.

4.1 Letters from P.Fouad

P.Fouad 86, 87, 88, and 89[42] are dated to the sixth century CE[43] and belong to the same dossier, which is certainly helpful for the reconstruction of the context;[44] they were written by four monks belonging to the same monastery

---

[40] The six letters under study are cited in their entirety along with an English translation and the BL references in the Appendix to this chapter.
[41] Papathomas (2007: 510) remarks that many of the letters dated to fourth century CE onwards were written by members of the clergy; before the fourth century CE there are only very few cases of correspondence between pagan priests.
[42] The four letters under study are included in the volume P.Fouad and were edited by Henri Marrou (in Bataille, Guéraud, Jouguet, Lewis, Marrou, Scherer, and Waddell 1939: 175–202). P. Fouad 87 is commented upon in detail by Gascou (1976: esp. 163–177; see BL VII 58); see also the commentary of P.Fouad 88 offered by Kim (2011: 115–119) focusing on the Christian elements of the letters.
[43] On the dating, see Marrou's remarks (1939: 175, 177); for a further precision, see Gascou (1976: 157 with fn. 2); also BL XI 82.
[44] For a definition of dossiers and archives, as well as the advantages of studying non-literary papyri belonging to such groups of texts, see Vandorpe (2009: 216–255); Papathomas (2016³: 258–269).

situated in Aphrodito and were sent to the same person, a certain *προεστώς* ('provost') Georgios, who is the Superior of the Monastery of Petinence (Μετανοίας) in Canope. Both monastic communities belong to the Pachomian Order.[45]

The content of all four letters reveals the power of the addressee: he seems to oversee the monastic community of Aphrodito (cf. P.Fouad 86 and 87) and is also considered as a very respectful religious person and spiritual father for the monks of this monastery (cf. P.Fouad 88 and 89). This is confirmed by the verso of the letters, where many honorific names and other nominal phrases denote the respect of the senders towards the recipient (see Appendix).[46] According to Henri Marrou (1939: esp. 176–177, 190), the monks who are connected to the monastery of Aphrodito, as well as the ones connected to the monastery of Stratonikis[47] are under the authority of Georgios, the superior of the monastery of Petinence, who serves as an intermediary between the two aforementioned monastic communities and the "common Father" of the Order.[48]

---

45 Information and bibliography on the two monasteries, as well as the monastery in Stratonikis mentioned in P.Fouad 87,11 is offered by Marrou in the general introduction of the edition (1939: 175–183); also in Gascou (1976), who focuses on the monastery of Μετανοία. The placement of this monastery seems to be problematic; see Marrou (1939: 176 and 178–183 [esp. 183]). Marrou believes that Ἀφροδιτώ should most probably be identified with Aphroditopolis of the Athribite nome of Lower Egypt, a place near the monastery of Stratonikis. This suggestion is questioned by Gascou (1976: 159–163; cf. BL VII 58). Gascou (1976: 160) believes that Ἀφροδιτώ might well be identified with the village of Aphrodito in the Antaiopolite nome, the current Kom Ichqaou; cf. Fournet (1999: 464; cf. BL XII 73).
46 In all four cases, the sender expresses his humbleness by belittling himself. On the relation between politeness and servility or self-devaluation in Greek papyrus letters of Late Antiquity, see Zilliacus (1953); Papathomas (2007); on the verso of P.Fouad 86, see Papathomas (1996); also BL XI 82.
47 Cf. fn. 45.
48 Cf. Marrou's remark: "ils [i.e. the monasteries of Aphrodito and of Stratonikis] sont soumis, eux, à l'autorité du supérieur de la Métanoia qui apparait comme un intermédiaire hiérarchique entre ces communautés et le supérieur général" ["they [i.e. the monasteries of Aphrodito and of Stratonikis] are subject to the authority of the superior of the Metanoia, who appears as a hierarchical intermediary between these communities and the general superior"] (1939: 177). Gascou (1976: 157 fn. 3) on the other hand remarks that this is not necessarily the case. He argues that, although the deference displayed towards Georgios and his influence on the senders are undeniable, neither his exact role nor the place of the monastery of Μετανοία in the Pachomian institutions are perfectly clear; what is more, the senders' exact position in the monastery of Aphrodito remains equally uncertain, and it is doubtful that they resided in this monastery on a permanent basis since they seem to move from place to place (cf. the relevant remarks in Marrou 1939: 184–185, 190). According to Gascou (ibid.), the content of P.Fouad 86 and 87 indicates that the letters of this small dossier were written by and sent to travelling monks, which, in his opinion,

4.1.1 P.Fouad 86

Both P.Fouad 86 and 87 are narrative letters that refer to issues of the monastery, and specifically to problems caused by unrighteous monks. Their context and the relation of the people involved in the stories told are complicated.[49] The sender of P.Fouad 86 informs the recipient, Georgios, about the wicked behaviour of an immoral monk. The fact that Georgios appears to be responsible for the solution of this problem and that he has the authority even to expel the monk in question from the convent (l. 18) indicates that he is certainly superior to the sender. The latter seems to play, though, an important role in the monastery of Aphrodito, which is why he is responsible for keeping Georgios informed. Nevertheless, he is not equal to the superior of the Monastery of Petinence (Μετανοίας), which is made evident by his deferential style of writing.[50]

The letter starts with the preparation for the directive (ll. 1–17; see Appendix). The detailed information offered to the recipient in this part of the text could be considered as indicative of the urgency of the situation and, consequently, as conveying a kind of imperative tone to the text. At the same time though, the fact that the sender informs the recipient in detail before formulating his request could be considered as a politeness strategy: it proves that the submission of the request, i.e. the expulsion of the immoral monk, is justifiable considering all the events he speaks of. The directive can be found in ll. 17–19:

> (2) **παρακληθῇ** οὖν ἡ ὑμ[ετέ]ρα πατρικὴ θεοφιλία κατὰ νοῦν ἔχειν | **περὶ τούτου πρὸς τῷ** τῇ ὑμετέρᾳ σπουδῇ **περιαιρεθῆναι** τὸν ἀνόσιον ἐκ τῶν | μοναστηρίων ἡμῶν.
>
> '**We beg**, therefore, **your paternal piety not to forget to remove** this unholy person from our monasteries.'
> (P.Fouad 86, 17–19; VI CE)

In general, the writer of this letter is largely dependent on politeness strategies. In the preparation of the request, we twice encounter the honorific name ἁγιοσύνη ('holiness') in combination with the 2nd person plural of politeness and specified in the first case by an adjective pointing to Christian faith (l. 1: τῇ ὑμετέρᾳ πατρικῇ ἁγιοσύνῃ; l. 7: ἡ ὑμετέρα ἁγιοσύνη ['your (paternal) holiness']).

In the formulation of the request, the prepositional phrase πρὸς τῷ τῇ ὑμετέρᾳ σπουδῇ περιαιρεθῆναι τὸν ἀνόσιον ἐκ τῶν | μοναστηρίων ἡμῶν (ll. 18–19)

---

should be rather attributed to "cette vie de relation développée qui caractérise le cénobitisme pachômien" ["this life of developed relationship that characterizes Pachomian cenobitism"].
49 See Marrou (1939: esp. 175–178, 184–185, 189–192).
50 See Marrou's remark in the introduction to the letter (1939: 184).

['to remove as soon as possible this unholy person from our monasteries'] which supplements the verbal phrase παρακληθῇ οὖν ἡ ὑμ[ετέ]ρα πατρικὴ θεοφιλία κατὰ νοῦν ἔχειν | περὶ τούτου (ll. 17–18) ['we beg, therefore, your paternal piety not to forget'], gives an imperative tone to the text, since it contains the noun σπουδή ('zeal'). This imperative tone is counterbalanced by many politeness strategies. First of all, the writer chooses a performative verb, the lexical sense of which is connected to the notion of politeness, i.e. παρακαλῶ, put in the 3rd person singular of the subjunctive (l. 17: παρακληθῇ), since the subject is an honorific name specified by a possessive pronoun in the 2nd person plural and the adjective πατρική (l. 17: ἡ ὑμ[ετέ]ρα πατρικὴ θεοφιλία ['your paternal piety']). The passive syntax also ensures that the 'ego' of the sender/requester is of less importance. In addition, the noun σπουδή (σπουδῇ, l. 18) is specified by a pronoun put in the 2nd person plural of deference (τῇ ὑμετέρᾳ σπουδῇ ['your zeal']).

Outside the textual unit of the directive (ll. 19–21), there are also some politeness strategies. Specifically, this part of the letter contains an extended version of the formula of salutation[51] including two verbs very closely connected to the notion of deference, i.e. προσκυνῶ ('to make reverences')[52] and ἀσπάζομαι ('to salute'), as well as the nominal phrase τὴν ὑμετέραν πατρικὴν ἁγιοσύνην ['your paternal holiness'] in l. 20, also attested in. l. 1 and enriched here by a phrase denoting the writer's deep Christian faith (ll. 20–21):

(3) πλεῖστα **προσκύνομεν (l. προσκυνοῦμεν)** καὶ **ἀσπαζόμεθα** | **τὴν ὑμετέραν πατρικὴν ἁγιοσύνην**, περιπτυσσόμενοι αὐτὴν τῇ τοῦ Πνεύματος | ἐνώσει.

'**We make you many reverences** and **salute your paternal holiness** embracing you **in the unity of the Holy Spirit**.'
(P.Fouad 86, 20–21; VI CE)

In sum, the sender of this letter clearly expresses his respect towards the recipient by combining several commonplace politeness strategies.

4.1.2 P.Fouad 87

Similarly to P.Fouad 86, this letter refers to issues of the monastery. Here again the sender writes about a problem the solution of which necessitates the addressee's intervention. The story hidden behind this letter is more complicated as

---

[51] For the thematic motif of salutation, see, among others, Koroli (2016: 67–68).
[52] On phrases containing προσκυνῶ καὶ ἀσπάζομαι, see the comment of Papathomas in CPR XXV (2006: 175–177 with fn. 3).

compared with the one to which P.Fouad 86 is related. The sender, Andreas,[53] asks Georgios to protect the monks living there from the vicious behaviour of their current superior. As already observed by Marrou (1939: 189–192), the relationship of the two correspondents is more complicated in comparison with P.Fouad 86, 88 and 89. Georgios is the superior of the monastery of Petinence, and therefore Andreas displays the appropriate respect; at the same time though Andreas is an important person of the monastery of Aphrodito, as well as the spiritual father of Georgios.[54]

The detailed information offered to the recipient in ll. 1–30 (see Appendix) functions as an indirect request. By means of this long list of complaints the writer clearly expresses his irritation for a third person and stresses the urgency of the situation. He writes that his intention is just to keep Georgios informed; cf. his statement in ll. 27–28, where the honorific name εὐτεκνία ('blessing of children'; 'fruitfullness'; 'blessedness'; for the first two meanings, see LSJ) is used specified by a possessive pronoun in the 2nd person plural, as well as the adjective θεοφιλής ('dear to God'): καὶ πρὸς εἴδησιν τῆς | ὑμετέρας θεοφιλοῦς εὐτεκνίας ταῦτα γέγραφα ['and I have written this text in order to keep your supreme blessedness, which is dear to God, informed']. Nevertheless, it is clear and easily understandable that the real intention of the sender is to make Georgios take action. This passage has a somewhat imperative tone due to its content. At the same time though the choice of the sender to submit an indirect request could be attributed to his effort to be polite by not asking explicitly for Georgios' intervention.

The direct request (l. 34), which is thematically irrelevant to the preceding indirect directive and supplemented by ll. 35–36 (see Appendix), is formulated in the 3rd person singular of the subjunctive; the subject is the honorific name θεοφιλία specified by the possessive pronoun in the 2nd person plural:

(4) μὴ ὀλιγορήσῃ (l. ὀλιγωρήσῃ) δὲ ἡ ὑμετέρα θεοφιλία κατὰ τοῦ γραμματηφόρου.

'**May your piety not be angry** with the letter-carrier.'
(P.Fouad 87, 34; VI CE)

---

53 On Andreas' status and relation to Georgios, see Marrou (1939: 190) and Gascou (1976: 157 fn. 3; 159).
54 Cf. l. 37 of the verso: τῷ τὰ πάντ(α) θεοφιλε(στάτῳ) **πν(ευματ)ικῷ υἱῷ** ['to my **spiritual son**, who is absolutely dearest to God']. On the reconstruction of the context of the letter, the persons involved and their relationship, see Marrou's remarks in the introduction to the letter (1939: 189–190).

Outside the two directives' thematic-textual units, we again find a version of the formula of salutation (ll. 30–33). The salutation is presented as the primary goal of the sender (cf. πρὸ πάντων ['first of all'] in l. 30). This passage, which includes the honorific name θεοφιλία ('the favour of God'; see LSJ; in this cotext: 'piety'), has a very striking religious content:

> (5) ἀσπάζομαι **πρὸ πάντων** τὴν σὴν ἀδελφικὴν | **θεοφιλίαν** ἐν Κυρίῳ, μετὰ πάντων τῶν {των} σὺν αὐτῇ καὶ ἀγαπούντω(ν) (l. ἀγαπώντων) | αὐτὴν ἀδελφῶν. οἱ σὺν ἐμοὶ ἀσπάζονται ὑμᾶς ἐν Κυρίῳ.
>
> '**First of all**, I salute your brotherly **piety** in the Lord, as well as all of the brothers who live with you and love you.'
> (P.Fouad 87, 30–33; VI CE)

In general, the sender resorts to several commonplace politeness strategies expressing his deferential attitude to the superior of the monastery of Petinence. Nevertheless, due to his sprititual superiority in comparison to the recipient he does not appear as submissive as the senders of the rest of the P. Fouad examples.[55]

4.1.3 P.Fouad 88

In P.Fouad 88 and 89, Georgios' influence on the monks connected to the monastery of Aphrodito is shown differently than in P.Fouad 86 and 87; Georgios is not asked to solve a problem but is the recipient of the sender's excessive deference.

What is particularly interesting in P.Fouad 88 is the content of the two directives it contains: the sender, a humble monk, asks the recipient to include him in his prayers and to always have good feelings about him (ll. 4–6; 9):

> (6) ἔπειτα δὲ καὶ παρακαλῶ | μνησθῆναι τῆς ἐμῆς βραχύτητος ἐν ταῖς πρὸς τὸν Θεὸν αὐτῆς | εὐπροσδέκτοις λιταῖς . . . παρακαλῶ αὐτὴν ταύτην βεβαίαν ἔχειν μέχρι παντός.
>
> 'Secondly, I beg you to remember me, the least of all, in the prayers that you address to God, which are accepted [by Him] . . . I beg you to keep it [i.e. your benevolence towards me] as strong as it is now for ever.'
> (P.Fouad 88, 4–6; 9; VI CE)

---

55 See Marrou's remark in the introduction to the letter (1939: 189–190).

In reality, these two directives are nothing more than an expression of the sender's deferential attitude towards the recipient.⁵⁶

Despite the particuliarity of the *petitum*, the writer organizes his text as a common request letter and writes as if he is asking for something of great importance. The two thematically relative directives are formulated by means of the performative verb παρακαλῶ. Their submission is justified by ll. 6–9 (see Appendix), which function as a supplement of the first directive and as preparation for the second one, as well as by ll. 10–11 (see Appendix), which function as the supplement of the second directive. The framing of the two directives stresses to an even greater extent the writer's respect, since it gives prominence to the recipient's piety and benevolence. This respect is displayed with the same intensity in the rest of the letter, which contains five attestations of the 2nd person plural of the possessive pronoun (ll. 3: τὴν ὑμετέραν; 6–7: τῶν | ὑμετέρων; 7–8: τῆς | ὑμετέρας; 10: τῶν ὑμετέρων; 11: ὑμετέρας).

In ll. 1–4, we come across two thematic motifs commonly attested in private papyrus letters. First of all, the sender refers to the opportunity he took advantage of to send the present letter to Georgios. He claims that his main goal was to prostrate and salutate the recipient. This passage is full of politeness markers, such as a nominal phrase including the honorific name ἁγιοσύνη ('holiness') in combination with the adjective πατρική ('paternal') and the second plural of politeness (l. 3: τὴν ὑμετέραν πατρικὴν ἁγιοσύνην ['your paternal holiness']), as well as the participles προσκυνῶν καὶ προσφθεγγόμενος (l. 4; ['making obeisance and saluting']):

(7) καὶ νῦν τῆς εὐκαιρίας δραξάμενος τοῦ γραμματηφόρου μονάζοντος | κατερχομένου μετὰ τῶν γραμμάτων τοῦ ὁσιοτάτου (l. ὁσιωτάτου) ἀββᾶ Ἀνδρέου | πρὸς **τὴν ὑμετέραν πατρικὴν ἁγιοσύνην** ⟦γε … φ.⟧ γέγραφα πρῶτον μὲν | **προσκυνῶν καὶ προσφθεγγόμενος** αὐτήν).

'Now also, finding an opportunity by the monk and letter-carrier, who descends towards **your paternal holiness** holding the letter of the most holy abbot Andreas, I have written this letter first and foremost **in order to make obeisance** to you **and salute** you.'
(P.Fouad 88, 1–4; VI CE)

---

56 Marrou characterizes this letter as a "bon specimen de la verbeuse politesse byzantine et de la vanité des jeux épistolaires où les chrétiens de la basse-antiquité se sont complu" ["a good specimen of the verbose Byzantine politeness and the vanity of the epistolary games in which Christians of the Roman and Late Antique period delighted themselves"] (1939: 197 with fn. 1, where literary parallels for this style of letter writing are offered); see also Gascou (1976: 158 fn. 2). The submission of directives of this kind is usually not the main communicative goal of the sender in private correspondence, but only a way of displaying reverence and religiousness; see indicatively Kim (2011: 45).

The letter closes in an equally submissive way, specifically with a long version of the salutation formula characterized by an intense religiousness and ending with the invocation θεοφιλέστατέ μου πάτερ ['my holiest spiritual father'] in ll. 11–14:

> (8) ἀσπάζομαι δὲ τόν τε | θεοφιλέστατον κοινὸν πατέρα, καὶ τὴν κοσμιωτάτην κοινὴν μητέρα, | καὶ πάντας τοὺς σὺν ὑμῖν ἐν Κ(υρί)ῳ, δέσπο(τα) **θεοφιλέστατέ μου πάτερ**.
>
> 'I salute our common Father, who is dearest to God, and our common mother, who is the most virtuous, and all the people who live with us in the Lord, **my** master and **most pious Father**'.
> (P.Fouad 88, 11–14; VI CE)

In reality, by means of the submission of two pseudo-directives, the writer displays in extremis his Christian virtues, so that he wins the favour of Georgios, who is both a man of power and his spiritual father.[57] It has to be noted that in other private papyrus letters, requests like the ones included in P.Fouad 88 are used only as subsidiary requests.[58]

The writer of this letter expresses not only an excessive politeness, reverence and admiration for Georgios himself and whatever is his (cf. ll. 5–8; 10–11; see Appendix), but also his unlimited humbleness and submission; he goes so far as to belittle himself not only in the verso but also in the main body of his letter.[59]

4.1.4 P.Fouad 89

This letter is very similar to the previous one in terms of both content and writing style. Once again, the text resembles a solicitation; in reality, the writer considers its writing and sending as proof of his deep religiousness and his deferential attitude towards the recipient and, consequently, as a means for winning his favour. The pseudo-request (ll. 4–8) is formulated again with the performative verb παρακαλῶ supplemented by the phrase τὸν ἐμὸν δεσπότην ['my lord']:

> (9) καὶ | **παρακαλῶ τὸν ἐμὸν δεσπότην μνησθῆναι** τῇ ἐμῇ ταπ<ε>ινώσει ἐν | ταῖς πανοσίαις καὶ εὐπροσδέκταις εὐχῆς (l. εὐχαῖς) **τῷ ἐμῷ ἀγαθῷ δεσπότῃ**, | ἄχρη (l. ἄχρι) ἀξιώσῃ μαι (l. με) ὁ Θεός καὶ κατὰ πρόσωπον προσκυνῆσαι τὸν | **ἐμὸν ἀγαθὸν δεσπότην**.

---

57 Cf. ll. 3: **πατρικὴν ἁγιοσύνην** ['paternal holiness']; 13: **θεοφιλέστατέ μου πάτερ** ['my most pious Father']; 15–16: πατρὶ | π(νευματι)κῷ ['spiritual Father'].
58 See Koroli (2016: 157–162, esp. 161).
59 Cf. ll. 5: τῆς ἐμῆς **βραχύτητος** ['me, **the least of all**']; 8–9: εἰς ἐμέ, τὸν **ἐλάχιστον** αὐτῆς ἀδελφὸν | καὶ υἱόν ['me, **the least of all** your brothers and your son'], as well as l. 17 of the verso: **ἐλάχ(ιστος)** ['**the least of all**']; cf. fn. 46.

'... and **I beg my lord to remember** my insignificance in his all-holy prayers, which are accepted by God, **for my virtuous lord** until God will think me worthy to make obeisance to **my virtuous lord** also in person.'
(P.Fouad 89, 4–8; VI CE)

The reference to the recipient as if he was a third person is an over-politeness strategy. In the supplement of the directive (ll. 8–11; see Appendix), the sender assures the recipient that he also prays for him all day and all night. In general, when the writer refers to the recipient, he never uses the second person (neither singular nor plural) but nominal phrases including the noun δεσπότης (ll. 3; 4; 5; 6; 8; 10; 11; see Appendix).

The letter opens again with the motifs of the chance for sending the letter (l. 1; see Appendix) and of the salutation (ll. 2–4). The latter is enriched by two clumsy repetitions expressing the boundless respect of the sender towards the recipient:

(10) προσκυνῶν καὶ ἀσπαζόμενος **τὰ εὐλογημένα ἴχνη τῶν εὐλογημένων | ποδῶν τῷ ἐμῷ ἀγαθῷ δεσπότῃ** μετὰ καὶ πάντων τῶν | συνόντων θεοφιλεστάτ(ων) ἀδελφῶν **τῷ ἐμῷ ἀγαθῷ δεσπότῳ** (l. δεσπότῃ).

'... in order to worship and salute **the blessed prints of the blessed feet of my virtuous lord**, and of all the brothers, who are the most pious, and who live with **my virtuous lord**.'
(P.Fouad 89, 2–4; VI CE)

The writer exalts the recipient and whatever is related to him;[60] at the same time, similar to P.Fouad 88, he expresses a limitless humbleness by devaluating himself.[61] Despite their similarities, P.Fouad 88 and 89 differ as far as the linguistic aptitude of the two senders is concerned.[62] The repeated use of nominal phrases containing the noun δεσπότης ('lord') in P.Fouad 89 is indicative not only of the sender's excessive deferential attitude but also of his inability to express it in good Greek.

---

60 ll. 2–3: τὰ εὐλογημένα ἴχνη τῶν εὐλογημένων | ποδῶν ['the blessed prints of the blessed feet']; 5–6: ἐν | ταῖς πανοσίαις καὶ εὐπροσδέκταις εὐχῆς (l. εὐχαῖς) ['in his all-holy prayers, which are accepted by God'].
61 cf. l. 5: τῇ ἐμῇ ταπ<ε>ινώσει ['my **insignificance**'], as well as ll. 12–13 of the verso: ἐλάχ(ιστος) | δοῦλος ['**the least of all slaves**']; cf. fn. 46.
62 Marrou attributes the sender's linguistic maladroitness, namely the syntactical and orthographical mistakes contained in the letter to his Coptic origin, manifested by his name (1939: 200); this view is questioned by Gascou (1976: 158 fn. 2), who attributes these features of the text to "la pratique du grec courant" ["the practice of then current Greek"].

4.2 Letters from P.Ness. III

4.2.1 P.Ness. III 47

This letter was sent to a deacon, Stephanos, by an abbot, Patrick, probably before 605 CE.[63] The position of Stephanos is mentioned on the verso of the papyrus (see Appendix). The title of the sender (ἡγούμενος, 'abbot') is mentioned in the letter preserved on the verso of the papyrus (l. 8). The verso also contains the reply of Stephanos to Patrick's letter. The content of the letter is not related to religious matters. The sender submits two thematically irrelevant directives. The basic directive is contained in ll. 2–5. The sender uses the structure θέλησον ['please'] + infinitive, which is a politeness strategy:

(11) **θέλεσων (l. θέλησον) δέξασθ[αι** παρ]ὰ [το]ῦ γραμ|ματεφώρου (l. γραμματηφόρου) σκάρου λ(ίτρας) ὠγδωέκωντα (l. ὀγδοήκοντα) κεφαλὰς μεγάλας ἔκωσι (l. εἴκοσι) | **καὶ** εἰς ταῦτα πρωκάλυμμα (l. προκάλυμμα) **ποιῆσε (l. ποιῆσαι)** τῷ ἀνθρώπῳ μου Ἀνακλᾷ | ὅτι ἐδέξου (l. ἐδέξω) αὐτά.

> '**Please accept** from the letter-carrier eighty pounds of sea fish, twenty large heads. In return **give** my man Anaklas the protection of a note that you have received them.'
> (P.Ness. III 47, 2–5; before 605 CE?)

In the second, formulaic directive (l. 5), the sender asks the recipient to pray for him. This is a subsidiary request increasing the perlocutionary force of the basic bipartite directive in an indirect way, since the two directives are thematically irrelevant:

(12) καὶ εὔχου ὑπὲρ ἐμοῦ διὰ τῶν (l. τὸν) κύριων (l. κύριον).

> 'Pray for me to the Lord.'
> (P.Ness. III 47, 5; before 605 CE?)

Furthermore, the sender makes use of a series of conventional politeness strategies. Specifically, in ll. 1–2 he writes a formula of obeisance and a salutation, in the framework of which he includes the recipient among his real friends, and uses the invocation δέσποτα ('lord') and of the verbs προσκυνῶ ('make obeisance') and ἀσπάζω ('salute'):

(13) πάντων πρότερων (l. πρότερον) γράφω **προσ[κ]υνῶ καὶ ἀσπ[άζω** σ]ε τὸν ἐμοῦ | **γνήσιων (l. γνήσιον) φίλων (l. φίλον) ὄντα, δέσποτα.**

---

[63] The two letters under study were published by Casper J. Kraemer in 1958. On their dating and provenance, cf. Kraemer (1958: 139, 144).

'Before writing anything else, **I send respectful greetings to you, sir, for you are my true friend.**'
(P.Ness. III 47, 1–2; before 605?)

The editor of the letter attributes the deferential attitude of the sender to the hierarchical distance between the two correspondents, which is obvious by the reply of the recipient on the verso: the latter makes no attempt to be excessively polite towards Patrick.[64]

4.2.2 P.Ness. III 50, 1–9

The sender of P.Ness. III 50, Georgios,[65] is also of a higher ecclesiastical and social status in comparison to the recipient, Zoninos; he is a bishop (ἐπίσκοπος), whereas the recipient is an abbot (ἀββάς). The position of the two correspondents in the clerical ranking is mentioned in the main body of the letter (ll. 1–2; 10–11; see Appendix). The content of this letter, written in the early seventh century CE, is clearly connected to religious – but practical – matters. The sender is ill and cannot attend a festival; so, he asks the recipient, in case he attends the festival in question, to request on his behalf an unnamed abbot to give a donation (εὐλογία) to another abbot, a certain Prokopios.[66]

The letter contains many linguistic choices giving the text an imperative tone. First of all, the sender submits two thematically relevant requests. The first, basic directive has three parts found in different parts of the text (ll. 2; 3–5; 9; see Appendix). Its third part (l. 9) closes the main body of the letter, which could also be considered as a marker of imperative tone:

(14) καὶ ἐάν μὲ (l. μὴ) ἐξέλθες (l. ἐξέλθῃς) γράψον αὐτῶν (l. αὐτῷ).

'If you do not go out, write him.'
(P.Ness. III 50, 9; early VII CE)

There is also a subsidiary request (ll. 7–8), repeating the basic directive:

(15) ἐπαρα|κλέθετι. (l. παρακλήθητι) χαρίσεν (l. χαρίζειν) με τῶ **(l. τὸ) καθῖκον (l. καθῆκον)** τοῦτο.

---

[64] See Kraemer's remark in the introduction to the letter (1958: 139), who, among others, notes the following: "The fact that Patrick calls himself simply ἡγούμενος . . . seems to indicate, unless he was not giving his full title, that he was not yet reader or priest . . . The tone of deference with which he addresses Stephan and the air of authority in which the reply is couched clearly reflects a considerable difference in rank between the two men".
[65] This Georgios is not the same person as the recipient of the letters P.Fouad 86–89.
[66] For more information on the context, see Kraemer's introduction to the letter (1958: 144).

> 'You are requested to grant me the favor, **which is my due**.'
> (P.Ness. III 50, 7–8; early VII CE)

The noun καθῖκον (l. καθῆκον) ('due') presents the satisfaction of the basic request as an obligation of the recipient. The sender exercises some pressure on the recipient because he is obviously worried about the arrangement of the issues of which he speaks. This is obvious from ll. 2–3, which supplement the basic request:

> (16) ἐπ<ε>ιδὴ ἀσθενῶ καὶ οὐ δύ|ναμε (l. δύναμαι) ἐξελθ<ε>ῖν εἰς τὴν ἑορτὴν τοῦ ἁγίου Σεργίου.
>
> 'Since I am sick and cannot go out to the festival of St. Sergios.'
> (P.Ness. III 50, 2–3; early VII CE)

Moreover, being superior to the recipient makes him feel free to ask him in a somehow persistent and implicitly strict way to satisfy his requests. However, although stressed and socially superior, he does not forget to use politeness strategies. In the textual unit of the request, we find the use of the imperative ἐπαρα|κλέθετι (l. παρακλήθητι) ['you are requested'] supplemented by the infinitive χαρίσεν (l. χαρίζειν) ['grant the favour']. Both words compensate for the formulation of the noun καθῖκον (l. καθῆκον), which is included in the same subsidiary directive.

There are also some politeness strategies outside the textual unit of the directives. The letter begins with the conventional form of salutation (l. 1), which is presented as the main communicative goal of the sender.

> (17) **πρ<ὸ> ʿμ´ὲν πάντων** γράφω κ[αὶ ἀ]σπάζομε (l. ἀσπάζομαι) τῶν (l. τὸν) ἀβ<β>ᾶν Ζόνι|νων (l. Ζόνινον).
>
> '**Before everything** I am writing to send greetings to Father Zoninon.'
> (P.Ness. III 50, 1; early VII CE)

Moreoever, the sender wishes the recipient to be healthy (l. 8):

> (18) ἀγυένον (l. ὑγιαίνων) διελθ[ε].
>
> 'Abide in good health.'
> (P.Ness. III 50, 8; early VII CE)

In conclusion, Georgios obviously does not want to displease the recipient of his request by seeming rude; furthermore, such a writing behaviour would not suit his status. Thus, he uses all the above-mentioned commonplace politeness strategies in order to display his respect to the recipient, who is also a member of the clergy.

4.3 The place of the selected texts in the politeness-imperative tone continuum

The place of the examples in the politeness-imperative tone continuum presented in Section 3 could be as follows:

Table 1: Politeness–imperative tone continuum.

The request letter per se as an expression of respect towards the recipient: **P.Fouad 88, P.Fouad 89**.
Requesting by counting greatly on over-politeness strategies; the sender is absolutely dependent on the recipient to solve an urgent problem (= solicitation).
The urgent tone or the critical mood of the sender are compensated by over-politeness strategies: **P.Ness. III 50; P.Fouad 86; P.Fouad 87**.
There is neither a problem nor any kind of emotional involvement. The tone is not at all imperative. The sender may use some common politeness strategies: **P.Ness. III 47**.
There is an imperative tone due to urgency. The sender may seem worried. Although he/she pays attention to not being rude, politeness strategies are not relied on.
There is (again) an imperative tone due to urgency. The sender displays over-strictness without blaming the recipient. Even if there are some politeness strategies, they certainly are not depended on.
There is a clear imperative tone due to the sender's intention to blame the recipient. The markers of the imperative tone are dominant.
The tone of the letter is severely critical or even threatening. No politeness strategies are used.

As can be seen in Table 1, imperative tone never prevails courtesy in the examined corpus; what is more, in two examples, P.Fouad 88 and P.Fouad 89, the expression of reverence itself was the primary goal of the writer. Cases like these could be regarded as a small but distinct category of papyrus request letters.

5 Conclusions

The analysis of the selected corpus revealed that each letter contains a variety of linguistic choices and strategies. Both politeness and imperative tone are codified in many different ways and interact to serve the main communicative goal of the sender. Each one of the senders of the six letters under study resorts to a different set of strategies depending on the content, the status of the correspondents and their relationship; cf. e.g. the case of P.Ness. III 50 and of P.Fouad 87 as opposed to P.Fouad 88 and 89.

The similarities observed in the selected examples allow us to assume that (male) members of the clergy or of monastic orders wrote in a distinct way differentiating them – to some extent – from other letter-writers. In all six letters, politeness constitutes a priority, whereas impoliteness markers seem to be completely inappropriate, especially when the recipient is higher in the ecclesiastical hierarchy.

An additional similarity between the six selected examples is the striking accumulation of honorific names, as well as words and phrases related to religiousness. Amphilochios Papathomas (2007: 508–510) attributes the abundance of these linguistic elements in clerical letters to the fact that these letters were obviously considered as proofs of the writer's deep Christian faith. Finally, letters like P.Fouad 88 and 89 show that religious persons could go so far as to write request letters only to display their respect to their superiors and, consequently, their absolute humbleness.[67] In this case, the request letter per se constitutes an expression of over-politeness and Christian virtues. This type of letter is similar in style to common solicitations, in the sense that the sender makes an effort to seem over-polite and appears to be completely dependent on the recipient. Nevertheless, the senders of these two letters do not ask the recipient to help them solve a problem; all they ask the recipient is to pray for them. Politeness here is something more than a priority – it is the *reason* for writing this letter.

All in all, the scrutiny of the interaction between politeness and imperative tone strategies as defined in Sections 2.1 and 2.2 in the selected epistolary texts leads to the assumption that these letters bear a set of common features; although the imperative tone is not absent, politeness strategies are always dominant. This "special" quota of imperative tone and politeness could be considered indeed as a Byzantine "ecclesiastical" style of letter-writing. A thorough examination of a larger corpus and the comparison of the papyrological evidence to the literary production coming from the same period may help us reach more concrete conclusions.

---

[67] P.Herm. 8 and 9 (IV CE; see BL X 85), as well as P.Lond. VI 1925, 1927 and partly 1924 (mid-IV CE), all sent to ascetic men and belonging to dossiers, offer close parallels to these request letters.

References

Bagnall, Roger S. & Raffaella Cribiore. 2006. *Women's letters from ancient Egypt, 300 BC–AD 800*. Ann Arbor: University of Michigan Press.
Bataille, André, Octave Guéraud, Pierre Jouguet, Napthali Lewis, Henri-Irénée Marrou, Jean Scherer & William Gillian Waddell. 1939. *Les papyrus Fouad I. Nos 1–89*. Le Caire: Institut français d'archéologie orientale.
Brown, Penelope & Stephen C. Levinson. 1987. *Politeness: Some universals in language usage*. Cambridge: Cambridge University Press.
Dickey, Eleanor. 1996. *Greek forms of address: From Herodotus to Lucian*. Oxford: Clarendon Press.
Dickey, Eleanor. 2001. Κύριε, δέσποτα, *domine*: Greek politeness in the Roman Empire. *Journal of Hellenic Studies* 121. 1–11.
Dickey, Eleanor. 2010. Latin influence and Greek request formulae. In Trevor V. Evans & Dirk D. Obbink (eds.), *The language of the papyri*, 208–220. Oxford: Oxford University Press.
Dickey, Eleanor. 2016a. Emotional language and formulae of persuasion in papyrus letters. In Ed Sanders & Matthew Johncock (eds.), *Emotion and persuasion in Classical Antiquity*, 237–262. Stuttgart: Steiner.
Dickey, Eleanor. 2016b. Politeness in ancient Rome: Can it help us evaluate modern politeness theories? *Journal of Politeness Research* 12. 197–220.
Fournet, Jean-Luc. 1999. *Hellénisme dans l'Égypte du VIe siècle. La bibliothèque et l'œuvre de Dioscore d'Aphrodité*. Cairo: Institut francais d'archéologie orientale.
Gascou, Jean. 1976. P. Fouad 87: Les monastères pachômiens et l'État byzantin. *Bulletin de l'Institut français d'archéologie orientale* 76. 157–184.
Grenfell, Bernard P., Arthur S. Hunt, & Harold I. Bell, 1924. *The Oxyrhynchus papyri. Part XVI*. London: Egypt Exploration Society.
Hagedorn, Dieter. 2008. Zu den Adressen einiger spätantiker Briefe. *Zeitschrift für Papyrologie und Epigraphik* 165. 129–132.
Handley, Eric W., Hariklia Grace Ioannidou, Peter J. Parsons & John E. G. Whitehorne (with contributions by H. Maehler, M. Maehler & M. L. West.). 1992. *The Oxyrhynchus papyri. Volume LIX*. London: Egypt Exploration Society.
Hornickel, Otto. 1930. *Ehren- und Rangprädikate in den Papyrusurkunden. Ein Beitrag zum römischen und byzantinischen Titelwesen*. PhD dissertation, Giessen University.
Iakovou, Maria. 1999. *Τροπικές κατηγορίες στο ρηματικό σύστημα της ΝΕ*. PhD dissertation, University of Athens.
Karlsson, Gustav H. & Herwig Maehler. 1979. Papyrusbriefe römisch-byzantinischer Zeit. *Zeitschrift für Papyrologie und Epigraphik* 33. 279–294.
Kim, Chan-Hie. 1972. *Form and structure of the familiar Greek letter of recommendation*. Missoula, MT: Scholars Press.
Kim, Chinook. 2011. *"Grüße in Gott, dem Herrn!": Studien zum Stil und zur Struktur der griechischen christlichen Privatbriefe aus Ägypten*. PhD dissertation, University of Trier.
Koroli, Aikaterini. 2014. Στρατηγικές αξιολόγησης στις ιδιωτικές παπυρικές επιστολές της ύστερης αρχαιότητας: η περίπτωση του αιτήματος. *Ελληνικά* 64. 41–53.
Koroli, Aikaterini. 2016. *Το αίτημα στις ελληνικές ιδιωτικές επιστολές σε παπύρους και όστρακα: από την εποχή του Αυγούστου έως το τέλος της αρχαιότητας*. Athens: Ινστιτούτο του Βιβλίου-Καρδαμίτσα.

Koskenniemi, Heikki. 1956. *Studien zur Idee und Phraseologie des griechischen Briefes bis 400 n. Chr.* Helsinki: Suomalainen Tiedeakatemie.
Kramer, Bärbel & Dieter Hagedorn. 1984. *Griechische Papyri der Staats- und Universitätsbibliothek Hamburg.* Bonn: Dr. Rudolf Habelt GMBH.
Kramer, Bärbel, Michael Erler, Dieter Hagedorn & Robert Hübner. 1980. *Kölner Papyri. Band 3. (Papyrologica Coloniensia, VII.).* Opladen: Westdeutscher Verlag.
Kraemer, Casper J. 1958. *Excavations at Nessana.* Vol. 3: *Non-literary papyri.* Princeton, New Jersey: Princeton University Press.
Leiwo, Martti. 2010. Imperatives and other directives in the Greek letters from Mons Claudianus. In Trevor V. Evans & Dirk D. Obbink (eds.), *The language of the papyri*, 97–119. Oxford: Oxford University Press.
Ljungvik, Herman. 1932. *Beiträge zur Syntax der spätgriechischen Volkssprache.* Uppsala: Almqvist & Wiksell.
Muir, John. 2009. *Life and letters in the Ancient Greek world.* London: Routledge.
Naldini, Mario. 1998. *Il cristianesimo in Egitto. Lettere private nei papyri dei secoli II–IV*, 2nd ed. Firenze: Nardini.
O'Callaghan. 1963. *Cartas cristianas griegas del siglo V.* Barcelona: Balmes.
Palme, Bernhard. 2002. *Corpus Papyrorum Raineri. Band XXIV. Dokumente zu Verwaltung und Militär aus dem Spätantiken Ägypten.* Wien: Hollinek Verlag.
Papathomas, Amphilochios. 1996. Korrekturen Tyche 217–220. *Tyche* 11. 246.
Papathomas, Amphilochios. 2006. *Fünfunddreissig griechische Papyrusbriefe aus der Spätantike. CPR XXV.* Munich & Leipzig: K. G. Saur.
Papathomas, Amphilochios. 2007. Höflichkeit und Servilität in den griechischen Papyrusbriefen der ausgehenden Antike. In Bernhard Palme (ed.), *Akten des 23. Internationalen Papyrologenkongresses, Wien, 22.–28. Juli 2001*, 497–512. Wien: Österreichische Akademie der Wissenschaften.
Papathomas, Amphilochios. 2009. Zur captatio benevolentiae in den griechischen Papyri als Zeugnis für die Mentalitätsgeschichte der Römerzeit: Die Verherrlichung des Adressaten und die Selbstherabsetzung des Ausstellers in den Petitionen an Herrscher und Behörden. In Eleni Karamalengou & Eugenia Makrygianni (eds.), Ἀντιφίλησις: *Studies on Classical, Byzantine and Modern Greek literature and culture in honour of John-Theophanes A. Papademetriou*, 486–496. Stuttgart: Steiner.
Papathomas, Amphilochios & Aikaterini Koroli. 2014. Subjectivité et stylistique dans l' épistolographie privée de l'Antiquité tardive: L'exemple de P.Oxy. XVI 1869. *Chronique d'Égypte* 89. 390–401.
Papathomas, Amphilochios. 2016. *Εισαγωγή στην παπυρολογία*, 3rd ed. Athens: self-publishing.
Rees, Brinley R. 1964. *Papyri from Hermopolis and other documents of the Byzantine period.* London: Egypt Exploration Society.
Risselada, Rodie. 1993. *Imperatives and other directive expressions in Latin: A study in the pragmatics of a dead language.* Amsterdam: Gieben.
Roberts, Colin H. 1950. *The Antinoopolis papyri.* London: Egypt Exploration Society.
Searle, John R. 1969. *Speech Acts.* Cambridge: Cambridge University Press.
Searle, John R. 1976. A classification of illocutionary acts. *Language in Society* 5. 1–23.
Shelton, John. 1977. Papyri from the Bonn Collection. *Zeitschrift für Papyrologie und Epigraphik* 25. 159–183.

Sifianou, Maria. 1992. *Politeness phenomena in England and Greece: A cross-cultural perspective*. Oxford: Oxford University Press.
Sifianou, Maria. 2014. Ευγένεια στον λόγο. In Marianthi Georgalidou, Maria Sifianou & Villy Tsakona (eds.), *Ανάλυση λόγου: θεωρία και εφαρμογές*, 261–294. Athens: Nisos.
Sirivianou, Maria G. (with contributions by H.-C. Günther, P. J. Parsons, P. Schubert et al.). 1989. *The Oxyrhynchus papyri. Volume LVI*. London: Egypt Exploration Society.
Steen, Henry A. 1938. Les clichés épistolaires dans les lettres sur papyrus grecques. *Classica et Mediaevalia* 1. 119–176.
Terkourafi, Marina. 2002. Politeness and formulaicity: Evidence from Cypriot Greek. *Journal of Greek Linguistics* 3. 179–201.
Terkourafi, Marina. 2005. An argument for a frame-based approach to politeness: Evidence from the use of the imperative in Cypriot Greek. In Robin Lakoff & Ide Sachiko (eds.), *Broadening the horizon of linguistic politeness*, 99–116. Amsterdam: Benjamins.
Terkourafi, Marina. 2008. Toward a unified theory of politeness, impoliteness, and rudeness. In Derek Bousfield & Miriam A. Locher (eds.), *Impoliteness in language: Studies on its interplay with power in theory and practice*, 45–74. Berlin: Mouton de Gruyter.
Tibiletti, Giuseppe. 1979. *Le lettere private nei papiri greci del III e IV secolo d.C.* Milano: Vita e Pensiero.
Trapp, Michael. 2003. *Greek and Latin letters: An anthology with translation*. Cambridge: Cambridge University Press.
Vandorpe, Katelijn. 2009. Archives and dossiers. In Roger S. Bagnall (ed.), *The Oxford handbook of papyrology*, 216–255. Oxford: Oxford University Press.
Watts, Richard J. 2003. *Politeness*. Cambridge: Cambridge University Press.
Zilliacus, Henrik. 1949. *Untersuchungen zu den abstrakten Anredeformen und Höflichkeitstiteln im Griechischen*. Helsingfors: Societas Scientiarum Fennica.
Zilliacus, Henrik. 1953. *Selbstgefühl und Servilität. Studien zum unregelmässigen Numerusgebrauch im Griechischen*. Helsingfors: Societas Scientiarum Fennica.
Zilliacus, Henrik. 1967. *Zur Abundanz der spätgriechischen Gebrauchssprache*. Helsingfors: Societas Scientiarum Fennica.

Appendix

P.Fouad 86 with BL VIII 133; X 77; XI 82

(Possibly Aphrodito, Antaiopolite nome [see BL VII 58; XII 73]; VI CE)

†

1 † γνωρίζο`μεν´ τῇ ὑμετέρᾳ πατρικῇ ἁγιοσύνῃ ὡς κατὰ τὴν εἰκάδα ἑβδόμην τοῦ
2 παρόντος μηνὸς Πέτρος ὁ Πενταπολίτης, ἐπιστὰς τῷ εὐαγεῖ μοναστηρίῳ
3 Ἀφροδιτοῦς ἀπὸ τῆς Ἀντινόου, ἐπιδέδωκεν τῷ θεοφιλεστάτῳ ἀββᾷ
4 Νόνᾳ γράμματα Μηνᾶ τοῦ Ἄρσᾶ, ἀπαντήσαντος αὐτῷ κατὰ τὸν Παβεείτ,
5 περιέχοντα αὐτὰ τὰ γράμματα ὅτι 'ποίησον ἀγάπην εἰπεῖν τῷ θεοφιλεστάτῳ
6 ἀββᾷ Ἀνδρέᾳ ὅτι προλαμβάνω καὶ ἀνέρχομαι εἰς Ἀντινόου καὶ πάντα τὰ

7 καινότερα μανθάνων γράψω ὑμῖν.' οἶδεν γὰρ ἡ ὑμετέρα ἁγιοσύνη τοὺς
8 τρόπους τοῦ ἀνδρός, κἂν μὴ γράψωμεν μάλιστα ὅτι οὐ μετρίως ἐλύπησεν ἡμᾶς
9 τὸ ἐμπόδιον τῆς ἀνόδου αὐτῆς· ἐὰν γὰρ εὕρῃ παρρησίαν πρὸς τὸν ὑπερ-
10 φυέστατον στρατηλάτην καὶ ὕπατον, οὐκ ἔχει ἡσυχάσαι, ἀλλὰ καὶ γονιορτὸν (l. κονιορτὸν) ἐγερεῖ
11 πάντως κατὰ τῶν μοναστηρίων καὶ καθ' ἑνὸς ἑκάστου ἡμῶν. πρὸ πολλῶν δὲ
12 οὐ πάνυ ἡμερῶν ἤμεθα γράψαντες τῷ θεοσεβεστάτῳ ἀββᾷ Μηνᾷ τῷ τοῦ οἰκονόμου
13 λαβεῖν γράμματα παρὰ τοῦ λαμπρο(τάτου) κυρίο[υ] Κομιτᾶ τοῦ Τζανκη πρὸς τὸν
14 [με]γαλοπ[ρ]ε(πέστατον) Πετέχωντα, ὑπομιμνήσκοντα αὐτὸν περὶ τῶν κακῶς πραχθέντων
15 [ὑπὸ .... μ]ετὰ Πελαγίου τοῦ μαγί[στρου] ἐν Λίνου πόλει (l. Νείλου πόλει) κατὰ τὸν πέρυσι χρόνον,
16 ἵνα μὴ εὕρῃ παρρησίαν, καὶ μ[έχρι τ]ῆς δεῦρο οὐδὲ ἀπόκρισιν ἐδεξάμεθα
17 περὶ τούτου. παρακληθῇ οὖν ἡ ὑμ[ετέ]ρα πατρικὴ θεοφιλία κατὰ νοῦν ἔχειν
18 περὶ τούτου πρὸς τῷ τῇ ὑμετέρᾳ σπουδῇ περιαιρεθῆναι τὸν ἀνόσιον ἐκ τῶν
19 μοναστηρίων ἡμῶν. ταῦτα γράφοντες, πλεῖστα προσκύνομεν (l. προσκυνοῦμεν) καὶ ἀσπαζόμεθα
20 τὴν ὑμετέραν πατρικὴν ἁγιοσύνην, περιπτυσσόμενοι αὐτὴν τῇ τοῦ Πνεύματος
21 ἑνώσει. †
verso
22 δεσπό(τῃ) ἡμῶν ὡς ἀληθ(ῶς) τὰ πάντα θεοφιλεσ(τάτῳ) κ(αὶ) ἁγιοτ(άτῳ) πατρ(ὶ) ἀββᾷ Γεωργίῳ προεστ(ῶτι) μο(ναστηρίου) Μετανοίας,
23 † Ἰωάγγης ἐλεειν(ὸς) προσκ(υνητής).

Translation

'We inform your paternal holiness that on the twenty-seventh of the present month, Petros from Pentapolis, who arrived at the holy monastery of Aphrodito (coming) from Antinoe, gave to the abbot Nonas, who is the dearest to God, a letter of Menas, son of Arsas, who replied to him on the issue of Paveeit. The content of this letter was the following: "Be so charitable as to tell the abbot Andreas, who is the dearest to God, that I'm taking the lead and I am going up to Antinoe, and I will write to you all the news that I will learn." For your holiness knows this man's character, even if we do not write to you first and foremost that the fact that you were impeded to come up here saddened us to a great extent; because if he [i.e. the above-mentioned person] finds the courage to speak out being near the most extraordinary *magister militum* and consul, he will not be able to remain quiet; instead he will raise dust by all means against the monasteries and each one of us separately. It was only a few days ago, when we wrote to Menas, the most pious abbot, the steward's son, asking him to receive by *vir clarissimus* lord Komita, son of Tzanke, a letter for *magnificentissimus* Petechon, reminding him of the bad actions committed by . . . [the aforementioned person] together with the magister Pelagios, in Neiloupolis, last year, so that he [the aforementioned person] will not find the audacity, and we have not received any reply about this issue so far. We beg, therefore, your paternal piety not to forget to remove as soon as possible this unholy person from our monasteries. In writing this, we make you many reverences and salute your paternal holiness embracing you in the unity of the Holy Spirit. (address) To our lord, who is truly dearest to God in all things and holiest Father, abbot Georgios, provost of the monastery of Repentence. Ioannes, the piteous worshipper.'[68]

P.Fouad 87 with BL VI 41; VII 58

(Possibly Aphrodito, Antaiopolite nome [see BL VII 58]; VI CE)

†

1 ℓκατὰ τὴν δευτέραν τοῦ παρόντος μηνὸς Φαμενὼθ
2 κατέλαβεν τὸν ὅρμον τοῦ μοναστηρίου Ἀφροδιτοῦς ὁ μεγαλοπρ(επέστατος)
3 κόμες Ἰωάννης, πέμψας μοι γράμματα τῆς σῆς θεοφιλοῦς εὐτεκνίας,
4 καὶ ἐκ τούτων γνοὺς τὴν ῥῶσιν αὐτῆς, ἐδόξασα τὸν δεσπότην Θεόν·
5 προετρεψάμην δὲ τὴν αὐτοῦ μεγαλοπρέπειαν ἀνελθεῖν (or ἀπελθεῖν) εἰς τὰ
6 μοναστήρια καὶ ἐπισκέψασθαι τὴν τούτων διοίκησιν. οὐκ ὑπέσχετο
7 τέως τοῦτο ποιῆσαι, ἀλ<λ>᾽ ὅμως ὡς ἐξήλθαμεν τῇ τρίτῃ ἕωθεν
8 εἰς τὸ κτῆμα τὸ λεγόμενον Περνίς, μετεστειλάμην αὐτὸν ἐκεῖσε,
9 ὀφείλων διαλεχθῆναι αὐτῷ τὰ εἰκότα ἰδιαζόντως πρὸ τοῦ ἀνάπλου
10 ἡμῶν, καὶ φθασάσης τῆς αὐτοῦ μεγαλοπρεπείας, κατέλαβαν (l. κατέλαβον) καὶ
11 οἱ εὐλαβέστατοι ἀδελφοὶ τοῦ μοναστηρίου Στρατονικίδος, κατα-
12 κράζοντες Ἰερημίου τοῦ προεστῶτος, καὶ λέγοντες μυρίας βίας
13 περὶ τῆς ἀνατροπῆς τοῦ μοναστηρίου, περί τε τῶν τούτου χρεῶν
14 ἐπὶ τοῦ χρόνου τῆς διοικήσεως αὐτοῦ, καὶ ἀκούσας ὁ αὐτὸς μεγαλοπρ(επέστατος)
15 ἀνὴρ τὰ παρ᾽ αὐτῶν λεχθέντα, μάλιστα ὅτι οὐκ ὑπάρχει σήμερον
16 τῷ μοναστηρίῳ ἐκείνῳ εἷς ξέστης ἐλαίου, καὶ ἓν κνίδιον οἴνου,
17 καὶ δέκα ἀρτάβας σίτου, ἠγανάκτησεν πάνυ κατὰ τοῦ αὐτοῦ Ἰερημίου,
18 καὶ οὐ συνεχώρησεν αὐτὸν ἀνελθεῖν μεθ᾽ ἡμῶν ἕως τῆς Βαῦ †,
19 ἀλλὰ ἀφῆκεν ἐν τῷ μοναστηρίῳ Ἀφροδιτοῦς, ἄχρι ἀποθέσεως
20 τῶν λόγων αὐτοῦ σὺν Θεῷ μετὰ τὴν διοίκησιν τοῦ πρώτου μοναστηρ(ίου)

---

68 A French translation is offered by Marrou (1939: 186–187).

21 τῆς Βαῦ. λοιπάζεται γὰρ ὁ λόγος αὐτοῦ τετρακόσια νομίσματα
22 μικρῷ ἢ πρός, ὑπὲρ μόνης τῆς διοικήσεως τοῦ μοναστηρίου
23 ἑνὸς ἐνιαυτοῦ τῆς πρώτης ἰνδ(ικτιῶνος), χωρὶς τῶν ἄλλων χρεῶν
24 τῶν δαν<ε>ιστῶν συντεινόντων εἰς ἕτε[ρ]α τριακόσια δεκατέσ<σ>αρ(α) νο(μίσματα)
25 καὶ κατ' αὐτὴν {αὐτὴν} ἡμέραν ἀντεπ[έ]ρασεν μετὰ τῶν θεοσεβεστ(ά)τ(ων)
26 ἀδελφῶν Ἰακώβου, Ἀγαθοῦ, Φοιβάμμωνος, βουλόμενος ἅμα αὐτοῖς
27 βερέτοις (l. βερέδοις) προλαβεῖν ἐπὶ τὴν Ἀντινόου, καὶ πρὸς εἴδησιν τῆς
28 ὑμετέρας θεοφιλοῦς εὐτεκνίας ταῦτα γέγραφα. ἀνέρχεται (or ἀπέρχεται) δὲ
29 μεθ' ἡμῶν Ἰερημίας, ὁ προεστὼς τοῦ μοναστηρίου Ἀφροδιτοῦς
30 ἕως τῆς Ἀντινόου. ἀσπάζομαι πρὸ πάντων τὴν σὴν ἀδελφικὴν
31 θεοφιλίαν ἐν Κυρίῳ, μετὰ πάντων τῶν {των} σὺν αὐτῇ καὶ ἀγαπούντω(ν) (l. ἀγαπώντων)
32 αὐτὴν ἀδελφῶν. οἱ σὺν ἐμοὶ ἀσπάζονται ὑμᾶς ἐν Κυρίῳ·
33 τὸ μοναστήριον τούτων ἀκάλως κεῖται. † Φαμενὼθ γ/, ἰνδ(ικτιῶνος) β/.
34 μὴ ὀλιγορήσῃ (l. ὀλιγωρήσῃ) δὲ ἡ ὑμετέρα θεοφιλία κατὰ τοῦ γραμματηφόρου·
35 ἐπειδὴ ἐκράτησα αὐτὸν ἐνταῦθα ἄχρι παρουσίας τοῦ μεγάλ(ου) κόμι(τος),
36 καὶ εἶθ'' οὕτως ἀπέλυσα αὐτὸν πρὸς ὑμᾶς †.
verso
37 † τῷ τὰ πάντ(α) θεοφιλε(στάτῳ) πν(ευματ)ικῷ υἱῷ ἀββᾷ Γεωργίῳ πρ`ο´εστ(ῶτι)
38 ⳨ ἀββ(ᾶ) Ἀνδρέας ἐλεεινός.

Translation

'On the second day of the present month Phamenoth, *magnificentissimus* comes Ioannes arrived at the port of the monastery of Aphrodito, and sent me a letter of your supreme blessedness, which is dear to God, and, after having learnt from this letter that you are well, I praised God, my lord. And I urged his magnificence to come up to (or: depart for) the monasteries and inspect their administration. He has not promised to do so up to this time; however, when we got out of the field called Pernis on the third [of Phamenoth], at earliest dawn, I sent him there, since I felt obliged to have a discussion with him in private about the right issues before our putting out to sea; and when your magnificence arrived [before we did], the most pious brothers of the monastery of Stratonikis also arrived and screamed against Ieremias, the provost, and told about [his] countless acts of violence, about the upheaval from which the monastery suffered, and about his debts during the year of his administration; and when the *magnificentissimus* man listened to their words himself, and in particular that today there is not even one sextarius of oil, one knidion of wine or ten artabae of grain in that monastery, he got furious with the afornentioned Ieremias and he did not permit him to come up with us until Bau; however, he allowed him to remain in the monastery of Aphrodito, until his words are recorded (?)[69] with God's help after the administration of the first monastery of Bau. His account has indeed less than forty solidi – or a bit more – than it should have for the sole administration of the monastery during the one and only year of the first indiction, without taking into account the other debts to the usurers, who will seek three hundred and fourteen solidi more; and on the same day, he passed to the other side of the river together with the most pious brothers Iacobos, Agathos, Phoibammon, planning to continue his route until Antinoe with the same post-horses; and I have written this text in order to keep your supreme blessedness, which is dear to God, informed. Ieremias, the provost of the monastery of Aphrodito, comes up with us until Antinoe. First of all, I salute your brotherly piety in the Lord, as well as all of the brothers who live with you and love you. The brothers who live with me greet you in the Lord; the monastery is unwell. 3 Phamenoth, 2nd indiction. May your piety not be angry with the letter-carrier; because I kept him here until the noble comes arrives, and only then I let him come back to you. (address) To my spiritual son, who is absolutely dearest to God, abbot Georgios, the provost. Abbot Andreas, the piteous man."[70]

P.Fouad 88

(Possibly Aphrodito, Antaiopolite nome [see BL VII 58]; VI CE)

†

1 ☧ καὶ νῦν τῆς εὐκαιρίας δραξάμενος τοῦ γραμματηφόρου μονάζοντος
2 κατερχομένου μετὰ τῶν γραμμάτων τοῦ ὁσιοτάτου (l. ὁσιωτάτου) ἀββᾶ Ἀνδρέου
3 πρὸς τὴν ὑμετέραν πατρικὴν ἁγιοσύνην ⟦γε...φ.⟧ γέγραφα πρῶτον μὲν
4 προσκυνῶν καὶ προσφθεγγόμενος αὐτήν, ἔπειτα δὲ καὶ παρακαλῶ
5 μνησθῆναι τῆς ἐμῆς βραχύτητος ἐν ταῖς πρὸς τὸν Θεὸν αὐτῆς

---

69 On the translation of ἀπόθεσις, see Gascou (1976, 168): "... l'ἀπόθεσις désigne normalement l'action et le résultat de rassembler, d'emmagasiner, et il en résulte que l'ἀπόθεσις τῶν λόγων ne se rapporte pas à la reddition des comptes, mais à leur rassemblement, soit dans des archives, soit auprès d'un service de verification comptable" ["...ἀπόθεσις normally designates the action and the result of gathering, of storing, and it follows that the ἀπόθεσις τῶν λόγων does not relate to the rendering of accounts, but to their collection, either in archives, or with an accounting audit service"].
70 A French translation is offered by Marrou (1939: 192–193); see also Gascou's remarks (1976: 163–177; see BL VII 58).

6 εὐπροσδέκτοις λιταῖς. ἔγνων γὰρ καὶ νῦν, πρὸς τὴν δύναμιν τῶν
7 ὑμετέρων γραμμάτων, τὸ σταθε⟦στε⟧ρὸν καὶ ἀμετακίνητον τῆς
8 ὑμετέρας ἀγαθῆς προαιρέσεως εἰς ἐμέ, τὸν ἐλάχιστον αὐτῆς ἀδελφὸν
9 καὶ υἱόν, καὶ παρακαλῶ αὐτὴν ταύτην βεβαίαν ἔχειν μέχρι παντός·
10 ἐπειδὴ οὐ μετρίως δέομαι οὐ μόνον τῶν ὑμετέρων εὐχῶν ἀλλὰ καὶ
11 συγκροτήσεως ὑμετέρας οὐκ ὀλίγης. † ἀσπάζομαι δὲ τόν τε
12 θεοφιλέστατον κοινὸν πατέρα, καὶ τὴν κοσμιωτάτην κοινὴν μητέρα,
13 καὶ πάντας τοὺς σὺν ὑμῖν ἐν Κ(υρί)ῳ, δέσπο(τα) θεοφιλέστατέ μου πάτερ. †
14 † Φαμενὼθ γ/†.
verso
15 † δεσπό(τῃ) ἐμῷ ὡς ἀληθ(ῶς) τὰ πάντα θεοφιλε(στάτῳ) (καὶ) ἁγιωτ(άτῳ) πατρὶ π(νευματι)κῷ ἀββᾷ Γεωργίῳ, προεστ(ῶτι) Μετ(ανοίας)
16 † Ἰωάννης, ἐλάχ(ιστος).

Translation

'Now also, finding an opportunity by the monk and letter-carrier, who descends towards your paternal holiness holding the letter of the most holy abbot Andreas, I have written this letter first and foremost in order to make obeisance to you and salute you; secondly, I beg you to remember me, the least of all, in the prayers that you address to God, which are accepted (by Him). Once again, thanks to the power of your letter, I came to know your stable and immovable benevolence towards me, the least of all your brothers and your son, and I beg you to keep it [i.e. your benevolence towards me] as strong as it is now for ever; because I am in great need not only of your prayers but also of your full approval. I salute our common Father, who is dearest to God, and our common mother, who is the most virtuous, and all the people who live with us in the Lord, my master and most pious Father. 3 Phamenoth. (address) To my lord, who is truly dearest to God in all things and holiest spiritual Father, Georgios, provost of the monastery of Repetence. Ioannes, the least of all.'[71]

---

[71] A French translation is offered by Marrou (1939: 198); see also Kim's commentary and German translation (2011: 115–119).

P.Fouad 89 with BL VII 58; XI 82

(Possibly Aphrodito, Antaiopolite nome [see BL VII 58]; VI CE)

✝

1 εὐκερίαν (l. εὐκαιρίαν) εὑρὼν τοῦ γραμματηφόρου ἀναγκέον (l. ἀναγκαῖον) ἡγησάμην γράφειν
2 προσκυνῶν καὶ ἀσπαζόμενος τὰ εὐλογημένα ἴχνη τῶν εὐλογημένων
3 ποδῶν τῷ ἐμῷ ἀγαθῷ δεσπότῃ, μετὰ καὶ πάντων τῶν
4 συνόντων θεοφιλεστάτ(ων) ἀδελφῶν τῷ ἐμῷ ἀγαθῷ δεσπότῳ (l. δεσπότῃ), καὶ
5 παρακαλῶ τὸν ἐμὸν δεσπότην μνησθῆναι τῇ ἐμῇ ταπ<ε>ινώσει ἐν
6 ταῖς πανοσίαις καὶ εὐπροσδέκταις εὐχῆς (l. εὐχαῖς) τῷ ἐμῷ ἀγαθῷ δεσπότῃ,
7 ἄχρη (l. ἄχρι) ἀξιώσῃ μαι (l. με) ὁ Θεὸς καὶ κατὰ πρόσωπον προσκυνῆσαι τὸν
8 ἐμὸν ἀγαθὸν δεσπότην. οὐ παύομαι γὰρ νύκτα{ν} καὶ ἡμέρα<ν>
9 εὐχόμενος πρὸς τὸν δεσπότην Χρ[ι]στὸν ὑπὲρ τῆς σωτηρίας καὶ
10 διαμονῆς τῷ ἐμῷ ἀγαθῷ δεσπότῃ, καὶ πάντων τῶν ἀγαπούντων (l. ἀγαπώντων)
11 τὸν ἐμὸν δεσπότην ἐν Κ(υρί)ῳ, δέσπο(τα). Φαμ(ενὼ)θ, β′, ἰ(ν)δ(ικτιῶνος) α′ ✝.
verso
12 σὺν Θ(ε)ῷ. τῷ ἐμῷ ἀγαθῷ δεσπότ(ῃ), μετὰ τ(ὸ)ν Θ(εό)ν, προεστ(ῶτι), ✝ Ψοῖος, ἐλάχ(ιστος)
13 δοῦλος.

Translation

'Now also, finding an opportunity by the letter-carrier I thought it was necessary to write to you, in order to worship and salute the blessed prints of the blessed feet of my virtuous lord, and of all the brothers, who are the most pious, and who live with my virtuous lord; and I beg my lord to remember my insignificance in his all-holy prayers, which are accepted by God, until God will think me worthy to make obeisance to my virtuous lord also in person. For I do not cease to pray night and day to Christ the Lord for the salvation and the perpetuity of my virtuous lord and of all those who love him in Lord, my master. 2 Phamenoth, 2nd indiction. (address) With God's help. To my virtuous lord, the provost, with God's help. Psoios, the least of all slaves.'[72]

---

[72] A French translation is offered by Marrou (1939: 201).

P.Ness. III 47 with BL IV 23

(Nessana, Palaestina; probably before 605 CE)

1 † πάντων πρότερων (l. πρότερον) γράφω προσ[κ]υνῶ καὶ ἀσπ[άζω σ]ε τὸν ἐμοῦ
2 γνήσιων (l. γνήσιον) φίλων (l. φίλον) ὄντα, δέσποτα. θέλεσων (l. θέλησον) δέξασθ[αι παρ]ὰ [το]ῦ γραμ-
3 ματεφώρου (l. γραμματηφόρου) σκάρου λ(ίτρας) ὠγδωέκωντα (l. ὀγδοήκοντα) κεφαλὰς μεγάλας ἔκωσι (l. εἴκοσι)
4 καὶ εἰς ταῦτα πρωκάλυμμα (l. προκάλυμμα) ποιῆσε (l. ποιῆσαι) τῷ ἀνθρώπῳ μου Ἀνακλᾷ
5 ὅτι ἐδέξου (l. ἐδέξω) αὐτά καὶ εὔχου ὑπὲρ ἐμοῦ διὰ τῶν (l. τὸν) κύριων (l. κύριον) †.
verso
6 † δεσπ(ό)τ(η) ἐμῷ [τὰ] π(άντα) θεοφιλ(εστάτῳ) (καὶ) πάσ(ης) τ[ι]μ(ῆς) (καὶ) πρ(οσκυνήσεως) [ἀξ(ίω) γνη(σίω) φί[λ(ῳ)]][73] † Στεφάνῳ Βικτωρίῳ
7 διακ(όνῳ).
8 † Πατρίκιος ἡγούμενος †.
9 ἐδεξάμην τὰ γράμ<μ>ατα τοῦ ἐμοῦ δεσπότου κ(αὶ) φίλου
10 δ(ιὰ) Πτολομέου ἅμα κ(αὶ) ὀψάρια ις (or κ) λιτρῶν ō ἐσταθμί-
11 σθεν (l. ἐσταθμίσθην) αὐ[τ]ὰ παρουσίᾳ Πτολεμέου ιφυλοποντη (perhaps: καὶ φυλότονται [l. φυλάττονται]) ἄχρις οὗ
12 ἔλθες (l. ἔλθῃς) ἔρε (l. αἶρε) δὲ κ(αὶ) τὰς ἄλλας εἴκωσει (l. εἴκοσι) λίτρας κ(αὶ) ὀλίγα ἁλικά.

Translation

'Before writing anything else, I send respectful greetings to you, sir, for you are my true friend. Please accept from the letter-carrier eighty pounds of sea fish, twenty large heads. In return give my man Anaklas the protection of a note that you have received them. Pray for me to the Lord. (address) To my Lord, greatly beloved of God, and my friend, worthy, with God's help, of all honor and reverence: Stephan son of Vicrorius, deacon. From Patrick, abbot.'

(The reply:)

'I received by Ptolemy the letter of my lord and friend, together with 16 (or 20) pickled fish, by weight 70 pounds. I weighed them in the presence of Ptolemy and . . . until you come. Get (?) the other 20 pounds, and a few salt fish.'[74]

---

73 On this reading, see Hagedorn (2008: 131); for a different reading, see BL XIII 203.
74 This translation is offered by Kraemer (1958: 140).

P.Ness. III 50

(Unknown provenance; early VII CE)

1 † πρ<ὸ> ˋμ΄ ἐν πάντων γράφῳ κ[αὶ ἀ]σπάζομε (l. ἀσπάζομαι) τῶν (l. τὸν) ἀβ<β>ᾶν Ζόνι-
2 νων (l. Ζόνινον), ἔπ<ε>ιτα παρακαλῶ σε ἐπ<ε>ιδὴ ἀσθενῶ καὶ οὐ δύ-
3 ναμε (l. δύναμαι) ἐξελθ<ε>ῖν εἰς τὴν ἑορτὴν τοῦ ἁγίου Σεργίου ἐὰν
4 ἐξέρχι (l. ἐξέρχῃ) {ε}ἵνα παρακαλέσες (l. παρακαλέσῃς) τῶν (l. τὸν) ἐγούμενων (l. ἡγούμενον) ὕνα (l. ἵνα)
5 δώσε (l. δώσῃ) τῶν (l. τῷ) ἀβᾶν (l. ἀββᾷ) Προκῶπιν (l. Προκωπίῳ) τὴν εὐλογίαν μου ὕνα (l. ἵνα)
6 μὴ ἀναγκασθῖ (l. ἀναγκασθῇ) μετὰ τὴν ἑορτή<ν> ἐξελ<θε>ῖν . καὶ αὐτὼς (l. αὐτὸς) ἐπα-
7 λάσετε (l. ἀπαλλάσηται) τοῦ ἀναλόματος (l. ἀναλώματος) καὶ μὲ ἀναπα<ύ>ειν. ἐπαρα-
8 κλέθετι (l. παρακλήθητι) χαρίσεν (l. χαρίζειν) με τῶ (l. τὸ) καθῖκον (l. καθῆκον) τοῦτο. ἀγυένον (l. ὑγιαίνων) δίελθ[ε]
9 καὶ ἐάν μὲ (l. μὴ) ἐξέλθες (l. ἐξέλθῃς) γράψον αὐτῶν (l. αὐτῷ). †
verso
10 (hand 2) τ(ῷ) ἀβ(βᾷ) Ζωνίνῳ Γεώργιος ἐλέει
11 θε(οῦ) ἐπίσκοπος.

Translation

'Before everything I am writing to send greetings to Father Zoninon.[75] Next I beg you, since I am sick and cannot go out to the festival of St. Sergios,[76] if you go, to beg the abbot to give Father Procopios my donation so that he will not be forced to come out after the festival. Thus he will himself be relieved of the expense, and I may rest in peace (?). You are requested to grant me the favor, which is my due. Abide in good health. If you do not go out, write him. (address) To Father Zoninon. From George, by the grace of God bishop'.[77]

---

75 I prefer this transliteration to 'Zunayn' proposed by Kraemer (see fn. 77).
76 I prefer the transliterations 'Sergios' and 'Prokopios' to 'Sergius' and 'Procopius', which are proposed by Kraemer (see fn. 77).
77 This translation is offered by Kraemer (1958: 145).

Victoria Fendel
5 Greek in Egypt or Egyptian Greek? Syntactic regionalisms (IV CE)

Abstract: The three structures analysed are the predicative possessive pattern with ὑπό 'by', support-verb constructions with the predicative noun χάριν 'gratefulness' and clause linkage by means of καί 'and'. In order to distinguish between features that are related to the internal evolution of Greek (modernisms), the production circumstances (colloquialisms), the impact of the writers' idiolect (interferences) and a regional variety (regionalisms), we analyse each structure by considering three aspects, that is grammaticality, type frequency, and convergence. Based on this analysis, it appears that the support-verb construction χάριν ὁμολογέω 'to be grateful' and the predicative possessive pattern with ὑπό 'by' have resulted from convergence and qualify as regionalisms, whereas clause linkage by means of multifunctional καί 'and' is closely related to the extra-linguistic circumstances and the syntactic developments in Greek which put pressure on semantically precise hypotactic structures.

1 Introduction

Personal letters from early Byzantine[1] Egypt confront us with an array of structures that seem incorrect at first glance, that is from a Classical Greek perspective, yet turn out to be regular on closer inspection, that is considering diachronic developments and internal variation.[2]

It is widely accepted that the language of early Byzantine (fourth to mid-seventh century) documentary texts from Egypt reflects (a) the internal evolution of Greek,[3] (b) the circumstances of production[4] and (c) writers' idiolects.[5] Bilingual interference occasionally impacted on the latter. Additionally, there is

---

[1] For common time ranges, see Pestman (1994: 6–13), Stolk (2015: 45).
[2] I owe particular thanks to Elizabeth Ramsey for her meticulous proofreading of this contribution and to Andreas Willi (Oxford) for his scrutiny of earlier versions of this contribution. All remaining mistakes are my own.
[3] See for instance Markopoulos (2009), Manolessou (2005), Stolk (2016, 2017), Bortone (2010).
[4] The production circumstances of a text are relevant in studies of register such as Bentein (2013; 2017a).
[5] Idiolects have been studied by Trevor Evans, especially in the Ptolemaic Zenon-archive, e.g. Evans (2010).

syntactic evidence that the long-term contact situation between Greek and Egyptian (based on its writing system called Demotic until the third century CE and called Coptic from the fourth century CE onwards) had by the fourth century resulted in (d) a regional variety in the sense of Adams' (2003: 426) "indigenised link-language".[6] This is corroborated by studies on phonology[7] and the lexicon[8], which have found Egypt to be a linguistically distinct area. Traces of a regional variety of Greek in Egypt in the areas of verbal, nominal and discourse syntax will be discussed in this paper.

In Section one, the concepts of standard, regionalism and interference are defined, the corpus of analysis is introduced and the selected case studies are outlined. In Section two, two full regionalisms and one partial regionalism are discussed. In Section three, the findings are summarised.

1.1 Regionalism, interference and standard

Distinguishing between a regional variety and an independent language is difficult. Indicators such as (a) mutual comprehensibility and (b) socio-political settings have been discussed in the past. However, even if we allow for degrees of comprehensibility[9] and for speakers' subjective view of their language as independent,[10] complete comprehensibility and the absence of an independence movement point to a regional variety rather than an independent language. Given that (a) our Greek texts from Egypt are generally comprehensible, relying on Greek grammar and lexis and (b) that we lack any indication that Greek-speakers in Egypt were striving for independence, we can leave aside the theory of an emerging independent language.[11]

Since two languages shared the geographical area of Egypt with Greek being the incoming "link-language", i.e. the language used for administrative purposes in a vast empire, we may adopt Adams' (2003: 426) concept of an "indigenised link-language": "[t]he link language may be said to be 'indigenised', as it takes

---

6 Supporters of the view that there is a distinct Egyptian variety of Greek include Torallas Tovar (2010: 253), Luiselli (1999: 17), Horrocks (2014: 111) and implicitly also Fewster (2002: 235). Conversely, Stolk (2015: 38) assumes that there is no significant difference between Greek in Egypt and other areas.
7 Cf. Bubenik (1993), Horrocks (2014: 111–113 and 165–170), Dahlgren (2016, 2017).
8 Cf. Torallas Tovar (2004a; 2004b).
9 Cf. Chambers & Trudgill (1998: 4).
10 Cf. Chambers & Trudgill (1998: 9–12).
11 Conversely, opinions differ with regard to Coptic (cf. Choat 2009: 354; Clackson 2010: 93).

on features of the different regions which may to some extent be due to interference from the first languages of the new speakers."[12] Indicative features include, in phonological terms, confusion between voiced and voiceless stops,[13] and, in lexical terms, the existence of dialect words.[14] A potential syntactic regionalism is discussed by Worp (2011–2012).

However, the adoption of Egyptian features into Greek underlies both genuine regionalisms and instances of bilingual interference. To distinguish between these two, three measures will be applied: grammaticality, type frequency[15] and convergence.[16]

Regionalisms are grammatically correct, occur with reasonable frequency and appear to have resulted form convergence of the structures of the two languages in contact. For instance, a Coptic structure is adopted into Greek and realised in a way that accommodates Greek syntax. The resulting structures appear across writers. Conversely, instances of bilingual interference are often ungrammatical, rare and have resulted from imposition. For instance, a Coptic structure is adopted into Greek and realised in a way that does not accommodate Greek syntax. The resulting structure appears only once or is limited to one writer or a very small group of writers.

For the application of our three measures, we need a standard[17] against which we can measure deviations. The grammar of early Byzantine Greek is still a desideratum.[18] Synchronically speaking, the standard is shaped by the internal evolution of Greek and the production circumstances from which our texts have emerged. As for the former, comparison with large Classical and Post-classical corpora, the language of which is well described,[19] is informative. Moreover, cross-linguistically common evolutional paths and comparison with the modern language may sometimes guide us.[20] As regards the production circumstances, it

---

12 Cf. also Bubenik's (1993: 19–21) "nativised Koine". For regions other than Egypt, see Bubenik (1993: 16–21), Brixhe (2010), Horrocks (2014: 110–114).
13 Cf. Bubenik (1993: 17), Fewster (2002: 235).
14 Cf. fn. 8.
15 Cf. Meurman-Solin (2014: 475).
16 Cf. Muysken (2010: esp. 272–273).
17 For the notion of "standard", see Versteegh (2002: esp. 55).
18 Cf. Wahlgren (2002), Evans & Obbink (2010: 11).
19 Examples are the corpus of Classical literary texts (cf. e.g. Kühner-Gerth 1890–1904), the corpus of the New Testament (cf. Moulton 1957–1976; Blass, Debrunner & Rehkopf 1990) and the corpus of Ptolemaic papyri to a certain extent (cf. Mayser; Mayser-Schmoll).
20 There are however also "dead ends" in the evolutional process (cf. Bortone 2010: 192–193; Bentein 2017b).

will prove beneficial to choose a context in which our writers were likely to put a regional variety into writing. Taking the slightly prejudiced view that a regional variety is the colloquial counterpart to the standard language, we will therefore be looking at private letters.

1.2 Corpus of analysis

Our analysis is primarily based on a corpus of 264 private letters belonging to bilingual (Greek–Coptic) papyrus archives that date from the fourth to mid-seventh centuries. The letters belong to the archives of Apa Paieous, Apa Nepheros, Apa John, the village of Kellis and the notary Dioscoros.[21] 127 letters are Greek (13,609 words in total) and 137 letters are Coptic. The former serve as the test group and the latter as the control group.

Table 1: The select corpus of texts (overview).

Archive owner	Abbreviation	Time range	Place (region and nome)[22]	Coptic dialect of the region[23]	Greek letters	Number of words	Coptic letters
Apa Paieous	AP	IV CE	Phator / ME U20	M	6	2219	4
Apa Nepheros	AN	IV CE	Phator / ME U20	M	18	2455	2
Apa John	AJ	IV CE	Hermopolis / ME U15	M	15	1307	12
Village of Kellis	PK (Greek)/ PKC (Coptic)	IV CE	Kellis, Wester desert / UE L16	L	19	2804	89
Dioscoros of Aphrodito	DA	VI CE	Aphrodito / ME U10	A	69	4824	30
TOTAL					127	13609	137
Apiones of Oxyrhynchos	AO	VI CE	Oxyrhynchos, ME U19	–	25	2869	∅

---

21 For descriptions of the archives, see TM Archives (accessed 7 September 2017).
22 Regions and nomes are according to Helck (1974).
23 Abbreviations are according to WKH: XIII–XXIV and Gardner et al. (1999: 84–84).

It is assumed that all letters from the corpus originate from bilingual surroundings because of their being part of bilingual archives.[24] The corpus is coherent in relation to genre, in that all the texts are letters, and register, in that all are private.[25] We do, however, encounter a range of styles, since stylistic variation is idiosyncratic.[26] Generally, classical patterns that were on the verge of disappearing in the early Byzantine period are considered more elaborate than modern patterns in line with Fleischman's (2000: 48) conceptualisation of development as decay. The relevance of this to our ancient setting is evident from the movements of Atticism and the Second Sophistic, which revived features that were deemed Classical.[27]

Two more sets of data have been consulted, the literary data of the TLG and the documentary data of the DDbDP. All the texts of the TLG corpus that date from the relevant period of time were considered. Similarly, all the texts of the DDbDP that date from the relevant period of time were considered yet with the data split into Egypt and outside of Egypt. Admittedly, the former corpus is much richer than the latter.

1.3 Selection of case studies

Three structures will be discussed in detail. They have been chosen since they represent three separate areas of syntax and since they clearly differ in Greek and Coptic.

Firstly, it is well known that Greek inflects cases and employs functionally rather narrow prepositions, whereas Coptic lacks the former feature,[28] but relies instead on some highly versatile prepositions. The Greek ὑπό was retreating in the Post-classical period. We may therefore wonder whether its frequent occurrence in predicative possessive patterns could be owing to bilingual interference or could be classified as a regionalism. Secondly, in Classical Greek some support-verb constructions with the predicative noun χάριν already existed; others emerged only in later periods. By contrast, Coptic employs a finely

---

24 Cf. Fewster (2002: 236).
25 Palme's (2009: 361–363) approach of labelling documents that are directly related to the government "official" and those that are not directly related to the government "private" has been adopted. Thus, the private register encompasses a variety of texts. On a continuum, we could say that some texts rather lean towards the colloquial end, whereas others rather tend towards the more formal end.
26 For the notions of genre, register and style, see Biber and Conrad (2009: esp. 15).
27 Cf. Lee (2013: 285).
28 Cf. Grossman (2015: 207).

nuanced system of support-verb constructions throughout its history. We must therefore consider possible internal and external factors for the emerging χάριν ὁμολογέω.

Finally, semantically imprecise clause-linkage has often been considered un-Greek.[29] On the one hand, authors sometimes leaving it to their readers to infer the exact link between clauses can be traced back as far as the Classical period; on the other, the comprehensive Greek system of semantically precise linking required a significant amount of processing from a writer. Moreover, semantic nuances were already beginning to blur in the Post-classical period. These observations shed a different light on our writers' extraordinarily frequent use of the multifunctional καί.

2 Analysis

2.1 The predicative possessive pattern with ὑπό

Husson (1982) identified instances of ὑπό with the following meanings as owing to bilingual interference from Egyptian based on the parallel Demotic ẖr:

(1) ὑπό with accusative:

(un animal) chargé de / portant quelque chose ['carrying (something)']
(un bâtiment) détenu / occupé par quelqu'un ['occupied by (someone)']
(une boîte) qui abrite / qui renferme quelque chose (des animaux ou des objets) ['which contains (something)']

Husson (1982: 229) wondered how marginal such Egyptian-Greek patterns were: "[c]e phénomène de contamination sémantique est à verser au dossier d'un 'grec égyptien'; peut-être apparaîtra-t-il moins isolé, si, à l'avenir, d'autres études mettent en lumière des faits analogues."[30] From the corpus, we can now add one more pattern that is closely linked to those in (1):

(2) ὑπ[ὲρ ἀρουρῶ]ν μὴ οὐσῶν **ὑπ' α[ὐ]τό[ν]**

'for the *arourae*, which he did not own'[31]
(P.Cair.Masp. II 67194, l. 6; VI/VII CE)

---

29 Cf. Hasznos (2006: 91–93).
30 "This phenomenon of semantic contamination is to be attributed to the text being in Egyptian Greek; perhaps it will be less isolated a phenomenon if in future other studies shed light on similar aspects."
31 All translations are my own.

(2) is an example of the predicative possessive pattern with ὑπό. Our data suggest that the predicative possessive pattern with ὑπό (a) appears too frequently to be a feature of someone's idiolect and (b) is grammatical in Greek given the existence of a feasible semantic path. Usually, locative patterns that profile close contact develop into possessive patterns in Greek.[32] While ὑπό may carry a spatial meaning and profile close contact,[33] ὑπό more often refers to having control over something or somebody.[34] (3) is a Classical Greek example of the control-metaphor expressed with ὑπό.[35]

(3) ὅταν ἄμφω μὲν **ᾖ ὑπὸ τὸ αὐτὸ γένος** γνωριμώτερον δὲ θάτερον ᾖ θατέρου

'When both are of the same kind – one is more notable than the other.'
(Aristot., *Rh.* 1357b29–30)

Example (3) shows that as early as in Classical Greek ὑπό would occasionally appear in a predicative possessive pattern rather than only in expressions of direct control (e.g. Th. 4.60.2).[36] Another example of moving beyond expressions of direct control is (4) taken from Kühner-Gerth (1890–1904, II.1: § 442.III):

(4) ὅσον ὑπὸ ὄρχησίν τε καὶ ᾠδήν

'when (it happens) alongside both dancing and singing'
(Pl., *Leg.* 670a1)

The patterns in (1), like that in (2), seem to reflect the control metaphor. In fact, a Greek pattern and a feasible semantic path did exist and the parallel Egyptian structure furthered the development of specific semantics. Hence, convergence seems to underlie ὑπό in the predicative possessive pattern.

Unlike the Greek pattern, the respective Coptic pattern is not one of the high-frequency predicative possessive patterns. This divergence may be because the pattern with ὑπό was apparently adopted in Demotic times and could thus develop in Greek independently of Egyptian.[37] Yet, in Greek the preposition ὑπό follows a general downward trend in the early Byzantine period except in the

---

32 Cf. Luraghi (2003: 326).
33 Cf. Luraghi (2003: 235 and esp. 242).
34 The control metaphor also accounts for expressions of inclusion (cf. Luraghi 2003: 237).
35 For ὑπό, see Luraghi (2003: 225–243). Example (3) is discussed by Luraghi (2003: 242 ex. (67)).
36 Husson (1982: 228) relied on Kühner-Gerth (1890–1904, II.1: §442.III) and stated that the construction can only be used to refer to people, collectives and territories which are under someone's power.
37 For Coptic predicative possessive patterns, see Müller (forthc. b) and Layton (2011: §§310 & 383–394).

predicative possessive pattern.[38] If we interpret the predicative possessive pattern with ὑπό as a regionalism in Greek, this could explain this seeming paradox. The pattern was an established regionalism that was independent of the general development of the preposition.

2.2 Support-verb constructions with χάριν

To begin with, support-verb constructions (SVCs) are constructions consisting of a support verb (SV) that primarily supplies the grammatical features and a predicative noun (PN) that primarily supplies the semantics. An English example is *to take a decision*. Often, an approximately synonymous base verb exists. The counterpart of *to take a decision* would be *to decide*. We are going to look at support-verb constructions with the predicative noun χάρις and variable support verbs.

2.2.1 Corpus data

In the corpus, five relevant structures appear. These fall into two groups: Group I comprises structures replacing the action-verb 'to thank somebody for something', while Group II comprises structures replacing the stative verb 'to be grateful to somebody for something'. Under Group I we can subsume the combination of χάριν with δίδωμι and under Group II those with ἔχω and ὁμολογέω. The one combination that does not neatly fit into either group is χάριν λαμβάνω. Essentially, the literal active meaning 'to receive thanks' and the less literal stative meaning 'to be grateful' coexist.[39] The semantic shift from active 'to receive thanks' to stative 'to be grateful' seems to parallel attested combinations such as φόβον λαμβάνειν 'to suffer from fear' and consequently 'to be afraid'.[40] In the corpus, χάριν λαμβάνω always carries a stative meaning as in (5).

(5) ἐγὼ γὰρ **χάριν λαμβάνω** ὅτε καταξιοῖς παρ' ἐμοῦ δέξασθαι ὁδήποτε

'For, I am grateful when you deign to receive anything whatsoever from me.'
(P.Neph. 4, ll. 23–25; IV CE)

---

38 ὑπό is otherwise mostly found in agent-expressions with lexical or grammatical passives.
39 Prepositional phrases meaning 'from someone' and datives, 'to someone', may indicate the intended meaning.
40 The respective base verb φοβεῖσθαι may carry stative or active semantics (cf. LSJ B.II.2 and 6). Incidentally, ἔχω occasionally adopts a meaning 'to have got' (LSJ A.I), which moves it closer to the duality outlined for λαμβάνω-combinations.

A passage resembling (5), but with another verb phrase is (6):

(6) **χάριν** καὶ νῦν **ἔσχον** ὅτι κατηξίωσας ἡμῖν γράψαι

'I am now grateful because you deigned to write to us.'
(P.Neph. 8, ll. 3–4; IV CE)

Here, we find χάριν ἔχω, which always has stative semantics. Instances of support-verb constructions accumulate in our fourth-century letters addressed to close friends or relatives. By contrast, the respective base verb εὐχαριστέω mainly appears in texts belonging to the sixth-century archive of the notary Dioscoros. εὐχαριστέω also appears in one fourth-century letter of the Paieous-archive, P.Lond. VI 1914. However, this letter seems to be more like an official report in epistolary form.[41] For the corpus, the respective distribution of support-verb constructions and base-verb constructions seems to indicate that the former were preferred in more colloquial contexts, whereas the latter prevail in more formal contexts.[42]

To return to the structural aspects of support-verb constructions, the predicative noun is bare in all instances of the corpus.[43] We will therefore focus on this most basic form of support-verb constructions. The absence of modifiers such as articles or adjectives related to the predicative noun underlines its dependent status. Were the predicative noun to be modified, it would assume a more independent status.

Four issues arise from the data-collection of support-verb constructions in the corpus. Which combinations of χάριν and a support verb are already classical? Do newly emerging combinations of χάριν and a support verb also appear in sources from outside Egypt? Is there a Coptic model for combinations of

---

[41] The contexts of εὐχαριστέω in P.Herm. 7, l. 2 and P.Herm. 10, l. 5, two fourth-century informal petitions addressed to Apa John, point to a learner, who may have held on to the standard language he was learning in school. The context of εὐχαριστέω in P.Herm. 8, another fourth-century letter addressed to Apa John, points to a proficient writer who held on to the standard language as an expression of skill.

[42] In modern languages support-verb constructions are often considered "stylistically inferior equivalents of corresponding base verb constructions" (Storrer 2009: 169). Conversely, Zilliacus (1956, 1967) subsumes support-verb constructions under the group of periphrases which he deems to reflect abundance of expression. This seems to be too superficial an account not least because of the fuzzy definition of periphrasis. For periphrasis, see Spencer (2006). For the distinctiveness of two-word formations as compared to the corresponding base verb, see Wild (2011) and Thim (2012) (on phrasal verbs), Storrer (2009) (on support-verb constructions). However, an in-depth study of support-verb constructions in Post-classical Greek does not exist yet so that the question of register must remain open as for now.

[43] Cf. Langer (2005: 4–5). Modification of the predicative noun is sometimes possible as in "to take an *important* decision". See also Hiltunen (1999). P. Kell. I 65, ll. 10–15 is discussed in §2.2.4.

χάριν and a support verb? In what contexts do support-verb constructions appear in the corpus? These four issues are addressed one by one in what follows.

2.2.2 Literary data

Support-verb constructions are close combinations of support verbs and predicative nouns, so that we expect the support verb and the predicative noun to appear close to one another. The online version of the TLG allows the running of proximity searches for χάριν and the lemma of each support verb. A reasonable maximum distance was set at five words. Since all instances in the corpus are active, middle and passive forms of the support verbs have been excluded. These settings result in a data collection of about a thousand instances (cf. column A in Table 2). We then need to manually identify instances in which the predicative noun is not bare[44] and instances in which the combination of noun and verb clearly carries its literal meaning (cf. column C in Table 2).[45] Furthermore, proximity searches disregard syntactic configurations so that in numerous instances the relevant verb and noun do not actually appear together. Sampling results in the following distribution of the data:[46]

Table 2: Support-verb constructions in literary sources.[47]

SV	(A) Total of hits in the TLG proximity search		(B) Total of SVCs (i.e. SV + PN)		(C) Total of combinations with a literal meaning (i.e. V + N)	
	CGr	PcGr	CGr	PcGr	CGr	PcGr
πληρόω	∅	9	∅	∅	∅	1
ὁμολογέω	∅	100	∅	69	∅	∅
λαμβάνω	19	181	∅	24	1	12

---

44 Relevant modifiers are (1) articles, demonstrative, indefinite and interrogative pronouns and (2) adjectives, participles and relative clauses that clearly refer to the predicative noun.
45 Relevant options are (1) χάριν ἔχω 'to have mercy', 'to be beautiful', (2) χάριν δίδωμι 'to grant a gift / favour' and (3) χάριν λαμβάνω 'to receive mercy'.
46 The Ptolemaic, Roman and Byzantine periods have been subsumed under the umbrella term 'Post-classical'. The total number of words for CGr is 2,958,284 (distributed over 230 documents) and for PcGr 9,792,438 (distributed over 723 documents).
47 CGr = Classical Greek; PcGr = Post-classical Greek; V = Verb; N = Noun

Table 2 (continued)

SV	(A) Total of hits in the TLG proximity search		(B) Total of SVCs (i.e. SV + PN)		(C) Total of combinations with a literal meaning (i.e. V + N)	
	CGr	PcGr	CGr	PcGr	CGr	PcGr
δίδωμι	42	244	6	50	∅	27
ἔχω	106	316	41	111	3	17
Total	167	850	47	254	4	57

Table 2 reveals that the total number of support-verb constructions is increasing in the Post-classical period. Table 2 also shows that combinations with ἔχω and δίδωμι already existed in the classical language and merely gained in frequency. Conversely, support-verb constructions with ὁμολογέω and λαμβάνω started to emerge in the Post-classical period with the former being more frequent than the latter.

2.2.3 Documentary data

Since the DDbDP does not allow us to search for lemmata reliably, the combinations of χάριν with the first person singular present active for all relevant support verbs have been checked. For a verb like 'to thank / to be grateful', this is the most probable form in documents that reflect interpersonal relationships. The data collection and sampling have been carried out in the same way as described for the literary data.

The documentary data from outside Egypt do not contain any relevant instances of support-verb constructions. However, even in the absence of this kind of comparative data, if a relevant letter of the corpus contains phonological peculiarities that are specific to Egypt, the letter is likely to have been written by someone who was familiar with Egyptian Greek.[48]

The documentary data from Egypt excluding our corpus resembles the distribution observed in the literary data (cf. §2.1.2).

---

[48] Sometimes we can determine that someone was familiar with Greek and Coptic based on other documents written by them. Examples are Paulos (archive of Apa Nepheros) and Pekysis (Papyri from Kellis). Cf. fn. 60 & 78.

Table 3: Support-verb constructions in documentary sources:[49]

Support-verb construction	Hits	Relevant	Text type, provenance, date
χάριν ἔχω	21	14	letter, Egypt, III BCE – IV CE
χάριν δίδωμι	3	1	letter, Egypt, III / IV CE
χάριν λαμβάνω	3	1	letter, Egypt, III CE
χάριν ὁμολογέω	4	1	contract, Egypt, VI CE
χάριν πληρόω	∅	∅	∅

To summarise, ἔχω was already in existence as an established support-verb construction to refer to a state and δίδωμι the alternative to refer to an action in Classical Greek.[50] In Post-classical Greek, λαμβάνω oscillated between a stative and an action meaning and may therefore have been less common. ὁμολογέω was a seemingly redundant newcomer. There is no evidence for χάριν πληρόω as an established support-verb construction.[51]

2.2.4 Irregular structures

In light of the above observations, two structures in the corpus are irregular. The first is the only instance in which πληρόω seems to function as a support verb. It must however be noted that χάριν is here modified by a definite article so that nothing but contextual inference makes one consider whether the writer intended a support-verb construction.

(7) ἐὰν δὲ ὁ θεὸς κελεύει σ' ἀπολῦσαι ἡμᾶς καὶ ζήσωμεν ἐγὼ **πληρώσω σοι τὴν χάριν σου**, ἐὰν δὲ μὴ ὁ θεός, **δίδωμί σοι τὴν χάριν**

---

[49] The numbers are smaller than those for the literary data as a consequence of the data collection. The total number of texts examined, that is texts dating from the relevant period of time, is 72,888. For 8204 of these, their provenance is uncertain. 723 come from outside Egypt.
[50] Support-verb constructions seem more common in drama than in prose, but χάριν ἔχω and χάριν δίδωμι were apparently acceptable in prose compositions. For χάριν ἔχω, see for instance Isocrates, *Aegineaticus*, 2; for χάριν δίδωμι, see for instance Plato, *Leges*, 877a2–b2.
[51] For ἔχω, cf. LSJ A.I.8 'of habits, states, or conditions, bodily or mental'; for δίδωμι, cf. LSJ A.I.5 'prose phrases'; for λαμβάνω, cf. LSJ A.II.3 'of persons conceiving feelings and the like'. For ὁμολογέω, cf. LSJ II.2 and *PGL* s.v. ὁμολογέω, 4 'to acknowledge gratitude, give thanks'.

'If God orders you to release us so that we live, I will reward you, if God does not, I will (still) reward you.'
(P. Kell. I 65, ll. 10–15; IV CE)

Example (7) contains several grammatical incongruities: First of all, the reference to the addressee is doubled in πληρώσω σοι τὴν χάριν σου. Secondly, the choice of πληρόω is unexpected. Perhaps our writer was insecure about the (correct) support-verb construction and therefore phrased more freely. The analogy between δίδωμι 'to give' and πληρόω 'to fulfil' is evident. Thirdly, our writer may have added an article to χάριν thinking of its basic meaning 'present / gift / reward'. Alternatively, if we assume a second-language learner, we may consider that the article is optional in some Coptic support-verb constructions. Compare, for instance, P.Kell.Copt. 73, l. 11 †-na-ϥι-ⲡⲥ-ⲣⲁⲅⲱ *ti-na-fi-ps-rauš* 'I will take care of her' with P.Kell.Copt. 84, l. 14 †-ϥι-ⲣⲁⲅⲱ ϫⲉ (. . .) *ti-fi-rauš d̠e* (. . .) 'I take care that (. . .)'. Finally, the elliptical ἐὰν δὲ μὴ ὁ θεός 'if God (does) not' replaces the regular ἐὰν δὲ μή 'if not'. The writer apparently wanted to describe two options, and hence needed the same conditional clause twice. This makes copying it reasonable. For an insecure writer, copying was a viable method in such cases.[52]

The second irregularity is the semantics of the newcomer ὁμολογέω χάριν as in (8). We would expect χάριν ὁμολογέω to align with χάριν δίδωμι rather than χάριν ἔχω.

(8) **χάριν ὁμολογῶ** τῇ θείᾳ προνοίᾳ ὅτι με τὸν ἐλάχιστο(ν) κατηξιώσατε ὑπουργῆσαι ὑμῖν

'I am grateful to the divine providence because you deemed me, the humblest one, worthy of serving you.'
(P. Neph. 9, ll. 4–6; IV CE)

χάριν ὁμολογέω carries a meaning that is not deducible from the sum of its parts.[53] It may however be noted that the support-verb construction mostly appears in formulaic sections such as (8).

2.2.5 Coptic data

In order to evaluate the status of emerging χάριν ὁμολογέω, we may turn to Coptic support-verb constructions.[54] The relevant predicative noun is ϩⲙⲟⲧ *hmot*

---

[52] P. Kell. I 65 comprises several struggles with Greek syntax and even the sender-addressee order in the internal address may have resulted from Coptic influence.
[53] Cf. Storrer (2009: 173–174 and 182–183).
[54] Cf. Layton (2011: §180).

'grace / favour'. It combines with (a) ϯ- *ti-* 'to give', (b) ⲉⲣ- *er-* 'to do', (c) ϣⲡ- *šp-* 'to accept' and (d) ϫⲓ- *dʲi-* 'to take / receive' in support-verb constructions. The Greek and Coptic ranges of combinations of support verb and predicative noun largely overlap as shown in Table 4:[55]

Table 4: Support-verb constructions with χάριν and ϩⲙⲟⲧ *hmot*.

	Greek	Coptic
	Action	
(a)	χάριν δίδωμι	ϯ-ϩⲙⲟⲧ *ti-hmot*
	State	
(b)	χάριν ἔχω	ⲉⲣ-ϩⲙⲟⲧ *er-hmot*
(c)	χάριν ὁμολογέω	ϣⲡ-ϩⲙⲟⲧ *šp-hmot*
	State / action	
(d)	χάριν λαμβάνω	ϫⲓ-ϩⲙⲟⲧ *dʲi-hmot*

The combination ⲉⲣ-ϩⲙⲟⲧ *er-hmot* in Table 4(b) is grammaticalised in Coptic and means 'to be grateful' (Layton 2011: § 180b).[56] ἔχω matches ⲉⲓⲣⲉ/ ⲉⲣ- *eire / er-* in grammaticalised support-verb constructions more widely. An example is χρείαν ἔχω and ⲉⲣ-ⲭⲣⲓⲁ *er-kʰria* 'to have need of'.[57] In Table 4(c) ϣⲡ- *šp-* and ὁμολογέω do not match semantically. Even so, the combinations ϣⲡ-ϩⲙⲟⲧ *šp-hmot* and χάριν ὁμολογέω appear in the same syntactic configurations and both carry a stative meaning in our corpus.[58]

2.2.6 Regionalism

If we apply the three parameters outlined in Section 1.1 to the support-verb construction χάριν ὁμολογέω with a dative 'to be grateful to someone', its status as a

---

[55] Given that πληρόω seems at best to be idiolectal, it stands outside of the system.
[56] ⲉⲣ- *er-* in support-verb constructions can either mean 'to have the function of / have the characteristic of' or 'to do / make'.
[57] Cf. Blass, Debrunner & Rehkopf (1990: §393.3 and 400.3), Mayser (2.2 §321.28 & 354), LSJ s. v. χρεία.
[58] The stative semantics of ϣⲡ- *šp-* 'to take, receive' in the support-verb construction may have resulted from the same path that was described for λαμβάνω (cf. §2.2.1).

regionalism becomes clear. The construction is grammatical in Greek since ὁμολογέω subcategorises for a direct object in the accusative and an indirect object in the dative.[59] The construction emerges in the Post-classical period and appears with sufficient frequency. The texts in which it appears are written by someone who seems to have been familiar with both Greek and Coptic.[60] It is not attested in texts from outside of Egypt. The construction seems to have resulted from the convergence of Greek and Coptic. Its meaning is not deducible from its parts.

Noticeably, the χάριν ὁμολογέω support-verb construction developed in a specific context, the formulaic section of letters. The need to express a specific semantic nuance may have triggered the choice of a support-verb construction in the first place.[61] The base verb was too unspecific since it carried a state *and* an action meaning. The χάριν ἔχω support-verb construction, the stative alternative, may have lacked the relevant semantic nuancing.

2.3 Discourse-organisation by means of καί

Formal parataxis that implies logical hypotaxis is often construed as a feature typical of Semitic languages,[62] a feature that has left an imprint on the language of the Greek New Testament, to name one example. Conversely, formal hypotaxis is said to be typical of Classical Greek (cf. §1.3). Our final case study concerns the preference for a semantically imprecise paratactic structure with καί over a semantically precise hypotactic structure.

2.3.1 Coptic

Coptic[63] shows a general preference for semantically imprecise multifunctional patterns over semantically precise patterns. For example, in the corpus hundreds of instances of multifunctional ϫⲉ *d̂e* 'that, so that, because' counter two

---

[59] It would be ungrammatical in Greek if support-verb constructions allowed for a direct object yet many Coptic ones do, cf. Layton (2011: §180a).
[60] Cf. fn. 48. Further for Paulos, see Kramer & Shelton (1987: 24–31). Construing χάριν ὁμολογέω as an idiolectal feature is impossible because of the literary data.
[61] Cf. Storrer (2009: 165).
[62] Cf. Lipinski (1997: §55.1–8).
[63] Egyptian does not share all common Semitic features (Allen 2013: 1–2).

instances[64] of more precise ετβε-ϫε *etbe-dʲe* 'because' in causal clauses. A further indicator is that Coptic borrows numerous semantically precise connectors from Greek.[65] An example is ϨⲓⲚⲀⲤ *hinas*, Greek ἵνα, in (9).

(9) ϫⲉⲕⲀ[ⲥ] ϬⲈ [ⲈⲨ-]ⲚⲀ-ϬⲰϢⲦ ⲈⲢⲞ-ϥ ϨⲓⲚⲀⲤ ϫⲈ ⲚⲚⲈ-ⲠⲈ-ⲠⲢⲈⲠⲞⲤⲒ ⲈⲢ-ⲖⲀⲨ Ⲙ-ⲠⲈ-ⲐⲞⲞⲨ ⲚⲀ-ϥ

dʲeka[s]	*kʲe*	*[e-u-]na-kʲōšt*	*ero-f*	**hinas**	*dʲe*
PTCL	then	FOC-they-FUT-watch.over	OBJ=him	so.that	so.that
nne-*pe-preposi*	*er-lau*	*m-pe-tʰoou*	*na-f*		
OPT-DET-praepositus	do=anything	of-DET-harm	to=him		

'They may then watch over him so that the *praepositus* may not do harm to him.' (P.Kell.Copt. 127, ll. 35–37; IV CE)

The borrowed connector is usually prefixed to an equivalent inherited pattern as in (9), or to an inherited multifunctional pattern (ϫⲉ *dʲe* 'that', the circumstantial conversion). Also, the distinction between main and subordinate clauses is syntactically less pronounced than in Greek. For example, ϫⲉ(ⲕⲀⲤ) *dʲe(kas)* with a verb in the optative is a regular pattern in main and subordinate clauses,[66] whereas ἵνα with a verb in the subjunctive only gradually became a deontic particle.

2.3.2 Classical Greek

In Classical Greek there is a clear syntactic distinction between main and subordinate clauses as well as an array of semantically precise subordinate-clause patterns. For instance, an infinitive with ὥστε only refers to a likely result and a future indicative is required in complement clauses only with verbs of concern. Nevertheless, classical literary sources also contain paratactic καί-structures in which καί has an additional semantic nuance that must be inferred from the context.[67] A particle such as γάρ may optionally accompany καί.

---

64 BM inv. P. 2724, l. 8–9; P.Kell.Copt. 25, l. 51.
65 Cf. Cook (2015), Müller (2009, 2012, forthcominga).
66 Cf. Layton (2011: §338.a.ii).
67 Cf. Bonifazi, Drummen, and De Kreij (2016: §94) utilise the term "enrichment". For the occasional use of καί (syndetic parataxis) instead of a complement clause, see Bentein (2015).

2.3.3 Post-classical Greek

In our Post-classical corpus, the paratactic καί commonly carries an additional semantic nuance. In (10), the particle γάρ clarifies that καί introduces a reason.[68]

(10) παρακαλοῦμεν οὖν εὔξασθαι ὑπὲρ τῆς ὁλοκληρίας ἡμῶν· **καὶ γὰρ** πρὸ τούτου τὰ παιδία ἡμῶν ἐνόσησαν καὶ διὰ τὰς εὐχὰς ὑμῶν ἐπαύσαντο

'We now beg (you) to pray for our health *because* our children were ill in the past but stopped (being ill) because of your prayers.'
(P. Neph. 1, ll. 12–14; IV CE)

In (11), the causal semantics of καί must be inferred from the context.

(11) ἐλθὲ σὺ **καὶ** χρείαν σου οὐκ ἔχει εἰς τοῦτο

'Come now *since* he does not need you for it (sc. his religious duties).'
(P. Kell. I 72, ll. 17–19; IV CE)

The writer is complaining that the addressee has not come yet. He politely suggested earlier in the same letter that the addressee might not have come *because* he was worried that he would be dragged into the religious duties of the writer's son. In (11), the writer insists that this worry is unfounded.

Besides the paratactic expression of reason, there is a support-verb construction in (11). In (10), the infinitive with ἐπαύσαντο is omitted. We saw in Section 2.2.1 that support-verb constructions tend to be preferred in more colloquial contexts; the same applies to omissions that do *not* obscure the meaning.[69]

By and large, three developments have moved Post-classical Greek towards the Coptic system. Firstly, many classical subordinate clause patterns were lost; for example, actual results may now be expressed by means of ὥστε with an infinitive.[70] Secondly, the distinction between main and subordinate clauses became blurred as classical connectors became grammaticalised and consequently came to be used as particles in main clauses; an example is ἵνα.[71] Thirdly,

---

[68] In the corpus, καί introduces an expression of reason twenty-five times, including three times where it is accompanied by γάρ and twice by διὰ τοῦτο.
[69] For "linguistic characteristics of conversation", see Biber and Conrad (2009: 88–92), Koch and Oesterreicher (1985: 27–29).
[70] Cf. Hult (1990: 139–141 and 145–146). The infinitive became the standard pattern, whereas the indicative became a stylistically marked alternative (cf. e.g. P.Lond. VI 1914, l. 14).
[71] Cf. Mandilaras (1973: §587), Hult (1990: 115), Sim (2011: 43–74). Sim's account is based on relevance theory but provides a wealth of examples. An example in the corpus is P.Kell. I 73, l. 21 (IV CE).

participles, the multifunctional Greek alternative to subordinate clauses, were retreating into higher registers.[72] Examples (12) and (13) appear in the same position in a letter: the writer attaches a personal comment concerning his own wellbeing to a formulaic greeting section.

(12) προηγουμένως πολλὰ τὴν σὴν εὐλάβειαν **προσαγορεύομεν** ἐγὼ καὶ ἡ σύμβιος καὶ οἱ υἱοὶ κατ' ὄνομα **εὖ ἔχοντες τέως προνοίᾳ τοῦ θεοῦ**

'First of all, we much greet your piety, (i.e.) I and (my) wife and (our) sons, each by name, *while* being well in the meantime because of God's providence.'
(P. Kell. I 71, ll. 4–8; IV CE)

In (12), the more variable verb of greeting,[73] the classical intransitive ἔχω with an adverb of manner and a variation in the phrase 'thanks to God' appear. καί is avoided in favour of a circumstantial participle.

(13) **ἀσπάζεταί** σε ὁ ἀδελφός σου Ὧρος καὶ Θε[όγ]νωστος καὶ Ψάις καὶ πάντες οἱ ἡμέτεροι **καὶ ἐρρωμένοι ἐσμὲν πάντες θεοῦ χάριτι**

'Your brother(s) Horos and Theognostos and Pshai and all those related to us greet you *and* we are all fine thanks to God.'
(P. Kell. I 72, ll. 7–11; IV CE)

In (13), the less variable verb of greeting, common ῥώννυμι in the perfect tense and the regular phrase 'thanks to God' appear. Here the writer opts for καί.[74] Consequently, there are syntactic reasons for preferring formal and semantic imprecision, namely the loss of patterns and the blurred distinction between main and subordinate clauses. But there are also situational reasons. A semantically imprecise paratactic structure requires less syntactic processing from the speaker than a semantically precise hypotactic structure. Koch and Oesterreicher (1985: 22) project the use of parataxis and hypotaxis on their notions of "Nähe-Diskurs", discourse in an informal context, and "Distanz-Diskurs", discourse in a formal context. Parataxis prevails in the former, whereas hypotaxis prevails in the latter.[75]

In light of these observations, to what extent can we assume syntactic interference from Coptic with regard to the use of multifunctional καί in our texts? Did the existence of a Coptic parallel increase the number of paratactic structures where Greek would have had means to employ hypotactic ones?[76]

---

72 Cf. Manolessou (2005).
73 Kim (2011: 158–159) observes that the number of forms in which a verb appears is significantly smaller for ἀσπάζομαι than for προσαγορεύω.
74 Cf. Mandilaras (1973: §901).
75 For paratactic complementation patterns in Greek, see Bentein (2015: 109–112).
76 Cf. Gignac (2013: 415 and 417) and Bortone (2010: 193) on the number of instances of instrumental ἐν in the New Testament. The instrumental ἐν is not entirely foreign to Greek grammar

2.3.4 Cross-linguistic evidence

Bisiada's study on the increase of parataxis at the expense of hypotaxis in German because of the influence of English may be informative here.[77] Greek, like German, has distinctive patterns for subordinate clauses (cf. word order, choice of mood). Coptic, like English, has no distinctive patterns for subordinate clauses. Compare the following sentences taken from Bisiada (2013: 125, example 52).

(14a) He couldn't learn to live with stress. He couldn't adjust.

(15a) Er lernte nicht, mit Stress umzugehen, **weil** er sich nicht anpassen konnte.

If we inserted a semantically precise connector in (14a), the syntax would remain unaltered:

(14b) He couldn't learn to live with stress **because** he couldn't adjust.

Conversely, if we removed the semantically precise connector *weil* from (15a), the syntax would have to be altered:

(15b) Er lernte nicht, mit Stress umzugehen. Er konnte sich nicht anpassen.

Bisiada (2013: 190) concludes from his study:

> The main aim of this study has been to find out whether German in business and management texts is becoming more paratactic in the expression of causal and concessive clause relations, and whether this may happen through language contact in translation. The answer to the first question is 'yes': a tendency to construct concessive and causal clause complexes paratactically rather than hypotactically has been shown to exist.

However, Bisiada (2013: 190) insists that he has not found any indication that hypotaxis was yielding to parataxis. If we project these findings on our data, we may assume that an accumulation of semantically imprecise paratactic structures in our Greek texts points to a bilingual writer. However, parataxis is also extremely common in colloquial discourse. The private register allows colloquialisms to encroach on our texts. Thus, only an accumulation of instances in combination with a context that displays instances of bilingual interference or insecurity in writing Greek can point us into the right direction.

(cf. also Luraghi 2003: 332), but the extraordinarily high number of instances is due to interference from Semitic languages, presumably the writers' first languages.

[77] In her study of the Greek translation of Hebrew *wa* 'and', Aejmelaeus (1982: esp. 145–147) made observations resembling Bisiada's. Greek καί 'and' is used as a multifunctional device. Moreover, it is overused to a degree that is unnatural in Greek.

2.3.5 Colloquialism or regionalism?

To return to the causal καί in (11) and the circumstantial καί in (13), which are both taken from P.Kell. I 72, does the use of καί in these represent a colloquialism or a regionalism? Consider the following observations: Firstly, P.Kell. I 72 is a private letter and the colloquial register is reflected in the entire structure of the two relevant sentences, even if we disregard καί. Secondly, the internal evolution of Greek made parataxis generally more favourable than in the classical period. Finally, the writer Pekysis seems to have known Coptic, judging from his use of epistolary formulae in P.Kell. I 72 and from his bilingual letter, P.Kell. Copt. 77.[78]

To conclude, if we adopt the view that a regional variety is more commonly found in lower registers, we may assume that parataxis and imprecision were common features – as they are of many spoken varieties.[79] However, we may wonder whether the extraordinarily frequent use of the multifunctional καί, as in P.Kell. I 72, instead of a semantically precise hypotactic structure, may be due to the influence of Coptic. For P.Kell. I 72, the internal and external contexts of the relevant instances would seem to suggest this.

3 Conclusion

The three structures we have analysed are the predicative possessive pattern with ὑπό, support-verb constructions with χάριν, and clause linkage by means of καί. In order to distinguish between features owing to the internal evolution of Greek (modernisms), the production circumstances (colloquialisms), the impact of writers' idiolects (interferences) and a regional variety (regionalisms), we have considered three aspects for each structure, namely grammaticality, type frequency and convergence.

The predicative possessive pattern with ὑπό is grammatical in Greek based on the control metaphor, very common in Post-classical texts from Egypt and seems to have resulted from the convergence of a Demotic and a Greek pattern.

Support-verb constructions with χάριν are grammatical in Greek, increasingly frequent and diversified in the Post-classical period and paralleled in

---

[78] For the brothers Pekysis and Pamour, see further Gardner, Alcock, and Funk (2014: 83–117).
[79] Cf. §2.3.3.

Coptic. In a specific context, one newcomer, χάριν ὁμολογέω 'to be grateful', seems to have resulted from the convergence of Greek and Coptic.

The multifunctional καί could occasionally substitute semantically precise hypotactic structures as early as in Classical Greek. Thus, it is grammatical. Instances are remarkably frequent in the corpus. Coptic aligns with other Semitic languages as regards its preference for formal parataxis as an expression of logical hypotaxis. However, the multifunctional καί is also favoured by both the internal evolution of Greek and the situational circumstances of our texts. Therefore, only an accumulation of relevant instances in combination with an internal and/or external context that points to a bilingual writer could point to a bilingual writer. With regional varieties mostly residing in the lower registers, it is however almost impossible to distinguish between colloquial and Coptic impact on our texts in many instances.

To conclude, the support-verb construction χάριν ὁμολογέω and the predicative possessive patterns with ὑπό seem to be regionalisms, whereas the use of the multifunctional καί is primarily related to the situational (extra-linguistic) circumstances and the syntactic developments in Greek that made more favourable semantically imprecise paratactic structures.

References

Adams, J.N. 2003. *Bilingualism and the Latin language*. Cambridge: Cambridge University Press.
Aejmelaeus, Anneli. 1982. *Parataxis in the Septuagint: A study of the renderings of the Hebrew coordinate clauses in the Greek Pentateuch*. Helsinki: Suomalainen Tiedeakatemia.
Allen, James. 2013. *The Ancient Egyptian language: An historical study*. Cambridge: Cambridge University Press.
Bentein, Klaas. 2013. Register and the diachrony of Post-classical and Early Byzantine Greek. *Revue Belge de Philologie et d'Histoire* 91. 5–44.
Bentein, Klaas. 2015. Minor complementation patterns in Post-classical Greek (I–VI AD): A socio-historical analysis of a corpus of documentary papyri. *Symbolae Osloenses* 89. 104–147.
Bentein, Klaas. 2017a. Finite vs. non-finite complementation in Post-classical and Early Byzantine Greek: Towards a pragmatic restructuring of the complementation system? *Journal of Greek Linguistics* 17. 3–36.
Bentein, Klaas. 2017b. Διά as a polysemous preposition in early Byzantine Greek: 'dead ends' and other uses in the Qurrah archive (VIII AD). *Symbolae Osloenses* 91. 1–25.
Biber, Douglas & Susan Conrad. 2009. *Register, genre, style*. Cambridge: Cambridge University Press.
Bisiada, Mario. 2013. *From hypotaxis to parataxis: An investigation of English–German syntactic convergence in translation*. PhD dissertation, University of Manchester.
Blass, Friedrich, Albert Debrunner & Friedrich Rehkopf. 1990. *Grammatik des neutestamentlichen Griechisch*, 17th ed. Göttingen: Vandenhoeck & Ruprecht.

Bonifazi, Anna, Annemieke Drummen & Mark de Kreij. 2016. *Particles in Ancient Greek discourse: Five volumes exploring particle use across genres*. Washington, DC: Centre for Hellenic Studies.

Bortone, Pietro. 2010. *Greek prepositions: From Antiquity to the present*. Oxford: Oxford University Press.

Brixhe, Claude. 2010. Linguistic diversity in Asia minor during the empire: Koine and non-Greek languages. In Egbert J. Bakker (ed.), *A companion to the Ancient Greek language*, 228–252. Malden: Wiley-Blackwell.

Bubenik, Vit. 1993. Dialect contact and koineization: The case of Hellenistic Greek. *International Journal of the Sociology of Language* 99. 9–23.

Chambers, Jack & Peter Trudgill. 1998. *Dialectology*, 2nd ed. Cambridge: Cambridge University Press.

Choat, Malcolm. 2009. Language and culture in late antique Egypt. In Philip Rousseau & Jutta Raithel (eds.), *A companion to Late Antiquity*, 342–356. Chicester: Wiley-Blackwell.

Clackson, Sarah. 2010. Coptic or Greek? Bilingualism in the papyri. In Arietta Papaconstantinou (ed.), *The multilingual experience in Egypt: From the Ptolemies to the Abbasids*, 73–104. Farnham: Ashgate.

Cook, Samuel. 2015. *Greek conjunctions in non-literary Coptic in the late Byzantine / early Islamic period*. Sydney: Macquarie University MA thesis.

Dahlgren, Sonja. 2016. Towards a definition of an Egyptian Greek variety. *Papers in Historical Phonology* 1. 90–108.

Dahlgren, Sonja. 2017. *Outcome of long-term language contact: Transfer of Egyptian phonological features onto Greek in Graeco-Roman Egypt*. PhD dissertation, University of Helsinki.

Evans, Trevor V. 2010. Identifying the language of the individual in the Zenon archive. In Trevor V. Evans & Dirk D. Obbink (eds), *The language of the papyri*, 51–70. Oxford: Oxford University Press.

Evans, Trevor V. & Dirk D. Obbink. 2010. Introduction. In Trevor V. Evans & Dirk D. Obbink (eds), *The language of the papyri*, 1–12. Oxford: Oxford University Press.

Fewster, Penelope. 2002. Bilingualism in Roman Egypt. In J.N. Adams, Mark Janse & Simon Swain (eds.), *Bilingualism in ancient society: Language contact and the written text*, 220–245. Oxford: Oxford University Press.

Fleischman, Suzanne. 2000. Methodologies and ideologies in historical linguistics: On working with older languages. In Susan Herring, Pieter Reenen & Lene Schøsler (eds.), *Textual parameters in older languages*, 33–58. Amsterdam: Benjamins.

Gardner, Iain, Anthony Alcock & Wolf-Peter Funk. 1999. *Coptic documentary texts from Kellis*. Vol 1. Oxford: Oxbow.

Gardner, Iain, Anthony Alcock & Wolf-Peter Funk. 2014. *Coptic documentary texts from Kellis*. Vol. 2. Oxford: Oxbow.

Gignac, Francis. 2013. Grammatical development of Greek in Roman Egypt significant for the New Testament. In Stanley Porter & Andrew Pitts (eds.), *The language of the New Testament: context, history, and development*, 401–419. Leiden: Brill.

Grossman, Eitan. 2015. No case before the verb, obligatory case after the verb in Coptic. In Eitan Grossman, Martin Haspelmath & Tonio Richter (eds.), *Egyptian-Coptic in typological perspective*, 203–225. Berlin: de Gruyter Mouton.

Hasznos, Andrea. 2006. A case where Coptic is more syndetic than Greek. *Acta Antiqua Academiae Scientiarum Hungaricae* 46. 91–97.

Helck, Wolfgang. 1974. *Die altägyptischen Gaue*. Wiesbaden: L. Reichert.
Hiltunen, Risto. 1999. Verbal phrases and phrasal verbs in early modern English. In Laurel Brinton & Minoji Akimoto (eds.), *Collocational and idiomatic aspects of composite predicates in the history of English*, 133–165. Amsterdam: Benjamins.
Horrocks, Geoffrey C. 2014. *Greek: A history of the language and its speakers*, 2nd ed. Malden: Wiley-Blackwell.
Hult, Katrin. 1990. *Syntactic variation in Greek of the 5th century CE*. Göteborg: Acta Universitatis Gotheburgensis.
Husson, Genevieve. 1982. Ὑπό dans le grec d'Égypte et la préposition égyptienne ḫr. *Zeitschrift für Papyrologie und Epigraphik* 46. 227–230.
Kim, Chinook. 2011. "*Grüße in Gott, dem Herrn!*": *Studien zum Stil und zur Struktur der griechischen christlichen Privatbriefe aus Ägypten*. PhD dissertation, University of Trier.
Koch, Peter & Wulf Oesterreicher. 1985. Sprache der Nähe – Sprache der Distanz: Mündlichkeit und Schriftlichkeit im Spannungsfeld von Sprachtheorie und Sprachgeschichte. *Romanistisches Jahrbuch* 36. 15–43.
Kramer, Bärbel & John C. Shelton. 1987. *Das Archiv des Nepheros und verwandte Texte*. Mainz am Rhein: von Zabern.
Kühner, Raphael & Bernhard Gerth. 1890–1904. *Ausführliche Grammatik der griechischen Sprache*, 3rd ed. Hannover: Hahnsche Buchhandlung.
Langer, Stefan. 2005. A formal specification of support verb constructions. In Stefan Langer & Daniel Schnorbusch (eds.), *Semantik im Lexikon*, 179–202. Tübingen: Gunter Narr.
Layton, Bentley. 2011. *A Coptic grammar: Sahidic dialect*, 3rd ed. Wiesbaden: Harrassowitz.
Lee, John A.L. 2013. The Atticist grammarians. In Stanley Porter & Andrew Pitts (eds.), *The language of the New Testament: Context, history, and development*, 283–308. Leiden: Brill.
Lipinski, Edward. 1997. *Semitic languages: Outline of a comparative grammar*. Leuven: Peeters.
Luiselli, Raffaele. 1999. *A study of high level Greek in the non-literary papyri from Roman and Byzantine Egypt*. PhD dissertation, University College London.
Luraghi, Silvia. 2003. *On the meaning of prepositions and cases*. Amsterdam: Benjamins.
Mandilaras, Basil. 1973. *The verb in the Greek non-literary papyri*. Athens: Hellenic Ministry of Culture and Science.
Manolessou, Io. 2005. From participles to gerunds. In Melita Stavrou & Arhonto Terzi (eds.), *Advances in Greek generative syntax: In honor of Dimitra Theophanopoulou-Kontou*, 241–283. Amsterdam: Benjamins.
Markopoulos, Theodore. 2009. *The future in Greek: From Ancient to Medieval*. Oxford: Oxford University Press.
Meurman-Solin, Anneli. 2014. Historical dialectology: Space as a variable in the reconstruction of regional dialects. In Juan Hernández-Campoy & Juan Conde-Silvestre (eds.), *The handbook of historical sociolinguistics*, 465–479. Malden: Wiley-Blackwell.
Moulton, James. 1957–1976. *A grammar of New Testament Greek*. Edinburgh: Clark.
Müller, Matthias. 2009. Contrast in Coptic I: Concessive constructions in Sahidic. *Lingua Aegyptia* 17. 139–182.
Müller, Matthias. 2012. Greek connectors in Coptic: A contrastive overview II. *Lingua Aegyptia* 20. 111–164.
Müller, Matthias. Forthcoming a. Greek connectors in Coptic: A contrastive overview I: Coordinating connectors. In Peter Dils, Eitan Grossmann, Tonio Richter & Wolfgang

Schenkel (eds.), *Language contact and bilingualism in Antiquity: What linguistic borrowing into Coptic can tell us about it.* Hamburg: Widmaier.

Müller, Matthias. Forthcoming b. Predicative possessive patterns in Bohairic: An overview. In Eitan Grossman & Stéphane Polis (eds.), *Possession in Ancient Egyptian.* Berlin: de Gruyter Mouton.

Muysken, Pieter. 2010. Scenarios for language contact. In Raymond Hickey (ed.), *The handbook of language contact*, 265–281. Malden: Wiley-Blackwell.

Palme, Bernhard. 2009. The range of documentary texts: Types and categories. In Roger Bagnall (ed.), *The Oxford handbook of papyrology*, 358–394. Oxford: Oxford University Press.

Pestman, Pieter. 1994. *The new papyrological primer*, 2nd edn. Leiden: Brill.

Sim, Margaret. 2011. *Marking thought and talk in New Testament Greek: New light from linguistics on the particles 'hina' and 'hoti'.* Cambridge: Clarke.

Spencer, Andrew. 2006. Periphrasis. In Keith Brown & Anne Anderson (eds.), *The encyclopedia of language and linguistics*, 287–294. Amsterdam: Elsevier.

Stolk, Joanne Vera. 2015. *Case variation in Greek papyri: Retracing dative case syncretism in the language of the Greek documentary papyri and ostraca from Egypt (300 BCE – 800 CE).* PhD dissertation, University of Oslo.

Stolk, Joanne Vera. 2016. Dative and genitive case interchange in Greek papyri. In Tomasz Derda, Adam Lajtar & Jakub Urbanik (eds.), *Proceedings of the 27th International Congress of Papyrology, Warsaw, 29 July – 3 August 2013*, 1305–1324. Warsaw: University of Warsaw.

Stolk, Joanne Vera. 2017. Dative and genitive case interchange in Greek papyri from Roman-Byzantine Egypt. *Glotta* 93. 182–212.

Storrer, Angelika. 2009. Corpus-based investigations on German support verb constructions. In Christiane Fellbaum (ed.), *Idioms and collocations: Corpus-based linguistic and lexicographic studies*, 164–187. London: Continuum.

Thim, Stefan. 2012. *Phrasal verbs: The English verb-particle construction and its history.* Berlin: de Gruyter Mouton.

Torallas Tovar, Sofía. 2004a. Egyptian lexical interference in the Greek of Byzantine and early Islamic Egypt. In Petra Sijpesteijn & Lennart Sundelin (eds.), *Papyrology and the history of early Islamic Egypt*, 163–198. Leiden: Brill.

Torallas Tovar, Sofía. 2004b. The context of loanwords in Egyptian Greek. In Pedro Bádenas, Sofía Torallas Tovar, Eugenio R. Luján & M. Ángeles Gallego (eds.), *Lenguas en contacto: El testimonio escrito*, 57–67. Madrid: Consejo Superior de Investigaciones Cientificas.

Torallas Tovar, Sofía. 2010. Greek in Egypt. In Egbert J. Bakker (ed.), *A companion to the Ancient Greek language*, 253–266. Malden: Wiley-Blackwell.

Versteegh, Kees. 2002. Dead or alive? The status of the standard language. In J.N. Adams, Mark Janse & Simon Swain (eds.), *Bilingualism in ancient society: Language contact and the written text*, 52–74. Oxford: Oxford University Press.

Wahlgren, Staffan. 2002. Towards a grammar of Byzantine Greek. *Symbolae Osloenses* 77. 201–204.

Wild, Kate. 2011. Phrasal verbs: 'a process of the common, relatively uneducated, mind'? *English Today* 27. 53–57.

Worp, Klaas. 2011–2012. (δια)φυλάσσω + DAT.: A linguistic regionalism in inscriptions from Christian Egypt? *Analecta Papyrologica* 23–24. 237–239.
Zilliacus, Henrik. 1956. Zur Umschreibung des Verbums in spätgriechischen Urkunden. *Eranos* 54. 160–166.
Zilliacus, Henrik. 1967. *Zur Abundanz der spätgriechischen Gebrauchssprache*. Helsingfors: Societas Scientiarum Fennica.

Sofía Torallas Tovar

6 In search of an Egyptian Greek lexicon in Ptolemaic and Roman Egypt

Abstract: While one expects a great deal of linguistic (including lexical) variation in a language spoken over a large geographical space, for languages of Antiquity its study represents a real challenge. The corpus of literary and documentary evidence is both fragmentary and complex. In this paper, I address the lexical variety of the Greek language written and spoken in Egypt in the Greco Roman period. One can expect that the Egyptian variant of Greek would present a large number of loanwords from the Egyptian language as a result of contact throughout centuries. In this paper, however, I only deal with the use of etymologically Greek terms deviating from the general use in Greek literature and in geographical spaces other than Egypt. I sketch what I consider useful strategies to search for information in these complex sources and present a number of examples that can be useful as case studies.

1 Introduction

Egyptian Greek is the geographical variety of the language spoken and written in Egypt between the Hellenistic period and the Arabic conquest.[1] This description is itself complicated. How should we assess a given definition of a speaker or writer of Egyptian Greek, or the nature of the Egyptian Greek language considered diachronically, beyond the basic concept of "Greek language written and spoken in Egypt from Antiquity to the Byzantine period"? There is moreover no such thing as a model speaker/writer: we know for certain that there was a great deal of bilingualism in the population at this time, but in different degrees.

In this paper I will address specifically the lexical part of that variety of Greek written and spoken in Egypt. One can expect that the Egyptian variant of Greek would present a large number of loanwords from the Egyptian language as a result of contact throughout centuries. In other works I have dealt with these kinds of terms appearing in Greek texts of diverse types, the adaptation

---

[1] I would like to thank Klaas Bentein and Mark Janse (UGent) for the invitation to participate in this exciting project. I am also indebted to the anonymous referee, to David Nirenberg (U. Chicago), Robert Ritner (U. Chicago) and Juan Rodríguez Somolinos (CSIC, Madrid) for their invaluable help and comments that have greatly contributed to this paper.

strategies to the morphology of Greek and the contexts in which the loanwords appear.² The use of etymologically Egyptian terms, however, is not exclusive of the language written and spoken in Egypt, but often and for a number of reasons was an attribute of Greek varieties in other parts of the Mediterranean,³ for example in terms used for typically Egyptian products, which were exported together with their names.

In this paper, however, I will not discuss further the Egyptian loanwords in Greek, but rather I will focus on the use of etymologically Greek terms deviating from the general use in Greek literature and in geographical spaces other than Egypt. While Egyptian loanwords are somehow easy to spot, identifying etymologically Greek words specifically used in Egypt, in comparison with other Greek speaking areas, is a greater challenge. These terms can be neologisms and they can be common Greek words, which however present a special and different semantic use.⁴ The sources at our disposal are not complete nor easy to interpret, and the risk of interpreting a term as typically Egyptian can often be based on lack of information from other areas, which is equivalent to an *argumentum ex silentio*. The fact that some of the deviations found in Egypt have parallels in later Greek is a proof of this "silence" of the sources. One could argue that Greek as used in Egypt was particularly influential upon later Greek, but the most likely explanation is that the abundance of documents from Egypt provides evidence for features not attested elsewhere due to the lack of positive evidence. For this reason, the coincidence with Byzantine and Modern Greek provides an excellent source for phenomena already present in Late Antiquity but absent from the sources.

With all these caveats in mind, I will sketch in this paper what I think are useful strategies to search for information and will present a number of examples that can be useful as case studies. I will proceed to do so in an assessment of each of the groups in which the evidence can be classified: 1) documentary texts (inscriptions, papyri, and ostraca) 2) literary texts including the biblical texts, and finally, 3) grammarians and lexicographers.

---

2 Most recent and systematic studies are Fournet (1989), Torallas Tovar (2004a, 2004b, 2017).
3 As an example I refer to Torallas Tovar (2017: 107–108) on the term κίκι in a variety of contexts.
4 Luján (2010).

2 Documentary texts (inscriptions, papyri and ostraca)

The first and natural source for Egyptian Greek is of course the immense wealth of documents preserved on papyrus,[5] from the Hellenistic period to the last documents produced in the first centuries of Arabic occupation. These documents are a fresh and direct attestation of the language spoken and written by the inhabitants of the land of the Nile. These "linguistic resources of extraordinary richness" (Evans and Obbink 2010: 2) do not come, however, without a few strings attached:[6] the administrative language is often very formulaic and thus is not a faithful representation of the natural language spoken by the people. Moreover, some of these formulas of administrative Greek can reflect uses external to Egypt. Nevertheless, an attentive inspection of this large corpus in recent years has produced a good number of extremely interesting approaches into the phonetics[7], morphology, and syntax[8] of the language of the papyri. I am dealing here with the lexicon, perhaps the most "visible" aspect, after the pronunciation, which would give away an Egyptian-Greek speaker and writer. I will refer in this section on terms attested by the papyri to two "types" of phenomena: 1) special Egyptian spellings (which might betray specific pronunciations) and 2) administrative terminology and other neologisms.

Part of the language use in the papyri is influenced by second language use by speakers of Egyptian as L1.[9] This specific situation could have caused different pronunciations of Greek words, which would later become standard in this geographical variant. This variant pronunciation might also have produced a variant spelling in the written word, strong enough to be used widespread.

(i) An example of this is the Greek term κόλπος, 'gulf or bosom', which in the papyri appears invariably as κόλφος (P.Cair.Isid. 63, l. 20 [297 CE]; P.Mich. VIII 514, l. 30 [III CE] –note that in both cases the editor has offered a

---

[5] For the linguistic approach to the papyri and technical development, see Vierros & Henriksson (2017).
[6] Some of the problems in dealing with the papyri have already been expressed by Bentein (2015).
[7] First approach in Mayser-Schmoll; first in depth, Gignac (1970a; 1970b; 1976); more recently, Horrocks (2010), Dahlgren (2016a).
[8] The most in detail studies mainly focusing on the impact of Egyptian on Greek have been performed in the Helsinki school: Vierros (2012), Leiwo (2005; 2010).
[9] Clarysse (1993), Vierros (2012), Dahlgren (2016b).

correction to the form with π).¹⁰ The Kahanes (1978: 208–209) consider this form typically Egyptian, with a change that "reflects the vagueness of boundaries between stops and aspirates, which is a typical feature of the Egyptian dialect within the Greek koine". The variant would later be exported from Egypt, perhaps as part of the Christian heritage that expanded throughout the Mediterranean in the first centuries.¹¹

(ii) A similar example with the same phonetic phenomenon is the term σπυρίδιον, 'basket, box', widely attested in the papyri as σφυρίδιον (see for example BGU VI 1296, ll. 16–17 [210 BCE] or P.Köln III 161, l. 13 [II CE]). In the Greek literature, this spelling is very scarcely attested, but it is interesting that it appears in Menander, *Samia* 297, a play preserved only through an Egyptian papyrus, and in the magical papyri (Suppl. Mag. II 86 col. ii, l. 12 [III-IV CE]).

(iii) The Egyptian spelling for the word 'beer', ζύτος, instead of the general spelling ζύθος, might be a good further example. There are 172 instances of the spelling with –τ– and only two with the general Greek spelling with –θ– in the documentary papyri.¹² (the "Egyptian" spelling appears, not unexpectedly, in another Egyptian source, the magical papyrus PGM IV 908 [IV CE]).

The use of specific terms related to the administration of Egypt has to be considered with great prudence. Some of these terms or semantic uses are only attested in the papyri, and thus can be considered typically Egyptian. But the lack of documents of the types we find in the papyri in other parts of the Roman Empire due to matters of material conservation needs to be taken into account.

(iv) This is the case for terms like: μονογράφος, 'notary', only attested in the papyri in the Ptolemaic period (examples are P.Enteux 54, l. 5 [218 BCE], or UPZ II 175, ll. 28–29 [145 BCE]),¹³ and

(v) ληστοπιαστής, 'thief-catcher', a branch of the local police in Egypt (O. Mich. I 102, ll. 10–12 [IV CE]; P.Flor. I 2, l. 168 [III CE]). The alternative term

---

10 Interchange of voiceless and aspirated stops, Gignac (1976: 86–95). For a recent extremely useful tool to detect these kinds of phenomena, see Depauw and Stolk (2015). As a follow-up to our example, search in TMTI, for "φ instead of π" to see the frequency of this exchange.
11 See the characteristically Egyptian sepulchral formula εἰς κόρφον τοῦ Ἀβρααμ, 'in Abraham's bosom' in P.Oxy. XVI 1874, l. 16 (VI CE). This spelling is only attested in Greek literature in the *Historia Alexandri Magni* (recensio R, 1160). It is remarkable that the interchange of *lambda* and *rho* is typical of the Fayumic dialect.
12 Papyri.info, last consulted May 2018.
13 I suspect this stands for νομογράφος, 'notary', widely attested in Egypt, though not exclusively Egyptian. See Pierce (1968: 69) with further bibliography.

ληστοδιώκτης, with the same meaning, is attested in an inscription from Pisidia, Asia Minor, in the third century (SEG 51: 1813).

Other types of terms that tend to be local are those referred to measures and weights:
(vi) for example διπλοκεράμιον, 'a measure for wine', only attested in the papyri (e.g. O.Theb 143 [III CE]; O.Wilck 1166 and 1479 [Roman period]; P.Oxy XIV 1735, l. 5 [IV CE]).

Three terms connected to administration bring us to the comparison with other types of sources: ἐπιστράτηγος, ἐνεχύρασμα and ἐντυχία. All three are transparent Greek terms, attested in the papyri and, interestingly, in LXX and other sources connected to Egypt.[14]

(vii) An administrative term such as ἐπιστρατηγία, with the meaning 'district under an ἐπιστράτηγος' is only attested in papyri and inscriptions (for example in BGU I 8, l. 26 [248 CE], or P.Bingen 107, l. 6 [250 CE]), while ἐπιστράτηγος, the title for the rank in the administration, is also attested in 1Macc 15:38, in Strabo 17.1.13.4 (his book on Egypt), in a description of the local Egyptian authorities, in Pseudo-Demetrius, *Formae epistolicae* 1.5, a work probably originating in Egypt,[15] and in a magical papyrus (PGM LXXVI.4).

(viii) In the case of the second term, ἐνεχύρασμα, 'pledge', 'thing pawned', it seems to be a synonym of the more frequently or more widely used ἐνεχυρασία. The term appears in P.Med. I 27 col. ii, l. 8 and P.Hamb. I 10, l. 42 (both II CE) and also in LXX, Ex. 22:25 and Ez. 33:15. It is no wonder that also Philo of Alexandria would reflect this use, perhaps Egyptian, in his works when commenting on the passage of the cloak as pledge from Exodus (*De somniis* 1.92).[16]

(ix) The third term, ἐντυχία, generally means 'meeting', 'conversation' or 'intercourse'.[17] In the papyri it seems to have a specific meaning, that of 'official petition or complaint' (e.g. BGU VIII 1767, l. 3 [I CE], or P.Köln V 234v, l. 1, [V CE], etc.). Again the term appears in LXX, 3Macc 6:40: τὴν ἐντυχίαν ἐποιήσαντο περὶ τῆς ἀπολύσεως αὐτῶν, 'they made the petition concerning their release', a text that many agree was produced in Alexandria (see below).

---

14 For a comparison of LXX with epigraphy, see Aitken (2014), where the author contends that while the papyri have been widely exploited in biblical Greek studies, the Greek inscriptions have been neglected.
15 Klauck and Bailey (2006: 194–195).
16 See also Clemens of Alexandria, *Stromata* 2.22.135 or Cyril of Alexandria, *De Adoratione* 68.564.39, on the same passage. This opens the question of the spread of biblical linguistic use through the expansion in Christian literature.
17 Cf. LSJ & *DGE* ss.vv., even in later Greek, cf. Sophocles (1910) & *LBG* ss.vv.

The terminology used for the hierarchy of the Egyptian temples has produced some shifts in the semantics of Greek words and some neologisms:[18]

(x) the term προφήτης corresponds to Eg. ḥm-ntr, literally 'servant of the god', a priest in the rank of the Egyptian clergy. It appears widely attested in the papyri and inscriptions with this same meaning (e.g. P.Tebt. I 6, l. 3 [II BCE]; BGU VIII 1795, l. 4 [I BCE]; OGI 56.59, Canopus [III BCE]), and is confirmed by its much later use in the magical papyri (PGM IV 2443, [IV CE]).

(xi) Lower in the rank, the term παστοφόρος, the bearer of the παστός, or 'shrine bearer', is used for Eg. wn or wn-pr 'opener (of the shrine)'. Its use in the papyri is widespread (e.g. BGU XVI 2577, l. 57 [I BCE-I CE]), and confirmed as Egyptian by the testimony of Diodorus Siculus 1.29 and Porphyry, *De Abstinentia* 4.8.

(xii) The term θεαγός, 'bearer of the god' (from θεός and ἄγω) corresponds literally to Eg. t3y ntr.w, a priest who carried images of the gods in Egypt, featured in more than thirty documents, among which BGU VIII 1855, l. 8 (I BCE), P.Col. X 249, l. 2–3 (9–10 CE), P.Count. 3, l. 188 and l. 190 (229 BCE), P.Giss.Univ. I 10, ii 4 (II BCE).

There are also derivatives, like the feminine form θεάγισσα, in the third century CE (P.Mert. I 26, l. 4; PSI IX 1039, l. 45), and even συνθεαγός, 'co-bearer of the god' (and συνπαστοφόρος, 'co-bearer of the shrine') (P.Hamb. IV 245, l. 8 [165 CE]).

(xiii) Among the terms used for the necropolis workers, χοαχύτης is a literal rendering of the Demotic w3ḥ-mw, 'water pourer'. It is very interesting that it probably presents a Doric vocalism (cf. e.g. χοηφόρος).[19] This indicates an early use of the term in Egypt, or an early rendering into Greek of a specialized term.

Two further terms, neologisms confirmed by their use in papyri and literature, are θαλαμηγός, 'house boat' and γρυλλισμός, 'Egyptian dance':

(xiv) The first one, 'house-boat or barge' (also πλοῖον θ.) (LSJ), is attested in the papyri since the Zenon archive in the third century BCE to the

---

18 On the temple hierarchy, Dieleman (2005: 205–211), and Clarysse & Thompson (2006: vol. 2, 179–181). Hesychius (see below) confirms the case of one of these Greek names of Egyptian priests (the feather bearers): (Π4206) πτεροφόροι· τέλος τι στρατιωτικόν, ἢ ὡς διὰ τὴν ἐν τοῖς λόφοις πτέρωσιν. καλοῦνται δὲ οὕτως καὶ τῶν ἐν Αἰγύπτῳ ἱερέων τινές 'feather bearers: military office, or because of the feathers on the back of the neck. Also so are called in Egypt some priests' (cf. P.Cair.Zen III 59512 [III BCE]; P.Dryton I 3 [126 BCE]). These are in Egyptian the ḥry-ḥ3b.t, 'carriers of the book'. On the attributions of these members of the priestly hierarchy, see Ritner (1993: 220–221).

19 I owe this observation to a personal communication by Prof. Emilio Crespo.

Roman period (e.g. BGU VIII 1882, l. 3 [I BCE]; P.Lond. VII 1940, l. 58 [257 BCE]; P.Oxy. XIV 1650, l. 20 [I CE]; P.Oxy. XXIV 2407, l. 56 [III CE]). Callixenus of Rhodes confirms its use in one of the fragments of his work on Alexandria, when he refers to Ptolemy Philopator's state-barge (frg. 1.62 κατεσκεύασε δ' ὁ Φιλοπάτωρ καὶ ποτάμιον πλοῖον, τὴν θαλαμηγὸν καλουμένην, 'Philopator equipped also a river-ship, the so called *thalamegos*'). Diodorus Siculus 1.85 and Strabo 17.1.15 also confirm this use.

(xv) The second one, γρυλλισμός,[20] is a typical Egyptian dance, and the γρύλλος is the dancer, as reported by Phrynicus (*Praep. Soph.* 58.17): ἡ μὲν οὖν ὄρχησις ὑπὸ τῶν Αἰγυπτίων γρυλλισμός καλεῖται, γρύλλος δὲ ὁ ὀρχούμενος, 'the dance is called *gryllismos* by the Egyptians, and the *gryllos* is the dancer'. Only one papyrus seems to confirm this use, the second century CE accounts of the expenses of a party, which include the payments for the flute player, καλαμαύλης, the dancer, γρύλλος, and the choir, χορός (SB XX 15029, l. 5).

(xvi) Finally, an example of a semantic shift in an already known Greek verb, παραναγιγνώσκω, 'compare, collate one document with another' (LSJ), with the meaning 'read publicly' can be found in the papyri (P.Baden II 43, l. 26 [III CE]; P.Ryl. II 234, l. 15 [II CE]; P.Tor. Amenothes 6 = P.Tor. 9 = UPZ II 194, l. 15 [119 BCE]) and both 2Macc 8:23 and 3Macc 1:12.

3 Literary texts

The examples in literary texts adduced in the previous section bring us to the question both of the utility or authenticity of literary sources for our inquiry[21] and of the apparent need of comparison to obtain some reliable results in establishing which terms belong to the Egyptian variety of Greek. I have argued elsewhere that when the evidence is so scarce it is not wise to leave out pieces of information that may be useful to reconstruct.[22] However, the literary sources present their own set of problems. Even texts produced in Egypt by Egyptian Greek speaking authors offer complexities to take into consideration before proceeding to use them as sources.

---

20 See Latte (1955: 190). See further Page (1957: 189–191) and Maas (1958: 71). There is no relation between γρύλλος, 'dancer', and γρῦλος 'pig, porker'.
21 For textual authenticity of literary texts, see Joseph (2000).
22 Example of the term κάκις in Strabo and the papyri in Torallas Tovar (2017: 106–107).

Some of the authors have reached us by indirect tradition through other authors. This calls for special attention, since textual transmission can produce leveling of the language. An author such as Manetho, a third cent. BCE Egyptian priest, who produced a work known as *Aegyptiaka*, seems to be a perfect source for the study of Egyptian. There is, however, only one papyrus, i.e. direct attestation, of his work known to date, a sixth cent. CE fragment (P.Baden IV 59 = LDAB 5970).[23] This means that our only source, apart from this papyrus, of the work of Manetho is indirect tradition, adapted and transformed by other later authors: Flavius Josephus (I CE), Eusebius (IV CE) and Syncellus (VIII–IX CE), who were also not from Egypt. His language has gone through the sieve of other authors and textual traditions, both factors that have probably affected the maintenance of any kind of variation in the language, including the vocabulary.[24]

Other "Egyptian" authors, such as Philo of Alexandria, wrote in a very formal and erudite prose, and thus avoided variants typical of the (popular) Greek of Alexandria or Egypt. Philo was probably a monolingual speaker of Greek,[25] a learned member of an upper class, who avoided any interference from the Egyptian language or the popular register current in Alexandria in his times. The three aspects of Philo's linguistic use that interest us here are his philosophical vocabulary – these "obscure and difficult terms"[26] often due to his own creativity,[27] his dependence on the lexicon of LXX,[28] and his reflection of

---

[23] Two more papyri attest the *Apotelesmata*, a poem ascribed to him too (P.Oxy. XXXI 2546 [III CE], and P.Amst. I 8 [III CE]).

[24] An interesting source to explore would be the hymns of Isidorus, preserved on inscriptions, thus not mediated by indirect tradition. On this, see Moyer (2016).

[25] On the debate of Philo's knowledge of Hebrew, see Sandmel (1956: 13; 1978–79: 107–112), Rajak (2014). Weitzman (1999: 39) states that Hebrew was not known in general by Hellenistic Jews in Egypt.

[26] Theodoros Metochites (*Miscellanea* 17) dedicates a few lines to describe the language of the "Egyptians" as 'rough' (τραχύτερον). He highlights characteristics of Alexandrian writers, among which he includes Philo, who use "obscure and difficult terms". On Philo, moreover, he would say that his language is not agreeable to the ears. For the text and translation, and commentary, see Fournet (2009: 68–71).

[27] Philo's debt to Plato is undoubtedly the source for much of his philosophical vocabulary, but he exceeded him in creativity. Terms like ἀκαλλώπιστος, 'unadorned', κοσμοπολίτης, 'citizen of the world', ἀγαλματοφορέω, 'to carry an image', and the terminology of creation of the cosmos: θεοπλάστης, 'maker of gods', κοσμοπλάστης, 'creator of the cosmos', κοσμοποιός, 'maker of the cosmos', are entirely his creation. See Siegfried (1875: III 31–137), Leopold (1983), Runia (1986: 399–402; 1992).

[28] Hanson (1959: 94) compares the lexicon in Philo and the Epistle to the Hebrews to propose a common lexical source for both in the Jews of Alexandria. See also Williamson (1970: 11–18). About a differentiated Jewish Greek variant, see Horsley (1989: 5–40), who surveys all theories

local "topolects". It is interesting that Philo does not reflect in general the terminology of administration in his descriptions of the army and the authorities, like for example in *Special Laws* 1.121. Unfortunately, few are the instances in which Philo might be reflecting a local use. One of them is in his "historical treatises", where he expounds a passionate discourse against the enemies of the Jewish people, following the persecutions of Alexandrian Jews under the reign of Caligula.[29] Many of the "insults"[30] he proffers can be explained, as much as the philosophical vocabulary just mentioned, as a literary legacy. The great creators of 'insults', Aristophanes and Demosthenes, are the inspiration for terms like the following:

(xvii) ταραξίπολις (*Against Flaccus* 20) 'city troubler', a philonic *hapax legomenon*, but most probably based on Aristophanes, ταραξιππόστρατον (*Knights* 247), a term used to refer to the 'army troubler' Cleon, or ταραξικάρδιον (*Acharnenses* 315), 'heart-troubling'.[31]

(xviii) The term γραμματοκύφων, 'scribbler', addressed by Philo to Lampo (*Against Flaccus* 20), is a Demosthenic inheritance. Demosthenes would dedicate it to his opponent Aeschines in *De corona* 209.2.[32]

(xix) There is, however, one Philonic appelative, καλαμοσφάκτης, 'pen-murderer', appearing in a specific context, which could be explained as a popular Alexandrian term:

(1) ὃν πολλάκις ὁ δῆμος ἅπας ὁμοθυμαδὸν εὐθυβόλως καὶ εὐσκόπως **καλαμοσφάκτην** ἐξεκήρυξεν, οἷς ἔγραφε μυρίους [καὶ] ἀνελόντα.

'Often the whole people unanimously denounced him, with an accurate and well-chosen expression, as the "pen-murderer", because by the things he wrote he had caused the death of numerous people.'
(Phil., *Flac.* 132) [tr. van der Horst]

---

to his date and concludes that while there was possible a specific vocabulary for their traditions and religious practice, there is no reason to believe there was a differentiated "dialect" spoken by the Jews; see also de Lange (2001).

29 Kasher (1985), Gambetti (2009).
30 On insult, see Bremmer (2000), Janse (2014). In Philo, Torallas Tovar (2013).
31 Degani (1987, 1993). López Eire (2000) observes that some of the insults in Aristophanes appear in epigraphy, and thus belonged to public use.
32 A scholion to *Ranae* confirms it is a creation of Demosthenes: *Schol.Ran.* 842b.4: ἔθος τοῖς ῥήτορσι πλάττειν ὀνόματα, ὡς καὶ ὁ θεολόγος· "Εἰδωλιανέ, καυσίταυρε", καὶ ὁ Δημοσθένης· "γραμματοκύφων", 'it was the habit of the rhetors to create terms, like the theologian (Greg. Nazianzenus): "idolater, bull-burner", and Demosthenes: "scribbler"'. See Burke (1972), Worman (2004), Muñoz Llamosas (2008: 33–49).

Philo seems to be reporting a popular lexical use on the streets of Alexandria. It is however very difficult to extract any further such instances from Philo, since he has a stronger connection to literary legacy than to the popular language of his environment.

Also in connection to the Hellenistic Jewish community of Alexandria is one of the most important sources for Alexandrian or Egyptian Greek: the translation of the Old Testament into Greek, known as the Septuagint, whose first "installment", the Pentateuch, can be dated to the third century BCE.[33] The importance of the text of the Septuagint in the history of the Greek language is based on its constituting not only an extensive corpus of translation Greek, but also an illuminating witness of the koiné of Ptolemaic Alexandria. In reference to the lexicon,[34] the comparison with the papyri can confirm, or alternatively, leave doubt open about the use of constructions in Egyptian Greek.

One of the semantic fields already explored within the study of the language of LXX is that of aulic and administrative terminology.[35]

(xx) Some examples of the usage of common terminology for administration in Ptolemaic and Roman times in the Septuagint are the expressions used to refer to responsible staff with the construction ἐπί + genitive.[36] This expression can be found in the LXX, in Gen. 43:16 τῷ ἐπὶ τῆς οἰκίας 'the overseer of the house, the butler', comparable to the terms for the hierarchy of the police forces in the papyri: ὁ ἐπὶ τῆς εἰρήνης 'the overseer of peace' (P.Cair.Isid. 130, l. 1 [IV CE], P.Rev. 2, 41, l. 24 [259 BCE]).[37]

---

[33] Janse (2002), Rajak (2009).

[34] See Muraoka (2009). A recent enterprise, the *Historical and Theological Lexicon of the Septuagint* will be groundbreaking in the assessment of the particular use of terminology in Greek considered "biblical". This project will also be impactful for the study of Egyptian Greek, since its purpose is to explore the connection of the Septuagint with, among other sources, the papyri in the belief that the language of the translators was very close to the popular koiné Greek of Alexandria.

[35] Different contributions collected in Lee (1983), Passoni dell'Acqua (1996; 1998; 1999), Cadell (1994), Montevecchi (1999), Fernández Marcos (1998: 17–42).

[36] This can also be compared to an Egyptian similar construction, e.g. ḥry-pr, 'overseer of the house' (Erichsen, *Demotisches Glossar*, 324).

[37] See Emmet (1913: 158): similar expressions are used to confirm this connection: οἱ/ὁ ἐπὶ τῶν προσόδων 'the overseer of public revenue' as in 3Macc 6:30 (see also BGU XVIII.1 2746, i, l. 5 [14–12 BCE] among many examples), or οἱ ἐπὶ πραγμάτων τεταγμένοι, 'those appointed for official positions', also in P.Tebt. I 5, l. 248 (118 BCE), and for example PSI XIV 1401, ll. 6–7 (118 BCE), which is also attested in 3Macc 7:1, 5:4. The use in later Greek may prove that this was a more generalized use than limited to Egypt.

Nevertheless, the Septuagint presents further problems. Being a translation,[38] the interference from a second language is double: from Egyptian by language contact in Alexandria and from the Hebrew language of the Vorlage.[39] The bilingual translators in fact made the effort to translate the Old Testament into understandable Greek, and even the words concerning Jewish realities were more or less literally rendered into Greek. Some of these realities required the creation of neologisms, semantic extensions or shifts in meaning, and the diffusion of the text of the Septuagint confirmed these new words or new uses in the Greek language. In most cases, this does not mean that these terms are typically Alexandrian or Egyptian, but instead a product of the process of translation that became popular through the spread of the Bible.[40]

(xxi) As an example, the rendering of *ephod*, a priestly garment, probably a linen sleeveless tunic, as ἐπωμίς tries to keep the relationship of the word with 'shoulder'. The Greek term was probably chosen because of the phonetic similarity with *ephod* and for being used in Classical times to refer to a piece of the women's tunic analogous to it.[41]

Other books of the Greek Old Testament were produced originally in Greek and most probably in Alexandria, as unanimously assumed in scholarship. It is the case, among others, of the Wisdom of Solomon,[42] or that of the third book of Maccabees,[43] "le plus alexandrin de tous les livres dont se compose la Bible d'Alexandrie" ["the most Alexandrian of all the books of which the Alexandrian Bible is composed"], as Modrzejewski (2008b: 159) states. The language has been described by Croy (2006: xiii-xiv) as presenting lavish

---

38 Another example of translation Greek is provided by the translations from Egyptian texts, like the *Prophecy of the Potter*, or the Myth of the *Eye of the Sun*, etc. In general see Tait (1994: 203–222). Depauw (1997: 98–99) provides references to specific texts, such as the prophecy of the potter or Nectanebo's dream.
39 Overview in Aitken (2016).
40 See for example, the term ἐγγαστρίμυθος, 'ventriloquist' (Maravela and Torallas Tovar 2001).
41 Le Boulluec & Sandevoir (1989: 251–252). In the papyri CPR XII 15, l. 2 (VII CE) (a Coptic list) and the diminutive in the margin of P.Oxy. LIX 3998 (IV CE): ἐπωμίδια.
42 Larcher (1969: 132–178), Reese (1970: 146–162), Winston (1979: 25), Grabbe (1997: 90), Hübner (1999: 16), Blischke (2007: 46, 203–223).
43 Emmet (1913: 156–157) collected a list of terms with the purpose of placing the composition in Alexandria. Modrzejewski (2008a), Hadas (1953), Johnson (2005: 129–169), for a discussion on date and authorship. The bibliography is enormous. I refer to these publications for more details. On 2 Macc. see most recently Domazakis (2018).

vocabulary and bombastic style, with neologisms, rare compound words, especially with privative alpha, and florid phrases.

(xxii) Precisely from this text, he extensively discussed ἀποτυμπανισμός (3Macc 3:27), 'crucifixion'(?), a term to refer to one of the instruments of torture or execution. Through a detailed scrutiny of the Ptolemaic legal system he proves that this term is not the product of the literary or lexical creativity of the author of 3Macc, but it conforms to the Ptolemaic legal system, and is probably a real local term.[44]

Emmet collected a number of words and expressions in 3Macc comparable to those found in the papyri:

(xxiii) for example, γραφικοὶ κάλαμοι (3Macc 4:20), 'writing reed-pen', appears in a letter about the purchase of scribal materials (P.Grenf. II 38, l. 7 [80 BCE]),[45]

(xxiv) or the verb καταχωρίζω[46] (3Macc 2:29, also *Letter of Aristeas* 36) bearing the meaning of 'enrolling or entering in a register or record'.

(xxxv) A metaphorical use of σκυλμός, literally 'mangling' or 'irritation', is found as 'vexation' or 'annoyance' in 3Macc 3:25, 4:6,[47] and in the papyri, like P.Tebt. I 16, l. 15 (115/114 BCE), P.Fay. 111, l. 5 (95–96 CE).

In sum, the Old Testament books produced in Greek or translated in Alexandria, together with some Hellenistic Jewish authors, who also lived in the same city, such as Philo or Pseudo-Phocylides,[48] provide a complex wealth of material, which can contribute to understanding the Egyptian and Alexandrian variety of Greek. The careful comparison with the papyri and inscriptions provides a firmer basis for the consideration of specifically Egyptian traits of the language.

---

44 P.Enteux 86, ll. 6 and 8; UPZ I 119, l. 37 (both Ptolemaic). For a full discussion, see Modrzejewski (2008a: 64–67, 2008b).
45 Found later in John Chrysostom, *In Joannem theologum* 59.611.50; Cyril Hier. *Catecheses ad illuminandos* 1.3.14
46 καταχωρισμός, 'registration, deposit in a registry' is a technical administrative term, found widely in the papyri, for example BGU I 2, l. 16 (209 CE) or P.Fay.108 fr. 2, l. 25 (170 CE).
47 And in fact, an Alexandrian author, Cl. Ptolemy, *Tetrabiblos* 4.206, μερίμνας τε καὶ σκυλμοὺς ἐμποιεῖ τῇ ψυχῇ καὶ τῷ σώματι. 'It (scil. Mars) induces worries and anxiety to the soul and the body'.
48 van der Horst (1978: 81–83).

4 Grammarians and lexicographers

After the papyri and inscriptions and the literary texts, which provide the main corpus for this inquiry, I venture to explore the grammarians and lexicographers in search of an Egyptian Greek lexicon. As already discussed, the Greek of Egypt is especially accessible to us through the abundant papyri found from north to south all along the river Nile in the deserted flanks beyond the cultivated area, where organic material was protected from humidity. Unfortunately, Alexandria and the whole Delta do not present the necessary conditions for the papyri to survive, and the little material we have from there was issued in Alexandria but sent elsewhere, and exceptionally preserved from decay. The grammarians and lexicographers described the language of the Alexandrians. The earliest of these is Demetrius Ixion from Adramyttium, a Homeric scholar from the school of Aristarchus of Samothrace, who produced a work περὶ τῆς Ἀλεξανδρέων διαλέκτου, 'On the language of the Alexandrians', in the second century BCE. He is quoted by Athenaeus,[49] but his work is unfortunately completely lost. Irenaeus Pacatus in the first century BCE wrote also seven books on the dialect of Alexandria, arranged alphabetically, that he moreover characterized as originating in Attic.[50] These two works would be enormously enlightening, if everything but their title was not completely lost. We hardly get any indirect reference or quotation from them, though there is also later material of the same kind, both grammatical and lexicographical. J.L. Fournet[51] has already devoted a very interesting monograph to the Greek of Alexandria, with special attention to the lexicon. He collects a list of more than sixty "topolects" (pp. 19–63) considered typically Alexandrian by the sources. Some examples are (xxvi) παγκαρπία (pp. 20–21), literally 'all-fruits', a kind of pastry; (xxvii) μενδήσιος (p. 21), a fish from the Delta, bearing a name connected to the toponym Mendes; (xxviii) vessels like βατάνιον (p. 24) 'flat dish' (cf. πατάνη); (xxix) βαύκαλις (pp. 25–26), 'bottle'; (xxx) καννίον (pp. 28–29) 'cup'; (xxxi) specimens of local flora, such as κιβώριον (pp. 33–34) 'kind of Nymphaea, Egyptian bean'; (xxxii) δαφνῖτις (p. 32) 'kind of bay', and a musical instrument; (xxxiii) φῶτιγξ (pp. 30–31) 'Alexandrian flute'. He remains skeptical about the value of these sources, since it is not clear what is meant by "Alexandrian", in sources that moreover refer to a very long span of time.

---

49 Mentioned by Athenaeus, *Deipnosphistae* 9.393b. He is also attested in Suda, D430, Staesche (1883).
50 See Suda, epsiloniota,190, pi 29. Fraser (1972: 470–471).
51 Fournet (2009). The first attempt was made already in (1808) by F. W. Sturz. See also the first modern approach by Fernández Marcos (1971).

The work of the Greek lexicographers can be traced through the remains of a number of lexica, some rightly attributed to specific authors and periods, some just preserved as *adespota*. These types of texts suffered a very turbulent textual history, being subject to change and adaptation as they were copied and belabored. One of the earliest fully preserved is that of Hesychius of Alexandria (V/VI CE.).[52] He composed a lexicon of obscure words based on the previous work by Diogenianus (second-century work, now lost). Hesychius' *Lexicon* consists of poetic and dialectal words and some short sayings. It is an extremely useful source for less attested languages, though with great problems of interpretation. While the most important lexicographer for this inquiry is Hesychius of Alexandria, other offer equally interesting material: ninth-/tenth-century Suda, or the *Etymologica*, ninth-century compilations of much earlier materials, Stephen of Byzantium in the sixth century or Photius' *Bibliotheca* and *Lexicon* in the ninth century and Zonaras in the thirteenth century. Athenaeus in the third century CE includes very useful lexicographical sources in his *Banquet of the Philosophers*.

The grammarians and lexicographers of Antiquity were not particularly interested in foreign languages, but they were indeed interested in recording some of their difficult or obscure vocabulary (sometimes without a clear reference to the place from which they culled it), and they provide testimonies of lost texts and languages. For example, Hesychius is the most important source of evidence for the lost Macedonian language. He has preserved between 150 and 200 entries with terms that he either classifies as Macedonian, or have been identified as Macedonian by later scholars.[53] This is the largest corpus we have for that language, complemented by inscriptions and numismatics.

One further problem is that the evidence that the lexicographers provide does not come with a clear explanation and context, and we cannot tell whether the terms belong or not to the specific Greek speaking population of Egypt or rather to the Egyptian language itself, real or imagined by the authors at stake.[54] For this reason, the only way of working through this wealth of information is by taking it with a pinch of salt, and applying careful analysis and comparison with other sources. Some of the terms found in the lexicographers may be of Egyptian origin used in Greek, some may be Greek terms specially used in Egypt, some

---

[52] Dickey (2007: 88–90).
[53] Crossland (1982), Masson (1996). The *Lexicon* of Hesychius has been exploited for other languages too: Tolman (1921), Sperber (1978).
[54] By imagined I refer to the representation of Egyptians in literature, often following stereotypes recognizable by an Athenian audience. For example, Aeschylus in *Supplices*. See Torallas Tovar (2004) and also Vasunia (2001).

may be just Egyptian terms not used in Greek, but appearing as foreign words in a piece of literature, as an exotic piece of information, or remain in the original rendering in a translation.[55]

Finally, even if the lexicographers and grammarians provide examples from a more general or popular background, their main interest is almost exclusively Classical literature and biblical texts. Among the terms we find in the lexicographers' works described as "Egyptian", many are found in the Septuagint. Here we have to ponder whether they refer to the real living Egyptians or the Biblical Egyptians as literary figures. As an example, we may compare the fate among the lexicographers of two Egyptian Greek words that appear in the papyri, the names of measures οἰφί and μάτιον:

(xxxiv) Μάτιον appears only in Suda as a kind of measure: (M 285) μάτιον: εἶδος μέτρου '*mation*: type of measure', but hardly in any other lexicographical source. The *scholia* to Aristophanes (*Clouds* 451b) include the same explanation as Suda for the term ματιολοιχός, 'devourer of meal', and Hesychius refers to an homonymous word without referring to this meaning. The term is indeed of Egyptian origin from Dem. *mḏ3t* a measure for dates, and is widely attested in the papyri in more than 250 hits in papyri.info from the third century BCE to the seventh century CE.

(xxxv) Οἰφί,[56] on the other hand, is much more extensively attested in the lexicographers than μάτιον: Hesychius O 435 (190) οἶφι: χοῖνιξ, '*oiphi*: a *choinix*' / (433) οἰφί· μέτρον τι τετραχοίνικον Αἰγύπτιον, '*oiphi*: Egyptian measure corresponding to four *choinices*', Photius O 166, Suda OI 190 and Ps-Zonaras O 1435, together with *Anon. Lex.* O 84, *Lex. Segueriana*, Epiphanius, *De mensuris* 131.23. When looking at the Greek papyri, we surprisingly find that the term is hardly attested in Greek.[57] The interest in the lexicographers is immediately explained when searching for the term in the Bible: it appears more than ten times in LXX (Leviticus, Numbers, Ruth, Judges, Kings, Ezechiel), and later in Philo and Clemens of Alexandria, and other later Christian authors,[58] while μάτιον never does.

---

55 On the latter, see Torallas Tovar (2017).
56 Also with an Egyptian etymology, *ip.t*, Achmimic Coptic, ⲟⲓⲡⲉ. Torallas Tovar (2004a: 191).
57 SB XX 14625, l. 31 (V-VI CE) presents an abbreviation, which in my opinion is not completely sure.
58 Philo, *De vita Mosis* 1.17; Flavius Josephus, *Contra Apionem* 1.287; Flavius Josephus, *Antiquitates Judaicae*, 2.228.2; Eustathius, *Commentarius in hexaemeron* 780.54; Clemens of Alexandria, *Stromata* I 23.152.3.

(xxxvi) Hesychius, moreover, and even other lexicographers, provide interesting false etymologies of "Egyptian words". This gives away immediately their main interests. Taking, for example, the Egyptian word for 'water', in Greek transliteration μῶυ, one finds in the lexicographers an explanation of the Egyptian etymology. There is only one reason this word is interesting for a Greek speaking audience, and it pertains to the etymology of the name of Moses (Ex. 2:10 'For out of the water I drew him'). We must remember that dating back to the Roman period there was a widespread practice among the Hellenistic Jewish interpreters of basing commentaries on (often false) etymologies of the terms pulled out of the biblical text itself.[59] Hesychius was the first to include the term in his lexicon, (μ 2076 μῶϋ: τὸ ὕδωρ, '*mou*: water') to which <παρ' Αἰγυπτίοις>, 'among the Egyptians' was added, based on Ps-Zonaras, who has the same entry (μ 1382.25 μῶς τὸ ὕδωρ παρ' Αἰγυπτίοις, καὶ μῶϋ, '*mos*: water among the Egyptians, also *mou*').[60] It is clear that the term is not used in Egyptian Greek. The general interest among Jewish and Christian scholars for this word and its etymology is clear as we find it in Philo of Alexandria, Flavius Josephus, Clemens of Alexandria, and has mainly to do with the explanation and interpretation of the biblical text, rather than any special interest in the language of the Egyptians or a popular use in Greek.

Finally I will provide a few examples of the lexicographical entries in Hesychius in which he describes "Egyptian uses" of Greek words. I discuss the contexts in order to provide an idea of the interpretative problems with which we are faced.

(xxxvii) The term κάλλαια is explained (κ 459) as the rooster's crest or tail feathers,[61] and probably conflated with a term like κάλλαϊς or καλάϊνος, 'blue-green, bluish.' The entry apparently attributes to the "Egyptians" the use of the term with the meaning of color: κάλλαια· οἱ τῶν ἀλεκτρυόνων πώγωνες καὶ πᾶν πορφυροειδὲς χρῶμα. ἔνιοι δὲ τὰ ποικίλα. καὶ παρ'

---

59 Grabbe (1988), Pépin (1976, 1987).

60 Etym. Gud. μ page 402.24–25 Μωϋσῆς, παρὰ τὸ μῶϋ, ὃ σημαίνει τὸ ὕδωρ Αἰγυπτιστί, καὶ τὸ σῆς, ὃ σημαίνει τὸ λαμβάνω, καὶ κατ' Αἰγυπτίους, ὁ ἐκ τοῦ ὕδατος ληφθείς 'Moyses stems from *mou*, which means "water" in Egyptian, and *ses*, which means "to take", also among the Egyptians: "he who was taken from the water".' The ending –σης is explained by Josephus (*Ant.* 2.9.6) as originating in the verb σῴζω, 'to save', because he was saved from the water. The etymology is based on the parallel of Ramses, born from Ra (true etymology, Divine name + -*mw-sw*, 'born of'), but cannot be applied to Moses in the same way.

61 Beekes (2016 s.v.): 'wattles' (Ar., Ael., Paus.), 'cock's crest' (Arist.), 'cock's tail feathers' (Ael. Dion.).

Αἰγυπτίοις χρῶμα. '*kallaia*: the beard of the roosters, and a completely purple-like color, some say they are variegated. Among the Egyptians, a color'.

(xxxviii) The plant called σαμψοῦχος (σ 156) 'marjoram' is said to mostly grow in Egypt, "although others call it *marathos*". It is not clear if the entry means that the first lemma is the term as used in Egypt. In any case, it appears in the magical papyri (among other sources). Sometimes, entries in Hesychius which do not specify any context, can be confirmed by other sources, like the following example:

(xxxix) σωχίς· εἶδος ἀμπέλου '*sochis*: type of vine' (σ 3112), which Pollux (6.82) specifies that it is an Egyptian vine: σωχὶς ἡ καὶ Αἰγυπτία '*sochis* also called Egyptian'.

These examples prove that even the context provided by Hesychius cannot be completely trusted.

5 Conclusions

When studying the typical vocabulary of Egyptian Greek there are very different, rich sources at our disposal. They all have, however, a number of problems of interpretation. My approach in this paper is an attempt at providing strategies to gather, analyze and compare the use of etymologically Greek terms in these sources, paying attention to the problems that each of them offers. The main issues can be summarized as follows:

The documentation we have for the use of Greek in Antiquity is fragmentary: although the papyri are an exceptionally rich source of information, the specific use in some registers (like the administrative) is not conclusive, due to the lack of evidence in other geographic areas that would confirm the hypothesis. Nevertheless, some terms can be safely attributed to an Egyptian Greek use, while others can be kept on the waiting list for the sake of caution.

Even in the case that an author or lexicon indicates that a term is used "by Egyptians" or "by Alexandrians", this specific indication is often difficult to interpret: Alexandrine can mean inhabitant of Alexandria or Alexandrian "philologist"; Egyptian can mean inhabitant of Egypt, speaker of Greek or Egyptian, bilingual or not, or Egyptian in the Bible.

Some terms could have been typically Egyptian in origin, but the later circulation of very popular texts, like the Bible, with large impact in biblical commentaries and other Christian literature, spread these uses at the same time, making it difficult to trace back to a specific geographical area.

References

Papyrus editions are cited according to J. Oates et al. Checklist of Editions of Greek, Latin, Demotic, and Coptic Papyri, Ostraca, and Tablets at: www.papyri.info/docs/checklist (last accessed 8 July 2018).

Aitken, James K. 2014. *No stone unturned: Greek inscriptions and Septuagint vocabulary*. Winona Lake: Eisenbrauns.

Aitken, James K. 2016. The Septuagint and Egyptian translation methods. In Wolfgang Kraus, Martin Maiser & Michaël van der Meer (eds.), *XV Congress of the International Organization for Septuagint and Cognate Studies, Munich 2013*, 269–293. Atlanta, GA: SBL Press.

Beekes, R.S.P. 2016. *Etymological Dictionary of Greek*. With the assistance of Lucien van Beek. Leiden: Brill.

Bentein, Klaas. 2015. The Greek documentary papyri as a linguistically heterogeneous corpus: The case of the katochoi of the Sarapeion-archive. *Classical World* 108. 461–484.

Blischke, Mareike V. 2007. *Die Eschatologie in der Sapientia Salomonis*. Tübingen: Mohr Siebeck.

Bremmer, Jan. 2000. Verbal insulting in Ancient Greek culture. *Acta Antiqua Hungarica* 40. 61–72.

Burke, Edmund Martin. 1972. *Character denigration in the Attic orators, with particular reference to Demosthenes and Aeschines*. Ann Arbor: Tufts.

Cadell, Hélène. 1994. Vocabulaire de l'irrigation: la Septante et les papyrus. In Bernadette Menu (ed.), *Les problèmes institutionnels de l'eau en Égypte ancienne et dans l' Antiquité méditerranéenne*, 103–117. Le Caire: Institut français d'archéologie orientale.

Clarysse, Willy. 1993. Egyptian scribes writing Greek. *Chronique d'Égypte* 68. 186–201.

Clarysse, Willy & Dorothy J. Thompson. 2006. *Counting the people in Hellenistic Egypt*. Cambridge: Cambridge University Press.

Crossland, R. A. 1982. The language of the Macedonians. In John Boardman, I.E.S. Edwards, N.G.L. Hammond & E. Sollberger (eds.), *Cambridge Ancient History*, vol. 3.1, 843–847. Cambridge: Cambridge University Press.

Croy, N. Clayton. 2006. *3 Maccabees*. Leiden: Brill.

Dahlgren, Sonja. 2016a. Towards a definition of an Egyptian Greek variety. *Papers in Historical Phonology* 1. 90–108.

Dahlgren, Sonja. 2016b. Egyptian transfer elements in the Greek of the Narmouthis ostraka. In Tomasz Derda, Adam Lajtar & Jakub Urbanik (eds.), *Proceedings of the 27th International Congress of Papyrology, Warsaw, 29 July – 3 August 2013*, 1257–1263. Warsaw: University of Warsaw.

Degani, Enzo. 1987. Insulto ed escrologia in Aristofane. *Dioniso* 57. 31–47.

Degani, Enzo. 1993. Aristofane e la tradizione dell'invettiva personale in Grecia. In Jan M. Bremmer & E.W. Handley (eds), *Aristophane: Sept exposés suivis de discussions*, 1–49. Genève: Fondation-Hardt.

Depauw, Mark. 1997. *A companion to Demotic studies*. Bruxelles: Fondation égyptologique Reine Elisabeth.

Depauw, Mark & Joanne Vera Stolk. 2015. Linguistic variation in Greek papyri: Towards a new tool for quantitative study. *Greek, Roman & Byzantine Studies* 55. 196–220.

Dickey, Eleanor. 2007. *Ancient Greek scholarship*. Cambridge: Cambridge University Press.

Dieleman, Jacco. 2005. *Priests, tongues, and rites*. Leiden: Brill.
Domazakis, Nikolaos. 2018. *The neologisms in 2 Maccabees*. Lund: Lund University.
Emmet, Cyril W. 1913. The third book of Maccabees. In R.H. Charles (ed.), *Apocrypha and pseudepigrapha of the Old Testament*. Vol. 1: *Gospels and related writings*, 155–173. Oxford: Clarendon Press.
Evans, Trevor V. & Dirk D. Obbink (eds.). 2010. *The language of the papyri*. Oxford: Oxford University Press.
Fernández Marcos, Natalio. 1971. Rasgos dialectales de la κοινή tardía de Alejandría? *Emerita* 39. 33–45.
Fernández Marcos, Natalio. 1998. *Introducción a las versiones griegas de la Biblia*. Madrid: Consejo Superior de Investigaciones Científicas.
Fournet, Jean-Luc. 1989. Les emprunts du grec à l'égyptien. *Bulletin de la Société de Linguistique de Paris* 84. 55–80.
Fournet, Jean-Luc. 2009. *Alexandrie: Une communauté linguistique? Ou: La question du grec alexandrin*. Le Caire: Institut franais d'archéologie orientale.
Fraser, P.M. 1972. *Ptolemaic Alexandria*. Oxford: Oxford University Press.
Gambetti, Sandra. 2009. *The Alexandrian riots of 38 C.E. and the persecution of the Jews: A historical reconstruction*. Leiden: Brill.
Gignac, Francis T. 1970a. The pronunciation of Greek stops in the papyri. *Transactions of the American Philological Association* 101. 185–202.
Gignac, Francis T. 1970b. The language of the non-literary Greek papyri. In Deborah. H. Samuel (ed.), *Proceedings of the 12th International Congress of Papyrologists, Ann Arbor, 13–17 August 1968*, 139–152. Toronto: Hakkert.
Gignac, Francis T. 1976. *A grammar of the Greek papyri of the Roman and Byzantine periods*. Vol. 1: *Phonology*. Milano: La Goliardica.
Grabbe, Lester L. 1988. *Etymology in early Jewish interpretation: The Hebrew names in Philo*. Atlanta, GA: Scholars Press.
Grabbe, Lester L. 1997. *Wisdom of Solomon*. Sheffield: Sheffield Academic Press.
Hadas, Moses. 1953. *The third and fourth books of Maccabees*. New York: Ktav.
Hanson, Richard P.C. 1959. *Allegory and event: A study of the sources and significance of Origen's interpretation of Scripture*. Richmond: John Knox Press.
Horrocks, Geoffrey C. 2010. *Greek. A History of the Language and its Speakers*, 2nd ed. London: Longman.
Horsley, G.H.R. 1989. *New Documents illustrating early Christianity*. Vol. 5: *Linguistic essays*. Sydney: The Ancient History Research Centre, Macquarie University.
Horst, Peter W. van der. 1978. *The sentences of Pseudo-Phocylides*. Leiden: Brill.
Horst, Peter W. van der. 2003. *Philo of Alexandria: Against Flaccus*. Leiden: Brill.
Hübner, Hans. 1999. *Die Weisheit Salomons*. Göttingen: Vandenhoeck & Ruprecht.
Janse, Mark. 2002. Aspects of bilingualism in the history of the Greek language. In J.N. Adams, Mark Janse & Simon Swain (eds.), *Bilingualism in ancient society: Language contact and the written word*, 332–390. Oxford: Oxford University Press.
Janse, Mark. 2014. Aischrology. *EAGLL* [online edition].
Johnson, Sara Raup. 2005. *Historical fictions and Hellenistic Jewish identity: Third Maccabees in its cultural context*. Berkeley: University of California Press.
Joseph, Brian D. 2000. Textual authenticity: Evidence from Medieval Greek. In Susan C. Herring, Pieter van Reenen & Lene Schøsler (eds.), *Textual parameters in older languages*, 309–329. Amsterdam: Benjamins.

Kahane, Henry & Renée Kahane. 1978. The role of the papyri in etymological reconstruction. *Illinois Classical Studies* 3. 207–220.
Kasher, Aryeh. 1985. *The Jews in Hellenistic and Roman Egypt: The struggle for equal rights.* Tübingen: Mohr Siebeck.
Klauck, Hans-Josef & Daniel P. Bailey. 2006. *Ancient letters and the New Testament: A guide to context and exegesis.* Waco: Baylor.
Lange, Nicholas de. 2001. Jewish Greek. In A.-F. Christidis (ed.), *A history of Ancient Greek: from the beginnings to Late Antiquity*, 638–645. Cambridge: Cambridge University Press.
Larcher, Chrysostome. 1969. *Études sur le Livre de la Sagesse.* Paris: Gabalda.
Latte, Kurt. 1955. Zur griechischen Wortforschung II. *Glotta* 34. 190–202.
Le Boulluec, Alain & Pierre Sandevoir. 1989. *La Bible d'Alexandrie: L'Exode.* Paris: Éditions du Cerf.
Lee, John A.L. 1983. *A lexical study of the Septuagint version of the Pentateuch.* Chico: Scholars Press.
Leiwo, Martti. 2005. Substandard Greek: Remarks from Mons Claudianus. In Nigel M. Kennel & Jonathan E. Tomlinson (eds.), *Ancient Greece at the turn of the millennium: Recent work and future perspectives: Proceedings of the Athens symposion, 18–20 May 2001*, 237–261. Athens: Canadian Archaeological Institute at Athens.
Leiwo, Martti. 2010. Imperatives and other directives in the letters from Mons Claudianus. In Trevor V. Evans & Dirk D. Obbink (eds.), *The language of the papyri*, 97–119. Oxford: Oxford University Press.
Leopold, John. 1983. Philo's vocabulary and word choice. In David Winston & John Dillon (eds.), *Two treatises of Philo of Alexandria: A commentary on De gigantibus and Quod Deus sit immutabilis*, 137–140. Chico: Scholars Press.
López Eire, Antonio. 2000. Reflexiones sobre la Comedia Aristofánica. *Myrtia* 15. 69–101.
Luján, Emilio R. 2010. Semantic change. In Silvia Luraghi & Vit Bubenik (eds.), *The Bloomsbury companion to historical linguistics*, 286–310. London: Bloomsbury.
Maas, Paul. 1958. The ΓΡΥΛΛΟΣ papyrus. *Greece and Rome* 5. 171–173.
Maravela, Anastasia & Sofía Torallas Tovar. 2001. The ἐγγαστρίμυθος in the Septuaginta: Between necromancers and ventriloquists. *Sefarad* 61. 419–438.
Masson, Olivier. 1996. Macedonian language. In Simon Hornblower & Anthony Spawforth (eds.), *The Oxford Classical Dictionary*, 3rd ed., 905–906. Oxford: Oxford University Press.
Modrzejewski, Joseph Mélèze. 2008a. *Trosième livre des Maccabées.* Paris: Cerf.
Modrzejewski, Joseph Mélèze. 2008b. Le troisième livre Des Maccabées: Un drame judiciare Judéo-Alexandrin. *Journal of Juristic Papyrology* 38. 157–170.
Montevecchi, Orsolina. 1999. *Bibbia e papiri: Luce dai papiri sulla Bibbia greca.* Barcelona: Institut de Teologia Fonamental.
Moyer, Ian. 2016. Isidorus at the gates of the Temple. In Ian Rutherford (ed.), *Greco-Egyptian interactions: Literature, translation, and culture, 500 BC–AD*, 209–244. Oxford: Oxford University Press.
Muñoz Llamosas, Virginia. 2008. Insultos e invectiva entre Demóstenes y Esquines. *Minerva* 21. 33–49.
Muraoka, Takamitsu. 2009. *A Greek-English lexicon of the Septuagint.* Louvain: Peeters.
Page, Dennis L. 1957. P.Oxy. 2331 and others. *Classical Review* 7(3–4). 189–191.
Passoni dell'Acqua, Anna. 1996. I LXX: Punto d'arrivo e di partenza per diversi ambiti di ricerca. *Annali di Scienze Religiose* 1. 17–31.

Passoni dell'Acqua, Anna. 1998. Notazioni cromatiche dall'Egitto greco-romano: La versione dei LXX e i papiri. *Aegyptus* 78. 77–115.
Passoni dell'Acqua, Anna. 1999. Il Pentateuco dei LXX testimone di istituzioni di età tolemaica. *Annali di Scienze Religiose* 4. 171–200.
Pépin, Jean. 1976. *Mythe et allégorie: Les origines grecques et les contestations judéo-chrétiennes.* Paris: Études augustiniennes.
Pépin, Jean. 1987. *La tradition de l'allégorie de Philon d'Alexandrie à Dante.* Paris: Études augustiniennes.
Pierce, Richard Holton. 1968. Grapheion, catalogue, and library in Roman Egypt. *Symbolae Osloenses* 43. 68–83.
Rajak, Tessa. 2009. *Translation and survival: The Greek Bible of the ancient Jewish Diaspora.* Oxford: Oxford University Press.
Rajak, Tessa. 2014. Philo's knowledge of Hebrew. In James K. Aitken & James Carleton Paget (eds.), *The Jewish-Greek tradition in Antiquity and the Byzantine Empire*, 173–187. Cambridge: Cambridge University Press.
Reese, James M. 1970. *Hellenistic influence on the Book of Wisdom and its consequences.* Rome: Biblical Institute Press.
Ritner, Robert K. 1993. *The mechanics of Ancient Egyptian magical practice.* Chicago: The Oriental Institute of the University of Chicago.
Runia, David T. 1986. *Philo of Alexandria and the Timaeus of Plato.* Leiden: Brill.
Runia, David T. 1992. Verba Philonica, ἀγαλματοφορεῖν, and the authenticity of the De Resurrectione attributed to Athenagoras. *Vigiliae Christianae* 46. 313–327.
Sandmel, Samuel. 1956. *Philo's place in Judaism: A study of conceptions of Abraham in Jewish literature.* New York: Ktav.
Sandmel, Samuel. 1978–79. Philo's knowledge of Hebrew: The present state of the problem. *Studia Philonica Annual* 5. 107–112.
Siegfried, Carl G. 1875. *Philo von Alexandria als Ausleger des alten Testaments.* Jena: Dufft.
Sophocles, E. A. 1910. *Greek lexicon of the Roman and Byzantine periods.* New York: Scribner.
Sperber, Daniel. 1978. Hesychius and rabbinic loanwords. *Scripta Classica Israelica* 4. 122–132.
Staesche, Traugott. 1883. *De Demetrio Ixione grammatico.* PhD dissertation, Halle University.
Sturz, Friedrich Wilhelm. 1808. *De dialecto Macedonica et Alexandrina.* Leipzig: Weigel.
Tait, W.J. 1994. Egyptian fiction in Demotic and Greek. In J.R. Morgan & Richard Stoneman (eds.), *Greek fiction: The Greek novel in context*, 203–222. London: Routledge.
Tolman, H.C. 1921. Persian words in the glosses of Hesychius. *Journal of the American Oriental Society* 41. 236–237.
Torallas Tovar, Sofía & Anastastia Maravela. 2001. The ἐγγαστρίμυθος in the Septuaginta: Between necromancers and ventriloquists. *Sefarad* 61. 419–438.
Torallas Tovar, Sofía. 2004a. Egyptian lexical interference in the Greek of Byzantine and early Islamic Egypt. In Petra M. Sijpesteijn & Lennart Sundelin (eds.), *Papyrology and the history of early Islamic Egypt*, 143–178. Leiden: Brill.
Torallas Tovar, Sofía. 2004b. The context of loanwords in Egyptian Greek. In Pedro Bádenas, Sofía Torallas Tovar, Eugenio R. Luján & M. Ángeles Gallego (eds.), *Lenguas en contacto: El testimonio escrito*, 57–67. Madrid: Consejo Superior de Investigaciones Científicas.
Torallas Tovar, Sofía. 2013. El orfebre del insulto: Filón y el griego de Alejandría. In Samir Khalil Samir & Juan Pedro Monferrer-Sala (eds.), *Graeco-Latina et Orientalia: Studia in honorem Angeli Urbani heptagenarii*, 384–399. Córdoba: CNERU.

Torallas Tovar, Sofía. 2017. The reverse case: Egyptian borrowing in Greek. In Pedro Dils, Eitan Grossman, Tonio Sebastian Richter & Wolfgang Schenkel (eds.), *Greek Influence on Egyptian Coptic: Contact-induced change in an ancient African language*, 97–113. Hamburg: Widmaier.

Vasunia, Phiroze. 2001. *The gift of the Nile: Hellenizing Egypt from Aeschylus to Alexander*. Berkeley: University of California Press.

Vierros, Marja. 2012. *Bilingual notaries in Hellenistic Egypt: A study of Greek as a second language*. Brussel: Koninklijke Vlaamse Akademie van België voor Wetenschappen en Kunsten.

Vierros, Marja & Erik Henriksson. 2017. Preprocessing Greek papyri for linguistic annotation. *Journal of Data Mining and Digital Humanities*, Episciences.org, 2017, Special Issue on Computer-Aided Processing of Intertextuality in Ancient Languages, <hal-01279493v1>.

Weitzman, Steve. 1999. Why did the Qumran community write in Hebrew? *Journal of the American Oriental Society* 119. 35–45.

Williamson, Ronald. 1970. *Philo and the Epistle to the Hebrews*. Leiden: Brill.

Winston, David. 1979. *The Wisdom of Solomon: A new translation with introduction and commentary*. New York: Doubleday.

Worman, Nancy Baker. 2004. Insult and oral excess in the disputes between Aeschines and Demosthenes. *American Journal of Philology* 125. 1–25.

Geoffrey Horrocks
7 Byzantine literature in "classicised" genres: Some grammatical realities (V–XIV CE)

Abstract: This chapter examines the phenomenon of interference from contemporary Medieval Greek in the classicising register of Greek traditionally used in the Byzantine period for literary genres with an ancient heritage (examples are taken from the fifth/sixth and thirteenth/fourteenth centuries). The focus lies on expressions of futurity and modality, and it is argued that, while authors are careful to replicate ancient morphology, which was consciously mastered and deployed, the actual uses of the relevant forms are heavily influenced by contemporary syntactic and semantic categories, which, being far more abstract, were subconsciously employed in even the most ancient-looking texts. Such interference was in fact almost inevitable in the absence of any thorough description of Classical Greek syntax in the grammatical tradition. Accordingly, Atticised Greek of the medieval period is best seen as a register of Medieval Greek in which the abstract syntactic and semantic properties of the contemporary language are conventionally realised by means of certain superficially obvious formal adaptations and the systematic substitution of ancient morphology.

1 Introduction

A great deal of research in recent years has focused on the literary registers of Byzantine Greek, and our understanding of writers' linguistic behaviour has been significantly advanced as a result.[1] This chapter will focus on a limited range of issues with a view to clarifying Byzantine writers' use of classicised Greek, i.e. on the highest levels of the spectrum of linguistic registers.

The discussion will focus on a comparison of specific aspects of the syntax of three high-register authors: Paul the Silentiary (VI CE: *Description of Hagia Sophia*), Anna Komnini (XII CE: *Alexiad*) and George Akropolitis (XIII CE: *History*) with the usage seen in texts by contemporary or near-contemporary writers in less elevated registers, specifically Callinicus (V/VI CE: *Life of Hypatius*), the anonymous "metaphrase" of Anna Komnini (XIV/XV CE), and some anonymous "vernacular" poems, specifically Digenes Akrites (version E, XII CE), the *Ptochoprodromika*

---
1 See especially the important collection of papers in Hinterberger (2014).

https://doi.org/10.1515/9783110614404-007

(XII CE, perhaps by Theodore Prodromos), *Spaneas* (version P, XII), an unpublished verse *Epithalamium* (probably XIII/XIV CE), and the *Chronicle of the Morea* (version H, XIV CE).

It is now widely accepted that few if any Byzantine writers sought to replicate the language of classical models in any precise way, and that varieties of high-register Greek had evolved with the passage of time, steadily allowing non-classical elements and usages into the contemporary literary "standard". This means that what are clearly "mistakes" from a strictly classical perspective should not be classified as such when they in fact represent the norms of usage of high-register writers of the relevant period. High-register Byzantine Greek, in other words, was in a very real sense a living language, used creatively by its practitioners and developing in the process its own internal peculiarities and conventions. It would not be entirely unreasonable to compare it, for example, with the highly specialised literary language of the early Greek epic tradition (the Homeric poems), which similarly retained many archaisms but also allowed their "original" usage to evolve alongside the steady incorporation of linguistic innovations.[2]

It is striking, however, that few of the innovations in Byzantine high-register writing involve morphology and that the majority involve syntax and semantics. The question is why this should be so. An examination of the surviving grammars inherited from antiquity (most notably the *Techne Grammatike* traditionally attributed to Dionysius Thrax [II/I BCE] but probably belonging to a later period in its current form), and of their later medieval or early modern adaptations (e.g. the well known grammar of Manuel Chrysoloras [XIV/XV CE], widely used in Italy for teaching Ancient Greek to early Renaissance scholars), provides an immediate answer. Standardly, there is a meticulous listing of forms and paradigms, but typically little or no attention is given to syntax – even to providing a simple description of the functions of the various forms in question, something that we might reasonably have expected to be important in later periods for teaching the use of the growing set of obsolete categories. And even where there is some attention to such matters (e.g. in the famous work of Apollonius Dyscolus [II CE] or later, that of Theodore of Gaza [XV CE]), the focus is largely theoretical rather than practical, i.e. focused on explaining the basis for various anomalies, whether real or apparent, while the selected examples are largely centred on the syntax of specific word forms rather than of larger constituents or clauses. There is, in other words, no real attempt at comprehensive coverage.

---

2 See, for example, Horrocks (2010).

We may briefly consider why this should be so. First and foremost, the earliest grammars were designed for the teaching of Classical Greek to speakers of the Koine who already controlled Greek syntax perfectly, at least in its contemporary form, which was still close enough to classical practice in most respects not to need extensive elaboration. This naturally led to a focus on morphology, where any diachronic differences were immediately apparent, and allowed those who did worry about syntax to concentrate primarily on abstract principles. For example, in resolving the apparent semantic conflict involved in the availability of perfect or aorist optatives for the expression of wishes, where the first component was widely seen as referring to the past and the second to the future, Apollonius developed an explanation which, though not without its difficulties,[3] represents one of the key early contributions to a proper characterisation of modality, time reference and aspect:

(1) 98. ἤδη καὶ περὶ τῆς ἐγγινομένης χρονικῆς διαθέσεως ἐν τῇ ἐγκλίσει διαποροῦσί τινες, ὡς μάτην εἰσκυκλεῖται ἡ τῶν παρῳχημένων χρόνων φωνὴ κατὰ τὴν ἔκλισιν . . . ἐκεῖνό φασιν· εἰ ἐν τοῖς οὐκ οὖσιν αἱ εὐχαὶ γίνονται εἰς τὸ ἐγγενέσθαι, πῶς τὰ γενόμενα εὐχῆς ἔτι δέεται;

98. 'Some are confused by the attribution of a temporal value to this mood, since the occurrence of the form of past tenses is without reason in this mood [. . .]. They say, "If wishes/prayers are for the fulfilment of something which does not exist, how can what is past have any need for wish?"'

99. πρὸς ὃ ἔστιν φάναι ὡς πᾶσα ἀνάγκη ὑπάρξαι καὶ τὴν ἐκ παρῳχημένου εὐχήν. φέρε γὰρ τὸν ἐπιβάλλοντα χρόνον τοῦ γινομένου ἀγῶνος Ὀλυμπίασι παρῳχῆσθαι, καὶ πατέρα εὔχεσθαι ὑπὲρ παιδὸς ἀγωνισαμένου περὶ τῆς τούτου νίκης· καὶ δῆλον ὡς οὔτε ποιήσεται εὐχὴν διὰ τῆς τοῦ ἐσομένου χρόνου οὔτε μὴν τοῦ κατὰ τὸν ἐνεστῶτα παρατεινομένου (τὰ γὰρ τοῦ παρῳχημένου ἀντίκειται), ἐξ οὗ ἂν ἀκολούθως γένοιτο ἡ εὐχὴ εἴθε νενικήκοι μου ὁ παῖς, εἴθε δεδοξασμένος εἴη . . .

99. 'To this statement we can reply that a wish in the past is absolutely necessary. Suppose that the appointed time for an Olympic contest has gone by and a father is praying for victory of a son who competed. Clearly he will not pray in the future tense or the present in extension (the past opposes it); consequently his wish would be: "May my son have won! [perfect]," "May he have been honoured! [perfect]".'

100. ἔστι καὶ οὕτως φάναι, ὡς ἀληθεύει ὅτι ἐπὶ τοῖς μὴ συνοῦσιν αἱ εὐχαὶ γίνονται· οὐ συνόντος γὰρ τοῦ φιλολογεῖν φαίημεν ἂν φιλολογοῖμι, οὐ συνόντος τοῦ πλουτεῖν τὸ πλουτοῖμι· χρὴ μέντοι νοεῖν ὡς τὸ ἐξαιτούμενον ἐκ τοῦ εὐκτικοῦ ἢ εἰς παράτασιν τοῦ ἐνεστῶτος παραλαμβάνεται, ἵνα ἐν αὐτῷ διαγίνηται, ὡς εἴ τις φαίη ζώοιμι ὦ θεοί, ἢ εἰς τελείωσιν τῶν μὴ ὄντων πραγμάτων, ὡς ὁ Ἀγαμέμνων εὔχεται, εἴθε ὦ θεοὶ πορθήσαιμι τὴν Ἴλιον· εὐχὴ γὰρ νῦν γίνεται . . . εἰς τὸ παρῳχημένον συντελὲς τοῦ χρόνου· τὴν γὰρ παράτασιν ἀπευκταίαν ἕξει· πορθοῦντι γὰρ αὐτῷ τὴν Ἴλιον· ἐννέα δὴ βεβάασι Διὸς μεγάλου ἐνιαυτοί, καὶ δὴ δοῦρα σέσηπε νεῶν καὶ σπάρτα λέλυνται

---

3 See e.g. Conti (2009).

> (B 134–135) καθότι πάλιν κατὰ τὸ ἐναντίον ἔστιν ἐπινοῆσαι ἐπὶ τοῦ ζώοιμι· οὐ γὰρ δή γέ τις παραλήψεται εἰς εὐχὴν τὴν τοῦ ζῆν συντέλειαν ἐν τῷ ζήσαιμι· ἡ γὰρ τοιαύτη συντέλεια τῆς εὐχῆς δυνάμει περιγράφει τὴν τοῦ βίου διατριβήν.
>
> 100. 'We can also say that it is true that wishes are for things not existing. It is when I am not busy studying that I could say "I hope to study [present]," and when I am not rich that I say "I pray to be rich! [present]" We must observe that what is requested in the optative can be used either for the extension of the present, so that it will go on, as when one says "O gods, may I continue to live [present]!" or for the accomplishment of something not existing, as when Agamemnon prays "Allow me, gods, to destroy [aorist] Troy!," the prayer in fact concerns the accomplishment and conclusion of the event, the prolongation being hateful; while he has been besieging Troy: "Already have nine years of great Zeus gone by, and the timbers of our ships have rotted, and the tackling has been loosed" (Iliad 2.134–135). We have to understand this in the opposite way, since no one will express in his desire the completion of life with "May I finish life [aorist]," for the fulfillment of the desire potentially delimits the continuation of life.'
> (Apollonius Dyscolus, *Syntax* 3.98–100)[4]

The grammatical tradition therefore evolved as one where morphology had to be learned but syntax, at least at the practical level, could be largely taken for granted. Even at the very end of the Byzantine era, the majority of those learning ancient varieties of Greek (albeit a tiny minority) were still native speakers of the language who, by definition, already knew its contemporary syntax. This enduring situation, in which the differences beween literary and colloquial Greek grew steadily greater over time, provided plenty of opportunity for what must have been largely subconscious innovation, many examples of which were then absorbed into the literary language as part of normal usage at that level.

Thus, for the privileged few, learning literary Greek was a matter of mastering morphological paradigms by rote and then learning to *use* the various forms, many of which were long obsolete, in some other way. In the absence of formalised syntactic rules abstracted from past usage, the only option available to would-be writers was the close examination of precedents under the guidance of a teacher. But both teacher and pupil - and this factor has till recently been seriously underestimated - must at least tacitly have exploited their own linguistic intuitions as native speakers of more "natural" varieties of contemporary Greek: "the vernacular" should not be seen as the exclusive property of the poor and uneducated, but rather as a set of colloquial registers ranging over the whole social spectrum. In other words, in the absence of explicit instruction to the contrary, what could be more natural than to view the distinctive morphological categories of Classical

---

4 All translations are my own.

Greek as alternative, albeit stylistically highly "marked", realisations of the familiar syntactic and semantic categories of the contemporary language?

2 Two examples

My own, admittedly limited, work in this field has focused on expressions of futurity and modality (Horrocks 2014, 2017a, 2017b), and this is the domain I have chosen here to provide material to justify these claims. The first example is taken from the famous poem composed by the 6th-century lawyer and court official Paul the Silentiary on the occasion of the reopening of Hagia Sophia after the restoration of its collapsed dome in 562 CE. It begins with 134 iambic verses praising the emperor Justinian (*panegyric)*, and then continues with the description (*ekphrasis*) proper in Homeric-style language and hexameters.

The poem as a whole is located firmly within the classical tradition in terms of its language, its metres, and its genres, yet even at this "highest" of literary levels Paul periodically allows non-classical alternatives to the regular Homeric or classical realisations of certain constructions. In (2), for example, the context makes it clear that we are dealing with a counterfactual, or at least an entirely hypothetical, situation:

(2) εἰ μὲν γὰρ ἐλπὶς ἦν τις εὐσθενεῖ λόγῳ
συνεξισοῦσθαι τῷ νεῷ τῷ παγκάλῳ,
σφαλερὸν **ὑπῆρχεν** ἐπαποδύεσθαι πάλαις
ἐν αἷς τὸ νικᾶν παρακεκινδυνευμένον

'For if there had been/were/were to be any prospect of some mighty discourse matching the most beautiful of churches [*but that's obviously impossible*], then it would have been/would be [*now or in future*] perilous to strip off for a match in which victory was at risk [*but given the impossibility of fulfilling the condition, that's something I didn't do/am not doing/would not do*].'
(Paul the Silentiary, *Description of Hagia Sophia* 104–107; V/VI CE)

Paul has completely discounted the possibility that his poem could ever match the glory of the church it describes, a concession that then allows him free rein to exercise his rhetorical skills in what follows! The only risk of failure would be if he really did try to match the wonders of Hagia Sophia in words. Despite the entirely classical lexicon and morphology, entirely appropriate to classical-style iambics, the apodosis of the counterfactual/hypothetical conditional contains an imperfect indicative without the regular classical particle ἄν. Furthermore, the bare imperfect is used in a temporally and aspectually neutral way, and can be interpreted as equivalent to a classical aorist with ἄν (past counterfactual), a classical imperfect with ἄν (past or present counterfactual), or to a classical optative with ἄν (future/hypothetical). This is in essence a version of the Modern Greek situation, subject to the later addition of the future-marker θα in the apodosis, but it is already available in high-register Greek of the sixth century. Its origins, however, are in the Koine of the Roman era, with examples already in papyri, in the New Testament and in the work of the early church fathers, as in the following example taken from Callinicus:

(3) εἰ γὰρ ἀνήγγειλας, **παρεκαλοῦμεν** καὶ ἡμεῖς

'For if you had appealed to us, we too would have comforted you.'
(Callinicus, *Life of Hypatius* 98.4; V/VI CE)

Details of the mechanisms promoting these changes can be found in Horrocks (1995). Here we can simply note that in more popular versions of the Koine ἄν came to be confused with the conjunction ἐάν 'if' and therefore disappeared from conditional apodoses, where the full array of classical options (aorist, imperfect, optative with ἄν) were eventually replaced by the modal imperfect, as we have just seen. This development was in turn accelerated by the general demise of the optative in the Koine, and the replacement of this mood in future/hypothetical protases with the imperfect, which could already have past and present time reference in this context. The imperfect thus came to be seen as an atemporal marker of hypotheticality/counterfactuality in protases, eventually largely replacing the aorist too in this context, and in this role it was quickly generalised to the corresponding apodoses, as seen in (2) and (3). In later times, even the most stylistically ambitious authors, such as the philosopher, historian and statesman Michael Psellos [1017/18 – *ca.* 1078], sometimes allow this construction.[5]

The second example comes from the later Byzantine period. Historiography of the Comnenian and Palaeologan periods is famous for its Atticising style, and in terms of lexicon and morphology this is for the most part a very fair description. Before considering this genre further, however, we must first establish the contemporary norms for the expression of futurity and modality.[6]

One striking feature of vernacular Greek in the Middle Ages is the extent to which expressions of futurity and modality came to overlap with each other, with conditional sentences once again playing a key role in the levelling process. First consider (4):

(4) From ca. the eleventh century reference to the future could be marked:
(a) ἵνα/νά + subjunctive.

---

[5] See Horrocks (2010, 233–8).
[6] For a full account of Medieval Greek syntax, including the expression of futurity and modality, see *CGMG* 4.

(b) infinitival periphrasis with μέλλω/ἔχω/θέλω; νά + subjunctive may be substituted for infinitive.

(c) νά + infinitival periphrasis with auxiliary ἔχω (a "low" innovation, mostly characteristic of the fourteenth-century *Chronicle of the Morea*).

All of these options can also convey a range of modal values (epistemic, volitional, dynamic and deontic) and in many cases clear distinctions are difficult or impossible to make, cf. (5):

(5a) τίς τῆς καρδίας του τὴν χαρὰν **νὰ ἰσχύσῃ** καταλέξειν

'Who will/can have the strength to describe the joy in his heart?'
(*Epithalamium*, lines 4 of MS Folio 7v.; XII or XIII/XIV CE?)

(5b) καὶ τότε δεῦτε πρὸς ἐμὲ καὶ κάτι **νὰ σᾶς εἴπω**

'And then come to me and I will/can/must tell you something.'
(*Spaneas* P 208; XII CE)

(5c) **περάσειν ἔχω**, Μαξιμού, ὡς διὰ σὲν τὸ ποτάμι

'(so) I will/can/must cross the river, Maximou, on your behalf.'
(*Dig.* E 1532; XII CE?)

Writers may exploit and combine the options more or less interchangeably, as the examples in (6), from the *Chronicle of the Morea* (H), demonstrate:

(6a) τὸ κάλλιον . . . ὅπου **ἔχομεν ποιήσει** . . .

'The best thing we can do.'; 'The best thing, which we shall/must do.'
(*Chronicle of the Morea*, 3647)

(6b) ἂν εὕρωμεν τὸν Βασιλέα . . . τὸν **θέλομεν πολεμήσει**

'If we find the king, we will/shall attack him.'
(*Chronicle of the Morea*, 3650–3651)

(6c) ἂν **θέλω** . . . **νὰ στείλω** ἐκεῖ φουσσᾶτα ἐδικά μου, . . . **νὰ τὸν ἐπάρουν** εὔκολα καὶ **νὰ τὸν ἔχεις χάσει**

'If I send my own armies there, they can/will take it [viz. your land] easily and you may/will lose it.'
(*Chronicle of the Morea*, 4233–4237)

Summarising, the later medieval vernacular had at its disposal a set of competing forms for referring to the future, all of which were also used to express a variety of modal notions, in part because the distinction between the two concepts, involving closely related domains of inherent uncertainty, was difficult to draw in a clear-cut way.

Let us begin our examination of later Greek in the high register with the proem to the *History* of the statesman George Akropolitis (XIII CE), which clearly owes a great deal rhetorically to ancient predecessors like Polybius, but where, we must assume, Akropolitis was also on his very best linguistic behaviour:[7]

(7) Τὸ τῆς ἱστορίας χρήσιμον καὶ πρὸ ἡμῶν οἱ συγγραψάμενοι διωρίσαντο, καὶ **ἅπερ ἂν ἐκείνοις ἐπῆλθεν εἰπεῖν, ταῦτ' ἂν καὶ ἡμεῖς ἐρεῖν ἔχωμεν**· τί γὰρ ἂν καὶ εὕροιμεν **καινότερον νόημα** τοσούτων ἱστορησάντων καὶ σύμπαν καλὸν τῆς ἱστορίας ἀποφηναμένων ἐν τοῖς σφετέροις συγγράμμασι; **τάχα δέ**, ὃ πλέον ἐκείνων ἐν τοῖς νῦν προκειμένοις ἡμῖν λέξειν ἄξιον, **τοῦτό γε ἂν τῆς ἡμετέρας συγγραφῆς προβαλούμεθα**.

'Historiographers long before us have defined what is useful in history, and we too will be able to say whatever it occurred to them to say - for what more novel thought can we come up with when so many have inquired into the past and expounded the general virtue of history in their work? But in defence of our book we can perhaps present in addition all that is noteworthy in the current situation.'
(George Akropolitis, *History* I.1–8; Heisenberg 1903)

The clauses that are important for our purposes are in bold. The first comprises a generic relative clause containing an aorist indicative that describes an indefinite series of past-time events, followed by a future referring main clause containing a subjunctive complemented by a future infinitive:

(8) ἅπερ ἂν ἐκείνοις ἐπῆλθεν εἰπεῖν, ταῦτ' ἂν καὶ ἡμεῖς ἐρεῖν ἔχωμεν

'Whatever it occurred to them to say, this we too will be able to say.'

The lexical items and morphology are impeccably ancient, as are the superficial aspects of its syntax (the preposed relative clause with a demonstrative pronoun used resumptively in the main clause), but "real" ancient Greek would have no ἄν in either clause, and would standardly employ either a bare optative or an imperfect indicative in the relative clause together with the future of ἔχω in the main clause complemented by a present or aorist (never a future) infinitive. By contrast, contemporary vernacular Greek would have a past indicative in the relative clause, either imperfect or aorist, though the latter must co-occur with an imperfective verb in the main clause, and is itself typically qualified by an overt indefinite-frequency adverb such as ποτέ 'ever'. The main clause could contain (i) a future referring infinitival periphrasis or (ii) νά + subjunctive:

---

7 For a fuller discussion see also Horrocks (2017a).

(9) ὅσα **πέρασαν** (ποτὲ) ἀπὸ τὸν νοῦν τοὺς νὰ εἰποῦν, αὐτὰ καὶ ἐμεῖς

'whatever crossed their mind to say, this we too . . .'

(i) **θέλουμε** (ἡ)**μπορέσει** εἰπεῖν / νὰ εἰποῦμε
(ii) **νὰ** (ἡ)**μπορέσουμε** εἰπεῖν / να εἰποῦμε

'. . . will be able to say.'

It is clear, therefore, that in (8) Akropolitis is simply following the tense usage of the contemporary language, namely aorist indicative in the subordinate clause and a future/modal expression in the main clause. The use of ἄν in the relative clause (permitted only with 'generic' subjunctives in Classical Greek) replicates in a high register the generalising adverbial used with indefinite frequency aorists in the vernacular; and in the main clause ἄν apparently replaces vernacular ἵνα/νά, inducing here the choice of subjunctive ἔχωμεν over future indicative ἔξομεν; once again, the "antiquing" of vernacular syntax has no solid foundation in Ancient Greek.

The remaining clauses of (7) marked in bold may be taken together:

(10a) τί γὰρ **ἂν** καὶ **εὕροιμεν** καινότερον νόημα . . .;

'For what more novel thought can we come up with. . .?'

(10b) τάχα δέ . . . τοῦτό γε **ἂν** τῆς ἡμετέρας συγγραφῆς **προβαλούμεθα.**

'But perhaps . . . we can present this [material] in defence of our book.'

While the optative in (10a), together with the particle ἄν in potential/epistemic use, is wholly classical, it is clear that the same meaning is also required in (10b), which contains instead a future indicative with ἄν (another impossible combination in Classical Greek). The key factor here is the presence of τάχα, which is often used in Ancient Greek with potential ἄν and the optative in the sense 'perhaps'. Evidently, it is not appropriate for the author to say that he *will* perhaps present certain material in defence of his book, which radically undermines the proem as a statement of authorial intent; evidently, Akropolitis wishes to express the hope that he "*can* perhaps present such material in defence of his book", as a modest way of saying he intends to do so. Given that these two expressions are used with equivalent potential meaning, it seems fair to conclude that Akropolitis is using both optative + ἄν and future indicative + ἄν exactly as he might have used ἵνα/νά + subjunctive in the vernacular, namely as expressions of futurity/ modality with the intended force to be determined by the requirements of the context (here epistemically).

Since we have already seen in (8) the subjunctive + ἄν used as an equivalent of ἵνα/νά + subjunctive (in this case with future force), it is clear that all three represent realisations of the functionally indeterminate vernacular future/subjunctive in this higher register.

Just in case this might be thought to be a strange quirk of Akropolitis' style, we can compare our conclusions with the evidence provided by the anonymous middle-register *metaphrase* of Anna Komnini's *Alexiad* (XII CE), which also belongs to the Palaeologan era.[8] In many cases the choice of forms in the metaphrase shows clearly how at least one native speaker of the period understood the classical forms used in high-register texts. Thus we find:

(i) Future indicatives interpreted modally (δύναμαι, core meaning 'being able', has no corresponding future use):

(11a) ἐγὼ μὲν τοῦ κάστρου παμμεγέθους ὄντος ἔν τινι τόπῳ **κρυβήσομαι**

'As the fortress is very large, I can/will hide myself in some place.'
(Anna Komnini, *Alexiad* 11.7.4)

(11b) ἐγὼ μέν, ἐπεὶ τὸ κάστρον μέγα ἐστί, **δύναμαι κρυβηθῆναι** ἐν μέρει τινὶ τοῦ κάστρου

'Since the fortress is large, I can hide myself in a part of the fortress.'
(*Metaphrase*, section 8)

(ii) Subjunctives read as futures (μέλλω + infinitive has no relevant modal functions):

(12a) ἄτερ χρημάτων ἴσθι ὡς οὐδὲ φρούριον **κατασχεῖν δυνηθῇς**

'But be sure you will never be able to take even a guard post without money.'
(Anna Komnini, *Alexiad* 11.11.6)

(12b) γίνωσκε ὅτι χωρὶς χρημάτων οὐδὲ ἓν καστέλλιον **μέλλετε ἐπαρεῖν**

'Be sure that without money you are not going to take even one little fort.'
(*Metaphrase*, section 100)

(iii) Optatives understood as futures (in (13b) as a strong denial with οὐ μή):

(13a) ἐκ τῆσδε τῆς Κορυφοῦς διαπέμπω . . . ἀγγελίας τῇ σῇ βασιλείᾳ, ἃς . . . οὐκ **ἂν** περιχαρῶς **ἀποδέξαιο**

---

8 See Horrocks (2014; 2017b) for a more detailed treatment.

'From this town of Corfu I send news to your Majesty that you will not receive with great joy.'
(Anna Komnini, *Alexiad* 11.12.6)

(13b) πέμπω σοι μηνύματα ἀπὸ τῆσδε τῆς πόλεως τῆς Κορυφώ . . . οὐ μὴ **δέξεσαι** ταῦτα μετὰ χαρᾶς

'I send you messages from this town of Corfu; you will not receive these with joy.'
(*Metaphrase*, section 114)

Whether or not we interpret Anna's own intentions as equivalent to the readings assigned by the metaphrast, it is clear that future, subjunctive and optative forms were potentially understood as functionally interchangeable future/modal expressions in environments where they could not be substituted one for another in the ancient language but where the medieval vernacular made no formal distinctions of function.

3 Conclusion

The argument that the writers of high-register works regarded the obsolete morphological resources of Classical Greek as contextually conditioned realisations of the regular syntactic/semantic categories of the contemporary colloquial language, and used them accordingly, implies that, at the appropriate level of abstraction (i.e. the level of construal), Medieval Greek in any given period had a largely common grammar in terms of its underlying "constructions", and that educated writers saw their principal task as one of choosing among different potential realisations, i.e. selecting the appropriate linguistic register for the genre in question - with each such genre characterised by specified sets of lexical, phraseological and (especially) morphological resources.

The reality of this situation is graphically illustrated in the *Ptochoprodromika* (XII CE), where the author (probably the court poet and writer Theodore Prodromos, *ca.* 1100 – *ca.* 1165/70) has great fun playing with different registers and indirectly revealing the difficulties that many speakers clearly had in conforming to the expected linguistic conventions with any conviction or consistency. Transposition of content between the full array of registers was an activity that only the most talented and very best educated could ever hope to control with confidence. From the following fragment it appears once again that the key markers were morphological and lexical rather than syntactic.[9] The elements in (14) that are discussed below are marked in bold.

(14) Ἀπὸ μικροῦ **μὲ** [μικρόθεν **μ'**] ἔλεγεν ὁ **γέρων** ὁ **πατήρ** μου,
τέκνον μου, μάθε γράμματα, καὶ ὡσάν' ἐσέναν **ἔχει**,
βλέπεις τὸν δεῖνα, **τέκνον** μου, πεζὸς **περιεπάτει**,
καὶ τώρα ἕν **διπλοεντέληνος** καὶ **παχυμουλαράτος**.
Αὐτός, **ὅταν** ἐμάνθανεν, ὑπόδησιν **οὐκ** εἶχεν,   60
καὶ τώρα, βλέπε τον, φορεῖ τὰ **μακρομύτικά** του.
Αὐτὸς μικρὸς **οὐδὲν** εἶδεν **τὸ τοῦ λουτροῦ κατώφλιν**,
καὶ τώρα λουτρακίζεται τρίτον τὴν **ἑβδομάδαν**·
ὁ κόλπος του ἐβουρβούρυζεν φθείρας ἀμυγδαλάτας,
καὶ τώρα τὰ νομίσματα γέμει τὰ μανοηλάτα·   65
τσάντσαλον εἶχεν στούπινον, **καβάδιν** λερωμένον,
κ' ἐφόρει το μονάλλαγος **χειμῶνα καλοκαίριν**,
καὶ τώρα, βλέπεις, **γέγονε** λαμπρὸς καὶ λουρικάτος,
παραγεμιστοτράχηλος, μεταξοσφικτουράτος.
Αὐτός, **ὅταν** ἐμάνθανε, **ποτέ του οὐκ** ἐκτενίσθην,   70
καὶ τώρα ἕν **καλοκτένιστος** καὶ **καμαροτριχάρης**.
Καὶ **πείσθητι** γεροντικοῖς καὶ πατρικοῖς σου λόγοις
καὶ μάθε γράμματα καὶ σὺ καὶ ὡσάν' **ἐσέναν ἔχει**.
Ἂν γὰρ **πεισθῇς ταῖς συμβουλαῖς καὶ τοῖς διδάγμασί μου**,
σὺ μὲν **μεγάλως τιμηθῇς**, πολλὰ **νὰ εὐτυχήσῃς**,   75
ἐμὲ δὲ τὸν **πατέρα** σου κἂν **ἐν τῇ τελευτῇ μου**,
νὰ θρέψῃς ὡς ταλαίπωρον καὶ **νὰ γηροτροφήσῃς**.
Ὡς δ' **ἤκουσα τοῦ γέροντος, δέσποτα, τοῦ πατρός μου**,
τοῖς γὰρ **γονεῦσι πείθεσθαι φησὶ** τὸ θεῖον γράμμα,
ἔμαθον [ἔμαθα] τὰ γραμματικὰ πλὴν **μετὰ κόπου πόσου**.   80
Ἀφοῦ δὲ **γέγονα** κἀγὼ γραμματικὸς τεχνίτης,
ἐπιθυμῶ καὶ τὸ **ψωμὶν** καὶ **τοῦ ψωμιοῦ** τὴν μάνναν,
καὶ διὰ τὴν πείναν τὴν πολλὴν καὶ τὴν στενοχωρίαν
ὑβρίζω τὰ γραμματικά, λέγω **μετὰ δακρύων**:
ἀνάθεμαν τὰ γράμματα, Χριστέ, καὶ **ὁπού** τὰ θέλει,   85
ἀνάθεμαν καὶ τὸν καιρὸν καὶ ἐκείνην τὴν ἡμέραν,
καθ' ἢν μὲ παρεδώκασιν [μ' ἐπαραδώκασιν] εἰς τὸ διδασκαλεῖον,
πρὸς τὸ νὰ μάθω γράμματα, **τάχα νὰ ζῶ ἀπ' ἐκεῖνα**.

'Ever since I was small, my old father used to say to me, "My child, learn your letters and then "it's all right for you". You see so-and-so, he used to go about on foot, but now he's wearing a double breast-plate and riding a fat mule. When he was a student, he didn't have shoes, but now just look at him, he's wearing his "long-toes". When he was a student, he hadn't ever seen the threshold of the bath-house, but now he takes three baths a week. His lap used to heave with lice the size of almonds, but now it's full of coins stamped with Manuel's head. He had rags of tow, a filthy

---

9 See also Horrocks (2010: 337–42).

overcoat that he wore without changing, winter and summer, but now, you see, he's become splendid in his armour, thick-necked, with tight silk drawers. When he was a student, he'd never combed his hair in his life, but now he's well-groomed with a bouffant style. Just obey your old father's words and learn your letters too, and then "it's all right for you". For if you follow my advice and my instructions, you will be greatly valued and enjoy much good fortune, while I your father, even at the end of my life, will be nursed by you in my misery and looked after in my old age." When I heard my old father, master (for holy scripture says one should obey one's parents), I learned to read and write - but what an effort! And ever since I too became an expert in letters, I've been longing for bread and even a crumb of bread, so in my great hunger and distress I curse my literacy and say with tears: "Damn letters, Christ, and all who want them, and damn the time and the day when they handed me over to the school to learn my letters, as if I could live on them."'
(*Ptochoprodromika* 3.56–88; tr. Eideneier)

The poems can be given a more colloquial or more conservative look according to the morphological choices made from the variant readings attested in the tradition, but the overall impression is one of modern syntax: cf. the vernacular positioning of clitic pronouns throughout, along with the Constantinopolitan preference for the accusative of the indirect object [56, 57, 73]; ἔχει = 'there is' [57, 73, literally 'there is a hosannah for you'] ; ἀφοῦ 'since' and ὅταν 'when' + indicative in temporal clauses [60, 70, 81]; idiomatic ποτέ 'ever' + genitive pronoun [70]; νά + subjunctive in future sense [75, 77]; ἐπιθυμῶ 'I long for' + accusative instead of genitive [82]; relative use of ὅπου 'whoever' [85]; νά -clause for infinitive in the nominalised clause after πρός 'to' [88]; idiomatic use of τάχα νά = 'as though' [88]; and ἀπό 'from' + accusative [88].

By contrast, the morphology remains quite traditional overall, always allowing for the usual, metrically helpful, variation in verb endings (e.g. 3pl present in –ουν/–ουσι, 3pl past in –αν/–ασι etc) and some modern inflections for plainly colloquial forms (cf. the neuters in –ιν [62, 66, 67, 82], the synizesis in ψωμιοῦ 'of bread' [82], and the addition of –ν to neuter ἀνάθεμαν 'curse' [85, 86]). Thus 3rd-declension consonant-stems normally retain their classical paradigm [56, 67, 76, 78], and adaptations involving accusative singular in –ν (e.g. ἑβδομάδαν 'week' [63]) might well be restored to their ancient form except where popular expressions are pointedly employed (e.g. with ἐσέναν 'you' [57, 73]). This blend of more or less conservative morphology with more or less contemporary syntax probably represents a stylised, perhaps gently parodic, version of the contemporary vernacular of the upper classes in Constantinople: note also the preference for οὐ(κ) 'not' [60, 70] over (οὐ)δέν [62, where it is arguably emphatic in the classical way], γέγονα 'I became' [68, 81] rather than ἔγινα, old-style "strong" aorists in –ον rather than regularised –α [80, at least as a variant], along with the occasional retention of aorist middles [not attested here], the use of inflected consonant-stem participles [ditto] and infinitival complements [79], and the retention of ancient government requirements involving the genitive or dative (e.g. after verbs [72, 74, 78, 79] and prepositions [76, 80, 84]).

The term 'mixed style' is often used to characterise the language of the *Ptochoprodromika,* in reference both to differences of register between sections (e.g. the introductory and concluding parts of the poems are typically composed in a higher register than the rest) and also to the use of traditional lexical and morphological options alongside their contemporary (and more popular) counterparts. The second case is relevant here, and it is noteworthy that the practice is sometimes carried over into direct speech, where modern forms normally increase in number in line with a speaker's passion and/or lower social status, cf. in particular the last four lines [85–88], where the language of the speaker's heated sentiments is contrasted with the learned language that has been so uselessly acquired: here we find neuter ἀνάθεμαν 'curse' with analogical –ν, relative ὁπού 'whoever', 3rd plural aorist ἐπαραδώκασιν 'they handed over' with external augment (at least as one variant), τό plus a να-clause, colloquial τάχα νά 'as if', and ἀπό 'from' + accusative. At the beginning of the passage addressed to the emperor [78 ff.], by contrast, the language is at first conspicuously more archaising: note the genitive after ἀκούω 'I hear' [78], the ancient φημί 'I say' [79] with its infinitival complement, the dative after πείθομαι 'I obey' [79], and the avoidance of synizesis in στενοχωρίαν 'distress' [83].

At other times more learned and more popular elements are combined deliberately to provide a laugh, as in the father's speech, where, especially but not exclusively in the peroration, the old man attempts, not entirely convincingly, to practice what he preaches: cf. the learned item τέκνον 'child' [57, 58], the internal augment in περιεπάτει 'he went about' [58], and the "sandwiched" genitive in τὸ τοῦ λουτροῦ κατώφλιν 'the threshold of the bath-house' [62, though the head noun is a vernacular term in a popular form], alongside the otherwise generally contemporary and colloquial syntax, phraseology and vocabulary, including the amusingly over-the-top compound adjectives so typical of colloquial speech [59, 61, 69]. Subsequently, a still more learned gloss is affected: cf. the aorist passive imperative πείσθητι 'obey' [72], the adverb in -ως [75] rather than –α, contrastive μέν and δέ [75/76], dative complements after πείθομαι 'I obey' [74] and ἐν 'in, at' [76] – but all alongside the repeated quotation of the colloquial expression "it's all right for you".

The language of the *Ptochoprodromika* is certainly mixed, but it is far from being a random mixture. It is wickedly contrived by the author, textual uncertainty and variation notwithstanding, to reflect perfectly, and often amusingly, the complexities and problems that characterised the "language question" of the time, and to satirise the often clumsy, imperfect and inappropriate use of different registers by those who strived to impress but lacked the resources to control the product in the manner approved (at least in theory, if not always in practice) by the educated urban elite.

References and selected bibliography

Browning, Robert. 1983. *Medieval and Modern Greek*, 2nd ed. Cambridge: Cambridge University Press.
Conti, Sara Eco. 2009. Reflections on the verb in Apollonius Dyscolus. *Quaderni del Laboratorio di Linguistica* 8. 1–22.
Davis, John C. 2010. Anna Komnene and Niketas Choniates 'translated': The fourteenth-century Byzantine metaphrases. In Ruth Macrides (ed.), *History as Literature in Byzantium: Papers from the Fortieth Spring Symposium of Byzantine Studies, University of Birmingham, April 2007*, 55–70. London: Routledge.
Eideneier, Hans. 1991. *Ptochoprodromos: Einführung, kritische Ausgabe, deutsche Übersetzung, Glossar Besorgt von Hans Eideneier*. Köln: Romiosini.
Goodwin, William Watson. 1890. *Syntax of the moods and tenses of the Greek verb*. Cambridge (Mass.): Sever and Francis.
Heisenberg, Augustus. 1903. *Georgii Acropolitae opera*. Vol. 1. Leipzig: Teubner.
Hinterberger, M. (ed.). 2014. *The language of Byzantine learned literature*. Turnhout: Brepols.
Horrocks, Geoffrey C. 1995. On condition. . .: Aspect and modality in the history of Greek. *Proceedings of the Cambridge Philological Society* 41. 153–173.
Horrocks, Geoffrey C. 1997. Homer's dialect. In Ian Morris and Barry B. Powell (eds.), *A new companion to Homer*, 193–217. Leiden: Brill.
Horrocks, Geoffrey C. 2010. *Greek: A history of the language and its speakers*, 2nd ed. Malden: Wiley-Blackwell.
Horrocks, Geoffrey C. 2014. High-register Byzantine Greek: Diglossia and what lay behind it. In Caterina Carpinato & Olga Tribulato (eds.), *Storia e storie della lingua greca*, 49–72. Venezia: Ca' Foscari.
Horrocks, Geoffrey C. 2017a. Georgios Akropolitis: Theory and practice in the language of later Byzantine historiography. In Andrea Massimo Cuomo & Erich Trapp (eds.), *Towards a historical sociolinguistic poetics of Medieval Greek*, 109–118. Turnhout: Brepols.
Horrocks, Geoffrey C. 2017b. 'High' and 'low' in Medieval Greek. In Klaas Bentein, Mark Janse & Jorie Soltic (eds.), *Variation and change in Ancient Greek: Tense, aspect and modality*, 210–241. Leiden: Brill.
Hunger, Herbert. 1978. *Die hochsprachliche Literatur der Byzantiner* (2 vols.). München: Beck.
Hunger, Herbert. 1981. *Anonyme Metaphrase zu Anna Komnene, Alexias XI–XIII: Ein Beitrag zur Erschließung der Byzantinischen Umgangssprache*. Wien: Verlag der Österreichischen Akademie der Wissenschaften.
Macrides, Ruth. 2007. *George Akropolites: The History, translated with an introduction and commentary*. Oxford: Oxford University Press.
Markopoulos, Theodore. 2009. *The future in Greek: From ancient to medieval*. Oxford: Oxford University Press.

Nuti, Erika. 2013. Reconsidering Renaissance Greek grammars through the case of Chrysoloras' Erotemata. *Greek, Roman and Byzantine Studies* 53. 240–268.

Reinsch, Dieter R. & Athanasios Kambylis (eds.). 2001. *Anna Comnenae Alexias* (Corpus Fontium Historiae Byzantinae 40). Berlin & New York: de Gruyter.

Sinclair, Kyle James. 2012. *War writing in Middle Byzantine historiography: Sources, influences and trends*. PhD dissertation, University of Birmingham. [http://etheses.bham.ac.uk/3977/]

Stone, Andrew Francis. 2009. The moods and tenses in Eustathian and late twelfth-century high-style Byzantine Greek. Βυζαντινά Σύμμεικτα 19. 99–145.

Wahlgren, Staffan. 2002. Towards a grammar of Byzantine Greek. *Symbolae Osloenses* 77. 201–204.

Wahlgren, Staffan. 2010. Byzantine literature and the classical past. In Egbert. J. Bakker (ed.), *A companion to the Ancient Greek language*, 527–538. Malden: Wiley-Blackwell.

Martin Hinterberger
8 From highly classicizing to common prose (XIII–XIV CE): The *Metaphrasis* of Niketas Choniates' *History*

Abstract: This chapter discusses the difference in register between the *History* of Niketas Choniates and the *Metaphrasis* of this same text. The first exhibits a learned (atticizing) language, whilst the second uses the more common Byzantine Koine. In the *History*, however, lexical and morphosyntactical forms of the learned variant as well as of the Koine variant occur, indicating that the two categories were not as rigid as is often purported. We must assume that a mixture of alternative forms from both registers was considered aesthetically superior. The chapter also proposes that the strict differentiation between classicizing and vernacular language is rather empty, since all Byzantine texts exhibit elements of both categories. It is therefore more useful to research how many classicizing and how many vernacular elements are to be found in a text and to investigate why this specific form is employed and not its variant(s).[1]

1 Introduction

During the first decade of the thirteenth century, the senior-ranking Byzantine dignitary Niketas Choniates wrote a highly classicizing history covering the last 50 years before the sack, and capture, of Constantinople by the participants of the Fourth Crusade.[2] Around 1340–50 this relatively popular text, which was however linguistically accessible only with substantial learning and effort, was "transposed" to a much simpler variety of Greek, the so-called *Metaphrasis*.[3]

Choniates' language usually is characterized as atticizing, (highly) classicizing or, simply, learned, whereas the *Metaphrasis* is regarded as representing

---

[1] I am indebted to John Davis for his critical comments and for emending my English. What I present here, is based on our joint work on the *Metaphrasis* of Choniates' *History* whose edition we hope to publish soon. The present contribution has considerably profited from the research project "The vocabulary of Byzantine classicizing and literary koine texts: A database of correspondences", conducted at the University of Cyprus, as well as from the project "El autor bizantino" FFI2015-65118-P_STI directed by Juan Signes Codoñer.
[2] On the text and its author see Simpson & Efthymiadis (2009) and Simpson (2013).
[3] On the Metaphrasis of Choniates' *History* see Davis (2004, 2009, 2010). On Metaphraseis in general see Hinterberger (2014b).

https://doi.org/10.1515/9783110614404-008

Byzantine written koine or "the common (written) language".[4] In all probability, the Byzantines themselves would have regarded Choniates' variety of written Greek as ἑλληνικά 'Greek', 'classicizing Greek' (or ἀτθίς 'Attic').[5] Anything else was categorized as κοινή 'common' or χύδην γλῶσσα 'loose language'. In this paper, I shall undertake a comparison of these two varieties, and at the end, suggest a different, more precise and more flexible way of categorizing the language of Byzantine texts.

In all likelihood, the linguistic differences between Choniates' *History* and its *Metaphrasis* are not due to the linguistic change that may have taken place during the 140 years that elapsed between the composition of the original text and the *Metaphrasis*. Most of Choniates' morphosyntactical features that the *Metaphrasis* replaced had already been obsolete in the spoken and simple written language of the Hellenistic and Imperial period. The editors of the forthcoming edition[6] suspect that the *Metaphrasis* may be based, to a larger or smaller extent, on interlinear or marginal notes accompanying the original text from a fairly early point on.

If we call this linguistic variety the language of "usual" or common prose (Ševčenko 1981), then we have to specify that this is the usual prose of historiography. In the case of, for instance, rhetorical texts, even in their simplified versions, e.g. the *Metaphrasis* of Nikephoros Blemmydes' *Basilikos Andrias*,[7] notwithstanding various common characteristics, a clearly distinguishable variety was used.

2 Niketas Choniates' *History* and its *Metaphrasis* compared: Differences and common features

Les us cast a glance over a short passage of Choniates' *History* and how it is rendered by the *Metaphrasis*.

(1) **Ἐπάνειμι** δ' **αὖθις** ἐπὶ τὰ **Παιονικά**, σαφηνείας δ' ἕνεκα τοῦ ἱστορεῖν προαναβαλοῦμαι ταυτί. τῷ τότε ἄρχοντι τῶν **Οὔννων** Ἰατζᾷ δύο ἦσαν **ὁμαίμονες**, Στέφανός τε καὶ Βλαδίσθλαβος, καὶ **παῖδες** Στέφανος καὶ Βελᾶς. τῶν ἀδελφῶν **τοίνυν** ὁ Στέφανος τὰς

---

4 Horrocks (2010: 264–268), in the context of "The written Koine in Byzantium". It also has been given the labels "the language of usual prose" (Ševčenko 1981: 309–310), *Umgangssprache* (Hunger 1981) or "written Byzantine Koine" (Schrift-Koine) (Eideneier 1982).
5 Various studies have shown that Byzantine ἀτθίς 'Attic' does not mean the Classical Attic dialect but a wide range of model texts spanning from Homer to Late antique/early Byzantine authors; see Hinterberger (forthcoming a: 4). Robert Browning (1978: 107) aptly speaks about "conceptual classicism" rather than the full imitation of classical models.
6 Davis & Hinterberger (forthcoming).
7 Hunger & Ševčenko (1988).

8 From highly classicizing to common prose (XIII–XIV CE) —— 181

ὁμογνίους ἐκφυγὼν χεῖρας κατ' αὐτοῦ **φονώσας** τὴν Κωνσταντίνου κατέλαβε, καὶ προσδεχθεὶς **ἀσπασίως** τῷ αὐτοκράτορι Μανουὴλ ἄλλης τε **φιλοφροσύνης** ὡς **πλείστης ἠύμοίρησεν,** ἀλλὰ δὴ καὶ Μαρίαν **ἔγημε** τὴν **τούτου** ἀνεψιάν, ἣν ὁ σεβαστοκράτωρ **ἐφύτευσεν** Ἰσαάκιος.

μετὰ δὲ βραχὺ καὶ ὁ τῶν ἀδελφῶν τρίτος Βλαδίσθλαβος κατ' ἴχνια βαίνων τῷ Στεφάνῳ τῷ Μανουὴλ **προσεχώρησεν,** οὐ τοσοῦτον Ἰατζᾶ καταγνοὺς ὡς μὴ **φιλοῦντος** ὅσον **εἰκὸς** ἢ ἐξ ἐκείνου ἐπιβουλὴν πτοηθείς, ὅσον τῇ τοῦ ἀδελφοῦ Στεφάνου φήμῃ γοητευθεὶς καὶ πρὸς αὐτὸν τὴν πορείαν τεινάμενος. **τῷ τοι** οὐδ' αὐτὸς ἐξέπεσε τῶν ἐλπίδων [. . .]

'I return once again to Hungarian affairs, and for the sake of historical clarity I shall put forward the following. The then ruler of the Huns (= Hungarians) Iatzas (= Géza II) had two brothers, Stephen (István IV) and Vladislav (Lásló II), as well as two sons, Stephen (István III) and Velas (Béla III). So, of the brothers it was Stephan who, after fleeing the kindred hands that tried to kill him, arrived at the (city of) Constantine where he was gladly received by the emperor Manuel and obtained numerous other benefits, but moreover married Maria, his (= the emperor's) niece whom the sebastrokrator Isaakios had begotten.

Shortly afterwards, also the third brother Vladislav, following in Stephen's footsteps, went over to Manuel, not so much because he accused Iatza of not loving him as much as he should or because he feared a plot by him, but rather because he was enticed by what he had heard about his brother Stephen and set his course in pursuit of him. And so it turned out that he too was not disappointed in his hopes.'
(Choniates, *History* 126.48–60; ed. van Dieten 1975) [tr. Magoulias 1984: 107]

(2) **Ἐπανέρχομαι** δὲ **πάλιν** ἐπὶ τὰ **Οὐγγρικὰ** καὶ τὴν ἱστορίαν ἄρχομαι λέγειν σαφέστερον. τῷ τότε ἄρχοντι τῶν **Οὔγγρων** Ἰατζᾶ δύο ἦσαν **ἀδελφοί,** Στέφανος καὶ Βλαδίσθλαβος, καὶ **υἱοὶ** δύο, Στέφανος καὶ Βελᾶς. ὁ γοῦν ἀδελφὸς Στέφανος **φυγὼν** ἀπὸ **τοῦ ἀδελφοῦ αὐτοῦ** τοῦ Ἰατζᾶ, ἐπεὶ **ἤθελε φονεῦσαι** αὐτόν, πρὸς τὸν βασιλέα Μανουὴλ κατέλαβε, καὶ προσδεχθεὶς **λαμπρῶς** παρ' αὐτοῦ, **πολλῆς εὐεργεσίας ἔτυχεν· ἔλαβε** δὲ καὶ εἰς γυναῖκα τὴν **αὐτοῦ** ἀνεψιὰν Μαρίαν, ἣν ὁ ἀδελφὸς αὐτοῦ ὁ Ἰσαάκιος **ἐγέννησε.**

μετ' ὀλίγον δὲ καὶ ὁ τρίτος ἀδελφὸς Βλαδίσθλαβος **προσῆλθε** καὶ αὐτὸς τῷ βασιλεῖ, οὐ τοσοῦτον καταγινώσκων τὸν Ἰατζᾶν ὡς μὴ κατὰ τὸ **πρέπον ἀγαπῶντα** αὐτόν, ἀλλὰ τὴν τοῦ ἀδελφοῦ ἀκούων παρὰ τοῦ βασιλέως ἀναδοχήν, ἔτι τε καὶ τὸν αὐτοῦ πλουτισμόν. **ὅθεν** οὐδὲ αὐτὸς ἀπέτυχε τοῦ σκοποῦ, οὐδὲ τῆς ἐλπίδος ἠστόχησεν [. . .]

'I return once again to Hungarian affairs, and shall tell the history in a clearer fashion. The then ruler of the Hungarians Iatzas had two brothers, Stephen and Vladislav, as well as two sons, Stephen and Velas. Well, the brother Stephen fled from his brother Iatza because he (= the latter) wanted to kill him, and arrived at the emperor Manuel; and he was splendidly received by him, and obtained many benefactions. Moreover, he married Maria, his niece, whom his brother the sebastrokrator Isaakios had fathered.

Shortly afterwards, also the third brother Vladislav, too, came to the emperor, not so much because he begrudged Iatzas for not loving him as he should, but because he had learnt of

his brother's favorable treatment by the emperor, and moreover that he had got rich. Thus, he too did not fail in his mission, nor was he disappointed in his expectations.'
(*Metaphrasis* 5.1.1; ed. Davis & Hinterberger forthcoming) [my translation]

If we juxtapose these two corresponding passages we observe that the *Metaphrasis* is almost a word by word transposition to the simpler variety, while some phrases are in fact left as they were in the original (e.g. τῷ τότε ἄρχοντι '(to) the then ruler' – usually a greater portion of text remains unchanged).

2.1 Differences in the vocabulary[8]

The most conspicuous changes regard vocabulary. In almost every line of Choniates' text several lexical items are replaced (all lexical correspondences are in bold); see e.g. in the above example: ἐπάνειμι > ἐπανέρχομαι 'to come back', αὖθις > πάλιν 'again', Παιονικά > Οὐγγρικά 'Hungarian (affaires)' etc. We may suppose that the words replaced had become entirely obsolete in the living language and therefore were not (readily) intelligible to a person lacking higher education, whereas the terms used in the *Metaphrasis* were commonly used. The words which were replaced fall into various categories. Archaizing ethnonyms and toponyms, a particular characteristic of classicized Greek, are substituted by modern terms (e.g. Λατίνος > Φράγγος 'westerner, Latin', Βυζάντιον > Κωνσταντινούπολις 'Constantinople', Μέανδρος > Μέντρος 'the Meander river'). Additionally, all compound verbs of the simple εἶμι 'to come' are replaced by forms of ἔρχομαι as are words with typical attic phonology such as νεώς, λεώς (> ναός, λαός, 'temple/church' and 'people' respectively) and the old personal pronouns οἱ, σφῶν, σφίσι(ν), σφᾶς (> usually αὐτῷ, αὐτῶν, αὐτοῖς, αὐτούς/ἑαυτούς). Moreover, all decidedly poetical words, mostly from the Homeric poems, but also from the tragedies and other texts, are replaced (or simply omitted), e.g. μόρος > θάνατος 'death', ὁμαίμων > ἀδελφός 'brother', ὁμόγνιος > τοῦ ἀδελφοῦ 'brotherly', φυτεύω > γεννάω 'to beget/father'. The same is true for the numerous hapax legomena and neologisms in Choniates' text (approximately 600!) which were created on the basis

---

[8] The analysis of the vocabulary of the two texts has been facilitated by the findings of the research project "The vocabulary of Byzantine classicizing and literary koine texts: A database of correspondences" conducted at the University of Cyprus and funded by the Leventis Foundation (see www.ucy.ac.cy/ byz/el/news-and-announcements). I would like to thank both institutions for their generous support.

of ancient word-formation patterns (e.g. ἀγκοίνησις, ἐκξιφισμός, κυλινδροφύλαξ, πρωτούργησις).⁹ None of Choniates' neologisms made it into the *Metaphrasis*. Apart from these categories, many more classical words are substituted, particularly those which had acquired a different meaning in the vernacular (e.g. φιλοῦντος > ἀγαπῶντα, the first meaning 'to kiss' in the common language).

On the other hand, clearly vernacular words appear in the *Metaphrasis* (clearly vernacular because of their characteristic phonetics, e.g. the combination τζ in μούντζα 'sooth', or word formation pattern, γλυκοσύντυχος 'soft-spoken' or both, as in τζουκαλολάγινα 'earthenware').

Despite these apparent differences between the vocabularies of the two texts, a considerable number of words is used in both texts. Most terms in the *Metaphrasis* which substitute terms of Choniates' *History*, are in fact used on occasions in the *History* (e.g. in the *Metaphrasis* πάλιν 'again' replaces αὖθις but πάλιν itself is used in Choniates' text). This means, therefore, that Choniates uses simple (though not decidedly vernacular) words as well, but in tandem with a multitude of high style synonyms, e.g. ἀδελφός, κασίγνητος, ὁμαίμων > ἀδελφός 'brother'; αὐτοκράτωρ, βασιλεύς, κρατῶν > βασιλεύς 'emperor'; ἐκτομίας, ὁ μὴ ἐνόρχης, εὐνοῦχος > εὐνοῦχος 'eunuch'. Those common lexical items which appear in both versions of the text (the passages which are retained without changes included) constitute the Byzantine core vocabulary (i.e. ἀδελφός, βασιλεύς, εὐνοῦχος, πάλιν etc.).

It is noteworthy that certain lexical items appearing in both texts have a distinctly different semantic value: παρακαλέω 'to comfort' (high) / 'to demand, ask for' (low), or τάξις 'military unit' (high) / 'social standing' (low).

Interestingly, there are two quite clearly distinguished registers within the *Metaphrasis*: the one used for narrative passages, the other for direct speech (or letters). In the latter, vernacular vocabulary as well as morphology and syntax are more frequent than in the rest of the text. Frequently, such passages of direct speech are based on indirect speech in Choniates, the conversion of indirect to direct speech being a characteristic trait of the "Metaphrastic"/transpositional process. Often these passages coincide with passages in which the Metaphrast deviates markedly from his model texts and appears to write in a more independent spirit than in most of his text. Compare, for instance, the following two passages (again, direct lexical correspondences are in bold):

(3) τό τε γὰρ **ξίφος** αὐτοῦ ἐκωμῴδησεν ὡς σκιατραφέσιν ὀξυνόμενον σώμασιν . . . καὶ αὐτὸν δὲ τὸν Ἰσαάκιον ὡς ἀπάλαμνον ἐμωκᾶτο· μηδὲ γὰρ **θυραυλῆσαί** ποτε καὶ ἐπὶ θυρεοῦ ἀφυπνῶσαι ἢ μαρύλλης ἀνασχέσθαι κράνους καὶ μολυσμὸν ὑπενέγκειν

---

9 For all these words see *LBG* (ss.vv.).

θώρακος, ἀλλὰ καπνῷ γραμμάτων προσανέχειν **ἐς γραμματιστοῦ φοιτῶντα ἐξ ἀπαλῶν ἔτι ὀνύχων** καὶ **δέρριν** ἐξημμένον περὶ ἀριθμῷ διεξιοῦσαν πινακίδιόν τε καὶ **γραφεῖον** ἀνὰ χεῖρας ἔχοντα τὴν σκυτάλην συχνὰ ὑποβλέπεσθαι καταφερομένην τῶν χειρῶν αὐτοῦ καὶ τῶν πυγῶν, καὶ ταύτης μόνης εἰδέναι καὶ **δεδιέναι** τὰ κροταλίσματα, ἀπειλὴν δ' Ἄρεος ὑφίστασθαι μηδαμῶς, μηδὲ **δοῦπον** ἀκόντων **ἐνηχηθῆναί** ποτε. οὐ ταῦτα δὲ μόνον ἐπικερτομῶν ἔγραφεν, ἀλλὰ καὶ **παραίφασιν** εἰσῆγε καὶ ἐχθρὸς ὢν συμφράδμων ἐγίνετο. καὶ ἐνῆγεν **ἀποθέμενον** τὸ βασίλειον **στεφάνωμα** [. . .]

'For he (= Baldwin) ridiculed his (= the emperor's) sword as being whetted on bodies grown in the shadow (= soft) . . . and he mocked Isaakios himself as being helpless. For (Baldwin said) he had never camped out and slept on a shield or endured a helmet covered with coal dust or abided a soiled coat of mail, but instead focused his attention on the smoke of letters, since he had been under the tutelage of a schoolmaster from a tender age and was often frightened of the cane cracking down on his hands and his buttocks when studying a parchment explaining numbers and holding a tablet and a pencil in his hands, and (Baldwin said) that he knew and feared only the rattle of this cane, but was never exposed to Ares' threat (= war/battle), nor had he ever heard the clash of lances. Not only did he write such things mocking (him), but he also gave him words of encouragement and, although an enemy, gave him counsel. And he suggested that he (= Isaakios) should set aside the imperial crown [. . .].'
(Choniates, *History* 365.67–366.80) [tr. Magoulias 1984: 202]

(4) οὐδὲ γὰρ οἶδας σὺ ποτὲ πόλεμον ἢ **σπάθην** γυμνὴν ἢ καὶ **στρατιωτικὴν κακοπάθειαν**, ἀλλ' **ἀπὸ μικρόθεν τὰ γράμματα μανθάνων** καὶ πινακίδιον καὶ **προβέαν** μετὰ **καλαμαρίου** γράφων συχνὰ ταύτην ἔβλεπες· καὶ λειώνων καὶ σφουγγίζων αὐτὴν καὶ εἰς ἀέρα κτυπῶν· καὶ ταύτης μόνους τοὺς κτύπους **ἐφοβοῦ**, μήποτε καὶ παρὰ τοῦ διδασκάλου **κωλοράβδια** λάβῃς· **κτύπον** δὲ σὺ **ἁρμάτων** ἢ ἀλόγων προσκρουσμοὺς ποτέ σου οὐκ **ἤκουσας**. καὶ **συμβουλεύομαί** σοι καὶ παραινῶ ἵνα τὴν [. . .] βασιλείαν **καταλείψῃς** καὶ τὸ **διάδημα** [. . .]

'You have never known battle or a naked sword or military hardship, but ever since you were young, studying letters and writing on your tablet and sheepskin [parchment] with a pen, your attention was quite focused on that [parchment]. And you would scrape and sponge it clean (the parchment), making strokes with it in the air, and you were concerned only to make these strokes, lest you receive strokes on your backside from the teacher. But you have never heard the clash of arms or the collision of horses. And I advise you and recommend you [. . .] to resign your realm and the crown.'
(*Metaphrasis* 12.3.4) [my translation]

Despite the clearly vernacular words in this specific passage (particularly κωλοράβδια 'strokes on the backside', λειώνω 'to make smooth' and σφουγγίζω 'to sponge') and its general "vernacular feeling", the *Metaphrasis*' overall linguistic character cannot be identified with the vernacular (if we regard vernacular morphology as a decisive criterion).[10]

2.2 Differences in phonology

The language of the *Metaphrasis* is still profoundly influenced by the written tradition and therefore clear phonological "innovations" are few and far between. We have already mentioned the cluster τζ /ts/ unknown to Classical Greek, which appears in various words of the *Metaphrasis* that replace Choniates' terms, such as μούντζα 'soot', τζακίζω 'to break', τζουκαλολάγινα 'earthenware'. In Choniates' *History*, however the cluster is not totally absent, but restricted to personal names or toponyms, mostly of foreign origin but not only (e.g. Ῥιτζάρδος, Καμύτζης, Βατάτζης, Τριάδιτζα, Βρανίτζοβα, Τζουρουλός).[11] Characteristically, in many cases of such toponyms Choniates characterizes them as 'so-called' (e.g. ὁ λεγόμενος or ὃ . . . κατονομάζεται).[12] The only exception to this general rule in Choniates is the compound word τζαγγρατοξότης 'crossbow-man'.[13]

Furthermore, atticist -ττ- in Choniates is regularly replaced with -σσ- in the *Metaphrasis* (mostly in verbal forms such as τάττω, φυλάττω and their derivative verbs; see also below), but also λύττα > λύσσα. An interesting difference is the avoidance of hiatus in Choniates (through e.g. apocope) whereas it is permitted in the *Metaphrasis*, e.g. ἡ μεθ' ὕβρεων ἀπαγωγή (Ch 587.87) > μετὰ ὕβρεως δίωξις (M 21.2.3) or οὐδ' αὐτὸς (Ch 126.60) > οὐδὲ αὐτὸς (M 5.1.1).

2.3 Morphosyntactical differences

Certain atticist nominal endings disappear in the Metaphrasis, such as the so-called attic declension νεώς, λεώς (> ναός, λαός, 'temple' and 'people' respectively) or the contracted comparative form πλείους > πλείονες 'more' (see also below).

---

[10] Van Dieten (1979) already demonstrated that this is not the vernacular used at the same time for literary texts in verse (see also Hinterberger 2016). Note, however, the various difficulties in defining "vernacular" Greek (Hinterberger 2006).
[11] More or less the same pattern is to be found in Anna Komnene's *Alexias*. On the history of τζ see *CGMG* (1.120–23).
[12] Choniates, *History* 359.4: ὁ τοῦ Δημητρίτζη λεγόμενος τόπος; 463.72–73 τὸ γὰρ φρούριον εἰσιών, ὃ Τζούγγρα κατονομάζεται.
[13] τζάγ(γ)ρα 'crossbow' being a loan word of Persian origin (cf. *LBG* s.v.).

When replaced, the dative corresponds with several periphraseis in the *Metaphrasis*, mostly μετά + genitive or διά + genitive. Frequently, however, the dative is retained, and it remains a fairly regular feature of the *Metaphrasis*, though considerably less frequent than in Choniates.[14]

The old monolectic perfect forms usually correspond with aorist forms in the *Metaphrasis*, both finite forms and participles, e.g. πέπομφε > ἀπέστειλε, ἠφάντωται > ἠφανίσθησαν, ἐξηπορηκώς > ἀπορήσας.[15] While a few perfect forms appear in the *Metaphrasis*, pluperfect forms disappear almost entirely (characteristically the form ἐγεγόνει with aorist meaning appears e.g. *Metaphrasis* 9.12.2). When they are replaced, they too correspond with the aorist: σέσωστο > ἐσώθην (ὁ βασιλεύς), ἠκηκόει > ἤκουσε.[16]

With a few exceptions, optative forms are rendered as subjunctives (Choniates alternates between the two forms).

The wide range of different participles in Choniates is generally reduced to certain morphological categories, particularly present and aorist participles in the *Metaphrasis*.[17]

The future participle, already rather rare in Choniates, corresponds with the aorist participle, e.g. ὀχήσοντα Ch 128.11–12 'the one who would/should administer' > προσενεγκόντα (M 5.1.5) or the aorist infinitive, e.g. συνέτρεχε ὀψόμενος 'he/she came running to see' (Ch 551.48) > συνέτρεχον θεάσασθαι (M 18.13) or a subordinate clause introduced with ὡς ἄν, e.g. τὰς πόλεις μετελευσομένη 'in order to punish the cities' (Ch 614.87) > ὡς ἄν διέλθωσι τὰς πόλεις (M 21.14.2).

Future infinitives are replaced with aorist infinitives: δράσειν 'to do' > ποιῆσαι, πείσεσθαι 'to suffer'> παθεῖν. However, a few new future infinitives

---

14 In the above short extract (texts 1 & 2) two out of five dative forms in Choniates are retained (τῷ ἄρχοντι, τῷ βασιλεῖ) in the *Metaphrasis*. In the 310 lines of Choniates' *History* (252.70–265.2), 158 dative forms (without articles) occur. In the corresponding part of the *Metaphrasis* (9.8.1–9.12.2) the number has dropped to 74.

15 In the 310 lines of Choniates' *History* (252.70–265.2), 24 perfect forms occur (six indicatives, three infinitives, 15 participles). In the corresponding part of the *Metaphrasis* (9.8.1–9.12.2) three of these forms are retained (one from each category), three perfect indicative forms as well as four perfect participles are replaced with aorist forms. Moreover, two new perfect forms appear (participles). More examples for the replacement of perfect forms with aorist forms are given in Hinterberger (2014a: 194).

16 Cf. Hinterberger (2007: 128–129).

17 In the 100 lines of Choniates' *History* (265.3–269.7), 76 participles occur. In the corresponding part of the *Metaphrasis* (9.12.3–7) the number has dropped to 47. Future participles (2 in Choniates) have disappeared, perfect participles have been reduced from 4 to 2. Already in Choniates nominative forms of the participle were dominant (62%), but in the *Metaphrasis* the percentage is even higher (71%).

appear in the *Metaphrasis* as an alternative for the aorist infinitive, particularly in combination with μέλλω (ἔμελλον) as a future (in the past) periphrasis.[18]

The frequent omission of the article before certain nouns (particularly ethnonyms and toponyms) must have been a quite disturbing feature in the *History* for anyone not very familiar with Ancient Greek texts. In these cases the article is regularly added (e.g. βασιλεύς 'emperor' > ὁ βασιλεύς, μετὰ Περσῶν 'with the Persians/Turks' > μετὰ τῶν Τούρκων, εἰς Ἱεροσόλυμα 'to Jerusalem' > εἰς τὰ Ἱεροσόλυμα). In comparison with the ancient language, Post-classical Greek had developed a need for 3rd person possessive pronouns even where they were semantically not necessary. This is reflected in the numerous additions of αὐτοῦ/αὐτῶν in the *Metaphrasis* (τῷ τεκόντι 'to the father' > τῷ αὐτοῦ πατρὶ 'to his father'). Interestingly, the language of the *Metaphrasis* required a different position for particles as well (οἱ δὲ βάρβαροι 'but the barbarians' (Ch 429.89) - οἱ βάρβαροι δέ (M 14.3.3), i.e. In the *Metaphrasis* the article cannot be separated from the noun by a particle).

On the other hand, in the *Metaphrasis* a few morphological features appear that are entirely alien to Choniates. The most frequent one is the vernacular nominal ending -ιν (e.g. φαρμάκιν 'poison').[19]

Occasionally verbal endings unknown to traditional grammar appear as well, such as the middle/passive 2nd person ending -εσαι, the indicative 3rd person plural -ωσιν or 3rd person middle/passive aorist -(θ)ην (identical with 1st person), e.g. ἐσώθην ὁ βασιλεὺς 'the emperor was rescued'.

The juxtaposition of Choniates' *History* and its *Metaphrasis* reveals how certain words or morphological categories were understood and used by Choniates (such as the pluperfect forms in the sense of an aorist). Similarly, this juxtaposition also sheds some light on the use of certain morphological categories in the *Metaphrasis*. The occasional final sense of the aorist participle in the *Metaphrasis*, as suggested by the context – a somewhat rare phenomenon outside of the *Metaphrasis*, I would say – is thus confirmed by the corresponding form in the *History*, a future participle. See e.g.:

(5) περιεσκόπουν τὸν τὴν θανατηφόρον κύλικα τῷ Στεφάνῳ ὀχήσοντα

'They were searching for someone to offer the death-bringing cup to Stephen' (Choniates, *History* 128.11–12) [tr. Magoulias 1984: 73]

---

18 E.g. *Metaphrasis* 13.6.7 μέλλει μὲν ἐλθεῖν καὶ εἰσελεύσεσθαι 'he will come and enter'; 13.2.1 ὡς δὲ παραχωρήσειν ἔμελλεν ὁ θεός 'since god would permit'; 13.3.5 καυχήσεσθαι ἔμελλον 'they would have boasted'.

19 E.g. *Metaphrasis* 9.10. The ending -ιν is used alongside the older alternative -ιον apparently without any semantic differentiation. On the phonological development leading to this ending see Horrocks (2010: 175–176) as well as *CGMG* (2.609–613).

(6) ἐγύρευον οὖν τὸν τὸ φάρμακον προσενεγκόντα αὐτῷ

'They were searching for someone to administer the poison to him' (*Metaphrasis* 5.1.5) [my translation]

2.4 Common features

Apart from the vocabulary that Choniates' *History* and the *Metaphrasis* have in common and which we have already mentioned, the vast majority of verbal and nominal endings are the same in both texts, too.

Despite their well-documented gradual disappearance from the living language, infinitives and participles are still in full use in the *Metaphrasis*, although formally and functionally restricted. Frequently, however, they are used in a way that violates syntactical rules of Ancient Greek (e.g. genitive absolute instead of a participle agreeing with a noun phrase in the main clause). Generally, there are many sentences which traditionally would be explained as anacoluthon constructions. In particular, there is a quite frequent appearance of nominative absolute constructions,[20] which recently have been interpreted as legitimate features of non-learned Medieval Greek.[21] Occasionally, participle and infinitive are combined in the same construction, indicating that their use was almost interchangeable (in certain contexts).

3 Levels/Varieties

From the comparison between the History and its Metaphrasis it becomes clear that both texts are closely related. Not only do they tell the same story, but also the sentence structure and word order (by and large) are generally the same in both texts. Until the beginning of the twentieth century the lower-level version was believed to be a draft version which Choniates later turned into his extremely artful *History*. Since the studies of van Dieten (1975), it has been firmly established that the second text is a later simplifying version based on the classicizing original.

---

[20] For examples see Hinterberger (2016: 142–143). On this kind of nominative absolute see also Horrocks (2010: 245–246).

[21] Cheila-Markopoulou (2003); see also Horrocks (2010: 246).

This parallel existence of two versions of the same text whose major difference consists in the linguistic composition has been regarded as quite characteristic of, and representing a general situation in, Byzantine literature, namely the coexistence of different registers or levels, be it linguistic or stylistic.[22] It is also broadly accepted that this diversity of linguistic levels is mainly a literary phenomenon, because the distribution of different varieties largely coincides with different literary genres. Historiography characteristically uses a high variety ("classicizing Greek"), whereas chronicle writing not only does not use a high variety, but very often shows clear traces of the influence of the spoken language (for this contrast see e.g. Prokopios and John Malalas who composed their texts, a history and a chronicle respectively, around the same time).[23] Clearly, in composing a historiographical work, the display of erudition was a *conditio sine qua non*.

Choniates' *History* belongs to the historiographical tradition; the *Metaphrasis*, as a result of simplification, could in some respects be seen as an attempt at the "chronicalization" of Choniates' text. In comparison with Choniates, the *Metaphrasis* not only omits and glosses over certain morphological and lexical categories, but it also dismisses almost all allusions to, and quotations from, Homer (which are very frequent in Choniates). Because of several erroneous renderings in the *Metaphrasis*, it is clear that the Metaphrast was neither especially familiar with Homeric language nor with the content of the Homeric poems. This indicates that within the Byzantine "educational system" he may not have progressed far beyond the first level of *grammatikê*/grammar.[24]

Geoffrey Horrocks (2014) has convincingly shown that the ubiquitous interchangeability of future indicative and aorist subjunctive forms, as well as optatives, in classicizing/learned texts reflect the status of the spoken language, in which futurity and modality were expressed by the same morphological categories. Following Horrocks (and motivated by my own findings)[25], it is my basic assumption that (at least morphosyntactically) all forms of the written language were essentially based on the spoken language (especially with regard to the deep structure of the texts). This means that even after many years of intensive literary study, Byzantines read Greek texts of previous centuries applying the linguistic competences which their spoken language provided them. They could, therefore, by imitation alone not obtain full command of those grammatical

---

[22] On varieties or levels in Byzantine Greek see Ševčenko (1981), Toufexis (2008).
[23] On Prokopios and John Malalas see Horrocks (2010: 231–233, 245–251).
[24] On education and language in Byzantium see Giannouli (2014).
[25] Hinterberger (2007; 2014a).

categories which once were elements of the spoken language, but had long disappeared from their mother tongue (e.g. dual, optative, pluperfect). Textbooks of standardized Classical Greek that traditionally supported the school curriculum were of little help in this respect, because they focused on morphology and contained very little syntax (mostly on prepositions and the *rectio verborum*). For the production of their own texts (when they were ambitious enough to aspire to write ἑλληνικά, "literary, stylistically and linguistically elaborate Greek", and not only to read it) authors often applied linguistic features present in older texts but absent in the spoken language, for stylistic reasons. These features served the "hellenization" of their texts (see the verbs ἑλληνίζω or ἐξελληνίζω).[26] As to how to use these "exotic" linguistic features, they followed the same principles by which they interpreted them when they encountered them in ancient or older Byzantine texts. Accordingly, they normally used pluperfect forms in the same way as aorist forms, i.e. as a marked variant or "morphological synonym" of aorist forms, because this is how they interpreted them in Ancient Greek texts (see e.g. Byzantine lexica), the aorist covering the same usage in contemporary spoken Byzantine Greek as did the pluperfect in Ancient Greek.[27] The same is true for optative forms functioning as future indicative or aorist subjunctive forms.[28] I believe that the same is the case for most of these atticizing/classicizing features that pop up in high style Byzantine texts such as in Choniates' *History*.

Since these classicizing elements were alternative forms marking the high variety of the written language, they do not constitute indispensable components of the language. They are therefore absent from such texts as the *Metaphrasis*. Thus, the question arises: by what criteria are these features used in the classicizing texts where they appear?

4 Classicizing markers (in Choniates and elsewhere)

When investigated diachronically, it becomes clear that the majority of the features which characterize our two varieties (Choniates – *Metaphrasis*), are to a

---

26 See e.g. Niketas Stethatos, *Life of Symeon the New Theologian* 2.25–27 (ed. Koutsas 1994): ἐλείπετο δὲ αὐτῷ ἐξελληνισθῆναι τὴν γλῶτταν τῇ ἀναλήψει παιδείας τῆς θύραθεν καὶ λόγου εὐμοιρῆσαι ῥητορικοῦ 'what he lacked was the hellenization of his tongue through the acquisition of outside/secular education as well as the acquisition of rhetorical discourse'.
27 Hinterberger (2007).
28 Horrocks (2014).

substantial degree identical with those features that are characteristic of the process to which Symeon the Metaphrast submitted the texts collected in his famous *Menologium* (second half of the tenth century; cf. Hinterberger 2014a, forthcoming c). This means that morphosyntactic features as well as vocabulary marking an elaborate variety of Byzantine Greek remain largely unchanged over many centuries. Because of their absence in the living language and because of the lack of clear rules pertaining to their use, the general appearance of all these features shows a high degree of inconsistency and diversity in Byzantine texts. Even a superficial investigation shows that they are used in very different ways by different authors (because – as I have already said – they are rather freely available, according to weakly defined rules, and they are not obligatory). Some authors use certain features frequently, others use the same features only rarely, and others not at all.

Most of these stylistically classicizing markers appear more frequently in Byzantine texts than they did in classical texts. Wahlgren (2005) has already demonstrated this for the dative.[29] The same is true for monolectic pluperfect forms.[30] On the other hand, certain features that are normal in classical Greek are avoided or relatively rare, because they are still in use in the usual, non-classicizing Byzantine language (such as μετά + genitive, cf. Hörmann 1938: 63–64). Due to their otherness, such markers of high-register language could develop other functions as well. Roderich Reinsch has recently shown that in Michael Psellos' *Chronographia* the frequently appearing dual often expresses irony or enhances a context emotively (Reinsch 2013).[31]

In the following pages I shall briefly present a few observations on how certain features that were regarded as characteristic of the Ancient Greek Attic dialect, and later of atticizing Greek, such as attic -ττ- and ξυν-, the attic declension and the personal pronouns σφῶν, σφίσι(ν), σφᾶς, were used by Choniates (and a few other authors).[32] With the exception of attic -ττ-, all these markers are entirely absent from the *Metaphrasis*.

4.1 Attic -ττ-

In the majority of verbal forms (κηρύττω/κηρύσσω 'to announce', πράττω/πράσσω 'to do', τάττω/τάσσω 'to array/order', φυλάττω/φυλάσσω 'to guard' and their

---

29 Cf. also Hörmann (1938: 85–105).
30 Hinterberger (2007).
31 Cf. also Horrocks (2010: 234).
32 As always the TLG is of invaluable help for such quantitative investigations.

compounds), Choniates uses -ττ- (134), but forms with -σσ- appear as well (20). In the case of θάλαττα/θάλασσα 'sea' the ratio is converse: -σσ- forms (53) are considerably more frequent than -ττ- forms (12). The adjective θαλάττιος, however, outnumbers its -σσ- alternative (18:3). Among the comparative forms ἐλάττων 'fewer/less', ἥττων 'worse', κρείττων 'better' Choniates clearly prefers the -ττ- variants (with the exception of κρεῖσσον all -σσ- forms are extremely rare).

4.2 Attic ἐς and ξυν-

The variant ἐς appears half as often as εἰς 'to' (630:1121), but ἐσ- is only exceptionally used as prefix instead of εἰσ-. Occasionally it can be observed that εἰς/ἐς alternate with each other for reasons of *variatio*; see e.g. τῶν δ' ἄλλων ἐς τὴν Ἀδριανοῦ συνδραμόντων ὡς εἰς σῶζον κρησφύγετον 'when the others gathered hastily in Adrianoupolis as if in a saving place of refuge' (Ch 614.9–10). On the other hand, Choniates does not use the preposition ξύν, but only the prefix ξυν- (though clearly less often than συν-).[33]

4.3 Attic declension

Forms of νεώς 'temple/church' are clearly more frequent than those of ναός (81:28), but the frequencies of λεώς 'people' and λαός are almost balanced (21:16).[34]

4.4 Contracted forms of the comparative

Usually uncontracted forms are more frequent than contracted forms. Yet in the case of χείρων 'worse', χείρω is more often (7) used than χείρονα (2). In a considerable number only contracted forms of πλείονες 'more'/πλείονας/ πλείονα are used. Both πλείους (33) and πλείω (18) clearly outnumber uncontracted πλείονες (3)/ πλείονας (7) and πλείονα (10). Contracted and uncontracted forms are obviously used without semantic differentiation as becomes clear from parallel passages

---

[33] Thucydides, *the* Attic historian, never uses εἰς and σύν only once. In Procopius the Attic forms still outnumber the Koine-forms (ἐς:εἰς 8:1, ξύν:σύν 12:1).
[34] It is particularly the genitive (νεώ 32) and accusative singular (νεών 35) forms of νεώς that are much more frequent than their ναός alternatives (ναοῦ 4, ναόν 9) whereas in the other cases the ratio is more balanced.

such as πρὸς ἅπαντας ἢ τοὺς πλείονας 'to all or most (of them)' (Ch 235.19–20) and τοὺς πλείους σχεδὸν ἢ τοὺς ἅπαντας 'almost most of them or all' (Ch 242.15). And again they are, at least occasionally, used for reasons of *variatio*; see e.g. στῆτε Ῥωμαῖοι· πλείους γὰρ πρὸς ἐλάττονας μαχεσόμεθα 'Stand your ground, Romans, for we who are more shall fight against fewer' (Ch 387.17–18).

4.5 Attic personal pronouns (plural forms σφῶν, σφίσι(ν), σφᾶς)

These personal pronouns disappeared from the living spoken language after the classical period.[35] They are entirely absent from texts composed in simple Hellenistic koine, such as the Septuagint and the New Testament. As typical features of Classical Attic prose, these forms are however used by atticist authors of the Imperial age.

Yet, even in the case of highly classicizing authors of the Early Byzantine period, such as Basil of Caesarea, these pronouns are surprisingly rare and are of course absent from non-classicizing authors of the Early Byzantine period (e.g. Romanos the Melode, John Malalas, Theophanes Confessor) and low-level saints' lives (e.g. the *Life* of Symeon Stylites the Younger). Nevertheless, Byzantine grammarians (e.g. George Choiroboskos [VIII–IX CE], Thomas Magistros [XIV CE]) treat them as normal 3rd person equivalents of the 1st and 2nd person pronouns ἡμεῖς and ὑμεῖς (without any further information on how or when they should be used).

A cursory investigation into later Byzantine texts shows that the plural forms are much more frequent than the corresponding singular forms (in Choniates e.g. only οἷ as well as οἱ are rarely used). In some authors (I restrict this investigation to highly learned authors, particularly of the eleventh–thirteenth century) σφῶν, σφίσι(ν), σφᾶς are practically absent (e.g. Psellos, or totally absent in Genesios), whereas in others they are very frequent (e.g. Pachymeres or the dative σφίσι(ν) in Kinnamos), which again confirms that they are not obligatory, i.e. a text can do without them, even rather learned ones. Among those authors who make frequent use of σφῶν, σφίσι(ν), σφᾶς, there is no consensus about their clitic or non-clitic

---

[35] It is noteworthy that already in Classical Greek the usage of these forms was not entirely consistent (as anaphoric and reflexive pronouns, occasionally even for the 1st and 2nd person). On their use in Ancient Greek see e.g. CGCG (89–91 = 7.2–3; 341 = 29.6), Cooper (2002: 2276–2280 = 2.51.1.14–2.51.2.4), Schwyzer (1950: 190–196; 1953: 607), Smyth (1920: 92 = §325.d), Jannaris (1897: 152 = §526), Kühner & Blass (1890–1892: I.2: 585, 588, 590–593, 596–599, especially §168).

status.³⁶ Both clitic and non-clitic forms are to be found in the same context, seemingly without semantic differentiation (e.g. in Choniates and Pachymeres).³⁷ Certain authors (such as George Akropolites) use σφῶν, σφίσι(ν), σφᾶς primarily in combination with αὐτός (i.e. emphatic forms), others (e.g. Theodore Prodromos), more rarely, use them together with ἑαυτός. In some cases, the overall profile of the usage of these pronouns appears to be quite characteristic for the author in case: it is a personal stylistic trait. During the age of late Byzantine high classicism these pronouns appear again as characteristic markers of a manneristic style, as *inter alia* the comparison of hagiographical texts of this period with their earlier models clearly shows.³⁸

Usually σφῶν, σφίσι(ν), and σφᾶς function as normal anaphoric or reflexive personal pronouns. As such they alternate with the less prestigious αὐτῶν, αὐτοῖς, αὐτούς/αὐτάς and ἑαυτῶν, ἑαυτοῖς, ἑαυτούς/ἑαυτάς respectively. In authors who make more than average use of σφῶν, σφίσι(ν), σφᾶς, the numbers for αὐτῶν, αὐτοῖς, αὐτούς/αὐτάς and ἑαυτούς, ἑαυτοῖς, ἑαυτῶν drop accordingly. Occasionally both variants are used side by side, apparently for no other reason than *variatio delectat* (see below). By certain authors, σφῶν, σφίσι(ν), and σφᾶς are also used for the 1st person plural. Not all cases are equally frequent. Generally, σφῶν functioning as a possessive pronoun appears in higher numbers than the other cases.

In Choniates σφῶν (33), σφίσι(ν) (70), σφᾶς (26) are rarer (129) than in Kinnamos' *History* (composed some 30 years before Choniates' *History*), but more frequent than in Anna Komnene's *Alexias* (composed some 50 years before Choniates' *History*).³⁹ Interestingly, these pronouns are much more

---

36 Already in Ancient Greek clitic and non clitic forms were barely distinguished; see e.g. Cooper (2002: 2273 = §2.51.1.4).

37 Here a more careful examination of the manuscripts is probably needed. Byzantine rules concerning the accentuation of clitics deviate considerably from Ancient Greek rules as they are traditionally taught in schools and universities (and therefore deviating accentuation tends to be tacitly corrected in modern editions). This has clearly been shown by Noret (2014). Since his meticulous investigation relied primarily on texts edited in the Corpus Christianorum series in which the appearance of σφῶν, σφίσι(ν), σφᾶς and their clitic equivalents is insignificant, no reliable data is available for clitic σφισι and σφας (σφῶν is never clitic).

38 Hinterberger (forthcoming b). Theodore Metochites but also Nicholas Kabasilas were particularly fond of attic personal pronouns.

39 In John Kinnamos' *History* σφίσι(ν) appears three times more often than in Choniates' text, whereas σφῶν and σφᾶς are equally frequent. Anna Komnene, whose *Alexias* is almost as long as Choniates' *History*, does not use the accusative form σφᾶς at all and σφίσι(ν) only twice. σφῶν is about as frequent as in Choniates.

frequent in the last part of Choniates' *History* (half of all attestations are in the last 100 pages), thus indicating a different date of composition for this section.⁴⁰

As already mentioned, σφῶν, σφίσι(ν), σφᾶς disappears in the *Metaphrasis*, being either totally omitted or replaced with more common pronominal forms.⁴¹ Here, again, the replacement of the classicizing pronouns in the *Metaphrasis* illuminates their use in Choniates' text. Whenever σφῶν, σφίσι(ν), or σφᾶς are replaced, they correspond with αὐτῶν, αὐτοῖς, αὐτούς (ἑαυτούς). This confirms their use as both anaphoric and reflexive pronouns, the simply anaphoric and the reflexive not being clearly distinguished in many medieval texts and perhaps in Medieval Greek in general.⁴²

Choniates, too, uses those pronouns which replace σφῶν, σφίσι(ν), and σφᾶς in the *Metaphrasis*, and much more often than the atticizing pronouns. Both are used side by side, as alternative forms. This raises the question whether we can establish a certain pattern or rule, when and why σφῶν, σφίσι(ν), σφᾶς are applied. In the following passage the classicizing forms appear alongside the common pronoun, for no other reason it seems, than to avoid repetition:

(7) ὡς μὴ συνᾷδον **αὐτοῖς** οὐ προσίενται, φιλοῦσι δὲ τὸ σαφὲς ὡς [. . .] συμβαῖνόν **σφισι** μάλιστα.

'They do not approach obscurity as something that does not fit them, but they cherish clarity as being particularly appropriate to them.'
(Niketas Choniates, *History* 3.36–38) [tr. Magoulias 1984: 3]

(8) οὐχ ὡς βασιλεὺς φίλοις, ἀλλ' ὡς ὑπηρέτης δεσπόταις προσδιαλέγεσθαι **σφίσιν** ἐν τοῖς πρὸς **αὐτοὺς** ἐπετάττετο γράμμασι.

'He had been instructed to address them in the letters to them not as an emperor (greets) his friends, but as a servant his masters.'
(Niketas Choniates, *History* 613.58–60) [tr. Magoulias 1984: 336]

---

40 On the various stages of composition of Choniates' *History* see Simpson (2006).
41 The same is the case in the *Epitome* of Georges Pachymeres' History (beginning of fourteenth century); see Failler (2004: 104–105). Being primarily an abbreviation rather than a *metaphrasis*, the *Epitome* occasionally retains the classicizing pronoun.
42 See e.g. Reinsch (2014: XXXIII) for Psellos' *Chronographia*.

The same is true for the next example where we observe one of the rare cases of the singular form:

(9) ᾤετο τοὺς ἐπὶ τῆς φρουρᾶς καταπροδοῦναί **οἱ** τὸ φρούριον καὶ σφᾶς προσαναθήσειν **αὐτῷ**.

'He thought that the guards would surrender the fortress to him and deliver themselves over to him.'
(Niketas Choniates, *History* 87.23–24) [tr. Magoulias 1984: 51]

As well as in a passage from Anna's *Alexias*:

(10) τὸ δὲ δὴ χεῖρον ὅτι οὐδὲ οἱ αὐτόχθονες τῶν τοιούτων ἀφίσταντο πράξεων, ἀλλ' οἷον ἐκλαθόμενοι **ἑαυτῶν** καὶ τὰ **σφῶν** ἤθη ἐπὶ τὸ χεῖρον ἀμείψαντες ἀνερυθριάστως καὶ αὐτοὶ ἅπερ οἱ βάρβαροι ἔπραττον.

'Indeed the worst feature was that not even the natives themselves abstained from these deeds but as though they forgot themselves and changed their manners for the worse, they shamelessly did themselves exactly the same things as the barbarians.'
(Anna Komnene, *Alexias* 2.10.4; ed. Reinsch and Kambylis 2001) [tr. Dawes 1928: 66]

The more subtle criteria for the use of σφῶν, σφίσι(ν), σφᾶς still have to be explored. Apart from their general classicizing function, they obviously appear when an alternative form is needed for various reasons. As in other cases of alternative forms, these reasons may be metrical (in poems) or generally rhythmical, as in rhetorical prose. Elsewhere it seems that by using them the author puts a certain emphasis on the personal pronoun, in contrast to a less emphatic variant.[43]

5 Conclusion

In Choniates' *History* both highly classicizing features and elements of the common written language are used side by side. Two, three or even more lexical and morphosyntactic variants give the text a particularly rich and colourful appearance. A well balanced mixture of alternative forms and alternative constructions (usual and less usual ones) seems to have been one of the author's aesthetic principles.

Returning to the initial question of how to characterize different varieties of written Byzantine Greek, I propose to use the Byzantine koine as the point of reference (rather than Ancient Greek). Through the centuries, this "common written language" can be defined by the absence of both decidedly outdated and

---

43 Cf. Reinsch (2013) for the dual.

innovative morphosyntactic elements. It constitutes a compromise between conservativism and modernism. Innovative elements are all those which are not recorded in traditional grammars. Obsolete are all those morphological categories which had disappeared from the living language for centuries already (e.g. dual, pluperfect, optative as well as the "attic" features discussed above). The vast majority of Byzantine texts are written in a linguistic variety that aims at such a compromise. Other texts, for various reasons, depart from this common written language, either by incorporating outdated linguistic material, taken from Ancient Greek, or by using forms that were totally alien to the written standard as defined by traditional textbooks.

For reasons of convenience and convention, we may continue to label these departures from the common written language as classicizing (or rather classicized) on the one hand, and vernacular on the other, but in both cases one should specify in which respect a specific text classicizes or is vernacular, and to what degree – because there is hardly a Byzantine text that is totally one or the other. In other words, we should explore which classicizing/ vernacular features appear, how often they appear (ideally in relation to the "normal" alternative forms, e.g. ναός : νεώς, σφᾶς : (ἐ)αυτούς, pluperfect : aorist; -ιν : ιον, -εσαι : -ου, future periphrasis : monolectic future), how they are distributed throughout the entire text, what are the exact semantics of these features, and finally, why they are used in the first place.[44] By posing these questions to our texts, we will probably observe that, for instance, a specific text displays some classicizing features, but not others, that in certain respects it is rather conservative, and in other respects (e.g. vocabulary) less so.[45] But before we can establish a definitive list of characteristic elements suitable for gauging the classicism or vernacularness of Byzantine texts, much more in-depth analysis of these texts in needed. One important step would be a thorough investigation of texts which are generally regarded as representative of the Byzantine written koine, for instance the great majority of saints' lives or chronicles.[46] Only when we properly understand how the common written koine works will we be able to appreciate fully the artful linguistic otherness of texts such as Choniates' *History*.

---

44 Karyolemou (2014).
45 On the use of vernacular vocabulary in otherwise learned texts see Trapp (1993).
46 See also the parallel investigation into Anna Komnene's *Alexias* and Michael Glykas' *Chronicle* undertaken by Hunger (1978).

References

Browning, Robert. 1978. The language of Byzantine literature. In Spyros Vryonis, Jr (ed.), *The past in Medieval and Modern Greek culture*, 103–133. Malibu: Undena.
Cheila-Markopoulou, Despoina. 2003. Προτασιακότητα και μετοχικές δομές στην Αλεξανδρινή και Μεσαιωνική Ελληνική. In Dimitra Theophanopoulou-Kontou, Chrysoula Laskaratou, Maria Sifianou, Michalis Georgiafentis & Vasilis Spyropoulos (eds.), *Σύγχρονες τάσεις στην ελληνική γλωσσολογία: μελέτες αφιερωμένες στην Ειρήνη Φιλιππάκη-Warburton*, 128–143. Athens: Pataki.
Cooper, Guy L. 2002. *Greek Syntax*. Vol. 3: *Early Greek poetic and Herodotean syntax*. Ann Arbor: University of Michigan Press.
Davis, John. 2004. *Η μετάφραση της Χρονικής Διηγήσεως του Νικήτα Χωνιάτη*. PhD dissertation, University of Ioannina.
Davis, John. 2009. The history metaphrased: Changing readership in the fourteenth century. In Alicia Simpson & Stephanos Efthymiadis (eds.), *Niketas Choniates: A historian and a writer*, 145–163. Genève: La Pomme d'Or.
Davis, John. 2010. Anna Komnena and Niketas Choniates 'translated': The fourteenth century Byzantine metaphrases. In Ruth Macrides (ed.), *History as literature: Papers from the 40th Spring Symposium of Byzantine Studies, University of Birmingham, April 2007*, 55–70. Farnham: Ashgate.
Davis, John & Martin Hinterberger. Forthcoming. *The Metaphrasis of Niketas Choniates' Chronike Diegesis*. Berlin: de Gruyter.
Dawes, Elizabeth A. (ed.). 1928. *The Alexiad of the Princess Anna Comnena: Being the history of the reign of her father, Alexius I, Emperor of the Romans, 1081–1118*. London: Routledge & K. Paul.
van Dieten, Ioannes A. 1975. *Nicetae Choniatae, Historia*. Berlin: de Gruyter.
van Dieten, Jan-Louis. 1979. Bemerkungen zur Sprache der sogenannten vulgärgriechischen Niketasparaphrase. *Byzantinische Forschungen* 6. 37–77.
Eideneier, Hans. 1982. Review of Hunger (1981). *Südostforschungen* 41. 589–90.
Failler, Albert. 2004. *La version brève des Relations Historiques de Georges Pachymérès III. Index*. Paris: Institut Français d'Études Byzantines.
Giannouli, Antonia. 2014. Education and literary language in Byzantium. In Martin Hinterberger (ed.), *The language of learned Byzantine literature*, 52–71. Turnhout: Brepols.
Hinterberger, Martin. 2006. How should we define vernacular literature? (paper delivered at the conference 'Unlocking the potential of texts: Interdisciplinary perspectives on Medieval Greek' held in Cambridge 18–19 July 2006, available at ucy.academia.edu/MartinHinterberger).
Hinterberger, Martin. 2007. Die Sprache der byzantinischen Literatur: Der Gebrauch der synthetischen Plusquamperfektformen. In Martin Hinterberger & Elisabeth Schiffer (eds.), *Byzantinische Sprachkunst: Studien zur byzantinischen Literatur, gewidmet Wolfram Hörandner zum 65. Geburtstag*, 107–142. Berlin: de Gruyter.
Hinterberger, Martin. 2014a. The synthetic perfect in Byzantine literature. In Martin Hinterberger (ed.), *The language of learned Byzantine literature*, 176–204. Turnhout: Brepols.

Hinterberger, Martin. 2014b. Between simplification and elaboration: Byzantine Metaphraseis in comparison. In Juan Signes Codoñer & Inmaculada Pérez Martín (eds.), *Textual transmission in Byzantium: Between textual criticism and Quellenforschung*, 33–60. Turnhout: Brepols.

Hinterberger, Martin. 2016. Bemerkungen zur Sprache der Choniates-Metaphrase. In Ulrich Moennig (ed.), «. . . ὡς ἀθύρματα παῖδας»: *Festschrift für Hans Eideneier*, 135–150. Berlin: Romiosini.

Hinterberger, Martin. Forthcoming a. The language of Byzantine literature. In Stratis Papaioannou (ed.), *The Oxford handbook of Byzantine literature*. Oxford: Oxford University Press.

Hinterberger, Martin. Forthcoming b. The hagiographical encomium as metaphrasis in the Paleologan period. In Christian Høgel & Stavroula Constantinou (eds.), *Metaphrasis: A Byzantine concept of rewriting and its hagiographical products*, 285–323. Leiden: Brill.

Hinterberger, Martin. Forthcoming c. Metaphrasis as a key for the understanding of different levels in Byzantine vocabulary. In Ann Alwis, Martin Hinterberger & Elisabeth Schiffer (eds.), *Metaphrasis in Byzantine literature*. Turnhout: Brepols.

Hörmann, Fritz. 1938. *Beiträge zur Syntax des Kinnamos*. PhD Diss., University of Munich.

Horrocks, Geoffrey. 2010. *Greek: A history of the language and its speakers*, 2nd ed. Malden: Wiley-Blackwell.

Horrocks, Geoffrey. 2014. High-register Medieval Greek: 'Diglossia' and what lay behind it. In Caterina Carpinato & Olga Tribulato (eds.), *Storia e storie della lingua greca*, 49–72. Venezia: Edizioni Ca' Foscari.

Hunger, Herbert. 1978. Stilstufen in der byzantinischen Geschichtsschreibung des 12. Jahrhunderts: Anna Komnene und Michael Glykas. *Byzantine Studies* 5. 139–170.

Hunger, Herbert. 1981. *Anonyme Metaphrase zu Anna Komnene, Alexias XI–XIII: Ein Beitrag zur Erschließung der byzantinischen Umgangssprache*. Wien: Österreichische Akademie der Wissenschaften.

Hunger, Herbert & Ihor Ševčenko. 1988. *Des Nikephoros Blemmydes Βασιλικὸς Ἀνδριάς und dessen Metaphrase von Georgios Galesiotes und Georgios Oinaiotes: Ein weiterer Beitrag zum Verständnis der byzantinischen Schrift-Koine*. Wien: Österreichische Akademie der Wissenschaften.

Jannaris, Antonius N. 1968 [1897]. *An historical Greek grammar chiefly of the Attic dialect as written and spoken from Classical Antiquity down to present time founded upon the ancient texts, inscriptions, papyri and present popular Greek*. Hildesheim: Georg Olms.

Karyolemou, Marilena. 2014. What can sociolinguistics tell us about learned literary languages? In Martin Hinterberger (ed.), *The language of learned Byzantine literature*, 34–51. Turnhout: Brepols.

Koutsas, Symeon. 1994. *Νικήτα τοῦ Στηθάτου Βίος καὶ Πολιτεία τοῦ ἐν ἁγίοις πατρὸς ἡμῶν Συμεὼν τοῦ Νέου Θεολόγου*. Athens: Akritas.

Kühner, Raphael & Friedrich Blass. 1890–1892. *Ausführliche Grammatik der griechischen Sprache*, vol. I.1–2, 3rd ed. Hannover: Hahnsche Buchhandlung.

Magoulias, Harry J. 1984. *O City of Byzantium, Annals of Niketas Choniatês*. Detroit: Wayne State University Press.

Noret, Jacques. 2014. L'accentuation Byzantine: En quoi et pourquoi elle diffère de l'accentuation «savante» actuelle, parfois absurde. In Martin Hinterberger (ed.), *The language of learned Byzantine literature*, 96–146. Turnhout: Brepols.

Reinsch, Diether R. 2013. Der Dual als Mittel literarischer Gestaltung in Michael Psellos' Chronographia. *Byzantinische Zeitschrift* 106. 133–142.
Reinsch, Diether R. 2014. *Michaelis Pselli Chronographia*. Berlin: de Gruyter.
Reinsch, Diether R. & Athanasios Kambylis. 2001. *Annae Comnenae Alexias*. Berlin: de Gruyter.
Ševčenko, Ihor. 1981. Levels of style in Byzantine prose. *Jahrbuch der Österreichischen Byzantinistik* 31. 289–312.
Schwyzer, Eduard. 1950–1953. *Griechische Grammatik: Auf der Grundlage von Karl Brugmanns griechischer Grammatik*. München: Beck.
Simpson, Alicia. 2006. Before and after 1204: The versions of Niketas Choniates' *Historia*. *Dumbarton Oaks Papers* 60. 189–222.
Simpson, Alicia. 2013. *Niketas Choniates: A historiographical study*. Oxford: Oxford University Press.
Simpson, Alicia & Stephanos Efthymiadis (eds.). 2009. *Niketas Choniates: A historian and a writer*. Genève: La Pomme d'Or.
Smyth, Herbert W. 1920. *Greek Grammar*. Cambridge: Harvard University Press.
Toufexis, Notis. 2008. Diglossia and register variation in Medieval Greek. *Byzantine & Modern Greek Studies* 32. 203–217.
Trapp, Erich. 1993. Learned and vernacular literature in Byzantium: Dichotomy or symbiosis? *Dumbarton Oaks Papers* 47. 115–129.
Wahlgren, Staffan. 2005. Modern Greek in 10th c. AD. In Vassilios Sabatakakis & Peter Vejleskov (eds.), *Filia: Studies in honour of Bo-Lennart Eklund*, 177–182. Lund: The authors and the editors.

Mark Janse

9 Back to the future: Akritic light on diachronic variation in Cappadocian (East Asia Minor Greek)

Abstract: Cappadocian is an East Asia Minor Greek variety most closely related to Pharasiot and Pontic. Having been cut off from the rest of the Greek-speaking world after the defeat of the Byzantine army by the Seljuk Turks in the battle at Manzikert (1071), Cappadocian was increasingly Turkicized, but the Greek component preserved its essentially Late Medieval Greek character. Unfortunately, our evidence for the historical development of Cappadocian is very scanty, consisting as it does of a few dozen inscriptions from the famous "rock-cut" churches of Cappadocia and the Greek poems written in Arabic script by the thirteenth-century Persian poet-scholar Rūmī and his son Sultan Walad. In this chapter I analyze new and hitherto unexplored evidence for diachronic variation in Cappadocian: Medieval Akritic songs orally transmitted through the ages in Cappadocia. The language of these songs, composed in the traditional Byzantine decapentasyllable or political verse, is a mixture of Late Medieval / Early Modern Greek and nineteenth-century Cappadocian, linguistically reminiscent of the Ancient Greek epic, which also combined archaic and innovative features in a set metrical framework. Apart from loanwords and grammatical patterns borrowed from Turkish, the so-called "Byzantine residue" of Cappadocian offers a unique glimpse of language variation and change in Late Medieval / Early Modern Greek.

1 Introduction: diachronic variation in Cappadocian

Cappadocian is perhaps the most famous representative of what is commonly referred to as "Asia Minor Greek", ever since it was presented as a prime example of heavy borrowing in Thomason and Kaufman's groundbreaking study of language contact (1988: 215–222).[1] Their use of the term was inspired by the

---

[1] Research for this chapter was done within the framework of a collaborative research project funded by the HERA network entitled 'Multilingualism and Minority Languages in Ancient Europe' (HERA.15.029). Embryonic versions of section 2 were presented at the U4 Winter School in Istanbul (2012), at the Seeger Center for Hellenic Studies of Princeton University (2017), at the Netherlands Institute at Athens (2019) and, obviously, at our 'Varieties' conference. I thank the

https://doi.org/10.1515/9783110614404-009

title of Dawkins' *Modern Greek in Asia Minor*, who explicitly restricted it to the dialects "native to Asia Minor" (D5), especially the dialects of Cappadocia, Pharasa and Pontus, which "must be regarded as having at one time formed a continuous linguistic area" (D205), referred to as "the medieval Greek dialect of eastern Asia Minor" (D213). It is therefore better to call this dialectal subgroup "East Asia Minor Greek" (Janse 2008: 190) and to use the term "Asia Minor Greek" exclusively as a geographic designation to include all the "varieties of Greek spoken in the Asia Minor peninsula" from the Middle Ages until the early twentieth century.[2] East Asia Minor Greek is a medieval descendant of the Asia Minor or Anatolian Koine.[3] Its subgrouping is a matter of controversy, the details of which need not detain us here.[4] The "accepted genealogical classification" (Karatsareas 2011: 50), based on Janse (2008: 191), is given in Figure 1 (where the dotted lines indicate contact zones). The subgrouping of the Cappadocian dialects is displayed in Table 1 (based on Janse 2008: 191).[5]

---

various audiences for insightful thoughts and comments, particularly Emmanuel Bourbouhakis and Brian D. Joseph. Special thanks are due to Marjolijne Janssen for her expert comments on an earlier version of this chapter, to Wolfgang de Melo and Federica Lazzerini for providing me with a digital photocopy of Levidis (1892), and to Nick 'Opoudjis' Nicholas for sending me a copy of Dedes (1993).

Abbreviations used in this chapter: AncGr = Ancient Greek, Cappa = Cappadocian, CC = Central Cappadocian, EMedGr = Early Medieval Greek, EModGr = Early Modern Greek, Lat. = Latin, LMedGr = Late Medieval Greek, MedGr = Medieval Greek, ModGr = Modern Greek, NEC = Northeast Cappadocian, NWC = Northwest Cappadocian, PcGr = Post-classical Greek, SEC = Southeast Cappadocian, SWC = Southwest Cappadocian, Tk. = Turkish.

2 Cf. Ralli (2019: 8–12), Manolessou (2019: 20).
3 On the Asia Minor or Anatolian Koine see Bubeník (1989: 237–252; 2014: 285), Brixhe (1987; 2010).
4 The controversy concerns the position of Pharasiot within the Proto-Cappadocian subgroup of East Asia Minor Greek. Dawkins (D206), followed by Andriotis (1948: 10), Anastasiadis (1975: 177; 1976: 16; 1995: 111–119), Janse (e.g. 2008: 190–191; 2020: §4) groups Pharasiot with Pontic; Kontosopoulos (1994: 10), followed by Janse in earlier publications (e.g. 1998b: 523), groups Pharasiot with Cappadocian; Karatsareas (2011: 53; 2013: 207–208) considers Pharasiot to be a subbranch separate from Cappadocian-Pontic. Instead of East Asia Minor Greek, Manolessou uses the term "Inner Asia Minor Greek" (2019: 20, 29), which is confusing, as it was used by Kontosopoulos to refer to Cappadocian-Pharasiot as a subbranch separate from Pontic (1994: 10; cf. Janse 1998b: 523).
5 The division between North, Central and South Cappadocian is due to Dawkins (D211), who also presents arguments to group Delmeso, geographically southwest, with Sinasos and Potamia, geographically northeast (D10 & D211). The consequential grouping of Silata, Anaku, Floïta and Malakopi is confirmed by Costakis (1964: 9). Dawkins considers Ulağaç and Semendere as a separate group within South Cappadocian (D18; cf. Kesisoglou 1951: 2–3), and also notes the intimate connection between Aravan and Ghurzono (D18; cf. Phosteris & Kesisoglou 1960: ι´).

9 Back to the future: Akritic light on diachronic variation in Cappadocian — 203

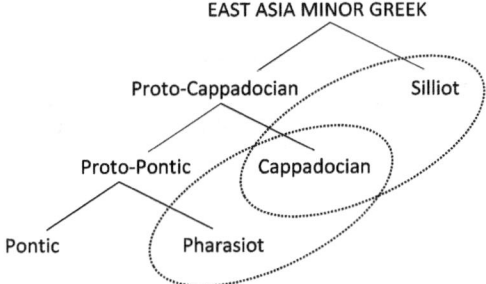

Figure 1: The accepted genealogical classification of the East Asia Minor Greek dialects.

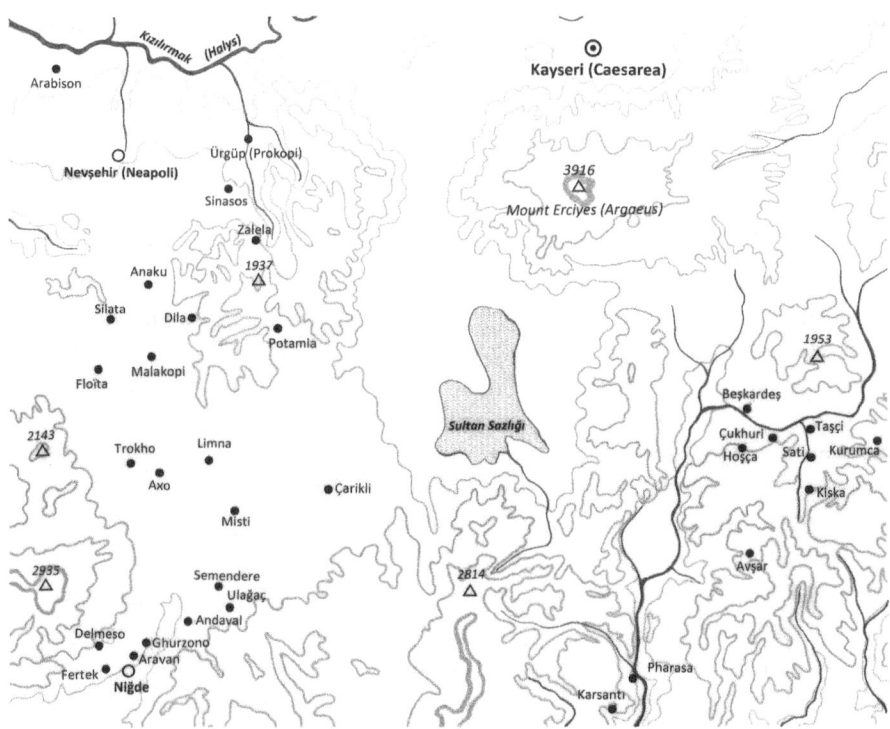

Map 1: Geographical distribution of Cappadocian and Pharasiot.

Our information about the historical development of Cappadocian is largely indirect. An interesting discussion of the evidence provided by loanwords is given by Dawkins (D193-197). Noting the "rarity of Italian words in the vocabulary", he concludes that Cappadocian was separated, culturally as well as geographically,

Table 1: Subgrouping of the Cappadocian dialects.

NORTH CAPPADOCIAN		
NORTHWEST CAPPADOCIAN – Floïta – Silata – Anaku – Malakopi		**NORTHEAST CAPPADOCIAN** – Sinasos – Potamia – Delmeso
	CENTRAL CAPPADOCIAN – Axo – Misti	
	SOUTH CAPPADOCIAN	
SOUTHWEST CAPPADOCIAN – Aravan – Ghurzono – Fertek		**SOUTHEAST CAPPADOCIAN** – Ulağaç – Semendere

from "the rest of Greek" during the long period of Italian domination, beginning with the Fourth Crusade (1202–1204) (D193).[6] The abundance of Latin loanwords, on the other hand, indicates that Cappadocian was "in full connexion with the rest of the Greek world in the early Byzantine period" and that "the separation came later, and before the appearance of the Italian words" and was "due to the arrival of the Turks in Asia Minor, where the Seljuks were fully settled by the latter part of the eleventh century" (D195), following the defeat of the Byzantine army at the battle of Manzikert (1071).[7]

The Turkicization of Cappadocian extended over a long period from the twelfth century until the exchange of populations between Greece and Turkey in 1923–1924. Writing in 1915, Dawkins has this to say about the extent of "the Turkish element" in Cappadocian: "as the language of dominant race, its influence is steadily increasing, even to the point of crowding the dialect out of existence altogether" (D197). The Turkicization of Cappadocian was such that Thomason

---

6 When Dawkins conducted his fieldwork (1909–1911), he noted an increase in Italian loanwords, "not in itself, but as part of the growing influence of the common Greek at such villages as Sinasos and Potamia" (D197).

7 The literature on the Turkish conquest of Asia Minor and its political and military consequences is abundant, but Vryonis' account remains a classic statement (1971: 69–142).

and Kaufman present it as their first case study, labelling it "an excellent example of heavy borrowing" (1988: 215), category 5 (the highest) in their borrowing scale (1988: 74–76).[8] They make the very interesting observation that most dialects "clearly retain enough inherited Greek material to count as Greek dialects in the full genetic sense," but "a few dialects may be close to or even over the border of nongenetic development" (1988: 93–94), an idea developed in more detail in Janse (2007).[9] Especially the Southeast Cappadocian dialects of Ulağaç and Semendere are typologically closer to Turkish than to Greek, having vowel harmony, agglutinative morphology and SOV-type word order.[10]

Extremely interesting as these Turkish features may be, much more relevant for the purpose of the present volume is what Vryonis calls the "Byzantine residue" (1971: 444–497) of Cappadocian, which Kitromilides considers "a form of idiomatic Medieval Greek" (1990: 5). This is immediately apparent from the great number of MedGr words in the Cappadocian lexicon (Janse 2020: §11), but also from the great number of grammatical archaisms, e.g. the retention of the so-called 'postpositive article' as relative pronoun,[11] the retention of the AncGr possessive adjectives ἐμός, σός, ἡμέτερος, ὑμέτερος in a variety of forms,[12] the retention of the AncGr interrogative pronoun τίς,[13] the retention of the aorist passive in -ην instead of -ηκα,[14] the retention of the PcGr / MedGr order of clitic pronouns,[15] the retention of να with the subjunctive to express a simple

---

[8] Cappadocian is also assigned a prominent position in Winford (2005: 402–409).
[9] Elsewhere, I have compared the Cappadocian language-dialect continuum with a creole continuum (Janse 2009: 38).
[10] For a general survey see Dawkins (D197–203), Janse (2009).
[11] Cf. Dawkins (D127), Janse (1999; 2020: §8.2.5.2). In LMedGr, the relative pronoun τόν, τήν, τό is "very frequent in lower-register texts" and has been called "the commonest form of the relative pronoun" (*CGMG* 2.1098).
[12] Cf. Dawkins (D122–124), Janse (2020: §7.4.2). These had become "residual forms" in LMedGr, as they "disappeared from spoken use in the first millennium" (*CGMG* 2.914).
[13] Cf. Dawkins (D126), Janse (2020: §7.4.7). In LMedGr and EModGr the ModGr interrogative pronoun ποῖος > ποιός "is fully synonymous with τίς, but is employed much more frequently" (*CGMG* 2.1004 & 2.1010).
[14] The actual endings are often active instead of passive, frequently a mixture of both, e.g. Delmeso (ἐ)λύθα, -θης, -θην, -θαμ', -θετε, -θαν (D145). The disappearance of the old endings in LMedGr was a "gradual process" (*CGMG* 3.1630).
[15] Cf. Janse (1993; 1994; 1998a; 2020: §8.2.3.1); for MedGr see Horrocks (1990), Mackridge (1993b; 2000), *CGMG* (4.2026–2037).

future.[16] Most of these archaisms are also attested in Pharasiot and Pontic and can safely be regarded as features of the East Asia Minor variety of MedGr.

Unfortunately, the written evidence for the diachronic development of Cappadocian is very scanty. Manolessou (2019: 29–34) provides a useful summary of the little we have: inscriptions from the Cappadocian rock-cut churches (9th-11th c.) and the Greek poems written in Arabic script by the Persian philosopher Rūmī and his son Sultan Walad (13th-14th c.), which have been identified as representing Cappadocian as spoken in the LMedGr period on the basis of a number of distinctive features,[17] e.g. the postalveolarization before [i] of [s] and [z] to [ʃ] and [ʒ] respectively,[18] the replacement of the dative by the accusative,[19] and many distinctive lexical items such as γιορών [joron] or γιόρος [jóros] 'old man'.[20]

Unfortunately, there is no other direct evidence for either. In the case of Cappadocian, we have to wait until the nineteenth century before we get the first reports about the villages and their dialects, usefully summarized by Dawkins (D11-12). Among these is a manuscript by Anastasios Levidis (1892), a schoolmaster from Zincidere near Kayseri (Caesarea), containing "a valuable collection of folk-songs", the publication of which he considered "greatly to be desired" (D32). Dawkins later acquired the manuscript from the author's heir and from it published a Byzantine carol in honour of St. Basil (1946) and four folk songs from Cappadocia (1934).[21] The manuscript is now part of the "Papers of Richard Dawkins" collection of the Bodleian Library at Oxford, on loan from Exeter College, of which Dawkins was a fellow.[22] In the next section, I discuss the importance of these folk songs for the history of Cappadocian and analyze one of them in detail in comparison with another version of the same song recorded by Pavlos Karolidis and published by Lagarde (1886: 17–18).

---

16 Cf. Dawkins (D626), Janse (2020: §7.6.1.5). "Futurative" (ἵ)να + subj. was used throughout the EMedGr and LMedGr periods, but "with decreasing frequency" in the EModGr period (*CGMG* 3.1768).
17 Cf. Theodoridis (2004: 433), Kappler (2010: 385), Manolessou (2019: 32).
18 Cf. Dawkins (D71), Janse (2020: §6.2.2.5.3).
19 Cf. Janse (2020: §8.2.1).
20 Dedes reads γιόρον (1993: 17), Theodoridis γιορών (2005: 437) for يورون ywrwn in Sultan Walad's *ġazal* 83.2b. Both forms are distinctively Cappadocian (D592 s.v. γέρος) ~ LMedGr γέρος (*LME*) < AncGr γέρων (LSJ).
21 The first of the four folksongs from Cappadocia is actually a Pontic song recorded at Karipler, a Pontic colony in the Akdağ ('White Mountain'), south of Tokat (Dawkins 1934: 113).
22 The Rector and Fellows of Exeter College have kindly granted me written permission in 2007 to publish, in whole or in part, the Levidis manuscript. For this reason I obtained a digital photocopy of the manuscript in 2017.

2 Akritic songs from Cappadocia: Variation and change

The four folk songs (δημοτικά τραγούδια)[23] published by Dawkins (1934) belong to the category of the so-called 'akritic songs' (ακριτικά τραγούδια):[24] heroic poems traditionally sung in 'political verse' (πολιτικός στίχος).[25] The name obviously suggests a relationship with the Late Byzantine epic-romance Διγενής Ἀκρίτης (Jeffreys 1998).[26] The hero's name is Basil (Βασίλειος), whose epithet διγενής means 'double-born' or 'of double descent': his father was an Arab emir who abducted the daughter of the governor of the Byzantine Theme of Cappadocia. His second epithet ακρίτης means 'frontiersman', not necessarily in a military sense, but more commonly to designate "inhabitants at the extremities of imperial territory" (Cappel 1991: 47). Basil's Cappadocian ancestry is often referred to:[27] ὁ θαυμαστὸς Καππάδοκας 'the marvellous Cappadocian' (*Dig.* E1092), τὸν Διγενῆ Καππάδοκα 'the Double-Blooded Cappadocian' (*Dig.* G3.106), τῶν Καππαδόκων ὁ τερπνὸς καὶ πανευθαλὴς ἔρνος 'the Cappadocian's delightful and all-flourishing offspring' (*Dig.* G7.2).[28]

It comes as no surprise, then, that akritic songs have always been very popular in Cappadocia,[29] where they continued to be sung until the population exchange in the 1920s. In the Pontic song from Karipler the hero's name is Ἀκρίτας (Dawkins 1934: 113), in the Cappadocian song from Potamia Ἀκρίτης (1934: 117), in other songs it is Διγενής or a related or even entirely unrelated form (Jeffreys 1991: 48), but the two are rarely found in combination (Jeffreys 1998: xv). What exactly counts as an akritic song or whether there even exists a separate such category is again a matter of much dispute.[30] Several themes have been identified as being truly 'akritic' (Jeffreys 1991: 48): the abduction of the bride,[31] the building of the castle, the wrestling with Charos (Charon) and

---

23 Levidis uses the term δημώδη ᾄσματα (1892: ch. Δ´ - the manuscript is unpaginated).
24 The best-known collections of akritic songs are Politis (1909) and Lüdeke (1994).
25 On the metrical structure of the decapentasyllable or political verse see Mackridge (1990), Lauxtermann (1999; 2019: 265–384), Jeffreys (2019).
26 The nature of the relationship has been the subject of much research and controversy which will not concern us here; see, for instance, Jeffeys (1991), Mackridge (1993a), Saunier (1993).
27 The epithet was included in the subtitle of Ioannidis' edition of the now lost Trebizond (T) version (1887; cf. Jeffreys 1998: xxi–xxii).
28 References are to the Escorial (E) and Grottaferrata (G) versions as edited by Jeffreys (1998).
29 As well as in Pontus, Cyprus and Crete (Jeffreys 1998: xv).
30 See especially Saunier (1993).
31 On this particular theme see Mackridge (1993a).

the ultimate death of the protagonist.[32] The last three themes are represented in the Pontic song from Karipler (Dawkins 1934: 113) and in the Cappadocian song from Potamia (1934: 117). The second Cappadocian song is very different, as Dawkins, an acknowledged expert in Greek folklore, acknowledges (1934: 119). Dawkins informs us that the hero is called 'George' (1934: 113), although his name does not appear in the song itself, but can only be gathered from the title provided by Levidis: Γεωργὸς καὶ Χάρων (Figure 2).[33]

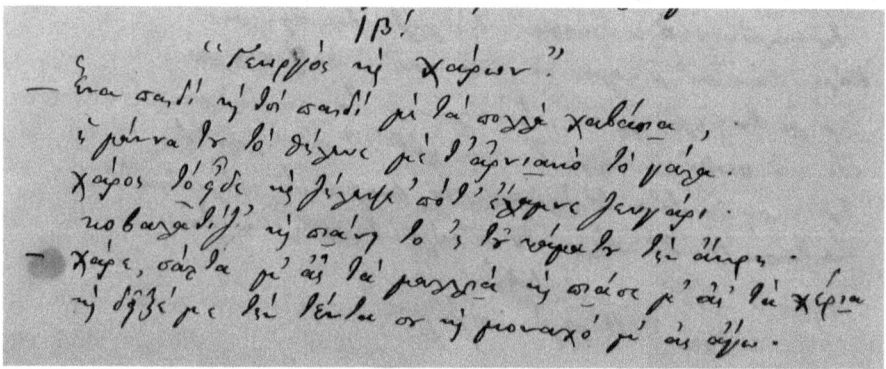

Figure 2: Γεωργὸς καὶ Χάρων, ll. 1–6 (Levidis 1892: ch. Δ΄, ιβ΄).

As Marjolijne Janssen astutely notes in her precious comments on a previous version of this paper, γεωργός [joryós] is a noun and not identical with the proper name derived from it, Γεώργιος [jórjos] > ModGr Γεώργος / Γιώργος [jóryos]. The meaning of the noun 'farmer' goes very well with the hero's agricultural activities described in the songs. As Dawkins observes: "in several of the Akritic songs the hero appears guiding his plough" (1934: 119). What is especially noteworthy is the fact that the noun lacks the definite article, which seems to suggest that it is a proper name after all, but the omission of the definite article with inherited masculine nouns in the nominative is a Cappadocian feature (cf. infra). This is not the place nor is it, indeed, my expertise to discuss the contents of this particular song from a comparative folkloristic perspective, either in comparison with other akritic songs in or with ModGr folk songs in general, for which the interested reader is referred to the brief but informative discussion by Dawkins (1934: 119). Instead, I

---

32 Saunier accepts "seven or eight important themes" as "truly [. . .] akritic" (1993: 148), but Politis (1909) and Lüdeke (1994) identify many more.
33 Cf. Levidis (1892: ch. Δ΄, ιβ΄), repeated in his παρατηρήσεις (ch. Ζ΄, ιβ΄).

will focus on the dialectological features of the song from a diachronic variationist perspective.

2.1 Critical edition

In his 'remarks' (παρατηρήσεις) on Γεωργὸς καὶ Χάρων, Levidis notes that it was "sung in Fertek and the neighbouring villages" (1892: ch. Z΄, ιβ΄).[34] Dawkins remarks that "the language in fact bears traces [. . .] of the dialects of Delmeso, Aravan, and Ghurzono, all villages only a very short distance from Fertek" (Dawkins 1934: 119; cf. Map 1), and concludes: "Though this song was taken down at Fertek, I think the informant must have come from one of these adjacent villages" (1934: 120). He admits that the song "is of a type I have not seen elsewhere" (1934: 119). This is very remarkable as a longer but otherwise very similar version was published by Lagarde (1886: 17–18), whose publication was known to Dawkins and described by him (D31). The song is part of a collection of songs and other texts from Cappadocia collected by Pavlos Karolidis, the author of a questionable comparative study of the Pharasiot vocabulary (Karolidis 1885). The collection was published by Lagarde with the following caveat: "Mir fällt nicht ein, die im folgende abgedrückten Texte für 'herausgegeben' anzusehen" (1886: 6).[35] Dawkins discusses Karolidis' work rather critically (D30) and Lagarde's very favourably (D31).[36] It is therefore all the more surprising that he should have missed this particular version of the song published in his article, which was recorded at Delmeso and called Χάρος καὶ ὁ ἄωρος ἀποθανὼν νέος 'Charon and the young man who died untimely' (1886: 17).[37] In what follows I present a critical edition of Levidis' transcription from the original manuscript (Figure 2) with reference to Karolidis' version as published by Lagarde, together with a thorough revision of

---

[34] "Τὸ ιβ΄ ᾆσμα « Γεωργὸς καὶ Χάρων » ᾄδεται εν Φερτακαίνοις καὶ τοῖς περιχώροις" (1892: ch. Z΄, ιβ΄). On the name of the village see Dawkins' remark: "Ferték, Grecised as Φερτέκι, is the Turkish name of the village; in the dialect it is called τὰ Βαρτάκαινα, and in literary Greek τὰ Φερτάκαινα" (D14).
[35] In his introduction to the glossary, Lagarde remarks: "Denn da Herr Karolides selbst an mehr als einer Stelle zugibt, daß er seine Lieder nicht verstehe, ich aber in einer noch weit schlimmeren Lage bin, als er, ist es das Klugste, die Leser sich auf eigene Gefahr in diese Wildnis hineinwagen zu lassen" (1886: 41).
[36] Lagarde's alphabetical arrangement (1886: 41–68) of Karolidis' γλωσσάριον συγκριτικόν (1885: 129–221) was judged "so much more convenient" than the latter's "chaotic" glossary that Dawkins refers only to Lagarde's work (D31).
[37] Henceforth referred to as K10, following the numbering in the manuscript, ~ L12 = Levidis (1892: ch. Z΄, ιβ΄).

Dawkins' translation (1934: 120–121).³⁸ The song is composed in the traditional decapentasyllable or political verse, with an obligatory caesura after the eighth syllable.

(1) ένα παιδί και τό̈ί παιδί | με τα πολλά χαϊβάνι̯α,³⁹
 éna peðí ce tʃi peðí | me ta polá xaináɲa
 a boy and what a boy, with his many cattle

(2) και μάννα του το θήλαινε | με τ' αρνι̯ακό το γάλα.⁴⁰
 i mána tu to θílene | me t arɲakó to ɣála
 his mother used to suckle him with lamb's milk

(3) Χάρος τό ει̯δε και ζήλεψε | 'ποτ' έλαμνε ζευγάρι.⁴¹
 xáros tóiðe ce ʒílepse | pot élamne zevɣári
 Charon saw him and desired him, as he was ploughing

(4) κοβαλατί̈ζ̌' και πι̯άνει το | σου κάματου τö̈ην άκρη.⁴²
 kovalatíʃ ce pçáni to | su kámatu t tʃin ákri
 he chases him and grabs him at the end of his field

(5) Χάρε, σάλτα μ' ας τα μαλλι̯ά | και πι̯άσε μ' ας τα χέρι̯α,⁴³
 xáre sálta m as ta maʎá | ce pçáse m as ta çérja
 Charon, let go of my hair and take me by the hands

---

38 Levidis' transcription contains very few capital letters, not even initials of proper names like Χάρων, as opposed to Dawkins', where every line starts with a capital. Interestingly, Levidis indicates synizesis of [i] > [j] by means of a horizontal line below ι + following vowel, e.g. χέρι̯α (Figure 2, l. 1), transcribed here as χέρι̯α, as elsewhere in this chapter. I have applied the 'monotonic' system of accentuation (cf. Horrocks 2010: xx) in my transcription, omitting breathings and replacing circumflex and grave with acute accents (cf. D40). I have added diacritics to distinguish postalveolar ŏ [ʃ] and ζ̌ [ʒ] from their alveolar counterparts, as well as Roman characters to represent the voiced plosives [b, d, g], following Dawkins (D39). Note that Lagarde writes Karolidis' "punktierte, š bedeutende, σ der Vorlage" as σσ (1886: 17).
39 = K[arolidis] 10.1 | χαϊβάνι̯α MJ : χαβάνι̯α L[evidis] ut vid., χαβάνια D[awkins] ~ ζουμπούλια K[arolidis].
40 = K10.2 | καὶ μάννα L ut vid. : καὶ μάνα K, ἡ μάννα D | θήλενε sive θήλευε sic pro τίλευε? L : θήλενε D : τίλευε K | ἀρνι̯ακό L D : ἀρνικό K.
41 = K10.3 | τὸ ε̂ι̯δε L, τὸ εἶδε D K | ζήλεψε L D : ζήλευσε K | έλαμνε L D : ἤλαυνε K.
42 = K10.4 | κοβαλατί̈ζ̌' καὶ πι̯άνει το L D : τὸ κώλησε καὶ τὸ 'πίασε K | σου MJ : σοῦ K : σ' τοῦ L | τö̈ην άκρη MJ : την ἄκρη L D : τὴν ἄκραν K.
43 = K10.5-6 | Χάρε L D : Χάρε μου K | σάλτα L D : ἄφες K | τὰ μαλλιά̯ L, τὰ μαλλιά D : ἀ [sic pro τὰ] καλλιά K | πι̯άσε L D : πιάς K | τὰ χέρι̯α L D : τὸ χέρι K.

(6) και δείξε με τŏην τέντα σου, | και μοναχό μ' αξ άγω.⁴⁴
    ce ðíkse me tʃin denda su | ce monaxó m aʃ áɣo
    and show me your tent, and let me go by myself

(7) εσάλτ'σεν τον ας τα μαλλιά, | και πιάν' τον ας το χέρι,⁴⁵
    esáltsen don as ta maʎá | ce pçán don as to çéri
    he let go of his hair, and takes him by the hand

(8) δείχνει σ' ετό τŏην τέντα του, | και μοναχό τ' πηγαίνει·⁴⁶
    ðíçni s etó tʃin dénda tu | ce monaxó t pijéni
    he shows him his tent, and he goes there by himself

(9) και δίνει και σα χέρια του, | τ' αμάθετα τα βό̦ι̦δι̦α,⁴⁷
    ce ðíni ce sa çérʝa tu | t amáθeta ta vóiðja
    and he gives into his hands the untamed oxen

(10) και δίνει και ŏη ράχη του | τ' ατέλειωτο <το> σπόρο.⁴⁸
    ce ðíni ce ʃi ráçi tu | t atéʎoto to spóro
    and he puts on his back the endless seed

(11) ένι τ' αλέτρι του χρυσό, | ζυγός του σαν αʃήμι,⁴⁹
    éni t alétri tu xrisó | ʒiɣós tu san aʃimi
    his plough is golden, his yoke as silver

(12) είνται και τα ζευλίτŏα του | παλληκαρ̦ι̦ού βραχιόνι̦α.⁵⁰
    índe ce ta zevlítʃa tu | palikarʝú vraçóɲa
    His [yoke's] collars are the arms of a brave young man

(13) λάμνει και παίνει κι̦ έρχεται, | σο γύρισμά του κλαίγει·⁵¹
    lámni ce péni c érçete | s to ʝirizmá tu kléʝi
    he is ploughing and going to and fro, at his turn he is crying

---

44 = K10.6 | τŏην τέντα MJ : την τέντα L : τὴν τέντα D : τὰ δένδρα K | μοναχό μ' L D : μόνος K.
45 = K10.7 | ἐσάλτσεν L D : ἀφῆκεν K | μαλλι̦ά L D : καλλιά K | καὶ πι̦άν' L D : κ' ἐπίασεν K.
46 om. K | ἐτό L : ἀτό D | τŏην MJ : τσῃ L D.
47 = K10.8 | καὶ δίνει καὶ L D : δῶκε K | ἀμαθέτα L D : ἀμάθητα K | βό̦ι̦δι̦α L, βοΐδία [sic] D, βωΐδια K.
48 = K10.9 | καὶ L D : om. K | σὴ L D : 'στὴ K | τ' ἀτελείωτο σπόρο L, τὸ suppl. D : τ' ἀτέλειωτο τὸ σπόρο K.
49 = K10.10 | χρυσό L D : χρουσό K | σὰν ἀσήμι L D : ἀς ἀσσῆμι K.
50 = K10.11 | εἴνται K : ἤνται L D | τα ζευλίτŏα MJ : τὰ ζευλίτσα K : ἡ ζευλίτσα L : ἡ ζευγλίτσα D | βραχι̦όνι̦α L D : βραχιόλια K.
51 = K10.12 | παίνει L D : πγαίνει K | καὶ 'ρχεται L D : κ' ἔρχεται K | σο γύρισμά του MJ : σ' τὸ γύρισμά του L D : κ' εἰς τὸ γύρισμα K | κλαίγει L : κλαίει D K.

(14) Χάρε, βρυχάται μάννα μου, | στριγγά με αδελφή μου.⁵²
xáre vrixate mána mu | striŋgá me aðelfí mu
Charon, my mother is crying, my sister is calling me

(15) μάννα σου ας μή βρυχηŏκεί, | κι αδελφή σ' μή στριγγήŏει.⁵³
mána su az mí vriçiʃcí | c aðelfí s mí striŋgíʃi
your mother should not cry and your sister should not call

(16) Χάρε, σάλτα μ' ας παραμώ, | ας μείνω κι αύρι' ας έρθω.⁵⁴
xáre sálta m as paramó | az míno ci ávri̯ as érθo
Charon, let me go back, let me stay [with them] and let me come tomorrow

(17) εδά 'μεναν Σαράκενοι, | εδά 'μεναν κι οι Τούρκοι,⁵⁵
eðá menan saráceni | eðá menan c i túrci
here Saracens have stayed, here the Turks have stayed as well

(18) εδά μικροί μεγάλωσαν, | μεγάλ' ήφεραν γένεια·⁵⁶
eðá mikrí meɣálosan | meɣál íferan ɟéɲa
here little ones have grown up, grown-ups have worn beards

(19) κάτσε κι έŏύ, κοντόχρονε, | με τους πολυχρονάτους.⁵⁷
kátse c eʃí kondóxrone | me tus polixronátus
sit down, you who is short-lived, with those who are long-lived

(20) νά σε είδα σε, Χάρε μου, | σ' ενα πλατŏύ λιβάδι,⁵⁸
ná se íða se xáre mu | s ena platʃí liváði
I wish I had seen you, my Charon, on a wide meadow

(21) ο μαύρος σου να βόσκεται, | κι εŏύ ν' αποκοιμάσαι,⁵⁹
o mávros su na vóscete | c eʃí n apocimáse
your black [charger] grazing and you asleep

---

52 = K10.13 | μάννα L D : μάνα K | με L D : ἡ K.
53 *om.* K | βρυχήŏκη MJ : βρυχήσκη [sic] L, βρυχίσκη [sic] D | κιἀδελφή L, κι ἀδελφή D | στριγγήση L D.
54 = K10.34 [sic] | Χάρε L D : Χάρε μου K | σάλτα μ' L D : ἄφες με K | παραμώ MJ : παρεμῶ K : πορέμαι L D | κι αὔρ' L, κι αὔρ' D : καὶ αὔριο K.
55 = K10.17 | ἐδά L D : ἐδῶ K bis | 'μέναν L D : μεῖναν K bis | Σαράκενοι L D : Σαράκηνοι K : Σαρακηνοί Lagarde *ad loc.* | κ' L D : *om.* K.
56 = K 10.35 [sic] | ἐδά L D : ἐδῶ K | μεγάλ' ήφεραν MJ : μεγάλοι 'φέραν L (D) : καὶ μεγάλοι ἔφεραν γένεια K.
57 = K 10.36 | κάτσε καὶ σύ L D : κάθου καὶ σύ K | κοντόχρονε L D : κοτόχρονε K | πολυχρονάτους L D : πολλοὺς χρονάτους K.
58 = K10.21 | εἶδα σε L D : ἰδῶ K | μου L K : μοι D | πλατύ L K : πλατύ K.
59 = K 10.22 | ὁ μαῦρος L K : τὸ μαῦρο K | βόσκεται L D : βόσκηται K | κ' ἐσύ L D : καὶ σύ K.

(22) να ήρθα αγάλια αγάλια, | να ήρθ' ενέσͅια ενέσͅια,⁶⁰
na írθa aɣáʎ aɣáʎa | na írθ enéʃ enéʃa
that I had come up very gently, that I had come up very quietly

(23) να παίρνισκα Χάρ' τα κλειδιά, | παράδεισ' τ' αναχτήρια,⁶¹
na pérniʃka xár ta kliðjá | paráðis t anaxtírja
that I would take Charon's keys, the keys of paradise

(24) ν' άνοιζα τον παράδεισο, | ν' ιδώ μέσα τσͅί είναι.⁶²
n ániza tom baráðiso | n iðó mésa tʃí íne
that I would open paradise, to see inside what is in it

(25) σͅη μέσͅη κείται μάννα μου, | σͅην άκρη αδελφή μου,⁶³
ʃi méʃi cíte mána mu | ʃin ákri aðelfí mu
in the middle sits my mother, at the end my sister

(26) αντζίς ακρής ακρούτσͅικα | κάθεται και γονιός μου.⁶⁴
andzís ákris akrútʃika | káθete ce ɣoɲóz mu
at the opposite end, at the very end, there sits my father as well

2.2 Linguistic analysis

The language of Γεωργὸς καὶ Χάρων is a fascinating admixture of LMedGr / EModGr and Cappadocian Greek, reminiscent of the *Kunstsprache* of the AncGr epic tradition.⁶⁵ The matrix language of Homer's *Iliad* and *Odyssey* is an archaic form of Eastern Ionic, interspersed with Aeolic elements and a number of archaisms not readily identifiable with any of the historical Greek dialects (Horrocks 2010: 44). The matrix language of this particular Akritic song is nineteenth-century Cappadocian interspersed with archaisms going back at least to the LMedGr Period.⁶⁶ Unfortunately, it is not always, if at all, possible to decide whether a particular archaism belongs to an earlier stage of Cappadocian, say,

---

60 = K10.23 | ἦρθα L D : ἦλθα K | ἀγάλια ἀγάλια L D : ἀγάλια ἀγάληνα K | ἦρθ' L D : ἦλθα K | ἐνέσͅια ἐνέσια L D : νέσσατζε K sic pro <ἀ>νέσια?
61 = K10.24 | παίρνισκα L D : ἐπῆρα K | Χάρ', τὰ κλειδιά L D : τοῦ Χάρου τὰ κλειδιά K | παράδεισ' τ' ἀναχτήρια L D : τοῦ παραδείσου τἀνοιχτήρια K.
62 = K10.25 | ν' ἄνοιζα L D : νὰ ἤνοιξα K | παράδεισο L D : παράδεισον K | ν' ἰδῶ L D : καὶ νὰ εἶδα K | μέσα L D : σὴ μέση του K | τσί L D : ποῖοι K | εἶνε L, εἶναι D : εἶνται K.
63 = K10.26 | κεῖται MJ : κεῖτ' ἡ L D : κάθεται K | σͅην άκρη MJ : σὴν ἄκρ' ἡ L D : σὴν ἄκρα ἡ K.
64 = K 10.27 | ἀντσὶς ἀκρῆς ἀκρούτσικα L D : καὶ ἀνακρούτζικα K | και γονιός MJ : ὁ γονιός L D : τἀγονιός *sic pro* καὶ γονιός? K.
65 More Akritic songs from Cappadocia are analyzed in Janse (forthcoming).
66 That is roughly the period covered by *LME* and *CGMG*.

'Early Modern' or 'Late Medieval', if we can borrow these terms from the history of Greek. In many cases, for instance, we can ascertain that a specific feature was absent from nineteenth-century Cappadocian and attested in LMedGr or EModGr, but these facts do not allow us to conclude that it must have been a feature of Late Medieval Cappadocian as well. In the case of γιορών or γιόρος discussed in section 1, we can in all likelihood conclude that they must be thirteenth-century Cappadocian variants of γέρων or γέρος, as both variants are attested in the modern dialects.[67] In the case of the other variants, γέρος and γέρων, also attested in the modern dialects as well as in varieties of LMedGr,[68] we cannot draw any conclusions as to whether it was already used as a variant in Late Medieval Cappadocian or whether it emerged at a later stage due to contact with other varieties of Greek as a result of the "constant population movements" during the seventeenth and eighteenth centuries (Manolessou 2019: 30) or the "close contact with Constantinople" in the nineteenth and early twentieth centuries (D194).

Especially in the case of the Akritic songs, which have been transmitted orally for very many centuries all over Asia Minor and the adjacent islands, there are theoretically many possible pathways by way of which particular linguistic features may have found their way back into Cappadocia, judging from the traditional formulaic phraseology attested in different versions in widely separated dialects. In addition, archaisms may have been retained for metrical reasons, just as in the AncGr epic tradition Aeolic words and inflections are used alongside their Ionic counterparts if the position in the verse requires a metrical alternative. Such considerations do not explain, however, the variation between ένι [éni] (11a) and είναι [íne] (24b), two metrically equivalent disyllabic penultimate words, in Levidis' version. The former is the inherited form which was still the most common form at the beginning of the LMedGr period, the latter one of several innovations often found side by side with ἔνι, including εἶν(αι) and ἔν(αι), often spelled εἶν(ε) and ἔν(ε) respectively (*CGMG* 3.1710–1727). Inherited ένι has survived in Pharasiot, Pontic, Cypriot and other ModGr dialects (Andriotis 1974: 239). At Pharasa ένι is used alongside είνι [íni], είναι [íne] and the Pharasiot innovation είνου [ínu] (Kostakis 1968: 77), which dramatically illustrates the possible extent of such variation.

In Cappadocian, on the other hand, ένι is not attested in any of the nineteenth-century dialects, except in Akritic and other traditional songs. Instead,

---

[67] γιόρος [jóros] Aravan (D592; PK23) < MedGr γέρος (*LME*); γιορών [jorón] Floïta, Malakopi (D592), Axo (MK99), Misti (Phates 2012: 157) < AncGr γέρων (LSJ).
[68] γέρος [jéros] Delmeso & Fertek (D592) < MedGr γέρος (*LME*); γέρων Axo (D592) < AncGr γέρων (LSJ).

the apocopated form έv' [én] is found in the majority of the dialects, including those of southwestern Cappadocia, where this particular rendition of the song is to be situated: Delmeso (D148), Fertek (Krinopoulos 1889: 38–39) and Aravan, where είv' [ín] is occasionally attested as a variant (PK152). As far as we know, the other dialects all have έv',[69] with the exception of Malakopi and Misti, where είv' is found.[70] These are the strong forms of the verb, which have a corresponding weak (clitic) form 'vαι [ne], or 'vι [ni] at Malakopi and Misti, where unstressed [e] is raised to [i].[71]

This seems to suggest that in Cappadocian έv' is the apocopated form of έvαι, one of the innovations of the LMedGr period, but the former is already attested in EMedGr as the apocopated variant of ἔvι, so the historical evolution of the forms in MedGr has to be reconstructed as ἔvι > ἔv' > ἔvαι > εἶvαι (CGMG 3.1720).[72] The variant είv' at Aravan seems to be the apocopated form of είvαι [íne], at Malakopi and Misti of είvι [íni]. These full forms are only found with any frequency in the folktales recorded by Dawkins at Floïta and Silata, as well as at Anaku,[73] which suggests that it may have been a feature of Northwest Cappadocian, although it cannot be excluded that such full forms are non-dialectal. This is certainly the case of είvι [íni] in present-day Mišótika, e.g. τί είvι; [tʰí íni?], reported by Phates (2012: 37) as opposed to τί είv'; [tí ín?] 'what is it?' in Dawkins' only folktale from Misti (D388).[74] The former is the Mišótika equivalent of ModGr είvαι, from which it is most likely borrowed, but normally the apocopated full forms are used, e.g. τί έv'; [tí én?] Potamia (D458), Ulağaç (Kesisoglou 1951: 150), τσί έv'; [tʃi én?] Aravan (PK67 & 122). If this interpretation is correct, the use of τσί είvαι; [tʃi íne?] in our song (L12.24b) is probably an archaism in disguise.[75] It may be noted that the weak (clitic) and not the strong forms of the verb are used after τίς [tís?] 'who?', e.g. τίς 'vαι (ι)τό; [tíz ne (i)tó?] 'who is this?' Ulağaç (D348 bis), τσίς 'σαι εσύ; [tʃis se eʃí?] 'who are you?' Aravan (PK74), τίς 'vι; [tʰíz ni?] 'who is it?' Mišótika (own fieldnotes).

The case of είvται [índe] (L12.12a) is different, as this form is not attested in LMedGr or EModGr (CGMG 3.1710). It is a typically Cappadocian 'agglutinative'

---

69 Axo έv' (MK58), Anaku έv' (Costakis 1964: 48), Ulağaç έv' (Kesisoglou 1951: 37).
70 Cf. Karphopoulos (2008: 96), Phates (2012: 37).
71 Cf. Dawkins (D64), Janse (2020: §6.2.1.3).
72 I owe this observation to Marjolijne Janssen (personal communication).
73 Cf. Dawkins (D410-452), Costakis (1964: 48).
74 Cf. Phates (2012: 37), who also quotes τί είv' ντου λές; [tʰí ín du les?] 'what is it that you are saying?' (ibid.). Voiceless plosives are often aspirated (Janse 2020: §6.1.2), as already noted by Thumb (1910: 297), but Dawkins admits to "have no record of this" (D70).
75 The disguise being the pronunciation of τί [tʰí] as τσί [tʃi], cf. infra.

formation (Janse 2009b: 98–103), which is best illustrated with the inflections from Fertek (D148) and Axo (MK58):

1sg	(έν)μαι		(én)me		(είν)μαι		(ín)me
2sg	(έν)μαι		(én)se		(είν)μαι		(ín)se
3sg	(έν)αι		(én)e		(έν)αι		(én)e
1pl	(έν)μεστε		(én)meste		(είν)μεστε		(ín)meste
2pl	(έν)οτε		(én)ste		(είν)οτε		(ín)ste
3pl	(έν)dαι		(én)de		(είν)dαι		(ín)de
	Fertek				**Axo**		

The full forms are ένμαι ~ είνμαι etc., the enclitic forms 'μαι etc., e.g. αστενάρ' 'μαι [astenár me] 'I'm sick' Fertek (Krinopoulos 1889: 39), Aravan (D148).[76] The entire paradigm was restructured on the basis of the 3sg:[77] έν' at Fertek, είν' at Axo, except that είν' was apparently no longer used there in the early twentieth century.[78] In the other dialects, the [n] of έν' ~ είν' has been assimilated or absorbed in the endings, but the innovative 3pl είνται is a silent witness of the process. It is attested everywhere, including at Delmeso. It is all the more remarkable that the version of the Akritic song recorded by Krinopoulos has είνται in a slightly different version of line 12 of Levidis', but two occurrences of ένται in a spurious line which is absent from the latter (K10.31). The variant ένdαι is not mentioned by Dawkins, who gives the full paradigm of the verb for Delmeso (D148), nor is it attested in the folktales recorded by him, as opposed to είνdαι which occurs five times (D304–320). Again we cannot exclude that ένdαι was used alongside είνdαι at Delmeso, as it would fit the agglutinative inflection even better than είνται in light of the 3sg έν(αι), but neither form occurs in any variety of LMedGr or EModGr, so both are clearly Cappadocian.

We are very fortunate to have Karolidis' alternative version of the same song, if only because it confirms that Levidis' version is in fact from Delmeso and not from Aravan or Ghurzono. As a matter of fact, Karolidis notes in his manuscript that this particular song was sung or dictated to him by more than

---

76 It is noteworthy that Krinopoulos writes αστενάρμαι 'ἀσθενῶ' as a single (phonological) word, whereas Dawkins hyphenates: αστενάρ-μαι, i.e. as a clitic group.

77 The restructuring of verbal paradigms on the basis of the 3SG, reanalyzed as having a zero ending, is attested cross-linguistically and known as Watkins' Law (Janse 2009b); see Joseph (1980) for ModGr evidence of Watkins' Law.

78 There is no trace of είν' in the folktales recorded by Dawkins (D388–402) and Mavrochalyvidis & Kesisoglou (MK186-220).

one informant from Delmeso.⁷⁹ There are only two lines in Levidis' version that do not occur in Karolidis', but the remaining 23 lines are almost without exception different and provide us with a fascinating view of variation and change in the oral transmission of traditional songs in Cappadocia.

Let me start with the Cappadocian features that identify the song as originating from Delmeso. I recall that Dawkins concluded that the singer could not have come from Fertek but from one of the adjacent villages, as some of the linguistic features of the song are only found in the dialects of Delmeso, Aravan and Ghurzono (1934: 120). The main evidence for this is the postalveolarization of the voiceless alveolar plosive [t] to the voiceless postalveolar affricate [tʃ] before [i] in these dialects as in τί [tí] > τσ̌ί [tʃî] (L12.1a), written τζί in Karolidis' version (K10.1a), την [tin] > τσ̌ην [tʃîn] (L12.6a & 8a, om. K), πλατύ [platí] (K10.21b) > πλατσ̌ύ [platʃî] (L12.20b). Similarly, [d] is postalveolarized to [dʒ] before [i] in αντίς [andís] 'opposite' > αντζ(ζ)ίς [andʒís] (L12.26a, written αντσίς).⁸⁰

A special case is the idiomatic phrase ας άγω 'let me go' (L12.6b = L10.6b), which should be read as αξ̌ άγω [aʃ áγo], with postalveolarization of [s] to [ʃ]. It is generally considered to be a variant of the aorist subjunctive 1sg of the verb παίνω [péno] (L12.13a), the Cappadocian variant of πηγαίνω [pijéno] (cf. infra), which is used alongside παίνω in Levidis' version of the song (L12.8b). Dawkins enumerates the various forms of the aorist subjunctive, some of which are contracted after the loss of the intervocalic fricatives [γ] or [j] (D137): 1sg πά(γ)ω [pá(γ)o] > πώ [pó], 2sg πά(γ)εις [pá(j)is] > πάς [pás], 3sg πά(γ)ει [pá(j)i] > πάει [páj], 1pl πά(γ)ωμ(ε) [pá(γ)om(e)] > πάμ' [pám], 2pl πάτ(ε) [pát(e)], 3pl πάν(ε) [pán(e)]. At Ghurzono (D634) and Aravan (PK185-186) the aorist subjunctive of παίνω is from υπάγω, which is of course the etymon of παίνω < πηγαίνω:⁸¹ 1sg υπά(γ)ω [ipá(γ)o], 2sg υπά(γ)εις [ipá(j)is] > υπάς [ipás], 3sg υπά(γ)ει [ipá(j)i] > υπάει [ipáj], 1pl υπά(γ)ωμ(ε) [ipá(γ)om(e)] > υπάμ' [ipám], 2pl υπάτ(ε) [ipát(e)], 3pl υπάν(ε) [ipán(e)].

For what is called "speaker-inclusive 'exhortation'" in the first person and "speaker-exclusive 'encouragement'" in the third person (*CGMG* 4.1878), the particle ας < άφες is used with, in the words of Dawkins, "a subjunctive without π, formed on the analogy of the imperative ἄμε, ἀμέτ(ε, which naturally serve

---

79 This can be deduced from the fact that l. 27 of Karolidis' version of the song was put between square brackets "διότι εἷς μόνον τῶν ᾀσάντων ἢ ὑπαγορευσάντων ἀπήγγειλε τὸν στίχον ἐκεῖνον" 'because only one of the informants who sang or dictated the song recited this particular verse' (Lagarde 1886: 17).
80 For this phonological change see Dawkins (D74), Janse (2020: §6.2.2.5.2), cf. αντίς [andís] Sinasos (Archelaos 1899: 223) < MedGr αντί(ς) (*LME*).
81 Cf. Andriotis (1974: 568; 1995: 279), *CGMG* 3.1391–1392, *LME* s.v. υπαγαίνω.

for the 2nd persons" (D137). He reports for Delmeso (D137): 1sg ας άω [aʃ áo], attested once in the folktales (D308) alongside ας άγω [aʃ áγo] (D310 & 322), 3sg ασ̌ άει [aʃ áj], 1pl ας άμ' [aʃ ám], 3pl ας άν' [aʃán]. Dawkins recorded 1pl ας άμ' [aʃ ám] also at Fertek (D137) and quotes Alektoridis' paradigm from the same village (1883: 501): 1sg ας άγω [aʃ áγo], 3sg ας άγει [aʃ áj], 1pl ας άμ(ε) [aʃ ám (e)], 3pl ας άν(ε) [aʃ án(e)].[82] The folktales recorded by Phosteris and Kesisoglou provide examples from Aravan: 1sg ας άγω [aʃ áγo] (PK118), 3sg ας άει [aʃ áj] (PK122), 1pl ας άμ' [aʃ ám] (PK98). Like Dawkins (D634), Phosteris and Kesisoglou refer to υπάγω and 'άγω under παίνω (PK171), suggesting that both are suppletive.

Dawkins was certainly on the right track when he claimed that the verbal forms "without π" were formed on the analogy of the imperative 2sg άμε [áme], 2pl αμέτ(ε) [amét(e)], which are used in all the dialects (D634). Krinopoulos, a native from Fertek who calls himself a 'philology student',[83] quotes the same forms as Alektoridis, but explains 1pl ας άμε [aʃ áme] from ας άγομεν (1889: 58), thus deriving the entire paradigm from AncGr άγω. Presumably άγομεν is a (not quite philological) typo for άγωμεν 'let us go' (e.g. *Ev.Marc.* 1.38): "the subjunctive form had undergone a remarkable semantic change from transitive 'bring, carry' to intransitive 'go' in the Hellenistic period, with multiple examples in the New Testament [. . .] probably with influence from άγε (see LSJ) and υπάγω" (*CGMG* 3.1369). In LMedG άγωμε(ν) (sometimes spelled άγομε(ν)) "came to be interpreted as a 2nd sg. imperative" and a "syncopated form άμε occurs from the 14th century onwards" (*ibid.*). It would seem, then, that the dialects of southwestern Cappadocian have preserved the "hortatory subjunctive" (*CGCG* 439) with the PcGr intransitive meaning of άγω 'go' in these grammaticalized phrases, including PcGr 1pl άγωμεν > (ας) άμ(ε) alongside the reanalyzed LMedGr aorist imperative 2sg άγωμε(ν) > άμε, 2pl αμέτ(ε). The idiosyncratic postalveolarization of [s] to [ʃ] may be due to conflation of the suppletive subjunctive ας υπάγω [as ipáγo] > ας υπάγω [aʃ ipáγo], where [i] is responsible for the postalveolarization of [s].[84] Finally, it may be noted that the other Cappadocian dialects use the regular subjunctive of παίνω: e.g. ας πάγω [as páγo] at Potamia (Levidis 1892: ch. Δ´, δ´; cf. Dawkins 1934: 25), Ghurzono (D340), Axo (MK186) and ας πάμ' [as pám] at Ulağaç (Kesisoglou 1951: 142), where Dawkins also recorded ας άμ' [aʃ ám] (D137).

---

82 We have to assume that Alektoridis spelling άς stands for ας [aʃ], as he did not distinguish alveolar [s] from postalveolar [ʃ], both being written as σ, as in most Greek publications. Dawkins' mention of 1pl ας άμ' [aʃám] at Fertek (D137) confirms this assumption.
83 The title page mentions the author as Σωκράτους Κρινοπούλου, φοιτητού τῆς φιλολογίας.
84 Cf. fn. 18.

Returning to the postalveolarization of [t] and [d] to [tʃ] and [dʒ]: these sound changes suffice in and by themselves to exclude Fertek as the place of origin of the singer of Levidis' song. Dawkins says they appear "a little" at Fertek, quoting τσ̌ίς [tʃís] "by the side of" τίς [tís], but mainly in the clusters τι̯ [tç] > τς̌ [tʃ] and δι̯ [dj] > τζ̌ [dʒ] (D74). Krinopoulos would surely have mentioned the sound change in the section entitled Παθολογία τῶν συμφώνων 'Pathology of the consonants' (1889: 35) and there is no trace of it in the glossary (1889: 64–65),[85] but he does quote σα σπίτι̯α [sa spítça] 'to the houses' instead of σα σπίτσ̌α [sa spítʃa] (1889: 39). Alektoridis' glossary does not contain a single word betraying the sound change either (1883: 504–505), but he does quote τίς, τίνος and τίνα and not τσ̌ίς, τσ̌ίνος and τσ̌ίνα as the interrogative pronouns (1883: 488). In the only folktale from Fertek recorded by Dawkins (D328-330) there is no trace of τσ̌ί, but instead two occurrences of τί[86] one occurrence of σπίτι τ' [spíti t] 'his house' and eleven of σπίτι̯α [spítça] 'houses' instead of *σπίτσ̌ι τ' [spítʃi t] and *σπίτσ̌α [spítʃa]. On the other hand, τζό [dʒó] instead of *δι̯ο [djó] < δύο [ðío] 'two' is attested once and listed as such in the glossary (D597). The folktale from Fertek recorded by Thumb (1910: 297–298) contains no traces of postalveolarization: σαχάτι μ' [saxátʰi m] 'my hour' ~ *σαχάτσ̌ι μ' [saxátʃi m],[87] άνδον με καντίεις [ándon me kandíis] 'if you believe me' ~ *καντζίεις [kandʒíis].[88]

Dawkins mentions only one feature that distinguishes the dialect of Delmeso from those of Aravan and Ghurzono: the change of ὅτι [ʃti] > ὅκι [ʃci] in ας μή βρυχηὅτεί [az mí vriçiʃtí] 'she should not cry' > βρυχηὅκεί [vriçiscí] (L12.15a, om. K), LMedGr βρυχηθεί.[89] This feature would in itself have sufficed to conclude that the singer must from Delmeso, but Dawkins nevertheless refrains from excluding Aravan and Ghurzono. There are, however, a number of features which clearly exclude the latter possibility. The inherited dental fricatives unvoiced [θ] and voiced [ð] are preserved only in Northwest and Northeast Cappadocian as well as at Delmeso, which belongs to the latter subgroup (Table 1). In all the other Cappadocian dialects, including Aravan and Ghurzono as well as Fertek, the dental fricatives have been

---

[85] And so we find τί καινά φέρετε [tí cená férete] 'what news are you bringing?' (Krinopoulos 1889: 21).
[86] The aspiration of initial [t] > [tʰ] is secured by Thumb (1910: 297).
[87] Compare σαάτσ̌' [saátʃ] > σαάσ̌' [saáʃ] at Aravan (PK7).
[88] κανδίζω [kandízo] 'believe' Fertek (Thumb 1910: 321), καντίζου [kandízu] Malakopi (Karphopoulos 2008: 114). The present subjunctive 2sg καντίεις [kandíis] is from καντίζεις [kandízis] by dissimilation (D84, 131).
[89] βρυχούμαι [vrixúme], aorist passive βρυ(χ)ήστα [vri(ç)iʃta] 'cry, shout' (Levidis Λεξ. ς´) < MedGr βρυχοῦμαι (*LME*).

replaced by various phonetically related sounds, depending (among other things) on the position of the original sound in the word, due to interference from Turkish, which lacks dental fricatives.⁹⁰

Initial [ð] becomes [d] at Aravan and Ghurzono (as well as at Fertek):⁹¹ δείξε [ðíkse] (L12.6a = K10.6a) ~ deíkse [díkse], δείχνει [ðíçni] (L12.8a, om. K) ~ deíχνει [díçni],⁹² δίνει [ðíni] (L12. 9a, om. K & L12.10a = K10.9a) ~ dίνει [díni].⁹³ Medial [ð] becomes usually [r], occasionally [d] (as at Fertek): είδε [íðe] (L12.3a = 10.3a) ~ είρε [íre], βόιδ' [vóið], pl. βόιδια [vóiðja] (L12. 9b = K10.8b) ~ βόρ' [vór], βόρια [vórja],⁹⁴ παιδί [peðí] (L12.1a = K10.1a) ~ παιρί [perí],⁹⁵ εδά [eðá] (L12.17 = K10.17) ~ ερά [erá],⁹⁶ λιβάδ(ι) [liváð(i)] (L12.20b = K10.21b) ~ λιβάρ' [livár],⁹⁷ κλειδί [kliðí] (L12.23a = K10.24a) ~ κλειρί,⁹⁸ but αδελφή [aðelfí] (L12.14b, 25b = K10.13b, 26b) ~ αδελφή [adelfí] at Aravan, Ghurzono and Fertek.⁹⁹ The Christian term παράδεισος [paráðisos] 'Paradise' (L12.24a = K10.25a) is attested in several Cappadocian dialects, but not at Aravan or Ghurzono, where it would probably have been παράγεισος [parájisos], as at Axo,¹⁰⁰ instead of *παράρεισος [parárisos], due to dissimilation.¹⁰¹

---

90 On the outcomes of the phonological substitutions in the various dialects see Dawkins (D74-80), Janse (2020: §6.2.2.6).
91 For Aravan and Ghurzono see Dawkins (D75-76), for Aravan in particular Mavrochalyvidis & Kesisoglou (MK5), for Fertek Dawkins (D75) and Krinopoulos, who notes that δ "προφέρεται πάντοτε ὡς τὸ γαλλικὸν d" (1889: 45).
92 δείχνω [ðíxno] 'show' NEC-NWC, deíχνω [díxno] Aravan (D595; PK5) < MedGr δείχνω (*LBG* & *LME*).
93 δίνω [ðíno] 'give' NEC-NWC, dίνω [díno] SEC & SWC (D596) < MedGr δίνω (*LBG* & *LME*).
94 βόιδ' [vóið] pl. βόιδια [vóiðja] 'ox' Delmeso, βόιτ' [vóit], pl. βόγια [vója] Fertek (D590) < MedGr βόιδι(ν) (*LME*); βόρ' [vór], pl. βόρια [vórja] Aravan, Ghurzono (D590; PK21) < MedGr βόδι(ν) (*LME*).
95 παιδί [peðí] 'boy' NEC-NWC, παιδί [pedí] Fertek, παιρί [perí] Aravan, Ghurzono, παι(γ)ί [pe(j)í] CC (D630) < MedGr παιδί(ν) 'child; boy' (*LME*).
96 εδά [eðá] 'here' NEC-NWC (D597), Anaku (Costakis 1964: 59), εδά [edá] Fertek (Krinopoulos 1889: 39), ερά [erá] Aravan (MK25), εγιά [ejá] Axo (MK77) < MedGr εδά (*LME*).
97 *λιβάδ' [liváð] NEC-NWC, λιβάρ' [livár] 'meadow' Aravan (PK32) < MedGr λιβάδι(ν) (*LME*).
98 κλειδί [kliðí] 'key' NEC-NWC, κλει(γ)ί [kli(j)í] Axo (D609; MK104), κλειρί [klirí] 'key' Aravan (PK29) < MedGr κλειδί(ν) (*LME*).
99 αδελφή [aðelfí] 'sister' NEC-NWC, αδελφή [adelfí] Aravan, Ghurzono, Fertek, αελφή [aelfí] Axo (D581), αϊλφή [ailfí] Misti (Kotsanidis 2005: 15) < AncGr ἀδελφή (*LSJ*).
100 Compare the saying at Axo: παραγείσ' πουλί [parajís pulí] 'bird of Paradise' (MK114 s.v. ουράνϊα), of the soul of a dead child who flies to heaven.
101 This is Dawkins' explanation for similar exceptions at Aravan (D75); compare MedGr Τετράδη [tetráði] 'Wednesday' > Τετράρ' [tetrár] Ghurzono (D76), Aravan (PK42) ~ Τετράχ' [tetráx] Aravan (D75).

Initial [θ] becomes [x] or [ç] at Aravan and Ghurzono (and [t] at Fertek),[102] but the verb θηλαίνω [θiléno] 'suckle' (L12.2a) is not attested in any of the Cappadocian dialects, which use βυζάνω [vizáno] instead (cf. infra). Medial [θ] becomes usually [r], sometimes [x] or [ç], occasionally [t] (as at Fertek): κάθομαι [káθome] (L12.26b = K10.27b) ~ κάρουμαι [kárume],[103] but έρθω [érθo] (L12.16b = K10.34b) ~ έρτω, ήρθα [írθa] (L12.22a–b) ~ ήλθα [ílθa] (K10.23a–b) ~ ήρτα [írta].[104] The adjective αμάθετο [amáθeto] 'unlearned: untamed' (L12.9b) is not attested in any of the dialects, but Levidis' variant must be Cappadocian, given the pronunciation of η as [e] instead of [i], the latter represented in Karolidis' variant αμάθητο [amáθito] (K10.8b).[105] At Aravan the form of the adjective would be αμάρετο [amáreto], cf. μαραινίσκω [mareníʃko] ~ μαθαίνω [maθéno].[106]

The other Cappadocian features of the song are non-distinctive and thus non-criterial for the identification of the matrix language of the song, e.g. the preposition ας 'from' (L12.5-7, 15–16 = K10.5-6, 10.34),[107] the personal pronoun ετό (L12.8a, om. K),[108] the progressive assimilation of [i] to [a] in ανοιχτήρια [aniçtírja] (K10.24b) > αναχτήρια [anaxtírja] (L12.23b),[109] the regressive assimilation of [a] to

---

102 For Aravan and Ghurzono see Dawkins (D75-76), for Aravan in particular Mavrochalyvidis & Kesisoglou (1960: 5–6), for Fertek Dawkins (D75) and Krinopoulos, who notes that θ "προφέρεται ὡς τ πάντοτε" (1889: 48).
103 κάθομαι [káθome] 'sit' NEC-NWC, κά(χ)ουμαι [ká(x)ume] Axo (MK261), κάχουμι [káxumi] Misti, Semendere (D605) < LMedGr κάθο(υ)μαι (*LME*).
104 On the variation between ήρτα and ήλτα cf. infra.
105 The "retention of 'Ionic' [e]" (*CGMG* 1.26-28) is usually considered to be an archaism of Cappadocian and especially Pontic (D67), but Horrocks considers it to be a case of vowel weakening, particularly in post-tonic syllables (2010: 400).
106 μαθαίνω [maθéno] 'teach' NEC-NWC (D621), μαραινίσκω [mareníʃko] Aravan (PK33) < MedGr μα(ν)θαίνω (*LME*).
107 "Used all over Cappadocia" (D586) as well as in Pontic; derived from ἀξ < ἐξ by Papadopoulos (1958–61: vol. 1, 148; cf. Andriotis 1974: 241 s.v. ἐξ).
108 Written as, or perhaps unwittingly corrected to, ατό by Dawkins (1934: 120), although ετό and ετά are the usual Cappadocian forms (D120). Just as ατό(ς) is derived from αὐτός, ετό(ς) is probably derived from εὐτός, a variant of αὐτός, rare in LMedGr and EModGr (*CGMG* 941), but well attested in Modern Greek dialects of the Ionian and Aegean Seas (Thumb 1910: 80).
109 Dawkins notes that Cappadocian αναχτήρ' "comes straight from ἀνοικτήριον, and not from it by way of Turk. anahtar" (D584). The Pontic forms ανοιχτάρι [aniçtári] and ανοιχτέριν [aniçtérin] (Papadopoulos 1958–61: vol. 1, 72) show that the Medieval Greek variants ἀνοιχτάρι(ν) (*LME*) and ἀνοικτήρι(ν) (*LBG*) may have coexisted in East Asia Minor as well. The former was borrowed in Turkish as *anahtar*, dialectal *anaḫtar*, the latter as dialectal *aneḫter, enetter* (Symeonidis 1976: 94), which exhibit regressive instead of progressive assimilations.

[e] in ανέσῐα [anéʃa]¹¹⁰ > ενέσῐα [enéʃa] (L12.22b].¹¹¹ The dissimilatory consonant reduction in the collocation of the preposition εἰς 'to' with the accusative definite article in στα > σα (L12.9a = K10.8a) and στου > σου (K10.4b) ~ σ' του (L12.4b) is also attested in the phrase εἰς σὴ ἑστία μου in Sultan Walad's *ġazal* 83.2a, if Dedes' reading of مواستیا اسی *sy 'sty' mw* is correct (1993: 17). The evolution of στη in Karolidis' version (K10.9a) to ση = ŏη [ʃi] in Levidis' (L12.10a) is again a distinctive feature of the dialect of Delmeso, as the feminine article is not preserved in the Southwest Cappadocian dialects of Fertek, Aravan and Ghurzono (D87-89). It is noteworthy that Karolidis writes ση(ν) = ŏη(ν) [ʃi(n)] elsewhere in his transcription of the song (K10.26a–b = L12.25a–b).

A distinctively Cappadocian feature is the formation of the imperfect of barytone verbs with a dedicated suffix attached to the present stem. The phonological shape of the suffix is -ισκ- [iʃk] in most dialects and so also at Delmeso.¹¹² The only example comes from Levidis' version: παίρνιŏκα [pérniʃka] (L12.23a), the imperfect indicative of παίρω.¹¹³ The imperfects without the suffix are not necessarily archaisms. Presents ending in -ζω, -αίνω, -ώνω, -εύω and -ίσκω are inflected as in MedGr and ModGr, e.g. άνοιζα [aníza] (L12.24a),¹¹⁴ έλαμνε [élamne] (L12. 3b) as opposed to ἤλαυνε [ílavne] (K10.3),¹¹⁵ which is definitely an archaism, and possibly θήλαινε [θílene] (L12.2a), although the verb is probably not Cappadocian (cf. supra). By contrast, the imperfect (ἐ)μεναν [(é)menan] (L12.17a-b) is definitely non-Cappadocian, as the verb μένω is not preserved in any of the dialects, only variants of the LMedGr prefixed verb ἀπομεινίσκω > ἀπομνίσκω¹¹⁶ > Cappadocian

---

110 Perhaps recoverable from Karolidis' reading ἦλθα (ἀ)νέσσατζε (K10.23b).
111 ενέσῐα [enéʃa] 'quietly' (hapax) < MedGr ανέσια « ἥσυχα, ἤρεμα » < ανέσι « ανάπαυση, ησυχία » (*LME*), cf. Dawkins' remark: "In all the villages an *i* tends to change *a* of the preceding syllable to *e* or less often to *aï*" (D65). For the reduplication cf. φιλεί, φιλεί με γαληνά, | κρατεί με ανέσι ανέσι 'he kisses me gently, he holds me tenderly' (*Erotop.* 401). Note that γαληνά 'gently' is usually taken to be the etymon of LMedGr αγάλια [aɣáʎa] 'gently' (Andriotis 1974: 192; 1995: 3; cf. *LME* s.v.), which is attested as such in Cappadocian (D580). It is therefore noteworthy that Levidis' αγάλια αγάλια [aɣáʎ aɣáʎa] (L12.22a) should appear as αγάλια αγάληνα [aɣáʎ aɣálina] in Karolidis' version (K10.23a).
112 For details on the variants of the suffix and the morphological restrictions on its use see Dawkins (D132–135), Janse (2020: §7.6.1.2).
113 παίρω [péro] 'take' Cappa (D630), rarely παίρνω [pérno] Aravan (PK66) < MedGr (ἐ)παίρνω (*LME*) < AncGr ἐπαίρω (LSJ).
114 ανοίζω [anízo] 'open' Cappa (D584), rarely ανοί(γ)ω [aní(ɣ)o] Anaku (Costakis 1964: 30) ~ MedGr ἀνοίγω.
115 λάμνω [lámno] 'plough' Cappa (D618), semantically narrowed from λάμνω ζευγάρι 'drive a yoke' < MedGr (ἐ)λάμνω < (ἐ)λαύνω (*LME*).
116 Dawkins derives the Cappadocian forms erroneously from απομένω (D585). On the productivity of the suffix -ισκ- to form new imperfective stems of nasal-stem verbs based on their

πομ(ν)ίσκω [pom(n)íʃko], aor. πόμ(ν)α [póm(n)a], which at Delmeso takes the form *πλομ(ν)ίσκω [plom(n)íʃko], aor. πλόμα [plóma] (D585). Consequently, the aorist (ἐ)μειναν [(é)minan] in Levidis' version (L12.17a–b) must be an archaism as well.

More challenging is the interpretation of Karolidis' επήρα [epíra] (K10.24a) versus Levidis' παίρνισκα [pérniʃka] (L12.23a). The aorist inicative of παίρω is πήρα "everywhere except at Ulağaç, where ἐπήρα, ἔπηρε and ἔπερα are used", as Dawkins notes, adding "ἐπήρα also at Delmeso" (D631). It is of course impossible to decide whether Karolidis' variant επήρα is here the Delmeso or the LMedGr form of the aorist indicative, as both are identical.[117] The same applies, *mutatis mutandis*, to the variation between ἤρθα [írθa] (L12.22a–b) and ἦλθα [ílθa] (K10.23a-b). Although the latter is historically an archaism and the former an innovation (*CGMG* 1.214–215), both forms are attested in LMedGr, EModGr and even Standard ModGr. The Cappadocian form is ἤρτα [írta], with a voiceless alveolar stop instead of a dental fricative, which is found "everywhere, except ἤλτα at Ax[o] and probably elsewhere by the side of ἤρτα" (D599), but there is no trace of the former in the Cappadocian folktales recorded by Dawkins, including those from Delmeso (D304–328) and Axo (D388–404).[118] The voiceless dental fricative [θ] is preserved at Delmeso, so it is difficult to make sense of Levidis' ἤρθα, that is whether it was actually pronounced as [θ] or as [t], and even more of Karolidis' ἦλθα.

This uncertainty applies to many other forms as well such as εδά [eδá] in Levidis' version (L12.17-18a) as opposed to εδώ [eδó] in Karolidis' (K10.17, 35a). Both are variants of the locative adverb 'here' in LMedGr, and both are attested, probably side by side, in Cappadocian (D597). The voiced dental fricative [δ] is of course only preserved in Northwest and Northeast Cappadocian, including Delmeso (cf. supra), and the fact that Karolidis has εδώ seems to suggest that both forms were used interchangeably at Delmeso as well, although Dawkins' folktales from the village (D304-328) contain only εδά (three times) and another variant, εδού [eδú] (eleven times).

Other variants are perhaps more easily explained as archaisms preserved in the oral tradition, assuming, of course, that Karolidis' and Levidis' transcriptions are accurate. Compare, for instance, the phrase στη ράχι του [sti ráçi tu] in Karolidis' version (K10.9a) with ὄη ράχη του in Levidis' (L12.10a). As explained

---

non-sigmatic perfective stems in LMedGr see *CGMG* (3.1295–1298), where μεινίσκω as well as the syncopated form μνίσκω are quoted (1296).
117 The variants πῆρεν (22x) and επῆρεν (4x) are used side by side in Dawkins' folktales from Delmeso (D304-328)
118 Nor, for that matter, in the folktales from Axo recorded by Mavrochalyvidis and Kesisoglou: the index of forms contains only delateralized forms (1960: 256–257).

above, the collocation στη(ν) became ŏη(ν) via στŏη(ν) at Delmeso, so στη is definitely an archaism.¹¹⁹ The noun ράχη 'back' was preserved as a feminine noun at Sinasos as well as at Anaku, where it appears as ρέδη [réʃi] with regressive assimilation of [a] > [e] and postalveolarization of [ç] > [ʃ]. In the Southwest Cappadocian dialects it became a neuter noun: ρέχ' [réç] at Aravan and, with a prosthetic [d] which is difficult to explain, δρέχ' [dréç] > δρέδ' [dréʃ] at Fertek. ¹²⁰ It is now clear that Karolidis' version of the phrase στη ράχι του is archaic, whereas Levidis' version ŏη ράχη του is innovative, but it cannot be decided whether ράχη was preserved as such at Delmeso, as one might have expected ρέχ(η) [réç(i)] with [e] instead of [a] as at Aravan and Fertek, because the regressive assimilation of [a] > [e] is well attested at Delmeso as well (D65).¹²¹

The phrase contains another archaism: the retention of unstressed final [u] in του. As is well-known, unstressed [u] is regularly apocopated in final position in Cappadocian (D62; Janse 2020: §6.2.1.1), but the song contains quite a few examples of non-apocopated forms of the possessive pronouns: μου (L12.14a-b, 20a, 25a-b, 26b = K10.13a-b, 21a, 26a-b, 27b), σου (L12.6a, 15a, 21a = K10.6a, 22a), του (L12.2a, 8a-13b = K10.2a, 8a-11b). Interestingly, however, there are also examples of apocopated forms: μάννα σου [mána su] ~ αδελφή σ' [aðelfí s] (L12.15a-b), μοναχό τ' [monaxó t] (L12.8) ~ μοναχό μ' [monaxó m] (L12.6b), but the latter can be explained as elision to avoid hiatus. The last two examples are interesting for another reason, as they illustrate another characteristic feature of Cappadocian: the use of neuter forms in adjectival agreement,¹²² in these cases μοναχό τ' [monaxó t] ~ μοναχός του [monaxós tu] and μοναχό μ' [monaxó m] ~ μοναχός μου [monaxóz mu].

Another non-apocopated form is κάματου [kámatu] (L12.4b = K10.4b), the meaning of which is 'trouble, fatigue' in all the Cappadocian dialects, just as it has always been in the entire history of the Greek language, but both Levidis and Karolidis gloss it here as 'field', which would be a hapax as far as its meaning is

---

119 It would have been pronounced [ʃci] at Delmeso, cf. βρυχήŏτει [vriçíʃti] > βρυχήŏκει [vriçíʃci] (L12.15a).
120 ράχη [ráçi] f. 'back' Sinasos (Archelaos 1889: 264), ρέδη [réʃi] Anaku (Costakis 1964: 23), ρέχ' [réç] n. Aravan (PK39), δρέχ(ι) [dréç(i)] Fertek (Alektoridis 1883: 494) > δρέδ' [dréʃ] Fertek (Krinopoulos 1889: 46) < MedGr ράχη (*LME*) < ράχις (*LBG*). Krinopoulos explains the successive changes in the Fertek forms as follows: τὸ ράχι > τ'ράχι > δρέχι > δρέδι > δρέδ' (1889: 46). Forms with prosthetic [t] or [d] are attested in other Cappadocian dialects and in Pharasiot (D641).
121 Examples include λιθάρ' [liθár] 'stone' > λιθέρ' [liθér] Delmeso > χτέρ' [çtér] Fertek > τερ' [tér] Aravan (D620) < MedGr λιθάρι(ν) (*LME*); Tk. *yular*, dialectal *yilar* (*DS*) > γιλάρ' [jilár] Ulağaç > ιλάρ' [ilár] Aravan > 'λέρ' [lér] Delmeso 'halter' (D688).
122 Cf. Dawkins (D115-116), Janse (2020: §8.1.2.1).

concerned.[123] Note that κάματος is a proparoxytone noun and that the stress remains on the antepenultimate in the genitive κάματου in both Levidis' and Karolidis' version. The same applies to παράδεισ' [paráðis] in Levidis' version (L12.23b) ~ παράδεισου [paráðisu] in Karolidis' (K10.24b). The same variation is attested in LMedGr (*CGMG* 2.288-289) and also in Cappadocian, notably at Delmeso, e.g. άθρωπος [áθropos], gen. αθρώπ' [aθróp] 'man' ~ δάσκαλος [ðáskalos], gen. δάσκαλ' [ðáskal] 'teacher' (D95).

Another reading in need of correction is Dawkins' rendering of Levidis' να παίρνισ̌κα, Χάρ' τα κλειδια [na pérniʃka xár ta kliðjá] (L12.23a) as να παίρνισκα, Χάρ', τα κλειδια, apparently interpreting Χάρ' as an apocopated form of the vocative Χάρε (L12.5a, 14a, 16a = K10.5a, 13a, 34a), suggested by the comma punctuation before Χάρ' in Levidis' transcription, but the comma added by Dawkins immediately after Χάρ' does not appear in the manuscript. It is therefore clear that Χάρ' is here the apocopated version of the genitive Χάρου, as appears from a comparison with Karolidis' version: να επήρα του Χάρου τα κλειδια [na epíra tu xáru ta kliðjá] (K10.24a). Levidis' is clearly innovative, as shown by the absence of the definite article, which "is not used at all in the genitive" (D87). Compare also the second colon in both versions, where the phrase from the first colon is paraphrased as του παραδείσου τ' ανοιχτήρια [tu paraðísu t aniçtírja] in Karolidis' version (K10.24b), but παραδείσ' τ' αναχτήρια [paraðís t anaxtírja] in Levidis' (L12.23b).[124]

The attentive reader will have noticed that Karolidis' version of this particular line is unmetrical, as in fact many of his lines are. The only way to turn the first colon into an octosyllable and the second one into a heptasyllable is to apocopate unstressed [u] in the genitive endings of του Χάρου > τ' Χάρ' [t xár] and του παραδείσου > τ' παραδείσ' [t paraðís].[125] In other cases, however, the apocopated and non-apocopated forms are simply variants which can be used

---

123 Although both Levidis and Karolidis have κάματου, it is tempting to read κομμάτου [komátu] 'of the field' or κομμάτου τ' [komátu t] 'of his field' instead, κόμμα being the usual word for 'field' in Cappadocian (D611). By simply adding the possessive pronoun του in its apocopated form τ' the retention of final [u] in κάματου τ' ~ κομμάτου τ' would be normal in Cappadocian (D62).

124 As Dawkins rightly notes: "The pagan view of death presented by the Modern Greek Charon songs is well known: here we have at least an attempt at a reconciliation with something more approaching Christian orthodoxy. The idea of Charon holding the keys of Paradise brings him close to St. Peter" (1934: 119). In a footnote he adds: "The usual approximation is that of Charon to St. Michael, who is in Greek iconography and tradition the angel who carries away the soul" (ibid.). For the phrase compare παραδείσου θυρῶν ανοικτήριον (TrypCant 32 ζ' 9).

125 At Axo apocopated του > τ' is in fact still regularly used as the genitive form of the definite article (MK81). It is very likely that the omission of the genitive article in the other

if the position in the verse requires a metrical alternative. Compare, for instance, και μοναχό μ' ας άγω [ce monaxó m aʃ áɣo] (L12.6b) ~ και μοναχό τ' πηγαίνει [ce monaxó t pi̯éni] (L12.8b). The latter example is also interesting for another reason, as the final unstressed [i] in πηγαίνει is not apocopated *metri causa*.[126] It is worthy of note, however, that the verb πηγαίνω [pi̯éno] is not attested as such in any of the Cappadocian dialects, where instead παίνω [péno] is the only attested form, cf. παίνει [péni] (L12.13a) but note πγαίνι [pi̯éni] in Karolidis' version (K10. 12a) which, if not a typo, may reflect a syncopated form πηγαίνει > π'γαίνει.[127] Obviously, an apocopated form of either variant would not fit the metre.

Another example of this variation *metri causa* is κοβαλατίʒ' και πι̯άνει το [kovalatíʒ ce pçáni to] (L12.4a) ~ και πι̯άν' τον ας το χέρι [ce pçán ton as to çéri] (L12.7b), where unstressed [i] is preserved in πι̯άνει (as well as in χέρι), but apocopated in κοβαλατίʒ' and πι̯άν'. It is worthy of note that the word order of Karolidis' version of the former half-verse is neither Medieval Greek nor Cappadocian Greek, as far as the preverbal position of the clitic pronouns is concerned:[128] το κόλησε και το 'πίασε [to kólise ce to píase] 'he chased him and grabbed him' (K10.4a), the latter part of which should probably be read και τό 'πι̯ασε [ce tó pçase].[129] The second colon, on the other hand, has the expected word order: κι̯ επίασεν

Cappadocian dialects is the result of cluster reduction, as apocopated τ' followed by an initial consonant in the noun yielded many clusters not normally found at the beginning of a word (Janse 2020: §6.2.2.9.1), e.g. τ' ναίκας [t nékas] 'of the woman', τ' μέρας [t méras] 'of the day'.

126 Other non-apocopated forms: ζευγάρι [zevɣári] (L12.3b), δείχνει [ðíçni] (L12.8a), δίνει [ðíni] (L12.9a & 10b), αʃήμι [aʃími] (L12.11b), κλαίγει [kléji] (L12.13b) στριγγήʃει [strinjíʃi] (L12.15b), Τούρκοι [túrci] (L12.17b), μεγάλοι [meɣáli] (L12.18b); αλέτρι [alétri] (L12.11) is normally not apocopated (Archelaos 1889: 221), but the usual form, also at Delmeso, is αλέτιρ [alétir] (D583).

127 Dawkins notes that πα(γ)αίνω [pa(ɣ)éno] is also found at Potamia, but "possibly not dialectic" (D634), because the "dialect has been a good deal influenced by the common Greek" (D29). In the folktales from Potamia I find παγαίν' [pajén] and παγαίνεις [pajénis] (D458 *ter*) as well as παγαίνιʃκαν [pajéniʃkan] (D464), but also παγαίν' [pajén] at Silata (D442 *ter*), where the "dialect is in common use" (D26). Πα(γ)αίνω is also attested at Sinasos (Archelaos 1889: 28), where "the old dialect largely gives way to the common Greek" (D27), as well as in Silliot and Pharasiot (D634), in the latter as a variant of παίνω (D634), which is clearly a contracted form of παaίνω [paéno].

128 For the position of clitic pronouns in Late Medieval and Early Modern Greek see Horrocks (1990), Mackridge (1993b; 2000), *CGMG* (4.2026–2037); for Cappadocian see Janse (1993; 1994; 1998a; 2020: §8.2.3.1).

129 Another Cappadocian song from Levidis' collection (1892: ch. Δ΄, δ΄), published by Dawkins (1934: 117) is riddled with preverbal clitic pronouns in contexts where postverbal position would be expected in Medieval Greek as well as in Cappadocian.

τον ας το χέρι [c epíasen ton as to çeri] 'and he took him by the hand' (K10.7b), but the verb phrase should probably be read και πιάσεν τον [ce pçásen ton].¹³⁰

There are other examples of archaims used for metrical reasons. As is well known, the definite article is not used in the nominative with inherited masculine and feminine nouns denoting animates in most of the dialects with the notable exception of Southeast Cappadocian.¹³¹ Examples include Χάρος (L12.5a = K10.3a), μάννα μου (L12.14a = K10.13a), μάννα σου (L12.15a), αδελφή σ' (L12.15b). An exception is ζυγός του [ʒiɣós tu], an inherited masculine but inanimate noun, but here the omission of the article can be explained as an extension of the rule by analogy with other masculine nouns.

Sometimes Levidis' and Karolidis' versions deviate from each other: στριγγά με αδελφή μου [striŋgá me aðelfí mu] (L12.14b) ~ στριγγά η αδελφή μου [striŋgá i aðelfí mu] (K10.13b). In other cases, a textual emendation seems possible: ὅη μέση κείτ' η μάννα μου [ʃi méʃi cít i mána mu] (L12.25a) > ὅη μέση κείται μάννα μου [ʃi méʃi cíte mána mu] ~ ὅη μέση κάθεται μάννα μου [ʃi méʃi káθete mána mu] (K10.26a); ὅην ἀκρ' η αδελφή μου [ʃin ákr i aðelfí mu] (L12.25b) > ὅην άκρη αδελφή μου [ʃin ákri aðelfí mu] ~ ὅην άκρα η αδελφή μου [ʃin ákra i aðelfí mu] (L12.25b) > ὅην άκρη αδελφή μου [ʃin ákri aðelfí mu]; εδά 'μεναν κ' οι Τούρκοι [eðá menan c i túrci] (L12. 17b) > εδά 'μεναν και Τούρκοι [eðá menan ce túrci] ~ κ' εδώ μεῖναν οι Τούρκοι [c eðó mínan i túrci] (K10.17b); κάθεται κ' ο γονιός μου [káθete c o ɣoɲóz mu] (L12.26b) > κάθεται και γονιός μου [káθete ce ɣoɲóz mu] ~ κάθεται καγονιός μου [káθete caɣoɲóz mu] (K10.27b) > κάθεται και γονιός μου [káθete ce ɣoɲóz mu].

A special case is ο μαύρος σου [o mávros su] in Levidis' version (L12.21a), which corresponds with το μαύρο σου [to mávro su] in Karolidis' (K10.22a). The phrase is formulaic and found many times in the Διγενὴς Ἀκρίτης.¹³² As a substantivized adjective it refers to a certain race of black horses, especially 'war horses' (*LME* s.v. μαύρος).¹³³ Levidis' ο μαύρος σου is therefore an echo of this formulaic usage, because the archaic masculine word ἵππος 'horse' underlying the phrase was unknown in nineteenth-century Cappadocia, where the word άλογο [áloɣo] was used, as in the rest of the Greek-speaking world. It should be noted, however,

---

130 For the accentuation see Dawkins (D138 & 634 s.v. πιάνω), Janse (1998b: 535–537). Karolidis' version τὸ 'πίασεν [to píase] cannot be read (or sung) with synizesis, as the metre requires an antepenultimate before the caesura (cf. *CGMG* 2.249-252).
131 On the use of the definite article in the nominative see Dawkins (D87), Janse (2004: 12–14; 2019: 100–102; 2020: §7.1.1), Karatsareas (2013: 211–221).
132 E.g. ἦτον δάος ὁ μαῦρός του | τὸ φέγγος ὡς ἡμέρα 'his black horse was swift, the moonlight like day' (*Dig.* G4.407) ~ ἦτον λαμπρὸς ὁ μαῦρός του | καὶ ἔφεγγεν τὸ φεγγάρι 'his black horse was gleaming, the moon shining bright' (*Dig.* E844).
133 ἀπόστρωσε τὸν γρίβαν μου | καὶ στρῶσέ μου τὸν μαῦρον 'unsaddle my grey horse, and saddle for me the black' (*Dig.* G4.376 = E798)

that άλογο is not the noun underlying Karolidis' το μαύρο σου, but rather the obscure word έθιο in the phrase μαύρο έθιο, which should probably be written μαύρο έτιο [mávro étço] (K10.14a), glossed as « ἵππος » in a footnote (Lagarde 1886: 17f) and in the glossary (Karolidis 1885: 81, 161). Lagarde correctly derives the word from Ottoman Turkish آت [at] (1886: 50), which was borrowed in Medieval Greek as άτι [áti] (*LME*), but in the song it appears with [e] instead of [a] due to the regressive assimilation so well attested at Delmeso (cf. supra). It is not attested at all in any of the Cappadocian dialects, but the phonological shape of the diminutive suffix -ιο instead of -ι at the end of the word gives it a particularly archaic outlook, as άτιο(ν) or even άτι(ν) is unattested in LMedGr.[134]

Another Cappadocian feature is also related to the use of the definite article: the multiple occurrence of the article in contexts of attributive adjectival modification, a phenomenon called 'determiner spreading' (Lekakou & Karatsareas 2016).[135] It is of course a phenomenon well-known from AncGr, where the article is obligatorily repeated when the adjective is used attributively in postnominal position (*CGCG* 331). It is very common as well in LMedGr, where the attributive adjective may also appear in prenominal position, an innovation called "reverse determiner spreading" in *CGMG* (4.1973). Whereas in LMedGr and EModGr the position of the adjective vis-à-vis the noun was thus "amenable to the rules of focalization" (*ibid.*), adjectives and other noun modifiers are obligatorily placed in prenominal position in Cappadocian, a word order pattern borrowed from Turkish.[136]

Levidis' version of our song contains one example of determiner spreading: τ' αμάθετα τα βόιδια [t amátheta ta vóiðja] (L12.9b ≈ K10.8b). The second colon of the following line reads τ' ατελείωτο σπόρο [t atelíoto spóro] (L12.10b), without determiner spreading, which prompted Dawkins to note: "probably a better reading would be τ' ἀτελείωτο τὸ σπόρο, with the double article" (1934: 120).[137] The reading in Levidis' manuscript actually lacks the second article, which is probably due to haplography of the syllable [to]. Fortunately, we have Karolidis' version of the same colon, which indeed reads τ' ατέλειωτο το σπόρο [t atéλoto to spóro] (K10.9b), with the double article and with the necessary synizesis

---

134 Kriaras only gives one reference (*Ptochol.* B 155), whereas the TLG yields eighteen results, four from the *Historia Alexandri Magni* and fourteen from Caesarius Dapontes, including the phrase ἅτι μαῦρον 'black horse' (5.8.2).
135 Cf. Dawkins (D116), Janse (2020: §8.1.2.1), Lekakou & Karatsareas (2016).
136 Cf. Dawkins (D200–202), Janse (2009a: ; 44–49; 2006; 2020: §8.2.3).
137 On the difference between Levidis' ἀτέλειωτο and Karolidis' ἀτελείωτο see the remarks on synizesis, stress shift and accent notation in *CGMG* 2.249–252.

ατελείωτο [atelíoto] > ατέλειωτο [atéλoto]. The second colon of the first line of the song seems to lack the double article as well: τα πολλά χαιβάνια [ta polá xaináɲa] (L12.1b ≈ K10.1b). In this particular case, the adjective is a quantifier and behaves like a numeral in this respect, as in the following examples from Delmeso: τα δυό φσάχα [ta ðjó ʃʃáxa] 'the two children' (D318 *bis*), τα τρία γκι̯ϋζέλια [ta tría ɟyzéλa] 'the three fair ones' (D304–326 *passim*).

The lexical variation in the two versions of the song is very interesting, as has already been shown on several occasions. Already in the second line of the song we are in for a surprise: Levidis reads θήλενε [θílene] (L12.2a) according to Dawkins (1934: 119). If Dawkins' reading is correct, the verb should be read as θήλαινε, a hapax by any standard, as it is not attested in Cappadocian nor in in any other variety of MedGr or ModGr, where the AncGr form θηλάζω is still used. It would be an example of the well-known variation between present stems in -άζω and -αίνω ~ -άνω, which can be appropriately exemplified with the Cappadocian word for 'suckle' βυζάνω [vizáno], which is identical with the first of two variants in MedGr βυζάνω (*LME*) ~ βυζάζω (*LBG*), the former corresponding with βυζαίνω in ModGr.[138] Karolidis, however, reads τίλευε [tíleve] (K10.2a), glossed as «τρέφω» (Lagarde 1886: 17d) and identified in his glossary as uniquely Cappadocian (Karolidis 1885: 217 = Lagarde 1886: 64).[139] The etymology of the verb is unknown,[140] but Dawkins recorded it at Delmeso, Aravan and Ghurzono, albeit with a voiced instead of an unvoiced initial alveolar plosive: διλεύω [dilévo] (D654). I tend to believe that Levidis actually wrote θήλευε [tʰíleve],[141] with θ to mark an aspirated voiceless alveolar plosive [tʰ]?[142]

An obvious crux is Levidis' reading πορέμαι [poréme] (L12.16a), which Dawkins considers "unmetrical", because he believes it stands for πορεύομαι, in Levidis' glossary of Zila and Sinasos glossed as «προσπορίζομαι» (Λεξ. Δ΄ *s.v.*) and translated by Dawkins as 'go forward' (1934: 118). This is really not appropriate, as is immediately apparent from the following context: our hero wants to go not forward but

---

138 On the variation between present stems in -άνω and -αίνω see *CGMG* (3.1294–1295). Compare πα(γ)άζω [pa(ɣ)ázo], a variant of πα(γ)αίνω [pa(j)éno] in Pharasiot (Andriotis 1948: 70), which is also attested at Ulagaç (Kesisoglou 1951: 85).
139 As opposed to Pharasiot, where the verb is ζουλεύω [zulévo], cf. Dawkins (D601), Andriotis (1948: 63).
140 Mavrochalyvidis & Kesisoglou (MK 147) and Phosteris & Kesisoglou (PK 60) list it in the section Λέξεις ανετυμολόγητες.
141 Both θήλενε (Dawkins' reading) and θήλευε (my alternative reading) are (neo)paleographically possible. Marjolijne Janssen confirms my alternative reading (personal communication).
142 Compare Karolidis' writing of έθι̯ο [étʰço?] with θ instead of τ, as opposed to Medieval Greek άτι (*supra*).

rather back, as he explicitly states that he wants to stay and come (= go) tomorrow (L12.16b). Archelaos glosses πορεύομαι for Sinasos as « ζῶ, ἔχω τι ὡς πόρον ζωῆς » (1899: 262) and likewise Karphopoulos for Malakopi (2008: 126) and Mavrochalyvidis & Kesisoglou for Axo (MK117). Obviously, then, Levidis' reading πορέμαι cannot be a corruption of πορεύομαι, as the idiosyncratic Cappadocian meaning of the verb does not fit the context. Moreover, we need an aorist subjunctive, not a present indicative, as is clear from ας μείνω and ας έρθω in the second colon. Karolidis' reading παρεμῶ (K10.34) offers the solution to the crux, although the corresponding line appears at the end of the song. The verb we are looking for is παραμαίνω, analyzed by Dawkins as "a compound of παρά and μαίνω (*i.e.* ε)μβαίνω)" and glossed as 'go away' (D632). The translation is not entirely accurate, as the verb is well attested and glossed as « ἀπέρχομαι εἰς τὴν οἰκίαν » by Karphopoulos (2008: 124) and « πηγαίνω σπίτι » by Mavrochalyvidis & Kesisoglou (MK115). The aorist indicative is παρέμα, subj. παραμῶ (*ibid.*). Karolidis' reading παρεμῶ, if correct, seems to represent an earlier form with both prefixes still visible: παρ-εμ-(π)ῶ.

Because of the formulaic nature of the Akritic songs, it is very interesting to take a closer look at the substitution of newer forms for older ones in both versions. In this respect, the use of Turkish loanwords is very interesting, as it is very unlikely that they were already in place when the songs started being transmitted. The case of χαϊβάνια [xainápa] 'cattle' (L12.1b) ~ ζουμπούλια [zumbúʎa] 'hyacinths' (K10.1b) is therefore not particularly revealing, as both are of Turkish origin.[143] More interesting is the use of the loanverb κοβαλατίζω [kovalatízo] 'run after, chase' in Levidis' version (L12.4a) vis-à-vis Karolidis' use of κολώ [koló] 'drive' (K10. 4a), a verb used all over Cappadocia but with unknown etymology.[144] Given the spread of the distinctively Cappadocian word κολώ, it is surprising that it should have been replaced by a Turkish loanverb.

Very intriguing as well is the use of the loanverb σαλτώ [saltó] 'let go' in Levidis' version: σάλτα [sálta] (L12.5a), εσάλτ'σεν [esáltsen] (L12.7a) versus Karolidis' use of αφήνω [afíno]: άφες [áfes] (K10.5a), αφήκεν [afícen] (K10.7a). Both verbs are used in Dawkins' folktales from Delmeso: the former appears as σαλδώ [saldó], with a voiced instead of an unvoiced alveolar plosive and

---

[143] χαϊβάν [xaiván] 'animal', pl. χαϊβάνια [xainápa] 'cattle' (D673) < Tk. *hayvan*; ζουμπουλ' [zumbul], perhaps to be read as ζϋμπϋλ' [zymbýl] 'hyacinth' Cappa (Lagarde 1886: 17c) < Tk. *sümbül*, Central Anatolian Tk. *zümbül* (*DS*).
[144] κολώ [koló] 'drive' Cappa (D611), etymology unknown, but see Karolidis (1885: 176) and Archelaos (1889: 245) for the spread of the verb and fanciful etymologies.

always in the sense of 'send'.¹⁴⁵ The aorist indicative is syncopated, as in Levidis' version, but with further cluster reduction: εσάλδησεν [esáldisen] > εσάλτ'σεν [esáltsen] > εσάλσεν [esálsen] or, without the augment, σάλσεν [sálsen] (both in the same text right after each other, D324). The present imperative σάλτα is apparently used as the equivalent of the aorist imperative άφες, but the reason is not metrical, but aspectual. That is to say, Cappadocian does not have an aspectual opposition between perfective and imperfective imperatives, barytone verbs having only perfective, oxytones only imperfective imperatives.¹⁴⁶

The case of σαλτώ [saltó] ~ σαλδώ [saldó] is interesting for other reasons as well, because the other Turkish loanverb is not an oxytone, but a barytone: κοβαλατίζω [kovalatízo] (L12.4a).¹⁴⁷ The borrowing of Turkish loanverbs takes place in the aorist, the perfective aspect being unmarked as opposed to the imperfective aspect. The basis for the borrowing process is the equivalent of the Greek aorist: the Turkish perfective or *dI*-past (Lewis 2000: 128). The basis for the borrowing is the 3sg of perfective past in accordance with Watkins' Law (Janse 2009b: 100–1003):¹⁴⁸ *sal-dı-Ø* [saldɯ] 'send-PFV-3sg' → aorist indicative 3sg (ε)-σάλ+δï-σ-εν [(e)sáldɯsen] > (ε)-σάλτ'σεν [(e)sáltsen] > (ε)-σάλσεν [(e)sálsen] (cf. supra), subj. 3sg σαλνδïσ(ει) [saldɯʃ(i)] or, without vowel harmony, σαλδίσ(ει) [saldíʃ(i)]. From the unmarked aorist two present stems can be formed, either oxytone σαλδώ [saldó] or barytone σαλδïζω [saldɯzo] or, without vowel harmony, σαλδίζω [saldízo]. According to Dawkins (D677), the oxytone variant is the only one attested in Cappadocian, including Delmeso and Aravan.¹⁴⁹ Phosteris and Kesisoglou, on the other hand, list σαλδïζω [saldɯzo] and σαλδώ [saldó] as variants for Aravan (PK55).¹⁵⁰ The reality is probably that the oxytone and

---

145 The verbal root *sal-* means 'let go' and in Anatolian Turkish also 'send' (*DS*); see also Dawkins (D677).
146 Cf. D139), Janse (2020: §7.6.1.6).
147 Dawkins translates κοβαλατίζ' incorrectly as 'strikes' (1934: 120), which is odd, as the verb is correctly translated as 'run after, chase' in his glossary (D682) < Tk. *kovala-*.
148 On the details of the borrowing process see Dawkins (D42¹, 129), Janse (2001: 477–478; 2009b: 100–103; 2020: §7.6.1.3, 9.4.2, 11.2.10).
149 Dawkins' folktales from Delmeso provide the present indicatives 3pl σαλδούν [saldún] (D320) and σαλδά [saldá] (D326), those from Aravan the present imperative 2sg σάλδα [sálda] (D336).
150 Their folktales, however, only contain examples of the oxytone variant: σάλδιναν [sáldinan] (PK114 *bis*).

barytone variants were often conflated, as the latter are found very frequently at Delmeso and elsewhere.[151]

As a matter of fact, oxytones and barytones in -ίζω were often conflated in MedGr as well. *CGMG* devotes a special section to this particular type of transfer and quotes numerous examples of barytone to oxytone and vice versa (3.1307–1311). They rightly emphasize that the availability of both oxytone and barytone forms of the same verbs is very convenient for poets composing political verse, because it allowed them to use oxytone or proparoxytone forms before the caesura, but paroxytone forms at verse end (1307). The oxtyone στριγγώ [striŋgó] (L12. 14b = K10.13b), attested in Cappadocia at Aravan (but only with reference to birds),[152] has a barytone variant στριγγίζω [striŋgízo] in MedGr. The fifteenth-century poet Leonardus Dellaportas uses present indicative 1sg στριγγίζω at verse end (1.796), but 2sg στριγγᾷς before the caesura (2.79). The barytone variant κοβαλατίζ̌ [kovalatíӡ] in Levidis' version (L12.4a) is of course metrically equivalent with its oxtyone counterpart κοβαλατά [kovalatá] / κοβαλαδά [kovaladá], the latter being attested at Malakopi (Karphopoulos 2008: 115), the former at Anakou (Kostakis 1963: 75).

Returning to Karolidis' use of αφήνω [afíno] instead of Levidis' σαλδώ [saldó], it is clear that both ἄφες (K10.5a) and αφήκεν (K10.7a) are archaic forms. The ancient aorist imperative ἄφες continued to be used in LMedGr and EModGr alongside the innovative sigmatic form ἄφησε, often apocopated before clitic pronouns (*CGMG* 3.1661–1662). The ancient aorist indicative ἀφῆκα continued to be used as well alongside two innovative forms: ἄφηκα (*CGMG* 3.1341) and ἄφησα (*CGMG* 3.1312[36]). The archaic forms in -κ- have been preserved in the Cappadocian aorist indicative: αφήκα [afíka] in Central, Northwest and Northeast Cappadocian, άφηκα [áfika] in Southeast and Southwest Cappadocian, often syncopated to άφ'κα [áfka], notably at Delmeso, which differs from the other Northeast Cappadocian dialects with respect to the stress.[153] The aorist imperative, on the other hand, has the sigmatic form: άφησε, but άφησ' before clitic pronouns.[154] It is therefore not clear whether Karolidis correctly transcribed the aorist imperative as ἄφες or should have written άφησ' instead.

---

151 E.g. pres. ind. 1sg αραδΐζω [aradǘzo] 'I am looking for' (D306, 308), 2sg αραδΐεις [aradǘis] (D308), 3sg αραδΐϊ' [aradǘʃ] (D306 *bis*, 308, 328).
152 E.g. το κοκονιός στριγγά [to kokoɲós striŋgá] 'the cock is crowing' (MK41).
153 Cf. Dawkins (D587), Janse (2020: §7.6.3). It may be noted that the Southwest Cappadocian dialects of Aravan and Ghurzono have metathesized forms: pres. ind. βαήνω [váino] ~ βαήκνω [vaíkno], aor. ind. βάφ'κα [váfka] ~ βάκα [váka] (PK21).
154 So still in present-day Mišótika (own fieldnotes) as well as at Axo (MK99, 169). At Aravan the metathesized form is βάης' το [váis to] (D139) or βάηš' το [váiʃ to] (PK104).

It is important to realize, however, that these lines belong to the oldest stratum of the song, as they appear in many other versions about the death of Digenis. Apart from the substitution of σάλτα with άφες and of χέρι with χέρα, line 5 in Levidis' version corresponds with 5b-6a in Karolidis', which is in turn identical with line 25 in a song from Potamia recorded by Levidis (1892: ch. Δ´, δ´) and published by Dawkins (1934: 117), with line 22 in a song from Sinasos recorded by Karolidis (Lagarde 1886: 26),[155] and with line 21 in another song from Sinasos recorded by Archelaos (1899: 160).[156] Likewise, lines 6–7 in Levidis' version appear in more or less the same form in the songs just quoted and in many others from other parts of Asia Minor and the adjacent islands. It is therefore not surprising that archaic forms should appear alongside less archaic and innovative forms and a study of formulaic variation in the Akritic songs is therefore a desideratum.

An important methodological caveat is in place, however. What we have at our disposal are transcriptions of songs and it is clear from Levidis' and Karolidis' versions that these transcriptions are not always reliable. Levidis' πορέμαι [poréme] (L12.16a) ~ Karolidis' παρεμώ [paremó] for παραμώ [paramó] (K10.34a) is a good example, already discussed above. Lagarde's warning that his publication of Karolidis' texts should not be considered definitive (1886: 6) is easily exemplified with a host of ghost readings. Some of these can easily be interpreted as misreadings, e.g. καλλιά [kaʎá] for μαλλιά [maʎá] (K10.5a & 7a), others are plain mistakes, e.g. νέσσατζε [néʃadʒe] for ενέσια [enéʃa] (K10.23). And even if the transcriptions we have are accurate, we have to take into account the possibility that the singer may have made mistakes, which is of course very likely in an oral setting, as we know very well from the AncGr epic tradition. One possible candidate is the enigmatic phrase αντζίς ακρής ακρούτσικα [andʒís akrís akrútʃika] (L12.25a) which, although perfectly interpretable, sounds like a distant echo of a formulaic colon found in several Pontic songs in Politis (1909): ακούσ' ακούσ' Ακρίτα μου [akús akús akríta mu] 'listen, listen, my Akritas'.[157] A similar echo can be found in the first line of another song from Delmeso recorded by Karolidis (Lagarde 1886: 18): ένα πουλί και τσί πουλί [éna pulí ce tʃí pulí] 'a bird and what a bird' (K11.1a). In this case, one wonders who came first: the boy or the bird?

---

155 = Politis (1909: 248, #37) = Lüdeke (1994: 174–175, #24).
156 = Politis (1909: 247, #36) = Lüdeke (1994: 175–176, #25).
157 E.g. #23.35, #24.10, #25.1; also in Levidis' song from Karipler (Dawkins 1934: 113, l. 9).

3 Conclusion

In this chapter I have presented a linguistic analysis of two orally transmitted Akritic songs as evidence for diachronic variation in Cappadocian. Although Akritic songs have been studied intensively from a comparative folkloristic and literary perspective, they have not yet been sufficiently explored and exploited linguistically, leaving aside the rather cursory remarks in Dawkins (1934). I hope to have shown that a comparative linguistic analysis of such songs sheds new light on linguistic variation, not just in Cappadocian but also in LMedGr and EModGr. The reason is that the Greek layer of Cappadocian is essentially LMedGr, with archaisms going back as far as the Asia Minor or Anatolian Koine. Many of the archaisms identified and studied in this chapter shed light on diachronic and diatopic variation in these older stages of the Greek language such as the retention of the AncGr 'postpositive article' as relative pronoun, the AncGr interrogative pronouns τίς, the possessive adjectives ἐμός, σός, ἡμέτερος, ὑμέτερος, the aorist passive in -ην instead of -ηκα, the PcGr / MedGr order of clitic pronouns, the use of να with the subjunctive to express the simple future etc.

The use of the traditional LMedGr decapentasyllable or political verse imposes metrical constraints on the use of certain forms and encourage the use of alternative forms. The centuries-long transmission of the Akritic songs have resulted in a unique admixture of archaic and innovative forms, comparable to the *Kunstsprache* of the AncGr epic tradition. Thus we find the older πηγαίνει [pijéni] (L12.8b) alongside the newer παίνει [péni] (L12.13a) and the syncopated intermediate π'γαίνει [pçéni] (K10.12a); remnants of the older hortative subjunctive 1sg ἄγω 'let me go' > ας ἄγω [aʃ áγo], 1pl ἄγωμε(ν) 'let us go' > ἄμε > ας ἀμ' [aʃ ám] alongside the reanalyzed LMedGr imperative 2sg ἄγωμε(ν) 'go!' > ἄμε > ἀμε [áme], 2pl αμέτ(ε) [amét(e)]; variation in the use of the nominative of the definite article with inherited masculine and feminine nouns denoting animates; lexical variation, with many lexical archaisms not found in other ModGr dialects etc.

I have not systematically reviewed every variant between Levidis' and Karolidis' version of the Akritic song, which would have resulted in a monograph-length chapter. This is just one suggestion for future research, which will include a comparative analysis of two more Akritic songs from Cappadocia (Janse forthcoming) and the critical and comparative edition of other traditional songs from the unpublished manuscript of Levidis (1892) and the published but unedited mansucript of Karolidis (Lagarde 1886: 15–40). One of my personal desiderata is the systematic study of the formulae in these traditional songs, which again reveal an unparallelled variation between the various versions.

References

D = Dawkins (1916) + page number(s).
DS = Türkiye'de Halk Ağzından Derleme Sözlüğü (Ankara: Türk Tarih Kurumu, 1963–82).
Λεξ. = Levidis (1892: Λεξιλόγιον Α'-Θ').
MK = Mavrochalividis & Kesisoglou (1960) + page number(s).
PK = Phosteris & Kesisoglou (1960) + page number(s).

Alektoridis, Anastasios S. 1883. Λεξιλόγιον τοῦ εν Φερτακαίνοις τῆς Καππαδοκίας γλωσσικοῦ ἰδιώματος. Δελτίον τῆς Ἱστορικῆς καὶ Ἐθνολογικῆς Ἑταιρείας τῆς Ἑλλάδος 1, 480–508.
Anastasiadis, Vasilios K. 1975. Ἱστορία καὶ γλῶσσα τῆς Καππαδοκίας καὶ τὸ ἰδίωμα τῶν Φαράσων. Μικρασιατικὰ Χρονικά 16, 150–184.
Anastasiadis, Vasilios K. 1976. Ἡ σύνταξη στὸ Φαρασιώτικο ἰδίωμα τῆς Καππαδοκίας σὲ σύγκριση πρὸς τὰ ὑπόλοιπα ἰδιώματα τῆς Μικρᾶς Ἀσίας, καθὼς καὶ πρὸς τὴν Ἀρχαία, τὴ Μεσαιωνικὴ καὶ τὴ Νέα Ἑλληνικὴ γλῶσσα. PhD dissertation, Aristotle University of Thessaloniki.
Andriotis, Nikolaos. 1948. Τὸ γλωσσικὸ ἰδίωμα τῶν Φαράσων. Athens: Ἴκαρος.
Andriotis, Nikolaos. 1974. Lexikon der Archaismen in der neugriechischen Dialekten. Wien: Verlag der Österreichischen Akademie der Wissenschaften.
Andriotis, Nikolaos. 1995. Ἐτυμολογικὸ λεξικὸ τῆς κοινῆς Ἑλληνικῆς. 3rd ed. Thessaloniki: Ἰνστιτοῦτο Νεοελληνικῶν Σπουδῶν (Ἵδρυμα Μανόλη Τριανταφυλλίδη).
Archelaos, Ioannis Sarantidis. 1899. Ἡ Σινασός: ἤτοι θέσις, ἱστορία, ἠθικὴ καὶ διανοητικὴ κατάστασις, ἤθη, ἔθιμα καὶ γλῶσσα τῆς ἐν Καππαδοκίᾳ κωμοπόλεως Σινασοῦ, ἐν ἐπιμέτρῳ δὲ καὶ σύντομος περιγραφὴ τῶν ἐν ταῖς ἐπαρχίαις Καισάρειας καὶ Ἰκονίου Ἑλληνικῶν Κοινοτήτων, ὡς καὶ τῶν ἐν αὐταῖς σωζομένων ἑλληνικῶν διαλέκτων ἐν σχέσει πρὸς τὴν ἐν Σινασῷ λαλουμένην. Athens: Ἰωάννης Νικολαΐδης.
Burgière, Paul & Robert Mantran. 1952. Quelques vers grecs du XIIIe siècle. Byzantion 22, 63–79.
Brixhe, Claude. 1987. Essai sur le grec anatolien au début de notre ère. Nancy: Presses Universitaires de Nancy.
Brixhe, Claude. 2010. Linguistic diversity in Asia Minor during the Empire: Koine and non-Greek languages. In Egbert Bakker (ed.), A companion to the Ancient Greek language, 228–252. Chichester: Wiley-Blackwell.
Bubeník, Vít. 1989. Hellenistic and Roman Greece as a sociolinguistic area. Amsterdam: Benjamins.
Bubenik, Vit. 2014. Koine, Origins of. EAGLL [online edition].
Cappel, Andrew J. 1991. Akritai. In Alexander P. Kazhdan (ed.), The Oxford dictionary of Byzantium, 47. Oxford: Oxford University Press.
Costakis, Athanase P. 1964. Le parler grec d'Anaku. Athens: Centre d'études d'Asie mineure.
Dawkins, Richard MacGillivray. 1910. Modern Greek in Asia Minor. The Journal of Hellenic Studies 30.109–132, 267–291.
Dawkins, Richard McGillivray. 1916. Modern Greek in Asia Minor: A study of the dialects of Sílli, Cappadocia and Phárasa with grammar, texts, translations and glossary. Cambridge: Cambridge University Press.
Dawkins, Richard McGillivray. 1934. Some Modern Greek songs from Cappadocia. American Journal of Archaeology 34, 12–122.

Dawkins, Richard McGillivray. 1946. A Byzantine carol in honour of St. Basil. *The Journal of Hellenic Studies* 66, 43–47.
Dedes, Dimitris. 1993. Τὰ ἑλληνικὰ ποιήματα τοῦ Μαυλανᾶ Ρουμῆ καὶ τοῦ γιοῦ του Βαλέντ κατὰ τὸν 13ον αἰῶνα. *Τὰ Ἱστορικά* 18–19, 3–22.
Horrocks, Geoffrey. 1990. Clitics in Greek: A diachronic review. In Maria Roussou & Stavros Panteli (eds.) *Greek outside Greece II*, 35–52. Athens: Diaspora Books.
Horrocks, Geoffrey. 2010. *Greek: A history of the language and its speakers*. 2nd ed. Chichester: Wiley-Blackwell.
Ioannidis, S. 1870. *Ἔπος μεσαιωνικὸν εκ τοῦ χειρογράφου Τραπεζοῦντος: Βασίλειος Διγενῆς Ἀκρίτης ὁ Καππαδόκης*. Constantinople: Κεφαλίδης.
Janse, Mark. 1993. La position des pronoms personnels enclitiques en grec néo-testamentaire à la lumière des dialectes néo-helléniques. In: Claude Brixhe (ed.): *La koiné grecque antique*. I. *Une langue introuvable*, 83–121. Nancy: Presses Universitaires de Nancy, 1993.
Janse, Mark. 1994. Son of Wackernagel. The distribution of object clitic pronouns in Cappadocian. In Irene Philippaki-Warburton, Katerina Nicolaidis & Maria Sifianou (eds.): *Themes in Greek linguistics: Papers from the First International Conference on Greek Linguistics, Reading, September 1993*, 435–442. Amsterdam: Benjamins.
Janse, Mark. 1998a. Cappadocian clitics and the syntax-morphology interface. In Brian D. Joseph, Geoffrey Horrocks & Irene Philippaki-Warburton (eds.): *Themes in Greek Linguistics II*, 257–281. Amsterdam: Benjamins.
Janse, Mark. 1998b. Grammaticalization and typological change : The clitic cline in inner Asia Minor Greek. In Mark Janse (ed.), *Productivity and creativity: Studies in general and descriptive linguistics in honor of E.M. Uhlenbeck*, 521–547. Berlin Mouton de Gruyter.
Janse, Mark. 1999. Greek, Turkish, and Cappadocian relatives revis(it)ed. In: Amalia Mozer (ed.): *Greek linguistics '97: Proceedings of the 3rd International Conference on Greek Linguistics*, 453–462. Athens: Ellinika Grammata.
Janse, Mark. 2001. Morphological borrowing in Asia Minor Greek. In Yoryia Aggouraki et al. (eds.), *Proceedings of the 4th International Conference on Greek Linguistics (Nicosia, 17–19 September 1999)*, 473–479. Thessaloniki: University Studio Press.
Janse, Mark. 2002. Aspects of Bilingualism in the History of the Greek Language. In J.N. Adams, Mark Janse & Simon Swain (eds.), *Bilingualism in ancient society: Language contact and the written text*, 332–390. Oxford: Oxford University Press.
Janse, Mark. 2004. Animacy, definiteness and case in Cappadocian and other Asia Minor Greek dialects. *Journal of Greek Linguistics* 5. 3–26.
Janse, Mark. 2006. Object position in Cappadocian and other Asia Minor Greek dialects. In Mark Janse, Brian D. Joseph & Angela Ralli (eds.), *Proceedings of the Second International Conference of Modern Greek Dialects and Linguistic Theory*, 115–129. Patras: University of Patras.
Janse, Mark. 2007. The Cappadocian language / dialect continuum. *Abstracts of the 4th International Conference on Language Variation in Europe (ICLaVE 2007), 17–19 June 2007, Nicosia, Cyprus*, 22. Nicosia: University of Cyprus.
Janse, Mark. 2008. Clitic doubling from Ancient to Asia Minor Greek. In Dalina Kallulli & Liliane Tasmowski (eds.), *Clitic doubling in the Balkan languages*, 165–202. Amsterdam: Benjamins.
Janse, Mark. 2009a. Greek-Turkish language contact in Asia Minor. *Études Helléniques / Hellenic Studies* 17, 37–54.

Janse, Mark. 2009b. Watkins' law and the development of agglutinative inflections in Asia Minor Greek. *Journal of Greek Linguistics* 5, 3–26.
Janse, Mark. 2019. Agglutinative noun inflection in Cappadocian. In Angela Ralli (ed.), *The morphology of Asia Minor Greek: Selected topics*, 66–115. Leiden: Brill.
Janse, Mark. 2020. Η Καππαδοκική διάλεκτος. In Chr. Tzitzilis (ed.), Νεοελληνικές διάλεκτοι. Thessaloniki: Ἰνστιτοῦτο Νεοελληνικῶν Σπουδῶν (Ἱδρυμα Μανόλη Τριανταφυλλίδη), in press.
Janse, Mark. Forthcoming. Ακρίτης κάστρον έχτισε: Variation and change in Akritic songs from Cappadocia. In preparation.
Janse, Mark & Johan Vandewalle. 2020. The history and etymology of Cappadocian *fšáx* 'child', Pharasiot *fšáxi* 'boy'. *Transactions of the Philological Society* 118, forthcoming.
Jeffreys, Elizabeth M. 1991. Akritic songs. *ODB* 48.
Jeffreys, Elizabeth M. 1998. *Digenis Akritis: The Grottaferrata and Escorial versions*. Cambridge: Cambridge University Press.
Jeffreys, Michael. 2019. From hexameters to fifteen-syllable verse. In Wolfram Hörandner, Andreas Rhoby & Nikos Zaglas (eds.), *A companion to Byzantine poetry*, 66–91. Leiden: Brill.
Jerphanion, Guillaume de. 1925–1942. *Une nouvelle province de l'art byzantin: Les églises rupestres de Cappadoce*. Paris: Geuthner.
Joseph, Brian D. 1980. Watkins' law and the Modern Greek preterite. *Sprache* 26, 179–184.
Kappler, Matthias. 2010. Die griechischen Verse aus dem *İbtidâ-nâme* von Sultân Veled. In Matthias Kappler, Mark Kirchner & Peter Zieme (eds.), *Trans-Turkic studies: Festschrift in honour of Marcel Erdal*, 379–397. Istanbul: Mehmet Ölmez Yayınları.
Karatsareas, Petros. 2011. *A study of Cappadocian Greek nominal morphology from a diachronic and dialectological perspective*. PhD dissertation, University of Cambridge.
Karatsareas, Petros. 2013. Understanding diachronic change in Cappadocian Greek: The dialectological perspective. *Journal of Historical Linguistics* 3, 192–229.
Karolidis, Pavlos. 1885. Γλωσσάριον συγκριτικὸν Ἑλληνοκαππαδοκικῶν λέξεων ἤτοι ἡ ἐν Καππαδοκίᾳ λαλουμένη Ἑλληνικὴ διάλεκτος καὶ τὰ ἐν αὐτῇ σῳζόμενα ἴχνη τῆς ἀρχαίας Καππαδοκικῆς γλώσσας. Smyrna: Ὁ Τύπος.
Karphopoulos, P. 2008. Γραμματικά; λεξιλόγιον. In Eleni G. Tzioutzia (ed.), *Μαλακοπὴ Καππαδοκίας: Μέσα ἀπό πηγές, ἔγγραφα καὶ μαρτυρίες*. Thessaloniki: ILP Productions
Kesisoglou, Ioannis I. 1951. *Τὸ γλωσσικὸ ἰδίωμα τοῦ Οὐλαγάτς*. Athens: Institut français d'Athènes.
Kitromilides, Paschalis M. 1990. Irredentism in Asia Minor and Cyprus. *Middle Eastern Studies* 26. 3–17.
Kontosopoulos, Nikolaos G. 1994. *Διάλεκτοι καὶ ἰδιώματα τῆς νέας ἑλληνικῆς*. 2nd ed. Athens: Γρηγόρης.
Kostakis, Athanasios P. 1963. *Ἡ Ἀνακού*. Athens: Κέντρο Μικρασιατικῶν Σπουδῶν.
Kostakis, Athanasios P. 1968. *Τὸ γλωσσικὸ ἰδίωμα τῆς Σίλλης*. Athens: Κέντρο Μικρασιατικῶν Σπουδῶν.
Kotsanidis, Lazaros. 2005. *Το γλωσσικό ιδίωμα του Μιστί Καππαδοκίας*. Kilkis: Γνώμη Κιλκίς-Παιονίας.
Krinopoulos, Sokratis. 1889. *Τὰ Φερτάκαινα: Ὑπὸ εθνολογικὴν καὶ φιλολογικὴν ἐποψιν εξεταζόμενα*. Athens: Δημ. Φέξης.
Lagarde, Paul. 1886. *Neugriechisches aus Kleinasien*. Göttingen: Dieterichsche Verlagsbuchhandlung.

Lauxtermann, Marc D. 1999. *The spring of rhythm: An essay on the political verse and other Byzantine meters*. Wien: Verlag der Österreichischen Akademie der Wissenschaften.
Lauxtermann, Marc D. 2019. *Byzantine poetry from Pisides to Geometres: Texts and contexts*. Vol. 2. Wien: Verlag der Österreichischen Akademie der Wissenschaften.
Lekakou, Marika & Petros Karatsareas. 2016. Marking definiteness multiply: Evidence from two varieties of Greek. In Mark Janse, Brian D. Joseph & Angela Ralli (eds.), *Proceedings of the 6th International Conference on Modern Greek Dialects and Linguistic Theory, Patras, 25–28 September 2014*, 189–203. Patras: University of Patras.
Levidis, Anastasios M. 1892. *Πραγματεία περὶ τῆς εν Καππαδοκίᾳ λαλουμένης γλώσσης: Μετὰ τῶν δημωδῶν ᾀσμάτων, αἰνιγμάτων, παροιμιῶν, ευχῶν, καταρῶν, ὅρκων, κυρίων ονομάτων, μύθων, ᾀσμάτων μεσαιωνικῶν, γραμματικῆς, καὶ γλωσσαρίων οκτώ, καὶ σημειώσεων*. Unpublished manuscript. Oxford: Bodleian Library [Arch.Z.Dawk.22].
Lewis, Geoffrey. 2000. *Turkish grammar*. 2nd ed. Oxford: Oxford University Press.
Lüdeke, Hedwig. 1994. *Ἑλληνικὰ δημοτικὰ τραγούδια: Τὰ ακριτικά / Neugriechische Volkslieder: Akritenlieder*. Athens: Ἀκαδημία Ἀθηνῶν.
Mackridge, Peter. 1990. The metrical structure of the oral decapentasyllable. *Byzantine & Modern Greek Studies* 14, 200–212.
Mackridge, Peter. 1993a. 'None but the brave deserve the fair': Abduction, elopement, seduction and marriage in the Escorial *Digenes Akrites* and Modern Greek heroic songs. In Roderick Beaton & David Ricks (ed.), *Digenes Akrites: New approaches to Byzantine heroic poetry*, 150–160. Aldershot: Variorum.
Mackridge, Peter. 1993b. An editorial problem in Medieval Greek texts: The position of the object clitic pronoun in the Escorial *Digenes Akrites*. In Nikolaos M. Panagiotakis (ed.), *Ἀρχές τῆς νεοελληνικῆς λογοτεχνίας: Πρακτικά του δεύτερου διεθνούς συνεδρίου "Neograeca Medii Aevi"*, 325–342. Venice: Instituto Ellenico di Studi Bizantini e Postbizantini di Venezia.
Mackridge, Peter. 2000. The position of the weak object pronoun in Medieval and Modern Greek. *Jazyk i rečevaja dejatel'nost'* 3. 133–151.
Manolessou, Io. 2019. The historical background of the Asia Minor dialects. In Angela Ralli (ed.), *The morphology of Asia Minor Greek: Selected topics*, 20–65. Leiden: Brill.
Mavrochalividis, Giorgios P. 1990. *Ἡ Ἀξὸ Καππαδοκίας*. Athens: Ἐστία Νέας Σμύρνης.
Mavrochalividis, Giorgios P. & Ioannis I. Kesisoglou. 1960. *Τὸ γλωσσικὸ ιδίωμα τῆς Ἀξοῦ*. Athens: Institut français d'Athènes.
Papadopoulos, Anthimos A. 1958–61. *Ἱστορικὸν λεξικὸν τῆς Ποντικῆς διαλέκτου*. Athens: Μυρτίδης.
Phates, Thomas. 201. *Χιογός α σι χαρίσ': Εκμάθηση του Μιστιώτικου ιδιώματος (άνευ διδασκάλου)*. Konitsa.
Phosteris, Dimitrios & Kesisoglou, Ioannis O. 1960. *Λεξιλόγιο τοῦ Ἀραβανί*. Athens: Institut français d'Athènes.
Politis, Nikolaos G. 1909. Ἀκριτικὰ ᾄσματα: ὁ θάνατος τοῦ Διγενῆ. *Λαογραφία* 1, 169–275.
Ralli, Angela. 2016. Strategies and patterns of loan verb integration in Modern Greek varieties. In Angela Ralli (ed.), *Contact morphology in Modern Greek dialects*, 73–108. Cambridge: Cambridge Scholars Press.
Ralli, Angela. 2019. Introduction. In Angela Ralli (ed.), *The morphology of Asia Minor Greek: Selected topics*, 1–19. Leiden: Brill.
Sarantidis Archelaos, Ioannis cf. Archelaos, Ioannis Sarantidis

Saunier, Guy. 1993. Is there such a thing as an 'akritic song'? Problems in the classification of Modern Greek narrative songs. Roderick Beaton & David Ricks (ed.), *Digenes Akrites: New approaches to Byzantine heroic poetry*, 139–149. Aldershot: Variorum.

Symeonidis, Charalambos. 1976. *Der Vokalismus der griechischen Lehnwrter im Türkischen*. Thessaloniki: Institute for Balkan Studies.

Theodoridis, Dimitri. 2004. Versuch einer Neuausgabe von drei griechischen Doppelversen aus dem *Dīwān* von Sulṭān Walad. *Byzantion* 74, 433–451.

Thomason, Sarah Grey & Terrence Kaufman. 1988. *Language contact, creolization, and genetic linguistics*. Berkeley: University of California Press.

Thumb, Albert. 1910. *Handbuch der neugriechischen Volkssprache*. 2nd ed. Strassburg: Trübner.

Vryonis, Speros, Jr. 1971. *The decline of medieval Hellenism in Asia Minor and the process of Islamization from the eleventh through the fifteenth cnetury*. Berkeley: University of California Press.

Winford, Donald. 2005. Contact-induced changes: Classification and processes. *Diachronica* 22. 373–427.

Part II: **Dimensions of variation in Post-classical and Byzantine Greek**

Carla Bruno
10 Tense variation in Ptolemaic papyri: Towards a grammar of epistolary dialogue

Abstract: This study investigates, through a qualitative approach, the distribution of finite verb forms expressing absolute time within a small corpus of Ptolemaic private papyrus letters, particularly focusing on the use of the present, perfect and aorist indicatives. Since sender and recipient do not share the same chrono-topic coordinates, compared to other forms of *discourse*, the epistolary communication, which is time-delayed and mediated by letters, offers an interesting perspective on the use of those tenses that are anchored to the moment of utterance. As a result, the sender's point of view may shift from his/her own present (i.e. the moment of the encoding) to the receiver's (i.e. the moment of the decoding), alternatively assumed as reference points for the statement. Scholars report similar cases in letters only for the past tenses (accordingly labelled as *epistolary*), through which – unexpectedly – sometimes the senders describe events occurring at the moment of writing. However, our survey highlights a number of inconsistencies in the anchoring of the verb not only in the past tenses, but also in the primary stems here under examination. In conclusion, the notion of *epistolary tense* – traditionally restricted to past tenses – may therefore represent a heuristic tool enabling a better understanding of the category of grammatical tense in letters.

1 Pieces of epistolary dialogues

Since the earliest attempts at establishing a textual typology, the dialogic attitude assumed by the sender in an exchange of letters has been variously captured by scholars. According to an often-quoted passage of the author of *De Elocutione*, a letter is, for instance, τὸ ἕτερον μέρος τοῦ διαλόγου 'the other half of a dialogue':

(1) Ἀρτέμων μὲν οὖν ὁ τὰς Ἀριστοτέλους ἀναγράψας ἐπιστολάς φησιν, ὅτι δεῖ ἐν τῷ αὐτῷ τρόπῳ διάλογόν τε γράφειν καὶ ἐπιστολάς· εἶναι γὰρ τὴν ἐπιστολὴν οἷον τὸ ἕτερον μέρος τοῦ διαλόγου.

Note: This project has received funding from the European Union's Horizon 2020 research and innovation programme under grant agreement No. 649307.

'Artemon, the editor of Aristotle's *Letters*, says that a letter ought to be written in the same manner as a dialogue, a letter being regarded by him as one of the two sides of a dialogue.'
(Demetr., *Eloc.* §223) [tr. W.R. Roberts]

In this passage, overtly recasting the words of Artemon, i.e. the editor of Aristotle's letters, the author associates the letter with the enunciative dimension that Benveniste (1974) called *discourse*,[1] where the speaker overtly presents himself as the source of the message. What is characteristic of the *discourse* is the speaker's overt orientation towards the recipient, as well as the anchoring of the message in the chrono-topic framework of the act of enunciation.

Alongside personal and spatial deictic markers, tense is one of the linguistic forms by means of which the speaker displays his relation to this act.[2] In particular, since the tense situates the statement with respect to the time of utterance, the speaker's discursive attitude can emerge in the use of spatio-temporal coordinates co-extensive with the moment of enunciation – anchored in the *hic et nunc* in which the verbal act occurs – as in oral dialogues (and in their theatrical mimesis) as well as in written correspondence.

However, unlike face-to-face conversations, in epistolary interaction, speaker and addressee are separated and they do not share the same spatio-temporal framework.[3] Every epistolary communication then involves a time gap between the encoding and the decoding of the message, which senders can ignore or take into account with obvious effects on the statement, especially on the tense stem alternation.

Consider for instance the passages compared below in (2) and (3), which – according to the diverse reference time assumed by the sender[4] – respectively

---

[1] *Story* and *discourse* are the two planes of the enunciation posited by Benveniste (1966). Unlike *discourse*, *historic enunciation* deals with "la présentation de faits survenus à un certain moment du temps, sans aucune intervention du locuteur dans le récit" ["the presentation of events that took place at a certain moment of time without any intervention of the speaker in the narration"] (Benveniste 1966: 239).
[2] According to Benveniste (1974), tense is one of the main linguistic markers "whose function is to put the speaker in a constant and necessary relation to his enunciation" (tr. D. Maingueneau). The "formal apparatus of enunciation" further includes: deictic markers referring to the interlocutors, demonstrative forms and modal markers.
[3] In mediated interaction, there is also a clear orientation of the addresser towards the addressee, but, unlike face-to-face communication, the two parts are separated (Thompson 1993: 82–84). Cf. also Altman (1982), who explores the artistic potential of the letter through the epistolary novel and singles out some recurrent linguistic patterns.
[4] To simplify the complex picture related to writing and literacy in the ancient world, the named sender is conventionally assumed to be also the author of the letter, apart from the

differ in presenting the topos of the delivery of the letter as an unaccomplished event (cf. κομίζοντι 'who carries', l. 9) and as an accomplished event (cf. ἀποδεδωκότι 'who has brought', l. 3).

(2) καλῶς ἂν οὖν ποιήσαις τὴμ πᾶσαν σπουδὴν| ποιησάμενος τοῦ συλληφθῆναι αὐτούς| [[ἵνα καὶ οια . . . οι]] καὶ παραδοὺς Στράτωνι| τῶι κομίζοντί σοι τὸ ἐπιστόλιον.

'Therefore, you would do well, making due haste that they be recovered, to hand them over to Straton who carries this note to you.'
(P.Cair.Zen. I 59015, ll. 6–9; 259–258 BCE) [tr. J.L. White, no. 6]

(3) καλῶς ἂν οὖν ποιήσαις δοὺς Νικάδαι| τῶι τὰ γράμματά σοι **ἀποδεδωκότι** (δραχμὰς) ρν.

'Therefore, you would do well to give 150 drachmas to Nikadas who has brought the letter to you.'
(P.Cair.Zen. I 59016, ll. 2–3; 259 BCE) [tr. J.L. White, no. 5]

Similar variations in the anchoring of the statement are not uncommon in letters. Scholars have especially labelled as *epistolary* those cases in which the sender – assuming the point of view of the recipient – describes the state of affairs located in their own present as past.[5] The tense stem alternation is thus shown to depend on the mode of interaction, which is – in the papyri language – mediated by letters and delayed time.

Accordingly, this study aims to deal with some aspects of the verb tense alternation, which can be traced back to the interaction mode (i.e. the epistolary mode) within a small corpus of early Ptolemaic private papyrus letters taken from White's (1986) collection. It consists of fifty-two documents ranging from the third to the second century BCE, which, despite the limited number of the items included, is sufficient for the emergence of regularities in the distribution of tense stems, given the stable frequency of the feature under examination. Additionally, due to

---

possible divergence between a sender, in whose name the letter is written, and a scribe, who has performed the act of writing (cf. Dossena 2012).

5 Cf., e.g. Mayser, who noted that "wo wir das Präsens erwarten, indem sich der Briefschreiber oder Bote zum voraus in die Lage des Empfängers versetzt" (2.1: 144). According to Naiden (1999), the practice – e.g. avoided in the letters in Herodotus' *Histories* – may not have been a very ancient one and maybe reflect the Aramaic letter writing tradition, according to which the preterite is reserved for the action of the writer and the present is employed for the reader. The earlier instance of the pattern is preserved within an ancient Attic letter, whose wording is not yet as strictly structured as the later epistolary patterns.

(i) Μνησίεργος| **ἐπέστειλε** τοῖς οἴκοι| χαίρεν καὶ ὑγιαίνεν·| καὶ αὐτὸς ἔφας[κ]ε [ἔχεν]
'Mnesiergos sends (lit. 'sent') to the people at home greetings and good health; he said that he too was like that'
(SIG³ 3, 1259, 1–4) [tr. Ceccarelli 2013: 352].

the editor's selection criteria, the collection is generally considered representative of the language variety of the period:[6] it is balanced according to the diversity of epistolary types included (i.e. letters of recommendation, family correspondence, petitions) and the producers' profiles, who were sampled according to gender, social status, education and ethnicity.[7]

Since letters are discursive acts, the present survey was limited to the verb stems expressing "the so-called *absolute time*" (Rijksbaron 2002: 4), i.e. the present, aorist and perfect indicative, which "locate the state of affairs relative to the moment of utterance". Modal and non-finite verb forms, which gain "their temporal value solely from their interaction with other verb forms" (Rijksbaron 2002: 5), were therefore excluded. The data were analysed from a basically qualitative perspective: accordingly, the argument will proceed from a selection of the most illustrative examples, which are discussed in the following sections.

2 Tense and time in epistolary exchanges

2.1 The unshared present

As in other *discourse* modes, in the letters under scrutiny, the present, which expresses the *hic et nunc* of the utterance, is also the most recurrent verb stem used.[8] The form can refer to events going on at the moment of writing, as in (4)–(5), but it is also used to refer to the letter structure, as in (6), where the present ὑπόκειται 'it is appended' introduces – as well as elsewhere – a document attached:

(4) **χρείαν ἔχομεν**| ὥστ' εἰς σίτευσιν ὀρνίθων υ καὶ τοκάδων ρ.

'We have need of four hundred fowls and of one hundred hens for fattening.'
(P.Mich. I 48, ll. 1–2; 251 BCE) [tr. J.L. White, no. 25]

(5) τὴν μὲν οὖν Ἀπολλωνίου εὔνοιαν καὶ τὴν σὴν **ἀναγγέλλει** μοι αὐτὸ τὸ παι[δά-]|| ριον ἣν ἔχοντες διατελεῖτε εἰς αὐτόν.

'Indeed, the boy informs me of the good will of Apollonios and of yourself which you always have for him.'
(P.Col. III 6, ll. 11–12; 257 BCE) [tr. J.L. White, no. 10]

---

6 Cf. Porter & O'Donnell (2010: 294).
7 Cf. White (1986: 3).
8 It accounts for almost 40% of the forms encountered.

(6) τῆς παρ' Ἀθηνοδώρου τοῦ διοικη[τοῦ]| **ὑπόκειταί** σοι τ' ἀντίγραφον.

> 'The copy of the (letter) from Athenodoros the dioiketes is appended below for you.'
> (P.Yale I 36, ll. 1–2; 232 BCE) [tr. J.L. White, no. 27]

Such presents – which have as their deictic centre the *hic et nunc* of the sender – are particularly common with psychological predicates (cf. οἶμαι 'I think' in (7)), also expressing the author's emotional states (cf. ἀηδίζομαι 'I am ill-pleased'[9] in (8)).

(7) οὐκ **οἶμαι** μέν σε ἀγνοεῖν περὶ Αἰσχύλου ὅτι οὐκ ἔστιν| ἡμῖν ἀλλότριος, ἀναπέπλευκεν δὲ πρὸς ὑμᾶς ἵνα συσταθῆι Κλεονίκωι.

> 'I do not think you are ignorant regarding Aischylos, that he is no stranger to us. He has now sailed up river to your company in order to be introduced to Kleonikos.'
> (P.Mich. I 6, ll. 1–2; 257 BCE) [tr. J.L. White, no. 11]

(8) ἐπὶ δὲ τῶι μὴ παραγίνεσθαί σε [π]ά[ντ]ων| τῶν ἐκεῖ ἀπειλημμένων παραγεγο[νό]τω\ν/| **ἀηδίζομαι**

> 'but when you did not come back when all of the others who had been in seclusion returned, I was unhappy'
> (UPZ I 59, ll. 12–14; 168 BCE) [tr. J.L. White, no. 34]

Predictably, they recur in performative expressions, such as συχωρῶ (for συγχωρῶ 'I agree') in (9), by which Eirene, a wealthy woman from the Arsinoite nome, agrees with three other contractors on the rent of an orchard, or ὀμνύο (metaplasm for ὄμνυμι 'I swear') in (10).

(9) **συχωρῶ** ὑμεῖν διαγράψαι Νικάνδρωι Συρακοσίωι| τὸν φό[ρον το]ῦ ὅλου παραδείσου χαλκοῦ τάλαντα τεσσαρά-| κοντα ὀκτὼ ἐν τοῖς κατὰ τὴν μίσθωσιν χρόνοις

> 'I agree with you that you are to pay off to Nikandros, Syracusan, the rent of the entire orchard, forty-eight talents of copper, in the times specified according to the lease'
> (P.Mich. III 183, ll. 3–5; 182 BCE) [tr. J.L. White, no. 30]

(10) **ὀμνύ-| ο** τὸν Σάραπιν, ἰ μὴ μικρόν| τι ἐντρέπομαι, οὐκ ἄν με| ἴδες τὸ πρ\ό/σωπόν μου| πόποτε

> 'I swear by Sarapis, if it were not that I still have a little reverence (for you), you would never see my face again'
> (UPZ I 70, ll. 2–6; 152–151 BCE) [tr. J.L. White, no. 42]

---

9 As translated by Bagnall & Cribiore (2006: 111), who – unlike White (1986) – maintain the present tense of the original text.

Moreover, they are the only form by which writers introduce their requests in petitions, where the present is regularly associated with the verbs δέομαι 'I beg', ἱκετεύω 'I beseech', or ἀξιῶ 'I ask', as illustrated in (11a) and (11b), both taken from the entreaty of Simale, an influential Greek woman, to Zenon, whom she begs to mediate between Apollonios and her son Herophantos.

(11a) εὐπρεπ[ή]ς **δέομαι** οὖν σου| καὶ **ἱκετεύω** ἐπιστροφὴν ποιήσασθαι περὶ τούτων

'Accordingly, therefore, I request and entreat you to bring about a correction of these things.'
(P.Col. III 6, ll. 6–7; 257 BCE) [tr. J.L. White, no. 10]

(11b) **ἀξιῶ** οὖν σε ἅμα δὲ καὶ **δέομαι** εἴ τι συντε[λεῖν τέ-]| ταχε Ἀπολλώνιος αὐτῶι ὀψώνιον ἀποδοθῆναί μοι.

'Therefore, I request and entreat you in this light that, if Apollonios has ordered that he be paid anything else (still outstanding), his wages be paid to me.'
(P.Col. III 6, ll. 12–13; 257 BCE) [tr. J.L. White, no. 10]

There is one request only in the corpus which is not inflected for the present, but for an curious *epistolary* past form (i.e. ἐνήτυχον 'I petitioned'). This is the petition of Senchons, an Egyptian widow, in which the spelling and morpho-syntactic deviations as well as some paleographic aspects, such as the use of the brush for writing, can be traced back to an Egyptian environment.[10]

(12) **ἐνήτυχ[όν]**| σοι περὶ τῆς ὄνου μου ἣν ἔλαβεν Νικί[ας].

'I petitioned you about my ass which Nikias took.'
(P.Mich. I 29, ll. 1–2; 256 BCE) [tr. J.L. White, no. 20]

Accordingly, the use of the thematic aorist ἐνήτυχ[όν] 'I petitioned' (l. 1) to introduce the object of the entreaty could – like the other inconsistencies – also be due to the scribe's poor mastery of both the Greek language and the Greek epistolary formulary, as historical tenses were generally avoided in similar contexts.

On the other hand, unlike the passages discussed so far, the present is available to senders in other circumstances, such as, for instance, when they refer to the moment in which the letter is read. An example is (13), taken from a later piece of correspondence, where the sender uses the present tense κελεύε[ι]ς 'you order'

---

10 Cf. Bagnall & Cribiore (2006: 103) on this letter. See Clarysse (1993) on some common characteristics of the early Ptolemaic papyri written by Egyptian scribes. On some aspects of the Greek-Egyptian interference see Evans (2012) on the Zenon archive and Vierros (2012) on the language of Hellenistic notarial contracts.

in order to refer to instructions that the receiver will dispatch after the delivery of the letter.

(13) τὰς μὲν (δραχμὰς) Α, ἃς δέδωκας Πετενήθι χῆνα ἀγωραζει‹ν›, τί **κελεύε[ι]ς** περὶ τούτων, ἀπόστιλόν μοι ἐπισ-| τόλιον ἔχων\τα/ Πολυδεύκην ταχὺ καὶ ἡ ἕτερον θέλις λέγειν, λέγε.

'Send me a letter quickly by means of Polydeukes, explaining what you want done with the one thousand drachmas (lit. 'what you order about the thousand drachmas') which you gave to Petenethis to buy a goose and if you have anything else you want to say, say it.'
(UPZ I 68, ll. 4–5; 152 BCE) [tr. J.L. White, no. 41]

Accordingly, the present tense, which is the default marking for the time of utterance, in a piece of correspondence, can range from the time in which the letter was written to the moment in which is read.

However, this does not exhaust the contexts in which the present tense occurs. In (14), for instance, by γράφεις 'you write' (l. 11) the writer refers to the content of a previous letter from the recipient.

(14) ἐκομισάμην τὴν παρου σου ἐπιστολὴν τοῦ Παχὼνς ιδ παρὰ Ζωίλου, ἐν ἧι **γράφεις**| θαυμάζων ὅτι οὐθέν σοι ἀπέσταλκα περὶ τῆς συντιμήσεως καὶ τῆς συναγωγῆς τοῦ σπόρου.

'I received your letter on Pachon 14 from Zoilos, in which you express astonishment that I have sent you no word about the valuation and the gathering of the crops.'
(PSI V 502, ll. 11–12; 257 BCE) [tr. J.L. White, no. 18]

Here, the present projects the words of the distant interlocutor in the sender's time frame, compensating for the time gap involved by the epistolary dialogue. It amplifies the moment of the utterance in order to contain both the writer and the reader and synchronize their delayed exchanges, producing a vivid realization of the topos of the *parousia* of the absent interlocutor.[11]

A similar attitude of the writer prevails also in P.Cair.Zen. I 59060, a piece of the correspondence between Zenon, the finance minister secretary, and Hierokles, the manager of a gym. The letter, about the training of a boy named Pyrrus, is mostly construed in the present tense, but as appears from a quick reading of the two excerpts in (15a) and (15b), the verb form does not always correspond to the same deictic centre.

---

11 This is another ideological theme of the classical epistolography. The letter not only allows exchanges with the distant correspondent, but also "transforms bodily absence in spiritual presence" (Klauck 2006: 189).

(15a) ἔ[γραψάς]| μοι περὶ Πύρρου, εἰ [μὲ]ν ἀκρει[βῶ]ς **ἐπιστάμεθα**, ἀλείφειν αὐτόν, εἰ δὲ μέ, μὴ συνβῆ[ι ἀνήλω]-| μά \τε/ μάταιον προσπεσεῖν καὶ [ἀ]πὸ τῶν γραμμάτων ἀποσπαθῆναι. π[ερ]ὶ μὲν οὖ[ν τοῦ με]| ἐπίσστασθαι οἱ θεοὶ μάλιστ' ἂν εἰδέησαν, Πτολεμαίωι δὲ **φαίνεται**, ὅσα κατ' ἄ[νθρωπον],| ὅτι τῶν νῦν ἀλιφομένων, οἳ προειλήφασιν χρόνον πολύν, πολὺ κρείττων π [......]| καὶ σφόδρα ὀλίγου χρόνου πολὺ ὑπερέξει αὐτῶν· **προσπορεύεται** δὲ καὶ πρὸς [ταῦτα]| καὶ πρὸς τὰ λοιπὰ μαθήματα· σὺν δὲ θεοῖς εἰπεῖν **ἐλπίζω** σε τεφανωθήσεσθαι.

'You wrote to me regarding Pyrrhos, (telling me) to anoint him (for gymnastic training), if we know with certainty (that he will be a success), but if not certain, to make sure that he not incur useless expense nor be distracted from his studies. Now, so far as my being certain is concerned, (only) the gods know for sure, but it seems to Ptolemy, so far as a man can tell, that Pyrrhos is much better than those presently being trained, who started training a long time before him, and that very soon he will be much beyond them; moreover, he is also pursuing his other studies; and to speak with the gods' leave, I hope to see you crowned.'
(P.Cair.Zen. I 59060, ll. 1–7; 257 BCE) [tr. J.L. White, no. 15]

(15b) ἔγραψας δέ μοι **θαυμάζεις** εἰ μὴ κατέχω ὅτι τούτοις πᾶσι τέλος ἀκ[ολουθεῖ].| **ἐπίσταμαι**, ἀλλὰ σὺ εἰκανὸς εἶ διοικῶν ἵνα ἀποσταλῆι ὡς ἀσφαλέστατα.

'You wrote to me that you were surprised that I did not realize that there is a tax on all these things. I know it, but you are well able to manage that it be sent with the greatest possible security.'
(P.Cair.Zen. I 59060, ll. 10–11; 257 BCE) [tr. J.L. White, no. 15]

Apparently, the sender, Hierokles, here groups the two sides of his (epistolary) dialogue with the recipient, Zenon, whose words are also reported in the letter. The present occurs in both sides, but it is relative to the time of utterance only in Hierokles' half of the dialogue (cf. φαίνεται 'it seems', προσπορεύεται 'he pursues (his studies)', ἐλπίζω 'I hope', in (15a); ἐπίσταμαι 'I know' in (15b)); in the other half, it recalls the content of the letter previously received from Zenon. In this regard, the sigmatic aorist ἔγραψας 'you wrote' (cf. l. 1 in (15a) and l. 10 in (15b)) regularly used to introduce Zenon's words, marks the switch from the one to the other round of conversation, overtly expressing the gap between the two times.

A picture thus emerges where, in epistolary dialogues, the grammar of the present tense makes possible the "impossible" dialogue in a present (time) between the separated correspondents, since "the present of the letter writer is never the present of his addressee" (Altman 1982: 129). What circumstances make impossible – i.e. the encounter with the other person – is made possible by the language by overcoming the distance between the sender and the receiver and outlining a common interactional framework.[12]

2.2 The perfect and the speech act

Despite at least a century of debate over the basic function of the Greek perfect stem, no real consensus has emerged among scholars: "it is still an open question whether this grammatical category constitutes an *aspect* [. . .], *tense* or *Aktionsart*, a mixture of these, or whether it represents a category of its own" (Bentein 2014: 46, where the diverse approaches to the matter are discussed with an examination of their critical issues). Nevertheless, there are some aspects of the perfect distribution on which scholars generally agree, i.e. its relation with the reference time and its stativizing value. Perfect forms can often be interpreted as present states resulting from a (prior) event. Scholars then disagree about the entity affected by the state[13] or about the relevance of discursive[14] and aspectual[15] features, but they all acknowledge the relevance of the enunciative dimension in defining the class.

---

12 Here, as elsewhere, the present indicative seems then to evoke a "pseudo-moment of utterance" shared by sender and receiver. According to Rijksbaron (2002: 22), this is the feature also underpinning the occurrences of the so-called "historic present", where "the narrator plays the role of an eyewitness" to a past event. Also in the letters selected, there are contexts in which the present combines with historical tenses in narrative sequences as e.g. ποιοῦμαι (l. 6) in the following excerpt from the report of Philotas to Zenon:

> (ii) ταύτην μ[ὲ]ν οὖν τὴν ὠνὴν **ἠρά-| μην**, ἄλλην δὲ **ποιοῦμαι** εἰς τὸ Ἀπολλοφάνους ὄνομα καὶ ἀπὸ τ[ο]ῦ συγκεχωρημένου| τέλους **ἀφεῖλον** (δραχμὰς) μ καὶ **συγκατέστησα** τὰ σώματα ἐπὶ τὸν λ[ι]μένα καὶ **εἰσηγάγομεν|** τὰ σώματα πρὸς Ἡρακλείδην καὶ **παρεδώκαμεν** Ἀπολλοφάνει
>
> 'Whereupon I annulled that (contract?) and made another in the name of Apollophanes and decreased the tax agreed upon by forty drachmas and I brought the slaves back to the harbor and I brought them in to Herakleides (the boat captain in whose ship the slaves were to be carried to Egypt) and handed them over to Apollophanes'
> (P.Cair.Zen. V 59804, ll. 6–9; 258 BCE) [tr. J.L. White, no. 9]

13 In studies drawing on the research of Wackernagel (1904) or Chantraine (1927), it is the object, while it is the subject for, among others, McKay (1965) or both – depending on the predicate type – for Rijksbaron (2002).
14 Cf. Gerö & Stechow (2003), who argue for an "extended now" approach to the Greek data or, among others, Orriens (2009) for an analysis in terms of "current relevance".
15 For an account of the perfect in terms of aspect, cf. McKay (1965, 1980) and Porter (1989), who consider the perfect as a stative present or Evans (2001), who regards the perfect as a imperfective stem.

In the following passages, for instance, the perfect consistently refers to (past) states of affairs, all of which are overtly related to the moment of utterance (i.e. the letter writing): in (16) the sender describes his current need of money because of the expenses he incurred in Tyre; in (17) – already discussed in (11a) – Simale traces back her son's present disease to the prolonged ill-treatment he suffered; in (18) Polemon informs his recipient of the tasks performed:

> (16) ἐν τῆι Τύρωι ἀγοράσματά τινα| λαβὼν **ἀνήλωκα** τὸ ἐφόδιον. καλῶς ἂν οὖν ποιήσαις δοὺς Νικάδαι| τῶι τὰ γράμματά σοι ἀποδεδωκότι (δραχμὰς) ρν.
>
> 'I have spent my travel allowance because of some purchases on Tyre. Therefore, you would do well to give 150 drachmas to Nikadas who has brought the letter to you.'
> (P.Cair.Zen. I 59016, ll. 1–3; 259 BCE) [tr. J.L. White, no. 5]

> (17) εὐπρεπ[ή]ς δέομαι οὖν σου| καὶ ἱκετεύω ἐπιστροφὴν ποιήσασθαι περὶ τούτων καὶ ἀναγγεῖλαι Ἀπολλωνίωι| ὃν [τινα]|| τρόπον μου ὑβριζόμενον τὸ παιδίον **διατετέληκεν** ὑπ' Ὀλυμπιχοῦ
>
> 'Accordingly, therefore, I request and entreat you to bring about a correction of these things and to report to Apollonios in what manner my boy has been so thoroughly mistreated by Olympichos'
> (P.Col. III 6, ll. 6–8; 257 BCE) [tr. J.L. White, no. 10]

> (18) περὶ τῶν| συμβόλων **γεγράφαμεν**| Κρίτωνι καὶ Καλλικλεῖ| ἵνα γένηται ὡς ἐπέ-|σταλκας.
>
> 'Concerning the receipts, we have written to Kriton and Kallikles that the matter be handled as you instructed.'
> (P.Hib. I 40, ll. 2–6; 261–260 BCE) [tr. J.L. White, no. 1]

Both the present and the perfect stem locate a state of affairs at the moment of the utterance, hence they often occur in the same passage (cf. (17)).[16] But, unlike the present, as in (16)–(18), the perfect can also deal with the process from which the state of affairs results.

In accordance with this, the perfect forms tend – within the letters under scrutiny – to mark those passages in which authors present themselves as *writers* or *senders* of the message, i.e. as the prompters of the enunciative act.[17]

---

16 On the discursive value of the perfect and its main use in monological or dialogical contexts "where the speaker's *base* (or: point of view) is located in his own present", cf. Orriens (2009: 231).
17 The perfect of ῥώννυμι (litt. 'I strengthen') has been excluded from the perfects encountered (84 tokens). This occurs only in the conventional opening health wish with the meaning

Consequently, they often associate with the verb forms of γράφω 'I write' (and compounds) or ἀποστέλλω 'I send off' showing a strong correlation with the first person.[18] In (19), from the *memorandum* of Kydippos to Zenon, e.g., the relation of γεγράφαμέν 'we have written' (l. 10) with the reference time is emphasized by its combination with νυνεί (for νυνί) 'now, at this moment'.

(19) νυνεὶ δὲ **γεγράφαμέν** σοι| ὧν χρείαν ἔχομεν, καθά-| περ Ἀπολλώνιος ᾤετο| δεῖν.

'but as it is we have written about what we need, since Apollonios considered it necessary.'
(PSI IV 413, ll. 9–12; 259–257 BCE) [tr. J.L. White, no. 8]

Also in the following excerpts from the letter of Toubias to Apollonios, in the Zenon archive, the perfect shows a strong relation with the circumstances in which the letter was written. Here, ἀπέσταλκα 'I have sent' occurs twice: at line 2 (cf. (20a)), where the sender, Toubias, introduces Aineas, the man entrusted with the delivery of the goods (and, presumably, of the letter too), and at line 5 (cf. (20b)), where he refers to the attachment of a letter addressed to the king. In particular, Toubias claims that he has sent Aineas 'on the tenth of Xandikos' (cf. τοῦ Ξανδικ[οῦ]|| τῆι δεκάτ[ηι, ll. 2–3 in (20a)), which is the day on which the letter was written according to the closing date (ἔτους) κθ, Ξανδικοῦ ι. '(Year) 29, Xandikos 10' at line 7.

(20a) καθάπερ μοι ἔγραψας ἀποστεῖλα[ι - ca.?-]| [-ca.?-] μηνί, **ἀπέσταλκα** τοῦ Ξανδικ[οῦ]|| τῆι δεκάτ[ηι ἄγοντα Αἰνέαν] \τὸν παρ' ἡμῶν/ ἵππους δύο

'Just as you wrote to me to send [gifts for the king] in the month [of Xandikos], I have sent our man [Aineas] on the tenth of Xandikos [bringing] two horses'
(P.Cair.Zen. I 59075, ll. 1–3; 257 BCE) [tr. J.L. White, no. 17]

(20b) **ἀπέσταλκα** δέ [σοι]| καὶ τὴν ἐπι[σ]τολὴν τὴν γραφεῖσαν παρ' ἡμῶν ὑπὲρ τῶν ξενί[ων]|| τῶι βασιλεῖ, ὁμοίως δὲ καὶ τἀντίγραφα αὐτῆς ὅπως εἰδῆις.| ἔρρωσο. (ἔτους) κθ, Ξανδικοῦ ι.

'Also, I have sent the letter which I wrote to the king about the gifts, along with a copy of it that you may know. Good-bye. (Year) 29, Xandikos 10.'
(P.Cair.Zen. I 59075, ll. 5–8; 257 BCE) [tr. J.L. White, no. 17]

'to be in good health'. Almost half of the tokens taken into account are forms of γράφω 'I write' (or compounds) and ἀποστέλλω 'I send'. More than two thirds of these plainly refer to the moment in which the letter was written.

18 On the use of the first-person plural markers – besides the singular ones – for the sender's self-reference in Ptolemaic papyri, cf. Bruno (2017).

Note also that, compared to the distribution of the perfect forms, the aorist ἔγραψας 'you wrote' (cf. (20a), l. 1), which refers to a previous exchange with the recipient, does not involve a reference to the situation at hand. Similarly, as shown by the excerpts in (21), taken from a report on the problems of Straton, Zenon's man, in order to recover the money loaned to an influential Palestinian landowner, the perfect occurs only where the sender, Alexandros, refers to the letter at hand (cf. γέγραφα οὖν σοι 'therefore, I wrote to you' in (21c)), while the aorist gives a detailed report of the prior exchanges among the parties involved: Alexandros and Oryas (cf. ἐκομισάμην 'I received' and ὑ]πέγρ[α]ψάς 'you appended' in (21a)) on the one hand, Alexandros and Jeddous (cf. συναπέστειλα 'I sent' and ἔγρ[α]ψα 'I wrote' in (21b)) on the other.[19]

(21a) **ἐκομισάμην** τὸ παρὰ σ[οῦ ἐ]πιστόλι[ον],| [ἐν ὧι **ὑ]πέγρ[α]ψάς** μοι τήν τε παρὰ Ζήνωνος πρὸς Ἰεδδοῦν γεγρ[αμμένην]

'I received your note, to which you appended a copy of what was written to Jeddous by Zenon'
(P.Cair.Zen. I 59018, ll. 1–2; 258 BCE) [tr. J.L. White, no. 7]

(21b) ἐγὼ μὲν [ο]ὖ ((ν| [ἄρρωστ]ος ἐτύγχανον ἐ\κ φαρμακείας ὤν, **συναπέστειλα** [δὲ Στ]ράτωνι| [παρ' ἡ]μῶν νεανίσκον καὶ ἐπιστολὴν **ἔγρ[α]ψα** πρὸς Ἰεδδοῦν.

'Since I myself happened to be sick because of some medicine, I sent a lad, a servant, to Straton and wrote a letter to Jeddous.'
(P.Cair.Zen. I 59018, ll. 4–6; 258 BCE) [tr. J.L. White, no. 7]

(21c) **γέγραφα** οὖν σοι.| ἔρρωσο.

'Therefore, I wrote to you (that you might know). Good-bye.'
(P.Cair.Zen. I 59018, l. 7; 258 BCE) [tr. J.L. White, no. 7]

Certainly, the strong correlation between the perfect and the verb γράφω 'I write' and ἀποστέλλω 'I send off' is also amplified by the frequency of the disclosure formulae γέγραφα οὖν σοι (ἵνα εἰδῇς) 'I have therefore written to you (in order that you know)' in Ptolemaic letters,[20] as in (20b) (cf. ἀπέσταλκα δέ [σοι] . . . ὅπως εἰδῇς 'I sent to you. . . in order that you know') and (21c) (cf. γέγραφα οὖν σοι 'therefore, I wrote to you').[21] It is nevertheless worth pointing out that other

---

19 Besides, the letter also mentions at line 2 in (21a) the exchange of letters between Zenon and Jeddous: τήν τε παρὰ Ζήνωνος πρὸς Ἰεδδοῦν γεγρ[αμμένην] 'what was written to Jeddous by Zenon'.
20 The formula conveys the sender's intent to inform the recipient about something. Cf. Porter & Pitt (2013) for an overview from the Ptolemaic papyri to the New Testament.
21 The formula occurs, e.g. inflected for the aorist, in (iii) where it refers to a previous exchange of letters between the sender, the native ill-treated by his Greek supervisors, and Zenon:

tenses tend to be excluded in similar contexts, where the speakers present themselves as the initiators of the enunciative act.²² As a result, the aorist occurs when the sender *narrates* his exchanges, and the perfect when he states his current involvement in them.

This picture seems to confirm, for the Ptolemaic papyri scrutinized here, the persistence of a strong correlation between the perfect stem and the moment of utterance. However, the same form – the perfect – seems to relate to this moment in different ways. While in (16)–(18), the perfect refers to states resulting from events accomplished by the time of utterance, in (19)–(21), the perfect of γράφω 'I write' and ἀποστέλλω 'I send off' refers to processes neither accomplished (i.e. writing the letter) nor started (i.e. sending the letter) at the time of utterance. These perfects are, therefore, rather anchored in the moment of the reading of the letter, by which time the acts of writing and sending have been accomplished.

Again, in accordance with the dislocated character of epistolary dialogue, the speaker's point of view can shift from his own present to the receiver's, alternatively assumed as reference points for their statements. In this regard, interestingly enough, the sender constantly chooses the point of view of the receiver when representing himself as the initiator of the interaction.

Since the Greek perfect is a primary tense, Evans (1999) excludes, for its indicative, an *epistolary* value such as the aorist and the imperfect. However,

---

(iii) ἐπεὶ δὲ τῶν ἀναγκαίων ἐν-| δεὴς ἤμην καὶ οὐθὲν ἠδυνάμην οὐθαμόθεν πορί-| ζειν ἠναγκάσθην ἀποτρέχειν εἰς Συρίαν ἵνα μὴ τῶι| λιμῶι παραπόλωμαι. **ἔγραψα** οὖν σοι ἵνα εἰδῆις ὅτι Κρό-| τος αἴτιος.

'But when I became in want of necessities and was unable to procure anything anywhere, I was obliged to run away into Syria lest I perish of hunger. Therefore, I wrote to you in order that you know that Krotos was the cause.'
(P. Col. IV 66, ll. 9–13; 256–255 BCE) [tr. J.L. White, no. 22].

22 Cf. (iv), where the present of γράφω 'I write' shows a generic value. The sender, the Greek soldier Esthlades, here recalls a common habit (cf. πλειονάκις 'several times') and the switch to the enunciative dimension is marked by the subsequent ἔτι καὶ νῦν 'also once again' (l. 6):

(iv) ἐπεὶ **πλειονάκις** σοι **γρά-| φω** περὶ τοῦ διανδραγαθήσαντα| σαυτοῦ ἐπιμέλεσθαι μέχρι τοῦ| τὰ πράγματα ἀποκαταστῆναι,| **ἔτι καὶ νῦν** καλῶς ποιήσεις παρα-| καλῶν σαυτὸν καὶ τοὺς παρ' ἡμῶν.

'Since I wrote to you often about acting consistently in a brave manner so as to take care of yourself until matters return to normal, so also once again please encourage yourself and our people.'
(P.Dryton 36, ll. 2–7; 130 BCE) [tr. J.L. White, no. 43]

what the perfect shares with the epistolary use of the historic tenses is not the reference to the past, but the prominence given to the present of the receiver as a reference point for the statement.

2.3 The lens of the past

Although principal tenses, which locate "a state of affairs *at* the moment of utterance (the "present")" (Rijksbaron 2002: 4),[23] tend to prevail within the sample of the letters collected, imperfect and aorist stems are also well represented.[24] In particular, they alternate when the sender shifts to a narrative attitude, as in the reporting of facts, which the recipient has to be informed of. In (22), for instance, another passage from the Simale petition, the aorist and the imperfect occur in the recount of the circumstances that induce the woman to address Zenon.

(22) ἀκούσασα ἠνωχλῆσθαί μου τ[ὸ παι-]‖ δάριον καὶ σφοδρότερον, **παρεγενόμην** πρὸς ὑμᾶς καὶ ἐλθοῦσα **ἤθελον** ἐντυχεῖν σοι ὑ[πὲρ] τῶν]‖ αὐτῶν τούτων. ἐπεὶ δέ με Ὀλυμπιχ[ὸ]ς **ἐκώλυσεν** τοῦ μὴ ἰδεῖν σε, ε̣[ἰ]σ̣ε̣κ̣ο̣μ̣ί̣σ̣θ̣η̣ν̣ πρό[ς τὸ]‖ παιδίον ὥς ποτ' **ἠδυνάμην**, καὶ ε̣ὗ̣ρον αὐτὸν καὶ μάλα γελοιώσα[σ]α δ[ι]ακείμενον καὶ ἤ[δη ι-]‖ κανομ μοι ἦν ὁρῶσαν ἐκεῖνον λυπεῖσθαι. ἀλλ' ἐπιπαραγενόμενος Ὀλυμπιχὸς **ἔφη** αὐτὸ[ν]‖ τύπτων σαπρὸν ποιή[σε]ιν ἢ πεπο[ί]ηκεν ὃς ἤδη σχεδὸ[ν] ἦ̃ν.[25]

'When I heard that my son was exceedingly distressed, I came to you and when I arrived I intended to complain to you about these same things. And when Olympichos hindered me from seeing you, I gained entry to the boy as well as possible and, though I laughed heartily, I found him lying (ill) and that was already enough to grieve me when I saw him. But when Olympichos arrived he said that he would beat him (until) he made him useless – or he had done so, since he already was nearly that.'
(P.Col. III 6, ll. 1–6; 257 BCE) [tr. J.L. White, no. 10]

Beyond their well-known aspectual (perfective vs imperfective) opposition, the two stems display a complementary distribution over different levels of discourse. Accordingly, the aorists mark the events that involve progress in the story-line (cf. παρεγενόμην 'I came', l. 2; ἐκώλυσεν 'he hindered', ε̣[ἰ]σ̣ε̣κ̣ο̣μ̣ί̣σ̣θ̣η̣ν̣ 'I was brought', l. 3; ε̣ὗ̣ρον 'I found', l. 4), whereas the imperfects introduce secondary details (as

---

23 They are also called "primary" tenses as opposed to "secondary" or "historical" stems, which locate "the state of affairs *before* the moment of utterance (the 'past')" (Rijksbaron 2002: 4).
24 They account for 40% of the indicative forms encountered. The aorist is slightly more frequent than the imperfect (24% vs 16%).
25 At line 4 others read καὶ μάλ' ἀγελοίως δ[ι]ακείμενον as, for instance, Bagnall & Cribiore (2006: 100), who translate the passage as 'I found him lying down in a hardly laughable state'.

ἤθελον 'I intended', l. 2, and ἠδυνάμην 'I was able', l. 5, respectively referring to the speaker's intents and conditions).[26]

As also elsewhere, verbs of saying (cf. ἔφη 'he said', l. 5) tend here to associate with the imperfective stem.[27] According to Rijksbaron (2002: 18–9), this occurs when the speaker expects a reaction from the addressee, whereas, as e.g. singled out by Bentein (2015), the aorist foregrounds the content of the speaker's words. Compared to the aorist, the imperfect then emphasizes the dialogic attitude of the speaker.[28]

In the following passage, taken from the letter that Panakestor addresses to the *dioikêtês* Apollonios, the imperfect likewise prevails in the report of the negotiation between the sender and the native workers on strike.

(23) οἱ δ' ἐπ[ὶ] μὲν τοῦ παρόντος **ἔφασαν** βουλευσάμενοι| ἀποφανεῖσθαι ἡμῖν, μετὰ δ' ἡμέρας δ καθίσαντες εἰς| τὸ ἱερὸν οὐκ ἔφασαν οὔτε δικαίως οὔτ' ἀδίκως| συντιμήσεσθαι, ἀλλ' **ἔφασαν** ἐκχωρήσειν τοῦ σπόρου·| ὁμολογίαν γὰρ εἶναι πρός σε αὐτοῖς ἐκ τοῦ γενήματος| ἀποδώσειν τὸ τρίτον.| ἐμοῦ δὲ καὶ Δάμιδος πολλὰ πρὸς αὐτοὺς εἰπάντων, ἐπειδὴ οὐθὲν **ἠνύομεν**, ᾠχόμεθα| πρὸς Ζωίλον καὶ **ἠξιοῦμεν** αὐτὸν συμπαραγενέσθαι· ὁ δ' **ἔφη** ἄσχολος εἶναι πρὸς τῆι τῶν ναυτῶν ἀποστολῆι.

'They said that after having deliberated for a while they would give us their answer and, after four days, taking up residence in the temple (i.e. they went on strike), they said they did not want to agree to any valuation, be it fair or unfair, but preferred to renounce their right to the crop. For they alleged there was an agreement between you and them that they would pay one-third of the produce. Moreover, when Damidos and I talked with them at length and accomplished nothing, we went away to Zoilos and asked him to assist us; but he said that he was busy in the dispatch of sailors.'
(PSI V 502, ll. 20–24; 257 BCE) [tr. J.L. White, no. 18]

Correspondingly, the imperfect also occurs when the sender introduces the content of the letter received through a verb of saying, as in (24), a later piece of correspondence from the Serapeum of Memphis.

---

26 On the correlation between perfectivity and foreground on the one hand, and imperfectivity and background on the other hand, cf. Hopper (1979: 215): "This correlation can be stated as a correlation between the lexical, intrinsic Aktionsart of the verb and the discourse-conditioned aspect". On the discourse function of the Greek imperfect and its diachronic continuity, cf. Rijksbaron (1988) and Gerö & Ruge (2008).
27 One-third of the imperfects encountered occur with verbs of saying. On the functional opposition, within this class, between aorist, imperfect and perfect, see Mandilaras (1973: 55): "all three tenses [. . .] can express similar (if not identical nuances of time). [. . .] The change from one tense to another involves questions of style".
28 On a similar usage of the Italian imperfect with *verba dicendi*, see Bertinetto (1986: 400), according to whom the pattern is typical of ordinary conversations and epistolary dialogues.

(24) κομισαμένη τὴν παρὰ σοῦ ἐπιστολήν| παρ' Ὥρου, ἐν ἧι **διεσάφεις** ε\ῖ/ναι| ἐν κατοχῆι ἐν τῶι Σαραπιείωι τῶι| ἐν Μέμφει, ἐπὶ μὲν τῶι ἐρρῶσθα[ί] σε| εὐθέως τοῖς θεοῖς εὐχαρίστουν

'When I received your letter from Horos, in which you make clear that you are held fast (i.e., in the possession of the god) in the Serapeum in Memphis, I gave thanks immediately to the gods that you are well'
(UPZ I 59, ll. 7–11; 168 BCE) [tr. J.L. White, no. 34]

Conversely, imperfects tend to be excluded when the sender – referring to a previous exchange of letters – uses the forms of the verb γράφω 'I write' (for what has been written) or of κομίζω 'I carry' (for what has been received), where sigmatic aorists are preferred (as in (21) above).

Such contexts, in which the aorist and the imperfect consistently locate an event in the past of the writer, consistently assume the present of the sender as the reference point of the statement. But, within the historic tenses too, variations in the reference time are encountered. In particular, when anchored in the present of the reader, the imperfect and the aorist refer to concurrent facts at the moment in which the letter is written, which are therefore located in the past of the recipient.

Under these circumstances, scholars – conveying the estrangement of the modern reader – have coined the label *epistolary* for passages such as the following in (25) and (26), where the senders use the imperfect tense to refer – according to the common opening formulaic health wish – to their current state of health.

(25) εἰ σύ τε ἔρρωσαι καὶ τὰ σὰ πάντα| καὶ τὰ λοιπά σο[ι κατὰ νοῦν ἐστὶν, πο]λλὴ χάρις τοῖς θεοῖς· καὶ αὐτὸς δὲ| **ὑγίαινον**, σοῦ διὰ π[αντὸς μνείαν ποι]ούμενος, ὥσπερ δίκαιον **ἦν**.

'If you are well and if all your affairs and everything else is proceeding according to your will, many thanks to the gods; we also are (lit. 'I was') well, always remembering you, as I should (lit. 'as it was right').'
(P.Cair.Zen. I 59076, ll. 1–3; 257 BCE) [tr. J.L. White, no. 16]

(26) εἰ ἔρρωσαι, εὖ ἂν ἔχοι· ἔρρωμαι δὲ καὶ ἐγὼ καὶ Ἀπολλώνιος **ὑγίαινεν** καὶ| τἄλλα **ἦν** κατὰ γνώμην. ὅτε δέ σοι **ἔγραφον**, **παρεγινόμεθα** εἰς Σιδῶνα, συμπεπορευμένοι τῆι βασιλίσσηι| ἕως τῶν ὁρίων, καὶ **ὑπελαμβάνομεν** ταχέως παρέσεσθαι πρὸς ὑμᾶς.

'If you are well, it would be excellent; I myself am also well and Apollonios is (lit. 'was') healthy and everything else is (lit. 'was') satisfactory. As I write (lit. 'I wrote') to you, we are (lit. 'were') arriving at Sidon, having escorted the princess to the border, and I assume (lit. 'we assumed') that we will soon be with you.'
(P.Cair.Zen. II 59251, ll. 1–3; 252 BCE) [tr. J.L. White, no. 24]

The pattern is often associated with the opening health wish (especially with the verb ὑγιαίνω 'I am healthy'),[29] but it is largely documented also in the body of the letter. In (26), for instance, the sender, the physician Artemidoros, inflects for the imperfect some of the verbs relative to the moment in which the letter is written (cf. ὅτε δέ σοι ἔγραφον 'when I wrote to you', l. 2); in (27), similarly, Apollodoros expresses in the imperfect his disappointment about Panakestor's management of the Fayoum estate.

(27) **κατεπλησσόμην** τὴν ὀλιγωρίαν σου ἐπὶ τῶι μηθὲν γεγραφέναι μήτε περὶ τῆς| συντιμήσεως μήτε περὶ τῆς συναγωγῆς τοῦ σίτου.

'I am astounded (lit. 'I was astounded') by your negligence in not having written either about the valuation or about the gathering of the crops.'
(PSI V 502, ll. 8–9; 257 BCE) [tr. J.L. White, no. 18]

Again, in (28) and (29), the sender presents his aim of writing to the recipient respectively with the imperfect and the aorist.

(28) ὁρῶντες δέ \σε/ καταραθυμοῦντα| **ᾤμην** δεῖν καὶ νῦν ἐπιστεῖλαί σ[οι].

'but seeing that you are remiss I thought it necessary to instruct you again.'
(P.Yale I 33, ll. 4–5; 253 BCE) [tr. J.L. White, no. 4]

(29) καλῶς δ' ἔχειν **ὑπέλαβον** καί σοι γράψαι ὅπως ἐάν τινά σου χρεί[αν τὰ πράγμα-]| τα ἔχηι συναντιλάβηι φιλοτίμως καὶ ἡμῶν ἕνεκεν καὶ Μενέτου.

'I have thought it advisable to write to you also in order that, if the matter requires your assistance, you may cooperate zealously both on your account and that of Menetos.'
(P.Col. III 9, ll. 6–7; 257 BCE) [tr. J.L. White, no. 13]

Compared to the aorist, the imperfect is more common in such contexts, where the speaker metaphorically aligns the reference time with the moment in which the letter is read. Unlike the aorist, which contributes to "a retrospectively distanced,

---

29 The topos of the health-wish (cf. Exler 1976[1923]) is curiously restated in the brief note addressed by Mnasistratos to Zenon (cf. v), where the sender informs the recipient of his poor state of health, instead of his well-being. It is in particular a collocation with the thematic aorist ἐνέπεσον 'I fell' that introduces the bad news.

(v) καλῶς ἂν ἔχοι εἰ ἔρρωσαι καὶ ὑγιαί-| [νεις τῶι σώματι. ἐ]γὼ εἰς μεγάλην δὲ ἀρρωστίαν **ἐνέπεσον** καὶ εἰς ἀπο-| ρίαν.

'It would be excellent if you are (feeling?) well and you are physically sound. I have fallen (lit. 'I fell') into a grave illness and into a difficult strait.'
(P.Col. III 10, ll. 1–3; 257 BCE) [tr. J.L. White, no. 14]

objective perspective on events" (Fleischmann 1990: 81), its inner focus on the ongoing process favours a subjective perspective on events. Accordingly, when the writer chooses to *narrate* the present situation from the reader's point of view, the imperfect – rather than the aorist – can be preferred.[30]

3 Conclusion

Apparently, as far as concerns the use of the *absolute* tenses, besides the expected patterns of variation (e.g. the use of the aorist for events not involving any current relevance vs the present and the perfect, and the aorist vs imperfect contrast to express the foreground vs background opposition), the language of the papyri displays a number of inconsistencies that can be traced back to aspects of the (epistolary) interaction between sender and recipient.[31] Like other forms of *discourse*, the letter is overtly oriented towards the addressee, immediately *implanted* by the addresser in his language appropriation.[32] However, unlike other forms of *discourse*, in letters, neither the addresser nor the addressee are present at the interaction. The epistolary dialogue is then governed by the sender's efforts to reach the distant receiver over space and time. In particular, the absence of the interlocutor, which is a defining feature of such an enunciative situation, can also be a determining factor in the expressive choices of the sender.[33]

---

30 Beyond epistolary practice, the imperfect has a similar "prospective" value also in Herodotus' *Histories*. According to Naiden (1999: 141–2), the "prospective imperfect" through which Herodotus describes objects or places which may no longer exist when his *Histories* are read, "is also remarkable as an authorial equivalent for the epistolary imperfect. [. . .] Similarly, the epistolary imperfect envisions the time in which the letter is read, and the prospective imperfect envisions the future of a literary text". The aorist cannot apparently trigger a similar *prospective* value and, as a matter of fact, the *epistolary* aorists are rarer than the imperfects. In the corpus, only a few thematic aorists (formally congruent with the morphology of the imperfect) were encountered. Interestingly enough, all these forms are, moreover, prone to a *resultative* interpretation (cf. e.g. (v) above and (29) in the text). Accordingly, an unequivocal *epistolary* value would be likely only for the imperfect.
31 Cf. e.g. Mandilaras (1973), who remarks that, in the language of papyri, the distinction of relative time is not always clearly expressed.
32 Or, in the words of Benveniste (1974), "as an individual realization, the enunciation can be defined in relation to language as a process of *appropriation*. [. . .] But, immediately, as soon as he declares himself as the speaker and assumes the language, he implants *the other* in front of him [. . .]. Any enunciation is, explicitly or implicitly, an allocution and it postulates an addressee" (tr. D. Maingueneau).
33 Altman (1982: 118) discusses the letter as a textual genre, defined by recurrent linguistic properties, such as the *polyvalence* of the epistolary statement: "The meaning of any epistolary statement is determined by many moments: the actual time that an act described is performed,

As far as tense usage in papyrus letters is concerned, the pervasive presence of the recipient is reflected in the possible variations of the deictic centre of the statement, which can be anchored not only to the time of writing, but also to the time of reading. Like every dialogic exchange, the letter is grounded in the enunciative context, from which it derives its attributes, particularly from the gap between the time of encoding and the time of decoding, which determines the possible shifts from the present of the sender to the present of the receiver. It follows that for each of the indicative tense stems evaluated – i.e. present, perfect, aorist and imperfect – there are two possible values, depending on the reference time assumed. In this regard, the notion of *epistolary tense* results in a heuristic device enabling the understanding of the category of grammatical tense in the letter. What particularly defines an *epistolary tense* is the anchoring of the statement in a – so-to-say – *amplified* moment of utterance that ranges from the time of encoding to the time of decoding.

Nevertheless, not all epistolary matters are likely to be prospected according to a twofold standpoint. There are contexts which tend to trigger the sender's present prominence – such as the psychological and performative presents (cf. §2.1) and the aorists for previous exchanges of letters (cf. §2.3) – and others that trigger an anchoring of the statement in the recipient's *hic et nunc*, such as the *authorial* perfect (cf. §2.2) or the imperfect to inform the recipient about his state of health (cf. §2.3). Under such circumstances, the point of view of the sender has been handed down through the ages, limited in its expression by a gallery of stereotyped situations codified by conventional epistolary wording.

References

Altman, Janet Gurkin. 1982. *Epistolarity: Approaches to a form*. Columbus, OH: Ohio State University Press.
Bagnall, Roger & Raffaella Cribiore. 2006. *Women's letters from Ancient Egypt: 300 B. C.–A.D. 800*. Ann Arbor: University of Michigan Press.
Bentein, Klaas. 2014. Perfect. *EAGLL* [online edition].
Bentein, Klaas. 2015. Aspectual choice with *verba dicendi* in Herodotus' *Histories*. *Emerita* 83. 221–245.
Benveniste, Émile. 1966. Les relations de temps dans le verbe français. In *Problèmes de linguistique générale* I, 237–250. Paris: Gallimard.
Benveniste, Émile. 1974. L'appareil formel de l'énonciation. In *Problèmes de linguistique générale* II, 79–88. Paris: Gallimard [English translation by Dominique Maingueneau.

---

the moment when it is written down, the respective times that the letter is mailed, received, read, and reread".

2014. The formal apparatus of enunciation. In Johannes Angermuller, Dominique Maingueneau & Ruth Wodak (eds.), *The discourse studies reader: Main currents in theory and analysis*, 140–145. Amsterdam: Benjamins].

Bertinetto, Pier Marco. 1986. *Tempo, aspetto e azione nel verbo italiano: Il sistema dell' indicativo*. Firenze: Accademia Della Crusca.

Bruno, Carla. 2017. Variations of the first person: Looking at the Greek private letters of Ptolemaic Egypt. In Piera Molinelli (ed.), *Language and identity in multilingual Mediterranean settings: Challenges for historical sociolinguistics*, 49–64. Berlin: Mouton de Gruyter.

Ceccarelli, Paula. 2013. *Ancient Greek letter writing: A cultural history (600 BC–150 BC)*. Oxford: Oxford University Press.

Chantraine, Pierre. 1927. *Histoire du parfait grec*. Paris: Champion.

Clarysse, Willy. 1993. Egyptians scribes writing Greek. *Chronique d'Égypte* 68. 186–201.

Dossena, Marina. 2012. The study of correspondence: Theoretical and methodological issues. In Marina Dossena & Gabriella Del Lungo Camiciotti (eds.), *Letter writing in late Modern Europe*, 13–30. Amsterdam: Benjamins.

Evans, Trevor V. 1999. Another ghost: The Greek epistolary perfect. *Glotta* 75. 194–221.

Evans, Trevor V. 2001. *Verbal syntax in the Greek Pentateuch: Natural Greek usage and Hebrew interference*. Oxford: Oxford University Press.

Evans, Trevor V. 2012. Complaints of the natives in a Greek dress: The Zenon Archive and the problem of Egyptian interference. In Alex Mullen & Patrick James (eds.), *Multilingualism in the Graeco-Roman worlds*, 106–123. Cambridge: Cambridge University Press.

Exler, Francis X. J. 1976 [1923]. *The form of the ancient Greek letter of the epistolary papyri (3rd c. B.C. –3rd c. A.D.): A study in greek epistolography*. Washington DC: Ares.

Fleischmann, Suzanne. 1990. *Tense and narrativity: From medieval performance to modern fiction*. Austin: University of Texas Press.

Gerö, Eva-Carin & Arnim von Stechow. 2003. Tense in time: The Greek perfect. In Regine Eckardt, Klaus von Heusinger & Christoph Schwarze (eds.), *Words in time: Diachronic semantics from different points of view*, 251–269. Berlin: Mouton de Gruyter.

Gerö, Eva-Carin & Hans Ruge. 2008. Continuity and change: the history of two Greek tenses. In Folke Josephson & Ingmar Söhrman (eds.), *Interdependence of diachronic and synchronic analyses*, 105–129. Amsterdam: Benjamins.

Hopper, Paul. 1979. Aspect and foreground in discourse. In Talmy Givón (ed.), *Discourse and syntax*, 213–242. New York: Academic Press.

Klauck, Hans-Josef. 2006. *Ancient letters and the New Testament: A guide to the context and exegesis*. Waco: Baylor University Press.

Mandilaras, Basil. 1973. *The verb in the Greek non-literary papyri*. Athens: Hellenic Ministry of Culture and Science.

McKay, Kenneth L. 1965. The use of the Ancient Greek perfect down to the second century A.D. *Bulletin of the Institute of Classical Studies* 12. 1–21.

McKay, Kenneth L. 1980. On the perfect and other aspects in the Greek non-literary papyri. *Bulletin of the Institute of Classical Studies* 27. 23–49.

Naiden, Fred S. 1999. The prospective imperfect in Herodotus. *Harvard Studies in Classical Philology* 99. 135–149.

Orriens, Sander. 2009. Involving the past in the present: the Classical Greek perfect as a situating cohesion device. In Stéphanie Bakker & Gerrie Wakker (eds.), *Discourse cohesion in Ancient Greek*, 221–239. Leiden: Brill.

Porter, Stanley. 1989. *Verbal aspect in the Greek of the New Testament with reference to tense and mood*. New York: Peter Lang.
Porter, Stanley & Matthew O'Donnell. 2010. Building and examining linguistic phenomena in a corpus of representative papyri. In Trevor V. Evans & Dirk D. Obbink (eds.), *The language of the papyri*, 287–311. Oxford: Oxford University Press.
Porter, Stanley & Andrew Pitt. 2013. The disclosure formula in the epistolary papyri and in the New Testament: Development, form, function and syntax. In Stanley Porter & Andrew Pitt (eds.), *The language of the New Testament*, 421–438. Leiden: Brill.
Rijksbaron, Albert. 1988. The discourse function of the imperfect. In Albert Rijksbaron, Hotze A. Mulder & Gerry Wakker (eds.), *In the footsteps of Raphael Kühner: Proceedings of the international colloquium in commemoration of the 150th anniversary of the publication of Raphael Kühner's Ausführliche Grammatik der griechischen Sprache, II. Theil: Syntax, Amsterdam, 1986*, 237–254. Amsterdam: Gieben.
Rijksbaron, Albert. 2002. *The syntax and semantics of the verb in Classical Greek: An introduction*, 3rd ed. Chicago: University of Chicago Press.
Thompson, John. 1995. *The media and modernity: a social theory of the media*. Stanford: Stanford University Press.
Vierros, Marja. 2012. *Bilingual notaries in Hellenistic Egypt: A study of Greek as a second language*. Brussel: Koninklijke Vlaamse Academie van België voor Wetenschappen en Kunsten.
Wackernagel, Jakob. 1904. Studien zum griechischen Perfectum. *Programm zur akademischen Preisverteilung*. 3–24. Göttingen [= *Kleine Schriften*, II, 1000–1021. Göttingen: Vandenhoeck & Ruprecht, 1953].
White, John. L. 1986. *Light from ancient letters*. Philadelphia: Fortress Press.

Jerneja Kavčič
11 The Classical norm and varieties of Post-classical Greek: Expressions of anteriority and posteriority in a corpus of official documents (I–II CE)

Abstract: This chapter examines how anteriority and posteriority are expressed in infinitive complement clauses as attested in a corpus of official papyrus documents (I–II CE). It is found that both the perfect and the aorist infinitive are used in the function of the perfective past, and that the future infinitive is relatively common despite the gradual omission of the Ancient Greek synthetic future. It is argued that these documents can also reflect Post-classical syntactic phenomena, in contrast to the view that Post-classical official documents closely follow the example of Classical Greek. In addition to official documents (such as receipts), which may display lower-register features, non-Classical phenomena can also be found in documents displaying no significant divergences from Classical Greek (namely, in mostly reports and applications). Furthermore, it is found that the Classical Greek construction of the aorist infinitive conveying anteriority is often a modern editor's suggestion rather than a certain reading, although it is sometimes attested in mostly higher-register documents from my corpus.

1 Introduction

This study discusses Post-classical official documents, focusing on official papyrus documents from the first and second centuries CE. This issue is subject to contradictory claims that primarily concern the impact of Classical (or Attic) Greek.[1] According to Horrocks (2010: 466–467), this language has much more in common with texts of no literary ambition than with literary texts, which more closely resemble Classical Greek. Official documents thus appear to display "a more practical, non-Atticizing Koine" (Horrocks 2010: 137). Moreover, Evans (2010: 205) has argued that, instead of assuming that Classical Greek was the norm for the authors

---

[1] The term *Classical Greek* refers to (mostly) Attic Greek of the fifth and the fourth centuries BCE. The term *Post-classical Greek* refers to Greek from the third century BCE to the fourth century CE.

https://doi.org/10.1515/9783110614404-011

of non-literary papyri, one should analyze internal relations between the varieties of the language of non-literary papyri in order to understand their linguistic norm. This norm, however, was perhaps not "the sort of usage we find in literary Attic prose of the classical period", as he claims elsewhere (Evans 2012: 117).

However, this may not necessarily mean that the authors of the texts investigated took no account of Classical Greek. It is noteworthy that Mandilaras (1973: 329) observes that official papyri documents reflect the "Attic norm", and this claim concerns the syntax of infinitive clauses, which is also the topic of this chapter. Similar observations can be found in recent studies. When discussing complement clauses in the Post-classical and Early Byzantine period, Bentein (2017: 23) thus mentions the phenomenon of formal (or official) texts "sticking closer to the Classical norm". Although he also mentions that this norm may be overridden (Bentein 2017: 33), he appears to assume that Classical Greek was the norm of these documents.

I discuss the impact of Classical Greek on the language of official documents by analyzing a particular aspect of their syntax; namely, expressions of temporal distinctions in declarative infinitive clauses. With this term I subsume complement infinitive clauses mostly dependent on verbs of saying and thinking that can convey temporal distinctions (anteriority, posteriority, and simultaneity); for instance, clauses after λέγω 'to say', νομίζω 'to believe', φημί 'to assert', and so on. I focus on expressions of temporal distinctions because they appear to have undergone significant changes in Post-classical Greek, as I have suggested in my previous studies.[2] These changes can mostly be observed in lower-register texts (e.g. in the New Testament). In this study, I examine whether they are also reflected in official papyrus documents and, thus, whether these documents follow the example of Classical Greek or instead display developments that appear to have taken place in later periods. It is noteworthy that verbs of saying can also govern the so-called dynamic infinitive clauses, which convey potential posterior events.[3] I do not discuss this construction because it does not seem to have undergone changes in Post-classical Greek equally extensive as those of declarative infinitive clauses.[4]

The corpus investigated contains some passages that display no significant divergences from Classical Greek. For instance, just as in Classical Greek, the future infinitive conveys posteriority in passage (1); namely, the event of taking

---

[2] Kavčič (2016, 2017a–b).
[3] Rijksbaron (2002: 97).
[4] Perhaps there was a difference, however, between the frequencies of these clauses in Classical Greek and Post-classical Greek. This is a suggestion in a recent study (Bentein 2018: 95, 98), which uses the terms *propositions/ proposals* instead of *declarative/dynamic infinitive clauses*.

over public land, which is expressed with the future infinitive ἀντιλήμψεσθαι (from ἀντιλαμβάνω 'to undertake'), is posterior with regard to the governing verb ὁμολογέω 'to acknowledge':

(1) ὁμολο-|γῶ ἀπὸ τοῦ νῦν ἀντιλήμψεσθαι τῆς| τ[αύ]της ἀναγραφομένης εἰς τὸν μετηλ-| [λαχότα σου] πατέρα Τεῶν [5]

'I agree that I will henceforward undertake all the public land registered in the name of your departed father Teos.'
(P.Oxy. VIII 1123, ll. 8–11; 158–159 CE) [tr. Hunt]

In passage (2), the event of noticing something, which is expressed with the aorist infinitive αἰσθέσθαι 'to notice', is anterior with regard to the governing clause:

(2) ἀπὸ μὲν τῆς Ἑρμιόνης οἰκίας ἐξιὼν οὔτ' ἔφη| πρός τινα αἰσθέσθαι οὐδενός

'When he came out of Hermione's house he did not tell anyone that he noticed anything.'
(P.Oxy. III 472, ll. 2–3; ca. 130 CE) [tr. Grenfell & Hunt]

This was also the function of the aorist infinitive in Classical Greek.[6] In what follows, I use the term "past-oriented aorist infinitives" for this construction.

Taking into account the process of the infinitive disappearing, which arguably was underway in the period investigated,[7] it is possible to claim that the use itself of the infinitive complement instead of the finite complement clause introduced with ὅτι 'that' indicates the impact of Classical Greek. Nevertheless, it is also interesting to observe that unlike examples of the first type, which are relatively frequent in the corpus investigated, past-oriented aorist infinitives are highly uncommon. This phenomenon seems particularly striking given that, in the period investigated, the Ancient Greek synthetic future appears to display a gradual decline, whereas no such process affected the aorist. This is one of the issues I address in my study, which supports the view that, rather than strictly following the example of Classical Greek, the corpus investigated also reflects developments that took place in the Post-classical period, at least to a certain degree. These developments appear to concern expressions of both anteriority and posteriority in the construction investigated.

First, I present how temporal distinctions were conveyed in the construction investigated in Classical Greek, as well as the diachronic processes that appear to

---

[5] The supplement in τ[αύ]της follows the suggestion of an anonymous reviewer, to whom I am grateful for many helpful remarks.
[6] E.g. Rijksbaron (2006: 97).
[7] Cf. Joseph (1983: 46–57).

have affected them in the Post-classical period (Section 2). After that, Section 3 specifies the method I adopt in this study. Section 4 explores whether the corpus investigated reflects the Classical Greek system of temporal distinctions or whether it is closer to what seems to have been the state of affairs in lower-register texts of later periods. Section 5 contains conclusions.

The corpus investigated is based on the DDbDP, from which I gathered examples of the construction investigated, introduced by very common governing verbs; namely, by λέγω 'to say', νομίζω 'to believe', φημί 'to assert', οἶμαι 'to think', ὁμολογέω 'to acknowledge', δηλόω 'to declare', (δια)βεβαιόω 'to confirm', ἀποκρίνομαι 'to answer', φάσκω 'to affirm', πυνθάνομαι 'to learn', προσφωνέω 'to utter', φαίνομαι 'to seem', and ἀκούω 'to hear'.[8] The corpus contains documents from the first and second centuries CE that are not specified in modern editions as private (e.g. contracts, receipts, reports, official letters, petitions, wills, decrees, etc.).[9] As stated, these are papyrus documents (except for one contract, which was written on parchment). I focus on this period because it displays the aforementioned changes concerning expressions of temporal distinctions in lower-register texts. The number of instances of the construction investigated amounts to around 1,500 in my corpus. Their distribution in different types of documents is shown in Table 1:

Table 1: The corpus investigated.

Type of document	Instances of complement infinitive clauses, n (%)
Receipts/acknowledgements	589 (38%)
Contracts	527 (34%)
Official letters/applications	186 (12%)
Reports/proceedings	139 (9%)
Wills	39 (2.5%)
Lists/registers	31 (2%)
Other documents	39 (2.5%)

---

[8] In the period investigated it is not uncommon to find an infinitive complement after a verb of perception (such as ἀκούω). It seems that the Post-classical period saw a spread of this construction (cf. Bentein 2017: 12).

[9] In distinguishing between private and official documents, I follow the characterizations of HGV.

2 Temporal distinctions in complement infinitive clauses

2.1 Classical Greek

As is well known, Classical Greek used the future infinitive in the function of conveying posteriority, the present infinitive in the function of conveying simultaneity, and the aorist infinitive in the function of conveying anteriority.[10] The future and the aorist infinitive have already been discussed; an example of a present infinitive is passage (3) below. In this case, the state of being difficult, expressed with the present infinitive εἶναι, is simultaneous with the governing verb:

(3) οἶμαι δὲ αὐτὸ χαλεπὸν εἶναι

'I think that it is difficult.'
(Pl., *Ap.* 19a4)[11]

In addition, the perfect infinitive could be used in complement infinitive clauses. However, this infinitive was a rare phenomenon, according to Rijksbaron (2002: 98), whereas the semantics of this infinitive (as well as the semantics of the perfect in general) have been subject to contradictory claims. A particularly complex issue concerns the relation between the perfect and the aorist infinitive. Rijksbaron (2002: 36) thus argues – in one of the generally rare discussions of this issue – that, whereas the aorist infinitive conveys completed (anterior) events, the perfect infinitive stresses the state resulting from anterior events; for example, in passage (4) from Sophocles' *Antigone*:

(4) Creon   Φῄς, ἦ καταρνῇ μὴ δεδρακέναι τάδε;
               'Do you admit or deny that you have done this?'

      Antigone   Καὶ φημὶ δρᾶσαι κοὐκ ἀπαρνοῦμαι τὸ μή
                'I admit that I did it and I do not deny it.'
                (Soph., *Ant.* 142–143)

According to Rijksbaron (2002: 36), the aorist infinitive δρᾶσαι in passage (4) refers to the completion of the anterior event (and means 'to have done'). On the other hand, he interprets the perfect infinitive δεδρακέναι in the preceding verse as 'to be responsible for this', in which case the emphasis lies on the resultant state of responsibility, with the anterior event in the background. The

---

10 See, for instance, Rijksbaron (2002: 97).
11 The translation is mine in all the cases where the translator is not specifically mentioned.

accuser, namely Creon, wants to stress Antigone's responsibility, which is why he uses the perfect infinitive δεδρακέναι rather than the aorist infinitive δρᾶσαι (which is used by Antigone when referring to the same events). According to some scholars,[12] the same distinction between the two infinitives is found in Post-classical official documents, which are the focus of this study.

However, it is also possible to find significantly different views. An example is Chantraine (1927: 187–189), who has argued that Classical Greek contains the earliest instances of the perfect infinitive manifesting "le rapprochement de l'aoriste et du parfait"[13] (e.g. διειλέχθαι 'to have discussed' in *Lys.* 8.15). He thus appears to suggest that there may not have been a clear-cut distinction between the perfect and the aorist infinitive in Classical Greek. Another and very influential modern approach goes back to Haspelmath (1992), who argues that Classical Greek saw the emergence of the so-called anterior perfect (or, in Haspelmath's terms, the "perfect"). This anterior perfect is to be distinguished from the resultative perfect and is believed to have much in common with the perfect in modern languages such as English, although there is no one-to-one correspondence between them. It is usually defined as the perfect referring to an anterior event with current relevance.[14] Because the emphasis in this type of perfect lies on the anterior event, it seems reasonable to assume that reference to anteriority could have been a prominent feature of the perfect infinitive in Classical Greek (and that it also contained a reference to the current relevance of the anterior event). An example that appears to allow for this interpretation, namely *Lys.* 32.27, is mentioned in Kavčič (2016: 269). In addition, the concept of the anterior perfect was adopted by Bentein (2012: 178–181; 2016: 153). It is thus not surprising that he argues, in a recent study, that the perfect infinitive conveyed anteriority in Classical Greek, in addition to the past-oriented aorist infinitive (without explicitly mentioning semantic differences between them; Bentein 2018: 88–89).[15] It is also worth noting that the concept of current relevance has met criticism, which primarily concerns the notion of relevance.[16] Nevertheless, this concept needs to be highlighted because current relevance may explain, as is sometimes argued, the use of the perfect in non-literary papyri. According to Bentein (2015a: 475), the perfect can thus be used in these documents in order to stress the current relevance of past events.

For the purposes of this chapter, which focuses on the Post-classical period, it must also be emphasized that, as is widely accepted, the temporal properties of

---

12 Especially McKay (1980).
13 "The convergence of the aorist and the perfect."
14 Haspelmath (1992: 190).
15 He uses the term *propositions* instead of *declarative infinitive clauses*; cf. fn. 4.
16 Cf. Fanning (1990: 111), Crellin (2016: 6).

the perfect (or its past-orientedness) became increasingly prominent in diachronic terms, leading to the perfect adopting the function of the perfective past and thus merging with the aorist in functional terms, and to a degree in formal terms as well.[17] However, the issue of when this process might have taken place is highly controversial. Whereas some scholars find its traces in the Hellenistic-Roman period, others place it much later, in the early Byzantine period.[18]

I adopt what appears to be the consensus view that, in Classical Greek, the aorist infinitive conveyed anteriority in infinitive complements. As a result, I also assume that, if a perfect infinitive is found in the function of conveying anteriority without containing any reference to subsequent state of affairs (i.e. in the sense of the state resulting from the anterior event or of its current relevance), this is a divergence from Classical Greek (in line with the aforementioned suggestions about the lack of distinction between the past-oriented aorist infinitive and the perfect infinitive, a suggestion that needs further corroboration).

2.2 Post-classical Greek

It appears that the aforementioned system of expressing temporal relations underwent significant change in the Post-classical period. As already mentioned, the Ancient Greek synthetic future experienced a gradual decline during this period, and this process seems to have affected its non-finite forms relatively early.[19] As a result, the future infinitive is highly uncommon in the New Testament and in contemporary private letters.[20] In addition, it has been observed that the New Testament and contemporary non-literary papyri avoid past-oriented aorist infinitives.[21] Recently, I suggested that this phenomenon could be related to the perfect infinitive adopting the function of conveying anteriority, which thus tended toward replacing the aorist infinitive in this function.[22] As is usually the case in the

---

17 Cf. Mandilaras (1972: 12–13), Horrocks (2010: 174–176), Bentein (2016: 153–156).
18 Cf. McKay (1980: 42), Gerö & Stechow (2003: 282–284), Horrocks (2010: 174–176).
19 E.g. Markopoulos (2009: 47, 53–54).
20 Blass, Debrunner & Rehkopf (2001: 284), Kavčič (2017b: 47).
21 Burton (1898: 53), Fanning (1990: 401), Kavčič (2017a: 36–41).
22 Kavčič (2016: 292–308). A different account is proposed in Kavčič (2017a) – which, however, is revisited in Kavčič (2016). As a careful reader may note, Kavčič (2016: 269) states that the third hypothesis of the paper (and this hypothesis is also adopted in this study) revisits Kavčič (Forthcoming b), which is cited in this study as Kavčič (2017a). Due to the publishing process, the 2017 article was published a bit later than the 2016 one. A recent discussion of the same developments is found in Bentein (2018), which was published after the completion of this study. He appears to accept the view that past-oriented aorist infinitives were very uncommon in

Post-classical period, this development is reflected in lower-register texts, whereas high-register texts (as well as the majority of literary texts) are closer to Classical Greek and display a much more frequent use of past-oriented aorist infinitives.

This hypothesis may seem counterintuitive and it may seem more reasonable to account for the lack of past-oriented aorist infinitives in terms of the infinitive disappearing.[23] Nevertheless, the hypothesis is supported by the high frequencies of the perfect infinitive in the texts avoiding past-oriented aorist infinitives,[24] which arguably convey anteriority given that they can be modified with past-oriented adverbials.[25] Second, the assumption that the perfect infinitive might have tended toward replacing the aorist infinitive in the function of conveying anteriority can be corroborated by a semantic distinction between the aorist and the perfect infinitive if it is taken into account that the aorist infinitive was an aspectual, augmentless form that encoded perfective aspect rather than tense,[26] whereas the reference to anteriority was a prominent feature of the perfect infinitive. As mentioned earlier, the perfect infinitive became increasingly past-oriented in Post-classical Greek. As a result, it was arguably more transparent in temporal terms than the aorist infinitive. This is reflected in the temporal ambiguity of the aorist infinitive, which can refer to posteriority or anteriority,[27] whereas no such ambiguity concerned the perfect infinitive, and this could have led to its preference over the aorist infinitive.[28]

According to this hypothesis, the process that affected the perfect and the aorist infinitives was (in one respect) different from that which affected the perfect and the aorist indicatives. The difference (as I argue below, it is also reflected in the corpus investigated) was that the tendency toward the perfect infinitive replacing the aorist infinitive in the function of conveying anteriority was much more prominent than the tendency toward the perfect indicative replacing the aorist indicative. As I suggested above, in the Post-classical period the perfect infinitive tended toward replacing the aorist infinitive in the function of conveying anteriority, with the past-oriented aorist infinitive mostly being used in high-register texts (which tend to follow the example of Classical

---

Post-classical Greek and that this was due to the availability of the perfect infinitive, providing further potential reasons for the situation in Post-classical Greek (see Bentein 2018: 95).
23 For a more detailed discussion of this issue, see Kavčič (2016: 279–280).
24 Cf. Kavčič (2016: 276).
25 Kavčič (2016: 291).
26 Although this may be the predominant modern view, the issue is controversial. A recent discussion is offered by Méndez Dosuna (2017).
27 Kavčič (2016: 293), Bentein (2017: 18).
28 Kavčič (2016: 293).

Greek). The process was different in the case of the indicative; namely, there are no reasons to think that the aorist indicative tended to be restricted to higher registers and that, in general, the perfect indicative was preferred over the aorist indicative. Modern Greek thus indicates that the aorist indicative prevailed over the perfect indicative. The large majority of Modern Greek perfective past tense forms are descendants of the ancient Greek aorist (e.g. έγραψα 'I wrote', νόμισα 'I thought', and έπεσα 'I fell', representing the Ancient Greek aorists ἔγραψα, ἐνόμισα, and ἔπεσον), with the perfect being represented in much fewer forms (e.g. βρήκα 'I found', a descendent of the Ancient Greek perfect εὕρηκα 'I have found').[29] This distinction can be explained if it is taken into account that the aorist infinitive stood in a different relation to the perfect infinitive than was the case with the aorist indicative in relation to the perfect indicative. Note that the aorist infinitive lacked the past-tense marker (namely, the augment), whereas the aorist indicative was augmented; on the other hand, no such morphological distinction concerned the perfect infinitive and the perfect indicative, which were both reduplicated. Thus in diachronic terms, the perfect infinitive tended toward replacing the aorist infinitive in the function of conveying anteriority because the aorist infinitive was unmarked for tense, whereas past-orientedness of the perfect infinitive became increasingly prominent. The aorist indicative, on the other hand, was an augmented form and was thus marked for tense; thus, when the perfect indicative tended toward adopting the function of the perfective past the tendency toward replacing the aorist indicative was significantly less prominent.[30]

3 Method

As already explained in Sections 1 and 2, I investigate whether in terms of expressing temporal distinctions my corpus reflects the Classical use of infinitives or whether it manifests phenomena that appear to concern Post-classical lower-register texts; namely, that the future infinitive is avoided and that, unlike in

---

[29] Further examples can be found in Jannaris (1968[1897]: 273; §222, on ποιέω 'to do'; 440).
[30] As an anonymous reviewer added, in this case the original perfect indicative replaced the original aorist indicative because the phonological change *eu* > *ev* in the first syllable of εὕρηκα 'I have found' resulted in a perfect indicative that seemed to be augmented, whereas the corresponding aorist indicative (εὗρον 'I found') seemed unaugmented. The replacement of the aorist indicative with the corresponding perfect indicative was thus a rare development, probably related to morphological/phonological factors.

Classical Greek, the perfect rather than the aorist infinitive tends to convey anteriority.

I examine this issue both from the perspective of statistical data and from the perspective of the semantics of the infinitives examined. A particularly intricate task, however, concerns the semantics of the perfect infinitive and its relation to the aorist infinitive. My analysis takes into account phenomena concerning the perfect in modern languages such as English and Dutch, as well as Ancient Greek of the period investigated, judging this from a recent study on the perfect in literary Koine.[31]

It has been observed that in English, in non-finite complements, the perfect infinitive can adopt the function of the simple (or perfective) past of a finite clause, in addition to the function of the present perfect indicative. An example is passage (5), taken from Comrie (1981: 55):

> (5) The security officer believes Bill to have been in Berlin before the war.

In such cases, according to Comrie (1981: 55), the perfect infinitive is paraphrased with a finite verb in the simple past if the infinitive clause is substituted by a finite one. The same phenomenon concerns the perfect infinitive in Dutch[32] and is reflected, among other things, in the behavior of time adverbials. Passage (5) thus shows that the perfect infinitive can be modified with a time specification of an anterior event. These adverbials can also modify verbs in the simple past, whereas they cannot modify the perfect indicative. This is consistent with the assumption that in infinitive complements the perfect infinitive can adopt the function of the simple past of finite clauses. In addition to the infinitive, in English time specifications can also modify the perfect participle and the past perfect.[33]

Similar phenomena have been observed in the Greek of the period investigated. According to Crellin (2016: 240–246), in literary Koine time specifications of anterior events can modify the perfect participle and the past perfect, whereas they cannot modify the perfect indicative. He mentions no instances of time specifications of anterior events modifying the perfect infinitive.

Based on these data, I first investigate variation in the use of infinitive and finite clauses. My basic assumption is that, if the corpus investigated suggests that infinitive clauses containing a perfect infinitive can be replaced with a finite clause containing an aorist indicative, this is an indication that the perfect

---

31 Crellin (2016).
32 ter Beek (2011: 43), Zwart (2014).
33 Comrie (1981: 55–56).

infinitive can be used in infinitive clauses in the function of conveying anteriority without containing a reference to subsequent state of affairs. In this case, the use of the perfect infinitive contrasts with Classical Greek because, as mentioned in Section 2.1, I assume that this used to be the function of the aorist infinitive. In the absence of native speakers (who could provide clear answers), I focus on the variation concerning complement infinitive clauses containing the perfect infinitive. I analyze complement clauses containing the perfect infinitive that frequently occur in (nearly) identical contexts (i.e. in the same parts of the same type of official documents) and display variation between infinitive and finite clauses. Recently, the importance of investigating such contexts was stressed by Bentein (2018: 93).

Second, I examine the behavior of time specifications of anterior events, assuming that, if they can modify the perfect infinitive and the aorist indicative but cannot modify the perfect indicative, this is an indication that the perfect infinitive can be used in infinitive complements in the function of the aorist indicative of finite clauses. If this is the case, the function of the perfect infinitive in the period investigated, contrasts with Classical Greek and literary texts of the period investigated (given that Crellin (2016: 240–246) mentions no such instances).[34]

Some of the phenomena I examine have also been observed by previous studies.[35] My analysis differs in the respect that it sheds light on them from the perspective of modern languages and the hypothesis about the decline of past-oriented aorist infinitives (§2.2).

As recent studies have shown, non-literary papyri may display low- or high-register features. Whereas low-register texts tend to contain non-Classical orthographic and morphological features, these features are avoided in higher registers. The distinctions between low and high registers also concern syntactic phenomena such as the use of particles, preference for certain complementation patterns, and so on.[36] This also applies to the corpus investigated. Some documents display lower-register features; for instance, non-Classical orthography and morphology such as ὑμεῖν 'to you' and καταχωρίσαμεν 'we assigned' (instead of ὑμῖν and κατεχωρίσαμεν) in P.Amh. II 69, 8 (154 CE). Other texts, however, appear to avoid such features, following Classical Greek more closely. It is worth stressing that my analysis concerns the corpus as a whole, which is why I also examine whether or not my findings concern both low- and high-register texts.

---

34 See also Bentein (2012: 176–181), whose overview mentions no such instances in Classical Greek.
35 E.g. Mandilaras (1972, 1973), McKay (1980), Bentein (2016: 154–155).
36 See especially Evans (2010), Bentein (2015a, 2015c, 2015d).

4 Temporal distinctions in the corpus investigated

Table 2 shows the frequencies of complement (infinitive) clauses containing the present, the future, the perfect, and past-oriented aorist infinitives. In this Table, eight instances of an aorist infinitive dependent on the verb ὁμολογέω were counted as uncertain instances of the past-oriented aorist infinitive because they can also be interpreted as future-oriented, as is explained below in Section 4.2.1.[37] Even if they are accepted as past-oriented aorist infinitives, however, there cannot be much doubt that the perfect infinitive is much more frequent in the corpus than the past-oriented aorist infinitive. This can be interpreted as an indication that, rather than following the example of Classical Greek, the documents investigated are closer to Post-classical lower-register texts. As stated in Section 2.2, the latter avoid the past-oriented aorist infinitive in addition to displaying high frequencies of the perfect infinitive.

Table 2: Frequencies of complement infinitive clauses.

	Pres. Inf.	Perf. Inf.	Fut. Inf.	Aor. Inf.
ἀκούω 'to hear'	0	1	0	0
ἀποκρίνομαι 'to answer'	3	5	0	0
δηλόω 'to declare'	99	126	6	0
(δια)βεβαιόω 'to confirm'	0	5	1	0
λέγω 'to say'	39	68	1	0
νομίζω 'to believe'	3	0	2	0
οἶμαι 'to think'	2	1	1	0
ὁμολογέω 'to acknowledge'	358	575	70	8 (?)
προσφωνέω 'to utter'	14	19	0	0
πυνθάνομαι 'to learn'	1	3	0	1
φαίνομαι 'to seem'	5	1	0	0
φάσκω 'to affirm'	7	17	1	0
φημί 'to assert'	25	74	2	6
Total	556	895	84	7–15 (< 1%)

On the other hand, frequencies of the future infinitive (approximately 5% of all complement infinitive clauses) seem high enough to argue that the documents

---

[37] An example of the past-oriented infinitive after this verb can perhaps also be found in a much later document; namely, in P.Oxy. LXIII 4397, ll. 133–137 (545 CE); see Bentein (2018: 95).

investigated follow the example of Classical Greek. Namely, they are higher than in lower-register texts of the period investigated, which tend to avoid the future infinitive (see §2.2).

However, it is also possible to raise the issue of whether the perfect infinitive follows the example of Classical Greek. Namely, it could be argued that it stresses the state resulting from the anterior event or its current relevance (if one adopts the concept of the anterior perfect). The view that official papyri documents reflect the Classical distinction between the perfect and the aorist has been supported by McKay (1980) and, if it is correct, the lack of past-oriented aorist infinitives could perhaps be attributed to the nature of these documents. Because they are official, there may have been a particular need for the authors to stress the state resulting from anterior events (or their relevance to the present). This is one of the issues addressed in the subsequent question, which, based on the method proposed in Section 3, discusses the semantics of the perfect infinitive in the corpus investigated.

4.1 The perfect infinitive

4.1.1 Variation between infinitive and finite clauses

As mentioned in Section 3, the construction investigated frequently occurs in the corpus investigated in (nearly) identical contexts. An example is passage (6). It is taken from a receipt in which the initial greeting formula is followed by a statement of acknowledgment; in this case, a phrase of the type ὁμολογέω 'to acknowledge' + perfect infinitive, which contains the perfect infinitive ἀπεσχηκέναι 'to have received':

> (6) Γάϊς Ἰούλις Ἀνθρωπᾶς πραγμα-|τευτὴς Οὐλπίου Μυγδονίου| Σεραπίωνι τῷ καὶ Ἀπολλωνι-| ανῷ Σπαρτᾶ γυμνασια[ρ]χήσαν-|τα τῆς Ὀξυρυγχειτῶν πόλεως| γενομένῳ ἐπισκέπτῃ Ὀάσε [-ca.?-]|..ς (Ἑπτανομίας(?)) χαίρειν. **ὁμολογῶ ἀπεσ-|χηκέναι** παρ' ἐσοῦ τὸ συμ-|πεφω[ν]ημένον φόλετρον
>
> 'Gaius Iulius Anthropas, agent of Ulpius Mygdonius, to Sarapion alias Apollonianus, son of Spartas, ex-gymnasiarch of the city of Oxyrhynchites, formerly surveyor of the Oasis of the Heptanomia (?) greeting. I declare that I have received from you the agreed transport charge.'
> (P.Oxy. XXXVI 2793, ll. 1–9; II/III CE) [tr. Grenfell & Hunt]

It is worth noting that the construction in question represents a widespread use of the perfect infinitive in the period investigated. According to Fanning (1990: 401–402), the New Testament displays the same use of the perfect infinitive (for which he uses the term *indirect discourse use*) "far more frequently" than any of its other uses. Furthermore, it appears that the construction remained relatively common even in subsequent periods, despite the gradual retreat of the Ancient Greek synthetic perfect.³⁸

It is also interesting to observe that it is uncommon for the infinitive to be substituted in such cases by a finite complement clause introduced with ὅτι 'that' (which is also attested in this period). According to Bentein (2017: 23), this avoidance of finite complements was a prominent feature of official documents.

Nevertheless passages such as (6) display a different type of substitution, which was also observed and commented on by McKay (1980: 39–41). Namely, in identical contexts and types of documents such as the one in passage (6) (i.e. after the initial greeting formula of a receipt) it is possible to find a simple clause containing an aorist indicative in place of the phrase ὁμολογέω + perfect infinitive. An example is passage (7), which contains the aorist indicative ἀπέσχον 'I received':

> (7) Νεῖλος Μύσθου Ἀρητίωνι Νά-|σωνος δι(ὰ) τοῦ υἱοῦ Χαιρήμονος| χαίρειν. **ἀπέσχον** παρὰ σοῦ τὸ ἐπι-|βάλλον σοι μέρος ὧν ὀφείλει μοι
>
> 'Neilos, son of Mysthes, to Aretion, son of Nason, through the son of Chairemon, greetings. I have received from you the appropriate part of what is owed to me.'³⁹
> (P.Princ. II 35, ll. 1–4; ca. 161 CE)

In addition, the same contexts display the use of the perfect indicative, as in passage (8), which contains the perfect indicative ἀπέσχηκα 'I have received':

> (8) Ἀρβῆχις Ἀγαθάμονος Παβοῦτι| Παβούτιο(ς) χα(ίρειν)· **ἀπέσχη(κα)** παρὰ σοῦ| τὸ τέλος ἁμάξ(ης) ἕως τοῦ Μεχ(εὶρ) \μη(νός)/.
>
> 'Harbechis son of Agathammon to Pabous son of Pabous, greeting. I have received from you the tax on wagon through the month of Mecheir.'
> (O.Leid. 49, ll. 1–3; 31 CE) [tr. Bagnall]

On the other hand, the corpus investigated contains no instances of the type ὁμολογέω + aorist infinitive in this context.⁴⁰ These passages suggest that the event of receiving something, which is expressed in passage (6) with the clause type ὁμολογέω + Perf. Inf. (ἀπεσχηκέναι 'to have received'), can also be expressed in basically the same context with the aorist indicative (ἀπέσχον 'I received') or

---

38 Compare Kavčič (2016: 301).
39 I have adapted the translation of this passage from the PN (accessed November 2017).
40 In addition, the clause type ὁμολογῶ + present infinitive occurs as well (e.g. BGU XI 2111, l. 5). I assume that its substitution is the clause type with the present indicative (e.g. BGU VII 1661, l. 3). For a somewhat different interpretation of a present infinitive from a later period, see Bentein (2018: 99).

with the perfect indicative (ἀπέσχηκα 'I have received'). Table 3 indicates how many instances of the verbs from the first column occur within each of the clause types represented in the passages above: ὁμολογέω + Perf. Inf. refers to the clause type represented in passage (6). Aor. Indic. refers to the clause type from passage (7), and Perf. Indic. refers to the clause type from passage (8). The table shows that the most common clause type in this case is the one containing the aorist indicative.

Table 3: Statements of acknowledgment in receipts: variation between infinitive/finite clauses.

	ὁμολογέω + Perf. Inf.	ὁμολογέω + Aor. Inf.	Aor. Indic.	Perf. Indic.
ἀπέχω 'to receive'	22	0	51	5
ἔχω 'to have'	12	0	119	4
λαμβάνω 'to get'	7	0	11	0
μετρέω 'to measure'	0	0	0	7
μισθόω 'to hire'	1	0	0	12
παραλαμβάνω 'to receive'	4	0	21	0
πιπράσκω 'to sell'	33	0	0	10
(προ)κίχρημι 'to lend'	25	0	0	0
τελωνέω 'to take toll'	0	0	1	2
Other verbs	11	0	13	10
Total	115 (30%)	0 (0%)	216 (57%)	50 (13%)

The fact that, in addition to the aorist indicative, the perfect indicative also occurs in this variation type could be interpreted in different ways. Assuming that the documents investigated may reflect the developments of the Post-classical period, it could be accounted for as a tendency of the perfect indicative toward adopting the function of the perfective past (see §2.2). Alternatively, the same fact could be seen as an attempt to stress the state resulting from the anterior event or its current relevance, in which case the perfect would be used as in Classical Greek. The latter view is adopted by McKay (1980: 39–41), who argues – with regard to the same variation type discussed here – that the aorist stresses the anterior event, whereas the perfect stresses the resulting state (e.g. the state of having sold/received something). This interpretation may also seem plausible in the case of the perfect infinitive: it can thus be argued that in passage (6) above it is used in order to stress the current state (of still having the agreed-upon transport change) rather than the anterior event (of having received it). However, this explanation seems particularly difficult to prove, which is why McKay (1980: 39) adds that "it may be that those who chose the aorist did so because of a feeling that neither of the other possibilities sufficiently characterized what to them was a very significant *action*", rather than that one necessarily has to assume this.

If it is assumed that the aorists stress anterior events, whereas the perfects stress the resulting state, it also seems difficult to explain why the authors of these documents stress the anterior event only in finite clauses, whereas this never happens in infinitive complements (given the absence of the type ὁμολογέω + Aor. Inf.), and the same objection can be raised if one assumes that, rather than the resulting state, the perfects refer to the current relevance of anterior events.[41] McKay appears to be aware of this problem because he notes that the perfect rather than the aorist infinitive is normally used in the function of conveying anteriority and that this is because "in indirect statements the perfect also avoids ambiguity as the aorist infinitive can (and in these contexts normally does) imply obligation" (McKay 1980: 41). This observation, however, is consistent with the hypothesis from Section 2.2; namely, that the perfect infinitive was more transparent than the aorist infinitive in temporal terms, which – as I suggested – could have led to its preference over the aorist infinitive. Furthermore, if it is assumed that the perfects stress the state resulting from the anterior event (or its current relevance), it seems difficult to explain why the perfect indicative is about four times less common than the aorist indicative in Table 3, and why the latter is by far the most common: given the official nature of the documents, a more prominent tendency toward stressing the state resulting from the anterior event (or its current relevance) would be expected.

Given the lack of evidence supporting the view that the corpus investigated reflects the Classical distinction between the perfect and the aorist infinitive, it seems at least equally plausible to claim that the variation examined in this section reflects the process in which the perfect infinitive tended toward adopting the function of conveying anteriority (see §2.2). This explanation is supported by the lack of complement clauses containing past-oriented aorist infinitives and by the high frequencies of aorist indicatives and perfect infinitives in this variation type. These data suggest that, just as in modern languages such as English and Dutch, the perfect infinitive was able, among other functions, to represent the function of the perfective past (aorist indicative) in infinitive complements. As for the perfect indicative, which also occurs in this variation type, it can represent the original Classical Greek function, although this view may lack evidence. If this view is correct, however, the perfect infinitive is arguably

---

41 For a more general critique of this concept, see Fanning (1990: 111) and Crellin (2016: 6).

able to represent both the functions of the perfective past (aorist) and the perfect indicative, and the situation is similar as in modern languages such as English and Dutch (see §3). If, on the other hand, it is assumed that the perfect indicatives are used in the same function as the aorist indicatives, this is an additional indication that in infinitive complements the perfect infinitive represents the function of the perfective past (aorist indicative). In both cases, however, the corpus investigated displays a departure from Classical Greek. Further evidence for this view is given below in Section 4.1.3.

4.1.2 Time specifications as modifiers of the perfect infinitive

The corpus investigated shows that the perfect infinitive can be modified by a time specification of past events. An example is passage (9), taken from what appears to be a fragment of an official report.[42] The adverbial η ἔτει 'in the eighth year' modifies the perfect infinitive γεγονέναι 'to have happened':

(9) Θεμιστοκλέους καὶ Ἥρωνος λεγόντων τὸ λεγόμενον **γεγο-|νέναι** πρᾶγμα **η (ἔτει) Δομιτιανοῦ** {γεγονέναι} καὶ τὴν Φιλουμένην τεθνηκέναι| μηδέποτε πρα<χ>θεῖσαν ὑπὸ τοῦ Διογένους, Μαξιμιανὸς ἔφη· πρᾶγμα παλαιὸν| ἐπιφέρεις·

'When Themistocles and Heron said that the thing they were talking about happened in the eighth year of Domitian and that Philoumene died without having been pressed for payment by Diogenes, Maximianus said: "You are bringing up an old issue".'
(PSI IV 281, ll. 44–47; 100–199 CE)

I found additional instances of this construction in twenty-one documents from the corpus investigated. In 3.5% of all complement clauses containing a perfect infinitive there is thus also a time specification of the anterior event.

This phenomenon places the language of the documents investigated in contrast both to Classical Greek and to contemporary literary texts (see §3). This view is further supported by passage (10) below, which is taken from a text of a contemporary literary author (namely, from Plutarch, 45–127 CE):

(10) ταῦτα δὲ πραχθῆναι λέγουσιν ἑβδόμῃ ἐπὶ δέκα μηνὸς Ἀθύρ

'They say that this was done on the seventeenth day of Athyr.'
(Plut., *Mor.* 356c–d)

In this passage, the past-oriented aorist infinitive (πραχθῆναι 'to be done') is modified by a time specification of the anterior event (namely, with ἑβδόμῃ ἐπὶ

---

42 Vitelli et al. (1917: 3).

δέκα μηνὸς Ἀθύρ, 'on the seventeenth day of Athyr'), speaking in support of the view that, when the time of the anterior event was specified, it was unlikely for a literary text adopt the perfect infinitive and that the perfect infinitive was in such cases a lower-register feature.

As suggested in Section 3, the use of the perfect infinitive with time specifications of anterior events is an indication that the perfect infinitive could adopt the function of the aorist indicative (or of the perfective past) of finite clauses (just as in English and in Dutch). Namely, there cannot be much doubt that the aorist indicative could be modified with time specifications of past events. An example is passage (11), in which the adverbial τῷ Φαῶφι μηνὶ 'in the month of Phaophi' modifies the aorist indicative ἐτελεύτησεν 'he died':

(11) [ὁ] πατρι[κό]ς μου| δοῦλος Πανομεως ἐτελεύτησεν| τῶι Φαῶφι μηνεὶ

'My slave Panomieus, inherited from my father, died in the month of Phaophi.'[43]
(C.Pap.Gr. II 1 19, ll. 5–7; 100 CE)

Nevertheless, there appears to be a difference between the corpus investigated and the aforementioned modern languages in the respect that the corpus also displays instances of time specifications modifying the perfect indicative. An example is passage (12), which contains the adverbial τῷ αὐτῷ κγ (ἔτει) 'in the same twenty-third year' and the perfect indicative πέπρακα 'I have sold':

(12) **πέπρα-|κα τῷ αὐτῷ κγ (ἔτει)** Ἁρποκρατίωνι| Σαραπίωνος Σωσικοσ(μίῳ) τῷ καὶ Ἀλθ (αιεῖ) | κάμηλον α ἄρρενα

'I sold in the same twenty-third year one male camel to Harpokration, son of Sarapion, of the Sosicosmian tribe and the Althaean deme.'
(BGU II 629, ll. 7–10; 161 CE)

The use of time specifications with the perfect indicative πέπρακα (as is the case in passage 12) is not uncommon in my corpus.[44] In addition to reflecting the use of the perfect indicative in the function of the perfective past, however, these

---

[43] The translation of this and the subsequent passage is taken from HGV (accessed in November 2017).
[44] Additional examples include O.Bodl. II 1094, l. 3 (21 CE), P.Lond. II 304, ll. 10–11 (144 CE), BGU I 51, l. 9 (143 CE), and BGU II 421, ll. 4–5 (160–161 CE).
[45] See, for instance, Jannaris (1968[1897]: 273) and Horrocks (2010: 154). In the period investigated, this aorist indicative is attested in only a few documents (e.g. P.Paris. 17, l. 2 (153 CE)), and it is significantly less frequent than the perfect πέπρακα 'I have sold'. It also appears that ἐπώλησα 'I sold', which eventually – as is suggested by Modern Greek – adopted the function of the aorist indicative of this verb, was highly uncommon in the period investigated (it is mostly attested in later periods). These data were gathered from the PN.

instances could also be explained in terms of avoidance of the corresponding irregular aorist indicative ἀπεδόμην 'I sold'.⁴⁵ This view is further supported by data concerning the verb πιπράσκω in Table 3 above, which suggest that, if a receipt contained a reference to an anterior event, it was very common to use the perfect indicative πέπρακα or the perfect infinitive πεπρακέναι 'to have sold', dependent on ὁμολογέω 'to acknowledge'. On the other hand, the corresponding aorist indicative – in contrast to other verbs that occur in the same context with some frequency (e.g. ἔχω 'to have', ἀπέχω 'to have, receive (in full)', and παραλαμβάνω 'to receive') – appears to have been avoided.

This example draws attention to morphological factors that may have played a role in the adoption of the perfect in the function of the perfective past. Scholars have also suggested that this phenomenon was related to the confusion between the augment and reduplication and, in more general terms, to the similarity between the aorist and the perfect indicative forms; the form ἠξίωκα 'I esteemed', for instance, can be seen as "a mixed form, whereby an aorist is combined with a perfect ending" and can also be explained as a result of 'the regularization of the verbal paradigm' (Bentein 2016: 154). This does not mean that morphological factors are behind every case in which a perfect indicative is modified with a time specification of the anterior event.⁴⁶ It should be emphasized, however, that they could not play the same role in the adoption of the perfect infinitive in the function of the perfective past because, first, the aorist infinitive was not augmented, which is why it was less likely for it to be confused with the perfect infinitive.⁴⁷ Moreover, my corpus shows that the perfect infinitive could be used with time specifications of anterior events even if – unlike in the case of πιπράσκω 'to sell' – the corresponding aorist infinitive was available, as well as arguably distinct enough from the corresponding perfect infinitive to exclude the possibility of confusion with another infinitive. For instance, γενέσθαι 'to become' is the corresponding (and very frequent) aorist infinitive of the perfect infinitive γεγονέναι 'to have become', which occurs in passage (9) above, whereas γαμηθῆναι 'to marry' and τελευτῆσαι 'to die' are the corresponding aorist infinitives of the perfect infinitives γεγαμῆσθαι 'to have married' and τετελευτηκέναι 'to have died', which are modified with time specifications of anterior events in P.Oxy. II 257, ll. 30–31 (94–95 CE), and in P.Harr. I 147, l. 7 (129 CE). This is an indication that the tendency toward the perfect infinitive adopting the function of the perfective past in the construction

---

46 See, for instance, Horrocks (2010: 176–178) and Bentein (2016: 155).
47 See also fn. 30: the perfect indicative could replace the aorist indicative because it was interpreted (in contrast to the aorist indicative) as augmented. No such process could have led to the replacement of the aorist infinitive with the perfect infinitive.

investigated was much more prominent than was the case with the perfect indicative in finite clauses. This tendency is consistent with the hypothesis in Section 2.2, and is reflected also in Table 4.

Table 4: Time specifications of anterior events.

	Aor. Ind.	Perf. Ind.	Aor. Inf.	Perf. Inf.
τῷ X ἔτει	148	9	0	21

The table shows that the corpus contains no instance of the adverbials of the type τῷ X ἔτει 'in the Xth year' modifying an aorist infinitive.[48] These adverbials can modify the aorist indicative and the aorist infinitive as well as (relatively rarely) the perfect indicative.

Whereas an example of the latter construction (with the perfect indicative) is passage (12) above passage (13) contains an example of the adverbial τῷ X ἔτει 'in the Xth year' modifying the aorist indicative (namely, κατέγραψεν 'he recorded'):

(13) κατέγ[ρ]αψέν μοι αὐτοὺς τῷ μα (ἔτει)

'He recorded them for me in the forty-first year.'
(Chr.Mitt 68, l. 9; 14 CE)

Furthermore passage (14), taken from P.Oxy II 257 (94–95 CE), which will be discussed in more detail in the subsequent section, contains an example of this adverbial (i.e. τῷ ζ ἔτει 'in the seventh year') modifying the perfect infinitive (namely, γεγαμῆσθαι 'to have married').

Unlike in the aforementioned modern languages, the perfect indicative could thus be modified (in Greek of the period investigated) by time specifications of anterior events. However, this tendency was much less prominent than was the case with the perfect infinitive in the construction investigated, which is consistent with the hypothesis from Section 2.2.

The phenomenon of time specifications modifying the perfect (infinitive and indicative) has been observed by Mandilaras (1972: 9–21; 1973: 226) and McKay (1980: 31). McKay's approach is the same as the one mentioned in Section 4.1.1; namely, that in such cases the aorist and the perfect follow the

---

48 A potential exception is P.Dura 17, ll. 2–3 and ll. 15–16 (180 CE), in which case, however, the time specification can be interpreted as modifying the participle γενόμενον (from γίγνομαι 'to become') rather than the aorist infinitive ἐκστῆναι 'to cede'.

example of Classical Greek and that, thus, the perfect stresses the state resulting from the anterior event, even when modified by a time specification of the anterior event. Nevertheless, this view seems difficult to maintain given that Post-classical literary texts, as well as Classical Greek, appear to display no instances of time specifications modifying the perfect indicative or infinitive (see §3).[49] In addition, McKay (1980: 31) notes that his explanation lacks evidence, adding that it is "one way of explaining the perfect" and that the context shows that "it is not necessary".

It thus seems more plausible to claim that, instead of following the example of Classical Greek, the phenomenon of time specifications of anterior events modifying the perfect infinitive reflects the Post-classical tendency of the perfect infinitive to replace the aorist infinitive in the function of conveying anteriority, whereas the (much less common) use of the perfect indicative with these types of adverbials is a reflection of its tendency toward adopting the function of the perfective past in finite clauses. A similar view is adopted by Mandilaras (1973: 227), who argues that the use of these types of adverbials with the perfect indicates that the perfect becomes "a mere preterite", with the phenomenon mostly found in private letters of the second century CE.[50] My data are consistent with those of Mandilaras in that the majority (more than 80%) of documents containing time specifications of anterior events modifying the perfect infinitive are from the same century. However, the corpus also shows that, rather than being restricted to private documents, this phenomenon also concerns official texts.

4.1.3 The register of the documents investigated

As already mentioned in Section 3, some documents display low-register features such as non-Classical orthography and morphology. This raises the question of whether the phenomena observed in the previous section concern only one part of the corpus investigated. It may seem reasonable to assume that they mostly occur in low-register texts because these texts in general reflect Classical Greek to a much lower degree than high-register texts and because the phenomena examined in Section 4.1.1–2 arguably diverge from Classical Greek.

---

49 According to Mandilaras (1972: 16), this construction is already attested in Classical Greek. However, the example he quotes contains the adverbial πρότερον 'before', which does not specify the time of the anterior event (see Crellin 2016: 241).
50 Recently, this view was also adopted by Bentein (2016: 154–155).

An example of a document displaying non-Classical and thus lower-register features is P.Oxy. XXXVI 2793 (II/III CE), quoted in passage (6), with non-Classical features including Γάϊς Λούλις 'Gaius Iulius' instead of Γάιος Λούλιος, ἐσοῦ '(from) you' instead of σοῦ, and a lack of agreement between the dative Ἀπολλωνιανῷ 'to Apollonianus' and the participle γυμνασια[ρ]χήσαντα 'ex-gymnasiarch' (which is in the accusative). Moreover, the corpus examined in Section 4.4.1 contains receipts, which contain additional instances of divergences from Classical Greek (this particularly is the case with ostraca from the Eastern Desert).[51] Examples include ὁμωλωγῶ ἀπιληφέναι 'I declare that I have received' (O.Claud. III 538, l. 3 (140–147 CE)) instead of ὁμολογῶ ἀπειληφέναι, μίσθωκα 'I hired' (P.Sarap. 27, l. 3 (125 CE)) instead of (probably) μεμίσθωκα, and τετελώνητε 'the toll has been paid' (O.Bodl. II 1084, l. 3 (84 CE)) instead of τετελώνηται. These low-register features are found in various clause types discussed in Section 4.4.1. Moreover, they are not uncommon in the two clause types containing the perfect indicative and the perfect infinitive ('Perf. Inf.' and 'ὁμολογέω + Perf. Inf.' in Table 3), also indicating their low register. These data are consistent with the view these two clause types reflect the non-Classical use of the perfect infinitive and the perfect indicative; that is, their use in the function of the perfective past (because non-Classical features, as stated in Section 3, tend to associate with lower registers). This may also suggest, however, that the non-Classical use of the perfect infinitive, as observed in Section 4.1.1, mostly concerned low-register texts from the corpus.

Furthermore passage (9), which contains a perfect infinitive modified with a time specification of the anterior event, is from another document containing low-register features. Although it follows classical orthography, it contains a present tense in the report of past events. Judging from Bentein (2015a: 477–479), this is a low-register feature (it is frequently used in drafts and omitted from the revised texts), and the same applies to the use of direct speech in this document.[52] In addition, a few other documents displaying the use of the perfect infinitive with time specifications of anterior events also display low-register features. The orthography is thus often non-Classical, examples including: ὁμολοκία 'agreement', ἰς 'in', μεταδεδώσθαι 'to have been distributed', and στολειστήν 'priest' (instead of ὁμολογία, εἰς, μεταδεδόσθαι, and στολιστήν) in P. Tebt II 295 (126–138 CE); and ἱμίσει 'to the half', γίτονες 'neighbours', ἴσοδος 'entrance', and ὑπάρχουσει 'they

---

51 Some documents display confusion between κ and γ, as well as between ρ and λ (e.g. ὁμολογῦ instead of ὁμολογῶ in O.Claud. III 449, l. 2 (137 CE), and φόλετρον 'expenses of transport' instead of φόρετρον in P.Oxy XXXVI, 2793, l. 9 (II/III CE)), also suggesting interference with Egyptian (cf. Horrocks 2010: 111–113, Dahlgren 2016: 92–105).
52 See Blass, Debrunner & Rehkopf (2001: 400), Bentein (2015c: 109).

exist' (instead of ἡμείσει, γείτονες, εἴσοδος, and ὑπάρχουσι) in P.Oxy VI 986 (131–132 CE). This is another indication that the construction in question might have mostly been associated with lower-register texts.

However, a different example is P.Oxy. II 257 (94–95 CE), an application in which the author tries to show that his son belongs to the privileged class, asking for a tax exemption. Although the name of the addressee is lost, the context suggests that the application was addressed to a higher-ranking official, in which cases high register is expected.[53] It is thus not surprising that the document displays high-register features, lacking any significant divergences from Classical orthography/morphology. In addition, it contains a finite complement clause introduced with ὡς 'that' (although the text is fragmentary and the reading is not entirely certain) and a few instances of particles, whereas its core consists of one long sentence (parts of which are cited below in passage 14). These are arguably high-register features.[54] However passage (14) also shows that the document contains perfect infinitives modified with time specifications of anterior events:

(14) δηλῶ κ[α]τὰ τὴν γενομένην τῷ ε [(ἔτει)] | θεοῦ Οὐεσπασιανοῦ . . . ἐπίκρισι[ν] | **ἐπικεκρίσθαι** [τ]ὸν πατέρα μου Διογένη[ν Θε-]|ογέ[ν]ους τοῦ Φιλίσκου μητρὸς Σινθοών[ιος]| Ἀχιλλέως . . . τὴν δὲ μητέρα μου| [Π]τολέμαν **γεγ[α]μ̣[ῆσθαι** τῷ π]α̣τρί μου **πρὸ| ζ (ἔτους) Νέρωνος** . . . τὴν δὲ| καὶ τοῦ υἱοῦ μη[τέρα] Ἰσιδώ[ραν **γ]εγαμῆ-|σθαι** μοι **τῶι ζ (ἔτει) Νέρωνος**

'I declare that my father Diogenes, son of Theogenes, son of Philiscus, his mother being Sinthoönis, daughter of Achilleus, was selected at the selection which took place in the fifth year of the deified Vespasian . . . that my mother Ptolema married my father before the 7th year of Nero . . . that my wife and the mother of my son, Isidora, married me in the seventh year of Nero.'
(P.Oxy. II 257, ll. 12–13, 15–18 , 24–26, 29–31; 94–95 CE) [tr. Grenfell & Hunt]

The passage contains several instances of a time specification of the anterior event modifying a perfect infinitive. The first is κ[α]τὰ τὴν γενομένην τῷ ε [(ἔτει)] θεοῦ Οὐεσπασιανοῦ . . . ἐπίκρισιν 'at the selection that took place in the fifth year of the deified Vespasian', which modifies the perfect infinitive ἐπικεκρίσθαι 'to have been selected' (ll. 12–13). Furthermore, the time specification πρὸ ζ (ἔτους) Νέρωνος 'before the seventh year of Nero' appears to modify the perfect infinitive γεγαμῆσθαι 'to have married' (ll. 24–26): although some letters are missing, the reduplication γε- suggests that this is a perfect infinitive. Finally, τῶι ζ (ἔτει)

---

53 Bentein (2015a: 468–469; 479).
54 Bentein (2015c: 111; 2015a: 471–476).

Νέρωνος 'in the seventh year of Nero' modifies the perfect infinitive [γ]εγαμῆσθαι 'to have married' (ll. 29–31).

This document indicates that complement clauses containing a time specification of an anterior event that modifies a perfect infinitive, which was an arguably non-Classical construction, were not incompatible with a relatively high register: in other words, this construction could be used in a document that in general displays no significant divergences from Classical Greek. Additional documents of similar contents and register that also contain time specifications of an anterior event modifying the perfect infinitive are P.Oxy. III 478, ll. 16–17 (132 CE), P.Oxy. VII 1028, ll. 19–21 (86 CE), and P.Oxy. XLVI 3283, ll. 9–12 (148–149 CE).

Section 4.1.2 also drew attention to the use of time specifications with the perfect indicative. Some (but not all) of the documents displaying this phenomenon also contain examples of (mostly orthographic) divergences from Classical Greek.[55] In general, however, the data in this section suggest that non-Classical uses of the perfect were not restricted to lower registers.

4.2 Past-oriented aorist infinitives

A few documents in the corpus investigated contain potential or certain instances of past-oriented aorist infinitives. As shown in Kavčič (2017b: 36–41), past-oriented aorist infinitives are highly uncommon in both official and private documents of the first century CE. In addition, at least some of them are suggestions of modern editors rather than certain readings (e.g. [ἐλθεῖν] 'to come' in P.Vindob.Bosw 1, l.37 (87 CE)). The corpus investigated, which also contains second-century documents, provides additional partially or fully restored past-oriented aorist infinitives, examples including [κομίσασθαι] 'to receive' in P.Ryl. II 78, l. 19 (157 CE), [ἄρξαι] 'to begin' in P.Muech. 3.1.66, 2, l. 23 (124 CE), ποιή[σα]σθε 'to do' in P.Oxy. XII 1472, ll. 23–24 (136 CE), ἐξαπατηθ[ῆναι] 'to be deceived' and [λαβεῖν] 'to take' in P.Oxy III 471, ll. 42–43 (II CE), as well as [πεσεῖν] 'to fall' and [ὑπορύξ]αι 'to dig under' in P. Oxy XLVI 3285, ll. 43–45 (150–200 CE). Although the final two letters in the latter case may indicate that this is an aorist infinitive, I take this instance as uncertain because the two letters are unclear. Except for the infinitive ἐξαπατηθ[ῆναι] in P. Oxy. III 471, l. 42 (II CE), where the certain reading of the final -θ indicates that this is an aorist infinitive,[56] none of these infinitives are counted in Table 2.

---

55 See BGU II 421 (160–161 CE) and O. Bodl. II 1094 (21 CE).
56 As an anonymous reviewer noted, a future infinitive is a possible reading as well. However, because the context does not support this view, I interpret this form as an aorist infinitive.

4.2.1 Time reference of the aorist infinitives

Table 2 also shows that past-oriented aorist infinitives are generally highly uncommon in the corpus. However, the exact number seems difficult to define, and this is mostly a result of the ambiguity of the aorist infinitive, which can refer to posteriority or to anteriority in Ancient Greek (see §2.2). Whereas an example of the former is passage (2) above, an example of the latter is passage (14). It contains two aorist infinitives dependent on the verb δηλόω 'to declare'. However, the context clearly shows that the infinitives refer to the obligations of the tenants of the vineyard and are thus future-oriented (and posterior). This is also seen in the modern translation:

(15) δεδήλω[τ]αι ἐν μὲν τῇ πρώτῃ τετραετίᾳ μηδὲν ὑπὲρ φόρου| τελέσ\αι/ ἀλλὰ μόνα [τ]ὰ δημόσια διαγράψαι

'(in which) it was stated that in the first four years he should be charged no rent but only pay the taxes on condition.'
(P.Oxy. IV 707, ll. 21–22; 136 CE) [tr. Grenfell and Hunt]

Although the time reference can usually be safely deduced from the context, some passages containing an aorist infinitive remain ambiguous between a past- and future-oriented reading (sometimes due to the fragmentary text). Modern translations may also suggest that an aorist infinitive is past-oriented; for example, in passage (16):

(16) [ὁ]μολογεῖ ἐν ἀγυι[ᾷ] τῇ αὐτῇ ἐγδοῦναι τὴν Θαΐδ[α

'. . . acknowledges in the same street that she has given away Thais in marriage.'
(P.Oxy. III 496, l. 5; 127 CE) [tr. Grenfell & Hunt]

However, aorist infinitives dependent on the verb ὁμολογέω, which is the case here, can also be interpreted as future-oriented. 'Agrees to give away' is thus a plausible interpretation of the phrase [ὁ]μολογεῖ . . . ἐγδοῦναι. As mentioned in Section 4.1.1, the aorist infinitive (when dependent on ὁμολογέω) usually refers to an obligation and is thus future-oriented according to McKay (1980: 41).[57] In the case of passage (16), this view can further be supported with the nature of the document: the passage is found in a marriage contract and it seems likely that such a document mostly refers to posterior events.

---

[57] Bentein (2018: 97) appears to support this view as well, arguing also that infinitive clauses that are dependent on ὁμολογέω and contain an aorist infinitive can be interpreted as propositions (or as declarative infinitive clauses) and may thus not necessarily refer to an obligation.

The corpus contains a few additional instances of the aorist infinitive dependent on the verb ὁμολογέω, which allow either for a future- or for past-oriented reading (e.g. BGU II 472, ll. 6–16 (139 CE), P.Prag I 31, l. 16 (139–160 CE), P.Tebt II 310, l. 3 (186 CE), P.Fay 34, ll. 3–5 (161 CE), P.Phil. 2, l. 5 (II CE), P.Babatha 18, l. 14 (128 CE)).[58] All of these instances are presented as uncertain in Table 2, except for the cases in which the context and the modern translation leave no doubt about the temporal reference of the aorist infinitive (e.g. P.Oxy. IV 707, ll. 21–22).

4.2.2 Certain instances of past-oriented aorist infinitives

The corpus also contains instances of past-oriented aorist infinitives that are much more certain. They represent less than 1% of all complement infinitive clauses. In these cases, the context leaves no doubt that the aorist infinitive conveys anteriority. An example is passage (2), quoted in Section 1. The documents containing these instances include a contract (P.Dura 18 l. 2; 7 (87 CE)), a decree by Emperor Hadrian (P.Oslo III 78, ll. 5–6 (136 CE)), an account of a debt (P.Fouad 54, ll. 4–8 (ca. 142 CE)), and two advocates' speeches (P.Oxy III 471, ll. 42–44 (II CE), P.Oxy III 472, ll. 2–3 (130 CE)).[59] These past-oriented aorist infinitives occur in high-register documents. An example is passage (17):

> (17) ἐξαπατηθ[ῆναι]| ἢ καὶ δωρεὰ[ς λαβεῖν]| φήσεις
>
> 'Will you say that you were deceived or that you took bribes?'
> (P.Oxy III 471, ll. 42–44; II CE) [tr. Grenfell & Hunt]

If ἐξαπατηθ- is accepted as a past-oriented aorist infinitive,[60] the distinction between this aorist infinitive and the perfect infinitives in the same document seems to reflect the Classical usage, observed in passage (4).[61] It thus seems possible to argue that the accuser uses the perfect infinitive when referring (in lines 46–48) to deeds of the accused: ἡμεῖς δ'οὐκ εἰληφέναι σε μισθὸν [ἀλλὰ δε] δωκέναι φαμέν 'But we say not that you took money but that you gave it.' On

---

58 The aorist infinitive (e.g. ποιήσασθαι 'to do' in BGU II 472, ll. 6–16 (139 CE)) may also be a result of a confusion between thematic vowels and can thus also represent the future infinitive (see Gignac 1981: 333). The rest of the cases quoted here can be interpreted with much more certainty as aorist infinitives.
59 The issue of whether the readings of past-oriented aorist infinitives are certain in P.Dura 18 (87 CE) is discussed in Kavčič (2017b: 38–39).
60 On this infinitive cf. fn. 56.
61 It is also noteworthy that the aorist infinitive is used within a coordinative construction, on which see Kavčič (2020).

the other hand, the aorist infinitive is used in passage (17), where the anterior events are presented from the perspective of the accused, just as appears to be the case in the Classical Greek passage (4), in which Antigone uses the aorist infinitive δρᾶσαι 'to do' in reference to her deeds.

According to Grenfell and Hunt (1903: 147), the accused was a high-ranking official and the speech was perhaps performed in front of the emperor himself.[62] As suggested in Section 4.1.3, the high register would be expected in such a case and the language of the document confirms this. As the editors note, it is "elaborately punctuated as a literary work" (Grenfell and Hunt 1903: 147) and contains a number of self-corrections. For instance, the non-Classical ἀναλημφθῆναι 'to be taken up' was corrected to ἀναληφθῆναι. It is worth noting that the future stem λημψ- appears to have become very frequent already by the time of the Septuagint,[63] whereas, according to Gignac (1981: 269), it was commonly used in non-literary papyri of the Roman period. This is an indication that this type of the future was a standard Koine form, and that, as a result, future forms in ληψ- were perceived in the period investigated as highly classicizing. Furthermore, the document contains the Atticistic form τοὔλαττον (τὸ ἔλαττον) 'at least'. In this case, ἔλασσον would be the expected Koine form. In addition, the text contains a number of particles, and some of them (μήν, τοίνυν) are typical of higher registers.[64]

The majority of other documents containing certain instances of the aorist infinitive display no significant divergences from Classical Greek. P.Oxy. III 472 (130 CE), P.Dura 18 (87 CE), and P.Oslo III 78 (136 CE) contain virtually no non-Classical orthographic or morphological features (an exception is the spelling μεγείστου 'of the largest' in P.Oslo III 78); P.Dura 18 also contains the participle μεταληψόμενος 'who will participate' with the future verb stem ληψ- (which was commented on above). In syntactic terms, P.Oxy III 472 contains additional examples of particles that are usually associated with higher registers. An example is ἄρα 'then', which is used in a positive context here (εἰ ἄρα τις καὶ ἐπεβούλευσεν 'if anyone really plotted against him'; P.Oxy. III 472, l. 8). According to Bentein (2015d: 745), this use of the particle ἄρα is in general highly uncommon in the non-literary papyri. Another example of a high-register particle is μήν (cf. above), and other particles from this text include μὲν . . . δὲ, γάρ, and μέντοι.

---

62 Grenfell and Hunt, loc. cit., also raise the issue of whether or not this was an actual speech. It could be considered a rhetorical exercise, for instance, which would also explain its high register. Nevertheless, later commentators appear to agree that the speech was delivered in an actual trial, noting also its high register (see Vout 2007: 141; Harper 2013: 29).
63 Examples from the Septuagint include Gen. 28.1, Ex. 6.7, Lev. 14.6, Num. 3.47, etc. I owe this observation to an anonymous reviewer of this study.
64 Bentein (2015d: 742–743, 746).

This also largely applies to the documents from Section 4.2.1, although an apparent exception – if these documents are taken into account – is P.Tebt. II 310 (186 CE). According to Grenfell and Hunt (1907: 105), this is "a very illiterate agreement". It contains a number of non-Classical forms and spellings; for instance, λεκομένας 'the aforementioned' instead of λεγομένας and ὥσα 'as much as' instead of ὅσα, in addition to the aorist infinitive ἐκχωρῆσαι 'to surrender' (spelled ἐκχωρῆσε̣), which is dependent on ὁμολογέω (spelled ὁμολοκῶ).[65] However, as suggested in Section 4.2.1, in the majority of cases when an aorist infinitive is dependent on the verb ὁμολογέω, the context also allows a future-oriented reading of the infinitive. As a result, the phrase ὁμολοκῶ ἐκχωρῆσε̣ can be interpreted as 'I agree to surrender' rather than 'I acknowledge that I have surrendered' and is thus an uncertain instance of a past-oriented aorist infinitive.

4.2.3 Anteriority and the Classical norm: Discussion

Previous sections showed that, in terms of expressing anteriority in complement infinitive clauses, the corpus investigated displays significant divergences from Classical Greek. First, this is indicated by the avoidance of past-oriented aorist infinitives, which are highly uncommon in the corpus, reaching around 1% of all complements clauses (even if uncertain instances are counted). It is also interesting to observe that the restored past-oriented aorist infinitives are about as frequent in the corpus as certain instances of this construction. This seems to be an indication of modern editors' view that official documents more strictly followed the example of Classical Greek than what might have been the case, and that such references to Classical Greek may not always be plausible.[66]

Another divergence from Classical Greek concerns phenomena indicating that the perfect infinitive could be used in the function of conveying anteriority (§4.1.2). It is noteworthy that perfect infinitives modified with time specifications of anterior events, which seem to be the clearest manifestation of this phenomenon, are about five times as common in the corpus as certain instances of past-oriented aorist infinitives.

Sometimes these non-Classical phenomena can be accounted for in terms of the generally low register of the documents. Nevertheless, this is far from true in all cases, which raises the issue of why the texts that in general display

---

[65] The confusion between κ and γ, as well some other misspellings in the document, suggest the Egyptian background of the scribe (cf. fn. 51).
[66] Cf. Depauw & Stolk (2015: 219).

no significant divergences from Classical Greek might have allowed a non-Classical use of the perfect infinitive.

A particularly significant feature of the perfect infinitive appears to be that it was less ambiguous in temporal terms than the aorist infinitive, as was stressed earlier (see especially §2.2). This could account for the spread of the perfect infinitive in the function of conveying anteriority, if one takes into account the definition of formality in Heylighen and Dewaele (1999). They define it as a tendency toward avoiding ambiguity and minimizing context-dependence of expression and, taking into account that the texts investigated are official (or, formal), it can be assumed that their authors might have been particularly prone to using a less ambiguous construction, which was the perfect infinitive. Alternatively, it is possible to argue, as Chantraine (1927: 187–189) did, that this function of the perfect infinitive was a relatively early development, originating from processes that already saw their emergence in Classical Greek. As already mentioned in Section 2.1, however, this assumption needs further corroboration.

On the other hand, past-oriented aorist infinitives mostly appear to be associated with high-register texts because they tend to follow the example of Classical Greek; this could be interpreted as an impact of Classical Greek on the corpus investigated.[67] It is also interesting to observe that five out of the six certain cases of past-oriented aorist infinitives are dependent on the same verb; namely, φημί 'to assert'. Perhaps this use of the aorist infinitive was mostly an archaic feature of one verb, and the choice of the construction in question could be related to the author's education level. This view is also supported by Bentein (2015b: 465), who claims that, in the period investigated, the very use of the verb φημί was a high-register feature. It is also noteworthy that two of the certain cases from the corpus investigated are found in advocate's speeches. In addition, P.Oxy. III 471 (II CE) contains elements of literary style, which is consistent with the initial assumption (§2.2) that past-oriented aorist infinitives tended to be used in the period investigated in literary texts.

As explained in Section 1, my corpus is heterogeneous, containing different types of documents. As a result, it also suggests that the past-oriented aorist infinitive was more likely to occur in some types of documents than in others. It is found, for instance, in a contract (i.e. in a deed of gift), in official speeches and in an emperor's decree, and these documents stand in contrast to receipts from my corpus that appear to avoid the past-oriented aorist infinitive despite

---

67 As an anonymous reviewer commented, this could be a reintroduction of the feature from the language of the literature or its survival from Classical Greek through higher registers. Much more research is needed, in my opinion, in order to clarify this issue.

the abundance of contexts in which this construction could be adopted. When conveying anteriority in the construction investigated, the perfect infinitive appears to have been preferred in these documents, the same as in applications and reports, which also contain instances of time specifications of anterior events modifying the perfect infinitive.

In general, many aspects of Post-classical registers remain unexplored, and future investigation may also show that non-classical syntactic structures – perhaps in contrast to orthographic and morphological features – were not uncommon even in higher registers. It is also interesting to observe, however, that of the five documents examined here one appears to originate from the capital city (P.Oslo III 78) and another one (P.Dura 18) from Dura-Europos. Other factors may have thus played a role in the choice of this construction as well because these data may indicate that the tendency toward using the perfect infinitive in the function of conveying anteriority was a particularly prominent feature of Egyptian scribes. Nevertheless, low frequencies of past-oriented aorist infinitives make it difficult to draw safe conclusions, and a more thorough investigation of this issue lies beyond the scope of this chapter.

4.3 The future infinitive: Further remarks

As suggested initially in Section 4, the frequencies of the future infinitive seem significant enough to assume the impact of Classical Greek. However, this claim stands in contrast with subsequent findings concerning the perfect infinitive, which showed differences between the corpus investigated and Classical Greek. Additional remarks concerning this contrast thus seem in place.

It is interesting to observe that, in the period investigated, the future infinitive is attested in unofficial documents.[68] An example is passage (18), taken from a private letter in which the sender (Zosimos) instructs the addressee (Paniscos) to purchase and deliver dates. The text also contains the verb form γυψιεῖν (from γυψίζω 'to plaster with gypsum'). It is noteworthy that this form appears distinct enough from other forms of the same verb to exclude the possibility of confusion

---

68 See also Bentein (2018: 92), who mentions examples of the future infinitive in non-literary papyri in general. Additional examples from private letters include P.Oslo II 62, l. 8 (III CE), P. Mil.Vogl. II 76, ll. 8–9 (II CE), P.Herm. 5, ll. 11–12 (IV CE), and P.Athen. 64, ll. 3–4 (II CE).

with another morphologically similar form (especially with the aorist infinitive).[69] As a result, it can safely be interpreted as a future infinitive:

(18) τὰ| γὰρ κεράμια τῶν ἐλαι-|ῶν οἶμαί σε ἀσφαλῶς| πάλιν γυψιεῖν.
'I believe that you will firmly seal the jars of olives again.'
(P.Mich XII 657, ll. 14–17; II–III CE)

It is often claimed that private documents tend to follow the example of Classical Greek much less strictly than official texts – although, as was argued in Section 1, even the assumption that Classical Greek was the norm of official documents is controversial.[70] In addition passage (18) occurs outside any formulaic expression; such expressions tend to retain archaic linguistic features.[71] As a result, it appears that, in the period investigated, the use of the future infinitive might not necessarily reflect a direct impact of Classical Greek. Furthermore, statistical data show that the frequencies of the future infinitive in the corpus investigated may be higher than in lower-register texts of the period investigated (see §4). However, they are also about four times lower than in Classical Greek, given that in Classical texts of different genres they amount to around 20% of all complement infinitive clauses.[72] Taking into account the process of the disappearance of the Ancient Greek synthetic future, this gradual decline seems expected for the Post-classical period.

As a result, these data suggest that the use of the future infinitive in the corpus investigated can be interpreted as an instance of continuation from earlier stages of the language, rather than reflecting an attempt to follow the example of Classical Greek.

5 Conclusion

This study first showed that not all of the documents in the corpus investigated equally follow the example of Classical Greek. In terms of the syntactic phenomena which I focused on, there appears to be a distinction between Classical Greek and the corpus investigated in at least one aspect; namely, in terms of expressing anteriority. There are reasons to believe that, unlike in Classical Greek and in

---

69 On this phenomenon see, for instance, Gignac (1981: 333) and Kavčič (2016: 283–285).
70 See, for instance, Depauw & Stolk (2015: 211–212) and Bentein (2017: 23) for the language of private documents, as well as works referred to in §1 (for official documents).
71 E.g. Bentein (2017: 23).
72 See Kavčič (2016: 284).

literary texts of the period investigated (as has recently been suggested by Crellin 2016: 240–246), the perfect rather than the aorist infinitive tended to adopt this function. This is best exemplified by the complement clauses that contain a perfect infinitive and a time specification of an anterior event, and place the corpus investigated in contrast to both literary Koine and Classical Greek. In addition to official documents that may seem to display lower-register features, such instances can also be found in documents displaying no significant divergences from Classical Greek (in orthographic, morphological, and syntactic terms), mostly in reports and applications. Past-oriented aorist infinitives, on the other hand, are very uncommon in the corpus investigated and appear to be restricted to higher-register documents. This situation is consistent with the hypothesis about the retreat of past-oriented aorist infinitives in the Post-classical period.

On the other hand, it could be argued, mostly based on statistical data, that the future infinitive displays a much stronger influence of Classical Greek. However, there is also evidence suggesting that, rather than being under direct influence of Classical Greek, it may also reflect the situation in Post-classical Greek, just as appears to have been the case with the use of the past-oriented aorist and the perfect infinitive.

References

Beek, Janneke ter. 2011. Two futures in infinitives. In C. Jan-Wouter Zwart & Mark de Wries (eds.), *Structures preserved: Studies in syntax for Jan Koster*, 41–48. Amsterdam: Benjamins.
Bentein, Klaas. 2012. The periphrastic perfect in Ancient Greek: A diachronic mental space analysis. *Transactions of the Philological Society* 110. 171–211.
Bentein, Klaas. 2015a. The Greek documentary papyri as a linguistically heterogeneous corpus: The case of the katochoi of the Sarapeion-archive. *Classical World* 108. 461–484.
Bentein, Klaas. 2015b. The Greek of the fathers. In Ken Parry (ed.), *The Wiley Blackwell companion to patristics*, 456–470. Chichester: Wiley-Blackwell.
Bentein, Klaas. 2015c. Minor complementation patterns in Post-classical Greek (I–IV AD): A socio-historical analysis of a corpus of documentary papyri. *Symbolae Osloenses* 89. 104–147.
Bentein, Klaas. 2015d. Particle-usage in documentary papyri (I–IV AD): An integrated sociolinguistically-informed approach. *Greek, Roman & Byzantine Studies* 55. 721–753.
Bentein, Klass. 2016. *Verbal periphrasis in Ancient Greek*. Oxford: Oxford University Press.
Bentein, Klaas. 2017. Finite vs. non-finite complementation in Post-classical and Early Byzantine Greek: Towards a pragmatic restructuring of the complementation system? *Journal of Greek Linguistics* 17. 3–36.
Bentein, Klass. 2018. The decline of infinitival complementation in Ancient Greek. *Glotta* 94. 82–108.

Blass, Friedrich, Albert Debrunner & Friedrich Rehkopf. 2001. *Grammatik des neutestamentlichen Griechisch*, 18th ed. Göttingen: Vandenhoeck & Ruprecht.
Burton de Witt, Ernest. 1898. *Syntax of moods and tenses in New Testament Greek*. Edinburg: Clark.
Chantraine, Pierre. 1927. *Histoire du parfait grec*. Paris: Champion.
Comrie, Bernard. 1981. *Aspect*. Cambridge: Cambridge University Press.
Crellin, Robert S. D. 2016. *The syntax and semantics of the perfect active in literary Koine Greek*. Chichester: Wiley-Blackwell.
Dahlgren, Sonja. 2016. Towards a definition of an Egyptian Greek variety. *Papers in Historical Phonology* 1. 90–108.
Depauw, Mark & Joanne Vera Stolk. 2015. Linguistic variation in Greek papyri: Towards a new tool for quantitative study. *Greek, Roman & Byzantine Studies* 55. 196–220.
Evans, Trevor V. 2010. Standard Koine Greek in third century BC papyri. In Traianos Gagos & Adam Hyatt (eds.), *Proceedings of the 25th International Congress of Papyrology, Ann Arbor, 29 July – 4 August 2007*, 197–206. Ann Arbor: Scholarly Publishing Office, University of Michigan Library.
Evans, Trevor V. 2012. The Zenon Archive and Egyptian interference. In Alex Mullen & Patrick James (eds.), *Multilingualism in the Graeco-Roman worlds*, 106–123. Cambridge: Cambridge University Press.
Fanning, Buist M. 1990. *Verbal aspect in New Testament Greek*. Oxford: Clarendon Press.
Gerö, Eva-Carin & Arnim von Stechow. 2003. Tense in time: The Greek perfect. In Regine Eckardt, Klaus von Heusinger & Christoph Schwarze (eds.), *Words in time: Diachronic semantics from different points of view*, 251–293. Berlin: de Gruyter.
Gignac, Francis T. 1981. *A grammar of the Greek papyri of the Roman and Byzantine period*. Vol. 2: *Morphology*. Milan: Cisalpino-Goliardica.
Grenfell, Bernard P. & Arthur S. Hunt (eds.). 1903. *The Oxyrhynchus papyri*. Part III. London: Egypt Exploration Society.
Grenfell, Bernard P. & Arthur S. Hunt (eds.). 1907. *The Tebtunis papyri*. Part II. London: Egypt Exploration Society.
Harper, Kyle. 2013. *From shame to sin: The Christian transformation of sexual morality in Late Antiquity*. Cambridge: Harvard University Press.
Haspelmath, Martin. 1992. From resultative to perfect in Ancient Greek. *Function* 11–12. 187–224.
Heylighen, Francis & Jean-Marc Dewaele. 1999. Formality of language: Definition, measurement and behavioral determinants. Internal Report, Free University of Brussels.
Horrocks, Geoffrey C. 2010. *Greek: A history of the language and its speakers*, 2nd ed. Malden: Wiley-Blackwell.
Jannaris, Antonius N. 1968 [1897]. *An historical Greek grammar chiefly of the Attic dialect as written and spoken from Classical Antiquity down to present time founded upon the ancient texts, inscriptions, papyri and present popular Greek*. Hildesheim: Georg Olms.
Joseph, Brian D. 1983. *The synchrony and diachrony of the Balkan infinitive*. Cambridge: Cambridge University Press.
Kavčič, Jerneja. 2016. The decline of the aorist infinitive in Ancient Greek declarative infinitive clauses. *Journal of Greek Linguistics* 16. 266–311.
Kavčič, Jerneja. 2017a. A diachronic perspective on the semantics of AcI clauses in Greek. In Lukasz Jedrzeyowski & Ulrike Demske (eds.), *Infinitives at the syntax-semantics interface: A diachronic perspective*, 81–111. Berlin: de Gruyter Mouton.

Kavčič, Jerneja. 2017b. Variation in expressing temporal and aspectual distinctions in complement clauses: A study of the Greek non-literary papyri of the Roman period. In Klaas Bentein, Mark Janse & Jorie Soltic (eds.), *Variation and change in Ancient Greek tense, aspect and modality*, 22–55. Leiden: Brill.

Kavčič, Jerneja. 2020. Examining a hypothesis about the past-oriented aorist infinitive in Post-Classical Greek. *Transactions of the Philological Society* 118, 1–28.

Mandilaras, Basil G. 1972. *Studies in the Greek language*. Athens: The Author.

Mandilaras, Basil. 1973. *The verb in the Greek non-literary papyri*. Athens: Hellenic Ministry of Culture and Science.

Markopoulos, Theodore. 2009. *The future in Greek: From Ancient to Medieval*. Oxford: Oxford University Press.

McKay, Kenneth L. 1980. On the perfect and other aspects in the Greek non-literary papyri. *Bulletin of the Institute of Classical Studies* 27. 23–49.

Méndez Dosuna, Julián. 2017. Syntactic variation with verbs of perception and the 'oblique imperfect': Once again on aspect, relative time reference and purported tense-backshifting in Ancient Greek. In Klaas Bentein, Mark Janse & Jorie Soltic (eds.), *Variation and change in Ancient Greek tense, aspect and modality*, 56–83. Leiden: Brill.

Rijksbaron, Albert. 2002. *The syntax and semantics of the verb in Classical Greek: An introduction*, 3rd ed. Chicago: Chicago University Press.

Vitelli, Girolamo & Medea Norsa (eds.). 1917. *Papiri greci e latini*. Vol. 4. Florence: Società italiana per la ricerca dei papiri greci e latini in Egitto.

Vout, Caroline. 2007. *Power and eroticism in imperial Rome*. Cambridge: Cambridge University Press.

Zwart, Jan-Wouter. 2014. The tense of infinitives in Dutch. In Jacob Hoeksema & Dirk Gilbers (eds.), *A Festschrift in honor of Frans Zwarts*, 363–387. Groningen: University of Groningen.

Joanne Vera Stolk
12 Orthographic variation and register in the corpus of Greek documentary papyri (300 BCE–800 CE)

Abstract: The corpus of Greek documentary papyri from Egypt consists of various types of documents, such as letters, contracts and accounts, showing different types of linguistic variation. The concept of register is applied here to examine the relationship between the presence of non-standard orthography and the situational context according to the situational variables setting, participants, genre and production circumstances. Quantitative study shows that the participants involved and the genre of the document are predictors for the amount of orthographic variation that is found in a document. Qualitative analysis of the documents in a number of archives reveals that there are also other important factors, such as the choice of scribe, method of production and the stage of composition of the text that is preserved to us, to explain the presence of orthographic variation in the corpus of documentary papyri.

1 Introduction

The corpus of Greek documentary papyri from Egypt is known as rich source for linguistic variation. This corpus of more than 50.000 texts is available online via the PN and includes documents of various types, such as letters, petitions, contracts, accounts and lists, mostly written in Egypt between 300 BCE and 800 CE. The attested variation in spelling has been used to reconstruct the pronunciation of the spoken language at the time,[1] but the distribution of orthographic variation within the corpus may also be governed by language external factors.[2] Documentary papyri do not form a homogeneous corpus: different types of variation at various levels of the language are found across variety of document types. The concept of register could be applied to explain the distribution of variation in more detail, but the variables governing the variation at the level of orthography and morphology may not be identical to those at the level of syntax and pragmatics (§1.1). One might expect that standard orthography is a feature of a higher register, but non-standard orthography does

---
1 E.g. Gignac (1976), Teodorsson (1977).
2 Cf. e.g. Rutkowska & Rössler (2012).

https://doi.org/10.1515/9783110614404-012

not exclusively appear in informal contexts in the papyrological corpus (§1.2). In this paper, I will test several situational variables to see to what extent they govern the distribution of orthographic variation in the corpus of documentary papyri. After a short introduction to the research question, the corpus and methodology will be explained in more detail in Section 2. The quantitative analysis of standard and non-standard orthography in Section 3 is based on the editorial regularizations provided in digital editions (TMTI) and followed by a qualitative analysis of the distribution of orthographic variation in several archives in Section 4. A conclusion and discussion of the results is provided in Section 5.

1.1 Register and linguistic variation

Register variation is often understood in the form of a continuum.[3] In some studies the whole corpus of documentary papyri is situated at the lower end of this register continuum,[4] whereas other studies have demonstrated that a register continuum can also be found within the corpus itself and even within sub-corpora such as papyrus archives. For example, Bentein (2015a: 479) concludes about the linguistic variation in the so-called archive of the "Katochoi of the Sarapieion" from the second century BCE (TM Archive ID 119): "In terms of the earlier-mentioned register-continuum, we can say that the language of the dreams is situated most to the left ('the low register'), followed by the letters and petitions respectively. This register-continuum itself can be seen as the sum of a number of linguistic dimensions (phonology, semantics, morphology, syntax)."

The concept of register to explain variation within the papyrological corpus has mainly been shown useful in the domains of syntax and pragmatics, such as for variation between complementation patterns[5] and the use of particles.[6] Comparison of features at other linguistic levels, however, does not always give the same results in individual texts.[7] This is also a concern expressed by Halla-aho (2010: 172) about the Latin language in the papyri: "There is often an implicit assumption that a given letter would, as a whole, belong to a certain linguistic variety [. . .] I shall argue that in a given letter, different levels of language

---

[3] Cf. Biber (1995: 31).
[4] Bentein (2012, 2013).
[5] James (2007), Bentein (2015c, 2017).
[6] Clarysse (2010), Bentein (2015b).
[7] Bentein (2015a: 479).

organization (phonological/orthographic, morphological, and syntactic) need not, and often do not, consistently relate to one linguistic variety (register or sociolect)." This inconsistency may be caused by a difference between the external factors governing the spread of syntactic and pragmatic features and the ones governing orthographic and morphological variation.

1.2 Language and context

Linguistic register is the result of an interplay between "linguistic behaviour" and the "sociolinguistic context".[8] James (2007: 35–36) defines three levels of language in the papyri, namely "high (official), middle (some official, business, and some personal), and low (personal texts which seem substandard even within the Koine)". The sociolinguistic context is here reduced to a cline of subject matters: from official and business related to personal texts. Linguistic behaviour is described in terms of its standardness or rather substandardness within the Koine. Characterisation of language in terms of vernacularity is not uncommon in historical linguistics, compare the following characterisation of the "formal" register by Hickey (2010: 8): "The lower this [vernacularity, JVS] is the more formal the register and hence the more standard the language will be [. . .] A high level of vernacularity implies a high incidence of non-standard features which are indicated by unexpected spelling and grammar."

More formal or "high" register texts are thus expected to show more standard language features, while non-standard spelling and grammar is taken as a sign of a "low" register text. These divisions across the register continuum are visualized in Table 1.

Table 1: Context-based and language-based approach to a register continuum.

Continuum	"high"	"middle"	"low"
Context-based	official texts	business texts	personal texts
Language-based	low number of non-standard features	average number of non-standard features	high number of non-standard features

---

8 Porter & O'Donnell (2010: 297).

One would assume that the results of the context-based approach largely overlap with the language-based approach, but this expectation is not always born out in the case of papyrus documents. James (2007: 36) mentions several problematic examples: "Some early texts, which are official in content, such as the copy of the letter of Claudius to the Alexandrians preserved in P.Lond. VI 1912 (= Sel.Pap. II 212), can show obviously low-level or 'late' orthography and morphosyntactic features."

Thus, individual examples show that non-standard language features can also be found in official contexts. In this paper I will test this relation between linguistic behaviour and sociolinguistic context in the whole corpus of published documentary papyri, focussing on the use of orthography. Are the documents that we would judge as formal or official in a context-based approach indeed the ones written with the most standardized orthography?

2 Approach to the corpus

Orthographic variation has not been annotated as such in digitalized papyrus editions, but the corpus offers an approximate measure of orthographic variation in the form of editorial regularizations (§2.1). This large scale identification of non-standard orthographic features allows us to do a quantitative analysis of the relation between orthography and the situational context. Different situational variables are selected (§2.2) and annotated in the corpus (§2.3) for this quantitative analysis (results in §3), whereas some other possibly relevant variables will be tested qualitatively in different sub-corpora in Section 4.

2.1 Counting orthographic variation

Digital editions of all published papyri are available in the PN, including regularizations of orthography and morphology in the text and apparatus. Together with Mark Depauw (KU Leuven), I collected and annotated more than 130.000 attestations of editorial regularization in a total corpus of almost 52.000 documentary papyri.[9] The results can be accessed through the TMTI. All regularizations have been categorized into the type of regularization (such as ο instead of ω, omission of ς, addition of ν) and annotated for linguistic level. For this study,

---

[9] See Depauw & Stolk (2015). All results are based on the state of the PN of January 2014 and the state of TM in November 2017.

I only used regularizations involving an interchange, omission or addition of a single character or diphthong. The majority of these are the result of phonological changes in Post-classical Greek.[10]

Standard linguistic features can be identified as "linguistic elements which have a regular distribution", but they can also be based on the "distribution according to occasion of use" (Milroy & Milroy 1985: 117). In orthography, the first type of standard features would be the form that is regularly used in contemporary sources and the second type is the form which is used in higher registers (e.g. more formal or literary language). Both types of definitions are used to regularize spelling in papyrus documents.[11] Editorial regularization has been applied to papyrus editions from the beginning of the twentieth century, initially meant to make papyrus editions easier to understand for readers used to Classical Greek. Editorial regularizations, therefore, tend to follow the norms of Classical Greek orthography (high register) and/or contemporary parallels (regular distribution). This means that they can give us an approximate measure for the amount of standard and non-standard orthographic features in a text. Of course, this method cannot have been entirely consistent throughout a century of scholarship and critical notes can be made to the linguistic accuracy of this old-fashioned system of annotation.[12] On the other hand, most of the volumes of papyrus editions contain a variety of documents and there seems no reason to think that the principles of regularization will differ significantly with respect to the original situational context of the document at hand. Qualitative analysis of a sample of texts from relevant archives (§4) will allow me to reassess and refine the quantitative conclusions based on these editorial regularizations (§3).

2.2 Selecting situational variables

The term register has been employed by Halliday, McIntosh and Strevens (1964: 87) in order to distinguish language varieties according to *use*, i.e. situationally defined varieties, from varieties according to *user*, such as dialects or sociolects. In this paper, I will follow the definition by Biber and Conrad (2009: 6): "a *register* is a variety associated with a particular situation of use (including particular communicative purposes). The description of a register covers three major

---

10 See Gignac (1976).
11 Stolk (2018: 130–131).
12 See Stolk (2018).

components: the situational context, the linguistic features, and the functional relationships between the first two components."

There are multiple ways to define the situational context and the term "register" can be applied with different levels of generality, although the basic features of the communicative setting and the roles of the participants seem to take an important place in many approaches.[13] Biber and Conrad (2009: 39–47) propose to describe the situational context according to the following parameters:

(1) participants, including the number of participants and their social characteristics
(2) the nature of the relationships among the participants
(3) channel: mode and medium of communication
(4) production and comprehension circumstances
(5) setting: time and place of communication and historical time period
(6) communicative purposes
(7) topic or subject matter

Not all of these characteristics are equally relevant in every corpus study. For example, the traditional dichotomy into a written and spoken mode of communication (category 3) is an irrelevant division for a corpus of historical documents. Similarly, not every characteristic of the situation can be easily identified for every text in a historical corpus. The social background of the sender of a papyrus document and their personal relationships cannot always be described in detail. Part of the process of identifying relevant variables for the corpus in its current state, therefore, is to select a practical and suitable approach to the data. In this paper, I will describe the context along the following combinations of situational variables:

(i) setting: date and context of use
(ii) participants: nature and direction of interaction
(iii) genre: communicative purpose and category
(iv) production circumstances: method of production and stage of composition

All texts are divided into three main periods (Ptolemaic 300–1 BCE, Roman 1–300 CE and Byzantine 300–800 CE) in order assess more general diachronic

---

[13] Compare for example the categories of a context of situation by Firth (1950: 42–43), the eight components of speech defined by Hymes (1967) or the sociosemiotic interpretation of language along the three dimensions "field", "mode" and "tenor" by Halliday, McIntosh & Strevens (1964).

differences. The setting also reflects the area of society in which the text is used, such as the private sphere or in the government administration.

The participants are classified according to their general role in society, the intended audience (or the lack thereof) and the direction of the interaction. Although the social and educational background of the participants involved is an important factor in explaining linguistic variation in papyri,[14] there is no reliable way to establish the educational background and social status of all participants in the corpus based on language-external characteristics. Furthermore, the author or sender of the document needs to be distinguished from the scribe in historical documents. Since orthographic features are more likely to be a reflection of the social background and competence of the scribe than that of the author,[15] the background of the scribe might be even more important than the social position of the author and addressee for the presence of orthographic variation. On the other hand, the intended register and general attitude towards standard orthography may also have been implied by the choices made by the author.[16] These types of differences can hardly be quantified for the whole corpus, but some relevant distinctions can be made by studying documents in archives (§4).

Genre is vaguely defined by Biber (1988: 68) as "text categorizations made on the basis of external criteria relating to author/speaker purpose" and further specified as "text categories readily distinguished by mature speakers of a language". This second notion is also reflected in the definition by Lee (2001: 46): "Genre is used when we view the text as a member of a category: a culturally recognised artifact, a grouping of texts according to some conventionally recognised criteria, a grouping according to purposive goals, culturally defined." Genre in this study is based on the groups of texts generally distinguished in ancient society according to papyrological studies, combined into several larger categories with a similar communicative purpose (see §2.3.3).

Production circumstances are not always considered in register studies, but they seem to me of particular relevance for the papyrological corpus. Biber and Conrad (2009: 40) distinguish "real time / planned / scripted / revised and edited" and add that written registers are usually different from spoken registers in these respects (2009: 43–44). Just as in modern times, the production circumstances of a written document may have had an impact on the linguistic features. Whether the

---

[14] Cf. Evans (2012).
[15] Halla-aho (2018: 231–233).
[16] Stolk (2019).

language of a particular papyrus has been produced freely at the spot, noted down from dictation, revised during a drafting process or copied from a written draft or model can make a significant difference to the type and amount of non-standard forms attested in a document.[17] The importance of the method of production and stage of composition for orthographic variation will be examined in more detail in Section 4.

2.3 Categorization of documents

Texts within a corpus can only be distinguished based on extensive knowledge of the corpus itself. Overviews of the document types commonly distinguished by papyrologists can be found in Montevecchi (1973), Turner (1968: 127–153) and Palme (2009: 358–394). Montevecchi (1973: 86–89) gives a detailed overview of the contents of the corpus, but her organization into groups is partly thematic rather than functional. For example, the categories "administration", "fiscal organization", "jurisdiction" and "business, transportation, trade" identify groups of documents concerned with specific topics rather than reflecting different settings and communicative purposes. The categorization by Palme is more useful for linguistic approaches, since the categories are divided within several larger domains, such as "private documents", "public life" and "interaction between state and individual". These larger categories are partly reflected in the characteristics "setting" and "participants" (see below §2.3.1 and §2.3.2).

The basis for this categorization of all digitalized papyrus documents is the information about the contents of the text available at papyri.info and within Trismegistos.[18] These content descriptions have been provided by the first editor (e.g. in the title of the edition), during entry of metadata in HGV and APIS, and/or by previous scholars working on specific genres within Trismegistos. Due to the extensive scale of the corpus it was not possible to consider every single text individually and the Greek text itself has only been consulted when the available metadata were insufficient or contradictory. Hence, this categorization relies to a large extent on the information that has been provided by

---

17 See Stolk (forthcoming), Stolk, Mihálykó & Grassien (forthcoming).
18 Paraliterary texts concerning religious and magical topics and school texts have been categorized, but they are not taken into account in this study. The same goes for very short texts such as name inscriptions on jars and mummy labels. Papyri without transcription and/or useful metadata and texts with uncertain contents are left out as well. In total, 45889 of the 51769 papyri with transcription in the database have been categorized into one of the seven genres and for 41977 of those the setting and participants could be determined as well.

previous scholars and aims only at a larger degree of unification and generalization at the level of the whole corpus.[19]

2.3.1 Setting

Traditionally, papyrus documents have been divided into private and public (or official) with respect to the context of use. This does not mean that these two domains were strictly separated in Greco-Roman Egypt, as government officials could produce both official and private documents and keep them together, such as the archive of Apollonios strategos (TM Archive ID 19). Private literate people would be in demand to take up public functions, especially from the later Roman period onwards.[20] Even though the same scribes and authors could use documents in both settings, the register requirements may have been different. Contracts can be produced for and used in more official or more private settings. Unless indicated otherwise, I assume for this paper that the majority of the preserved contracts originate from a private context of use rather than being solely produced for official archives. A private setting excludes texts that are used by the government, but it may contain documents from a professional, juridical or commercial context. The category of official documents includes documents related to public administration, justice and the military. Most of them were used at the level of the local administration (in the village or district capital), but few also relate to matters important to higher levels of the government.

2.3.2 Participants

Various types of relationships may exist between the people involved in the act of communication, such as between author and audience or sender and addressee. The author is taken to be the person in whose name the document is drawn up,

---

19 The basic level division into different genres (and subordinate topics) has been made available through the Trismegistos portal (see e.g. www.trismegistos.org/words). Previous mistakes may not have been noticed and the information gathered by different people could have been misleading in some cases. Documentary papyri are often fragmentarily preserved and their initial interpretation could be subject to revision. It is expected that the large amount of data and the generally abstract level of categorization will limit the consequences of possible misinterpretations. However, if anyone notices a mistake, please inform the author of this chapter or Trismegistos to help improving this resource.
20 Ast (2015).

i.e. the sender of a letter or the acknowledging party of a contract, and the audience is the intended reader or addressee of the document. The relationships between the participants are defined with respect to the two different domains of society: private and official. These lead to four basic relationships and directions of communication:
(1) interaction between officials
(2) interaction between private persons
(3) interaction from official to private
(4) interaction from private to official
(5) private administration
(6) official administration

Documents in these last two groups are not primarily meant for communication but rather for the purposes of recording and archiving. They may or may not be read later by the scribe himself or his associates. Only the texts concerned with the interaction between private persons and private administration are expected to be produced in a private setting. Of course, there are many more relationships and more detailed social levels to be distinguished within private and official settings, such as positions in government, social classes and professions. This type of detailed information, however, is not readily available for the full corpus of documentary papyri.

2.3.3 Genre

The identification of genres is intended to stay close to the traditional divisions made by papyrologists to distinguish the different genres that existed in ancient society. As these labels have a tendency to become fuzzy, a prototype approach is applied to distinguish different levels of generalization (cf. Lee 2001: 48):

Table 2: Example of a prototype approach applied to genres of documentary papyri.

Superordinate	contract			declaration			
Basic level	contract	testament		petition		notification	
Subordinate	sale lease	will	donatio mortis causa	enteuxis	petition to prefect	epicrisis declaration	notification of death

An infinite amount of topics can be reflected in the lowest level of the individual instances, while the basic level distinguishes the genres as they are generally recognized in society.[21] Document types which share a similar communicative function are combined into the seven superordinate genres. Inevitably, these genres bear a strong relationship with the setting in which they are commonly produced and the relations between the participants involved. The relations between the different variables have also been indicated in the characterisations below.

1) **Letters** are concerned with correspondence between private people or between government officials. Communication from private people to officials or vice versa often takes often a more specialized form, such as a declaration or pronouncement (see below). Orders for arrest and payment orders are also considered as a form of correspondence.
2) **Contracts** are produced as proof of a juridical agreement. Although they can be used in official settings, they usually concern a (juridical) relationship between private people. There are numerous different subtypes, such as a sale, loan, lease and marriage contracts, donations and testaments.
3) **Declarations** are letters to request or notify the government of (private) events. The largest group consists of petitions, but also other notifications to authorities, such as applications to *epicrisis* and *census*, notifications of birth, death, property returns, are included.
4) **Pronouncements** are formal announcements to inform government officials and citizens about rules and regulations. These pronouncements often originate in the higher level of the government and are only passed on through the lower levels of administration.
5) **Reports** are documents produced to collect and record information. Official registration was important in ancient society.[22] These include council minutes and court proceedings as well as diaries of officials, land inspections, registers of official correspondence and abstracts of contracts to be kept in archives.
6) **Receipts** provide proof of delivery, payment or the execution of work. They form a continuum with contracts that can also be used to prove an exchange of money, such as an acknowledgement of debt or deposit, but they are generally shorter with fewer legal precautions. Documents to prove that work has been done, such as the *penthemeros* certificates, are also counted.

---

21 Taylor (1989: 48). Almost all papyrological texts apply some fixed formulas, but certain genres (such as contracts and certificates) are largely pre-composed, while others, such as letters, may contain more elements of free composition. As this study is focussed on the situational context, the direct linguistic context (specific terminology or fixed formulas) is not given special attention at this stage.
22 Palme (2009: 374–375).

7) **Lists** are mainly defined by their form as itemized collection of information. The documents in this group can be difficult to place in a social setting due to a lack of context.

3 Quantitative results

For this study, the presence of non-standard orthography as well as the total number of words per text is calculated in the Trismegistos Irregularities database. A maximum of one non-standard orthographic feature is counted per word. The normalized frequency (Nf), then, is the number of non-standard spellings per 1000 words for every text.[23] The normalized frequency is used as a dependent variable and the situational variables setting, participants and genre as independent variables in the following test. The results for each of these variables are presented and interpreted in Section 3.1, while other factors are considered in Section 3.2. The remaining situational variables, such as the social background of the scribe and the production circumstances will be addressed in Section 4.

3.1 Comparison of the situational variables

The average frequency of occurrence of non-standard orthographic features generally increases over time in the papyri from 14 per 1000 words in the Ptolemaic period to 31 per 1000 words in the Byzantine period. It is important to distinguish between the frequencies in the Ptolemaic and Byzantine period in this study, since the highest levels of non-standard features (16 per 1000 words) for any category during the Ptolemaic period are identical to the lowest average frequencies during the Byzantine period. These differences are highly significant (p.<2.71e-157) in comparison with the other variables.[24] Table 3 presents the predictors for standard orthography in documentary papyri in Egypt in each of these three periods separately.[25]

---

[23] In order to limit the effects of outliers from very short texts on the normalized frequency, only documents with a reliable word count and a minimum length of 10 words are taken into account.
[24] Based on linear regression analysis in a fixed effects model with the other independent variables.
[25] From the documentary texts for which all three situational variables could be determined (cf. fn. 18) with a minimum length of 10 words (cf. fn. 23), securely dated to the Ptolemaic (300–1 BCE), Roman (1–300 CE) or Byzantine (300–800 CE) period are counted (total 35024 texts).

12 Orthographic variation and register in Greek documentary papyri — 311

Table 3: Linear regression analysis on three situational variables.[26]

	Ptolemaic (300–1 BCE)			Roman (1–300 CE)			Byzantine (300–800 CE)		
Total texts (T)	6597			19004			9423		
Overall mean (Nf)	14			26			31		
	coef	T	Nf	coef	T	Nf	coef	T	Nf
Setting	p.<3.01e−05			p.<6.49e−103			p.<5.43e−25		
private	1.401	2772	15	7.507	5910	26	5.083	4461	36
official	−1.401	3825	13	−7.507	13094	21	−5.083	4962	26
Participants	p.<1.21e−16			p.<3.95e−192			p.<1.92e−14		
private people	4.157	3099	16	13.171	8067	36	5.690	6584	33
officials	−0.721	693	11	10.174	1044	33	4.975	614	32
private to official	3.693	1002	16	−1.727	2068	21	5.035	608	32
official to private	−2.205	987	10	−7.164	6067	16	0.161	877	27
private admin.	0.392	447	12	−6.570	394	16	−5.151	191	21
official admin.	−5.315	369	7	−7.885	1364	15	−10.710	549	16
Genre	p.<1.72e−07			p~0			p.< 5.74e−32		
letter	2.206	2282	15	23.998	3613	49	10.099	2749	38
contract	3.753	774	16	7.402	2552	33	−3.177	2314	25
pronouncement	−1.811	44	11	0.524	259	26	7.268	111	35
declaration	2.973	1002	16	−4.125	2069	21	3.954	608	32
receipt	−0.651	1682	12	−7.833	8756	18	3.695	2901	32
list	−2.733	667	10	−10.338	949	15	−9.623	531	18
report	−3.737	146	9	−9.628	806	16	−12.217	209	16

---

26 The results in Table 3 are computed in R with the package Rbrul (see Johnson 2009). The absolute number of texts is given under T and the Nf shows the mean of the normalized frequency of the number of nonstandard words per 1000 words in those texts. The p-value per independent variable (p.) and the effect-size coefficients (coef) for each subcategory are added to show whether the effect of the variables is significant. A p-value < 0.05 is taken as a significant effect. The coefficients show the relative strength of the prediction between the subcategories. A larger coefficient (positive or negative) indicates a stronger effect than a smaller coefficient.

All situational variables have significant effects (see the p-values and effect size coefficients in Table 3) on predicting the number of non-standard features. A fixed effects model combining all three variables (log.likelihood -180948.7) shows that the variables genre (p.<8.51e-84) and participants (p.<1.47e-05) are the best predictors for orthographic variation in this corpus, while the setting does not provide a significant contribution to the other two.[27] Documents produced in a private setting generally contain a higher number of non-standard features than those from an official setting across all periods, but this difference is minimal in the Ptolemaic period (15 vs. 13 per 1000 words per text) and gets only more pronounced in the Byzantine period (36 vs. 26 per 1000 words per text).

As perhaps expected, texts produced as part of the interaction between private people contain a high number of non-standard features across all three periods (16, 36 and 33, respectively), while official administration produces the lowest numbers (with 7, 15 and 16 non-standard spellings per 1000 words). It should be noticed, though, that the frequency of non-standard spellings in documents directed from private to official is equally high during the Ptolemaic period (also 16 per 1000 words). During the Roman and Byzantine periods, the interaction between officials yields a particularly high number of non-standard features (33 and 32, respectively), not much below the average number of non-standard features in documents between private people.

These observations are confirmed by the results according to genre. Letters and contracts – which contain most of the interaction between private people and between officials – have the highest numbers of non-standard features in the Roman period (up to 49 per 1000 words). Administrative lists and reports tend to have the lowest number of non-standard features of all genres during these three periods, which is comparable to the low average frequencies found for documents used in private and official administration.

Combination of the situational variables allows us to specify in more detail in which situational context non-standard features appear most commonly. During the Ptolemaic period, contracts (Nf=16) and declarations (Nf=16) share the same high level of non-standard orthography as the private letters (Nf=16). During the Roman period, not only the letters between private people (Nf=56), but also contracts (Nf=33) and letters between officials (Nf=32) have a higher number of non-standard features than average. In the Byzantine period, letters

---

27 The added value of testing these three predictors together in a multi-effect model is limited, since they are partly dependent on each other (see §2.3). A variable rule analysis of the three fixed effects together does not give any significant model for the Ptolemaic period.

(Nf=40) and receipts (Nf=34) between private people as well as pronouncements and nominations by officials (Nf=35) show the highest frequencies.

3.2 Writers and register

Although the combination of the variables participants and genre proves to be a reasonable predictor for the amount of orthographic variation in the corpus, this does not mean that this is the only or even most important explanation for the distribution of orthographic variation in papyri. Register-dependent linguistic features are typically identified in the lexical and grammatical domains of language rather than at the level of orthography.[28] It has been suggested that the use of non-standard orthography is mainly the result of the level of education of the individual scribe.[29] For example, Vierros (2012) has shown that there can be large differences in linguistic competence between scribes producing contracts in very similar situational contexts. Thus, the level of orthography achieved in these circumstances may be in the first place writer-dependent rather than register-dependent.

The importance of this factor for the general interpretation of the data can also be observed in the above quantitative results by comparing the standard deviation of each of the different genres. The high level of non-standard orthography in (private) letters, in particular, obscures a high level of variation within the category itself. While the standard deviation from the reported means lies between 26 and 36 for all other genres, letters show a standard deviation of 58 and letters between private people even 62. That means that private letters cannot straightforwardly be identified as a "low" register, even though it seems that an informal situational context coincides here with a high average number of non-standard orthographic features. Instead, different registers may need to be identified within this group of letters between private people. A drastic refinement of the variables covering the social background of the participants, including the scribe, seems necessary to explain whether the distribution of orthographic variation is dependent on the level of education of the scribe, the social status of the addressee or both (see also §4.1 and §4.2). Only a more detailed comparison of different types of texts written by the same scribe may reveal whether the variation is primarily related to *use* or to the *user* (see §4.1).

---

28 Biber & Conrad (2009: 6).
29 Evans (2012).

4 Registers in archives

The quantitative results show a relation between the occurrence of non-standard orthography and the situational context of the text (§3.1). Although general tendencies can be observed, there is a large degree of variation within some of the categories (§3.2). Archives can often provide more information about the role of individuals and the process of text production (cf. §2.2). Comparison of the results within and between several known archives allows us to address the role of the scribe and the production circumstances of the text in more detail and establish whether any of these other variables are relevant to explain the occurrence of orthographic variation in the corpus of documentary papyri. Below I examine the occurrence and distribution of non-standard orthography in several genres in the third century BCE Zenon archive (TM Archive ID 256), the second century BCE archive of the Katochoi of the Sarapieion (TM Archive ID 119), the first century CE archive of Kronion son of Apion, head of the *grapheion* of Tebtynis (TM Archive ID 93) and the sixth century CE archive of Dioscorus from Aphrodito (TM Archive ID 72).[30]

4.1 Petitions, requests and lists in the Zenon archive

According to the results of the quantitative survey in Section 3, non-standard orthography seems most common in declarations, contracts and private letters during the Ptolemaic period. In the Zenon archive, dating to the mid third century BCE, all seven genres are represented and declarations have indeed the highest average frequency of non-standard features of all (Nf=23). The low level of orthography in the declarations in the Zenon archive could perhaps be explained by the nature of these requests and the roles of their participants. The majority (98 out of a 148 declarations) are in fact letters expressing a request or complaint to Zenon (or occasionally to one of the other protagonists of the archive). A well-known example is the petition of an Egyptian lady Senchons to Zenon (P.Mich. I 29) in which she complains that her she-ass has been taken and begs him to help her to get it returned. This Greek text has been painted with a brush by a native Egyptian scribe[31] and contains one of the highest numbers of non-standard features in the group (Nf=189). These requests for help

---

[30] More information about these (and other archives) can be found through the Trismegistos portal, at www.trismegistos.org/arch/index.php, see also Vandorpe, Clarysse & Verreth (2015).
[31] See Clarysse (1993: 196–199).

addressed to Zenon as the manager of the estate or just as a person in a higher position may not have required the same level of orthography as an official petition or *enteuxis* addressed to the king of Egypt. The wide variety of backgrounds of the writers of these petitions does not allow for a high average level of standardization and this was apparently not a major factor for the recognition of the submitted request. The linguistic variety in the requests to Zenon can be contrasted to the relative uniformity of the *enteuxeis* in the official archive of Diophanes, *strategos* of the Arsinoite district from the later third century BCE (TM Archive ID 80). Non-standard orthography occurs in this archive as well, but the frequencies are well below the average for the Ptolemaic period (Nf=8). Petitions to the king or a high official are also found in the Zenon archive, but the mere fact that they were found in the archive suggests that these were probably not official or final versions of the text.[32] Some of them concern petitions by a third party that were copied (sometimes as part of a letter) and forwarded to Zenon or Apollonios. The general level of orthography in these copied petitions (Nf=26) is comparable to the requests addressed to Zenon (Nf=24).

Another small group contains drafts of petitions written in the name of Zenon. One might think that orthographic variation would be acceptable in such a preliminary version of a document, perhaps even expected to some extent, but the frequency of non-standard orthographic features in this group is the lowest of the petitions in the archive (Nf=12). That Zenon was a highly educated and conservative writer can also be observed from his other texts. When archaisms, such as *sandhi* and *crasis*, are left out, only very few non-standard spellings are found in the documents written in his own hand.[33] If anything can be concluded from this small group of autographs, it seems that non-standard orthographic features occur particularly in Zenons accounts, personal notes and to-do-lists (e.g. P.Col. III 58; P.Cair. Zen. IV 59787). These may represent the situations in which standard orthography was least important to Zenon. This potentially register-based difference, however, is not reflected in the quantitative results of the papyrological corpus, where private administration, accounts and lists are categories attracting generally low levels of orthographic variation (see 3.1).

The Zenon papyri thus show the significance of the level of education of the writer for the occurrence of non-standard orthography. When a writer is able to produce standard orthography without difficulties, he is less likely to

---

[32] Pestman (1981: 190–191).
[33] Clarysse (2009: 38–44).

produce non-standard features in any situational context. On the other hand, studying documents by the same writer – even a well-educated one – shows that the notion of register could be relevant to explain orthographic variation in different situations, albeit with slightly different results than attested in the full corpus written by numerous writers with various levels of competence.

4.2 Petitions and letters in the archive of the Katochoi of the Sarapieion

The highest average frequency of non-standard features in the Ptolemaic period (Nf=50), is found in the archive of the Katochoi of the Sarapieion[34] from the second century BCE. Bentein (2015a: 481) concludes that we can situate the documents in this archive on a register continuum from dreams and letters to petitions, where dreams contain "the largest amount of orthographical mistakes" and petitions the smallest. His ranking was based on a combination of linguistic features at various levels of the language, but the average frequencies of non-standard orthography (Nf=43 for declarations and Nf=58 for letters) give the same impression. The petitions addressed to the king (*enteuxeis*, Nf=20) seem to show a more standardized orthography than those addressed to a *strategos* or other official (Nf=53), but the genre and the status of the addressee are not the only factors responsible for the distribution of non-standard orthography in this archive.

The writer of the document and the version of the document at hand may also play a role, as briefly observed by Bentein (2015a: 469). In fact, when all petitions and letters in the archive are categorized based on the hand writing (following the identification by Wilcken in UPZ I), it becomes clear that the average frequency of non-standard features in the petitions (Nf=43) is mainly lowered by the petitions written by professional scribes in chancery hands (Nf=12), who are also responsible for most of the *enteuxeis*. The average number of non-standard features is much higher in the petitions written by Ptolemaios' younger brother Apollonios (Nf=91). When we compare the orthography of the petitions and letters written by Apollonios, we find that Apollonios even produces more non-standard orthographical features in his petitions than in his letters (Nf=69). However, this should not automatically lead to the conclusion that Apollonios' letters represent a "higher" register than his petitions. While the preserved letters by Apollonios are copies of official letters (UPZ I 23, I 26, I 37, I 38) and final versions of private

---

34 On this archive, see also Vierros (this volume), Bentein (this volume).

letters to his brother Ptolemaios (UPZ I 65, I 68, I 70, I 93), the majority of the petitions produced by Apollonios are preliminary drafts of petitions surviving in multiple copies (e.g. UPZ I 18, I 33, I 39). His copies of official letters by other scribes are more standardized (Nf=46) than the final versions of his own private letters (Nf=78), but his private letters seem again more standardized than these drafts of petitions (Nf=91). Hence, the level of education and experience of the writer (Apollonios or chancellery scribe), method of production (copy or draft) and the stage of composition of the text in question (preliminary or final product) count as important factors to explain the presence of non-standard orthographic features in this archive.

4.3 Contracts, lists and reports in the *grapheion* archive

The contracts from the archive of Apion and his son Kronion, heads of the record office (*grapheion*) of Tebtynis between 7 and 56 CE, have been used to show that "the majority of the professional scribes associated with the Tebtynis grapheion do not seem very concerned with the maintenance of standard orthography" (Bucking 2007: 237). This may be the case at a personal level, or perhaps even more generally among scribes at the lower levels of administration, as Bucking (2007) assumes, but what are the consequences of this for the levels of orthography generally achieved in juridical documents? Less focus on using standard orthography during scribal training and in scribal practice could explain the observed increase in non-standard forms in contracts during the Roman period. However, the average frequency of non-standard orthography in the contracts preserved in the *grapheion* archive (Nf=99) is well above the average for contracts during that period and this may be related to the stage of production of these contracts.

The village record office had two main tasks: to compose contracts for their private customers and to keep a register of all produced contracts for the official administration. For the first stage of the production of a new contract, the contracting parties convened at the *grapheion* and a contract was drawn up by one of the scribes from the office.[35] After that, the contracting parties added their subscription to the bottom half of several papyrus sheets in order to provide each party with its own copy of the whole contract at a later stage. The parties subscribed the contract themselves, if needed with help from a relative or one

---

35 For the procedure see Husselman et al. (1944: 3–11).

of the scribes often called upon.³⁶ The majority of the contracts preserved in the archive comprise in fact these subscriptions on partial contracts that still needed to be completed and collected by the customer. Not only the fact that these particular documents were never finished, but especially the part of the document that is preserved may explain the frequent occurrences of non-standard orthography. When compared, the average frequency of non-standard spellings (Nf=114) is much higher in the documents that contain only the subscriptions of the parties than in the other contracts in which also (part of) the body of the document is preserved (Nf=69). Subscriptions to contracts are generally produced by people with various levels of (orthographic) competence.³⁷ The fact that a signature was supposed to be written in the hand of the party itself rather than added by someone else was clearly considered more important than the correct use of orthography in this part of the document. The abnormally high ratio of partial documents and papyri containing subscriptions only contributes to the high frequency of non-standard features in the *grapheion* archive.

Apart from producing the contracts for their customers, the *grapheion* also had to forward all contracts to the central administration (in a τόμος συγκολλήσιμος 'pasted roll'), compile a document with abstracts to these contracts (εἰρόμενον) and provide a list of all contracts by title (ἀναγραφή). Parts of the latter two types of registers have been found in the archive as well. The average frequency of non-standard forms in these reports (Nf=72) is comparable to the numbers encountered in the more complete versions of the contracts.³⁸ However, the preserved lists and reports represent again different stages in the production of the final report. As Husselman (1970: 237) illustrates, preliminary entries of various types were made by Kronion in P.Mich. II 128, to be transferred later to P.Mich. II 123 and P.Mich. V 238, and again copied and put in a chronological order in P.Mich. V 240. During the compilation of the final report, the contents were checked and adjusted where necessary, but also minor changes were made to the orthography. For example, in the draft entries by Kronion in P.Mich. II 128, ii, ll. 19, 23 and 25, the words γεοργίας (instead of γεωργίας) 'of cultivation', κομογρ(αμματέως) (instead of κωμογραμματέως) 'of a village scribe' and ἐνυκήσεω(ς) (instead of ἐνοικήσεως) 'of lodging', seem reproduced in identical (non-standard) spellings in the chronological list in P.Mich. V 240, ll. 14, 17 and 19, while the words

---

36 See Husselman et al. (1944: 21–22).
37 See Youtie (1971).
38 Based on the published reports listed by Husselman (1970: 227–230).

ἁλοπολῶ(ν) 'of salt merchants', περαχορή(σεως) 'of cession' and φυνικό(νος) (instead of φοινικῶνος) 'of a palm-grove' in P.Mich. II 128, iii, ll. 10, 13, 22 become (partially) corrected to ἁλοπω(λῶν), παραχο(ρήσεως) and φυνικῶνο(ς) in P.Mich. V 240, ll. 31, 33 and 42.

The frequency of non-standard spellings in the registers and accounts of expenses of the *grapheion* is mainly the result of a limited set of lexemes for which the supposedly non-standard orthographic variant is used consistently.[39] P.Mich. II 122 contains a model for the registration of contracts which Kronion may have produced as an example for another scribe in the office.[40] In this document all names are replaced by the indefinite pronouns, such as ὁ δεῖνα τοῦ δεινοῦ 'NN son of NN', and these are almost consistently spelled as ὁ δῖνα τοῦ δῖνος or τοῦ δίνατος. This word on its own makes up the majority of the non-standard spellings in this text.

Furthermore, the high number of abbreviations in registers and accounts lowers the potential number of candidates for non-standard spellings. As more than half of the words in these registers are abbreviated, the number of non-standard spellings pertaining to morphemes (often word-final) is reduced to 5 per 1000 words, compared to 23 in the contracts from the archive. The same phenomenon applies to all lists and reports in the Roman period. While letters, contracts and receipts have non-standard spellings exclusively in morphemes in respectively 10, 6 and 5 words out of a 1000, the lists and reports count only 3 and 2, respectively. The repetitive nature of the registers and accounts combined with their relatively limited vocabulary and fixed syntactic structures should make the orthography of these genres easier for scribes to master and potentially reduce the number of non-standard orthographic features compared to contracts and letters. On the other hand, as observed in the *grapheion* archive above, when a certain non-standard spelling of a frequent word is used repeatedly in the same text, they could still add up to large numbers for single documents.

4.4 Pronouncements and petitions in the Dioscorus archive

Pronouncements in the form of edicts by the Roman emperor or the prefect of Egypt are rarely transmitted to us in their original version. When they surface

---

39 See also Bucking (2007: 237, Table 3) for the variation between πρόκειται and πρόκιται in this archive.
40 Cf. Bucking (2007: 237, Table 4).

on a papyrus in a village in Egypt, the orthography cannot straightforwardly be taken to reflect the standards of the imperial chancery. This has been shown by Bucking (2007: 233) for the letter of the emperor Claudius to the Alexandrians in P.Lond. VI 1912 (see also §1.2) and the same can be assumed for many other examples. P.Yale I 61 contains an edict by Soubatianus Aquila, the prefect of Egypt between 206 and 210 CE, announced by Sarapion, the *strategos* of the Arsinoite district. The text is written in an impressive chancery hand, but contains several non-standard orthographic forms. The contents, morphology and syntax have been revised by the same hand as the one who approved of the whole text, probably the *strategos* himself. This procedure of (re)composing, copying and distributing important messages throughout the provinces, inevitably led to linguistic variation between the different versions of the text.

During the Byzantine period, the procedure to compose imperial documents can be observed in more detail in the archive of Dioscorus of Aphrodito from the middle of the sixth century CE. The imperial rescripts P.Cair.Masp. I 67024–67025, 67026–67027 and 67028 are drafts written by Dioscorus himself and his companion.[41] During their visit to Constantinople, they produced their own rescripts, i.e. answers to their own requests.[42] Several versions of these rescripts have been preserved in the archive, such as the reformulation of 67024 recto on the verso by Dioscorus, copied and revised again by his companion in 67025. The various stages of drafting of the rescripts show a high level of skill. A generally high level of orthographic standardization is visible in these drafts and revision is mainly aimed at stylistic refinement.

While these drafts for imperial rescripts left very little to be desired from an orthographic point of view, the same cannot be said of all petitions in Dioscorus' archive. Some petitions contain particularly high frequencies of non-standard spellings, for example P.Cair.Masp. I 67002, 67006, 67020 and P.Lond. V 1674. Their apparently lower orthographic standards co-occur with a high frequency of scribal corrections. P.Cair.Masp. I 67002 and P.Lond. V 1674 were written by Dioscorus himself[43] and are likely to be drafts.[44] The corrections consist almost entirely of superlinear additions of words and short phrases. Hardly any orthographic of morphological corrections are made, while there are several possible candidates, e.g. ἐπί 'upon' for ἐπεί 'when' in margin of P.Lond. V 1674, l. 21, ἐπραίτευσεν for ἐπραίδευσεν 'he plundered' in P.Cair.Masp. I 67002, ii, l. 24 (cf. πραιδεύουσι in iii 13) and ὑπολέλιπται for ὑπολέλειπται 'is left' in 1674, l. 94

---

41 Perhaps his cousin Dioscorus, see Van Minnen (2003), Zuckerman (2004).
42 Van Minnen (2003), Feissel (2004).
43 See Del Corso (2008).
44 Fournet & Gascou (2004: 145–146, 168–169), Keenan (2008: 173).

(cf. ὑπο|λέλειπται in 67002, iii, ll. 11–12). P.Cair.Masp. I 67006 and 67020 were not written by Dioscorus himself, but he did make corrections to these texts.[45] Orthographic corrections are more frequent than stylistic corrections in these two petitions, especially in 67020, which Fournet and Gascou (2004: 153) assume to have been dictated to the scribe by Dioscorus. Not only omitted vowels and consonants are inserted by Dioscorus in this document, but also interchanged consonants and itacisms are corrected this time, e.g. ἐπεί 'when' corrected to ἐπί 'upon' in l. 3, τοτῆρες corrected to δοτῆρες 'givers' in l. 12, χαλκῖς corrected to χαλκεῖς 'smiths' in l. 17. While non-standard orthography does not seem to be the focus of attention in preliminary drafts, Dioscorus did make orthographic corrections to copies of more complete petitions produced by his scribes.[46] Thus, the scribe, method of production and stage of composition of these documents is highly relevant to explain the presence or absence of orthographic variation.

5 Conclusions and discussion

In this paper, I set out to examine the relationship between the use of non-standard orthography and the situational context in the corpus of Greek documentary papyri from Egypt. Based on quantitative testing, non-standard orthography generally seems to occur in documents related to the interaction between private people, such as letters and contracts. It is also frequently encountered in declarations to the government during the Ptolemaic and Byzantine periods, letters between officials in Roman period and pronouncements and nominations by officials in the Byzantine period. The lowest frequencies of non-standard orthography are found in lists and reports in private and official administration. The distinction between private and official settings is therefore not an essential parameter to explain the distribution of non-standard orthography, but the participants and genre are relevant factors. Some (linguistic) characteristics of the genres themselves may help to explain these differences. The fixed structure, repetitive vocabulary and frequent use of abbreviations could potentially reduce the number of non-standard orthographic features in lists and reports. On the other hand, the registers and accounts of expenses in the *grapheion* archive show that a repetitive use of certain non-standard forms, especially in a (short) text with a limited range of vocabulary, could also easily increase the normalized frequency of non-standard features. Even though contracts

---

45 Fournet & Gascou (2004: 148, 153).
46 See also Stolk (forthcoming).

also contain many fixed formulas, non-standard orthography is more common in this genre than in others during the Ptolemaic and Roman periods. This may be related to the way in which contracts and their subscriptions are produced, the level of education of the writers involved and, perhaps, the general attitude towards standard orthography in scribal offices.

Although the setting, the participants and the genre may explain part of the distribution of orthographic variation, closer analysis reveals several other important factors. The particularly high level non-standard orthography in private letters across all periods co-occurs with a high level of variation within the group itself. Because levels of education could differ greatly between individuals, the level of orthography is always closely related to the choice of scribe. The variety of backgrounds of the writers of requests to Zenon shows why these documents generally have a lower standard than for example official *enteuxeis* to the king during the same period. A more experienced scribe could be employed to increase the level of orthography in petitions, as was shown by the differences between the petitions written by Apollonios and those written by professional scribes in Ptolemaios' archive. Official contracts are typically produced by multiple writers and the different levels of experience may also create a difference between the orthographic variation in the body of the text and in the subscriptions, as shown in the partially completed documents in the *grapheion* archive. In documents written by the same writer, register-based variation can be identified more clearly. The highly-educated secretary Zenon produces standard spelling in almost every situation, but this attention to detail may drop slightly in lists and notes for personal use. The well-educated notary Dioscorus also manages to produce a higher standard of orthography in imperial rescripts than in his other genres.

Since many scribes had to make an effort to produce a document in standard orthography, the method of production and version of the text that is preserved to us seem important variables for orthographic variation. Apollonios produces more standard orthography in his copies of letters by other scribes than in his own letters, while his final versions of private letters are again more standardized than his drafts of petitions. The amount of linguistic variation, especially at the level of orthography, could increase or decrease during the production process. Kronion shows that orthography can be improved in the process from draft to the final version and Dioscorus makes multiple orthographic corrections to documents, potentially increasing the level of orthographic standardization. When documents produced at the highest levels of society, such as official texts sent to and from Alexandria or imperial correspondence, surface in little villages in the Egyptian countryside, they are most likely versions handed down to us through several stages of copying by various scribes, possibly decreasing the level of standardization. Still, the high standards pursued by Dioscorus by means of corrections in his drafts and in the documents produced by his scribes show that standard orthography was still highly valued in rescripts and petitions, despite their sometimes different appearance in the versions preserved to us.

Apart from the register expectations related to the genre of the document and the participants involved, the choice of scribe and the process of textual production thus seem important factors to explain the presence of non-standard orthographic features in the corpus of documentary papyri. It would be advisable, therefore, to take account of the method of production and stage of composition of the text in question in future studies of linguistic variation.[47]

References

Papyrus editions are cited according to J. Oates et al. Checklist of Editions of Greek, Latin, Demotic, and Coptic Papyri, Ostraca, and Tablets www.papyri.info/docs/checklist (accessed 22 December 2017).

Ast, Rodney. 2015. Writing and the city in later Roman Egypt: Towards a social history of the ancient scribe. *CHS Research Bulletin* 4.1 <nrs.harvard.edu/urn-3:hlnc.essay:AstR. Writing_ in_the_City_in_Later_Roman_Egypt.2016>.

Bentein, Klaas. 2012. Perfect periphrases in Post-classical and Early Byzantine Greek: An ecological-evolutionary account. *Journal of Greek Linguistics* 12. 205–275.

Bentein, Klaas. 2013. Register and the diachrony of Post-classical and Early Byzantine Greek. *Revue Belge de Philologie et d'Histoire* 91. 5–44.

Bentein, Klaas. 2015a. The Greek documentary papyri as a linguistically heterogeneous corpus: The case of the katochoi of the Sarapieion-archive. *Classical World* 108. 461–484.

Bentein, Klaas. 2015b. Particle-usage in documentary papyri (I–IV AD): An integrated, sociolinguistically-informed approach. *Greek Roman and Byzantine Studies* 55. 721–753.

Bentein, Klaas. 2015c. Minor complementation patterns in Post-classical Greek (I–VI AD): A socio-historical analysis of a corpus of documentary papyri. *Symbolae Osloenses* 89. 104–147.

Bentein, Klaas. 2017. Finite vs. non-finite complementation in Post-classical and Early Byzantine Greek: Towards a pragmatic restructuring of the complementation system? *Journal of Greek Linguistics* 17. 3–36.

Biber, Douglas. 1988. *Variation across speech and writing*. Cambridge: Cambridge University Press.

Biber, Douglas. 1995. *Dimensions of register variation: A cross-linguistic comparison*. Cambridge: Cambridge University Press.

---

[47] My research was funded by the Research Foundation - Flanders (FWO), at Ghent University, and The Research Council of Norway (NFR COFUND), at the University of Oslo.

Biber, Douglas & Susan Conrad. 2009. *Register, genre, and style*. Cambridge: Cambridge University Press.
Bucking, Scott. 2007. On the training of documentary scribes in Roman, Byzantine, and early Islamic Egypt: A contextualized assessment of the Greek evidence. *Zeitschrift für Papyrologie und Epigraphik* 159. 229–247.
Clarysse, Willy. 1993. Egyptian scribes writing Greek. *Chronique d' Égypte* 68. 186–201.
Clarysse, Willy. 2009. The Zenon papyri thirty years on. In Guido Bastianini & Angelo Casanova (eds.), *100 Anni di Istituzioni Fiorentine per la Papirologia: Atti del convegno internazionale di studi Firenze, 12–13 giugno 2008*, 31–43. Firenze: Istituto papirologico G. Vitelli.
Clarysse, Willy. 2010. Linguistic diversity in the archive of the engineers Kleon and Theodoros. In Trevor V. Evans & Dirk D. Obbink (eds.), *The language of the papyri*, 35–50. Oxford: Oxford University Press.
Depauw, Mark & Joanne Vera Stolk. 2015. Linguistic variation in Greek papyri: Towards a new tool for quantitative study. *Greek, Roman & Byzantine Studies* 55. 196–220.
Del Corso, Lucio. 2008. Le scritture di Dioscoro. In Jean-Luc Fournet & Caroline Magdelaine (eds.), *Les archives de Dioscore d'Aphrodité cent ans après leur découverte*, 89–115. Paris: de Boccard.
Evans, Trevor V. 2012. Linguistic and stylistic variation in the Zenon Archive. In Martti Leiwo, Hilla Halla-aho & Marja Vierros (eds.), *Variation and change in Greek and Latin*, 25–42. Helsinki: Suomen Ateenan-Instituutin säätiö.
Feissel, Denis. 2004. Pétitions aux empereurs et formes du rescrit dans les sources documentaires du IVe au VIe siècle. In Denis Feissel & Jacques Gascou (eds.), *La pétition à byzance*, 33–52. Paris: Association des Amis du Centre de recherche d'histoire et civilisation de Byzance.
Firth, John Rupert. 1950. Personality and language in society. *The Sociological Review* 42. 37–52.
Fournet, Jean-Luc & Jacques Gascou. 2004. Liste des pétitions sur papyrus des Ve-VIIe siècles. In Denis Feissel & Jacques Gascou (eds.), *La pétition à byzance*, 141–196. Paris: Association des Amis du Centre de recherche d'histoire et civilisation de Byzance.
Gignac, Francis T. 1976. *A grammar of the Greek papyri of the Roman and Byzantine periods*. Vol. 1: Phonology. Milano: La Goliardica.
Halla-aho, Hilla. 2010. Linguistic varieties and language level in Latin non-literary letters. In Trevor V. Evans & Dirk D. Obbink (eds.), *The language of the papyri*, 171–183. Oxford: Oxford University Press.
Halla-aho, Hilla. 2018. Scribes in private letter writing: Linguistic perspectives. In Jennifer Cromwell & Eitan Grossman (eds.), *Scribal repertoires in Egypt from the New Kingdom to the Early Islamic Period*, 227–239. Oxford: Oxford University Press.
Halliday, Michael A. K., Angus McIntosh & Peter Strevens. 1964. *The linguistic sciences and language teaching*. London: Longman.
Hickey, Raymond. 2010. Linguistic evaluation of earlier texts. In Raymond Hickey (ed.), *Varieties of English in writing: The written word as linguistic evidence*, 1–14. Amsterdam: Benjamins.
Husselman, Elinor M., Arthur E.R. Boak & William F. Edgerton. 1944. *Papyri from Tebtunis II (Michigan papyri V)*. Ann Arbor: University of Michigan Press.

Husselman, Eleanor M. 1970. Procedures of the record office of Tebtunis in the first century A.D. In Deborah Hobson Samuel (ed.), *Proceedings of the 12th International Congress of Papyrology, Ann Arbor, 13–17 August 1968*, 223–238. Toronto: Hakkert.

Hymes, Dell. 1967. Models of the interaction of language and social setting. *Journal of Social Issues* 23. 8–28.

James, Patrick. 2007. *Retention and retreat: Complementary participles and infinitives with verbs of perception and declaration in the Roman and Byzantine documentary papyri*. PhD dissertation, University of Cambridge.

Johnson, Daniel E. 2009. Getting off the GoldVarb Standard: Introducing Rbrul for mixed-effects variable rule analysis. *Language and Linguistics Compass* 3. 359–383.

Keenan, James G. 2008. 'Tormented Voices': P.Cair.Masp. I 67002. In Jean-Luc Fournet & Caroline Magdelaine (eds.), *Les archives de Dioscore d'Aphrodité cent ans après leur découverte*, 171–180. Paris: de Boccard.

Lee, David Y. W. 2001. Genres, registers, text types, domains, and styles: Clarifying the concepts and navigating a path through the BNC jungle. *Language Learning & Technology* 5(3). 37–72.

Milroy, James & Lesley Milroy. 1985. *Authority in language: Investigating language prescription and standardisation*. London: Routlegde & Kegan Paul.

Montevecchi, Orsolina. 1973. *La papirologia*. Torino: Società editrice internazionale.

Palme, Bernhard. 2009. The range of documentary texts: Types and categories. In Roger S. Bagnall (ed.), *The Oxford handbook of papyrology*, 358–394. Oxford: Oxford University Press.

Pestman, Pieter W. 1981. *A guide to the Zenon archive (P. L.Bat. XXI)*. Leiden: Brill.

Porter, Stanley E. & Matthew B. O'Donnell. 2010. Building and examining linguistic phenomena in a corpus of representative papyri. In Trevor V. Evans & Dirk D. Obbink (eds.), *The language of the papyri*, 287–311. Oxford: Oxford University Press.

Rutkowska, Hanna & Paul Rössler. 2012. Orthographic variables. In Juan Manuel Hernández-Campoy & Juan Camilo Conde-Silvestre (eds.), *The handbook of historical sociolinguistics*, 221–244. Chichester: Wiley-Blackwell.

Stolk, Joanne Vera. 2018. Encoding linguistic variation in Greek documentary papyri: The past, present and future of editorial regularization. In Nicola Reggiani (ed.), *Digital papyrology II: Case studies on the digital edition of Ancient Greek papyri*, 119–137. Berlin: de Gruyter.

Stolk, Joanne Vera. 2019. Itacism from Zenon to Dioscoros: Scribal corrections of ‹ι› and ‹ει› in Greek papyri. In Sofia Torallas Tovar & Alberto Nodar (eds.), *Proceedings of the 28th International Congress of Papyrology, Barcelona, 1–6 August 2016*, 690–697. Barcelona: Publicacions de l'Abadia de Monstserrat, Universitat Pompeu Fabra.

Stolk, Joanne Vera. Forthcoming. Scribal revision in the process of text production: A linguistic typology of scribal corrections in Greek documentary papyri. In Martti Leiwo, Sonja Dahlgren, Hilla Halla-aho and Marja Vierros (eds.), *Act of the scribe: Interfaces between scribal work and language use: A workshop, The Finnish Institute at Athens, April 6–8, 2017*.

Stolk, Joanne Vera, Ágnes Mihálykó & Céline Grassien. Forthcoming. The language of the liturgy: Greek used by Theban scribes. In Anastasia Maravela & Ágnes Mihálykó (eds.), *New perspectives on religion, education, and culture at Christian western Thebes (VI–VIII)*.

Taylor, John R. 1989. *Linguistic categorisation: Prototypes in linguistic theory*. Oxford: Clarendon Press.

Teodorsson, Sven-Tage. 1977. *The phonology of Ptolemaic Koine*. Göteborg: Acta Universitatis Gothoburgensis.

Turner, Eric G. 1968. *Greek papyri: An introduction*. Oxford: Clarendon Press.

Vandorpe, Katelijn, Willy Clarysse & Herbert Verreth. 2015. *Graeco-Roman archives from the Fayum*. Leuven: Peeters.

Van Minnen, Peter. 2003. Dioscorus and the law. In A.A. MacDonald, M.W. Twomey & G.J. Reinink (eds.), *Learned antiquity scholarship and society in the Near East, the Greco-Roman world, and the Early Medieval West*, 115–133. Leuven: Peeters.

Vierros, Marja. 2012. *Bilingual notaries in Hellenistic Egypt: A study of Greek as a second language*. Brussel: Koninklijke Vlaamse Akademie van België voor Wetenschappen en Kunsten.

Youtie, Herbert C. 1971. Βραδέως γράφων: Between Literacy and Illiteracy. *Greek, Roman & Byzantine Studies* 12. 239–61.

Zuckerman, Constantin, 2004. *Les deux Dioscore d'Aphroditè ou les limites de la pétition*. In Denis Feissel & Jacques Gascou (eds.), *La pétition à byzance*, 75–92. Paris: Association des Amis du Centre de recherche d'histoire et civilisation de Byzance.

Emilio Crespo
13 The Greek phonology of a tax collector in Egypt in the first century CE

Abstract: This chapter gathers the examples of deviating spellings found in four documentary papyri written by Nemesion, a tax collector for the Egyptian village of Philadelphia, in the first century CE, with the aim to ascertain the features of the phonemic system of Greek spoken by the writer. The main conclusion is that such spellings evidence a number of phonemic features of an idiolect of Koine Greek characterized by a pronunciation with interferences from the Egyptian vowels and consonants. The phonemic Greek idiolect of Nemesion most probably reflects the sociolect of many adults who lived in Egypt at that time and were bilingual in Greek and Egyptian.

1 Introduction

Graphic variations in writing provide important information when reconstructing the phonological system of both corpus languages and past states of languages, such as Ancient Greek. While Greek literature and public inscriptions that post-date the spread of the so-called Milesian alphabet typically use standardized spellings, Greek documentary papyri from Egypt quite often show deviations from the standard writing norm. These deviations have various causes, including insufficient knowledge or imperfect use of writing norms, the desire to reproduce pronunciation, the stock of available signs in the writing system, the influence of textual context on the psychological process of setting words to writing (e.g. the similarity of different graphemes), or simple carelessness due to fatigue or other factors. Only variations arising from an attempt to reproduce pronunciation using the standard writing system are relevant for the purpose of reconstructing the phonological system.[1]

It is not always easy, however, to distinguish between graphic variations that are relevant in determining a phonological system and variants that stem

---
[1] Research for this chapter was done within the framework of a collaborative research project entitled 'Multilingualism and Minority Languages in Ancient Europe' and funded by the HERA network Uses of the Past (HERA.15.029). I am grateful to Professor L. Gil, who drew my attention to the papyrus containing the letter from Claudius a long time ago, to the audiences of the earlier versions read at Ghent and Thessaloniki, and to an anonymous reviewer for their insightful comments and criticisms. The abbreviation l. stands for Latin *lege* ('read'), C for consonant and V for vowel.

https://doi.org/10.1515/9783110614404-013

from carelessness or other factors. The former are usually very frequent or even systematic, which means that the more examples we find of a particular graphic alternation, the more likely it is that it is relevant for the purpose of determining pronunciation. Study of an archive of papyri is thus more likely to unveil the phonological system underpinning the writing than graphic variants that are only documented in a single text.

Nemesion's archive contains a document of note from a historic perspective as well as in terms of writing, as it shows many variants. It is thus expedient to compare said document to others from the same archive, as if they show similar misspellings it would lend support to the view that they are due to the pronunciation of the person who wrote the texts.

In view of the foregoing, the objective of this paper is twofold: first, it aims to ascertain the features of the phonemic system of Greek that underpin the graphic variations employed by Nemesion, son of Zoilos, a tax collector for Philadelphia (modern Gharabet el-Gerza), in four documents written in his own hand and dated from 40 to 60/1 CE; and second, it attempts to determine whether the phonemic system of Greek reflected by the deviant spellings found in such documents represents an individual variety – either Nemesion's personal idiolect or a register linked to a certain setting or topic – or a dialect (geographical or social) that is shared with other speakers.

The structure of the paper is as follows. Section 2 briefly outlines some information about Nemesion gleaned from the papyri that make up his archive, which is the only source of information on this individual that has come down to us, and from several studies cited in the list of references, mainly by A. Hanson and W. Clarysse. Section 3 lists and summarizes the contents of four documents belonging to this archive which were very likely written by Nemesion himself, before going on to consider their graphic interchanges. Section 4 focuses on the deviant spellings found in these four documents. While many of their graphic variations attest to phonemic shifts that occurred in Koine Greek before medieval times, we see that some spellings do not coincide with the developments of Greek in other geographical areas and point to close parallels in Egyptian. They are thus likely to be related to interference from the Egyptian language.[2] This was probably due to

---

[2] For the sake of convenience, "Egyptian" in this chapter refers to the language spoken by the majority of the population in Ancient Egypt up until the Arabic conquest. This language was commonly written with the Demotic script from Alexander's conquest to the end of the Julio-Claudian dynasty. "Coptic" denotes the script which, based on the Greek alphabet with additional characters derived from Demotic, is attested from the third century CE onwards (see Bagnall 2011: 32–39 for the writing in the Hellenistic period, and 74–94 for the emergence of Coptic).

Nemesion being bilingual in Greek and Egyptian rather than to the influence of the Egyptian adstratum on the pronunciation of a monolingual speaker of Greek. Section 5 shows the close correlation between scribal errors made by Nemesion and mistakes found in other documents written by Egyptians who were assuredly bilingual and inhabited Philadelphia and other parts of Egypt, in Nemesion's time and afterwards. This allows us to infer that Nemesion's pronunciation of Greek reflects a sociolect shared by others who spoke and wrote in Greek in Philadelphia and elsewhere and used spellings that reveal a pronunciation of Greek with phonemic bilingual interference from Egyptian. Although the archive provides no definite clues enabling us to deduce that Nemesion spoke, wrote and read Egyptian, phonemic interference due to his bilingualism is the most likely explanation for several graphic variations found in the documents considered. This explanation is substantiated for a small number of graphic variations, and only tentative for other deviant spellings. Finally, Section 6 summarizes the conclusions.

2 Nemesion, son of Zoilos

Nemesion (also called Νεμίων, Νεμείων and Νεμεσᾶς[3]), son of Zoilos, lived in Philadelphia, a village in the Herakleides division (*merís*) of the Arsinoite province (*nomós*) of Egypt, in the first century CE.[4] He probably married Thermouthis and had three sons.[5] "He lent money on interest and farmed and raised sheep" (Clarysse 2015: 257). He also served as a collector of money taxes "during at least seven different years over a thirteen-year period" (Hanson 1994: 218) under the principates of Tiberius, Claudius and Nero.[6] Tax collectors were also peasant taxpayers who were chosen by the governor (*strategós*) of the nome to

---

[3] Νεμίων Ζωΐλου (P.Princ. I 1, dated after April 17th, 51 CE); Νεμείωνος (P.Corn. 24 recto, 56 CE); Νεμεσᾶς, πράκτωρ λα[ογ]ραφίας κώμης Φιλαδελφείας 'Nemesas, collector of poll tax for the village of Philadelphia' (SB IV 7461, dated April 18th, 45 CE).
[4] Hanson (2015: 21–29).
[5] A letter sent by Thermouthis to Nemesion (SB XIV 11585 (July 7th, 59 CE)) informing him of some private affairs implies that the addressee was her husband. Another letter sent by a man named Servilius to "his brother" Nemesion (P.Graux II 10 (30–61 CE)) asks him "to take care of the children, Thermoutis (*sic*) and everybody at home". Another letter (P.Graux II 11 (30–61 CE)) addressed by someone to "his brother" Nemesion contains the farewell message: ἀσπάζου Θερμουθιν καὶ Διωγένην (l. Διογένην) καὶ Ἀμμώνου (l. Ἀμμονοῦν) καὶ Ṇεεμεσου (l. Νεμεσοῦν) 'my greetings to Thermuthis, Diogenes, Ammonous and Nemesous'.
[6] Nemesion appears as a collector of taxes in the second document written on P.Mich. X 582 (50 CE) (see §3.3) and is probably the sender who is referred to as one of the λογευτῶ[ν λαογ] ραφίας Φιλαδε[λφεία]ς τῆς Ἡρακλείδου μερίδος [τ]οῦ Ἀρ[σινοΐ]του ν[ομοῦ 'tax-collectors of

carry out this function. The provincial authority assigned this job as a form of tax (*leitourgía*), upon proposal of the village secretary (*komogrammateús*). Logically, the *strategós* entrusted this *leitourgía* to members of society able to perform the service, which leads us to suppose that Nemesion was an influential man in his village.

The Greek names borne by both Nemesion and his father do not assure us that they were native speakers of Greek. It is widely known that bearing a Greek name and speaking Greek in Egypt during this era did not mean that a person spoke the vernacular Greek. Some of Nemesion's closest colleagues, for example, have Greek names and another has an Egyptian name. A papyrus in Nemesion's archive containing a letter from Herakleides, secretary of the village of Philadelphia, to Ammonius, *strategós* of the Herakleides and Polemon *merídes* (P.Gen. II 91 (dated to 50/51CE); see §5 below), lists three collectors of poll tax (πράκ[τωρ] λαογραφίας) in Philadelphia. Two of them bear Greek names and can write (εἰδὼς γράμματα). The third is called Horion, son of Petosiris, and it is not specified whether he can write.[7] We find this same Horion in one of the papyri that we will consider as written in Nemesion's hand (see §3.3 below).

Nemesion seems to have had a broad network in his village. Most people mentioned in his archive have Egyptian names and are described as being subject to or having paid a money tax. Nemesion was in close contact with the population and went house-to-house, along with soldiers and other associates, to collect capitation taxes, as shown by the repeated sequences of personal names listed in the same order in several documents.[8] Several documents in Nemesion's archive mention people bearing Latin names. One of them is the local centurion Lucius Cattius Catulus, who is mentioned in the draft of a request addressed to an unnamed official (P.Mich. X 582 (50 CE); see §3.3 below) and in P.Sijp. 15 (50/51 CE) and is referred to by the single name Λοῦκις in the letter sent by Thermouthis to Nemesion (cf. footnote 5; SB XIV 11585, July 7th, 59 CE; also SB XX 14526 = P.Princ. III 152 (60/61 CE) on which see §3.4 below) and whose agents took oaths from certain debtors (see P.Thomas 5 (July 24th, 46 CE)). In this letter, Thermouthis informs Nemesion about matters relating to his business with Lucius and about items of clothing and tools that each have of the other's, implying a certain degree of familiarity. Persons referred to only by a Latin *praenomen*

---

poll tax at Philadelphia of the Herakleides division of the Arsinoite province' of a request addressed to the prefect Aulus Avilius Flaccus (P. Graux II 9, dated after 33 CE).
7 See Hanson (1979, 1992: 134–135).
8 See Hanson (1994: 218).

or *cognomen* rather than by the *tria nomina* may have been Egyptians who adopted Latin names.⁹

Sixty-four certain and two uncertain documents have come down to us from Nemesion's archive. All of them are written in Greek. "Half of the texts in the archive are lists of taxpayers, year lists of payments due, day books and lists of arrears, in different classifications (by area and village, alphabetically by name of the taxpayers, by type of taxes)" (Clarysse 2015: 256). There are also drafts of official requests. About ten of the documents are Nemesion's private business letters. The papyri that are dated range from 30 to 60/1 CE, and more than half of them are published.

3 Four documents written in Nemesion's hand

Turning now to graphic variations, an attempt will be made to identify features of the phonemic system underlying Nemesion's pronunciation, using deviations from the regular spelling of Greek as a guide.¹⁰ Consideration will be given to four published documents from his archive. According to Hanson (2010: 310–311; 1992: 139, fn. 30; 1992: 136, 144), three of them are demonstrably written in Nemesion's hand, and, in any case, in the same hand. The remaining document (P.Mich. X 582; see §3.3 below) is a draft of a request sent by Nemesion, for which I have not found any references that explicitly state that it is written in Nemesion's hand. For the text of these papyri we follow the PN. Other documents in the archive were also probably written by Nemesion himself, but they consist of lists of Egyptian personal names written in Greek and they either lack alternative spellings or such spellings are rare, and they thus do not suit our objective.¹¹ The four documents considered are as follows.

---

9 Hanson (1992: 135).
10 Deviant spellings are generally due to an insufficient command of spelling conventions on the part of the writer, which may or may not be combined with accommodation of the spelling to his/her pronunciation, and to the availability of different signs for a given sound in the script (see Teodorsson 1977: 209–212). For a quantitative study of variations, see Depauw & Stolk (2015), Stolk (2019) and the section on text irregularities at TMTI.
11 Further papyri from Nemesions's archive such as P.Ryl. IV 595 (ca. October 28ᵗʰ – November 26ᵗʰ, 57 CE) (list of missing persons), P.Princ. I 14 (after 48–49 or 62–63 CE) (register of taxes), SB XIV 11481 (ca. 38–48 CE) (list of taxpayers), P.Corn. 24 recto (56 CE; the author' name is Νεμείωνος) (list of names of delinquent taxpayers) and P.Mich. XII 638–642 (41–54 CE) (lists of names) are all written by the same hand (see Hanson 1974; Oates 1976, 1978), but it is uncertain whether the writer is Nemesion himself or one of his scribes. The same applies to P. Coll.Youtie I 20 (56 CE) (verso of P.Corn. 24).

3.1 Letter of the Emperor Claudius to the Alexandrians

The letter from the Emperor Claudius to the Alexandrians is the lengthiest and, from a historical and linguistic viewpoint, most prominent document in the archive. The papyrus contains a copy of a letter from the Emperor Claudius to the Alexandrians (P.Lond. VI 1912), preceded by a command by the prefect L. Aemilius Rectus to publish it. The copy was written on the back of a papyrus sheet not long after its promulgation on November 10th, 41 CE.[12] The recto of the papyrus, not yet published, includes a year ledger of payments for regnal year 2 of Gaius, corresponding to 37/8, and was written by the same hand in Philadelphia.[13] The letter from Emperor Claudius deals with various topics. The one that has attracted the most attention concerns the feud and riots between Jews and other inhabitants of Alexandria and the Emperor's efforts to maintain peace.[14] As it is a copy of a document written in the official style, the letter only provides information about the author's pronunciation and indirect information about the phonemic system behind the spellings, not about other linguistic aspects of Nemesion's Greek.

Since the text is full of graphic deviations, it is highly unlikely that the document that has come down to us was copied directly from the official texts of the prefect's command and the attached letter, which were doubtlessly written with standard spellings. The papyrus was either taken in dictation or is a copy of a copy, and there may even have been several intermediate copies. This raises the question of whether the spelling in our copy should be attributed to Nemesion himself, to the reader of the text dictated to him or to the author of any intermediate copy there might have been. In my opinion, this is an insurmountable difficulty which leaves a margin of uncertainty to any conclusions that may be drawn from our analysis. Nemesion did, however, make nineteen corrections, which probably indicates that he was to some degree responsible for the text's final spelling. Moreover, there are several similarities, as we will see below, between the nature of the deviant spellings attested by Claudius' letter and the nature of those found in the other documents considered in this chapter. Of the twenty-five types of variations that will be listed and described (§4.1–4 below), six are coincident in at least two of the documents. A difference is seen, of course, in the number of deviant spellings and the proportion of words that contain them. While the

---

[12] See Hanson (1992: 138; 2010: 310–311), Clarysse (2015: 257).
[13] The papyrus sheet also contains a list of personal names between columns 2 and 3 of the verso in the opposite direction.
[14] In a letter sent on August 4th of the same year, 41 CE (BGU IV 1079, l. 24), Sarapion advises Herakleides to be cautious with the Jews: καὶ σὺ βλέπε σατὸν (l. σαυτὸν) ἀπὸ τῶν Ἰουδαίων 'And look for yourself away from the Jews' (see Hanson 1992; Harker 2008: 25–28).

letter from Claudius attests roughly one hundred and fifty words that display corrections or deviations from the standard spelling, the number of deviations in each of the other documents studied ranges from twelve to fourteen. This difference is partly due to the subject matter. While the other three papyri considered –two of which are accounts and the third a draft petition– pertain to matters associated with customary tax collector duties, the content and linguistic register of Claudius' letter fall outside the sphere of common tax collector duties. Furthermore, the draft petition and the account of expenses are much shorter than Claudius' letter.

3.2 Fragmentary ledger recording payments for the *syntáximon*

The second document considered is an account dated January 14th, 43 and 46/47 CE (SB XX 14576 = P.Princ. I 13; see Hanson 1990), consisting of twenty columns of a ledger recording payments for a tax called *syntáximon*. The text is much longer than the letter from Claudius. It consists of a list of personal names of people who have paid the *syntáximon* and displays many abbreviated forms.[15]

3.3 Draft of a petition addressed by Nemesion

The third document studied (P.Mich. X 582) contains a draft of a petition addressed by Nemesion as πράκτορος [ἀρ]γυρικῶν ἀπὸ Φιλαδελφείας τ(ῆς) Ἡρακ[λείδου] μερίδος τοῦ Ἀρσινοείτου (l. Ἀρσινοίτου) ν[ο]μοῦ 'collector of the taxes paid in money from Philadelphia of the Herakleides division of the Arsinoite province' to an unnamed official. In his petition, Nemesion complains or reports that his colleague Horion (see §2 above) has abandoned his office and requests that the unnamed official write to the centurion Lucius Cattius Catulus (see §2 above) to get him to compel Horion to perform his duties. The draft is dated to 50 CE and is written on a reused papyrus sheet, next to a tax list written in a different hand. Another papyrus (SB VI 9224, dated to 50/51 CE) reports that by the next year Horion belonged to the class of farmers who had been released from service.

---

15 P.Princ. I 13, on the verso of P.Princ. I 8 (27–32 CE) (see Hanson 1974: 231, fn. 9), was written by Nemesion himself (see Hanson 1992: 139, fn. 30).

3.4 Account recording expenditure for wages and other costs

The fourth document, written in Nemesion's hand according to Hanson (1992: 136, 144), contains an account covering two years and records expenditure for wages and other costs (SB XX 14526 = P.Princ. III 152). It is dated to shortly after 60/61 CE.[16]

4 Deviant spellings in the four documents written by Nemesion

The documents show many deviations from the regular spelling of Koine Greek. As mentioned above, misspellings are particularly abundant in the copy of the prefect's command and Emperor Claudius' letter to the Alexandrians. The graphic deviations found in this copy contrast with its official style and reveal that its writer generally adapted his spelling to his pronunciation of Greek.

With few exceptions (see §4.4 below), the deviations from the common orthography of Ancient Greek reveal that two or more different graphemes stand for the same sound. While one of them is the inherited standard spelling, the other was employed in an earlier stage for a different sound that underwent a shift causing it to approach to the sound rendered by the inherited grapheme or even to merge with it. Thus, the alternative spelling <ε> in ἐξερέτως rather than ἐξαιρέτως 'specially' shows an identification of <ε> with the digraph <αι>, which had the value of /ai/ in Greek orthographic tradition.

The graphic interchanges with phonological relevance found in these documents written by Nemesion can be divided into three groups. The first consists of interchanges also attested in other Greek-speaking areas outside of Egypt, which are the result of sound shifts also undergone in other areas in which the Koine was spoken and retained in later phases of the history of the Greek language, in some cases even up to the present. Several of them seem to reflect a pronunciation like that of present-day standard Greek. To cite one example, the numerous

---

[16] The draft of a request probably addressed by Nemesion and one or more tax collectors to Aulus Avilius Flaccus (P.Graux II 9 (33 CE)) offers deviating spellings that are also found in one or more of our four documents, suggesting that Nemesion was its author: 6, 7, 10–11 ἐ]ωρτῆ[ς] (l. [ἑ]ορτῆς) 'feast' (genitive case) (see 4.1 (f) below), 10 and 15 βυβλιοφύλακος, -ι (l. βιβλιοφύλακος, -ι) 'keeper of archives' (see 4.3 (m) below), 18 τειμῆς (l. τιμῆς) 'price' (see 4.1 (h) below), 19 μοσχηίαν (l. μοσχείαν) 'for the planting of a sucker', 21 παρεπράκθημεν (l. παρεπράχθημεν) 'we were wrongly charged' (see 4.3 (x) below).

confusions between ἡμεῖς 'we' and ὑμεῖς 'you' in the copy of the letter from Emperor Claudius to the Alexandrians might initially be accounted for as concealing an identical pronunciation of the two pronouns, as /i'mis/ (see §4.3 (p) below). In such cases, the graphic variations found in the documents provide the *terminus ante quem* for the dephonologization of a phonemic distinction or for the transphonologization of a phoneme in Nemesion's phonological system of Greek, with the result that two or more graphemes that had stood for different phonemes before a given sound shift took place became available for the same sound in the ensuing stage. This is the case with the diphthong /ai/, which lost its phonemic character when it developed into /e/ in Nemesion's pronunciation, as shown by ἐξερέτως instead of ἐξαιρέτως 'specially'.

The remaining anomalous spellings which seem to have phonological relevance and appear to be attested in one or more of our four documents are dealt with in Sections 4.2 and 4.3. They point to sound shifts which in Nemesion's time are attested only or mainly in papyri written in Egypt and were not retained in later phases of Greek. At least one of these interchanges is due to the interference of Egyptian with Greek (§4.2). This opens the possibility that the other spellings point, with varying degrees of probability, to a pronunciation resulting from the interference of Egyptian on Greek (§4.3).

4.1 Misspellings as the result of internal developments of Koine

The following graphic variations are attested in one or more of the four documents considered, as well as in other Greek-speaking areas outside of Egypt in Nemesion's time, and were retained in later stages of the Greek language:
(a) The single consonants <σ>, <λ> and <τ> alternate with their corresponding geminates <σσ>, <λλ> and <ττ>: P.Lond. VI 1912, 3.40 ἴσσως instead of ἴσως 'perhaps', 3.43 Πολείωνος (l. Πωλλίωνος) 'Pollio'; 1.1 Αἰμίλλιος and 4.70 Αἰμιλλίωι 'Aemilius'; P.Mich. X 582, 2.21 ἔλατον instead of ἐλάττον 'worse'. This alternation indicates that for Nemesion there was no phonological difference between single and geminate consonants. This interchange is frequent in papyri of the Roman period.[17] Similar examples are documented in Attic inscriptions.[18] In the documents from Nemesion's archive studied, alternation between single and geminate consonants is restricted to σσ/σ, ττ/τ

---

17 See Gignac (1976: 155).
18 See Threatte (1980: 513–514).

and λλ/λ. This limitation is probably due to these geminates being, along with -ρρ-, -μμ- and -νν-, the most frequent in Greek. It is plausible that the spelling <λλ> also reflects the palatal pronunciation of the liquid consonant.

(b) The consonant <τ> in the group <πτ> is omitted in P.Lond. VI 1912, 3.41, 3.43: Αἰγύπ<τ>ου (l. Αἰγύπτου) 'Egypt', "reflecting a tendency to simplify consonant clusters in colloquial speech" (Gignac 1976: 66–7).[19]

(c) –ν word-finally: P.Lond. VI 1912, 1.5: ἠδυνήθην (l. ἠδυνήθη) '(the city) was not able'. This hypercorrect spelling reflects that the writer did not pronounce the final –ν which was pronounced by other speakers in other verbal forms in the third-person singular and has added it in this third-person singular of the passive aorist, where there was no –ν in standard Greek. The interchange has phonetic relevance because it reveals that the writer dropped the final –ν in other verbal forms. The erroneous addition of final –ν shows that the nasal phoneme was dropped regardless of the nature of the following sound.[20]

(d) <ν> instead of <γν>: P.Lond. VI 1912, 1.8 ἀναγεινόσκων (l. ἀναγιγνώσκοντες) 'reading', 3.53 γεινώσκωι (l. γιγνώσκω) 'I decide'. This is the habitual spelling in Roman-era papyri, indicating assimilation or loss of /g/ in this context.

(e) In the documents considered, ancient long diphthongs with second element /i/ alternate with spellings without second element /i/: while <ᾱι> is not attested, <η> (η in editions) instead of <ηι> is regular: SB XX 14576 = P.Princ. I 13, v,3,22, v,10,225 χιριστῇ (l. χειριστῇ) 'collector' (dative). The diphthong <ηι> is only found in P.Lond. VI 1912, 5.105 πάσηι 'complete' (fem. sing. dative). <ωι> occurs instead of <ω> in P.Lond. VI 1912, 2.26 εἴπωι (l. εἴπω) 'in order to say', 2.30 and 3.43 ἐπιτρέπωι (l. ἐπιτρέπω) 'I grant', 2.32, 3.46 συνχωρῶι (l. συγχωρῶ) 'I agree', 2.32 ὁρῶι (l. ὁρῶ) 'I see', 3.39 συνπομπευέτωι (l. συμπομπευέτω) 'let it accompany in the procession', 3.53 γεινώσκωι (l. γινώσκω) 'I decree', 3.54 διαφυλάσσωι (l. διαφυλάσσω) 'I protect', 4.67 ἔχωι (l. ἔχω) 'I have', 4.79 προσαγορεύωι (l. προσαγορεύω) 'I announce', 5.87, 5.103 ἐγώι (l. ἐγώ) 'I', 5.89 κελεύωι (l. κελεύω) 'I order', 5.89 πλήωι (l. πλήω) 'more', 5.103 ἀνατάτωι (l. ἀνωτάτω) 'most upwards', 5.105 μαρτυρῶι (l. μαρτυρῶ) 'I bear witness'; P.Mich. X 582, 2.13 ἀξιῶι (l. ἀξιῶ) 'I demand'. These spelling alternations reveal that Nemesion didn't pronounce the second element of the long diphthongs with second element /i/. Monophthongization of ancient

---

[19] Ἑρμαίσκος 'Hermaiscos' is corrected from Ἑρμαικος in P.Lond. VI 1912, 2.19. Further examples in Gignac (1976: 130).
[20] See Gignac (1976: 111–114).

long diphthongs is documented earlier in Attic inscriptions[21] and has carried into Modern Greek.

(f) There are numerous interchanges of <o> instead of <ω>: P.Lond. VI 1912, 1.2 ἱεροτάτης (l. ἱερωτάτης) 'holiest', 1.8 ἀναγεινόσκων (l. ἀναγινώσκοντες) 'reading', 2.17 Λεονίδου (l. Λεωνίδου) 'Leonidas', 2.24 γνόριμον (l. γνώριμον) 'well-known', 2.29 πρότα (l. πρῶτα) 'first', 2.37 φορτικότε[ρο]ς (l. φορτικώτερος) 'too arrogant', 3.38 ἐπονύμαις (l. ἐπωνύμοις) 'named after someone', 3.49 ἀνθρόποις (l. ἀνθρώποις) 'human beings';[22] SB XX 14576 = P.Princ. I 13, v,6,89 δεδοκ (l. δέδωκεν) 'he gave'; <ω> instead of <o>: P.Lond. VI 1912, 3.53 ἐφηβευκώσει (l. ἐφηβευκόσι) 'those who became *epheboi*' (dative), 4.64 φώβωι (l. φόβωι) 'out of fear' (dative), 4.69 πρῶτων (l. πρῶτον) 'first', 5.92 ὦ (l. ὅ) 'what'; SB XX 14576 = P.Princ. I 13, v,13,308 Ἡλιωδ (l. Ἡλιόδωρος) 'Heliodorus'; P.Mich. X 582: 2.8 πρακτωρεύσας (l. πρακτορεύσας) 'who acted as collector', 2.20 δημωσίων (l. δημοσίων) 'public'. These alternations show that Nemesion didn't make the vowel quantity distinction characteristic of Classical Greek. The loss of quantity opposition is in line with documents in other Greek-speaking areas, but the disappearance of vowel quantity opposition in Attic is seen "especially after 100 CE" (see Threatte 1980: 385).[23]

(g) <ε> instead of <αι>: P.Lond VI 1912, 2.24 ἐξερέτως (l. ἐξαιρέτως) 'specially', 2.32 ποιήσασθε (l. ποιήσασθαι) 'to make', 3.45 ἀφιδρῦσέ (l. ἀφιδρῦσαί, corr. ex αφυδρυσε) 'to set up', 3.49 παρετοῦμε (l. παραιτοῦμαι) 'I deprecate', 3.51 ἐξέρετα (l. ἐξαίρετα) 'exclusive', 3.57, 4.61 βούλομε (l. βούλομαι) 'I wish', 4.71 δηλῶσε (l. δηλῶσαι) 'to show', 4.82 διαμαρτύρομε (l. διαμαρτύρομαι) 'I bear witness', 4.83 προσφέροντε (l. προσφέρωνται) 'they behave' (subjunctive), 5.86 λοιμένωνται (l. λυμαίνωνται) 'they are disrespectful', 5.88 Ἰουδέοις (l. Ἰουδαίοις) 'Jews', 5.98 ἀνανκασθήσομε (l. ἀναγκασθήσομαι) 'I shall be forced', 5.105, 108 ἑτέρωι (l. ἑταίρωι) 'companion', 5.107 κέχρ[ητε] (l. κέχρ[ηται]) 'he has advocated'; SB XX 14576 = P.Princ. I 13, v,4,42 ἀπετη (l. ἀπαιτήσεως) 'by claim', v,19, 553, 554 μαχερο, 554 μαχεροφο (l. μαχαιροφόρῳ) 'armed guard'; P.Mich. X 582, 2.18 ἀντέχεσθε (l. ἀντέχεσθαι) 'to undertake';

---

21 See Teodorsson (1978: 79–80), Threatte (1980: 353–368).
22 Remaining instances: φιλανθρόποις (3.55; l. φιλανθρώποις) 'indulgences', νεοκόρους (4.60; l. νεωκόρους) 'wardens of the temple', κληροτούς (4.61; l. κληρωτούς) 'chosen by lot', Κανόπωι (4.61; l. Κανώπωι) 'Kanopos', πρότων (4.69; l. πρῶτον) 'for the first time', φιλάνθροπος (4.81; l. φιλάνθρωπος) 'benevolent', προσφέροντε (4.83; l. προσφέρωνται) 'they behave' (subjunctive), ὦ (5.92; l. ὅ) 'what', φιλανθροπείας (5.102; l. φιλανθρωπίας) 'kindness', των ἀγῶνα (5.107; l. τὸν ἀγῶνα) 'the contest'.
23 The early date of sound shifts in papyri from Egypt may reflect a lower register in which the change had occurred at an earlier date, or interference from Egyptian. If the latter hypothesis is correct, these spelling alternations should be grouped with those listed in §4.3.

SB XX 14526 = P.Princ. III 152, 2.19 καταλείπετε (l. καταλείπεται) 'it is left'; see also 4.3 (w). <αι> instead of <ε>: P.Lond. VI 1912, 2.23, 4.68 εἴχεται (l. εἴχετε) 'you had', 2.30–31 προείρησθαι (l. προείρησθε) 'you proposed', 2.34 σπουδασαται (l. <ἐ>σπουδάσατε) 'you were eager', 3.40, 43, 45 βούλεσθαι (l. βούλεσθε) 'you wish', 3.54 βαί[[βον]]βαιον (l. βέ[[βον]]βαιον) 'firm', 4.64 δοκεῖται (l. δοκεῖτε) 'you seem', 4.71 ται (l. τε) 'and', 4.79 καταπαύσηται (l. καταπαύσητε) 'you put a stop', 5.109 ἔρρωσθαι (l. ἔρρωσθε) 'farewell'. There are occasional alternations between <αι> and <ε> in Attic inscriptions[24] and in papyri[25] at earlier dates, but they are only common after the first century CE.[26]

(h) Interchange of <ει> and <ι> before consonant or front vowel is the most common spelling variation in Greek papyri from Egypt and shows that both spellings stand for /i/. Thus, we see <ει> instead of <ι> and <ι> instead of <ει> in the following instances: P.Lond. VI 1912, 1.3: ἰς (l. εἰς) 'into', 1.3, 1.10, 4.84 πόλειν (l. πόλιν) 'city', 1.4 πόλεις (l. πόλις), 1.8 ἀναγεινόσκων (l. ἀναγινώσκοντες) 'reading', 2.15, 2.26 μέγειστος (l. μέγιστος) 'greatest', 2.15 ἀποδεδιγμένος (l. ἀποδεδειγμένος) 'designated', 2.22 εἶστε (l. ἴστε) 'you know', 2.25, 4.82 εἶνα (l. ἵνα) 'in order that', 2.30, 3.58, 4.67 ὑμεῖν (l. ὑμῖν) 'you' (dative), 2.36 προσελειπάρη[σ]εν (l. προσελιπάρησεν) 'he entreated', 2.37 ἐπεὶ (l. ἐπὶ) 'upon';[27] SB 20.14576 = P.Princ. I 13, v,3,22, v,10,225 χιριστῇ (l. χειριστῇ) 'armed guard', v,5,81, v,5,82, v,5,87 ἰς (l. εἰς) 'into'; P.Mich. X 582, 2.3 Ἀρσεινοείτου (l. Ἀρσινοίτου) 'Arsinoite', 2.4 ἀκθίς (l. ἀχθείς) 'assigned', 2.5 ἔτι (l. ἔτει) 'year', 2.8–9 ἀριθμήσις (l. ἀριθμή|σεις) 'accounting periods', 2.10 ἰσπράξεως (l. εἰσπράξεως) 'collection'; SB XX 14526 = P.Princ. III 152, 1.8, 2.32, 2.33 ποιμένει (l. ποιμένι) 'shepherd' (dative), 2.23, 2.26, 2.28, 2.29, 2.31 τειμῆς (l. τιμῆς) 'of the price', 2.31 ἰς (l. εἰς) 'into'. Similar examples occur in

---

24 See Threatte (1980: 294–299).
25 See Teodorsson (1977: 222–225).
26 See Gignac (1976: 193).
27 Further instances of interchange of <ει> and <ι> in P.Lond. VI 1912: 3.41 τειμάς (l. τιμάς) 'honours', 3.41 καταδίξαι (l. καταδεῖξαι) 'to establish', 3.43 Οὐειτρασίου (Οὐιτρασίου) 'Vitrasius', 3.53 γεινώσκωι (l. γινώσκω) 'I decide', 3.53 ἐφηβευκώσει (l. ἐφηβευκόσι) 'those who became *epheboi*', 3.53 ἄχρει (l. ἄχρι) 'up to', 3.55 πολειτείαν (l. πολιτείαν) 'citizenship', 3.56 πάσει (l. πᾶσι) 'all' (dative), 4.62-3 πολειτεικάς (l. πολιτικάς) 'political', 4.63 τριετῖς (l. τριετεῖς) 'triennial', 4.65 ἡμεῖν (l. ὑμῖν) 'you' (dative), 4.70 πράγμασει (l. πράγμασι) 'affairs' (dative), 4.71 συνείστασθαι (l. συνίστασθαι) 'to establish', 4.75 φιλοτειμηθέντων (l. φιλοτιμηθέντων) 'who strove for great honour', 4.78 πάλειν (l. πάλιν) 'again', 4.81 δῖξαι (δεῖξαι) 'to show', 4.84 οἰκοῦσει (l. οἰκοῦσι) 'inhabitants' (dative), 5.90 δυσεί (δυσί) 'two' (dative), πόλεσειν (l. πόλεσιν) 'cities' (dative), 5.93 ἀγώσει (l. ἀγῶσι) 'contests' (dative), 5.96 προσείεσθαι (l. προσίεσθαι) 'to let come', 5.100 τεινα (l. τινα) 'some', 5.107 φιλοτειμεία (l. φιλοτιμίᾳ) 'zeal for honour'.

Attic inscriptions[28] and in other areas where Greek was spoken in the first century CE.

(i) The alternation of <Cιο> and <Cειο> and of <Cια> and <Cεια>, which appears in μεγαλιότητα (P.Lond. VI 1912, 1.8; l. μεγαλειότητα) 'majesty', γενεθλείαν (2.30; l. γενεθλίαν) 'birthday', Πολείωνος (3.43; l. Πωλλίωνος) 'Pollio',[29] likely reflects confusion of <ει> with <ι> before a back vowel, which Teodorsson (1977: 214) dates "at the middle of the 3rd century" in most speakers.

(j) <o> instead of <οι>: P.Lond. VI 1912, 4.83 Ἰουδαίο<ι>ς (5.88 Ἰουδέοις); 5.103 ποήσομαι, 5.106 ποιουμένωι. According to Gignac (1976: 199–201; see also Teordorsson 1977: 227–228), the fact that there is an interchange of <οι> and <υ> in some words rules out the possibility that alternation of <οι> and <o> indicates retention of the diphthong /oi/. Ἰουδαίο<ι>ς is likely a *lapsus calami*, but we cannot say for certain that it does not document the interchange of /o/ and /y/ or /i/ (see 4.3 (o) below).

(k) <α> instead of <αυ>: ἀπολάοντας (P. Lond. VI 1912, 6.94). This alternation may indicate that the second element of the diphthong has disappeared or has evolved into the sound /w/ or /β/ but isn't written because there is no way to reflect these sounds in the inherited writing system. The latter interpretation is more plausible, as <αυ> also alternates with <αου>, revealing that the diphthong's second element had not disappeared (see Gignac 1976: 229–233).

4.2 Errors due to bilingual interference from Egyptian

The four documents considered show further graphic variations that share the following features: they are relatively frequent in Greek papyri written in Egypt but unknown or rare in other Greek-speaking areas in Nemesion's time, they differ from the general development from Koine to Medieval Greek and they tend to mask phonological distinctions existing in Greek but not in Egyptian. These graphic interchanges are as follows.[30]

---

28 See Teodorsson (1978: 58–60), Threatte (1980: 299–323).
29 Remaining instances of interchanges of ει and ι before o or α in P.Lond. VI 1912: ἠγε-μονείας (3.54; l. ἡγεμονίας) 'Principate', τειμείοις (3.55; l. τιμίοις) 'privileges', οἰκῖα (5.94; οἰκεῖα) and οἰκίας (5.104 οἰκείας) 'of their households', φιλανθροπείας (5.102; l. φιλανθρωπίας) 'kindness', φιλοτειμείᾳ (5.107; l. φιλοτιμίᾳ) 'zeal'.
30 The graphic alternations listed in 4.2-3 are common in Greek papyri. According to the TMTI, their frequency ranges from 42 instances of the use of <α> instead of <ω> to 938 instances of <τ> instead of <δ>, which ranks as the most frequent. The high frequency of such graphic variations reinforces the view that they reflect pronunciation.

(1) Interchange of <δ> and <τ>: P.Lond. VI 1912, 2.31, 3.42 τε (l. δέ) 'and' (τε in 2.31 is responsive to μέν, and in 3.42 links substantive clauses); 3.44 'δὲ corr. from τε'. Alternations of <δ> and <τ> show that, with respect to pronunciation, Nemesion identified the voiced dental stop with the corresponding voiceless stop. The correction made in 3.44 shows that Nemesion was attempting to adapt his spelling to the customary norm in Greek. In our four documents there are no instances of the use of the voiceless velar stop <κ> instead of the voiced <γ> and of <π> instead of <β>. The use of the voiceless bilabial stop instead of the voiced bilabial stop is less frequent in papyri.[31] Spelling alternations of voiceless and voiced stops are documented in various Classical-era Greek dialects such as in Pamphylian, Thessalian and, specially, Macedonian.[32] They indicate that voiceless stops evolved into voiced stops. In late Greek there are instances of spirantization of voiced stops, which also occurred in Western romance languages and the insular Celtic languages, wherein the softening of voiced stops is respectively called weakening and lenition. In contrast, the spelling that appears in our documents from Nemesion's archive does not document a weakening of the voiceless dental stop into a voiced stop and its confusion with the voiced dental, but rather fortition of the voiced dental stop, which Nemesion pronounced as voiceless. Nevertheless, the evolutionary path to Modern Greek shows that voiceless stops have generally held stable, while voiced stops developed into fricatives. The graphic variations between <δ> and the corresponding voiceless stop <τ> (and between <γ> and <κ> in other documents) are due to bilingual interference from the phonological system of Egyptian.[33] Egyptian lacked voiced plosives and the Coptic graphemes corresponding to Greek <δ> and <γ> (and <ζ>) are mainly used for Greek borrowings.[34] This explains the common substitution of voiced for voiceless plosives in many documentary papyri from Egypt.

---

[31] According to Gignac (1976: 63–64, 66–86) and Horrocks (2010: 112), the paucity of instances of confusion between <π> and <φ> is due to the opposition between /p/ and /f/ in Egyptian.
[32] See Méndez Dosuna (2014), Hatzopoulos (2018), Crespo (2018).
[33] Vierros (2014: 235–236).
[34] See Gignac (1976: 85–86), Loprieno (1995: 40–41), Allen (2013: 18–19).

4.3 Further graphic interchanges in the documents under consideration

The interpretation of other phonologically relevant graphic interchanges which are found in our documents from Nemesion's archive but are not described above are more controversial. Alternative spellings can be interpreted, with varying degrees of likelihood, as stemming from a phonetic change common to all of the Koine, albeit one which occurred earlier in Egypt, or as a change that was specific to Egyptian speakers and could have been caused by the Egyptian language's interference on Greek. There are advantages and drawbacks to both interpretations. The drawback of interpreting some spelling alternations as resulting from a shared evolution of the Koine is that it pushes back the dates generally agreed upon for various phonetic developments in Greek and does not account for the time lag between the dates of these developments in Egypt and in other areas. On the other hand, the graphic variations among vowels in our four documents can hardly be proved to be the outcome of bilingual interference of Egyptian on Greek for several reasons. First, the vowel system of the Egyptian language in the two first centuries CE is reconstructed on the basis of developments from the previous historical phase of Egyptian as well as the correspondence between the characters of the later Coptic script with their models in the Greek alphabet.[35] Furthermore, Coptic as attested from the third and fourth centuries CE is split into several dialects, and in this period "stressed vowels show considerable variation both among and within dialects" (Allen 2013: 13), though the Coptic characters that correspond to Greek <α, ε, ο> are generally associated with closed stressed syllables, and <η, ι, ω> with open stressed ones.[36] Finally, the distinction between the Coptic graphemes corresponding to Greek <ε> and <η>, on the one hand, and <ο> and <ω>, on the other, has been interpreted in terms of length (with <ε> and <ο> standing for short vowels and <η> and <ω> for long ones) or in terms of vowel height (with <ε> and <ο> standing for closed-mid vowels and <η> and <ω> for open-mid ones).[37] In spite of such difficulties, it is reasonable to interpret all or some of the following graphic variations attested by one or more of the four documents studied as resulting from Egyptian interference.

---

[35] Allen (2013: 11).
[36] Allen (2013: 14).
[37] Loprieno (1997: 452–454), Peust (1999: 201–211), Allen (2013: 11–22).

(m) <υ> instead of <ι>: ὑδρόσασθαι (l. ἰδρύσασθαι; P.Lond. VI 1912, 2.34) 'to set up'.³⁸ This graphic alternation of <υ> instead of <ι> is open to at least two interpretations. One is that /y/ had lost its roundness and merged with /i/ in the Koine of the first century CE. The difficulty with this hypothesis is that the literature generally takes the view that the evolution of /y/ > /i/ in other geographic areas only concluded centuries later.³⁹ An alternative hypothesis is that <υ> is a hypercorrection for <ι>. The /i/ pronunciation reflected by the spelling of <υ> for <ι> in our document is the result of interference from Egyptian and occurred much earlier than the spread of the identification of /y/ and /i/ as /i/ in other geographic regions where Koine Greek was spoken, and perhaps in Egypt itself. Egyptian lacked the phoneme /y/, as evidenced by the fact that the Coptic grapheme corresponding to <υ> was only used for the notation of Greek loanwords. There is also a parallel confusion of <ι> with <υ> when writing Greek loanwords in Coptic.⁴⁰

(n) <o> instead of <υ>: ὑδρόσασθαι (l. ἰδρύσασθαι; P. Lond. VI 1912, 2.34) 'to set up'. This alternation, which in Greek is rare and only appears as a conditioned change in several classical dialects in which the value /u/ had been kept and was noted by means of <υ>,⁴¹ could be explained as an approximate spelling of /y/ by means of <o>. Two factors might have contributed to the under-differentiation: the vicinity of the vibrant consonant and the accent.

(o) Alternation of <υ> and <οι>, both before a vowel and before a consonant, is frequent in the documents from Nemesion's archive studied: <υ> instead of <οι>: P.Lond. VI 1012, 2.20, 4.61, 4.64 ὑ (l. οἱ) 'the' (article), 4.72 δέυ (l. δέοι) 'it should be right', 4.81 ὗον (l. οἷόν) 'of which sort', 4.87 ὗς (l. οἷς) 'which'; <οι> instead of <υ>: 5.86 λοιμένωνται (l. λυμαίνωνται) 'they are disrespectful' (subjunctive). Interchanges, which appear in various phonetic contexts from the first century CE in papyri from Egypt, and only later before a consonant in other parts of the Greek-speaking world,⁴² show that both spellings represent a single phoneme. According to the literature, this spelling alternation in documents written in Koine indicates that the phoneme represented by <υ> and <οι> is /y/. However, the spelling alternations of <ι> and <υ> (see (m) above) and of <η> and <υ> (see (p) below) found in our documents from Nemesion's archive seem to imply that <υ> in Nemesion's pronunciation stands for /i/ at least in some contexts, which would indicate that also in this

---

38 The infinitive ἀφιδρῦσε (l. ἀφιδρῦσαι) 'to set up' with ι corrected from υ appears in the same document (3.45). συνοίσει 'it will be useful' (from συμφέρω) is corrected from σινοισει in 4.69–70.
39 See Teodorsson (1978: 73–74), Threatte (1980: 261).
40 See Gignac (1976: 273).
41 Gignac (1976: 293–294), Threatte (1980: 217–218).
42 See Gignac (1976: 197), Threatte (1980: 323–324).

context <οι> and <υ> may represent /i/. The identification of /y/ and /i/ as /i/ in Nemesion's pronunciation would precede by several centuries[43] that which eventually spread to all Greek speakers in the ninth century CE. The earlier merger of /oi/ and /y/ into /i/ in the Nemesion's documents could be a result of interference from Egyptian, which lacked the phoneme /y/. As pointed out above, the phonological system of Egyptian lacked the close front rounded vowel /y(:)/, as shown by the fact that the Coptic grapheme corresponding to <υ> only appears in Greek loanwords.[44]

(p) η instead of υ: P.Lond. VI 1912, 2.28, 5.106 ἡμῶν (l. ὑμῶν) 'you' (genitive case), 2.33 ἡμετέρας (l. ὑμετέρας) 'your', 4.65 ἡμεῖν (l. ὑμῖν) 'you' (dative case), 4.75 ἡμετέρων (l. ὑμετέρων) 'your'; <υ> instead of <η>: 5.104 ὑμῖν (l. ἡμῖν, corr. ex υμων) 'to us'. It is generally held that /y/ concluded its evolution into /i/ in the ninth century CE and that in earlier Koine <υ> thus stands for the phoneme /y/, such as in Attic[45] and Ptolemaic papyri.[46] According to Gignac (1976: 267), examples of spelling alternations of <υ> and <η> are more frequent in the Byzantine period than in the Roman Empire. This seems to indicate that confusion of /y/ with /i/ spread during the Byzantine Empire. Spelling alternations between <υ> and <η> in some documents from the Roman Empire era thus represent /i/, which might be attributed to assimilation from the following labial nasal and to the pretonic position of the vowel.[47] Such assimilation is rare in Greek and is probably caused by bilingual interference. As described above, the Egyptian phonological system lacked /y/ and <η> was restricted to accented syllables. The hypothesis that <η> and <υ> stand for /i/ in the documents from Nemesion's archive studied raises the following issue: if the graphemes <η, ι, οι> stand for /i/, one would expect interchanges of <η> and <ι> and of <οι> and <ι>, but this doesn't occur. The absence of examples of such variations may indicate that the graphemes <η> and <οι> stand for /i/ only under certain conditions (see (w) below). It is significant that <η> appears in lieu of <υ> only in pretonic syllables and before a bilabial nasal, because the Coptic grapheme corresponding to Greek <η> occurred only in accented syllables.[48] Furthermore, it is likely that the spelling <η> reflected a more open vowel than /i/, because <η> alternates with <ε> and <αι> in the documents considered (see (g) and (w) below), but not with <i>.

---

43 See Threatte (1980: 337–338).
44 See Gignac (1976: 267), Horrocks (2010: 112).
45 See Teodorsson (1978: 73–74), Threatte (1980: 267).
46 See Teodorsson (1977: 225–226).
47 Horrocks (2010: 118–119).
48 See Gignac (1976: 242).

(q) <ηω> instead of <ειω>: πλήωι (P.Lond. VI 1912, 5.89; l. πλήω) 'more'. The interchange of <ηω> and <ειω> occurs frequently in all phonetic conditions throughout the Roman and Byzantine periods,[49] although in our documents it only appears in the example cited. The spelling <ηω> instead of <ειω> also appears in Attic inscriptions contemporaneous with the documents from Nemesion's archive studied. Threatte (1980: 205)[50] interprets the variant grapheme as "good evidence that ει has remained a long e-vowel in prevocalic position in contrast to its alteration to [i:] elsewhere". This variant spelling seems to be a result of an evolution of the Koine in general.

(r) Omission of a vowel between consonants occurs in ἐπακλουθῆσαι (l. ἐπακολουθῆσαι; P.Mich. X 582, 2.22) 'to accrue'. This spelling is more common in Egypt than in other Greek-speaking areas, and may likely be attributed to the more popular register that is attested particularly in Egyptian papyri and to bilingual interference from the heavy stress accent of the Egyptian language.[51] Coptic shows a strong tendency towards vowel reduction or loss in unstressed syllables,[52] though a Greek internal cause for the omission of unstressed <o> cannot be ruled out.

(s) Unstressed <α> instead of <ω>: ανατατωι (l. ἀνωτάτω, corr. ex ανατωτωι; P.Lond. VI 1912, 5.103) 'most upwards'. This change is also attested outside of Egypt, especially in association with liquids, but less frequently and interpreted as a purely graphic error.[53] This suggests that the change in Nemesion's papyrus might be due to under-differentiation of unaccented phonemes caused by bilingual interference.[54] In Coptic, some vowels in unaccented syllables partially neutralized the timbre and were pronounced /ə/.

(t) Unstressed <ε> instead of <α>: τέσσαρες for τέσσαρας (P.Mich. X 582, 2.9) 'four'.[55] Interchanges of α and ε occur frequently, especially before /r/.[56] This spelling alternation also appears outside of Egypt,[57] but nowhere else is it as frequent or as unrestricted to particular phonetic contexts or lexical elements. For some time now, bilingual interference has been posited as an explanation

---

49 See Gignac (1976: 239–247).
50 See also Teodorsson (1977: 219), Horrocks (2010: 168).
51 See Gignac (1976: 306).
52 Allen (2013: 13).
53 See Threatte (1980: 130).
54 Gignac (1976: 288–289).
55 P.Lond. VI 1912, 2.23 ὑπάρχοντες (corr. ex υπαρχοντας) 'being' may be due to syntactic causes. Note δει' ἒ̓ δῖ (l. δι' ἃ δεῖ) 'for these reasons it is necessary' in a letter written by Nemesion (P.Mich. XII 656, 8).
56 See Gignac (1976: 278).
57 See Threatte (1980: 120–130).

for this frequency, especially in accented syllables. The spelling alternation likely reflects the reduction of the vowel in an unaccented syllable to /ə/.[58]

(u) Unstressed <o> instead of <ε>: σπουδασθέντος (l. σπουδασθέντες; P.Lond. VI 1912, 2.25) 'being the object of my eagerness'.[59] This change also appears in Attic inscriptions,[60] but less often than in papyri, where it usually occurs when <o> precedes a /s/ or /n/, suggesting that the sound represented by /o/ was of the sort /ə/. The confusion is caused by bilingual interference, as in Coptic <o> only occurred in stressed syllables.[61]

(v) <υ> instead of <ε>: Θύωνι (Hanson; Θυωνί PN) instead of Θέωνι (SB XX 14526 = P.Princ. III 152, 2.31) 'Theon'. This alternation is rare in Attic inscriptions.[62] Gignac (1976: 273–274) states that "examples in accented syllables occur almost exclusively before a back vowel, a nasal, or /s/, in which positions there was also an interchange of ε with ι and ει". Such examples suggest that the vowel was unstressed and pronounced /ə/ or that <υ> stands for /i/ (see (m) above). Interference from Egyptian is possible.

(w) Unstressed <η> or <ε> instead of <αι>: συνερεμα and συνηρεματο (l. συναιρέμα(τος)) (SB XX 14576 = P.Princ. I 13, v,3,27, v,9,216, v,19,529) 'total'. In contrast with the documents here considered, the grapheme η frequently alternates with /i/[63] suggesting that the sound originally represented by <η> merged with /i/ by the second century CE. Nevertheless, "the interchange of η and ε is commonly found in documents showing other evidence of bilingual interference" (Gignac 1976: 249).

(x) The spelling <κθ> instead of χθ in P.Lond. VI 1912, 4.65 προσενεκθήσονται, 5.92 ἐπράκθη and P.Mich. X 582, 2.4 ἀκθίς (l. ἀχθείς) poses a difficult question.[64] The spelling <πθ> (e.g. ἀπθόνων, l. ἀφθόνων) is attested in other papyri, but not in the four documents taken into account in this chapter. The traditional view in Greek grammar is that the first of two aspirates lost its aspiration and became the corresponding voiceless stop, as suggested by spellings such as ἐκθρός in dialects, Latin transcriptions as *dipthongus* and

---

58 See Gignac (1976: 285).
59 A syntactic reason for the interchange is unlikely as the participle in passive voice is coordinated with the participle of the same verb in active voice: καὶ σπουδάσαντες καὶ σπουδασθέντος 'being eager about my house and being the object of my eagerness'.
60 See Threatte (1980: 214–217).
61 See Gignac (1976: 291–292).
62 See Threatte (1980: 267).
63 See Gignac (1976: 235–242).
64 Another papyrus (P.Graux II 9, dated to after 33 CE) which was probably written by Nemesion attests παρεπράκθημεν instead of παρεπράχθημεν 'we were wrongly charged' and βυβλιοφύλακος, -ι instead of βιβλιοφύλακος, -ι 'keeper of archives' (see (m) above and fn. 16).

Coptic ἀπθαρτος.⁶⁵ Gignac (1976: 86) and Teodorsson (1977: 238–243) accept this view. However, the most prevalent hypothesis at present holds that the inherited Greek aspirates had developed into spirants by the time the documents studied were written. This leads us to assume that the spellings <κθ> and <πθ> do not reflect the ancient values that the graphemes <π, τ, κ> and <φ, θ, χ> originally had in Greek as not aspirated and aspirated voiceless plosives, but rather an internal development of Egyptian Greek in the context of two spirants in contact with each other. This internal development of Greek may have been reinforced by the Egyptian language of the time.⁶⁶ Excluding the Bohairic variety, which may have differed from the other dialects,⁶⁷ the Coptic graphemes that correspond to the Greek consonants <φ, θ, χ> were realized as voiceless or as aspirated depending on their environment, or were used as monograms for the sequences /ph, th, kh/, respectively.⁶⁸ In other words, voiceless stops in most dialects of Egyptian were aspirated or unaspirated depending on the environment. The variations observed in the representation of the first consonant of the sequence in the documents considered in this chapter might reflect a phonetic distribution. According to Gignac (1976: 95), "the unconditioned interchange of aspirated and voiceless stops is caused by bilingual interference".

4.4 Etymological writing and morphological shifts

The last group of graphic interchanges in the documents considered seems to lack phonetic relevance:
(y) The spelling <χιι> instead of <χι> in ἀρχιερεύς and ἀρχιερέα (P.Lond. VI 1912, 2.14, 3.48) 'Pontifex' seems to be an etymological spelling that distinguishes the two elements that make up the compound word. If this is the case, the grapheme has no phonetic relevance. An alternative possibility is that <χι> indicates the palatal pronunciation of <χ> (see 4.1 (b) above).
(z) It is highly unlikely that the spelling <ν> before a velar stop instead of -γκ- in ἀνανκαῖον 'necessary', ἐξελένξαι 'to put to the proof' and ἀνανκασθήσομε (1. ἀναγκασθήσομαι) 'I shall be forced' (P.Lond. VI 1912, 1.6, 4.77, 5.98) and ἐπανανκάσαι (P.Mich. X 582, 2.17) 'to compel', as well as in ἐνπόρῳ (SB XX 14526 = P.Princ. III 152, 2.17; l. ἐμπόρῳ) 'trader' instead of -μπ- in

---
65 See Schwyzer (1939: 210–211), Threatte (1980: 570–571).
66 Horrocks (2010: 112).
67 Loprieno (1997: 447), Allen (2013: 18).
68 Loprieno (1995: 34).

simple words, represents dissimilation of the velar nasal /ŋ/ before a velar stop or of the labial nasal before a bilabial stop. Rather, the spelling <ν> almost certainly results from analogy with environments in which <ν> is written without assimilation, such as when it is in word-final position (e.g. φυλὴν Κλαυδιανὰν 'Claudian tribe' in P.Lond. VI 1912, 3.41) or in compounds, as in συνχωρῶι 'I agree' (P.Lond. VI 1912, 2.32 and 3.46) and ἐνπόρῳ.[69]

The omission of unstressed <o> in the sequence <Vo> is limited to personal names in our documents: Κλαύδις (P.Lond. VI 1912, 1.19)[70] 'Claudius', Ἀπολλώνις (P.Lond. VI 1912, 1.19, 2.16) 'Apollonios'. The abbreviated form in –ις instead of –ιος for personal names is a morphological and lexical feature rooted in the tendency of personal names to be shortened. The feature has no phonetic significance.[71]

5 Register, idiolect, geographical dialect or sociolect?

As to the question of whether the spellings of the four documents considered reflect a register, an idiolect, a geographical dialect or a sociolect, it seems most likely that they represent a sociolect.

Although the four documents that we have considered differ in that those containing lists of taxpayers provide very few examples of spellings not retained in later Greek, it is unlikely that Nemesion's pronunciation was influenced by the register of the documents. The differences between the documents are content-dependent rather than register-dependent. Documents that consist of lists of personal names and sums and use abbreviations show hardly any graphic variations offering clues as to pronunciation.

---

69 See Gignac (1976: 172). In other contexts and registers, the spelling <ν> cannot be explained as standing for a nasal whose place of articulation is unspecified. Rather, it reflects "a form of lento speech characterized by artificial intersyllabic pauses", a feature which is common in "dictation style" (Méndez Dosuna 1993: 97–99; 2017: 374–375). This explanation accounts for the fact that <ν> was the only nasal permitted before a pause in Greek, and hence word-finally in words that were not borrowings from a foreign language.
70 Κλαύδιος is used to refer to the Emperor several times and to other envoys from the Alexandrians.
71 See Gignac (1981: 25–29). ἑκατασ\σ/ταχοῦ for ἑκασταχοῦ 'everywhere' (P.Lond. VI 1912, 2.31) is a purely graphic mistake.

The graphic variations found in other documents belonging to Nemesion's archive show that the four documents considered do not reflect a personal idiolect. Documents in his archive written by someone other than Nemesion attest sound changes that did not crystallize in later Greek, as well as pronunciations like those of Egyptian. Despite its brevity, the letter from Thermouthis (SB XIV 11585; dated to July 7th, 59 CE), who was Nemesion's wife, provides two examples of interchange between unstressed <α> and <ε> (άπανο for ἐπάνω 'some time ago' and στ[α]τῆρες for στατῆρας 'staters') which parallel those described in 4.3 (t) above, and one example of stressed <ου> for <ῳ> (αὐτοῦ for αὐτῷ 'to him'), an interchange unattested in the four documents analysed and rare elsewhere in Greek, but paralleled in Greek loanwords in Coptic and explained by Gignac (1976: 213–214) as being rooted in bilingual interference. If such deviant spellings have phonological relevance, they would attest to sound shifts not retained in later Greek and may therefore be the result of Egyptian interference.[72]

The documents written in Nemesion's hand do not represent a geographical dialect either, as other papyri belonging to his archive written by other people based in Philadelphia only attest spellings that evidence developments that were retained in subsequent stages of Greek and they do not reveal sound changes that point to interference from Egyptian. This is the case with two documents written by Herakleides, secretary of the village of Philadelphia during Nemesion's time. In a letter dated to the reign of Claudius (41–54 CE), Herakleides asks Nemesion to lend his support to six men whose names he gives and to some of their associates until he returns from a place where he has been retained by many pending matters (SB XIV 12143). The letter shows spellings attesting to various kinds of iotacism, but no example of the graphic deviations listed in Section 4.2–3 above. A note sent by the same Herakleides to Ammonius, *strategós* of the divisions of Herakleides and Polemon, which contains a list of capitation tax collectors (P.Gen. II 91, dated to 50/51 CE), is along the same lines.

---

72 Thermoutis' letter also attests the following graphic interchanges that are not attested in the four documents studied written by Nemesion himself: η instead of ι (γηνόσκειν for γιγνώσκειν 'to know'), ε for η (παραμεμένεκε for παραμεμένηκε 'is still in place'), and ε for η (ἔτησο for ᾐτήσω 'you asked'). In addition, Thermouthis' letter attests the following deviant spellings, which are also found in one or more of our four documents: ε for αι (καταβένις for καταβαίνεις 'you come down'); ει for ι or vice versa (ὄτει for ὄτι 'that', ἥκι for ἥκει 'has come'); ο for ω (θέλο for θέλω 'I want'); υ for οι (πυμένον for ποιμένων 'shepherds' twice); and probably morphological omission of unstressed /o/ in Λουκις 'Lucius'. Nemesion's wife's name is spelled Θερμοῦθις by herself (SB XIV 11585), but Θερμουτις by the sender of a letter to Nemesion (P. Graux II 10).

However, spellings that illustrate sound shifts not retained in later Greek are also found in papyri written in other parts of the Fayum and elsewhere in Egypt.[73] To cite a single example, P.Tebt. II 390 (167 CE?) contains an agreement between a certain Helene and three brothers with Egyptian names, to whom she lends a sum of money. The papyrus is written in four different hands. The first is Helena's and uses the traditional spelling of Greek. The second shows ἑκατέν for ἑκατόν 'hundred' (paralleled in §4.3 (u) above), δώκου for τόκου 'interest' and τημοσίων for δημοσίων 'taxes' (analogous to §4.2 (m) above), and ἀρουρων for ἄρουραν 'aroura of land' (similar to §4.3 (s) above). The third mistakes ἐγατόν for ἑκατόν (see §4.2 (m) above), and the fourth uses ἑκατέν for ἑκατόν like the second hand and τέσαρος for τέσσαρες 'four'.

Interpretation of some graphic variations as resulting from Egyptian interference does not presuppose that Nemesion was bilingual in Egyptian and Greek. Unfortunately, given that all the documents in Nemesion's archive are written in Greek, there are no clues in his archive that would enable us to determine whether he read and spoke Egyptian. The graphic interchanges are also compatible with the hypothesis that Nemesion's pronunciation of Greek was due to the influence of the Egyptian adstratum, even if he was not bilingual.[74] The most likely hypothesis, however, is that he was.[75]

6 Conclusions

The main conclusion that can be drawn from the above discussion of the graphic variations found in four documents written by Nemesion, a tax collector for Philadelphia in the first century CE, is that they evidence a number of features of an idiolect of Koine Greek characterized by a pronunciation with interferences from Egyptian. Nemesion was probably bilingual in Greek and Egyptian, and this was likely the source of such interferences, but we should

---

73 See Vierros (2012).
74 According to Hanson (1992: 136; 2001), only the verso of one papyrus in the archive (P.Thomas 5; see §2 above) contains "fourteen much effaced lines" in Demotic "without apparent connection to the text on the recto". Accordingly, there is no evidence indicating whether Nemesion could read and write Demotic.
75 If the word ταβούριος, attested only twice in Greek in P.Princ. III 152 (see §3.4. above), is a loanword from the Semitic root *tbn/tbr* with the meaning of 'hay' which was taken up by Nemesion in Greek, the implication would be that Nemesion could speak Egyptian. The word is used in relation to the farmer Theon, who receives a payment for having cut the fodder (Hanson 1992: 136).

not rule out the possibility that such interferences resulted from the influence of the Egyptian adstratum.

The following graphic variations that are found in the documents written by Nemesion are rarely witnessed in Greek outside of Egypt and lack of continuity in later Koine: the voiced stop <δ> occasionally alternates with the corresponding voiceless <τ>; the sequence <κθ> is used instead of the common <χθ>. With regard to the vocalic system, <υ> is occasionally used instead of <ι> in unaccented syllables; <ο> sometimes alternates with <υ> in accented syllables; <υ> interchanges with <οι> in accented and unaccented syllables and with <η> only in unaccented syllables; <α> alternates with <ω> and with <ε> in unaccented syllables; and <ε> alternates with <ο> in unaccented syllables.

Such graphic variations point to the Egyptian language. Nemesion identified the Greek voiced dental stop <δ> with the corresponding voiceless <τ>. As known, Egyptian lacked the voiced plosives /d/ and /g/ and the Coptic graphemes corresponding to Greek <δ> and <γ> are mainly used for Greek borrowings. Although there are no examples of graphic variations between <γ> and <κ> in the documents considered, it is plausible that Nemesion also pronounced the Greek voiced velar stop <γ> as a voiceless /k/, as the alternation of <γ> and <κ>, analogous to the existing alternation of <δ> and <τ>, is documented in other papyri which display similar graphic variations to those found in the documents from Nemesion's archive studied. It is also likely that the ancient aspirated plosives were pronounced by Nemesion as aspirated or as voiceless depending on the contexts. Nemesion also represented the Greek phoneme /y/, which didn't exist in Egyptian, with various spellings that depended in part on whether the vowel appeared in an accented or unaccented syllable, and he represented the Egyptian phoneme /ə/, which didn't exist in Greek, with various Greek graphemes.

Many of the graphic deviations found in the documents considered here are due to the fact that the Greek writing system had graphemes for phonemes that did not exist in Egyptian and lacked characters for phonemes that existed in Egyptian. The Coptic symbols corresponding with the Greek letters <δ>, <γ> and <υ> were used in Coptic only for Greek loanwords. This indicates that the phonemes /d/, /g/ and /y/ didn't exist in Egyptian. On the contrary, the Egyptian language had a phoneme /ə/ in unstressed syllables which the Greek lacked.

The features of Nemesion's pronunciation of Greek that have been ascertained may represent not a mere idiolect but rather a sociolect shared with other speakers, who were probably bilingual in Greek and Egyptian, as documentary papyri written by other people at various times, both nearby and in other parts of Egypt, evidence similar clusters of deviant spellings, suggesting a similar pronunciation of Greek characterized by the interference from Egyptian.

References

Allen, James P. 2013. *The Ancient Egyptian language: An historical study*. Cambridge: Cambridge University Press.
Bagnall, Roger S. 2011. *The Oxford Handbook of Papyrology*. Oxford: Oxford University Press.
Clarysse, Willy. 2015. Nemesion son of Zoilos. In Katelijn Vandorpe, Willy Clarysse & Herbert Verreth (eds.), *Graeco-Roman archives from the Fayum*, 256–258. Leuven: Peeters.
Crespo, Emilio. 2018. The softening of obstruent consonants in Macedonian. In Georgios K. Giannakis, Emilio Crespo & Panagiotis Filos (eds.), *Studies in Ancient Greek dialects: From Central Greece to the Black Sea*, 329–348. Berlin: de Gruyter.
Depauw, Mark & Joanne Vera Stolk. 2015. Linguistic variation in Greek papyri: Towards a new tool for quantitative study. *Greek, Roman & Byzantine Studies* 55. 196–220.
Gignac, Francis T. 1976. *A grammar of the Greek papyri of the Roman and Byzantine periods*. Vol. 1: *Phonology*. Milano: La Goliardica.
Gignac, Francis T. 1981. *A grammar of the Greek papyri of the Roman and Byzantine periods*. Vol. 2: *Morphology*. Milano: La Goliardica.
Hanson, Ann Ellis. 1974. Lists of taxpayers from Philadelphia (P.Mich.inv. 879 and P. Princ. I 14). *Zeitschrift für Papyrologie und Epigraphik* 15. 229–238.
Hanson, Ann Ellis. 1979. Documents from Philadelphia drawn from the census register. In Jean Bingen & Georges Nachtergael (eds.), *Actes du XV Congres International de Papyrologie, Bruxelles – Louvain, 29 août – 3 septembre 1977*, vol. II: *Papyrus inédites*, 60–74. Bruxelles: Fondation égyptologique Reine Élisabeth.
Hanson, Ann Ellis. 1990. P. Princeton I 13: Text and context revised. In Mario Capasso, Gabriella Messeri Savorelli & Rosario Pintaudi (eds.), *Miscellanea papyrologica in occasione del bicentenario dell'edizione della Charta Borgiana*, vol. I, 259–283. Firenze: Gonelli.
Hanson, Ann Ellis. 1992. Egyptians, Romans, *ARABES* and *IOUDAIOI* in the first century A.D. tax archive from Philadelphia: P. Mich. inv. 880 recto and P. Princ. III. 152 revised. In Janet H. Johnson (ed.), *Life in a multicultural society: Egypt from Cambyses to Constantine and beyond*, 133–148. Chicago: Oriental Institute of the University of Chicago.
Hanson, Ann Ellis. 1994. Topographical arrangement of tax documents in the Philadelphia tax archive. In Adam Bülow Jacobsen (ed.), *Proceedings of the 20th International Congress of Papyrologists, Copenhagen, 23–29 August 1992*, 210–218. Copenhagen: Museum Tusculanum Pess.
Hanson, Ann Ellis. 2001. Sworn declaration to agents from the centurion Cattius Catullus: P.Col. inv. 90. In Traianos Gagos & Roger S. Bagnall (eds.), *Essays and texts in Honor of J. David Thomas*, 91–97. Oakville: American Society of Papyrologists.
Hanson, Ann Ellis. 2010. Revisions for P. Mich. X 578 (census list). In Traianos Gagos & Adam Hyatt (eds.), *Proceedings of the 25th International Congress of Papyrology, Ann Arbor, 29 July – 4 August 2007*, 307–312. Ann Arbor: Scholarly Publishing Office, University of Michigan Library.
Hanson, Ann Ellis. 2015. Papyri and efforts by adults in Egyptian villages to write Greek. In Elizabeth P. Archibald, William Brockliss & Jonathan Gnoza (eds.), *Learning Latin and Greek from Antiquity to the present*, 10–29. Cambridge: Cambridge University Press.
Harker, Andrew. 2008. *Loyalty and dissidence in Roman Egypt: The case of the Acta Alexandrinorum*. Cambridge: Cambrige University Press.

Hatzopoulos, Miltiades B. 2018. Recent research in the Ancient Macedonian dialect: Consolidation and new perspectives. In Georgios K. Giannakis, Emilio Crespo & Panagiotis Filos (eds.), *Studies in Ancient Greek dialects: From Central Greece to the Black Sea*, 299–328. Berlin: de Gruyter.
Horrocks, Geoffrey C. 2010. *Greek: A history of the language and its speakers*, 2nd ed. Malden: Wiley-Blackwell.
Loprieno, Antonio. 1995. *Ancient Egyptian: A linguistic introduction*. Cambridge: Cambridge University Press.
Loprieno, Antonio. 1997. Egyptian and Coptic phonology. In Alan S. Kaye (ed.), *Phonologies of Asia and Africa including the Caucasus*, vol. 1, 431–460. Winona Lake: Eisenbrauns.
Méndez Dosuna, Julián. 1993. Los griegos y la realidad psicológica del fonema: κ y ϙ en los alfabetos arcaicos. *Kadmos* 32. 96–126.
Méndez Dosuna, Julián. 2014. Macedonian. *EAGLL* 2.392–397.
Méndez Dosuna, Julián. 2017. Once again on allophonic spellings in Ancient Greek. In Ivo Hajnal, Daniel Kölligan & Katharina Zipser (eds.), *Miscellanea Indogermanica: Festschrift für José Luis García Ramón zum 65. Geburtstag*, 487–498. Innsbruck: Institut für Sprachen und Literaturen der Universität Innsbruck, Bereich Sprachwissenschaft.
Oates, John F. 1976. Census totals: Nemesion's notes. In Ann Ellis Hanson (ed.), *Collectanea papyrologica: Texts published in honor of Herbert C. Youtie*, 189–196. Bonn: Habelt.
Oates, John F. 1978. More of Nemesion's notes: P. Corn. inv. 18. *Illinois Classical Studies* 3. 81–89.
Peust, Carsten. 1999. *Egyptian phonology: An introduction to the phonology of a dead language*. Göttingen: Peust und Guttschmidt.
Schwyzer, Eduard. 1939. *Griechische Grammatik: Auf der Grundlage von Karl Brugmanns Griechischer Grammatik*. Bd. I. *Allgemeiner Teil, Lautlehre, Wortbildung, Flexion*. München: Beck.
Stolk, Joanne Vera. 2019. Itacism from Zenon to Dioscoros: Scribal corrections of ‹ι› and ‹ει› in Greek papyri. In Sofía Torallas Tovar, Alberto Nodar, María Jesús Albarrán, Raquel Martín, Irene Pajón, José Domíngo Rodríguez, Marco Antonio Santamaría & Amalia Zomeño (eds.), *Proceedings of the 28th Congress of Papyrology, Barcelona, 1–6 August 2016*, 690–697. Barcelona: Publicacions de l'Abadia de Monstserrat, Universitat Pompeu Fabra.
Teodorsson, Sven-Tage. 1977. *The phonology of Ptolemaic Koine*. Göteborg: Acta Universitatis Gothoburgensis.
Teodorsson, Sven-Tage. 1978. *The phonology of Attic in the Hellenistic period*. Göteborg: Acta Universitatis Gothoburgensis.
Threatte, Leslie. 1980. *The grammar of Attic inscriptions*. Vol. 1: *Phonology*. Berlin: de Gruyter.
Vierros, Marja. 2012. *Bilingual notaries in Hellenistic Egypt: A study of Greek as a second language*. Brussel: Koninklijke Vlaamse Akademie van België voor Wetenschappen en Kunsten.
Vierros, Marja. 2014. Bilingualism in Hellenistic Egypt. *EAGLL* 1.234–238.
Youtie, Herbert C. 1977. P. Mich. Inv. 855: Letter from Herakleides to Nemesion. *Zeitschrift für Papyrologie und Epigraphik* 27. 147–150.

Julie Boeten
14 Metrical variation in Byzantine colophons (XI–XV CE): The example of ἡ μὲν χεὶρ ἡ γράψασα

Abstract: In this chapter, several metrical varieties in a corpus of Byzantine book epigrams are explored. More specifically, we look into a number of varieties in metrical colophons of the type ἡ μὲν χεὶρ ἡ γράψασα 'the hand that wrote [this]', which was a very popular colophon throughout the entire Byzantine period. In its canonical form, these epigrams follow a dodecasyllabic metrical pattern, but many scribes freely experimented with the wording and the metrical structure of these colophons, which gives us a unique insight into the mechanics behind the colometrics of these texts and, by expansion, of Byzantine texts in general. The modern cognitive-linguistic theory of Information Units provides a fitting framework to interpret these varieties and to see them in a way that is different from the traditional reading of written texts. Indeed, the specific characteristics of these texts allow us to attribute certain oral characteristics to them, while still maintaining their written status. From this point of view, multiple reoccurring "mistakes" in the metre turn out to be varieties in disguise, originating from a wrongful pairing of correct metrical units (cola).

1 Introduction: Metrical colophons

In this paper, I will investigate the varieties to be found in Byzantine colophons, and more specifically the metrical varieties therein. Even though these texts display a number of interesting linguistic features – most notably orthographical and morphological varieties – this chapter will focus solely on the metre. Indeed, the metre of Byzantine colophons and/or epigrams has not been studied before, even though this may provide new insight into the use and perception of metre in Byzantine texts in general, because of the *ad hoc* character of many of these texts. I will investigate this by means of a closer inspection of the varieties in one specific case study, the ἡ μὲν χείρ-colophons, within the framework of the linguistic theory of Information Units and the concept of metrical pairing (or ταίρισμα).

A modern definition of a colophon is "an inscription at the end of a book or manuscript usually with facts about its production" (Kleinedler *et al.* 2005: 227). In a more Byzantine context, it can be defined as a brief statement, usually at the beginning or end of the main text, containing information about the production of the manuscript, such as the scriptorium where it was copied, the patron who ordered the manuscript, the date of the production, the scribe who copied the manuscript etc. Colophons can sometimes also be book epigrams, but this is not necessarily so. Book epigrams are inscriptions "in and on books" (Kominis 1966: 38), with a clear connection to manuscript production[1] and with the main characteristic of being written in verse, i.e. in metre. The case study of this paper stands at the crossroad between a colophon and a book epigram, since it is both at once. It contains information about the scribe and the production of the manuscript, but it is also a poem and is therefore written in verse. A more correct way of referring to it may therefore be "metrical colophon".

Byzantine colophons are very often metrical – much more often than they are in western, Latin manuscripts.[2] This tendency for metrical texts is not only noticeable in manuscripts, but also in other inscriptions that are scattered throughout the Byzantine world, since Byzantines had the custom to inscribe everything that had some importance to them with a text in verses.[3] Paul Magdalino touches upon this when he speaks of the "Byzantine epigrammatic habit" (Magdalino 2012:32). But why did the Byzantines bother with this metricality so much that even hardly literate scribes produced (or attempted to produce) verses?

Through the investigation of the metre in our case study, I hope to provide an answer to this question – or at the least to give a clearer and deeper insight into the production of Greek metrical texts in the Middle Ages.

2 The case study

Many Byzantine colophons circulated in the form of pre-set verses, on which scribes relied to produce their own version of the colophon. These were not set in stone, but could be varied upon elaborately. Two popular examples of such adaptable colophons are the following ones:

(1a) ὥσπερ ξένοι χαίρουσιν ἰδ(εῖν) πατρίδα,
οὕτω καὶ οἱ γράφοντες βιβλίου τέλος.

---

1 Lauxtermann (2003: 197).
2 Bernard & Demoen (2019).
3 Bernard & Demoen (2019).

'Just like strangers rejoice in seeing their fatherland,
so do writers in seeing the end of the book.'[4]
(DBBE 3004 [Firenze - Bibl. Medicea Laurenziana - Plut. 86, Cod. 7, f. 217v]; XII CE)[5]

(1b) Θεοῦ τὸ δῶρον καὶ Ἰωάννου πόνος.

'The present is God's and the toil is John's.'
(DBBE 4165 [Athos - Monê Megistês Lauras
Λ 122 (Eustratiades 1613), f. 16v]; XV CE)

Our case study is another popular and frequently used example of such a colophon. In its most basic form, it looks like this:

(1c) ἡ μὲν χεὶρ ἡ γράψασα σήπεται τάφω,
γράφη δε μένει εἰς πληρεστάτους χρόνους.

'The hand that wrote this rots in a grave,
But the writing remains until the end of time.'
(DBBE 2456 [Athos - Monê Batopediou 1486, f. 299r]; 1291 CE)

In the *Database of Byzantine Book Epigrams*, sixty occurrences[6] of this type have been collected today, but this number will most likely grow in the future, as the *DBBE* is a work in progress. Of course, not all texts that were produced in medieval times are still available for us today, and this number suggests that the formula was quite widely spread in the Byzantine world. Moreover, the exact same formula occurs in Syriac and Arabic manuscripts (McCollum 2015), indicating its wide popularity even across the boundaries of language and culture. The colophon must therefore have been very well known to anyone who had anything to do with manuscripts. This was presumably enhanced by the fact that these metrical colophons had no or little connection to the main texts of the manuscript and could thus easily migrate from manuscript to manuscript and from scribe to scribe.

---

4 All translations are my own.
5 All DBBE-numbers used in this chapter refer to the number of the occurrence in the DBBE. The database distinguishes between "occurrences" and "types", with the occurrences being the exact reproduction of the text as it is found in the manuscript, with all peculiarities and punctuations kept intact, while the types are a sort of hyper-texts, collecting identical or near-identical occurrences into one, normalised text (Bernard & Demoen 2019). This paper will only deal with the occurrences, that is, with the faithful reproductions of the manuscript texts.
6 In this paper, the term "occurrence" is used in the technical meaning, in the way it is employed in the DBBE, contrasted with the term "type" (cf. fn. 2).

A well-known epigram like this typically exhibits a wealth of variation (lexical, orthographical, grammatical and metrical) in its numerous occurrences. This great variety is tightly connected to the wide circulation of the colophon. As was mentioned, our case study must have been quite well known, which means that most scribes must have had some kind of blueprint of what the text looked like in the back of their minds. They knew the standard shape of the epigram and usually produced their own version of it from memory, rather than copying it from parchment. The vast amount of variation in the occurrences can only be explained through this assumption. Christine Thomas has studied something similar in her study on the *Acts of Peter* and she has called these texts "fluid texts" (Thomas 2003). She notes that they behave "similarly to oral tradition, with each manuscript representing a new 'performance' of the work in another context. Yet this occurs on the level of written text" (Thomas 2003: 40). Peter Van Nuffelen has also described the excerpts of John of Antioch in these terms. He calls them "living texts" in that "they could often be rewritten and adapted to new needs" (Van Nuffelen 2012: 446). These texts are thus primarily written, but they exhibit certain characteristics of oral texts in the variation that they display. This variation is often dispelled as being mere mistakes made by scribes who were hardly literate or simply ignorant. In this paper, I aim to refute this and prove that we are dealing with variants rather than mistakes.

3 The dodecasyllable

The metre of our case study is the very popular dodecasyllable, which – as its name suggests – consists of twelve-syllable verses. This is a typically medieval, Byzantine metre, since it is isosyllabic[7] and thus no longer (primarily) focuses on the length of syllables, but rather on the number of syllables.[8] This is in contrast to the hexameter or elegiac, which are still used in Byzantine times, but

---

[7] This refers to metres that are composed of an equal amount of syllables in each verse.
[8] Some dodecasyllables still maintain the old prosodic rules of the iambic trimeter (with some adaptations), which suggests that the scribe in these cases had enjoyed a thorough education. The difference between long and short syllables had long been lost to the Byzantine ear, which means that the rules for each syllable had to be learned by heart. However, the rules of prosody were not always heeded and are in most cases not the most prominent feature of the dodecasyllable. It is therefore first and foremost an isosyllabic metre.

only in a very artificial way and only by the more educated scribes. A similarly isosyllabic metre of Byzantine times is the political verse (πολιτικὸς στίχος).

In the isosyllabic metres, a very important, if not fundamental, feature is the caesura or breathing pause.[9] In the dodecasyllable this occurs after either five or seven syllables, in the political verse after eight syllables. This caesura subdivides the verse into two (or sometimes more) verse-halves or metrical cola. The caesura must be conceived as being a pause in pronunciation, thus giving these metrical cola a distinct intonational character. As such, the cola are circumvented by two pauses and form one intonational whole. They do not only have intonational features, but they have also been shown to function in the same way as so-called "information units" of Cognitive Linguistics.[10]

Wallace Chafe is the main investigator of information units (henceforth IUs) in spoken English and the Native American languages.[11] He asserts that oral, spontaneous language is not produced in one long sequence or sentence, but is chopped up into smaller "chunks" of information. These chunks have been given all sorts of names in the literature, going from "sentence segment" (Janse 1991), "intonation groups" (Cruttenden 1997: 1) and "intonation(al) phrases" (Selkirk 1984) to "tone units" (Crystal 1975, Brazil 1997) and "tone groups" (Halliday 1985). Chafe often uses "intonation units" (Chafe 1987, 1988, 1993, 1998, 2001) as well, but for so-called dead languages the term "information units" is usually applied (Slings 1999: 2).[12] These units have an intonational unity, which often means that they are bracketed by pauses of different lengths, but they also have syntactic and semantic unity, which means that words that syntactically and/ or semantically belong together will usually be joined in one unit. They moreover function on a cognitive level, since they allow the speaker to cognitively structure what he is about to say, and at the same time enable the listener to process what is being said.

The metrical cola of Byzantine isosyllabic metres function very much in the same way. They allow the scribe to structure his verses and group syntactically/ semantically connected words together within one colon. Moreover, the audience, whether they were reading the text or listening to it being read, must have

---

9 Maas (1903) called this the "Binnenschluβ". The caesura in Byzantine metre must not be conceived of in exactly the same way as the caesura in ancient metre, because of the fundamentally different character of the metres, but we have retained the term "caesura" in this paper for reasons of simplicity and custom. In accordance with Maas' term "Binnenschluβ", however, the abbreviation "B" is often used to annotate the caesura, followed by the number of syllables preceding the caesura (e.g. "B7" stands for a caesura after the seventh syllable).
10 Boeten & Janse (2018).
11 Chafe (1976, 1980, 1987, 1993, 1994).
12 For more about the difference between 'intonation group' and 'information group', see Halliday & Greaves (2006).

benefitted from this structuring, since it allowed them to easily comprehend the content of these poems. This is presumably also the reason why the commatic style was so popular in Byzantine rhetorical texts.[13] It made the dodecasyllable and political verse very easy to produce, even for less literate scribes, since it resembled the natural way of speaking so much. This is very different from metres like the hexameter or the elegiac, which could only be produced by scribes who had enjoyed a more thorough education.

However, this is not to say that there do not exist high-brow dodecasyllables. High-brow dodecasyllables take the old prosodic rules of the iambic trimeter (from which the dodecasyllable emerged, Maas 1903, Rhoby 2011) into account and often use archaic wordings, much like hexametrical and elegiac epigrams do.[14] But whereas the Byzantine hexameter is by definition high-brow, the dodecasyllable can vary greatly from author to author and from text to text. Indeed, quite often dodecasyllabic epigrams do not exhibit any consciousness of prosody and display a variety of orthographical mistakes. These are low-brow dodecasyllables (that are however still very different from the vernacular texts in political verses) which were written by scribes who had enjoyed a less thorough education. The epigrams of our case study belong to this latter group, which makes them interesting to study from a linguistic and cognitive point of view.

4 The variation

Let us now take a closer look at the metrical deviations ("mistakes") in the different occurrences of our case study. At first glance, these texts have very little literary value, since no less than 60% (36 out of 60) of all occurrences of the ἡ μὲν χείρ-colophon contain metrical irregularities. As mentioned, however, I will show that they must not simply be considered mistakes, but rather be seen as variation in the low-brow dodecasyllable.

We find three large groups of irregularities in our case study that frequently recur, thus suggesting that we are not dealing with random mistakes but rather with some sort of pattern. The irregularities in question are octosyllables

---

[13] Valiavitcharska (2013). The commatic style entails a rather abrupt writing style, with small semantic units (κόμματα) being juxtaposed, in order to underline and highlight an antithesis or a parallellism.

[14] A good example of such a high-brow dodecasyllable is DBBE 5719 (ATHOS - Monê Ibêron 159, f. 64r). It contains words like μελωδέει and Δαμασκόθεν, which remind one of Homeric texts.

(eight-syllable verses), decasyllables (ten-syllable verses) and decatetrasyllables (fourteen-syllable verses). These deviating verses always occur on their own in an otherwise dodecasyllabic epigram. Our corpus contains one epigram with an octosyllable, five epigrams with a decasyllable, two more with both an octo- and a decasyllable, and six epigrams with a decatetrasyllable. Together they comprise 23% of all ἡ μὲν χείρ-occurrences. One might perhaps assume that these variants were each based on an early testimony where the mistake occurred once, which was then copied several times. However, as we have seen, evidence indicates that so-called fluid texts, such as our case study, were usually cited from memory (based on a rough knowledge of what the epigram should look like) rather than copied from parchment, which makes the automatic copying of an error less likely. Moreover, not one of the deviating lines is the same twice, meaning that each mistake is a new one. This is illustrated by the decasyllabic lines in our case study, which are cited below. As was mentioned, these are each irregular (decasyllabic) lines in an otherwise perfectly dodecasyllabic epigram, which are cited on their own here, but which are each part of a ἡ μὲν χείρ-occurrence:[15]

(2a) (. . .) γραφεὶ δὲ μένη· προς χρώνους πολλοῦς·

(DBBE 202 [Paris - BnF - gr. 375, f. 193r]; 1021 CE)

(2b) (. . .) Θεοδώρου λέγω δὶ καὶ αὐτην·
(. . .) τυρεὶ αὐτοῦς· ἐν ταίλοὶ αἰώνων· (. . .)

(DBBE 1129 [Vaticano - Biblioteca Apostolica Vaticana - Vat. gr. 1853, f. 124r]; 1173 CE)

(2c) (. . .) γραφὴ μόνιμος ἐστὶν ἐνθάδε:

(DBBE 1767 [Athos - Monê Xêropotamou 221, f. 201v]; 1329 CE)

(2d) (. . .) γραφῇ (δὲ) ἕως τέλους διαμένει

(DBBE 5301 [Sankt-Peterburg - Rossijskaja Nacional'naja biblioteka (RNB) - Ф. № 906 (Gr.) Gr. 71 (Granstrem 195), f. 169r]; 1020 CE)

(2e) (. . .) τί συνε περ(ὶ) σε κύψον βλέψον (. . .)

(DBBE 5305 [Meteora - Monè Metamorphoseos 84, f. 113v]; 1408 CE)

---

15 No translation has been provided of these verses, since it would make little sense trying to translate them isolated from their context.

(2f) (. . .) ἡ δὲ γραφὴ μένει εἰς αἰῶνας:-

(DBBE 5327 [Vaticano - Biblioteca Apostolica Vaticana - Vat. gr. 52, f. 212v]; 1415 CE)

(2g) (. . .) ἡ δὲ γραφὴ μένει εἰς αἰῶνας (. . .)

(DBBE 5362 [Venezia - Bibl. Naz. Marc. - gr. app. X 5, f. 124v]; 1394 CE)

Some verses resemble one another, but it is quite clear that they are in fact different lines and can never have been based on one and the same mistake by an earlier scribe. Did all of these separate scribes then make the same mistakes? Or were they in fact even meant to be metrical? These numbers are not even close to the original twelve syllables anymore, so one may wonder if we are not dealing with some sort of rhythmical prose here instead. But in fact, we can be certain that these are metrical verses, because of the rather consistent paroxytonic verse ending in these lines[16] and because the same numbers of syllables (8, 10, 14) keep on recurring, which would not be the case if we were dealing with rhythmical prose. Moreover, we even find the same colometrical divisions frequently coming back.

Three times, we see the colometry of 5 + 5 recurring in the decasyllable, as it is here in the second line of the epigram:

(3a) ἡ χεὶρ μὲν ἡ γράψασα σύπετε τάφω,
γραφεὶ δὲ μένη· ||[17]***προς χρώνους πολλοῦς·***

'The hand that wrote this rots in a grave,
But the writing remains for a long time.'
(DBBE 202 [Paris - BnF - gr. 375, f. 193r]; 1021 CE)[18]

Three times, we find a colometry of 6 + 4, as in the following example:

(3b) ἡ μὲν χεὶρ ἡ γράψασα σήπετ(αι) τάφω,
ἡ δὲ γραφὴ μένει || εἰς αἰῶνας:-

'The hand that wrote this rots in a grave,
But the writing remains for centuries.'
(DBBE 5327 [Vaticano - Biblioteca Apostolica Vaticana - Vat. gr. 52, f. 212v]; 1415 CE)[19]

---

16 A paroxytonic verse ending entails that the second-last syllable of each verse is accentuated. This is a consistent and typical rule in the dodecasyllable as well as in the political verse, and may therefore be considered a criterium to decide whether something is metrical or not.
17 The double vertical lines indicate the location of the caesura.
18 The other ones are: DBBE 1767 (Athos - Monê Xêropotamou 221, f. 201v) and DBBE 5305 (Meteora - Monè Metamorphoseos 84, f. 113v).
19 The other ones are: DBBE 1129 (Vaticano - Biblioteca Apostolica Vaticana - Vat. gr. 1853, f. 124r) and DBBE 5362 (Venezia - Bibl. Naz. Marc. - gr. app. X 5, f. 124v).

And twice, there is a colometry of 7 + 3:

(3c) Ἔγραψε ταυτ(α) χεῖρ μιχαῆλ (μον)αχ(οῦ)·
(καὶ) χεῖρ μὲν σίπετε τάφω·
γραφῇ (δὲ) ἕως τέλους || διαμένει

'The hand of the monk Michael wrote these things,
And his hand rots in a grave,
But the writing remains till the end.'
(DBBE 5301 [Sankt-Peterburg - Rossijskaja Nacional'naja biblioteka (RNB) - Ф. № 906 (Gr.) Gr. 71 (Granstrem 195), f. 169r]; 1020 CE)[20]

The decatetrasyllables, on the other hand, almost always have the caesura at B7, resulting in a colometry of 7 + 7:

(3d) Ἡ μὲν χεὶρ ἡ γράψασα τήνδε τὴν βίβλον
σαπήσεται φεῦ καὶ γενήσετ(αι) κόνις·
τάφω προσεγγίση τὲ· σωματο|φθόρω
ἡμεῖς δὲ ἅπαντ(ες), οἱ τοῦ χ(ριστο)ῦ μερίδος·
εὔχεσθε πρὸς κ(ύριο)ν || εὑρεῖν σφαλμάτ(ων) λύσι(ν)·
(. . .)

'The hand that wrote this book
Alas! will rot and will be dust
And will bring near the body-damning grave.
All of us who have part in Christ,
Let us pray to the lord in order to find salvation from our sins'
(. . .)
(DBBE 5319 [Paris - BnF - gr. 1553, f. 301r]; XV CE)[21]

There are two exceptions, however, where the colometry is 6 + 8.[22] The octosyllables do not have a clear caesura and were probably meant to be pronounced as one unity.

Despite the fact that these verses seem very incorrect, most of them are built up out of correct metrical cola. This has everything to do with what Peter Mackridge and Marc Lauxtermann have called "ταίρισμα" or the "principle of pairing" (Mackridge 1990, Lauxtermann 1999). This is a principle that explains the emergence of the medieval dodecasyllable and political verse as the result of the consistent pairing of shorter verse-types. In this scenario, the dodecasyllable has arisen

---

[20] The other one is: DBBE 1129 (Vaticano - Biblioteca Apostolica Vaticana - Vat. gr. 1853, f. 124r).
[21] The other ones are: DBBE 5321 (Sinai - Monè tès Hag. Aikaterinès - gr. 50, f. 163r), DBBE 5396 (PARIS - BnF - gr. 96, f. 264v), DBBE 5605 (Sankt-Peterburg - Rossijskaja Nacional'naja biblioteka (RNB) - Ф. № 906 (Gr.) Gr. 102 (Granstrem 427), f. 345v).
[22] DBBE 5338 (Vaticano - Biblioteca Apostolica Vaticana - Palat. gr. 159) and DBBE 5339 (Vaticano - Biblioteca Apostolica Vaticana - Palat. gr. 256).

from the pairing of a pentasyllable and a heptasyllable, and the political verse through the pairing of an octosyllable and a heptasyllable. Indeed, as we have seen, the caesura in the dodecasyllable is positioned either at B5 or at B7. This means that the metrical cola in the dodecasyllable are always a pentasyllabic colon and a heptasyllabic colon, in either order. The same goes for the political verse, where the caesura is positioned at B8. We must therefore assume that the pentasyllable, heptasyllable and octosyllable are the three correct and accepted cola in Byzantine isosyllabic metres.

If this is true, then there is in fact nothing wrong with the decasyllables that have a colometry of 5 + 5 and the decatetrasyllables with a colometry of 7 + 7. In fact, Lauxtermann (1999: 51) even mentions a ninth-century manuscript with a hymn that consists of paired heptasyllables, which suggests that the idea of pairing whichever metrical cola was indeed present in earlier Byzantine times and may therefore have survived into later centuries as well. Of course, we must not suppose these decasyllables and decatetrasyllables to be perfectly correct metres, since there are no epigrams written entirely in deca- or decatetrasyllables. However, they must not be done away with as simple ignorant mistakes either. Their frequent occurrence, not only in this formula but also in others,[23] suggests a new pattern, that is, simply of a different combination of these three traditional units.

So what about the verses with other colometrical divisions? Most of them can be explained in a very similar way, but through a more thorough analysis of the Byzantine caesura. Indeed, the main caesura in the dodecasyllable is either at B5 or B7, but Lauxtermann has briefly touched upon secondary pauses which he calls "diereses" (Lauxtermann 2018). These diereses[24] are not as strong as the main caesura, but must have been audible in pronunciation (at least in some cases) nonetheless. Lauxtermann situates a dieresis at B4 when the main caesura is at B7, and a dieresis at B8 when the main caesura is at B5. This results in a colometry of 4 + 3 + 5 and 5 + 3 + 4, respectively. Or in other words, the heptasyllable can be split up into a trisyllable and a tetrasyllable. So if we add these two new cola to the ones we already had (pentasyllable, heptasyllable and octosyllable), then we see that the other colometries of the decasyllables and decatetrasyllables are in fact to be explained in quite the same way as was already mentioned – this is through a different combination of accepted units (e.g. a decasyllable which consists of a trisyllable and a heptasyllable).[25]

---

[23] Cf. Boeten & Janse (2018) about the "Ὥσπερ ξένοι"-colophon.
[24] Not to be confused with the dieresis in the hexameter or other classical metres.
[25] DBBE 5301 (Sankt-Peterburg - Rossijskaja Nacional'naja biblioteka (RNB) - Ф. № 906 (Gr.) Gr. 71 (Granstrem 195), f. 169r). The other one is: DBBE 1129 (Vaticano - Biblioteca Apostolica Vaticana - Vat. gr. 1853, f. 124r).

If we look back at the resemblance between IUs and metrical cola, then this different combination of cola makes even more sense, especially in consideration of the low-brow dodecasyllables that are used in our case study. Metrical cola were used in the same way as IUs and could therefore easily be strung together to make a verse or a sentence. It is this resemblance with spoken language that enabled less educated scribes to produce verses. For them, it was not the exact number of syllables in the verse that was the most prominent feature of their text, but the stringing together of these units and the general rhythm that came about by concatenating them.

The appearance of octosyllables can be explained through the theory of IUs as well. Instead of being paired with a heptasyllable, as it usually is in the political verse, the colon occurs on its own here. It is because it functions as a prosodic, syntactic and semantic unity, just like an IU, that it has some degree of independence. It was therefore not felt to be problematic if the colon appeared on its own. According to the "principle of pairing", moreover, the political verse first came into being through the pairing of an independent octo- and heptasyllable. The existence of an independent octosyllable in later Byzantine times can therefore not quite be done away with as a mere mistake, simply because it does not fit into the normative pattern of any of the metres of this time. A good corroboration of this are the four book epigrams in the DBBE (that are not of the ἡ μὲν χείρ-type, however) that are written entirely in octosyllables,[26] as though it were a metre on its own.

5 The six-syllable colon

However, this still leaves us with 37% of the epigrams, which are irregular and do not fall into the categories of octo-, deca- and decatetrasyllables. All of these epigrams are either eleven or thirteen syllables in total and do not seem to lend themselves to a gratifying explanation at first sight. They look as follows:

(4a) ἡ μὲν χεὶρ ἡ γράψασα, σήπετε τάφω·
τὸ δὲ γράμμα μένη εἰς χρόνους πληρεστάτους

'The hand that wrote this rots in a grave,
But the letter remains until the end of time.'
(DBBE 130 [Athena – EBE 180, f. 393r]; 1089 CE)

---

26 DBBE 938 (Vaticano - Biblioteca Apostolica Vaticana - Palat. gr. 367, f. 136r-v), DBBE 4770 (Vaticano - Biblioteca Apostolica Vaticana - Palat. gr. 367, f. 68v), DBBE 7269 (Athos - Monê Ibêron 1384, f. 126r), DBBE 7270 (Athos - Monê Ibêron 1384, f. 1r).

(4b) χεὶρ μ(ὲν) ἡ γράψασα, σίπεται τάφῳ·
γραφὴ δὲ πᾶσα μένει, εἰς τοὺς αἰῶν(ας)

'The hand that wrote this rots in a grave,
But the entire writing remains for centuries.'
(DBBE 1110 [Vaticano - Biblioteca Apostolica Vaticana - Vat. gr. 920, f. 221v]; 1340 CE)

There is no plausible way in which a synizesis can make the 13-syllable verse into a correct dodecasyllable or that the 11-syllable verse can be magically made into twelve syllables. Surely, these must all be mistakes?

First of all, it is interesting to note that several instances in this category of "unexplainable" epigrams can in fact be explained in the very same way as the octo-, deca- and decatetrasyllables, i.e. through the wrong pairing of correct cola. We are talking about the following epigrams:

(5a) **ὀτὶ χεῖρ μὲν ἡ γράψασα ǁ σίπεται τάφω·**
γραφῇ δὲ μένοι· εἰς μάκρους φεῦ μοι χρ(όνους)·

'Because the hand that wrote this rots in a grave,
But the writing remains, poor me!, for a long time.'
(DBBE 1877 [Vaticano - Biblioteca Apostolica Vaticana - Barb. gr. 455, f. 145r]; 1276 CE)

(5b) ἡ μὲν χεὶρ ἡ γράφουσα σήπεται τάφω·
γραφὴ δὲ μένει ǁ εἰς αἰῶ(νας) ἀπεράντους

'The hand that wrote this rots in a grave,
But the writing remains for endless centuries.'
(DBBE 958 [Vaticano - Biblioteca Apostolica Vaticana - Vat. gr. 67, f. 256r]; XIV–XV CE)

(5c) Οἱ μὲν χεὶρ ἡ γράψασα σήπεται τάφω·
ἡ δὲ βίβλος παῐφῆκεν ǁ χρο|νους πλῆστους·

'The hand that wrote this rots in a grave,
But the book produces many years (much time).'
(DBBE 7971 [Athos - Monê Dionusiou 10, f. 518]; X CE)

As you can see, these epigrams display a colometry of respectively 8 + 5; 5 + 8; and 7 + 4 syllables. All of these cola are correct cola, but through a wrong combination, we end up with irregular verses.

Then what about all of the other "inexplainable" epigrams? They are merely "inexplainable" because they all exhibit a colon of six syllables, which is not among the accepted or available cola in Byzantine metre. Let us retake the epigrams in (4) (= (6)):

(6a) ἡ μὲν χεὶρ ἡ γράψασα, σήπετε τάφω·
τὸ δὲ γράμμα μένῃ ǁ εἰς χρόνους πληρεστάτους   6 + 7 syllables

(6b) **χεὶρ μ(ὲν) ἡ γράψασα, ‖ σίπεται τάφῳ·**   6 + 5 syllables
γραφὴ δὲ πᾶσα μένει, εἰς τοὺς αἰῶν(ας)

We cannot somehow make these six syllables into five or seven syllables to make it fit, and it is also not possible to split the colon of six syllables into two smaller cola of three syllables, because there are no word(group) boundaries to facilitate this. Yet, no less than 25 verses with a six-syllable colon can be found in the "ἡ μὲν χείρ" occurrences.

A possible explanation for the existence of these six-syllable cola is the re-interpretation of smaller cola into larger units. To understand this concept, we must reiterate the "principle of pairing" which was discussed earlier. According to this principle, the pairing of shorter cola has resulted into the emergence of the medieval verse forms as we know them. This means that, at a certain point in time, the two shorter cola were not considered to be two separate units anymore, but became two subparts of a larger whole. This is a re-interpretation of the cola into a larger unit (i.e. the verse). We can also see that, from a certain point in time, for some authors the entirety of the verse prevails over the cola in that verse. This becomes apparent when there is no clear caesura anymore, as is illustrated in the following epigrams:

(7a) Τὸ παρὸν τετραευάγγελον, ὑπάρχ(ει)
ἐμοῦ Γρηγορίου ἱερομονάχου·

'These four gospels belong
To me, the holy monk Gregory.'
(DBBE 1761 [Athos - Monê Xêropotamou 107, f. 553r]; XIII CE)

(7b) ἐλενη ἐκ θεοῦ ἐυρεμα ἐδόθη.

'Helen was given an invention from God.'
(DBBE 319 [Firenze - Bibl. Medicea Laurenziana - Plut. 11, Cod. 9, f. 282r]; 1020 CE)

(7c) τὴν χειροχορδοβροντόκρουστον κιννύραν.
τὴν ἀσματοδοψαλμοσύνθετον βίβλον.
τὴν θειοκοσμοψυχόσωστον πυξίδα
προφητοτερπνόφθογγον ἔφρασε στόμα
καὶ κρατοῦσαν καὶ λαλοῦσαν (καὶ) ψάλλουσάν σε

'The kinor, its strings struck by a mortal hand,
The book, consisting of songs and psalms,
The tablet, saving the divine cosmos and soul,
Of these things this delightfully sounding prophet-tongue speaks,
Both controlling and talking and singing about you'
(DBBE 8301 [Athos - Monê Dionusiou 60, f. 6r]; XIII CE)

In these cases, the combination of two cola is re-interpreted as one, more or less unbroken verse. We have seen that the trissyllable is an acceptable colon in Byzantine metre and it is not unthinkable that two trissylables were sometimes combined into a six-syllable colon. Later, in the same way as the entire verse emerged out of two (or more) cola, the six-syllable colon was then re-interpreted as being one colon and the separation into two trissyllables becomes forgotten. This would explain why there are not that many occurrences of six-syllable cola, since the combination of two trissyllables is rather rare and they are generally not considered to be correct, but why there are still enough of them to form a noticeable group. Once again we are dealing with something not entirely "wrong" (yet more wrong than any combination of the acceptable cola) and at the same time not correct at all either.

6 Conclusion

We must look at Byzantine metre in a different way in order to appreciate the many varieties in the corpus of book epigrams. We have to first of all understand that the texts of our case study were most likely cited from memory, rather than being copied from parchment. Indeed, certain colophon types circulated throughout the Byzantine world (and even beyond) and left the scribe with a more or less set notion of what these colophons should look like. As a result, the reproductions of these texts often have a distinct oral characteristic, despite the fact that they are written texts. What is more, the metrical cola in the dodecasyllable function in the same way as IUs do in spoken language. The theory of IUs has originated through the investigation of oral languages and as such this similarity between metrical cola and IUs gives our texts an extra oral dimension. Despite their fundamentally written character, we must therefore study and appreciate the ἡ μὲν χείρ-epigrams in a different way than we usually do with written texts.

Therefore, the metrical mistakes in the case study should not be discarded as being simple mistakes. The wrong combination of traditional cola has led to some irregularities, which can however not be considered entirely wrong. Rather, their frequent occurrence indicates that the stringing together of units was often deemed more important than the resulting number of syllables. In other words, the general rhythm of these texts prevailed over the metrical rules.

Because of the oral dimension to these texts and the fact that their units (metrical cola) function in the same way as the units of spoken language (IUs) do, it was perhaps quite easy for Byzantine scribes to produce metrical texts.

Indeed, the only steps in the production process were basically to assemble several syllables to form units (cola), which in turn needed to be strung together in the same way as they were in everyday spoken language. Deviations were most likely not felt to be gross transgressions, as long as the general rhythm of the text was not compromised, which is why they occur so frequently in our corpus of book epigrams and which made the production of metrical texts seem more accessible to those who had less metrical competence. After all, breaking the metrical rules happened all the time! All of this must have been a contributing factor to the abundance of metrical texts throughout the Byzantine world and what Magdalino (2012:32) called the "Byzantine epigrammatic habit".

In conclusion, this different approach to Byzantine metrical texts has given us a deeper insight into the mechanics behind Byzantine metre in general. Not only were penta-, hepta- and octosyllables considered to be correct cola, but we may assume that the heptasyllable could be split up into a tetra- and a trissyllable. These trissyllables, in turn, could then be reinterpreted as a six-syllable colon. In short, the scope of accepted metrical units seems to have become infinitely wider than it was, which opens the door for future research of this subject.

References

Bernard, Floris & Kristoffel Demoen. 2019. Book epigrams. In Wolfram Hörandner, Andreas Rhoby & Nikolaos Zagklas (eds.), *A companion to Byzantine poetry*, 404–429. Leiden: Brill.

Boeten, Julie & Mark Janse. 2018. A cognitive analysis of metrical irregularities in the Ὥσπερ ξένοι book epigrams. *Byzantine and Modern Greek Studies* 42. 79–91.

Brazil, David. 1997. *The communicative value of intonation in English*, 2nd ed. Cambridge: Cambridge University Press.

Chafe, Wallace L. 1976. Givenness, contrastiveness, definiteness, subjects, topics and point of view. In Charles N. Li (ed.), *Subject and topic*, 27–55. New York: Academic Press.

Chafe, Wallace L. 1980. The deployment of consciousness in the production of a narrative. In Wallace L. Chafe (ed.), *The Pear stories: Cognitive, cultural and linguistic aspects of narrative production*, 9–50. Norwood: Ablex.

Chafe, Wallace L. 1987. Cognitive constraints on information flow. In Russell S. Tomlin (ed.), *Coherence and grounding in discourse: Outcome of a symposium, Eugene, Oregon, June 1984*, 21–52. Amsterdam: Benjamins.

Chafe, Wallace L. 1988. Linking Intonation Units in spoken English. In J. Haiman & S. A. Thompson (eds.), *Clause combining in grammar and discourse*, 1–27. Amsterdam: Benjamins.

Chafe, Wallace L. 1993. Prosodic and functional units of language. In Jane A. Edwards & Martin D. Lampert (eds.), *Talking data: Transcription and coding in discourse research*, 33–43. Hillsdale: Erlbaum.

Chafe, Wallace L. 1994. *Discourse, consciousness and time: The flow and displacement of conscious experience in speaking and writing*. Chicago: University of Chicago Press.

Chafe, Wallace L. 1998. Language and the flow of thought. In M. Tomasello (ed.), *The new psychology of language: Cognitive and functional approaches to language structure*, 93–111. Hillsdale: Erlbaum.
Chafe, Wallace L. 2001. The analysis of discourse flow. In D. Schiffrin, D. Tannen & H. E. Hamilton (eds.), *The handbook of discourse analysis*, 673–687. Oxford: Blackwell.
Cruttenden, Alan. 1997. *Intonation*, 2nd ed. Cambridge: Cambridge University Press.
Crystal, David. 1975. *The English tone of voice: Essays in intonation, prosody and paralanguage*. London: Arnold.
Halliday, M. A. K. 1985. *An introduction to functional grammar*. London: Arnold.
Halliday, M. A. K. & William S. Greaves. 2006. *Intonation in the grammar of English*. London: Equinox.
Janse, Mark. 1991. La phrase segmentée en grec ancien: Le témoignage des enclitiques. *Bulletin de la Société de Linguistique de Paris* 86. 14–16.
Kleinedler, S. J. Pickett & Christopher Leonesio. 2005. *The Riverside dictionary of biography*. Oxford: Houghton Mifflin.
Kominis, Athanasios. 1966. *Τὸ βυζαντινὸν ἱερὸν ἐπίγραμμα καὶ οἱ ἐπιγραμματοποιοί*. Athens: Τυπογραφείον Αδελφών Μυρτίδη.
Lauxtermann, Marc D. 1999. *The spring of rhythm: An essay on the political verse and other byzantine metres*. Wien: Verlag der Österreichischen Akademie der Wissenschaften.
Lauxtermann, Marc D. 2003. *Byzantine poetry from Pisides to Geometres: Texts and contexts*. Vol. 1. Wien: Austrian Academy of Sciences Press.
Lauxtermann, Marc D. 2019. *Byzantine poetry from Pisides to Geometres: Texts and Contexts*. Vol. 2. Wien: Austrian Academy of Sciences Press.
Maas, Paul. 1903. Der byzantinische Zwölfsilber. *Byzantinische Zeitschrift* 12. 278–323.
Mackridge, Peter. 1990. The metrical structure of the oral decapentasyllable. *Byzantine & Modern Greek Studies* 14. 551–574.
Magdalino, Paul. 2012. Cultural change? The context of Byzantine poetry from Geometres to Prodromos. In Floris Bernard & Kristoffel Demoen (eds.), *Poetry and its contexts in eleventh-century Byzantium*, 19–36. Burlington: Ashgate.
McCollum, Adam C. 2015. The rejoicing sailor and the rotting hand: two formulas in Syriac and Arabic colophons. *Journal of Syriac Studies* 18. 67–93.
Rhoby, Andreas. 2011. Vom jambischen Trimeter zum byzantinischen Zwölfsilber. Beobachtung zur Metrik des spätantiken und byzantinischen Epigramms. *Wiener Studien* 124. 117–142.
Selkirk, Elisabeth O. 1984. *Phonology and syntax: The relation between sound and structure*. Cambridge, MA: MIT Press.
Slings, Simon R. 1999. Information unit and metrical unit. In Ilja Leonard Pjeijffer & Simon R. Slings (eds.), *One hundred years of Bacchylides: Proceedings of a colloquium held at the Vrije Universiteit Amsterdam*, 61–75. Amsterdam: V.U. University Press.
Thomas, Christine. 2003. *The Acts of Peter, gospel literature and ancient novel: Rewriting the past*. Oxford: Oxford University Press.
Valiavitcharska, Vessela. 2013. *Rhetoric and rhythm in Byzantium, the sound of persuasion*. Cambridge: Cambridge University Press.
Van Nuffelen, Peter. 2012. John of Antioch, inflated and deflated, or how (not) to collect fragments of early Byzantine historians. *Byzantion* 82. 437–450.

Staffan Wahlgren
15 Arguing and narrating: Text type and linguistic variation in tenth-century Greek

Abstract: Linguistic variation in Byzantine literary Greek has normally been attributed to differing levels of education and competence, or stylistic choice. In this paper it is suggested that some variation may be due to discursive factors and communicational needs. A corpus taken from the *Letters* and the *Chronicle* of Symeon the Magistros and Logothete (X CE) is investigated, and variation with regard to the occurrence, and use, of verb forms, subordinating conjunctions and particles is discussed.

1 Introduction

Despite progress made in recent years, it still holds true that linguists of Byzantine Greek pay only little attention to formal, literary, Greek.[1] Instead, they tend to focus on forms of the language supposedly close to the vernacular.

The focus of this paper lies on the mid-Byzantine period and, more specifically, on the tenth century. The reason for this choice is the fact that this is a period in which the vernacular, or a language form close to this, is no option for use in literature. This makes the mid-Byzantine period special: in earlier periods there are, in addition to high-level language, varieties neighbouring on the vernacular, and in Late Byzantium, after a period of comparative unity, Greek may be said to be split into two again: on one hand a high-level language, and on the other a language variety, or set of varieties, with traits of Modern Greek. In other words, it seems that the mid-Byzantine centuries constitute a period of a particularly narrow range of linguistic variation in written Greek.

The question now presents itself as to what variation there is in the tenth century, and to what it is due. The hypothesis presented in this paper, is that much of the existing variation is due neither to differing levels of education and competence, nor to stylistic choice. Instead, the variation can be explained as being due to discursive factors and ruled by the communicational needs the author wishes to meet.

---

[1] For general background reading and bibliography the reader is referred to Hinterberger (2014) and Wahlgren (2010).

In order to substantiate this statement, and to give a picture of how communicational needs influence usage, I am going to employ certain kinds of text linguistics as my framework. First of all, I will operate with the concept of *text types*, and in particular, the types we may call *argumentation* and *narration*, that is, whether the author is arguing a case or narrating a series of past events.[2] In doing so, I will pay particular attention to the manner of establishing links and dependencies within texts and of connecting sentences and phrases so as to create coherence. Here my starting point is the hypothesis that argumentative and narrative texts are likely to differ from each other in their use of connectives and other means of linking information.

1.1 Corpus

Ideally, in an investigation of the kind presented below, bias conditioned by individual choice (on the part of the Byzantine writers) and by different levels of education and competence should be ruled out.

Consequently, I have turned to texts of clearly different kinds but (probably) written by one and the same person. Such works do not exist in abundance from this period. The chosen works are parts of the *Chronicle* of Symeon the Magistros and Logothete and some of the *Letters* presumably written by the same man.[3] In the *Chronicle*, we encounter passages mainly of a narrative kind, that is, relating a progressive action and introducing new topics and participants with a minimum of comment. (There are, in fact, some speeches in the *Chronicle*, and also other non-narrative, argumentative passages; however, this is not the case in the corpus investigated below). In contrast, the *Letters* – as is fairly typical of medieval letters – are almost without any specific information at all, and involve very few participants. There is one main theme in the *Letters*, in two variations: First: "You do not write to me – why?". And, secondly: "I have not written to you – my apologies! (but I have my reasons)". In sum, the *Letters* are almost pure argumentation and contain hardly any narrative at all.

Now, there are many difficulties of a philological and historical kind, with which the path of research into Byzantine Greek is fraught.

---

[2] For background reading on theory the reader is referred to Adamzik (2004) and Revuelta (2015).
[3] The texts are taken from Wahlgren (2006) and Darrouzès (1960) respectively (see below for the passages used). All translations are by myself. For further bibliography and discussion of the philological and historical problems touched upon in this section, see Wahlgren (2006).

The first of these is that of the transmission of texts of the kind represented by the *Chronicle*. These texts tend to be transmitted in *open traditions*, which means: they are seldom copied faithfully and, in almost every instance of the production of a new manuscript copy, there is considerable room for intentional change. Thus, the genealogical relationship between manuscripts is blurred, and it is difficult for us to reconstruct what manuscripts earlier than the existing ones may have looked like, and, consequently, what the original manuscript – that of the chronicler himself – may have looked like.

Secondly, there is the problem of textual homogeneity. Usually, the genre is compilatory. Chroniclers take large pieces of text from previous works, more or less wholescale, without paying tribute to their predecessors, and they add their own, original, contribution only at the end of the text. Therefore, it is very hard to be sure how much, and what parts of a chronicle were written by one and the same author.

In the case of the *Chronicle* of Symeon the Magistros and Logothete, it is my claim that the problems outlined above, while considerable, remain manageable for the purpose of the present investigation, and that we can isolate segments of the text which are likely to have been written by one person. Thus, it is likely that the text covering the years from about 913 until 948 was written by one court official, Symeon, active shortly after the middle of the century. This, therefore, is the part of the text that I will use in the present investigation.

This takes us to one last point, that of the identity of the author. This is a thorny matter, which has attracted much speculation. In sum, there is a remote possibility that the *Letters* are written by more than one person, and that Symeon the chronicler was an altogether different individual.[4] However, no doubt remains that all of the text used in this paper was written in the tenth century and in very much one and the same linguistic environment, that is, that of the Byzantine elite, presumably in the capital of Constantinople.

2 Verb forms: Participles, infinitives, finite forms

Our main focus lies on the interplay between participial constructions, infinitives, and finite clauses, and how these are connected with each other (through

---

[4] In this case, the reader may object, bias due to individual choice has not been successfully ruled out (cf. above, where I state that such bias should be ruled out).

coordination and subordination, for instance). The distribution of different verb forms is given in Table 1:[5]

Table 1: Number of verb forms in a corpus of 4000 words per text investigated.

	Chronicle	Letters
Participles	363	268
Infinitives	79	136
Finite forms	269	335
indicatives	229	240
imperfects/pluperfects	33	19
imperatives	2	23
subjunctives	3	18
optatives	2	35
Sum total	711	739

As can be seen, the total frequency of verb forms is almost one and the same in the *Chronicle* and the *Letters*, with 711 instances in the former, and 739 in the latter (in both cases in samples of approximately 4000 words). Nevertheless, several differences between the texts are striking and call for explanation.

First, participles are significantly more common in the *Chronicle* (363 occurrences) than in the *Letters* (268 occurrences), and the higher frequency of these in the *Chronicle* almost balances the lower frequency of infinitives and finite verb forms in the same text. The discussion below, focusing on the alternatives to participles, will, I hope, contribute towards an explanation as to why these differences exist. In short, my belief is that the differing needs of argumentative vs. narrative texts are the key to our understanding, and I argue that participles neither do provide the kind of explicitness which is given by finite clauses (an explicitness which is clearly desirable in an argumentative text), nor do they fit into the semantic context where the infinitive is needed. Participles make for tempo, which is desirable in a narrative.

As for infinitives, these are more frequent in the *Letters* (136 occurrences) than in the *Chronicle* (79 occurrences). While not ruling out that this is a matter of stylistic ambition (that is, that the lack of infinitives in the vernacular is more

---

[5] The texts used here and in the following are Ch. 135, §1–136, §26 of the *Chronicle* and *Letters* 1–21.

compensated for in texts with higher stylistic ambition than in texts with less stylistic ambition), I would suggest that one reason for the differences between the texts is a certain preference of the *Letters* for infinitives such as the following:

(1) ἀληθῆ σπούδασον **θέσθαι** τὴν ἐπαγγελίαν·

'Do your best to make your promise come true.'
(Sym. Mag. et Log., *Letter* 1)

(2) Περὶ δὲ τῶν καινοτομιῶν ὧν μοι ἔγραψας . . . ἐβουλόμην **γράψαι** τῷ ταύτας ποιοῦντι κτλ.

'Regarding the innovations you wrote to me about . . . I was going to write to the one who instituted them (etc.).'
(Sym. Mag. et Log., *Letter* 5)

In the first of these cases, the infinitive θέσθαι 'to make' depends upon the imperative σπούδασον 'do your best', and, in conjunction, these two forms amount to about the same as an imperative of the verb τίθημι. In the second case, the infinitive γράψαι 'to write' depends upon ἐβουλόμην 'I intended', which reminds us of the construction with θέλω 'I want' + infinitive (which is becoming increasingly common in the vernacular as a (neutral) reference to the future). The kind of emphasis conveyed by the almost periphrastic construction seems to fit nicely with the argumentative character of the *Letters*, and the author's desire to show the fervour of his love for his addressee. At the same time, there is a certain long-windedness in the construction, with a change neither of topic nor of participant, and, therefore, it may be less useful in narrative.

Turning to finite clauses, several differences between the texts call for comment. Imperfects and pluperfects (all of them synthetic) are somewhat more common in the *Chronicle* (33 occurrences, vs. 19 in the *Letters*). Also the aorist indicative is, relatively speaking as well as in absolute numbers, much more common in the *Chronicle* (aorist indicative 157, present indicative 57) than in the *Letters* (aorist indicative 68, present indicative 104). The obvious explanation for this is that a text narrating bygone events, such as the *Chronicle*, more often needs verb forms such as the imperfect and the aorist indicative, which (in many contexts) provide an unequivocal reference to the past.

A further, striking difference between the texts lies in their employment of modal forms, which are ten times more common in the *Letters* than in the *Chronicle* (76:7). Examples of this are instances of the imperative, e.g.:

(3) **Παρακλήθητι** οὖν . . . καὶ **ἐπίνευσον** τὴν τοιαύτην ἡμῶν αἴτησιν γενέσθαι κτλ.

'Be asked herewith . . . and give your consent, so that this request of ours may be fulfilled (etc.).'
(Sym. Mag. et Log., *Letter* 6)

Not so different from a semantical point of view and equally independent are most occurrences (in the *Letters*) of the optative, e.g.:

> (4) **Χαρίσαιτό** μοι Κύριος μετὰ τῶν ἁγίων εὐχῶν καὶ τὴν ἁγίαν ἀγάπην σου καὶ **ἀξιωθείημεν** κτλ.
>
> 'May the Lord grant not only the fulfillment of your saintly prayers, but your saintly love, and let us be worthy of this (etc.).'
> (Sym. Mag. et Log., *Letter* 5)

Subjunctives, on the other hand, seem mostly to be dependent (they are, for instance, used in final clauses). Once, however, there is the subjunctive παράσχῃ 'may he grant' together with the optative ἀντιδοίη 'to give in recompense':

> (5) Ἀλλ' **ἀντιδοίη** σοι Κύριος, ὁ τὴν ἀγάπην νομοθετήσας, τῆς ἀδόλου φιλίας τὸ μίσθωμα ἔγκαρπον καὶ **παράσχῃ** ἀλλήλοις συνεισελθεῖν κτλ.
>
> 'But may the Lord, who instituted love, give you fruit-bearing recompense for your guileless friendship, and may He grant us to meet (etc.).'
> (Sym. Mag. et Log., *Letter* 9)

It seems justified to take this as an indication of not only the syntactic but also the semantic equivalence of the optative and the subjunctive.

Modal forms, especially the optative, remain fairly exclusive in Medieval Greek. It is therefore possible (as suggested above with regard to the infinitives) that we should take the existence of optatives in a text as a sign of stylistic ambition (that is, that a higher frequency of the optative means a higher stylistic ambition). At the same time, it seems reasonable to think that this and other differences between our texts as to mood are due to different communicational needs. Thus, imperatives by definition argue, and the same holds true for most subjunctives and optatives encountered with here. Therefore, without ruling out that stylistic ambition is at play, it seems more than probable that subject matter and argumentative needs play a large role in accounting for the modal differences of our texts.

2.1 Subordination and its equivalents

An even more striking difference between the texts is perhaps that there are so many more examples of subordinate finite verb clauses in the *Letters* than in the *Chronicle*. No doubt, subordination is a problematic concept, and, in a language such as Greek, with so little of a true subordinating syntax, there can, in a number of cases, be no unambiguous interpretation as to what is subordinate and what is not. Some categories marked by formal elements are included in Table 2:

Table 2: Number of subordinate phrases in a corpus of 4000 words per text investigated.

	Chronicle	Letters
Relative pronouns and adverbs	28	37
Final-consecutive and temporal expressions with the infinitive ὡς ὥστε πρίν	3 3 0	4 1 1
True subordination (adverbial and object clauses with a finite verb)	εἰ: 1; εἰ μή: 4; ἐπεί: 2; ἐπειδή: 1; ἐπειδήπερ: 1; μή: 3; ὅπως: 1; ὅτι: 1; ὡς: 4; ὡσάν: 1; ὥστε (with ind.): 2 = 21	εἰ: 30; ἐπεί: 6; ἐπειδή: 1; ἵνα: 7; καθὼς ἄν: 1; κἄν: 3; μήποτε: 2; ὅπως: 2; ὅτε: 2; ὅταν: 1; ὅτι: 22; ὡς: 1; ὡσάν: 2 = 80
Sum total	55	123

Although there is a somewhat higher number of relative pronouns in the *Letters* than in the *Chronicle*, the more considerable difference between the texts lies in the distribution of adverbial and object clauses with a finite verb: in the *Letters* there are about four times as many examples of this as in the *Chronicle* (80.21). A remarkable difference lies in the scarcity vs. frequency of εἰ and ὅτι: these hardly occur in the *Chronicle*, whereas there are many instances in the *Letters*. Further, considering the fact that the *Chronicle* narrates a story in time, it is rather surprising that ὅτε and ὅταν do not occur (at least not in the present sample).

Under what circumstances, then, does the *Chronicle* employ subordinate clauses with a finite verb? There are a number of occurrences of ἐπεί and ἐπειδή (περ). As far as I can see, all of these have a slightly causal ring, although it is perfectly legitimate to read a temporal meaning into them as well. See e.g.:

(6) **ἐπεὶ** δὲ τήν τε τῶν τειχῶν κατέμαθεν ὀχυρότητα τήν τε ἐκ τοῦ πλήθους καὶ τῶν ὅπλων καὶ τῶν πετροβόλων ἀσφάλειαν, τῶν ἐλπίδων σφαλεὶς ἐν τῷ λεγομένῳ Ἑβδόμῳ ὑπέστρεψεν εἰρηνικὰς σπονδὰς αἰτησάμενος.

'However, since/when he realised the strength of the City walls and the degree of safety provided by the mass of people and the weapons and the catapults that were employed, he lost hope and retreated to the area called Hebdomon and asked for a truce.' (Sym. Mag. et Log., *Chron* 135.10)

Further, there are four cases of εἰ μή, e.g.:

(7) καὶ ταύτην [sc. Στρόβηλον νῆσον] παρέλαβεν ἄν [sc. Δαμιανὸς ἀμηρᾶς], **εἰ μὴ** νοσήσας ἐτελεύτησεν.

'. . . and, had he [sc. the emir Damian] not fallen ill and died, he would have captured it [sc. the island of Strobilos].'
(Sym. Mag. et Log., *Chron* 135.17)

The reason for the employment of a conjunction and a subordinate clause in cases like these is, I believe, that other constructions, such as those with participles, are not sufficiently precise. Thus, the irreality expressed by εἰ μή is not readily expressed by any other construction; also ἐπεί and ἐπειδή seem more precise than any alternative causal construction. To sum up the whole argument so far: the *Letters* vividly explain and argue, and the preferred linguistic means in order to connect the links in the argument are subordinate clauses expressing causal or concessive relationships, conditions and the like, often introduced by conjunctions with a high degree of transparency. On the other hand the *Chronicle* narrates, and this is done by participles which express relationships between the links in the argument less explicitly.

3 Particles

In this section we will explore how another element capable of creating a coherence between clauses and other constituents, namely particles, is used, and how this fits into the picture painted above. Table 3 gives an overview of the usage:

Table 3: Particles in a corpus of 4000 words per text investigated.

	Chronicle	Letters
	ἀλλά: 9; ἄρα: 2; ἅτε: 3; γάρ: 7; γε: 1; δέ: 121; δή: 4; μέν: 8; οὖν: 39	ἀλλά: 35; γάρ: 31; γε: 4; γοῦν: 1; δέ: 57; δή: 4; μέν: 13; οὖν: 10; πλήν: 1
	καίτοι: 1	καίτοι: 2; μέντοι: 1; τοιγαροῦν: 1; τοίνυν: 3
		δέ τοι: 1; δ' οὖν: 4; μὲν οὖν: 1
	-δέ (μηδέ, τάδε): 2; -δή: 2 (ἐπειδή); -περ: 3	-δε: 6 (μηδέ, ὅδε, οὐδέ); -δέ γε: 1 (οὐδέ γε); -δή: 2 (ἐπειδή, δηλαδή); -περ: 14; -περ δή: 1
Sum total	202	193

As to the overall frequency of particles there is no great difference between the *Chronicle* and the *Letters*, although the *Chronicle* has a slightly smaller variation than the *Letters*. δέ alone accounts for over 60% of the instances in the *Chronicle*, compared to 30% in the *Letters*.[6] Of other particles, ἀλλά (adversative) and γάρ (explanatory) are more common in the *Letters*, the higher frequency of these being, I think, a testimony to the argumentative character of the *Letters*. On the other hand, οὖν as a weak connective (somewhere between δέ and γάρ, similar to *igitur* in Medieval Latin) is very common in the *Chronicle*. See for example:

(8) Θεόδωρος **οὖν**, ὁ τοῦ βασιλέως Κωνσταντίνου παιδαγωγός . . . ὑπέθηκε Κωνσταντίνῳ βασιλεῖ Ῥωμανὸν δρουγγάριον προσλαβέσθαι . . . ὡς ἂν σύμμαχον ἔχει καὶ βοηθόν. πολλάκις **οὖν** περὶ τούτου λαληθεὶς Ῥωμανὸς ἀπείπατο. γραμματεῖον **οὖν** ὁ βασιλεὺς Κωνσταντῖνος . . . ἀπέστειλεν αὐτῷ κτλ.

'Theodore, who was the emperor Constantine's tutor, suggested to the emperor Constantine that he should take the droungarios Romanos into his private service . . . to be his ally and assistant. This had often been mentioned to Romanos, but he had always rejected the idea. Now the emperor Constantine wrote a letter . . . and sent it to him (etc.).'

(Sym. Mag. et Log., *Chron* 135.24)

In this case, three successive sentences employ οὖν. The first of these sentences is at the beginning of a new paragraph,[7] and the connection with the preceding sentence, which is never strong, is here particularly loose.

In sum, it is clear that particles are capable of creating some kind of coherence in our texts. Only a more thorough investigation could tell us more about how this works. Tentatively I would suggest that they are perceived as somewhat devoid of content, syntactically and semantically. Therefore they do not work on a par with conjunctions in order to indicate argumentative structure, and this is why they are not more common in the *Letters*.

4 Case syntax and coherence: the dative case

Finally, I would like to turn to an item of case syntax. As observed elsewhere, the dative case is remarkably common in a wide range of Byzantine texts, even

---

[6] Particles are here defined in the most conventional way (for this see Denniston 1954). For a recent treatment of particles and cohesion/coherence in Ancient Greek, see Revuelta (2015). For particles in learned Byzantine Greek, see Bočková Loudová (2014).
[7] In the modern edition, of which I am the editor (Wahlgren 2006: I have also introduced the paragraphs).

of a modest linguistic level.[8] This applies to the *Chronicle* discussed here as well as to the *Letters*. However, the dative is significantly more common in the *Chronicle* than in the *Letters*, as can be seen in Table 4:

Table 4: Number of datives in a corpus of 4000 words per text investigated.

	Chronicle	Letters
Separate phrases	258	279
Spatial phrases	78	7
Temporal phrases	33	2
Sum total of occurrences	486	371

No doubt the higher frequency of the dative in the *Chronicle* may be due to several factors and, as was the case with the optative and the infinitive (see above), there may be reason to suspect that stylistic ambition is one part of the equation. As can be seen, the number of separate phrases does not to any great extent differ from text to text to any great extent (in Table 4, a phrase like ταύτῃ τῇ ἡμέρᾳ 'on this day' counts as three occurrences, while it is regarded as only one separate phrase). One matter where the texts differ most clearly from each other is in the use of the dative in spatial and temporal expressions, which are much more common in the *Chronicle* than in the *Letters*. This higher frequency I think we can connect very nicely with the discussion about argumentative structure and means of creating coherence. Such temporal and spatial expressions occur precisely where a chronicle needs clarity of expression in order to create the kind of coherence necessary in such a text. In other words, expressions in the *Chronicle* like ταύτῃ τῇ ἡμέρᾳ 'on this day', or τρίτῃ ἰνδικτιῶνος 'in the third year of the indiction', or ἐν τούτῳ τῷ τόπῳ 'in this place' serve as a kind of beacons, or as cohesive elements, similar to the elements (such as conjunctions) employed in the *Letters* in order to create argumentative coherence.

5 Conclusion

Variation in literary Greek, often put down to stylistic ambition, varying levels of education and competence or individual preference, may have other explanations.

---

8 Wahlgren (2014).

My suggestion is that we should take into account whether a text is concerned with arguing a case, telling a story, or something different: in short, with the text type.

In the case of the interplay between various kinds of verb forms, I think the differences between the *Chronicle* and the *Letters* do tell us something about the needs of an argumentative text as opposed to a narrative one. The use of modal forms as well as subordinate clauses introduced by a conjunction is typical of the *Letters*, and I would argue that these constructions ensure a certain explicitness. On the other hand, the *Chronicle* strives for a quicker flow of information and a quicker change of topics and participants. For this, participial constructions, which are less explicit, serve a useful purpose.

In contrast, it is difficult to see that either of the text types favours particles in any way. Perhaps this is due to a certain semantic-syntactic voidness on their part. For the *Letters*, particles simply do not convey enough meaning, and they do not provide a sufficiently transparent argumentative structure. On the other hand, the *Chronicle* does not need to prioritise them either, since the characteristic lack of explicitness of this text is equally well achieved without them.

Finally, the higher frequency of the dative case in the *Chronicle* can be explained in a similar way. Expressions with the dative are employed precisely at the points where a chronicle must have explicitness: when it comes to stating the time and place of occurrences.

In conclusion, this is an investigation of limited scope, and it has been conducted on a small corpus only. Hopefully, it demonstrates a need for further research, and shows that text type, and whether an author is arguing or narrating, might be a factor to keep in mind if we want to explain certain kinds of linguistic variation.

References

Adamzik, Kirsten. 2004. *Textlinguistik: Eine einführende Darstellung*. Tübingen: Niemeyer.
Bočková Loudová, Kateřina. 2014. On the category of particles in Byzantium. In Hinterberger (ed.), *The language of Byzantine learned literature*, 147–169. Turnhout: Brepols.
Darrouzès, Jean. 1960. *Epistoliers byzantins du Xe siècle*. Paris: Institut français d'études byzantines.
Denniston, John Dewar. 1954 [1934]. *The Greek particles*, 2nd edn. Oxford: Clarendon Press.
Hinterberger, Martin (ed.). 2014. *The language of Byzantine learned literature*. Turnhout: Brepols.
Revuelta, Antonio R. 2015. Particles and discourse cohesion in Ancient Greek. In Giorgos K. Giannakis, Maria Baltazani, Giorgos I. Xidopoulos & Tasos Tsagalidis (eds.), *Proceedings*

of the 8th International Conference on Greek Linguistics, University of Ioannina, Greece, August 30th-September 2nd 2007, 394–405. Ioannina: University of Ioannina.
Wahlgren, Staffan. 2006. *Symeonis magistri et logothetae chronicon*. Berlin: de Gruyter.
Wahlgren, Staffan. 2010. Byzantine literature and the classical past. In Egbert. J. Bakker (ed.), *A companion to the Ancient Greek language*, 527–538. Malden: Wiley-Blackwell.
Wahlgren, Staffan. 2014. Case, style and competence in Byzantine Greek. In Hinterberger (ed.), *The language of Byzantine learned literature*, 170–175. Turnhout: Brepols.

Klaas Bentein
16 The distinctiveness of syntax for varieties of Post-classical and Byzantine Greek: Linguistic upgrading from the third century BCE to the tenth century CE

Abstract: Specialists of the history of Ancient Greek scholarship and modern-day sociolinguists alike have made observations regarding the seemingly "distinctive" status of syntax: the former have argued there is no coherent theory of syntax in Ancient grammatical treatises, and the latter that syntactic variation is much less prominent in modern languages than lexical or phonetic/orthographic variation. The aim of this contribution is to confront these two perspectives by studying linguistic variation in three different types of sources: petitions in the Katochoi of the Sarapieion archive (II BCE), Phrynichus' *Ecloga* (II CE), and the *Life of Euthymius* and its later metaphrasis (VI/X CE). It appears that syntactic variation plays a different role in these three types of sources, which I explain by referring to the cognitive status of syntax, which is more schematic and complex than lexis, and therefore less easily focused upon in "observer-centered" sources such as the *Ecloga*. At the same time, I suggest that culture-specific explanations should be taken into account, too.

> "It seems . . . that there is a difference between syntax and the rest of language which needs to be explained" (Hudson 1996: 43)

1 Introduction: The distinctive status of syntax

The absence of syntactic observations[1] is well-known among those who study the history of Ancient Greek scholarship.[2] As Donnet (1967: 27) writes, "la

---

[1] I would like to thank Andrea Cuomo for his insightful comments on a draft version of this chapter, as well as Martin Hinterberger for suggesting to study the life of Euthymius. Evidently, any remaining errors and inconsistencies are entirely my own doing. My work was funded by the Research Foundation - Flanders (FWO Grant Nr 12B7218N) and the European Research Council (Horizon 2020 research and innovation programme, Starting Grant Nr 756487). Parts of this contribution were presented at the *Beyond Standards: Attic, the Koiné and Atticism* conference (Cambridge, September 14, 2018) and the Metaphrasis workshop (Nicosia, October 13, 2018).
[2] As Swiggers and Wouters (2003: 35–36) note, syntactic observations are not entirely absent in ancient sources, but there is no coherent syntactic perspective form which these observations

https://doi.org/10.1515/9783110614404-016

syntaxe n' pas été, dans l'Antiquité et au Moyen Age, érigée en branche autonome de la grammaire."[3] Even Apollonius Dyscolus, the author of a separate treatise *On syntax*, was more interested in morphology and semantic/logical distinctions than syntax properly speaking.[4] Similarly, in the tradition of writings on language correctness (so-called *hellenismos*),[5] "the available documentation suggests they addressed such issues as the correct meaning of words, prosody, choice among phonetic-orthographic variants, use of etymological and dialectal considerations, as well as the pursuit of linguistic regularities on the basis of analogical reasoning, *whereas no reference attests that these works also dealt with syntax*" (Pagani 2015: 816 [my emphasis]).[6]

The separate status of syntax has also been emphasized in a quite different area of research, that is, modern-day sociolinguistics. Sociolinguists have separated syntax, together with lexis and morphology, from pronunciation/orthography on the basis of the fact that there is invariance of meaning between phonological/orthographic variants, but that this is not necessarily the case with syntactic, lexical or morphological variants (an issue which is known as "the sociolinguistic variable").[7] Such invariance of meaning is typically postulated by (historical) sociolinguists, who want to study the social factors behind linguistic variation, and thereby assume that semantic and discourse-factors do not play a significant role. As Berruto (2004: 314) notes, such an assumption "tends to become increasingly problematic and difficult to establish once we change the level of analysis and move form phonetics/phonology to morphology to lexicon to syntax to pragmatics."

More interesting for our present purposes is the fact that syntax has also been contrasted on its own with the other linguistic levels on the basis of the fact that syntax would display less variation than lexis or phonology/orthography, and would therefore be less marked. As Berruto (2009: 21) writes, scholars tend to think of syntax as "il livello di analisi piu 'duro', meno sensibile e meno coinvolto nella variazione."[8] The most specific proposal that has been made in

---

are made. Orthography, morphology, and lexis, on the other hand, were well studied (see e.g. Valente 2015).

3 "Syntax was not established in antiquity and the Middle Ages as an autonomous branch of grammar."
4 Cf. Lallot (1994), Sluiter (1997: 209–210), Swiggers & Wouters (2003: 26–27). For an overview of Alexandrian syntax, as represented by Apollonius Dyscolus, see Lallot (2015).
5 See e.g. Schenkeveld (1994: 281–292).
6 Compare Schenkeveld (1994: 290).
7 For further discussion, see e.g. Romaine (1982: 31–37).
8 "The most 'difficult' level of analysis, less sensitive and less involved in variation." Compare Hess-Lüttich (2004: 496): "Soziolekte wurden bislang überhaupt zumeist als primär lexikalisch

this regard is that by Hudson (1996),[9] who hypothesizes that the different linguistic levels, and the variants that can be found along these levels, have different relations to society: Hudson considers syntax to be "the marker of cohesion in society", "with individuals trying to eliminate alternatives in syntax from their individual language" (Hudson 1996: 45). Lexis, on the other hand, is a "marker of division in society", with individuals "actively cultivat[ing] alternatives in order to make more subtle social distinctions" (Hudson 1996: 45). Pronunciation, finally, "reflects the permanent social group with which the speaker identifies" (Hudson 1996: 45).[10]

Studies in Greek linguistics have only partly confirmed the picture drawn by Hudson (1996) and other sociolinguists. Torallas Tovar (this volume), for example, considers orthography and vocabulary to be the most "visible" aspects of a text, which goes along the lines of Hudson's proposal. At the same time, many studies have highlighted the existence and significance of syntactic variation in the Post-classical and Byzantine periods, commenting on issues of textual coherence (particles), case, aspect, tense, word order, etc.[11] The main aim of this chapter will therefore be to analyze what role the traditionally recognized linguistic levels (pronunciation/orthography, lexis, morphology, and syntax) play in different types of sources from Antiquity, in other words, to investigate what importance people in Antiquity attached to different types of variation.

The chapter is structured as follows: in Section 2, I briefly discuss the sources that can help us clarify whether syntax had, indeed, a distinctive position for users of Greek in Antiquity; in Section 3, I analyze the different sources, discussing orthography, morphology, syntax, and lexis in detail. Before concluding the chapter in Section 5, I discuss some of the difficulties that one encounters in classifying items according to the traditionally recognized linguistic levels, and propose to reinterpret these levels in terms of a "syntax-lexis" continuum (§4). Such a reinterpretation, I argue, also explains the distributional differences which we find in our sources.

---

zu identifizierende beschrieben" ["So far, sociolects have generally been described as primarily lexically identifiable."]

9 Hudson's (1996) argumentation is to a large extent based on earlier work by Gumperz and Wilson (1971).

10 Hudson (1996) does not say much about morphology. Berruto (2009: 21) considers morphology, together with syntax, to be more stable than vocabulary and orthography. Hudson (1996: 43), on the other hand, writes that "it is certainly the case that examples of syntactic differences within a variety are much less frequently quoted in the literature than differences in either pronunciation or morphology, which are in any case hard to keep separate."

11 See e.g. some of my recent publications (Bentein 2015b, 2016, 2017).

2 Primary sources: A reconceptualization

Scholars studying (the development of) the Greek language have often noted the difficulty of working with the primary sources that have survived.[12] Browning (1983: 4–5) for example has noted that, "in spite of the large number of texts surviving from all periods, it is often difficult to trace the development of the language as it was actually used in most situations. The real process of change is masked by a factitious, classicizing uniformity." Browning (1983: 4–5) therefore distinguishes texts and genres which display "features of the spoken language", such as non-literary papyri, world chronicles, tales of ascetics, and lives of saints,[13] from others which do not. The language of the latter type of texts is considered to be "equivalent" to that of Classical Greek, and therefore without interest.[14] In one recent volume (Herring, Van Reenen and Schøsler 2000), these texts and the linguistic features they contain have been qualified as "non-authentic", whereas "spoken-like", "oral" textual data are qualified as "authentic".

Others scholars, however, have reacted against this dichotomy and the viewpoint it implies, by noting that "authentic" texts, too, must have contained archaic features, and that vice-versa "non-authentic" texts, must have contained innovative features. A new generation of scholars has set it as its goal to study the entire Greek language – "[to] look at Greek in all its varieties", as Horrocks (2010: 4) writes. Register is a key term in this context: the differences that have been noted by previous scholars can be referred to in terms of "higher" and "lower" registers, which need to be compared to each other. In this context, one can refer to the "register-continuum" which I have proposed for Post-classical Greek in a number of publications, as illustrated in Figure 1.[15]

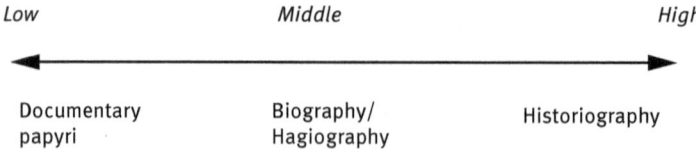

Figure 1: The Post-classical Greek register-continuum (from Bentein 2013).

---

12 Part of the discussion in this section is based on Bentein (2013).
13 Browning (1983: 5) notes, however, that "none of these works is in any sense a reproduction of contemporary spoken Greek; they are mixtures of living speech and dead tradition".
14 Cf. Wahlgren (2002).
15 For further qualification, see Bentein (2015a). For the register continuum, see also Stolk (this volume, §1.1).

One of the disadvantages of a continuum like this is that it does not really take into account the wide range of sources that have actually been preserved. We do not only possess higher- and lower-register literary and non-literary texts, but also texts which offer a fascinating first-hand perspective towards the social evaluation of linguistic features. To be more specific, I am referring to sources such as schoolbooks, grammatical treatises, lexica, annotated manuscripts, documentary texts with scribal corrections, stylistically revised texts, *metaphraseis*, etc. Whereas some of these sources have started to be taken into account in recent linguistic research,[16] much more remains to be done with them. I suggest that they, too, can be placed on a continuum, which ranges from "user-centered" sources to "observer-centered" sources, with at one extremity texts which do not show any explicit social evaluations, and at the other texts which deal explicitly with such evaluations, such as schoolbooks, grammatical treatises and lexica. In between, we can locate annotated manuscripts, stylistically revised texts, and documentary texts with scribal corrections, as shown in Figure 2.

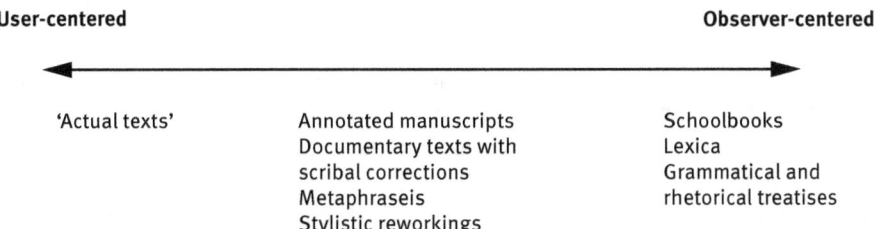

Figure 2: The user-observer continuum.

In what follows, I will analyze the role that syntax plays in texts which display social evaluations more or less explicitly. For this purpose, I have selected three different types of sources, spanning the time-period from the third century BCE to the tenth century CE, all of which are concerned with linguistic upgrading:[17] (i) documentary petitions from the so-called "Katochoi of the Sarapieion archive" (III BCE); (ii) Phrynichus' Atticist lexicon, the *Ecloga*, and (iii) the metaphrasis of the *Life of Euthymius* (VI/X CE).

---

16 See e.g. Luiselli (2010), Cuomo (2017), Stolk (this volume).
17 Note that the reverse phenomenon, linguistic downgrading, is also attested in later Byzantine times. See e.g. Wahlgren (2010: 537).

3 Linguistic upgrading from the third century BCE to the tenth century CE

3.1 The Katochoi of the Sarapieion archive (II BCE)

The first collection of texts that I want to have a closer look at is the so-called "Katochoi of the Sarapieion archive",[18] which is dated to the second century BCE (164–151 BCE). The main figures of this archive are the brothers Ptolemaios and Apollonios, sons of Glaukias, an officer of Macedonian origins. The eldest son, Ptolemaios, was born around the end of the third century BCE in a village called Psichis. After a rudimentary Greek education in the village, he became a recluse in the Great Sarapieion in Memphis in 172 BCE, where he entered in service of the God Sarapis, and probably remained so until his death.[19]

Ptolemaios was especially close to one of his four siblings, his younger brother Apollonios. Since Apollonios was only eight when their father died (164 BCE), Ptolemaios became a kind of substitute father, relying not only on Apollonios as a liaison to the outside world, but also as a scribe: about half of the documents in the archive are written in the hand of Apollonios. Apollonios was able to write fast, but his education must have been quite basic. As Lewis (1986: 76) notes: "his writing is uneven and unattractive in appearance, his spelling even worse than his older brother's, and his grammar rudimentary and erratic."[20]

At the age of fifteen/sixteen, Apollonios joined his brother as a recluse in the Great Sarapieion. After physical violence against the brothers by some Egyptians with anti-Greek feelings, Ptolemaios petitioned the King in order to secure for his brother a military appointment in the Graeco-Macedonian corps stationed at Memphis, which was granted. The texts in the archive show that after this appointment, Apollonios frequently visited his brother in the Sarapieion, bringing food supplies or simply visiting. At the Sarapieion, Ptolemaios also took care of the twin girls Thaues and Taous, who could not write Greek, and therefore needed a representative in their correspondence with Greek officials. Having been thrown out of the house by their mother, the twins were able to enter into the service of Sarapis too, where they remained for seven or more years.[21]

---

18 For historical background, see a.o. Wilcken (1927: 104–116), Lewis (1986: 69–87), Hoogendijk (1989), Legras (2011: esp. 169–89), Bentein (2015a), Vierros (this volume). This archive is also known as the "Ptolemaios archive" (Hoogendijk 1989: 47).
19 Cf. Lewis (1986: 75).
20 For a linguistic analysis of the archive, see Bentein (2015a), Vierros (this volume).
21 Cf. Lewis (1986: 80).

In its present state, the archive contains little over one hundred texts,[22] which have been classified by Wilcken (1927) in terms of four major texts types: letters, petitions, dreams and accounts. In the context of this contribution, I want to have a closer look at the petitions in the archive: these form interesting source material, because on several occasions we have multiple versions of one and the same text, earlier versions having been linguistically upgraded. I will focus on four sets of related texts:[23] (i) UPZ I 5 and UPZ I 6 (from Ptolemaios to the *strategos* Diodotus/the King, against Amosis and his companions); (ii) UPZ I 18 and UPZ I 19 (from the twins to the King, against Nephoris);[24] (iii) UPZ I 35 and UPZ I 36 (from Ptolemaios to the *hypodioikêtês* Sarapion on behalf of the twins);[25] (iv) UPZ I 52 and UPZ I 53 (from Ptolemaios to the *hypodioikêtês* Sarapion on behalf of the twins).

Figure 3 gives a general overview of the types of changes that have been made in these four sets of texts.

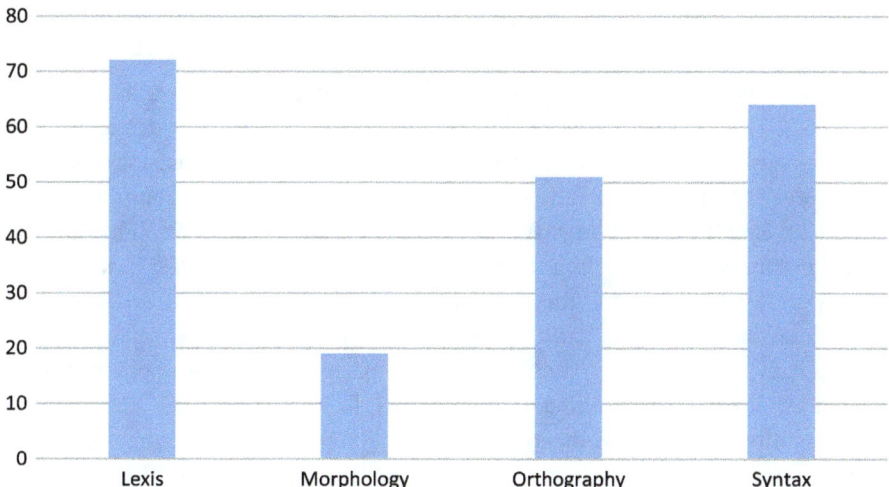

Figure 3: Linguistic changes in the Katochoi of the Sarapieion archive.

---

22 117 texts, according to the Trismegistos portal (last accessed 11 September 2018). The texts were edited and translated by Wilcken (1927).
23 For other related texts, see the overview given in the appendix to Bentein (2015a) and Vierros (this volume, Table 1).
24 Interestingly, a second hand has made additional corrections in UPZ I 19. My comparison is with the first hand in UPZ I 19.
25 There are two copies of UPZ I 35: UPZ I 33 and I 34.

3.1.1 Lexical changes

As Figure 3 shows, most of the linguistic changes that have been made in the petitions are lexical in nature. Almost half of these changes concern verbs, many of which express movement (or absence thereof): so, for example, ἐν κατοχῇ εἰμι > ἐνκατέχομαι 'I am in katochè' (UPZ I 5, l. 9; UPZ I 6, l. 8), ἀπεπήδησε 'he leaped off' > ἀποκολυμβήσαντος 'having jumped (into)' (UPZ I 18, l. 9; UPZ I 19, l. 11), ἔλθη εἰς νῆσον 'he went to an island' > ἀνασωθέντος ἐπί τινα νῆσον 'having been saved on an island' (UPZ I 18, l. 10; UPZ I 19, l. 12), πορεύονται 'they went' > ἀναπλευσάντων 'having sailed up' (UPZ I 18, l. 13; UPZ I 19, l. 15), ἀνεχορημεν (l. ἀνεχωρή<σα>μεν) 'we went up' > ἀναβᾶσαι 'to go up' (UPZ I 18, l. 17; UPZ I 19, l. 23). In one case, a verb of movement is changed into a nominal expression: ἐκπορ[ευ]ομ<έν>ων 'while going out' > ἐν τεῖ ἐξόδωι 'during the exit' (UPZ I 5, l. 11; UPZ I 6, l. 9). Several verbs of giving and taking have also been altered. So, for example, ἐξενέγκαι 'to carry off' > προσ[εσ]ύλησεν 'he plundered in addition' (UPZ I 5, l. 22; UPZ I 6, l. 19), ἐνοίκιον λαμβάνει > ἐνοικιολογεῖ 'she receives rent' (UPZ I 18, l. 16; UPZ I 19, l. 19), δέξασθαι > προσλαβέσθαι 'to take on' (UPZ I 18, l. 26; UPZ I 19, l. 25), διδοῖ 'may he give' > [ἀν]δαποδῷ 'may he give back' (UPZ I 52, l. 26; UPZ I 53, l. 30), and ἀποδοῦναι 'to return'> προσαποδοῦναι 'to pay as a debt besides' (UPZ I 34, l. 10; UPZ I 35, l. 22). On a couple of occasions, we also find more extensive reformulations of verbal expressions. So, for example, ἄταφός ἐστειν 'he is unburied' > οὐ τετόλμηκεν αὐτὸν ἡ Νεφόρις θάψαι 'Nephoris has not had the courage to burry him' (UPZ I 18, l. 15; UPZ. I 19, ll. 16–17), καὶ ταῦτα ἐξήνεγκαν 'these things too they carried off' > οὐδὲ ταῦτά γε ἡμῖν ἀπέλιπον 'not even these they left for us' (UPZ I 5, ll. 39–40; UPZ I 6, ll. 28–29), and εὑρόντες ἐξερημωμένον τὸν τόπον 'having found the place deserted' > μηθὲν εὑρόντες χρήσιμον 'having found nothing of use' (UPZ I 5, ll. 36–37; UPZ I 6, l. 28).

Less often, nouns have been altered in the archive. So, for example, τὰ δύο μολύβδινα 'the two leaden (items)' > τὰ ποτήρια 'the drinking cups' (UPZ I 5, l. 44; UPZ I 6, l. 32), εἰς Ἡρακλήους πόλειν > τὸν Ἡρακλεοπολίτην '(to) Herakleopolis' (UPZ I 18, l. 12; UPZ I 19, l. 13), ὑπὸ τῆς λύπης 'because of grief' > ὑπὸ τῆς ἀθυμίας 'because of hopelessness' (UPZ I 18, ll. 12–13; UPZ I 19, l. 14), τὴν δὲ οὐσίαν αὐτοῦ 'his property' > τὰ δ' ἐκείνου ὑπάρχοντα 'his possessions' (UPZ I 18, ll. 15–16; UPZ I 19, l. 17), and οἱ δὲ γνώριμοι αὐτῆς 'her acquaintances' > τῶν δὲ τῆς μητρὸς φίλων '(of) friends of our mother' (UPZ I 18, l. 22; UPZ I 19, ll. 24–25). Interestingly, the way people and places are referred to is also subject to lexical change, references being either more or less specific: so e.g. τῶν πτωχῶν '(of) the beggars' > τῶν ἄλλων ἐνκατό[χ]ων '(of) the others in katochè' (UPZ I 5, l. 21; UPZ I 6, ll. 18–19), τινος τῶν πτωχῶν '(of) one of the beggars' > Ἁρμαῖς (l. Ἁρμάιος) δέ τινος '(of) a certain Hermais' (UPZ I 5, l. 22; UPZ I 6, l. 19), Φιλίππωι Σωγένου 'with Philippus son of Sogenes' > Φιλίππωι τινὶ 'with a certain Philippus' (UPZ I 18, l. 4; UPZ I 19, l. 7), τὸν πατέρα ἡμῶν 'our father' > αὐτὸν 'him' (UPZ I 18, l. 6; UPZ I 19, l. 8), and εἰς τὴν νεκρ<ί>αν 'to the necropolis' > εἰς τὰς κατὰ Μέμφιν νεκρίας 'to the burying grounds at Memphis' (UPZ I 18, l. 14; UPZ I 19, l. 16). Infrequently, adjectives and adverbs have been changed. Some examples include ἐξενι<αύ>του 'yearly' > ἑκάστου ἐνιαυτοῦ 'every year' (UPZ I 34, l. 5; UPZ I 35, ll. 10–11) and ἔτει (l. ἔτι) καὶ νῦν 'even now' > μέχρι τοῦ νῦν 'until now' (UPZ I 18, l. 15; UPZ I 19, l. 16). Numbers, too, are involved in lexical changes. So, for example, alphabetic notation is replaced by an adjective on one occasion (ιζ '17' > τῆι [ἑ]πτακαιδεκάτηι 'on the seventeenth' (UPZ I 5, l. 19; UPZ I 6, l. 17)), and vice versa on another (ἑνδέκατον 'eleventh' > ια '11' (UPZ I 52, l. 4; UPZ I 53, l. 4)).

To conclude, we also see that function words are subject to lexical changes. Some examples include ἐν Μέμφει > πρὸς Μέμφει 'in Memphis' (UPZ I 18, l. 1; UPZ I 19, l. 3), εἰς νῆσον > ἐπί τινα νῆσον 'to an island' (UPZ I 18, l. 10; UPZ I 19, l. 12), ἐνγὺς τοῦ ποταμοῦ > πρὸ[ς] τῶι ποταμῶι 'near the river' (UPZ I 18, ll. 8–9; UPZ I 19, l. 10) (prepositions); [τὸν υ]ἱὸν αὐτῆς > τὸν ἐκείνης υἱὸν 'her son' (UPZ I 18, l. 22; UPZ I 19, l. 25), αὐτὸν > τοῦτον 'him' (UPZ I 5, l. 25; UPZ I 6, l. 21) (pronouns); μὴ > μήποτε '(I fear) that' (UPZ I 35, l. 17; UPZ I 36, l. 15) (complementisers); δὲ > τε (UPZ I 5, l. 11; UPZ I 6, l. 10), καὶ 'and' > οὐ μὴν [ἀ]λλὰ καὶ 'not only but also' (UPZ I 5, l. 26; UPZ I 6, l. 22), οὖν > διόπερ 'so' (UPZ I 5, l. 46; UPZ I 6, l. 32) (particles).

3.1.2 Syntactic changes

Syntactic changes occur second most frequently in our archive. Two types of syntactic changes are particularly often attested. First, in the area of word order, we see a conscious effort to place the syntactic "head" after, rather than in front of, its complements, which had become the usual word order in Postclassical Greek.[26] Some examples of verb phrases include εἰσελθόντες εἰς τὸ τῆς θεᾶς ἄδυτον > εἰς τὸ ἄδυτον τῆς θεᾶς εἰσελθὼν 'having entered the sanctuary of the goddess' (UPZ I 5, ll. 26–27; UPZ I 6, l. 22), εἰς τὴν νεκρ<ί>αν καθειστῶσιν 'they brought him to the necropolis' > παρακομισάντων αὐτὸν εἰς τὰς κατὰ Μέμφιν νεκρίας 'having conveyed him to the burying grounds at Memphis' (UPZ I 18, l. 14; UPZ I 19, ll. 15–16), καιθειστᾷ αὐτὸν εἰς Ἡρακλήους πόλειν '(the boat) set him down in Herakleopolis' > εἰς δὲ τὸν Ἡρακλεοπολίτην χωρισθέντος 'having gone off to the Herakleopolite nome' (UPZ I 18, ll. 11–12; UPZ I 19, ll. 13–14), and ἀποθνήσκει ἐκεῖ ὑπὸ τῆς λύπης 'he died there because of grief' > ὑπὸ τῆς

---

26 See e.g. Levinsohn (2000), Horrocks (2007).

ἀθυμίας μετήλλαχεν τὸν βίον 'he departed life because of hopelessness' (UPZ I 18, ll. 12–13; UPZ I 19, ll. 14–15). We see the same phenomenon at a lower syntactic level, that of the noun phrase: στάμνον αὐτοῦ > τ[ὸ]ν αὐτοῦ στάμνον 'his storage jar' (UPZ I 5, l. 23; UPZ I 6, l. 20), τοῦ δὲ πατρὸς ἡμῶν > ἡμῶν . . . τοῦ πατρὸς '(of) our father' (UPZ I 18, l. 19; UPZ I 19, l. 22), and [τὸν υ]ἱὸν αὐτῆς > τὸν ἐκείνης υἱὸν 'her son' (UPZ I 18, l. 22; UPZ I 19, l. 25). In two cases, however, we see the opposite syntactic movement: τὸ τῆς θεᾶς ἄδυτον > τὸ ἄδυτον τῆς θεᾶς 'the sanctuary of the godess' (UPZ I 5, ll. 26–27; UPZ I 6, l. 22) and τὸν ἐπιστάτην τῶν ἱερῶν Ψινταῆν > Ψινταῆν τὸν ἐπιστάτην [τ]ῶν ἱερῶν 'Psintaes overseer of the priests' (UPZ I 52, l. 2; UPZ I 53, ll. 23–24).

Another major type of syntactic change concerns participial syntax.[27] Very often, main verbs in the indicative mood are changed into participles (genitive absolute constructions in particular). Some examples include: παραλαβόντες φυλακίτας εἰσῆλθον 'having taken *phylakitai* they entered' > παραλαβόντων φυλακίτας καὶ εἰσελθόντων 'having taken *phylakitai* and having entered' (UPZ I 5, ll. 7–8; UPZ I 6, l. 7), ἀδεικούμεθα ὑπὸ Νε[φό]ρυτος 'we are being wronged by Nephoris' > ἀδικούμεναι ὑπὸ Νεφόριτος 'being wronged by Nephoris' (UPZ I 18, l. 2; UPZ I 19, l. 4), οἱ δελφοὶ (l. ἀδελφοὶ) αὐτοῦ πορεύονται 'his brothers went' > τῶν δὲ ἀδελφῶν αὐτοῦ ἀναπλευσάντων 'his brothers having sailed up' (UPZ I 18, l. 13; UPZ I 19, l. 15), and ἄγουσιν καὶ εἰς τὴν νεκραν καθειστῶσιν αὐτόν 'they went to fetch him and brought him to the necropolis' > [[ἀγαγόντων]] καὶ παρακομισάντων αὐτὸν εἰς τὰς κατὰ Μέμφιν νεκρίας 'having brought and conveyed him to the burying grounds at Memphis' (UPZ I 18, ll. 14–15; UPZ I 19, ll. 15–16). In two cases, however, we see the reverse syntactic movement, whereby a participle in the first version is changed into a main verb in the indicative in the second version: συνοικήσασα Φιλίππωι Σωγένου 'having set up house with Philippus son of Sogenes' > συνώικησε Φιλίππωι τινὶ 'she lived with a certain Philippus' (UPZ I 18, l. 4; UPZ I 19, l. 6) and ἐκβάλλουσα ἡμᾶς 'throwing us out' > ἐξέβαλεν ἡμᾶς 'she threw us out' (UPZ I 18, l. 17; UPZ I 19, l. 20). It is interesting to note that in the first of these two instances a second hand has stricken through the main verb συνώικησε and changed it into the participle συνοῦσα 'living together'.

Next to word order and participial syntax, various other types of syntactic changes are made. For example, we see that the active voice is sometimes changed into the passive voice: so, e.g., Ψῦλιν . . . ἀπέσταλκεν 'Psulis has sent' > ἀπ[ε]στάλθα[ι] ὑπὸ Ψοῦλιν 'to have been sent by Psulis' (UPZ I 5, ll. 42–43; UPZ I 6, l. 31), and εἴληφεν 'she took' > ἀναληφθέντα 'having been confiscated' (UPZ I

---

27 For some observations, see also Vierros (this volume, §3.3).

18, l. 16; UPZ I 19, l. 17). Definiteness is also an area where changes are made: the indefinite pronoun is added in cases such as εἰς νῆσον > ἐπί τινα νῆσον 'to an island' (UPZ I 18, l. 10; UPZ I 19, l. 12), Θέωνι > Θέωνι τινὶ 'to (a certain) Theon' (UPZ I 5, 26; UPZ I 6, 21), and τῷ (l. τῶ<ν>) ἐν κατοχῇ > τινα τῶν ἐν κατοχῇ ὄντων 'one of the people living in katochè' (UPZ I 18, ll. 18–19; UPZ I 19, l. 22), and in one case the definite article is added: Θέωνι Παῦτος > Θέωνι . . . τῶι Παῆτ [ος] 'Theon son of Paes' (UPZ I 5, l. 26; UPZ I 6, l. 21). In the area of complementation/ subordination, too, we see a number of interesting changes, which cannot be easily grouped under one heading. So, for example, there is a change from direct to indirect speech in πυθομένων δὲ ἡμῶν αὐτῶν· τίνος χάριν ἐπισπορεύεσθε 'when we asked: why do you intrude' > πυνθανομένων δ' ἡμῶν τοῦ τίνος χάριν εἴησαν εἰσπεπορευμένοι 'when we asked why they had entered' (UPZ I 5, ll. 40–41; UPZ I 6, ll. 29–30); a change from the bare infinitive to ὡς with the future indicative: ἐπέταξαν αὐτῷ ἀποκτῖναι 'they ordered him to kill' > ἐξηργά\ζε/το ὡς ἐπανελεῖται 'she contrived that he would destroy' (UPZ I 18, l. 6; UPZ I 19, l. 8); a change from ἵνα with the subjunctive to the bare infinitive: εἶνα δειακονεῖ ἡμῖν > διακονεῖν ἡμῖν 'to serve us' (UPZ I 18, l. 23; UPZ I 19, l. 25); and a change from a participle to ὥστε with the infinitive: πινῶντες 'starving' > ὥστ' ἂν κ[ι]νδυνεύειν τῶι λιμῶι διαλυθῆναι 'so that we are in danger of perishing from starvation' (UPZ I 18, l. 17; UPZ I 19, ll. 20–21).

3.1.3 Orthographic changes

Orthographic changes are also quite prominent in the archive. Most of these concern vowels, reflecting changes in pronunciation that were ongoing already in the Early Ptolemaic period,[28] such as the loss of quantitative distinctions, the convergence of ει, ι, η, etc. in pronunciation towards /i/ ("itacism"), and the reduction of diphthongs to simple vowels. Some examples include: χάρειν > χάριν 'grace' (UPZ I 35, l. 13; UPZ I 36, l. 11), ἐπὶ > ἐπεὶ 'since' (UPZ I 35, l. 17; UPZ I 36, l. 14), τώπους > τόπους 'places' (UPZ I 35, l. 18; UPZ I 36, l. 16), ἰκοστοῦ > εἰκοστοῦ '(of) the twentieth' (UPZ I 35, l. 19; UPZ I 36, l. 16), ἀπέδοκα > ἀπέδωκα 'I delivered' (UPZ I 35, l. 5; UPZ I 36, l. 5), βοιηθείας > βοηθείας '(of) help' (UPZ I 5, l. 53; UPZ I 6, l. 38), προεῒ > πρωὶ 'early in the day' (UPZ I 5, l. 20; UPZ I 6, l. 17), ὀφιλομένας > ὀφειλομένας 'required' (UPZ I 52, l. 24; UPZ I 53, l. 25), αἰδικοῦνται > ἀδικοῦνται 'they are being wronged' (UPZ I 52, l. 9; UPZ I 53, l. 10), and ἀδεικούμεθα 'we are being wronged' > ἀδικούμεναι 'being wronged' (UPZ I 18, l. 2; UPZ I 19, l. 4).

---

28 For further discussion, see Mayser-Schmoll, Teodorsson (1977), Horrocks (2010: 160–188).

As can be expected, the second version in each set of petitions tends to correct irregular orthography, but on some occasions it introduces additional mistakes and hypercorrections: so, for example, ἐν τούτοις > ἐν τούτος 'in these matters' (UPZ I 35, l. 16; UPZ I 36, l. 14), οὐκ > εοὐκ 'not' (UPZ I 52, l. 11; UPZ I 53, l. 12), ἥμυσι > ἥμυσυ 'half' (UPZ I 52, l. 15; UPZ I 53, l. 17), Μακεδώνος > Μαικεδόνος 'Macedonian' (UPZ I 52, l. 2; UPZ I 53, l. 2), and σοι > σι 'to you' (UPZ I 52, l. 26; UPZ I 53, l. 30). As can be seen, all of these additional misrepresentations occur in the two sets of texts addressed to Sarapion the *hypodioikêtês*, which is probably not a coincidence. Paleographical evidence shows that these two sets of texts were written by the same hand, that of Apollonios.[29] In trying to upgrade these petitions himself, Apollonios must have introduced new mistakes.

Orthographic misrepresentations are much less prominent when it comes to consonants.[30] Here, too, misrepresentations reflect pronunciation changes that are in progress, such as the confusion between voiced and voiceless consonants (e.g. τ for δ), the confusion between voiceless and aspirated voiceless consonants (e.g. π for φ), and consonant cluster reduction (e.g. τ for ντ). Some examples include διαρπάσζεται > διαρπάζεται 'it is robbed' (UPZ I 52, l. 20; UPZ I 53, l. 21), νομίζαντα > νομίσαντα 'having considered' (UPZ I 35, l. 20; UPZ 36, l. 17), and βασιλίσης > [β]ασιλ[ί]σσ[η]ς '(of) the queen' (UPZ I 35, l. 6; UPZ I 36, l. 6). Occasionally, misrepresentations that can be less easily connected to the changes in pronunciation are corrected. So, for example, ἐταναγκάσαι > ἐπαναγκάσαι 'to compel' (UPZ I 52, l. 23; UPZ I 53, l. 24) and ἀξιουνμεν > ἀξιοῦμεν 'we ask' (UPZ I 52, l. 21; UPZ I 53, l. 22).

3.1.4 Morphological changes

Least often, morphology is involved in the linguistic changes that have been made. In the area of verb morphology, the archive contains a couple of examples where one type of aorist formation is changed into another. So for, example, we find ἐξηνέγκαντο 'they carried off' > ἐξήνεγκεν 'he carried off' (UPZ I 5, l. 18; UPZ I 6, l. 16), σκύλαντες > σκυλήσας 'having robbed' (UPZ I 5, l. 18; UPZ I 6, l. 15), and ἔσκυλαν 'they robbed' > ἐσκύλη[σε]ν 'he robbed' (UPZ I 5, l. 27; UPZ I 6, l. 22). Interestingly, there are also examples where one aspectual stem is changed into the other: διδοῖ > δοῖ 'may he give (UPZ I 35, l. 12; UPZ I 36, l. 11), πυθομένων 'having inquired' > πυνθανομένων 'while inquiring' (UPZ I 5, l. 40;

---

29 Cf. Wilcken (1927: 115).
30 Cf. Bentein (2015a: 467).

UPZ I 6, l. 29), and ἠνομημένον 'having been used lawlessly' > ἀνουμο\ύ/μενον 'being used lawlessly' (UPZ I 5, l. 47; UPZ I 6, l. 34). In one case, the aorist endings of the verb γίγνομαι are changed from middle to passive: γενομένου > ἐπιγενηθέντος 'having occurred' (UPZ I 18, l. 20; UPZ I 19, l. 23).

In the area of nominal morphology, even less changes can be noted. In one case, a plural form is changed into a singular form: εὐτυχίαι > εὐ]τυχία 'success(es)' (UPZ I 35, l. 30; UPZ I 36, l. 25). In a number of other cases, we see that endings are changed: παν τὸν τόπον > πάντα τὸν τόπον 'the entire place' (UPZ I 5, l. 11; UPZ I 6, l. 11), ἐπαφροδισίαν > ἐπαφροδισία 'charm' (UPZ I 35, l. 28; UPZ I 36, l. 24), ἀντιπεσον > ἀντιπεσόντα 'having resisted' (UPZ I 35, l. 26; UPZ I 36, l. 21), and ἔλαιον 'olive oil' > ἐλαίου '(of) olive oil' (UPZ I 35, l. 24; UPZ I 36, l. 20).

To conclude the discusion on the Katochoi of the Sarapieion archive, it is worth drawing attention to some noticeable differences between the texts included in our archive: in the last two sets of petitions, UPZ I 35/36 and UPZ I 52/53, orthographic changes are much more common than in the other texts in the archive. This becomes clear in the following Figure, which graphically represents the types of changes made only in these two sets of texts (compare with our earlier Figure 3).

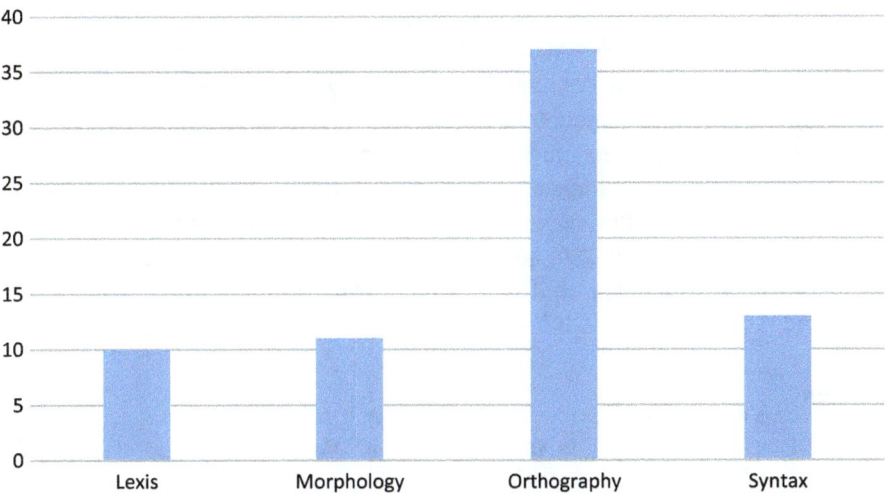

Figure 4: Linguistic changes in UPZ I 35/36 and UPZ I 52/53.

As I mentioned before, this noticeable difference between the first two sets of petitions and the last two sets of petitions can be connected to paleographical differences: the first two sets of petitions are written by an elegant chancery hand,

and in these texts orthography is much less an issue. The last two sets of petitions, on the other hand, are written by the hand of Apollonios, indicating that he himself was responsible for the linguistic upgrading. In doing so, Apollonios mainly focused on orthography, making only a couple of changes in the areas of syntax, morphology, and the lexicon. That changes are much less thoroughgoing can perhaps also be connected to the social status of the respective addressees: the first two sets of petitions are addressed to the King, whereas the last two sets of petitions are addressed to Sarapion the *hypodioikêtês*, a lower official.

3.2 Phrynichus' *Ecloga* (II CE)

The second source which I consider here is a lexicographical treatise from the second century, by the hand of Phrynichus.[31] Phrynichus was a rhetorician from the later second century CE, and one of the strictest Atticists.[32] Swain (1996: 55) connects this to Phrynichus' origins: Photius calls him an "Arabian",[33] which would have meant that he was a non-Greek speaker by birth, who had to learn the rules by hard work, and was therefore opposed to anyone challenging those rules.

Two of Phrynichus' works survive, both of them dealing with proper Atticist usage. The first is called Σοφιστικὴ προπαρασκευή (*Praeparatio Sophistica*),[34] a lengthy work of thirty-seven books, which is preserved only in an epitome, fragments, and a summary by Photius. The second is called Ἐκλογὴ Ἀττικῶν ῥημάτων καὶ ὀνομάτων (*Ecloga*)[35] and is much shorter, comprising only two books. It was originally considered an epitome, but is now thought to be more or less complete. It was dedicated to the imperial secretary, Sulpicius Cornelianus, and can be dated back to 178 CE. Phrynichus' two works have much the same purpose, although, as Lee (2013: 288–289) notes, not entirely: the *Ecloga* is primarily a list of what needs to be avoided, and what needs to be used instead,[36] whereas the

---

[31] On Phrynichus, see e.g. Swain (1996: 54–56), Dickey (2007: 96–97), OCD, s.v.
[32] Phrynichus finds "mistakes" in writers such as Demosthenes (CCXXIII), Lysias (CCCXXXI), Sophocles (CLXIII), and Xenophon (LXXI).
[33] The Suda, on the other hand, says that Phrynichus was born in Bithynia. As Swain (1996: 55) notes, this statement need not be contradictory, since the sophists travelled around quite a bit.
[34] Edited by de Borries (1911).
[35] Text editions include Rutherford (1881) (with commentary) and Fischer (1974). In what follows, references are made to Rutherford's (1881) edition.
[36] While this is standard practice in the *Ecloga*, it is not always the case: for example, Phrynichus will sometimes start with a good word, and then give the bad alternative (e.g. CCXC). On other occasions, he does not give an alternative (e.g. XLVIII), simply mentions that

Praeparatio Sophistica aims to suggest or explain a useful Attic expression, without necessarily naming the equivalent feature that needs to be avoided.

Since both of Phrynichus' works are arranged in the form of a lexicon, Phrynichus is traditionally characterized as a "lexicographer", and his works as "lexica".[37] As several scholars have noted, however, their purpose was much wider: Swain (1996: 54), for example, describes the purpose of Phrynichus' *Praeparatio Sophistica* as "to provide guidance on vocabulary, grammar, and style for literature, rhetoric, and conversational purposes, as well as for satirical writing . . . and, interestingly, for the language of love." In similar vein, Kim (2010: 477) has noted that lexica such as Phrynichus' *Ecloga* "[cover] more than vocabulary; many entries deal with phonology, morphology, and occasionally syntax".[38] As the following Figure shows, Kim's judgment is quite right: about 60% of the entries are lexical in nature, while the rest of the entries deal with morphology, syntax and orthography.

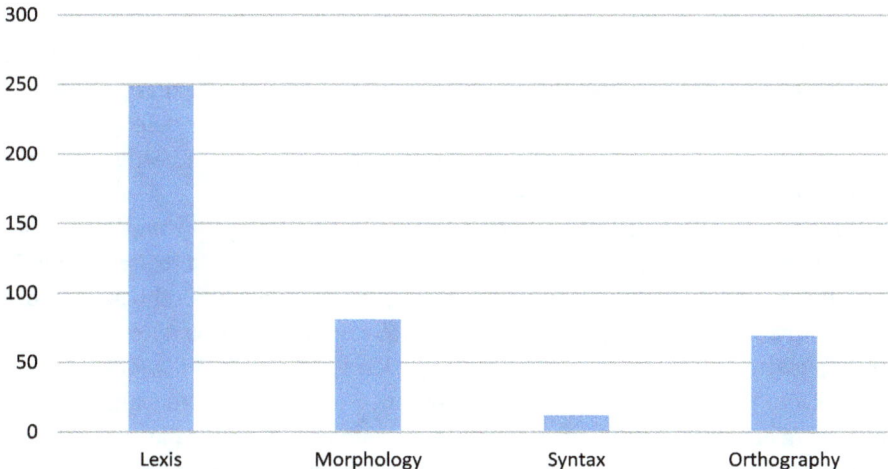

Figure 5: Entries in Phrynichus' *Ecloga*.[39]

---

a word is "to be deleted" (e.g. CCCLXVIII), or does not mention a good alternative, leaving the lemma open for further comments (e.g. CCL).
37 So also Dickey (2007). Contrast Lee (2013), who explicitly speaks of "the Atticist grammarians".
38 For a typology of "lexica", see Tosi (2015), who discusses Phrynichus' *Ecloga* under the heading of "lexica whose content is more properly morphological and orthographical" (Tosi 2015: 632).
39 Entries that concern more than one linguistic level have been counted double.

3.2.1 Lexical entries

Most of the lexical entries in the *Ecloga* concerns nouns and verbs. Nouns are discussed most often: there are about twice as many entries on nouns as there are on verbs (approx. 125 vs. 66). Many of these involve the replacement of one term, which is to be avoided, with its proper "Attic" variant: so, for example, ἐρεύγεσθαι > ἐρυγγάνειν 'to belch' (XLV), ἀναιδεύεσθαι > ἀναιδίζεσθαι 'to behave impudently' (XLVII), κοράσιον > κόριον '(little) girl' (LVI), λιθάριον > λιθίδιον 'pebble' (CLVIII), ἀρτοκόπος > ἀρτοποιός 'baker' (CXCVIII), πάπυρος > βίβλος 'papyrus' (CCLXXI), and φάγομαι > ἔδομαι 'I eat' (CCCI). In other cases, Phrynichus gives a comment about the proper semantic usage of specific lexical items, without suggesting an alternative. So, for example, he comments that αὐθέντης (XCVI) should never be used in the sense of 'master' (δεσπότης), but always with the sense of 'murderer' (αὐτόχειρ φονέως).[40]

Interestingly, Phrynichus sometimes attributes improper usages to specific social groups, such as doctors (XIX, CXCIV), orators (XCVIII), farmers (CLXXXI), stoics (CCXLVII, CCCIV, CCCLII), and gymnasts (CCLXXIX). On a couple of occasions, he also gives comments about proper male vs. female usages: he notes, for example, that νὴ τὼ θεώ 'by the goddesses' (CLXXI) is used for female oaths, and should be avoided by men, and that one should reserve the adjective μέθυσος 'drunk' for women, using μεθυστικός for men (CXXIX).

In many of Phrynichus' suggestions, compounding plays an important role. So, for example, he has a whole range of suggestions about verbal compounds which are used with the wrong preposition: ἐμπτύει > καταπτύει 'he spits upon' (IX), ἀνεῖναι > διεῖναι 'to saturate' (XIX), ἐπιτροπιάζειν > ὑποτροπιάζειν 'to recur' (LXV), ἀνατοιχεῖν > διατοιχεῖν 'to roll from side to side' (CXXXIX), ἀφιερῶσαι > καθιερῶσαι 'to dedicate' (CLXVIII), ἐξυπνισθῆναι > ἀφυπνισθῆναι 'to wake up' (CC), etc. There are also a couple of examples with nouns. So, for example, he suggests: ὑπόδειγμα > παράδειγμα 'example' (IV), βασκάνιον > προβασκάνιον 'amulet' (LXVIII), συμπολίτης > πολίτης '(fellow) citizen' (CL), etc. Compounds where a verb is combined with a noun, an adverb, or an adjective, have to be avoided entirely, it seems: καλλιγραφεῖν > εἰς κάλλος γράφειν 'to write beautifully' (XCIX), εὐκαιρεῖν > εὖ σχολῆς ἔχειν 'to have leisure' (CIII), σιτομετρεῖσθαι > σῖτον μετρεῖσθαι 'to deal out portions of corn' (CCCLX), χρησιμεῦσαι > χρήσιμον γενέσθαι 'to be useful' (CCCLXVII), αἰχμαλωτισθῆναι > αἰχμάλωτον γενέσθαι 'to be captured' (CCCCVII), etc. Again, there are a couple of examples with nouns: compounds consisting of a

---

[40] For similar examples, see e.g. XL, LV, LXXXI, LXXXIII, CX, CCXVI, CCCLI, CCCLV (nouns); LXXVI, LXXX (verbs).

noun and an adjective or second noun are to be avoided. So, for example μεσοδάκτυλα > τὰ μέσα τῶν δακτύλων 'spaces between two fingers or toes' (CLXXII) and οἰκοδεσπότης > οἰκίας δεσπότης 'master of a house' (CCCXLVIII).

The *Ecloga* also contains quite a few entries on adjectives and adverbs. Some representative entries include ἀπόπαλαι > ἐκ παλαιοῦ 'from of old' (XXXI), ἀρχῆθεν > ἐξ ἀρχῆς 'from the beginning' (LXXV), ἀκμήν > ἔτι 'still' (C), ἐξεπιπολῆς > ἐπιπολῆς 'on the top' (CIV), μονόφθαλμον > ἑτερόφθαλμον 'one-eyed' (CXII), γελάσιμον > γελοῖον 'laughable' (CCV), and βιωτικόν > χρήσιμον ἐν τῷ βίῳ 'lively' (CCCXXXII). Function words such as prepositions, particles, pronouns, etc. are almost entirely absent. One exceptional entry is ὀνδηποτοῦν > ὀντινοῦν 'whoever' (CCCXLIX). Occasionally, Phrynichus discusses entire phrases/expressions. So, for example, ἀνατέλλει ὁ ἥλιος, ἐπιτέλλει δὲ ὁ κύων 'the sun rises, but the dog-star comes up' (CII), ἔνδον εἰσέρχομαι > εἴσω παρέρχομαι 'I go inside' (CV), κατὰ κοιλίας ποιεῖν > ὑπάγειν τὴν γαστέρα 'to purge the belly' (CCLXXIX), and τὰ ἴδια πράττω > τὰ ἐμαυτοῦ πράττω 'I do my own things' (CCCCV). On various occasions, Phrynichus connects the stems of lexical items across word classes. So, for example, he notes that the adjective ἀναίσθητος 'not perceptible by sense' can be used by the Atticist, but its derivative verb ἀναισθητεύομαι 'I do not sense' not (CCCXXIX), the correct usage being οὐκ αἰσθάνομαι.

3.2.2 Morphological entries

As Figure 5 shows, quite a few entries in the *Ecloga* deal with morphology. Both nominal and verbal morphology are well represented. In the former area, there are quite a few entries dealing with gender,[41] whereby the male article is typically replaced by the female article.[42] So, for example, ὁ ὄμφαξ > ἡ ὄμφαξ 'the unripe grape' (XXXVII), ὁ χάραξ > ἡ χάραξ 'the palisade' (XLIII), ὁ φάρυγξ > ἡ φάρυγξ 'the throat' (XLVI), ὁ ὕσπληξ > ἡ ὕσπληξ 'the cord' (LIV), ὁ ῥώξ > ἡ ῥάξ 'the grape' (LVII), and οἱ χόλικες > αἱ χόλικες 'the bowels' (CCLXXXIII).

In a number of other entries, Phrynichus rejects female endings on the noun in favor of male endings: ἀσβόλη > ἄσβολος 'soot' (XC) and αἰθάλη > αἴθαλος 'thick smoke' (CXI). Elsewhere, he argues in favor of a different noun formation: θερμότης > θερμασία 'heat' (XCII), ἀτταγήν > ἀτταγᾶς 'francolin' (XCIII), or of different endings in the nominative or other cases: υἱέα > υἱόν 'son' (XLIX), Ἡρακλῆν

---

[41] I classify gender here as morphological. This may be debated.
[42] But note τὸ ῥύπος > ὁ ῥύπος 'the dirt' (CXXVII), ὁ ἐπίδεσμος > τὸ ἐπίδεσμον 'the outer bandage' (CCLX), and τὴν κόριν > τὸν κόριν 'the bug' (CCLXXVII).

> Ἡρακλέα 'Heracles' (CXXXIV), αἱ ναῦς > αἱ νῆες 'the ships' (CXLVII), χρύσεα > χρυσᾶ 'golden' (CLXXXIII), δυσί > δυοῖν '(with) two' (CLXXXV), ὤτοις > ὠσί '(with) ears' (CLXXXVI), etc. A couple of entries also deal with number, whereby Phrynichus proposes to replace a plural form by a singular one. So, for example, κατὰ χειρῶν > κατὰ χειρός 'at hand' (CCC) and χρηστὸς τὰ ἤθη > χρηστὸς τὸ ἦθος 'well-mannered' (CCCXLIV). Degrees of comparison are another hot topic in the *Ecloga*. So, for example, τελευταιότατον > τελευταῖον (L), ἐσχατώτατον > ἔσχατον 'farthest' (LI), κορυφαιότατον > κορυφαῖον 'at the top' (LII), τάχιον > θᾶττον 'quicker' (LVIII), ἀγαθώτερος > ἀγαθὸς μᾶλλον 'better' (LXXIV), καλλιώτερον > κάλλιον 'more beautiful' (CXI), and ἔγγιον > ἐγγύτερον 'nearer' (CCLXV).

When it comes to verbal morphology, proper tense formation is the most discussed issue. Several entries deal with the formation of the perfect, future, aorist and imperfect. So, for example, ἀπελεύσομαι > ἄπειμι 'I will go away' (XXVI), ἐπεξελευσόμενος > ἐπεξιών 'to be marching out' (XXVII) (future); κατώρυκται > κατορώρυκται 'he is buried' (XXIV), ὤμοκε > ὀμώμοκε 'he has sworn' (XXV), τέτευχε > τετύχηκε 'he has obtained' (CCCLXXIII) (perfect); ἧς > ἦσθα 'you were' (CXXIV), ἔφης > ἔφησθα 'you said' (CXXV), ἤμην > ἦν 'I was' (CXXX) (imperfect); εὕρασθαι > εὑρέσθαι 'to have found' (CXV), ἀφείλατο > ἀφείλετο 'he has taken away' (CXVI), ἵνα ἄξωσιν > ἵνα ἀγάγωσιν 'so that they bring' (CCLII), ἐκλείψας > ἐκλιπών 'having abandoned' (CCCXLIII) (aorist). In one case, the perfect tense is preferred to the present tense: γρηγορῶ > ἐγρήγορα 'I am awake' (XCV). A couple of other entries deal with the augment, e.g. περιέσσευσεν > ἐπερίσσευσε 'it was more than enough' (XX) and τεθεληκέναι > ἠθεληκέναι 'to have wanted' (CCCVII).

An issue that is addressed multiple times in the *Ecloga* is contract verb formation: so, for example, πεινᾶν > πεινῆν 'to be hungry' (XLII), λούομαι > λοῦμαι 'I bathe' (CLXV), ῥέει > ῥεῖ 'it flows' (CXCV), ἐδέετο > ἐδεῖτο 'he begged' (CXCVI), προσδέεσθαι > προσδεῖσθαι 'to need besides' (CXCVII), γαμῴη > γαμοίη 'may he marry' (CCCXXIV), and διδῴη > διδοίη 'may he give' (CCCXXV). Other entries deal with voice: so, for example, ἀνέῳγεν ἡ θύρα > ἀνέῳκται ἡ θύρα 'the door has opened' (CXXXV) and διεφθορὸς αἷμα > διεφθαρμένον αἷμα 'destroyed blood' (CXXXVI).

3.2.3 Orthographic entries

The orthographic and orthoepic entries in the *Ecloga*, which are about as frequent as the morphological entries, concern both vowels and consonants.[43]

---

43 For a more comprehensive account, see Vessella (2018).

They reflect changes in pronunciation that were ongoing during the Post-classical period, as I also noted with regard to the Katochoi of the Sarapieion archive, although Phrynichus also has an awareness of dialectal differences in the Classical period.[44] In the case of vowels, many of Phrynichus' entries concern interchanges between long and short vowels: so, for example, ἔνυστρον > ἤνυστρον '(fourth) stomach' (CXL), νήστης > νῆστις 'fasting' (CCXCIX), Διονυσεῖον > Διονύσιον 'the temple of Dionysus' (CCCXLVI), χρέως > χρέος 'obligation' (CCCLXX), ἀνυπόδετος > ἀνυπόδητος 'barefoot' (CCCCIX), and εὕρεμα > εὕρημα 'invention' (CCCCX). There are a couple of comments on interchange between α and ε/η: θέρμα > θέρμη 'heat' (CCCVI) and πεντάμηνος > πεντέμηνος 'five months old' (CCCLXXXVI).

Other entries concern diphthongs: οἰκοδόμηκεν > ᾠκοδόμηκεν 'he has built' (CXXXI), ἀπίναι > ἀπιέναι 'to go away' (VII), νούδιον > νοίδιον 'mind' (LXIX), ἐλαῖαι > ἐλᾶαι 'olives' (XCIV), Διόσκουροι > Διόσκοροι 'Dioscori' (CCXII), etc. There are also some comments on double vowels and the contraction of vowels: Ἀλκαϊκόν > Ἀλκαιικόν 'used by Alcaeus' (XXVIII), ἐπαοιδή > ἐπῳδή 'enchantment' (CCXIX), νεομηνία > νουμηνία 'the first of the month' (CXXIII), νοσσός > νεοττός 'young bird' (CLXXXII), βαλαντοκλέπτης > βαλαντιοκλέπτης 'cutpurse' (CCI).

When it comes to consonants, one of the main issues is the wrongful insertion or dropping of consonants such as β, γ, ν, and σ: so, for example, ὄπιθεν > ὄπισθεν 'behind' (II), μέχρις > μέχρι 'until' (VI), ὀρθρινός > ὄρθριος 'at daybreak' (XXXIV), ὀψινός > ὄψιος 'late' (XXXV), σμῆγμα > σμῆμα 'soap' (CCXXVIII), βόλβιτον > βόλιτον 'cow-dung' (CCCXXXV), and ἀντικρύς > ἀντικρύ 'opposite' (CCCCVIII). There is also frequent discussion of wrongful interchange between two consonants: between voiceless and aspirated voiceless consonants: ἐφιόρκους > ἐπιόρκους 'perjured' (CCLXXX), πανδοχεῖον > πανδοκεῖον 'inn' (CCLXXVI), μόκλος > μόχλος 'bar, lever' (CCLXXVIII); between voiced and voiceless consonants: ποταπός > ποδαπός 'where born?' (XXXIX), διώρυγος > διώρυχος '(of a) trench' (CCX), κρύβεται > κρύπτεται 'it is being hidden' (CCXCI); between *liquidae*: κλίβανος > κρίνανος 'vessel' (CLVI), νίτρον > λίτρον 'sodium carbonate' (CCLXXIII); between bilabial consonants: πύελος > μυελός 'marrow' (CCLXXXII); and between sibilant fricatives and alveolar stops, or sibilant and non-sibilant fricatives: ἱκεσία > ἱκετία 'supplication' (III), ὀδμή > ὀσμή 'smell' (LXXI), βαθμός > βασμός 'threshold' (CCXCVI). On a number of occasions, Phrynichus also comments on double consonants: so, for example, ἀνειλεῖν > ἀνείλλειν 'to back' (XXII), γρυλλίζειν > γρυλίζειν 'to grunt' (LXXX), and σάκκος > σάκος 'bag' (CCXXIX).

---

[44] So e.g. Ionic (CXCIII), Doric (CCXVII), and Aeolic (CCLXXIII).

Interestingly, Phrynichus also discusses syllabification, which was considered to be one of the major constituent parts of orthography in antiquity. On various occasions, Phrynichus suggests to reduce the number of syllables, as in the following examples:[45] εὐέριος > εὔερος 'of good wool' (CXXII), ἐδεδίεσαν > ἐδέδισαν 'they feared' (CLIX), στυππέϊνον > στύππινον 'of tow' (CCXXXIII), and ἐνιαυσιαῖος > ἐνιαύσιος 'annual' (CCCXL).

3.2.4 Syntactic entries

The syntactic entries in Phrynichus' *Ecloga* are limited and difficult to group under one heading. A couple of entries deal with proper case usage: so, for example, κληρονομεῖν τόνδε > κληρονομεῖν τοῦδε 'to be an heir of someone' (CVI), ὑστερίζειν τῷ καιρῷ > ὑστερίζειν τοῦ καιροῦ 'to come too late' (CCXIII), εὐαγγελίζομαί σε > εὐαγγελίζομαί σοι 'I bring good news to you' (CCXXXV), and τίνι διαφέρει > τί διαφέρει 'in which respect does it differ?' (CCCLXXII). In one entry, he suggests that a prepositional phrase should be replaced by a bare case: τὸν ἀκολουθοῦντα μετ' αὐτοῦ > τὸν ἀκολουθοῦντα αὐτῷ 'the one following him' (CCCXXXI).

Isolated remarks can also be found with regard to participial complementation: φίλος μοι τυγχάνεις > φίλος μοι τυγχάνεις ὤν 'you are my friend' (CCXLIV); the definite article: κατ' ἐκεῖνο καιροῦ > κατ' ἐκεῖνο τοῦ καιροῦ 'at that time' (CCXLVI); word order: μὲν οὖν τοῦτο πράξω > τοῦτο μὲν οὖν πράξω 'so I will do this' (CCCXXII); and tense usage: ἔμελλον ποιῆσαι > ἔμελλον ποιεῖν/ἔμελλον ποιήσειν 'I intended/was going to do' (CCCXV and CCCXVI).

Finally, a couple of entries deal with collocations, mostly adverbs and verbs. So, for example, Phrynichus notes that ἑκὼν εἶναι 'willinglyh' should only be used with verbs which contain a negative element in them, as in ἑκὼν εἶναι οὐ μὴ ποιήσω 'I will never do it'; a collocation such as ἑκὼν εἶναι ἔπραξα 'I did it willingly', he considers a grave error (CCXLI). So, too, he notes that ἄρτι 'just now' should always be combined with a present or past tense, and never with the future tense (ἄρτι ἥξω 'I'll be coming now' > ἄρτι ἥκω 'I've come just now', XII), and that ἔνδον 'inside' should never be used with a verb of motion (ἔνδον εἰσέρχομαι > εἴσω παρέρχομαι 'I will go inside', CV).

---

45 Note, however, ὕπαιθρον > ὑπαίθριον 'under the sky' (CCXXVI).

3.3 *The Life of Euthymius* (VI/X CE)

The last text which I consider here, the *Life of Euthymius*, was written at a later time, that is, the sixth century CE. Its author, Cyril of Scythopolis,[46] was probably born around 525 CE[47] in the city of Scythopolis, a city which was not only known as a commercial center producing fine linen,[48] but also as a city of monks, because of the association of the area with John the Baptist.[49] As we know from his writings, Cyril grew up in an ecclesiastical milieu, and was educated in the bishop's house. He was tonsured as a monk in 543 CE, and soon after went to Jerusalem. After a short period as a hermit, he entered the cenobitic monastery of St. Euthymius the Great at Jericho in 544 CE, where he spent ten years. He moved to the New Lavra of St. Sabas in 555, where he started writing a number of biographies of Palestinian monks (seven in total).[50] His literary activity came to an abrupt end with his untimely death in 558/559 CE at the Great Lavra of St Sabas.

Cyril's writings were linguistically revised during the tenth century by Symeon the Metaphrast. Relatively little is known about Symeon's life: he was born in Constantinople in an aristocratic family under the reign of Leon VI (886–912 CE), held several high-level administrative posts in the Byzantine civil service, and became a monk towards the end of his life. He died around 987 CE. His major achievement is a voluminous collection of Saints' Lives, which was organized according to the feasts of the ecclesiastical calendar (hence it is called "menologion").[51] Many of the texts in Symeon's *Menologion* had existed earlier, but their stylistic quality varied, which made them seem intolerable or even ridiculous to a highly-educated audience. As Høgel (2002: 138) notes, "in the new cultural climate of the Macedonian renaissance the old-fashioned phrases and word (sic), combined with helpless syntax and sentence structure of the old texts did much to destroy the pious reverence that was the saint's due." They were therefore standardized and purified by Symeon, as well as rhetorically embellished.[52]

---

[46] For further details, see ODB s.v.
[47] Cf. Price (1991: xxxviii).
[48] Price (1991: xxxviii).
[49] As Price (1991: xxxix) notes, archaeological research has uncovered the remains of five monasteries active in the sixth century in the city of Scythopolis.
[50] The lives have been edited by Schwartz (1939), and translated by Festugière (1961–1965) in French, and Price (1991) in English.
[51] The standard edition is still that by Migne (PG 114–116). For a translation of selected lives, see recently Papaioannou (2017).
[52] Peyr (1992) has argued that Symeon's reworking was not just limited to language, since he added historical details, and made the structure of the narrative more logical and vivid.

Because of the popularity of Symeon's version (his *Menologion* becoming standard reading in monastic circles from the eleventh century onwards), many of the older versions disappeared. In some cases, however, as with the *Life of Euthymius*, both the older and more recent versions have been preserved, giving us a unique opportunity to gain insight into the contemporary linguistic standard.[53] For the purposes of this contribution, I have linguistically analyzed twenty-one sections in Migne's edition (IV–XXIV), representing eleven pages of Greek text in Schwartz' (1939) edition. The picture that emerges from my analysis is that again, lexis plays a (much) more important role than syntax or morphology, as shown in Figure 6:

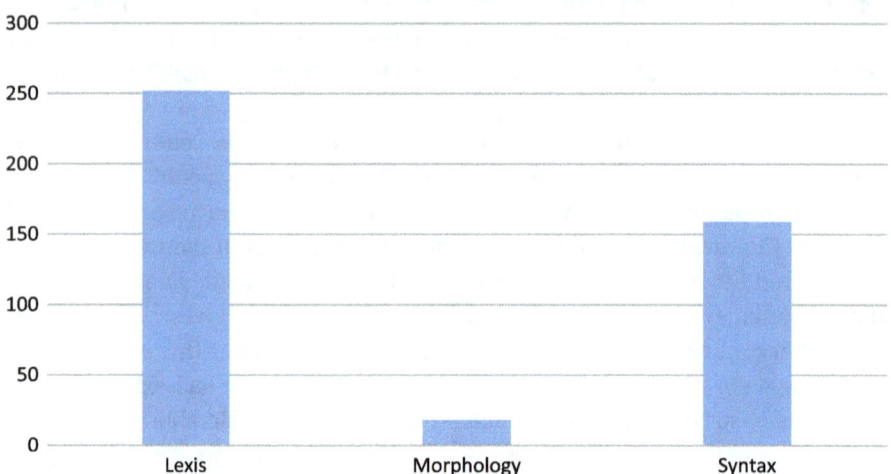

Figure 6: Linguistic changes in the metaphrasis of the *Life of Euthymius*.

3.3.1 Lexical changes

Almost half of the lexical changes concern verbs.[54] Quite often, this concerns verbs which imply a certain movement (or absence thereof): so, for example,

---

[53] For previous studies, see esp. Zilliacus (1938), Peyr (1992), Høgel (2002: 135–149).
[54] My database also contains about 30 examples of short reformulations, where the phrasing is very similar, but it is difficult to make a clear-cut classification in terms of word class. So e.g. ἔχοντα τὸν πώγονα μέγαν > βαθὺν τὸν πωγώνα καθειμένον 'having a long beard' (20.9; XXI). I will not further discuss these reformulations here.

προσήγαγεν 'she presented' > ἐπαγομένη 'bringing forward' (10.11; IV),⁵⁵ διεξελθών 'having gone through' > ἐλθών 'having gone' (13.14; IX), ᾤχετο > φοιτᾷ 'he went' (14.1; X), ἦλθεν 'he came' > καταλαμβάνει 'he reached' (14.9; X), παρερχόμενοι > παριόντες 'passing through' (15.12; XII), ἔμειναν 'they stayed' > ποιοῦνται τὴν κατοικίαν 'they made it their dwelling-place' (15.18; XII), ἀγαγεῖν 'to have led' > προσάγουσι 'they led to' (15.23; XIII), οἰκοῦμεν 'we inhabit' > οἰκεῖν προειλόμεθα 'we have preferred to inhabit' (16.4; XIII), ἀπῆλθον > ὑπέστρεψον 'they went away' (16.6; XIII), διαδραμούσης 'having spread' > διαβαινούσης 'spreading' (16.17; XIV), ἦλθεν 'he went' > ἀφικνεῖται 'he arrived' (19.12; XIX), and καταμένων > οἰκῶν 'residing' (20.13; XXI). Another category which is frequently altered are verbs of communication. So, for example, εἶπεν > φησίν 'he said' (10.18; V), ἀπαγγέλλοντες 'reporting' > διεσάφουν 'they made clear' (16.7; XIII), μὴ λαλεῖν 'not to talk' > τὴν εὔκοσμον ἀσπάζεσθαι σιωπὴν 'to embrace decorous silence' (18.2; XVII), παρήγγελλεν 'he instructed' > παρῄνει 'he exhorted' (18.2; XVII), ἀπήγγειλεν 'he announced' > διηγεῖται 'he described' (19.10; XIX), ἔλεγον 'I said' > διωμίλουν 'I spoke' (19.26; XX), and παρεκάλουν 'they demanded' > δέονται 'they begged' (20.26; XXIII). As these examples show, Symeon had a number of strategies for verbal changes: he could change the preposition in compound verbs, opt for an entirely different verb, or choose a periphrastic alternative.

Nouns are less frequently altered. Examples include abstract concepts such as τὴν τῶν μοναχῶν φροντίδα 'the care of the monks' > τὴν τῶν μοναστηρίων ἐπιστεσίαν 'the care of the monasteries' (13.26–27; IX) and πραότητι τρόπων > τῇ τῶν τρόπων ἁπλότητι 'in the simplicity of his ways' (15.5; XI); professions such as αἰπόλοι 'goatherds' > ποιμένες 'shepherds' (16.4; XIII), ἰατρὸς 'physician' > ἐπιμελητὴς 'curator' (17.4; XV), στρατηλάτης > στρατηγὸς 'commander' (19.7; XVIII); and places such as μοναστήριον > σεμνεῖον 'monastery' (13.19; IX) and ἐν ἐκκλησίαι 'in the church' > ἐν ναῷ Κυρίου 'in the temple of the Lord' (18.2; XVII). The word for 'child', 'son', is also conspicuously often altered. So, for example, μειράκιον > παιδίον (10.19; V), ὁ νέος > ὁ παῖς (19.10; XIX), τὸν υἱὸν > τὸν παῖδα (19.5; XVIII), and παῖδα > υἱὸν (19.21; XIX). There are a couple of examples of adjectives and adverb(ial)s being changed: so, for example, ὁμωνύμως > ἀκολούθως τοῖς ὀνόμασι 'in accordance with the name' (11.7; V), ἀκριβῶς 'carefully' > εὖ 'well' (11.14; VI), θαυμασίου 'wonderful' > οὐκ ἀθαύμαστον 'not without wonder' (13.22; IX), παλαιοὶ > πρεσβύτεροι 'the elders' (18.12; XVIII), ἐκτενῶς > θερμῶς 'fervently' (20.22; XXII), and ὑγιῆ > ἐρρωμένον 'healthy' (20.23, XXII).

---

55 The first term of each pair is the one in Cyril's version, the second that in Symeon's version. Quotations refer to the editions of Schwartz (1939) and Migne (1857–1866).

Interestingly, there are a couple of examples where one word class is changed into another. So, for example, we find ἀσκητικοὺς ἀγῶνας 'ascetic struggles' > διὰ Χριστόν ἀγῶνας 'struggles because of Christ' (11.15; VI), προσκυνήσας 'having venerated' > κατὰ προσκύνησιν 'for veneration (of)' (14.5; X), φιλήσυχος ὢν 'being fond of silence' > πρὸς ἡσυχίαν 'for silence' (14.10; X), γηΐνης φροντίδος '(of) worldly concern' > τῶν γηΐνων φροντίδος '(of) concern of worldly matters' (14.14; X), and φυγεῖν 'to flee' > τὴν φυγήν 'the flight' (19.3; XVIII).

Finally, there are also changes concerning function words such as particles and prepositions. So, for example, καὶ 'and' > εἶτα 'and then' (10.19; V), δὲ 'and' > οὖν 'so' (10.22; V), γὰρ 'for' > τοιγαροῦν 'therefore' (12.22; VIII), δὲ 'and' > μέντοι 'but' (15.4; XI), μέντοι > ἀλλὰ 'but' (16.19; XIV); ἐπὶ τὰ Ἱεροσόλυμα > εἰς Ἱεροσόλυμα 'to Jerusalem' (14.1; X), κατὰ τὴν ἔρημον > ἐπὶ τῆς ἐρήμου 'in the desert' (14.7; X), πρὸς αὐτούς > ὡς αὐτούς 'towards them' (16.5; XIII), εἰς τοὺς Χριστιανοὺς 'towards the Christians' > κατὰ Χριστιανῶν 'against the Christians' (18.26; XVIII), and εἰς τὴν γῆν > ἐπ' ἐδάφους 'on the ground' (20.26; XXIII).

3.3.2 Syntactic changes

At the syntactic level, most of the changes that have been made by Symeon concern word order. Sententially, we see a tendency to place the verb after its complements. So, for example, ἐπεθύμουν οἰκῆσαι 'they desired to live with him' > ἕκαστος . . . συνοικεῖν ἐδεῖτο 'everyone wanted to live with him' (16.17; XIV), συνήρχοντο πολλοὶ πρὸς αὐτὸν 'many came together to him' > πολλοὶ πρὸς αὐτὸν συνέρρεον 'many streamed together to him' (16.17–18; XIV), διηγήσαντό μοι > μοι διηγήσαντο 'they told me' (18.1; XVIII), λαβὼν τὸν υἱὸν > τὸν παῖδα παραλαβὼν 'having taken his son' (19.5; XVIII), ἀπήγγειλεν τῶι πατρὶ 'he announced to his father' > τῷ πατρὶ διηγεῖται 'he described to his father' (19.10–11; XIX), and συνέθου τῶι θεῶι > τῷ θεῷ ἐπηγγείλω 'you have offered to the Lord' (20.11; XXI). The same tendency can be seen at lower and higher levels. In the noun phrase, for example, we find changes such as κατοικητήριον θηρίων 'a dwelling-place for wild animals' > θηρίων καταφυγή 'a place of refuge for wild animals' (15.19–20; XII), ποιμένας τινὰς τοῦ Λαζαρίου > τινες τῶν τοῦ Λαζαρίου ποιμένων 'some herdsmen of Lazarium' (15.23; XIII), and τῆς ἐπαγγελίας κληρονόμους > κληρονόμους τῆς ἐπαγγελίας 'heirs of the promise' (21.9; XXIV). Direct speech forms an interesting parallel at the higher, discourse-level: here we see that Cyril consistently places the verb of saying before the speech, whereas Symeon always places it in the middle or at the end of the speech. So, for example, ἔλεγον· μὴ φοβεῖσθε 'they said: do not fear' > μὴ φοβεῖσθε . . . ἔλεγον 'do not fear . . . they said' (16.2 ; XIII).

A second word-order tendency which is noteworthy is the splitting of nominal groups. Symeon is quite fond of hyperbaton, much more so than Cyril. So, for example, we find πάσης ἀνθρωπίνης συναναστροφῆς χωριζόμενοι > πάσης ἀνθρωπίνης χωριζόμενοι συναυλίας 'being separated from all human intercourse' (14.27; XI), ἦν ἰατρὸς ψυχῶν 'he was a doctor of souls' > ψυχῶν ἦν ἐπιμελητής 'he was a curator of souls' (17.4; XV), τὴν πληγὴν ταύτην ... δεξάμενος > ταύτην δεξάμενος τὴν πληγήν 'having received this affliction' (19.22; XX), and ἐλθὼν εἰς τὴν πολιτείαν ταύτην 'having come to this region' > εἰς τὴν Ἀράβων ἤλθομεν ταύτην 'when we came to this Arabic region' (19.24–25; XX).

A number of other syntactic changes are worth mentioning. Quite frequently, Symeon has changed the tense of verb forms. Much more so than Cyril, he employs the historic present[56] at dramatic moments in the narration.[57] So, for example, τέλει τοῦ βίου ἐχρήσατο > καταλύει τὸν βίον 'he brought his life to an end' (10.5–6; IV), εἶπεν > φησίν 'he said' (10.18; V), ἐχειροτόνησεν > χειροτονεῖ 'he ordained' (11.1; V), εὗρον > καταλαμβάνουσι 'they found' (15.15; XII), and ἦλθεν 'he went' > καταλαμβάνει 'he reached' (14.9; X). Another frequent phenomenon concerns the omission of the article: on various occasions, Symeon drops the article in the original version. So, for example, τῶν γραμμάτων > γραμμάτων '(of) (the) letters' (11.11; VI), τὰ Ἱεροσόλυμα > Ἱεροσόλυμα 'Jerusalem' (14.1; X), ἡ μελέτη > μελέτη '(the) meditation' (18.8; XVII), and ἡ διάκρισις > διάκρισις '(the) discernment' (18.8–9; XVII). There is only one exception: Ἀσπεβέτωι > τῷ Ἀσπεβέτωι '(to) Aspebetus' (19.9; XVIII). In the areas of complementation and relativization, some changes have also been made: among others, Symeon avoids substantivized participles and replaces them with ordinary relative clauses. So, for example τὸν γεγονότα τῆς ἐρήμου ταύτης μέγαν κοινοβιάρχην 'the one who became a great cenobitic superior of this desert' > ὃς τῶν κατὰ τὴν ἔρημον ἐξηγήσατο κοινοβίων 'who was a leader of the cenobitic monks in this desert' (16.14–15; XIV) and τὴν μέχρι τοῦ νῦν σωιζομένην 'the one preserved even now' > ἥτις καὶ εἰς τόδε χρόνου μένει συνισταμένη 'which up until this time remains in existence' (21.1; XXIV). He also has a distinct preference for indirect over direct speech.[58] So, for example, καὶ λέγει· τί ἐστιν ὃ ζητεῖτε 'and he said: what is it that you search' > τὴν χρείαν ἥτις αὐτοὺς ἀγάγοι διεπυνθάνετο 'he inquired about the

---

56 Cf. Zilliacus (1938: 342).
57 On a couple of occasions, however, Symeon changes an original historical present form into an imperfect or aorist. So, for example, λέγει 'he said' > διεπυνθάνετο 'he inquired' (19.17; XIX), θεωρῶ 'I saw' > ἐδόκουν ὁρᾶν 'I seemed to be seeing' (20.9; XXI), λέγει > εἶπεν 'he said' (20.10; XXI), and λέγει > ἔφη 'he said' (20.13; XXI).
58 Cf. Zilliacus (1938: 349).

need that brought them' (19.17; XIX) and ἐμοῦ δὲ πάλιν εἰπόντος· ὅσα ὑπεσχόμην τῶι θεῶι, πληρῶ 'when I said again: "all that I have promised tot he Lord, I will fulfill"'> πληρώσειν ὑποσχομένου 'having promised to fulfil' (20.12; XXI). Finally, various changes have also been made in the area of case: one case can be replaced by another case, or by a prepositional expression in Symeon's version. So, for example, ἐξῆλθεν τὴν πόλιν 'he left the city' > ἐξελθὼν τῆς πόλεως 'having gone out of the city' (14.1; X), ἐμαυτῶι > πρὸς ἐμαυτὸν 'to myself' (19.26; XX), and τῆς ὁδοῦ Ἱεριχούντων > τῆς πρὸς Ἱεριχοῦντα ὁδοῦ 'of the road to Jericho' (20. 14–15; XXI). In other examples, a prepositional expression is replaced by a bare case. So, for example, μετὰ γέλωτος καὶ ψιθυρισμοῦ > γέλωτι καὶ ψιθυρισμῷ 'with laughter and slandering' (12.13; VI), διὰ πάσης ἰατρικῆς ἐπιστήμης καὶ μαγικῆς περιεργίας 'through all medical science and magical arts' > πολλαῖς ἰατρικαῖς τε καὶ μαγικαῖς τέχναις 'by all medical and magical arts' (19.22–23; XX), and τὴν ἐν Χριστῶι σφραγίδα 'the seal in Christ' > τῇ τοῦ Χριστοῦ σφραγίδι '(with) the seal of Christ' (20.26; XXIII).

3.3.3 Morphological changes

To conclude, the passages which I have analyzed also contain a number of morphological changes. Compared to lexis and syntax, however, these changes are quite minimal, as Figure 6 shows. Most of the morphological changes concern number: in various cases, Symeon has changed singular into plural. So, for example, τῶι ἐκκλησιαστικῶι καταλόγωι > τοῖς ἐκκλησιαστικοῖς καταλόγοις '(in) the list of the clergy' (11.2; V), περὶ τὸ τέλος > περὶ τὰ τέλη 'towards the end' (18.21; XVIII), and δι' ἐμοῦ 'through me' > δι' ἡμῶν 'through us' (20.16; XXI). The reverse phenomenon is also attested: so, for example, ταύταις καὶ ταῖς τοιαύταις διδασκαλίαις 'by these and other teachings' > τοιαύτης . . . τῆς διδασκαλίας '(of) such teaching' (18.9–10; XVII). Only in one case is a dual form used: ἀμφοτέρους > ἄμφω 'both' (21.5; XXIV). Pronouns are also sensitive to morphological change. The main tendency here seems to be to avoid the morphologically heavier generalizing forms. So, for example, οἵτινες > οἵ 'who' (11.25; VI), ἅπαντες > πάντες 'all' (18.12; XVIII), and οὕστινας > οὕς 'who' (19.6; XVIII).

4 Linguistic levels: A reconceptualization

Traditionally, the different linguistic levels are thought of as being strictly separated. Language is then viewed as a dictionary (the lexicon) with a set of rules that allow us to decline and inflect idiosyncratic forms (morphology), and to put them together in a sentence (syntax). Applied to the sources outlined in Section 3, however, it is not always easy to a make a strict distinction between these different levels: for example, do we consider function words such as particles to be part of the lexicon, or rather of syntax? Do we consider subtle changes in verb stem relevant to morphology, or rather to syntax? Is the use of prepositions a lexical matter, or more a matter of avoiding cases? Is voice a morphological phenomenon or rather a syntactic one, etc.[59]

It should thus come as no surprise that various Functionally and Cognitively oriented linguistic frameworks have proposed to re-interpret these traditional labels: Systemic Functional Linguistics, for example, speaks about "lexico-grammar", lexical items being viewed as "most delicate grammar".[60] Cognitive linguists, too, speak of the "syntax-lexicon" continuum,[61] the main unit of analysis being "constructions", which can be defined very generally as "pairings of form and meaning".[62] Together, all of these constructions, whether they be words, idioms, endings, or syntactic constructions, make up what has been called the "Constructicon".

Cognitive linguists propose to view lexico-grammatical knowledge in terms of two dimensions/continua. The first of these is the schematicity continuum, which ranges from the "substantive" to the "schematic" (contrast e.g. a lexically filled construction such as [kick the bucket] with the much more abstract ditransitive construction [S V IO DO]).[63] The second dimension involves the complexity continuum, which ranges from "atomic" to "complex" (contrast e.g. the simple adjective [green] with the expression [kick the bucket], consisting of multiple words).[64] Using these two dimensions, we can characterize any construction. Particles, for example, can be characterized as atomic and partially schematic. Aspectual morphology, too, can be considered atomic and partially schematic. This type of conceptualization is of interest from another point of view, too. To be more specific, I hypothesize that the two continua proposed by Cognitive Linguistics can be related to the user-observer continuum which I proposed earlier in this chapter. This relationship is illustrated in Figure 7.

My hypothesis is that observer-centered sources will naturally focus more on constructions that are substantive and atomic, because they are so tangible,

---

59 In the figures and discussion, I have consistently chosen the first option.
60 See e.g. Hasan (1987).
61 See e.g. Croft & Cruse (2004: 256).
62 See e.g. Goldberg (2003: 219).
63 See e.g. Croft & Cruse (2004: 255). 'S' stands for subject, 'V' for verb, 'IO' for indirect object, and 'DO' for direct object.
64 See e.g. Croft & Cruse (2004: 255).

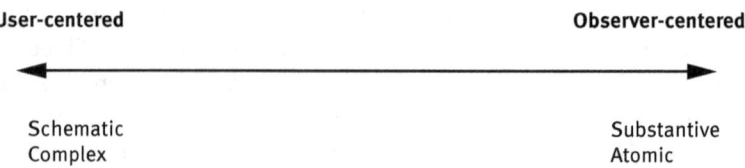

Figure 7: Relating continua to each other.

than user-centered sources, which are not constrained by such motivations. One can observe relevant differences even between the different types of sources discussed in the context of this chapter: it is quite noticeable that syntax (or, in other words, what is complex and schematic) is almost entirely absent in Phrynichus' *Ecloga*, whereas it is much more prominent in other sources such as the petitions from the Katochoi of the Sarapieion archive or the *metaphrasis* of the *Life of Euthymius*. In fact, I would go even further and argue that due to the fact that observer-related sources pay little attention to syntax in Antiquity, syntactic variation may become more prominent in user-related sources, even more prominent than lexical or morphological variation.[65]

This type of explanation fits well with previous observations on the position of syntax in Ancient grammatical treatises: Donnet (1967), for example, has argued that when Ancient grammarians address questions of syntax, they do so by concentrating on isolated words, rather than developing a theory of relationships between words.[66] For example, Dionysius Thrax presents detailed classifications of word classes such as nouns and adverbs, which he subdivides into thirty-one and twenty-six types respectively, but does not go further than that: the meaning of the enunciation is viewed as that of the combination of the individual words.[67]

Since in Indian and Arabic grammatical traditions there was a firm syntactic tradition,[68] it seems necessary to look at the cognitive status of syntax in combination with culture-specific explanations,[69] such as the educational

---

[65] Cf. Horrocks (this volume).
[66] Donnet (1967: 39). Robins (1997: 31) notes that "the framework of grammatical description in western Antiquity was the word and paradigm model."
[67] Cf. Desbordes (1986: 354–355).
[68] See e.g. Swiggers and Wouters (2003: 27).
[69] Next to culture-specific explanations, scholars have also drawn attention to language-specific explanations: (i) when discussing one's mother-tongue, it is natural to focus less on

system.[70] As Schenkeveld (2000) dicusses, Hellenistic education consisted of three stages: in the first stage, the pupil would learn to read and write; in the second stage, grammar proper, that is, phonology and morphology, together with reading the poets; and in the third and final stage, he would take lessons in rhetoric by a rhetorician, also making compositions of his own. Schenkeveld (2000: 16) observes that pupils at no stage needed a proper training in syntax, and that the development of a syntactic theory was therefore unnecessary. Moreover, one can add that because of this "ascendant" type of formation, syntax was naturally backgrounded: one first started with the letters and individual words, and progressively moved on to the enunciation.[71] Donnet (1967) has also drawn attention to the presence of a philosophical (Stoic) tradition.[72] Philosophers discussed matters related to the sentence, but primarily from a logical, rather than a syntactic, point of view. In Antiquity, people never learned to make a distinction between these two different approaches: affronting the sentential level, they immediately turned to the philosophical approach.

5 Conclusion

To conclude, it may be clear that Hudson's (1996) hypothesis of syntax functioning as a "marker of cohesion in society" does not hold for Ancient Greek: otherwise, the extensive amount of syntactic variation that I have outlined in this contribution would be difficult to explain. Nevertheless, there seems to be good ground to distinguish between the different linguistic levels: lexis plays a crucial role in all of the sources discussed, whereas morphology and syntax are often less prominent.[73] Orthography, too, plays an important role, but only in certain contexts: in literary texts, we see fewer orthographic changes. To claim,

---

syntax (Schenkeveld 2000); (ii) because of the fact that Ancient Greek is an inflectional language, it is natural to put a lot of emphasis on morphology (Swiggers & Wouters 2003: 36).
70 Horrocks (this volume), in a similar fashion, has suggested that students learned proper syntax "some other way", that is, simply by reading texts of Classical models.
71 Cf. Swiggers & Wouters (2003: 37).
72 For further details, see Egli (1978), Taylor (1993), Robins (1997: 20–22, 34–36), Swiggers & Wouters (2003: 2–30), Basset (2003), Van Ophuijsen (2003).
73 From this point of view, one could agree with Kim (2010) that Atticism was mainly a matter of vocabulary.

therefore, that the features which are likely to mark social distinctions are *completely* arbitrary, and that social markedness is not a property inherent to the manifestations of the linguistic system, but rather is mediated through the social group which realizes such manifestations, as Berruto (2003: 144) does, is probably a bridge too far.

I have argued that the sources which I have analyzed show signs of variation vis-à-vis the different linguistic levels: "observer-related sources" such as Phrynichus' *Ecloga* tend to pay a lot less attention to syntax than "user-related sources" such as the petitions in the Katochoi of the Sarapieion archive and the metaphrasis of the *Life of Euthymius*.[74] This I have attributed to the fact that syntax is more schematic and complex, making it less "tangible" for sociolinguistic observations and evaluations. Tentatively, I would argue that it is the same fact which has driven much of the history of modern-day linguistics, which, as Hymes (1974: 89–90) notes, started with the "conquest of speech sounds", then proceeded to morphology in the 1930s and 1940s, and in the 1960s expanded to syntax. Only in a later stage did scholars come to study what is most abstract, that is, pragmatics and (discourse) semantics.

To conclude, it is perhaps ironic that while pronunciation/orthography and especially lexis played a crucial role in Antiquity, these are not the domains which nowadays receive most interest in Classical studies.[75] In papyrology, for example, the standard lexicon remains Preisigke (1925–1927) (followed by various supplements), documentary examples having only been added piecemeal to the main lexicons of Ancient Greek such as LSJ. This, I think, can be attributed to a different mindset: as we are not native speakers of Ancient Greek, we have to invest a lot of time in morphology and syntax, so much so that we are naturally inclined to pay more attention to variation at these levels. On a higher level, academics nowadays largely seem to prefer what is schematic and complex to what is atomic and simple, following current trends in linguistics. At the same time, however, scholars more and more strive towards a more holistic picture, incorporating multiple linguistic theories, different linguistic levels, and various types of sources, as I have tried to do in this chapter.

---

74 From this perspective, one could agree with Sinner (2013: 127–128) that first-hand observers are bad sources.
75 It is worth signaling, however, recent projects such as the *Lexicon of the Zenon archive* (led by Trevor Evans), the LBG (led by Erich Trapp), and the *Database and Dictionary of Greek Loanwords in Coptic* (led by Sebastian Richter).

References

Basset, Louis. 2003. Aristote et la syntaxe. In Pierre Swiggers & Alfons Wouters (eds.), *Syntax in Antiquity*, 43–60. Leuven: Peeters.
Bentein, Klaas. 2013. Register and the diachrony of Post-classical and Early Byzantine Greek. *Revue Belge de Philologie et d'Histoire* 91. 5–44.
Bentein, Klaas. 2015a. The Greek documentary papyri as a linguistically heterogeneous corpus: The case of the katochoi of the Sarapeion-archive. *Classical World* 108. 461–484.
Bentein, Klaas. 2015b. Particle-usage in documentary papyri (I–IV AD): An integrated, sociolinguistically-informed approach. *Greek, Roman & Byzantine Studies* 55. 721–753.
Bentein, Klaas. 2016. διό, διὰ τοῦτο, ὅθεν, τοίνυν, οὖν, or rather asyndeton? Inferential expressions and their social value in Greek official petitions (I–IV AD). *Acta Classica* 59. 23–51.
Bentein, Klaas. 2017. Finite vs. non-finite complementation in Post-classical and Byzantine Greek: Towards a pragmatic restructuring of the complementation system? *Journal of Greek Linguistics* 17. 3–36.
Berruto, Gaetano. 2003. *Fondamenti di sociolinguistica*. Roma: Laterza.
Berruto, Gaetano. 2004. The problem of variation. *Linguistic Review* 21. 293–322.
Berruto, Gaetano. 2009. Περί συντάξεως: sintassi e variazione. In Angela Ferrari (ed.), *Sintassi storica e sincronica dell'italiano: Subordinazione, coordinazione, giustapposizione*, vol. 1, 21–58. Firenze: Cesati.
Borries, Ioannes de. 1911. *Phrynichi Sophistae praeparatio sophistica*. Leipzig: Teubner.
Browning, Robert. 1983. *Medieval and Modern Greek*, 2nd ed. Cambridge: Cambridge University Press.
Croft, William & Alan D. Cruse. 2004. *Cognitive linguistics*. Cambridge: Cambridge University Press.
Cuomo, Andrea Massimo. 2017. Medieval textbooks as a major source for historical sociolinguistic studies of (highregister) Medieval Greek. *Open Linguistics* 3. 442–455.
Desbordes, Françoise. 1986. Elementa: Remarques sur le rôle de l'écriture dans la linguistique antique. In: Henri Joly (ed.), *Philosophie du langage et grammaire dans l' antiquité: Actes du colloque international, Grenoble, 3–6 septembre 1985*, 339–355. Bruxelles: Ousia.
Dickey, Eleanor. 2007. *Ancient Greek scholarship: A guide to finding, reading, and understanding scholia, commentaries, lexica, and grammatical treatises, from their beginnings to the Byzantine period*. Oxford: Oxford University Press.
Donnet, Daniel. 1967. La place de la syntaxe dans les traités de grammaire grecque, des origines au XIIe siècle. *L'Antiquité Classique* 36. 22–48.
Egli, Urs. 1978. Stoic syntax and semantics. In Jacques Brunschwig (ed.), *Les Stoïciens et leur logique*, 135–154. Paris: Vrin.
Festugière, André Jean. 1961–1965. *Les moines d'Orient*. Paris: Cerf.
Fischer, Eitel. 1974. *Die Ekloge des Phrynichos*. Berlin: de Gruyter.
Goldberg, Adele E. 2003. Constructions: A new theoretical approach to language. *Trends in Cognitive Sciences* 7. 219–24.
Gumperz, John J. & Robert Wilson. 1971. Convergence and creolization: A case from the Indo-Aryan/Dravidian border in India. In Dell Hymes (ed.), *Pidginization and creolization of languages*, 151–167. Cambridge: Cambridge University Press.

Hasan, Ruqaya. 1987. The grammarian's dream: Lexis as most delicate grammar. In M.A.K. Halliday & Robin P. Fawcett (eds.), *New developments in systemic linguistics*, vol. 1, 184–211. London: Pinter.

Herring, Susan C., van Reenen, Pieter & Lene Schøsler. 2000. On textual parameters and older languages. In Susan C. Herring, Pieter van Reenen & Lene Schøsler (eds.), *Textual parameters in older languages*, 1–31. Amsterdam: Benjamins.

Hess-Lüttich, E.W.B. 2004. Die sozialsymbolische Funktion der Sprache. In Ulrich Ammon, Norbert Dittmar, Klaus J. Mattheier & Peter Trudgill (eds.). *Sociolinguistics: An international handbook of the science of language and society*, vol. 1, 2nd ed. 491–502. Berlin: de Gruyter.

Høgel, Christian. 2002. *Symeon Metaphrastes: Rewriting and canonization*. Copenhagen: Museum Tusculanum Press, University of Copenhagen.

Hoogendijk, Francisca A.J. 1989. Ptolemaios: Een Griek die leeft en droomt in een Egyptische tempel [Ptolemaios: A Greek who lives and dreams in an Egyptian temple]. In P.W. Pestman (ed.), *Familiearchieven uit het land van Pharao* [Family archives from the land of Pharao], 47–69. Zutphen: Terra.

Horrocks, Geoffrey C. 2007. Syntax: From Classical Greek to the Koine. In A.-F. Christidis (ed.), *A history of Ancient Greek: From the beginnings to Late Antiquity*, 618–631. Cambridge: Cambridge University Press.

Horrocks, Geoffrey C. 2010. *Greek: A history of the language and its speakers*, 2nd ed. Malden: Wiley-Blackwell.

Hudson, R. 1996. *Sociolinguistics*, 2nd ed. Cambridge: Cambridge University Press.

Hymes, Dell H. 1974. *Foundations in sociolinguistics: An ethnographic approach*. Philadephia: University of Pennsylvania Press.

Kim, Lawrence. 2010. The literary heritage as language: Atticism and the Second Sophistic. In Egbert J. Bakker (ed.), *A companion to the Ancient Greek language*, 368–482. Malden: Wiley-Blackwell.

Lallot, Jean. 1994. Les fonctions syntaxiques chez Apollonius Dyscole. In Jan De Clerq & Piet Desmet (eds.), *Florilegium historiographiae linguisticae: Études d'historiographie de la linguistique et de grammaire comparée à la mémoire de Maurice Leroy*, 131–141. Leuven: Peeters.

Lallot, Jean. 2015. Syntax. In Franco Montanari, Stephanos Matthaios & Antonios Rengakos (eds.), *Brill's companion to Ancient Greek scholarship*, 850–895. Leiden: Brill.

Lee, John A.L. 2013. The atticist grammarians. In Stanley E. Porter & Andrew W. Pitts (eds.), *The language of the New Testament: Context, history and development*, 283–308. Leiden: Brill.

Legras, Bernard. 2011. *Les reclus Grecs du Sarapieion de Memphis: Une enquête sur l'Hellénisme égytien*. Leuven: Peeters.

Levinsohn, Stephen. 2000. *Discourse features of New Testament Greek: A coursebook on the information structure of New Testament Greek*, 2nd ed. Dallas: Summer Institute of Linguistics.

Lewis, Naphtali. 1986. *Greeks in Ptolemaic Egypt: Case studies in the social history of the Hellenistic world*. Oxford: Oxford University Press.

Luiselli, R. 2010. Authorial revision of linguistic style in Greek papyrus letters and petitions (AD I–IV). In Trevor V. Evans & Dirk D. Obbink (eds.), *The language of the papyri*, 71–96. Oxford: Oxford University Press.

Migne, Jacques Paul. 1857–1866. *Patrologia Graeca*. Paris: Imprimerie catholique.

Pagani, Lara. 2015. Language correctness (*hellenismos*) and its criteria. In Franco Montanari, Stephanos Matthaios & Antonios Rengakos (eds.), *Brill's companion to Ancient Greek scholarschip*, 798–849. Leiden: Brill.
Papaioannou, Stratis. 2017. *Christian novels from the Menologion of Symeon Metaphrastes*. Cambridge, MA: Harvard University Press.
Peyr, Elisabeth. 1992. Zur Umarbeitung rhetorischer Texte durch Symeon Metaphrastes. *Jahrbuch der österreichischen Byzantinistik* 42. 143–155.
Preisigke, Friedrich. 1925–1927. *Wörterbuch der griechischen Papyrusurkunden mit Einschluss der griechischen Inschriften, Aufschriften, Ostraka, Mumienschilder usw. aus Ägypten*. Berlin: Selbstverlag der Erben.
Price, R.M. 1991. *Lives of the Monks of Palestine by Cyril of Skythopolis*. Collegeville: Liturgical Press.
Robins, Robert Henry. 1997. *A short history of linguistics*, 4th ed. London: Longman.
Romaine, Suzanne. 1982. *Socio-historical linguistics: Its status and methodology*. Cambridge: Cambridge University Press.
Rutherford, William G. 1881. *The new Phrynichus, being a revised text of the Ecloga of the grammarian Phrynichus*. London: Macmillan and Co.
Schenkeveld, Dirk M. 1994. Scholarship and grammar. In Franco Montanari (ed.), *La philologie grecque a l'époque hellenistique et romaine*, 263–306. Genève: Droz.
Schenkeveld, Dirk M. 2000. Why no part on syntax in the Greek school grammar? Solecisms and education. *Histoire, Épistémologie, Langage* 22. 11–22.
Schwartz, Eduard. 1939. *Kyrillos von Skythopolis*. Leipzig: Hinrichs.
Sinner, Carsten. 2013. *Varietätenlinguistik: Eine Einführung*. Tübingen: Narr.
Sluiter, Ineke. 1997. The Greek tradition. In Wout J. van Bekkum, Jan Houben, Ineke Sluiter & Kees Versteegh (eds.), *The emergence of semantics in four linguistic traditions*, 147–224. Amsterdam: Benjamins.
Swain, Simon. 1996. *Hellenism and empire: Language, classicism, and power in the Greek world AD 50–250*. Oxford: Oxford University Press.
Swiggers, Pierre & Alfons Wouters. 2003. Réflexions à propos de (l'absence de?) la syntaxe dans la grammaire gréco-latine. In Pierre Swiggers & Alfons Wouters (eds.), *Syntax in Antiquity*, 25–41. Leuven: Peeters.
Taylor, Daniel J. 1993. Desperately seeking syntax: Rewriting the history of syntactic theory in Greece and Rome. *Language & Communication* 13. 265–285.
Teodorsson, Sven-Tage. 1977. *The Phonology of Ptolemaic Koine*. Göteborg: Acta Universitatis Gothoburgensis.
Tosi, Renzo. 2015. Typology of lexicographical works. In Franco Montanari, Stephanos Matthaios & Antonios Rengakos (eds.), *Brill's companion to Ancient Greek scholarschip*, 622–636. Leiden: Brill.
Valente, Stefano. 2015. Typology of grammatical treatises. In Franco Montanari, Stephanos Matthaios & Antonios Rengakos (eds.), *Brill's companion to Ancient Greek scholarschip*, 600–621. Leiden: Brill.
Van Ophuijsen, Jan. 2003. Parts of what speech? Stoic notions of statement and sentence, or: How the dialectician knew voice and begat syntax. In Pierre Swiggers & Alfons Wouters (eds.), *Syntax in Antiquity*, 77–94. Leuven: Peeters.
Vessella, Carlo. 2018. *Sophisticated speakers: Atticistic pronunciation in the Atticist lexica*. Berlin: De Gruyter.

Wahlgren, Staffan. 2002. Towards a grammar of Byzantine Greek. *Symbolae Osloenses* 77. 201–204.
Wahlgren, Staffan. 2010. Byzantine literature and the Classical past. In Egbert J. Bakker (ed.), *A companion to the Ancient Greek language*, 527–538. Malden: Wiley-Blackwell.
Wilcken, Ulrich. 1927. *Urkunden der Ptolemäerzeit (Ältere Funde)*. Berlin: de Gruyter.
Zilliacus, Henrik. 1938. Zur stilistischen Umarbeitungstechnik des Symeon Metaphrastes. *Byzantinische Zeitschrift* 38. 333–350.

Index locorum

Anna Comnena
Alexias
    2.10.4   196
    11.7.4   172
    11.11.6   172
    11.12.6   173
Metaphrasis
    8   172
    100   172
    114   173

Anonymous
Lex.
    O 84   155

Apollonius Dyscolus
Syntax
    3.98-100   165–6

Aristophanes
Acharnenses
    315   149
Nubes
    451b   155
Equites
    247   149
Ranae (schol.)
    842b   149

Aristophanes Byzantinus
    fr.24   20

Aristoteles
Rhetorica
    1357b   121
    1480a   19

Athenaeus
Deipnosphistae
    9.393b   153

Bible
New Testament

Mark
    1.38   218
Septuagint
Genesis
    28.1   291
    43.16   150
Exodus
    2.10   156
    6.7   291
    22.25   145
Ezechiel
    33.15   145
Leviticus
    14.6   291
1 Maccabees
    15.38   145
2 Maccabees
    8.23   147
3 Maccabees
    1.12   147
    2.29   152
    3.25   152
    3.27   152
    4.6   152
    4.20   152
    5.4   150
    6.30   150
    6.40   145
    7.1   150
Numeri
    3.47   291

Caesarius Dapontes
    5.8.2   228

Callinicus
Vita Hypatii
    98.4   168

Chronicle of the Morea
    3647   169
    3650-3651   169
    4233-4237   169

Clemens Alexandrinus
Stromata
    I.23.152.3   155
    II.22.135   145

Cyrillus Hierosolymitanus
Catecheses ad illuminandos
    1.3.14   152

Cyrillus Alexandrinus
De Adoratione
    68.564.39   145

Demosthenes
De corona
    209.2   149

Digenes Acrites
    E 798   227
    E 844   227
    E 1092   207
    E 1532   169
    G 3.106   207
    G 4.376   227
    G 4.407   227
    G 7.2   207

Diodorus Siculus
    1.29   146
    1.85   147

Epigrams
DBBE
    130   363
    202   359–60
    319   365
    938   363
    958   364
    1110   364
    1129   359, 360–2
    1761   365
    1767   359–60
    1877   364
    2456   355
    3004   355
    4165   355
    4770   363
    5301   359, 361–2
    5305   359–60
    5319   361
    5321   361
    5327   360
    5338   361
    5339   361
    5362   360
    5396   361
    5605   361
    5719   358
    7269   363
    7270   363
    7971   364
    8301   365

Epiphanius
De mensuris
    131.23   155

Epithalamium
    Folio 7^v, 4 169

Erotopaegnia
    401   222

Eustathius
Commentarius in hexaemeron
    780.54   155

Flavius Josephus
Antiquitates Judaicae
    2.228.2   155
    2.9.6   156
Contra Apionem
    1.287   155

Herodotus
    2.154   42

Hesychius
    K 459   156

Index locorum — **417**

M 2076	156	
O 435	155	
Π 4206	146	
Σ 156	157	
Σ 3112	157	

Historia Alexandri Magni
Recensio R
    1160   144

Historia Ptocholeontos
    B 155   228

Inscriptions
OGI
    56.59   146
SEG
    51.1813   145

Isidorus
Origines
    2.14   19

Johannes Chrysostomus
In Joannem theologum
    59.611   152

Leonardus Dellaportas
    1.796   232
    2.79   232

Letter of Aristeas
    36   152

Menander
Samia
    297   144

Nicetas Choniates
Historia
    3.36-8   195
    87.23-4   196
    126.48-60   181
    235.19-20   193
    242.15   193

359.4	185
365.67–366.80	184
387.17-8	193
463.72-3	185
613.58-60	195
614.9-10	192

Metaphrasis
    5.1.1   182
    9.10   187
    12.3.4   184
    13.2.1   187
    13.3.5   187
    13.6.7   187

Nicetas Stethatus
Vita Symeonis
    2.25-7   190

Ostraka
    K227   27
    M1191   24
O.Bodl.
    II 1094   282, 288
O.Claud.
    II 224–242   32
    II 239   28
    II 243–254   32
    II 299   28
    III 449   286
O.Did.
    386   33
    393   33
O.Krok.
    I 70   29
    I 73   30
    I 74   29
    I 96   29
O.Leid.
    49   278
O.Mich.
    I 102   145
O.Theb
    143   145
O.Wilck
    1166   145
    1479   145

Papyri

BGU
- I 2 — 152
- I 8 — 145
- I 51 — 282
- II 421 — 282
- II 472 — 290
- II 629 — 282
- VI 1296 — 144
- VII 1661 — 278
- VIII 1767 — 145
- VIII 1795 — 146
- VIII 1855 — 146
- VIII 1882 — 147
- XI 2111 — 278
- XVI 2577 — 146
- XVIII 1.2746 — 150

BM inv. P.
- 2724 — 130

C.Pap.Gr.
- II 1.19 — 282

Chr.Mitt
- 86 — 284

CPR
- XII 15 — 151
- XXIV 31 — 84

P.Amh.
- II 69 — 275

P.Amst.
- I 8 — 148

P.Ant.
- I 45 — 83, 86

P.Athen.
- 64 — 294

P.Babatha
- 18 — 290

P.Baden
- II 43 — 147
- IV 59 — 148

P.Bingen
- 107 — 145

P.Cair.Isid.
- 63 — 143
- 130 — 150

P.Cair.Masp.
- I 67002 — 320–1
- I 67006 — 320–1
- I 67020 — 320–1
- I 67024 — 320
- I 67025 — 320
- I 67026 — 320
- I 67027 — 320
- I 67028 — 320
- I 67064 — 83
- II 67194 — 120

P.Cair.Zen.
- I 59015 — 245
- I 59016 — 245, 252
- I 59018 — 254
- I 59060 — 250
- I 59073 — 249–50
- I 59075 — 253
- I 59076 — 258
- II 59251 — 258
- III 59512 — 146
- IV 59787 — 315
- V 59804 — 251

P.Col.
- III 6 — 246, 248, 252, 256
- III 9 — 259
- III 10 — 259
- III 58 — 316
- IV 66 — 21, 255
- X 249 — 146

P.Count.
- 3 — 146

P.Dryton
- 3 — 146
- 36 — 255

P.Dura
- 18 — 290–1, 294

P.Enteux
- 54 — 144
- 86 — 152

P.Fay
- 34 — 290
- 108 — 152
- 111 — 152

P.Flor.
- I 2 — 144

P.Fouad
- 54 — 290
- 86 — 89–94, 99, 101, 105–7

87	89, 90–4, 99, 101–2, 107–9	P.Med.	
		I 27.ii	145
88	89–90, 93–7, 99, 101–2, 109–10	P.Mert.	
		I 26	146
89	89–90, 93–4, 96–7, 99, 101–2, 111	P.Mich	
		I 2	168
P.Giss.Univ.		I 6	247
I 10	146	I 29	248, 314
P.Graux		I 48	246
II 9	330, 334, 345	II 122	319
P.Grenf.		II 123	318
II 38	152	II 128	318–9
P.Hamb.		III 183	247
I 10	145	V 238	318
III 228	83	V 240	318–9
II 245	146	VIII 514	143
P.Harr.		X 582	329, 330–47
I 159	86	(passim)	
P.Herm.		XII 657	295
5	294	P.Mil.Vogl.	
7	123	II 76	294
10	123	P.Neph.	
17	84	1	131
P.Hib.		4	122
I 40	252	8	123
P.Kell.		9	127
I 65	123, 127	P.Ness.	
I 71	132	III 47	98–9, 101, 112
I 72	131–2, 134	III 50	99–102, 113
P.Kell. Copt.		P.Oslo	
25	130	II 62	294
73	127	III 78	290–1, 294
77	134	P.Oxy	
127	130	II 257	283–4, 287
P.Köln		III 471	288, 290, 293
III 161	144	III 472	267, 290–1
III 166	83	III 478	288
V 234^v	145	III 496	289
P.Leid.		IV 707	289–90
406	46, 49	VII 1028	288
P.Lond.		VIII 1123	267
II 304	282	IX 1187	22
V 1674	320	XII 1472	288
VI 1912	302, 320, 332–47	XII 1480	23
VI 1914	123, 131	XII 1481	24
VII 1940	147	XII 1482	26

XIV 1650	147
XIV 1735	145
XIV 1775	84
XVI 1838	85
XVI 1847	83
XVI 1849	84
XVI 1868	81
XVI 1869	81
XVI 1874	144
XVI 1935	84
XXIV 2407	147
XXXI 2546	14
XXXVI 2793	277, 286
XLVI 3283	288
XLVI 3285	288
LVI 3869	78
LIX 3998	151
LIX 4000	85
LXIII 4397	276

P.Phil.
2	290

P.Prag
I 31	290

P.Princ.
I 13	330–347
II 35	278
III 152	330–347

P.Rev.
II 41	150

P.Ryl.
II 78	288
II 234	147

P.Tebt
I 5	150
I 6	146
I 16	152
II 310	290, 292
II 390	349

P.Tor.
9	147

P.Vindob.Bosw.
1	288

P.Yale
I 33	259
I 36	247
I 61	320

PGM
IV 908	144
IV 2443	146
LXXVI 4	145

PSI
IV 281	281
IV 318	85
IV 413	253
V 502	249, 257, 259
IX 1039	146
XIV 1401	150

SB
XIV 11585	329, 330, 348
XIV 12123	78
XIV 12143	348
XVI 12573	83
XX 14463	82
XX 14576	330–47
XX 14526	330–47
XX 15029	147

SIG^3
III 1259	245

Suppl.Mag.
II 86 col. ii	144

UPZ
I 1	42
I 2	44, 47
I 3	44, 47
I 4	44, 47
I 5	44, 387–92
I 6	44, 387–93
I 7	43–4, 49
I 8	43–4, 49
I 9	44, 47
I 10	44
I 11	44
I 12	44, 47, 70
I 13	44, 47, 69
I 14	44, 47, 49
I 15	44, 47
I 16	44, 47
I 17	44, 47
I 18	44, 47, 317, 387–91, 393
I 19	44, 387–391, 393
I 20	44–5
I 21	44–5, 47

I 22	44	I 67	44, 48
I 23	44, 47, 316	I 68	44, 249, 317
I 24	44	I 69	44
I 25	44	I 70	44, 247, 317
I 26	44, 47, 316	I 71	44
I 27	44, 45, 47	I 72	44
I 28	44	I 73	44
I 29	44	I 74	44, 48
I 30	44	I 75	44, 47
I 31	44, 47	I 76	44
I 32	44	I 77	45, 47
I 33	44, 48–9, 317, 387	I 78	45, 48
I 34	44, 48–9, 50, 387–9	I 79	45, 48
I 35	44, 387–93	I 80	45, 48
I 36	44–5, 49, 387–93	I 81	45
I 37	44, 316	I 82	44, 47
I 38	44, 316	I 83	44, 48
I 39	44, 48, 317	I 84	44, 48
I 40	44	I 85	44, 48
I 41	44	I 86	44, 47
I 42	44	I 87	44
I 43	44–5, 48–50	I 88	44
I 44	44, 48–50	I 89	44, 47
I 45	44	I 90	44, 48
I 46	44	I 91	44
I 47	44, 48	I 92	44
I 48	44	I 93	44, 317
I 49	44, 48–9	I 94	44
I 50	44, 48–9	I 95	44
I 51	44	I 96	44, 48
I 52	44, 47, 387–92	I 97	44, 47
I 53	44, 387–92	I 98	44
I 54	44, 48	I 99	44
I 55	44, 48	I 100	44, 47
I 56	44, 48	I 101	44, 48
I 57	44, 48	I 102	44
I 58	44, 48	I 103	44, 48
I 59	44, 247, 258	I 104	44, 48
I 60	44	I 105	44
I 61	44	I 119	152
I 62	44	I 144	45
I 63	44, 48	I 145	45
I 64	44	I 147	45
I 65	44, 317	II 175	144
I 66	44	II 194	147

Paulus Silentiarius
Descriptio Hagiae Sophiae
    104-7   167

Philo
In Flaccum
    20   149
    132   149
De somniis
    1.92   145
De specialibus legibus
    1.121   149
De vita Mosis
    1.17   155

Photius
    O 166   155

Phrynichus
Praeparatio sophistica
    58.17   147

Plato
Apologia
    19a   269
Leges
    670a   121
    877a2–b2   126

Plutarchus
Moralia
    356c–d   281

Porphyrius
De abstinentia
    4.8.   146

Pseudo-Demetrius
Formae epistolicae
    1.5   145

Pseudo-Zonaras
    M 1382   156
    O 1435   155

Ptochoprodromica
    3.56-88   174–5

Ptolemaeus
Tetrabiblos
    4.206   152

Sophocles
Antigone
    142–143   269

Spaneas
    208 (P)   169

Strabo
    17.1.13.4   145
    17.1.15   147

Suda
    M 285   155
    OI 190   155
    D 430   153

Symeon
Epistulae
    1   373
    5   373–4
    6   373
    9   374
Chronicon
    135.10   375
    135.17   376
    135.24   377

Theodorus Metochites
Miscellanea
    17   148

Thucydides
    IV.60.2   121

Index nominum

Ancient authors

Apollonius Dyscolus 164–6, 382
Aristarchus Grammaticus 153
Aristophanes Byzantinus 20
Aristoteles 19, 244
Athenaeus 153–4

Chrysoloras, Manuel 164
Clemens Alexandrinus 145, 155–6
Cyrillus Alexandrinus 145

Demetrius Ixion 153
Diodorus Siculus 146–7
Diogenianus 154
Dionysius Thrax 164, 408

Eusebius 148
Eustathius 155

Georgius Acropolites 163, 170–2, 194
Georgius Choeroboscos 193
Georgius Pachymeres 193–5

Irenaeus Pacatus 153

Johannes Chrysostomus 152
Johannes Malalas 189, 193

Lucretius 30

Manetho 148
Michael Psellus 168, 191

Nicephorus Blemmydes 180

Paulus Silentiarius 163, 167
Photius 154–5, 394
Polybius 170
Procopius Caesariensis 189, 192, 113
Pseudo-Phocylides 152

Romanus Melodus 193
Rūmī 201, 206

Stephanus Byzantinus 154
Sultan Walad 201, 206, 222
Syncellus 148

Theodore Gazensis 164
Theodorus Metochites 148
Theodorus Prodromus 164, 173, 194
Theophanes Confessor 193
Thomas Magister 193

Zonaras 154–6

Modern persons/editors/writers cited

Altman 244, 250, 261
Andriotis 202–34 (*passim*)

Bentein 1–13 (*passim*), 62–3, 65–8, 251,
  257, 266, 270–1, 275, 278, 283, 286,
  291, 293–5, 300, 316, 381–414 (*passim*)
Benveniste 244, 260
Berruto 4–6, 382, 410
Biber 7, 301, 303–5
Brown 76–7
Browning 7, 180, 384

Chafe 357
Coseriu 4–6

Dahlgren 18, 53–7
Dawkins 201–34 (*passim*)
Dickey 2
Dittmar 4

Evans 2, 5, 255, 265–6

Fishman 19
Fournet 29, 153

Gignac 30–1, 55, 57, 291, 336–48 (*passim*)

Halla-aho 6, 300
Halliday 3–4, 303–4, 357

Hinterberger 2, 9, 179–200 (*passim*)
Horrocks XV, 7–9, 51, 53–8, 61, 117, 164–78
    (*passim*), 187–91, 221–2, 265, 286, 384
Hudson 3–4, 6, 381, 383, 409

James 6, 301–2
Janse 206–34 (*passim*)
Janssen 202, 208, 215, 229
Joseph 8, 147

Karolidis 206–34 (*passim*)
Kaufman 201–5
Klein 4
Koroli 75–114 (*passim*)
Koskenniemi 77

Labov 1, 7, 18, 39–40
Lagarde 206–34 (*passim*)
Lasswell 19
Lauxtermann 361–2
Leiwo 2, 5, 8–9, 17–37 (*passim*)
Levidis 206–34 (*passim*)
Lüdtke & Mattheier 5

Maas 357–8
Mackridge 361

Magdalino 354, 367
Manolessou 202, 206

Nabrings 6

Obbink 2, 117, 143

Palme 306
Papathomas 102

Reinsch 191
Rijksbaron 246, 251–2, 256–7, 269

Searle 78

Teodorsson 53, 55–6, 331–6 (*passim*)
Thesleff 2
Thomason 201–5
Thompson 41–3
Trenkner 2

Valiavitcharska 358
Veisse 43

Wahlgren 191, 369–80 (*passim*)
Wilcken 41, 49, 59, 316

Index rerum

accent xvi, 30-2, 51–5, 57, 59, 62, 65, 194, 210, 215, 224–6, 227–8, 341–45, 347–8, 350, 360
addressee 10, 63, 67, 77, 78, 90, 92, 127, 131, 244, 250, 257, 260, 287, 294, 305, 307–8, 313, 316, 329, 373, 394
adjective 123–4, 176, 205, 227–9, 234, 389, 396–7, 403, 407
adverbs / adverbials 84, 132, 170–1, 176, 223, 272, 274, 281–5, 375, 389, 396–7, 400, 403, 408
agglutination inflection
Acritic songs 201–234 *(passim)*
ambiguity 87, 272, 280, 289, 293, 374
ancient grammars 281, 408
anteriority 10, 265–95
(passim)
application 78, 117, 265, 268, 287, 294, 296, 309
article 61, 64, 126–7, 187, 208, 222, 225, 227–9, 234, 342, 391, 397, 400, 405
– 'postpositive' 205, 234
aspect
– imperfective 170, 222, 231, 251, 256–7
– perfective 223, 231, 256, 265, 271–4, 279–83, 285– 6
augment 176, 231, 272–3, 283, 398
author vs. writer 40, 42, 44

background vs. foreground 257, 260, 269
bilingualism 34, 45, 55, 62, 66, 72, 115, 117–20, 133–5, 141, 151, 157, 328–9, 339–50
book epigram 353–67 *(passim)*

caesura 210, 227, 232, 357, 360–2, 365
case
– accusative 7, 24, 27, 33, 61–5, 81–2, 120, 129, 175–6, 192, 194, 206, 222, 286
– confusion of cases 58, 62
– dative 26–7, 33–4, 57–8, 62–4, 122, 128–9, 176, 186, 191, 193, 206, 286, 336–8, 343, 377–9

– genitive 7, 27, 54, 58–9, 62 70, 150, 175–6, 186, 188, 191–2, 225, 334, 343, 390
– genitive absolute 69–70, 188, 390
– nominative 27, 33–4, 59, 61–2, 64–5, 70, 72, 186, 188, 208, 227, 234, 397
– nominative absolute 188
– vocative 64, 225
clause linkage 115, 120, 134
code switching 46
colloquialism 1–2, 7, 9, 21, 115, 118–9, 123, 131, 133–5, 166, 173–6, 336
colon / colometry 225–33, 357, 360–7
colophon 10, 353–67 *(passim)*
commatic style 358
comparative 185, 192
complement clause 130, 265–7, 275, 278, 280–1, 287–8, 295
conditional sentence 83, 168
conjugation See inflection
conjunction 51, 66, 71, 77, 168, 369, 373, 376–9
consonants xv–xvi
– aspirated 31, 53, 59, 144, 215, 229, 346, 350, 392, 399
– alveolar 210, 217–8, 223, 229, 230, 399
– dental 54, 61, 219–20, 223, 340, 350
– fricative 26, 31, 217, 219–20, 223, 340, 346, 399
– liquid 53, 56, 336, 344, 399
– nasal 54–5, 57, 64, 222, 336, 343, 345, 347
– palatal 336, 346
– postalveolar 224
– plosive 30–1, 34, 53, 61, 69, 88, 117, 144, 149, 155, 210, 215, 217, 223, 229, 230, 340, 345–7, 350, 399
– spirant See fricative
– stop See plosive
– voiced 30–1, 34, 53, 59, 61, 117, 210, 219, 223, 229, 230, 340, 350, 392, 399
– voiceless 30–1, 34, 59, 61, 117, 219, 229, 230, 340, 350, 392, 399
convergence 116–7, 121, 129,134, 270, 391

coordination 129, 130, 132–5, 372
Coptic 30–1, 54–5, 97, 115–139 *(passim)*,
    151, 155, 328, 340–6, 348, 350
correction 8, 19, 21, 23, 25–6, 34, 44, 49, 57,
    65–6, 144, 225, 248, 252, 291, 283, 300,
    302–3, 320–3, 332–3, 340, 342, 385,
    387, 392
crasis 58, 315

declension See inflection
deference 86, 90, 92, 94, 99
deictic centre 10, 167, 169, 177, 247,
    249, 261
Demotic 20, 41, 45–8, 116, 120–1, 134, 146,
    328, 349
deontic 79, 83–4, 130, 169
determiner spreading 228–9
dialect See lect
dieresis 362
dimension 2, 4–6, 8, 244, 251, 255, 304,
    366, 407
diphthong xv, 12–3, 336–7, 339, 391, 399
direct/indirect speech 149, 176, 183, 286,
    391, 404–5
directive 75–113 *(passim)*
discours vs. *récit* 164, 179
discourse 9, 66–7, 72, 116, 129–34, 243,
    246, 256–7, 260, 278, 382, 404, 410
discursive 244, 246, 251–2, 370
dual 196

enunciation/enunciative 244, 251–2, 255,
    260–1, 408–9
epistolary 10, 75–7, 95, 102, 123, 134, 165,
    168, 170, 175, 179, 243–64 *(passim)*
etymological writing 346–7

finite clause 274–5, 277–81, 282, 284–5,
    371–3
fluid texts 356, 359
formula 9, 31, 33, 35, 69, 72, 77, 83–4, 87,
    92, 94, 98, 127, 129, 132, 134, 143, 144,
    214, 227, 230, 233–4, 254, 258, 277–8,
    295, 309, 322, 355, 362
fortition 340

future 7, 10, 31, 65, 71, 79, 83, 130, 165,
    170–3, 175, 186–7, 189–90, 197, 206,
    234, 265–7, 269, 271, 273, 276–7, 288,
    290–1, 294–6, 391, 398, 400
futurity 9, 163, 167–8, 171, 189, 276, 289

gender
– biological 1, 89, 246
– grammatical 397
grammarians 142, 153–7, 193,
    394–400, 408
grammaticality 115, 117, 134
grapheme 51, 57, 327, 334–5, 340–6, 350
Greek 14, 18, 24, 26
– Asia Minor Greek 201–3
– Attic 10, 21, 23–4, 29, 33, 35, 59, 119, 153,
    163, 168, 179–80, 182, 185, 190–96,
    197, 245, 265, 291, 335, 337–9, 343–5,
    385, 394–400
– Atticising Greek See Attic
– Biblical Greek 2, 117, 129, 132, 142, 146,
    150–2, 155–7, 168, 193, 218, 254, 266,
    271, 277
– Byzantine Greek See Medieval Greek
– Cappadocian 9, 201–234 *(passim)*
– Classical Greek See Attic
– Doric 146, 399
– East Asia Minor Greek See Asia Minor
    Greek
– Aeolic 213, 399
– Early Modern Greek 201–34 *(passim)*
– Egyptian Greek 8–9, 17–37, 39–74,
    76–113, 115–39, 141–62, 243–63,
    386–94, 265–98, 299–326, 327–52
– *Hellēnika* 146, 154
– Ionic 65, 213–4, 221, 399
– Koine Greek See Koine
– Medieval Greek 1–13 *(passim)*, 76– 113,
    163–78, 179– 200, 201–34
    (passim), 300–26, 353–68, 369–80,
    401–06
– Modern Greek 81, 142, 168, 221, 273, 282,
    337, 340, 369
– New Testament Greek See Biblical Greek
– Pharasiot 201–34 *(passim)*

- Pontic 201–34 *(passim)*
- Post-classical Greek 1–13 *(passim)*, 394–400 See also Egyptian Greek; Koine
- Septuagint Greek See Biblical Greek

hand(writing) 39–74 *(passim)*
Hebrew 133, 148, 151
hypercorrection See correction
hypotaxis See subordination

idiolect See lect
imperative tone 75–102 *(passim)*
inflection
- agglutinative 205, 215–6
- nominal 54, 61–5, 156, 175, 185, 191–2
- verbal 65–6
infinitive 7, 10, 27, 65, 79, 84, 98, 100, 130–1, 169–70, 172, 175, 186, 187–9, 265–98, 342, 371–4, 375, 378, 391
information unit 353, 357
innovator 40
insult See speech acts
intonation unit 357
iota 55, 57–9
itacism 321, 391
Italian 203–4, 257

Koine 1–2, 10, 146 See also Egyptian Greek
- Asia Minor Koine 202
- Byzantine Koine See Medieval Greek
- Egyptian Koine See Egyptian Greek

language change 6, 17–20, 22–3, 27, 29, 31, 35, 39, 51, 71, 168, 180, 191, 201, 213–33, 266, 271, 273, 303, 337, 341–9, 384, 387, 388–94, 394–400, 402–9
language contact 18, 20–1, 29–31, 35, 40, 116–7, 121, 133, 142, 151, 201–2, 214
lects 1, 8, 17–37, 72
- chronolect 1
- dialect 1, 3, 10, 149, 30, 328
- doculect 8, 20, 34
- ethnolect 1, 8, 20–1, 24, 30–1, 34
- genderlect 1

- idiolect 1–2, 5, 8–10, 20, 23, 27, 29, 31–4, 39–74, 115, 128–9, 134, 327–8, 347–9, 350
- officialese 18
- regiolect 1, 9, 115–35 *(passim)*, 328, 347–9
- sociolect 1, 3, 6, 10, 29, 303, 327–9, 347–9, 350, 383
- technolect 1
- topolect 149, 153
lenition 340
lexicographers See grammarians
living texts See fluid texts
loanwords 9, 341–2, 201, 203–4, 230, 342–3, 348, 350, 410

Macedonian 154, 340
metaphrasis 9, 163, 172–3, 179–200, 381, 385, 401–6, 408, 410
modality 9, 79, 83, 163, 165, 167–8, 171, 189
mood
- imperative 65, 71, 79, 83, 86, 100, 176, 217–8, 231–2, 234, 372–4
- indicative 10, 24–5, 27, 31, 130–1, 167, 170–2, 175, 186–7, 189–90, 222–3, 230–2, 243, 246, 251, 255–6, 261, 272–5, 278–85, 288, 372–3, 390–1
- optative 7, 130, 165–6, 168, 170–3, 186, 189, 190, 197, 372, 374, 378
- subjunctive 27, 31, 57, 79, 83, 86, 92–3, 130, 168–73, 175, 186, 189–90, 205, 217–9, 230, 234, 337, 342, 372, 374, 391
moment of enunciation 164, 166, 168, 170–1, 174–5, 180

norm 10, 87, 164, 265–6, 295, 303 See also standard

orthography 14, 18–21, 24, 28, 299–326

parataxis See coordination
parousia topos 249
participle 24, 31, 51, 63–6, 68–70, 84, 95, 124, 132, 141, 176, 186–8, 274, 284, 286, 291, 345, 371–6, 379, 390–1, 400, 405

particle 10, 51, 66–8, 72, 130–1, 167, 171, 187, 217, 275, 287, 291, 300, 369, 376–7, 379, 383, 389, 397, 404, 407
Phoenician 46
phonology 2, 6, 18, 25, 29–31, 51, 57, 64, 71, 116–7, 125, 182, 185, 187, 217, 220, 222, 228, 273, 300–1, 303, 327–50, 382, 395, 409
politeness 9, 21, 31, 75–102
postalveolarization 206, 217–9
posteriority 10, 265–95 *(passim)*
pragmatics 299–301, 382, 410
predicative possessive pattern 9, 116, 119, 120–2, 134–5
preposition 61, 63–4, 70, 91, 119, 121–2, 176, 190, 192, 221–2, 389, 396–7, 403–4, 406–7
principle of pairing 361, 363, 365
pronoun 397, 406
– clitic 175, 205, 226, 232, 234
– demonstrative 170
– indefinite 319, 391
– interrogative 124, 205, 219, 234
– personal 182, 191, 193–6, 221, 335, 389
– possessive 92–3, 95, 187, 224–5
– relative 62, 205, 234, 375
pronunciation xv–xvi, 10, 25, 27, 39, 51, 53, 63, 72, 143, 215, 221, 299, 327–9, 331–2, 334–6, 339, 340, 342–3, 346–50, 357, 362, 382–3, 391–2, 399, 410

reanalysis 65, 70
reduplication 222, 283, 287
regionalism See regiolect
register 2–3, 6–7, 8–10, 18–9, 21–5, 34, 42, 68, 71–2, 115, 119, 123, 132, 133–5, 148, 157, 163–77 *(passim)*, 179–97 *(passim)*, 205–96 *(passim)*, 299–323 *(passim)*, 328, 337, 344, 347–9, 384–5
regularization See correction
request See directive

semantics 9, 121–3, 127–8, 131, 146, 164, 197, 269, 274, 277, 300, 410

social dialect See sociolect
sociolect See lect
speech acts 78–81, 98, 149, 246
spelling See orthography
standard 19, 20, 25–7, 29, 31, 32, 34–5, 51–5, 63, 65, 69, 72, 116–8, 123, 131, 143, 164, 190, 197, 291, 299–323 *(passim)*, 327, 332, 333–4, 336, 356, 401–2
subordination 5, 7, 10, 79, 84, 115, 129–35, 171, 186, 307–8, 374–6, 379, 391
support-verb construction 115, 119–20, 122–9, 131, 134–5
syllable 52–4, 57, 59, 61–2, 65, 221, 228, 273, 341, 343–5, 350, 353–67 *(passim)*, 400
synizesis 175–6, 210, 227–8, 364

tense 70–1, 243–61, 265–96
– aorist 10, 24–5, 27, 31, 65, 70, 83, 165–8, 170–1, 175–6, 186–7, 189, 190, 197, 205, 217–9, 223, 230–3, 243, 246, 248, 250, 254–61, 265–95 *(passim)*, 336, 373, 392–3, 398, 405
– absolute 164, 166, 179
– future
– imperfect 24, 27, 65, 167–8, 170, 222, 231, 255–61, 372–3, 398, 405
– perfect 7, 10, 27, 65–6, 70–1, 132, 165, 186, 244, 246, 251–6, 257, 260–1, 265–95 *(passim)*, 398
– pluperfect 186–7, 190–1, 197, 372–3
– present 373, 398, 400, 405
text type 41–3, 126, 369–79
time of enunciation See moment of enunciation
Turkish 201–34 *(passim)*

variable 1, 4, 29, 299–300, 302–4, 309–14, 322, 382
verse
– decapentasyllable 201, 207, 210, 234
– decasyllable 359
– decatetrasyllable 359, 361–2, 364
– dodecasyllable 353–67 *(passim)*

– heptasyllable 225, 362, 367
– octosyllable 358–9
– pentasyllable 362
– political verse See decapentasyllable
– tetrasyllable 362
– trissyllable 366–7
vowels xv–xvi, 22, 24, 31–2, 34, 51, 53–5, 57–9, 62, 321, 327, 337–9, 341–5, 350, 391, 398–9

– vowel harmony 205, 231

Watkins' Law 216, 231
word order 21, 133, 188, 205, 226, 228, 383, 389–90, 400, 404–5
– position of adjectives 228
– position of clitic pronouns 175, 205, 226, 234
– position of markers of politeness 82–6

www.ingramcontent.com/pod-product-compliance
Lightning Source LLC
Chambersburg PA
CBHW052041220426
43663CB00012B/2404